Modern Cryptography with Proof Techniques and Implementations

Modern Cryptography with Proof Techniques and Implementations

By

Seong Oun Hwang

Intae Kim

Wai Kong Lee

CRC Press
Taylor & Francis Group
Boca Raton London New York

CRC Press is an imprint of the
Taylor & Francis Group, an **informa** business

[First] edition published [2021]
by CRC Press
6000 Broken Sound Parkway NW, Suite 300, Boca Raton, FL 33487-2742

and by CRC Press
2 Park Square, Milton Park, Abingdon, Oxon, OX14 4RN

© 2021 Taylor & Francis Group, LLC

CRC Press is an imprint of Taylor & Francis Group, LLC

ISBN: 9781138584082 (hbk)
ISBN: 9780367723231 (pbk)
ISBN: 9781003152569 (ebk)

Typeset in Computer Modern font
by KnowledgeWorks Global Ltd.

To Moonja, Miyeon, and Hyunjun

Contents

III   Post-Quantum Cryptography   411

Preface

Security is critical in modern society, particularly in the Internet era, where things as well as people are interconnected. Cryptography plays a critical role to ensure the security of the society by serving as a primitive and building block.

The goal of this book is to introduce the foundations of cryptography to students, researchers, and practitioners so that they design their own secure systems, analyze the existing cryptographic schemes, or apply the provably secure cryptographic schemes to the real world.

Features of the Book Compared to other subjects, cryptography is generally accepted as "difficult to understand," mainly because the underlying proofs are kind of mental games, which may be hardly understandable. To ease the understanding of cryptography, we introduced detailed-and-intuitive explanations, relevant implementations, and extensible applications in this book. Particularly, sometimes, but not always, we found that detailed-and-intuitive explanations are especially helpful for beginners to figure out the structural flow of security proof of cryptographic schemes; it becomes easier to understand a specific complex theoretical concept by implementing itself or constructing relevant applications. Specifically, this book is designed to have the following in mind in detail:

1. giving a big picture of cryptography, wide and deep

   (a) the basic building blocks
   (b) various cryptographic schemes
   (c) applications to the real world

2. providing fundamentals on cryptography

   (a) formal definitions of security
   (b) complexity assumptions of computational problems
   (c) proof techniques

3. giving practice on how to implement cryptographic schemes efficiently

   (a) fundamental mathematical tools for efficient implementation
   (b) efficient techniques to optimize the implementation based on specific hardware

    (c) trade-off to be made during implementation (e.g., memory versus speed)

Structures of the Book In line with the above design purposes and features of the book, the whole book comprises the following four parts:

1. **Part I:** Fundamentals of classical and modern cryptography are explained including the structure of security proofs, private-key encryption, message authentication code, hash function, basic number theory, public-key encryption, and digital signature.

2. **Part II:** Identity-based encryption can use any arbitrary data for an identity as public keys, which is one of the big differences from traditional public-key encryption, which makes identity-based encryption easier to use, less expensive, and more practical.

3. **Part III:** Post-quantum cryptography has emerged recently to prepare for the near future, as existing conventional cryptography is expected to be broken by advanced algorithms executed on quantum computers. Two representative post-quantum approaches, lattice-based and code-based, are explored.

4. **Part IV:** Various popular cryptographic schemes are implemented using the MIRACL library, which is based on C/C++ programming language. Some post-quantum schemes are implemented with plain C codes and evaluated on the Graphics Processing Units (GPU) with massively parallel architecture. Mathematical tools like Montgomery reduction, Chinese remainder theorem (CRT), and number theoretic transform (NTT) are used to optimize the performance.

Guide to the Book Readers will get much help if they study considering the following guidelines:

1. **Proof:** One of the key design issues of this book is how to introduce seemingly hard security proofs of cryptographic schemes to readers, particularly beginners and self-learners, in an intuitively easy and detailed method so that they could completely understand them by just following the book. Readers are first recommended to grasp the big picture of security proofs by taking a look at Chapter 2 and revisit this chapter whenever they study a specific security proof techniques. Particularly, they are encouraged to walk through the proofs in each chapter of Part 1 in sequence, which comprises the fundamentals of cryptography. Readers will get many benefits by referring to intuitions or outlines, if any, underlying a specific proof before going deeper into the proof itself. When they go deeper into a specific proof, they can easily understand it by just following the detailed step-by-step explanations of the proof, unique feature quite different from the other cryptography textbooks. If readers

fully understand the key proof techniques in Parts 1 and 2, they can easily understand more complex proof techniques.

2. **Implementation:** Most of the implementations in this book are based on the MIRACL library with detailed guidance on setting up the compilation. The readers can first explore the implementation of ECDSA and Paillier, which are fundamental cryptography. Next, readers may implement more advanced cryptographic schemes including IBE, BE, CP-ABE, and PE. The implementation of RSA involves parallel programming using GPU, which can be explored at the later stage. The readers can explore the implementation of lattice-based and code-based cryptography, wherein various optimization techniques are presented. Finally, the readers can also explore the implementation of AES and SSL. **All implementation source code can be accessible at https://ai-security.github.io.**

Comments and Errata We would appreciate it if you email any comments or errata to sohwang@gachon.ac.kr. A list of errata will be maintained at https://ai-security.github.io.

Seong Oun Hwang, Ph.D., Gachon University, Korea
Intae Kim, Ph.D., The University of Wollongong, Australia
Wai Kong Lee, Ph.D., Universiti Tunku Abdul Rahman, Malaysia

List of Figures

List of Tables

Part I

Fundamentals of Cryptography

1

Introduction to Cryptography

CONTENTS

The chapter begins with the history of cryptography. Cryptography is divided into two main classes, classical and modern cryptography. Classical cryptographic schemes are mostly designed in an ad hoc way that they cannot provide security proofs. In the modern cryptography, schemes are designed in a structured way so that they could provide security proofs, which are commonly based on rigorous definitions and hardness assumptions of underlying mathematical problems. One-time pad, a special example of classical cryptographic scheme, provides perfect security, while modern cryptographic schemes pursue computational security. The differences between the perfect and computational security are explained further with the basic mathematical background used in the computational security.

1.1   History of Cryptography

We classify cryptography into classical cryptography and modern cryptography roughly according to the time of before and after the 1980s. In classical cryptography, cryptographic schemes are designed in a *non-rigorous* way that they are commonly breakable with an exemption of one-time pad which will be explained shortly. Representative historical classical ciphers include shift ciphers and substitution ciphers. A cipher means an algorithm for performing encryption or decryption. In contrast to classical cryptography, modern cryptographic schemes are designed in a *rigorous* way that they can provide proofs of security, which are based on definitions and hardness assumptions of underlying mathematical problems.

1.1.1 Classical Cryptography

Let us first formally define what an encryption scheme (i.e., cipher) is as follows.

The syntax of encryption Let $\mathcal{K}, \mathcal{M}, \mathcal{C}$ be the key, plaintext message, ciphertext message spaces, respectively. A basic encryption scheme Π is comprised of three algorithms.

1. The key-generation algorithm Gen is a probabilistic algorithm that outputs a key $k \in \mathcal{K}$ chosen according to some distribution that is deterministic by the scheme.

2. The encryption algorithm Enc takes as input a key k and a plaintext message m and outputs a ciphertext $c \in \mathcal{C}$. We denote by $Enc_k(m)$ the encryption of the plaintext m using the key k.

3. The decryption algorithm Dec takes as input a key k and a ciphertext c and outputs a plaintext $m \in \mathcal{M}$. We denote the decryption of the ciphertext c using the key k by $Dec_k(c)$.

The above scheme is also called the private-key encryption or the symmetric encryption scheme.

Unlike the other classical ciphers, one-time pad (OTP, *aka* Vernam's cipher [97] in 1917) is *perfectly secure* regardless of the adversary's computational power in the sense that a ciphertext reveals nothing about the underlying plaintext, or *information-theoretically secure* in the sense that the adversary simply does not have enough "information" to succeed in its attack. Intuitively, the one-time pad is perfectly secure because given a ciphertext, there is no way an adversary can know which plaintext it originated from.

The syntax of one-time pad Let $\mathcal{K}, \mathcal{M}, \mathcal{C} = \{0,1\}^l$ (that is, the set of all binary strings of length l). The one-time pad is as follows.

1. $Gen \rightarrow k$ chosen uniformly at random from $\{0,1\}^l$ (i.e., each of the 2^l strings in the space is chosen as the key with probability exactly 2^{-l}).

2. $Enc_k(m) = m \oplus k = c$.

3. $Dec_k(c) = c \oplus k = m$.

Correctness is established by verifying that $c \oplus k = (m \oplus k) \oplus k = m$. Since we got some insight on perfect security of one-time pad, we can formally define the exact notion of perfect security and explore some properties as follows.

Definition 1 *An encryption scheme (Gen, Enc, Dec) over a message space $\mathcal{M}$ is **perfectly secure** if for every probability distribution over $\mathcal{M}$, every message $m \in \mathcal{M}$, and every ciphertext $c \in \mathcal{C}$: $Pr[M = m | C = c] = Pr[M = m]$.*

The above definition can be interpreted as: A scheme is perfectly secure if the distributions over messages and ciphertexts are *independent*. The following lemmas give equivalent formulations of Definition 1.

Lemma 1 *An encryption scheme (Gen, Enc, Dec) over a message space $\mathcal{M}$ is perfectly secure if for every probability distribution over $\mathcal{M}$, every message $m \in \mathcal{M}$, and every ciphertext $c \in \mathcal{C}$: $Pr[C = c | M = m] = Pr[C = c]$.*

Lemma 2 *An encryption scheme (Gen, Enc, Dec) over a message space $\mathcal{M}$ is perfectly secure if and only if for every probability distribution over $\mathcal{M}$, every $m_0, m_1 \in \mathcal{M}$ and every ciphertext $c \in \mathcal{C}$: $Pr[C = c | M = m_0] = Pr[C = c | M = m_1]$.*

The above lemmas imply that it is impossible to distinguish an encryption of $m_0 \in \mathcal{M}$ from an encryption of $m_1 \in \mathcal{M}$ because for every $m_0, m_1 \in \mathcal{M}$, the distributions $\mathcal{C}(m_0)$ and $\mathcal{C}(m_1)$ are identical. That is, the ciphertext contains no information about the plaintext.

Adversarial indistinguishability is another equivalent definition of perfect security (*aka perfect secrecy*). This definition is based on hypothetical, interactive *experiment* or *game* where an adversary tries to break a cryptographic scheme and an imaginary tester (i.e., challenger) wishes to see if the scheme is secure by computing the adversary's success probability. Through the experiment as follows, we prove the security of the underlying scheme by showing that no adversary can succeed with probability higher than one half, indicating that randomly guessing the plaintext is the best it can do.

The eavesdropping indistinguishability experiment $PrivK_{\mathcal{A},\Pi}^{eav}(n)$

1. The adversary $\mathcal{A}$ outputs a pair of messages $m_0, m_1 \in \mathcal{M}$.

2. The challenger generates a random key k by running *Gen*, and chooses a random bit $b \in \{0, 1\}$. Then, a ciphertext $c \to Enc_k(m_b)$ is computed and given to $\mathcal{A}$.

3. $\mathcal{A}$ outputs a bit b'.

4. The output of the experiment is defined to be 1 if $b = b'$ (in this case, $\mathcal{A}$ was right) and 0 otherwise. We write $PrivK_{\mathcal{A},\Pi}^{eav}(n) = 1$ if the output is 1, and in this case we say that $\mathcal{A}$ succeeded in breaking the scheme Π.

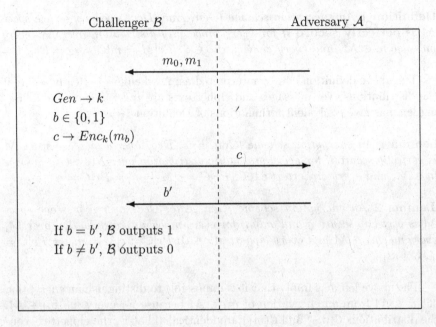

Definition 2 *An encryption scheme (Gen, Enc, Dec) over a message space $\mathcal{M}$ is* **perfectly secure** *if for every adversary $\mathcal{A}$ it holds that $Pr[PrivK_{\mathcal{A},\Pi}^{eav}(n) = 1] = \frac{1}{2}$.*

Note that the perfect security of one-time pad is established by showing that $Pr[C = c | M = m] = (\frac{1}{2})^l$ as follows.

Proposition 1 *Let (Gen, Enc, Dec) be an encryption scheme over a message space $\mathcal{M}$. That is, (Gen, Enc, Dec) is perfectly secure with respect to Definition 1 if and only if it is perfectly secure with respect to Definition 2.*

In the above, we note that there is no limitation whatsoever on the computational power of $\mathcal{A}$ (e.g., probabilistic polynomial time adversary). Compare this definition with that of Definition 2 in Chapter 3.

Limitations of one-time pad and perfectly secure schemes makes the one-time pad or any other perfectly secure scheme unusable (i.e., impractical).

1. The key space should be as large as the message space (i.e., $|\mathcal{K}| \geq |\mathcal{M}|$).

2. The key should be used only once. Otherwise, encrypting more than one message with the same key leaks information about the messages.

It seems necessary to compromise on perfect security in order to achieve

TABLE 1.1

Comparison of info-theoretic security and computational security.

Info-theoretic Security (Perfect security)	Computational Security (Practical security)
Adversary has unbounded computational resources	Adversary has bounded computational resources
Pursuing zero success probability	Negligible success probability is allowed
Ideal	Practical

practical cryptographic schemes, which could arguably provide sufficient security in the real world.

1.1.2 Modern Cryptography

Modern cryptography is based on complexity theory (i.e., the theory of how easy or difficult is to solve a given problem computationally). It should not matter whether a ciphertext reveals information about the message. What matters is whether this information can be efficiently extracted by an adversary.

Modern cryptography takes computational approach which is weaker than perfect (i.e., information-theoretic) but sufficient (i.e., practical) security. The main differences between perfect security and computational security are summarized in Table 1.1

"Practical" means that computationally secure schemes can be broken given enough time and computation, but under certain assumptions, the amount of time and computation needed to break the scheme would take more than a person's lifetime, for example.

The computational approach incorporates two relaxations of the notion of perfect security.

1. Security is only guaranteed against "efficient" adversaries that run in a feasible amount of time, and

2. Adversaries can potentially succeed with some "very small probability" (that is, small enough so that we are not concerned with the probability that it will ever really happen).

How can we formally or rigorously define what is meant by the above? There are two common approaches: the concrete approach and the asymptotic approach.

The concrete approach explicitly specifies the maximum success probability of any adversary running for at most some specified amount of time. It takes the following form.

> *A scheme is (t, ε)-secure if every adversary running for time at most t*
> *succeeds in breaking the scheme with probability at most ε.*

For example, no adversary running for at most 2^{80} CPU cycles can break the scheme with probability better than 2^{-64}.

The asymptotic approach, rooted in complexity theory, views the running time of the adversary as well as its success probability as functions of some parameter n (that is, security parameters which are determined during initialization of a scheme, for example, key length) rather than as concrete numbers.

1. We equate the notion of "feasible strategies" or "efficient algorithm" or "practical algorithm" with probabilistic algorithms running in time polynomial in n (PPT stands for probabilistic polynomial time).

2. We equate the notion of "very small probability of success" with success probabilities smaller than any inverse polynomial in n. A function that grows slower than any inverse polynomial is called negligible.

It takes the following form which is employed in the book.

> *A scheme is secure if every PPT adversary succeeds in*
> *breaking the scheme with only negligible probability.*

Modern cryptography takes a rigorous approach to security based upon the following, which is the main theme of Chapter 2:

1. exact (i.e., formal) definitions of security including the attack goal and model

2. precise assumptions on both the resources given to the adversary and the hardness of the underlying computational problem(s)

3. proof techniques

1.2 Background Review

Background knowledge useful in computational security is presented in this section.

1.2.1 Big Oh Notation

Suppose we have a function $f(n) : \mathbb{N} \to \mathbb{N}$. Then we say that $f(n) = O(g(n))$ if and only if there exist constants $d, n_0 \in \mathbb{Z}$ such that $\forall n \geq n_0, f(n) \leq d \cdot g(n)$. Big oh notation is a representation to show the time complexity of an algorithm. It represents a worst-case time complexity. The highest leading term determines the complexity of an algorithm.

Examples

As a simple example, we take $f(n) = 3n^2 + 3n$, as the purpose of big oh notation is to find the dominant factor in the polynomial or the function as the value of variable reaches to infinity. In this case, the variable is n. If we look at the function, some factors are more important than the others. As n goes to infinity, n becomes less prominent as compared to n^2. Other terms become less prominent. We neglect the less prominent terms. The only term that defines the complexity is the highest leading term, which in this case is n^2. The final complexity of $3n^2 + 3n$ is $O(n^2)$. Similarly final complexity for $3n + 3$ is $O(n)$.

Properties

1. If $k_1 \in O(f_1)$ and $k_2 \in O(f_1)$, then $k_1 k_2 \in O(f_1 f_2)$.
2. If $k_1 \in O(f_1)$ and $k_2 \in O(f_1)$, then $k_1 + k_2 \in O(max(f_1, f_2))$.

1.2.2 Polynomial

We say that $f(n) : \mathbb{N} \to \mathbb{N}$ is a polynomial if and only if $f(n) = O(n^c)$ for some $c \in \mathbb{Z}$. In general, we say that an algorithm is efficient if its complexity can be expressed as a polynomial of input size n.

Examples

1. $F(n) = 3n^2 + 3n$ is a polynomial as $F(n) = O(n^2)$, where $c = 2$.
2. $G(n) = 3n + 3$ is a polynomial as $G(n) = O(n)$, where $c = 1$.
3. $P(x) = 2x^4 + x^3 - 2x^2 + 1$ is a polynomial with integer coefficients of degree $c = 4$.

Properties

1. A polynomial cannot have fractional powers of the variable.

2. Exponents of the variables should not be negative.

3. Any two polynomials can be added, subtracted, or multiplied, and the result will be a polynomial, too.

1.2.3 Super Polynomial

A function that is not polynomial is super polynomial.

Examples

1. $F(x) = 8x^{-2} + 1$ is a super polynomial as it has negative exponent, which does not satisfy a property of a polynomial.

2. $F(x) = 5x^{1/2} + 4$ is a super polynomial as it has fractional exponent, which does not satisfy a property of a polynomial.

3. $F(x) = (5x^3 - 1)/3x$ is a super polynomial as it is in fractional form, which does not satisfy a property of a polynomial.

Properties

1. A super polynomial may have fractional powers of the variable.

2. In super polynomial, exponents of the variables may be negative.

3. Any two super polynomials can be added, subtracted, or multiplied and the result will be a super polynomial, too.

1.2.4 Negligible

We say that a function is negligible (negl) if for all polynomials p, there exists $n_0 \in \mathbb{Z}$ such that $\forall n \geq n_0, f(n) < \frac{1}{p(n)}$. Note that $p(n)$ is not a specific polynomial, but assumed to be an arbitrary one.

A negligible function is a function $f(n) : \mathbb{N} \to \mathbb{R}$ such that for every positive integer n there exists an integer n_o such that for all $x > n_o, |f(x)| < \frac{1}{x^n}$.

Examples

1. $f(x) = x^{-n}$ is negligible for any $x \geq 2$.

2. $f(x) = 2^{-\sqrt{x}}$ is negligible.

Properties

1. If f and h are two negligible functions, the sum $(f + h)$ of the two function is also negligible.

2. If f is non-negligible and h is negligible function, the difference $(f - h)$ of the two function is also non-negligible.

3. If f is a polynomial and h is a negligible function, (fh) is negligible.

Exercises

1.1 Prove that Definition 1 implies Definition 2.

1.2 Prove that Definition 2 implies Definition 1.

1.3 Explain why the one-time pad scheme is not perfectly secure if

1. The key space is shorter than the message space (i.e., $|K| < |M|$).
2. The key is not used only once.

1.4 Prove Lemma 1.

1.5 Prove Lemma 2.

2

Structure of Security Proof

CONTENTS

This chapter provides an overview of the structure of security proofs. In modern cryptography, one establishes a formal security notion of the scheme to be designed, makes precise computational assumptions, builds the scheme based on some existing atomic primitive(s), and finally proves its security by exhibiting the so-called reduction between an algorithm which breaks the security notion and an algorithm that contradicts the assumptions. In relation to security notion, security goals are defined for the encryption and signature schemes, against which attack models are also described for the types of attack scenarios. We discuss how higher cryptographic schemes could be built by assembling the lower cryptographic schemes. The next part of the chapter discusses reduction and various security proof techniques based on reduction including the random oracle methodology, sequence of games, and the generic group model. Readers are recommended to refer this chapter as frequent as possible whenever encountering relevant security proof techniques.

2.1   Overview of Security Proof

In this chapter, we will look at the basic concepts of security proof and various proof techniques.

2.1.1   Why Proving Security?

To answer this question, we consider different paradigms taken by classical and modern cryptography. Classical cryptography takes an iterated design approach, where tries to design a cryptographic scheme by endless iteration of the process "attack found ⇒ revision to the scheme." The problems with this approach is that one never knows if things are right, and when damaging attacks emerge, it is difficult or impossible to effectively fix them. On the other hand, modern cryptography takes a completely different approach called the provable security, where one tries to design a cryptographic scheme by proving that no attack exists under some assumptions. In this approach, one establishes a formal security notion of the scheme to be designed, makes precise computational assumptions, builds the scheme based on some existing atomic primitive(s), and finally proves its security by exhibiting the so-called reduction between an algorithm which breaks the security notion and an algorithm that contradicts the assumptions. A security notion is defined by pairing a security goal of the designed scheme with an attack model, which describes what means or information are available to attackers. You can see an example of security notion in the eavesdropping indistinguishability experiment $PrivK_{A,\Pi}^{eav}(n)$ in Chapter 1, where indistinguishability corresponds to security goal and eavesdropping does attack model. Figure 2.1 shows the comparison of the iterated design and provable security.

2.1.2   Security Goals

1. Security goals for encryption schemes

    (a) **Unbreakability** It should not be feasible for an adversary to compute the secret key from the public key (denoted UBK).

    (b) **One-wayness** It should not be feasible to invert the encryption function over any ciphertext under any given key (denoted OW).

    (c) **Indistinguishability**[1] It should not be feasible to distinguish which of the two messages are encrypted given a ciphertext (denoted IND).

---

[1] Ciphertext indistinguishability is known to be equivalent to the so-called semantic security. It is the computational complexity analogue to perfect secrecy, which means that the ciphertext reveals no information at all about the plaintext, whereas semantic security implies that any information revealed cannot be feasibly extracted.

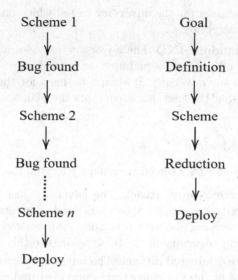

FIGURE 2.1
Comparison of iterated design and provable security.

   (d) **Non-malleability** It should not be feasible to transform some ciphertext into another ciphertext such that plaintext are meaningfully related (denoted NM).

2. Security goals for signature schemes

   (a) **Unbreakability** It should not be feasible to compute the secret key from the public key (denoted UBK).

   (b) **Universal unforgeability** It should not be feasible to produce a valid signature of any message in the message space (denoted UUF).

   (c) **Selective unforgeability** It should not be feasible to produce a valid signature of a message an attacker committed to before knowing the public key (denoted SUF).

   (d) **Existential unforgeability** It should not be feasible to produce a message and a valid signature of it (likely not of his choosing) (denoted EUF).

   (e) **Non-malleability** It should not be feasible to construct another signature for the same message when given a pair of message and signature (denoted NM).

Indistinguishability comes in different equivalent flavors:

1. **Left-or-Right IND** The adversary chooses two plaintexts. One is selected at random and its encryption is given to the adversary.

It should be hard for the adversary to tell which one was selected given the encryption.

2. **Real-or-Random IND** The adversary provides a plaintext. An encryption of either this plaintext or a randomly selected one is returned to the adversary. It should be hard for the adversary to decide whether the encryption encrypts the plaintext or not.

2.1.3   Attack Models

1. Basic types of attack scenarios against encryption schemes

   (a) **Ciphertext-only attack** The adversary just observes a ciphertext (or multiple ciphertexts) and attempts to determine the underlying plaintext (or plaintexts)(denoted COA). Eavesdropping adversary in the book belongs to this category.

   (b) **Known-plaintext attack** The adversary learns one or more pairs of plaintexts/ciphertexts encrypted under the same key. The aim of the adversary is then to determine the plaintext that was encrypted in some other ciphertext (denoted KPA).

   (c) **Chosen-plaintext attack** The adversary has the ability to obtain the encryption of plaintexts of its choice. It then attempts to determine the plaintext that was encrypted in some other ciphertext (denoted CPA).

   (d) **Chosen-ciphertext attack** The adversary has the ability to obtain the decryption of ciphertexts of its choice. It then attempts to determine the plaintext that was encrypted in some other ciphertext (denoted CCA, *aka lunchtime*, or midnight attack).

   (e) **Adaptive chosen-ciphertext attack** The adversary has the ability to obtain the decryption of ciphertexts of its choice adaptively (that is, it chooses next ciphertexts after viewing the decryption of the previously selected ciphertexts). It then attempts to determine the plaintext that was encrypted in some other ciphertext (denoted CCA2).

2. Basic types of attack scenarios for signature schemes

   (a) **Key-only attack** It should not be feasible to compute the secret key from the public key (KOA).

   (b) **Known-message attack** The adversary obtains signatures for a set of known messages (KMA).

   (c) **Chosen-message attack** The adversary chooses a set of messages and are given the corresponding signatures. The choice of the set of messages are non-adaptive (CMA).

(d) **Adaptive chosen-message attack** The adversary is able to obtain signatures on arbitrary messages chosen adaptively (that is, it chooses the next message after viewing the signature of the previous message) during its attack (Adaptive CMA).

As mentioned above, any notion (or definition) of a scheme consists of two distinct components.

1. a specification of the adversary's power (attack types such as eavesdropping attack, chosen plaintext attack, chosen ciphertext attack, etc.; it runs in polynomial time; the number of queries is polynomial, etc.)

2. a description of what constitutes a "break" of the scheme (indistinguishable encryption, existential unforgeability, etc.)

2.1.4 How Can We Build a Cryptographic Scheme? Lego Approach!

We construct higher level schemes by assembling and connecting lower level schemes or atomic primitives as

1. pseudorandom generators, pseudorandom functions
2. one-way functions, one-way trapdoor functions, one-way trapdoor permutations
3. hash functions (e.g., SHA1, MD5)
4. private-key permutations (e.g., DES, AES)
5. message authentication codes
6. arithmetic or Boolean operations
7. and so on.

We typically design high-level primitives from the atomic ones and history shows that the transformer is usually a weak link. The atomic primitives are secure yet the higher-level primitives are insecure. This enables us to get the transformers for which we can guarantee the atomic primitives are secure and the high-level primitives are also secure. Figure 2.2 shows that how the atomic primitives are linked to the high-level primitives through the transformers.

2.1.5 Computational Assumptions

Cryptographic primitives are connected to plenty of supposedly intractable problems as

1. discrete log is hard
2. factoring is hard

3. RSA is hard

4. computational/decisional Diffie-Hellman is hard

5. computing residuosity classes is hard

6. deciding residuosity is hard

7. finding shortest lattice vector is hard

8. etc.

2.2   Proof by Reduction

Motivation A cryptographic scheme that is computationally secure (but not perfectly secure) can always be broken given enough time. Then how can we prove it? To prove that some scheme is computationally secure requires a lower bound on the time needed to break the scheme, which is very hard to achieve in the current state of the art. Instead, we take the following approach as

> *Assume that some low-level problem is hard to solve, and then prove that the scheme in question is secure under this assumption.*

Then how can we relate the scheme in question with the low-level problem? It is by the concept of reduction which originates from complexity theory. Now we walk through a high level outline of security proof by reduction.

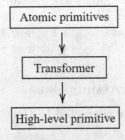

FIGURE 2.2
Lego approach.

2.2.1 What Is Reduction?

Suppose we want to build some cryptographic scheme Π and show that an adversary $\mathcal{A}$ attacking Π under some security notion, e.g., IND-CPA, can be used as a black box tool to answer some supposed hard problem, e.g., X, with non-negligible probability (In this case, we say that Π is *reducible* to X). This, however, contradicts to the computational assumption. Therefore, we could conclude that Π is provably IND-CPA secure in the presence of the attacker under the assumption that X is hard.

Note 1: The reduction has to simulate the attacker's environment in a way that preserves (or does not alter too much) the distribution of all random variables which it interacts with.

Note 2: A reduction shows that the only way to defeat the scheme is to break the underlying atomic primitive.

2.2.2 Outline of Security Proof by Reduction

1. Begin with an assumption that some problem X cannot be solved by any polynomial time algorithm except with negligible probability.

2. Fix some efficient (i.e., probabilistic polynomial time) adversary $\mathcal{A}$ attacking Π with success probability $\epsilon(n)$, where n is the input size of the problem.

3. Construct an efficient algorithm $\mathcal{B}$ (called the "reduction," "challenger," or "simulator") that attempts to solve the problem X using $\mathcal{A}$ as a sub-routine. So, given some input instance x of X, $\mathcal{B}$ simulates for $\mathcal{A}$ an instance of Π such that

   (a) As far as $\mathcal{A}$ can tell, it interacts with Π. More formally, the view of $\mathcal{A}$ when it is run as a sub-routine by $\mathcal{B}$ should be distributed identically to (or at least close to) the view of $\mathcal{A}$ when it interacts with Π itself.

   (b) If $\mathcal{A}$ succeeds in "breaking" the instance of Π that is being simulated by $\mathcal{B}$, this should allow $\mathcal{B}$ to solve the instance x, at least with inverse polynomial probability $1/p(n)$.

4. Combining (a) and (b) together implies that if $\epsilon(n)$ is not negligible, then $\mathcal{B}$ solves problem X with non-negligible probability $\epsilon(n)/p(n)$, which contradicts the initial assumption.

5. We conclude that Π is computationally secure under the assumption.

A high level overview of a security proof by reduction is shown in Figure 2.3.

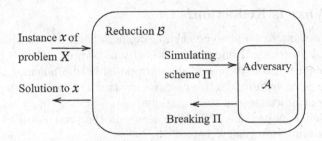

FIGURE 2.3
A high level overview of a security proof by reduction.

2.3   Random Oracle Methodology

When designing and validating cryptographic schemes, we use two kinds of models, standard model, where no random oracle is presented, and random oracle model. Cryptographic schemes are usually based on complexity assumptions, which state that some problem, for example, factorization, cannot be solved in polynomial time. Schemes which can be proven secure using only complexity assumptions are said to be secure in the standard model. Under the random oracle model, we construct and prove a scheme under the assumption that the world contains a random oracle. A random oracle is a powerful (i.e., producing deterministic, efficient, and uniform output, that is, computationally indistinguishable from the uniform distribution), imaginary (output of a random oracle has an entropy greater than that of its input; by Shannon's theory, deterministic function cannot amplify entropy; therefore a random oracle does not exist) function. However, the difficulty arises when we instantiate the scheme in the real world (for example, when replacing the random oracle by a concrete hash function). In fact, it is known that there exist contrived schemes that can be proven secure in the random oracle model but are insecure no matter how the random oracle is instantiated.

For these reasons, a proof of security in the random-oracle model should be viewed as providing evidence that a scheme has no "inherent design flaws," but is not a rigorous proof that any real world instantiation of the scheme is secure.

Therefore, proofs of security in the random oracle model are less desirable and less satisfying than those in the standard model. However, the random oracle model continues to be widely used. Why? Notwithstanding of limitations in the random oracle model, it has some benefits as

1. It enables the design of substantially more efficient schemes than those we know how to construct in the standard model.

2. The schemes in the random oracle model are comparatively easier to prove than in the standard model.

2.3.1   Security Proof in the Random Oracle Model

In the standard model, a definition of security for Π takes the following general form: a scheme Π is secure if for any probabilistic polynomial-time (PPT) adversaries $\mathcal{A}$, the probability of some "bad" event is below some threshold (for encryptions $\gamma = \frac{1}{2}$ and for signatures $\gamma = 0$), in other words, we have

$$Pr[\text{Experiment}_{\mathcal{A},\Pi}(n) = 1] \leq \gamma + negl(n), \qquad (2.1)$$

where this probability is taken over the random choices of the parties running Π and those of the adversary $\mathcal{A}$. Assuming the honest parties who use Π in the real world make random choices as directed by the scheme, satisfying a definition of this sort guarantees security for real-world usage of Π.

In the random oracle model, in contrast, a scheme Π may rely on an oracle H. As before, Π is secure if for all PPT adversaries $\mathcal{A}$ the probability of some "bad" event is below some threshold, in other words,

$$Pr[\text{Experiment}_{\mathcal{A}^H,\Pi^H}(n) = 1] \leq \gamma + negl(n), \qquad (2.2)$$

where $\mathcal{A}^H$ denotes that $\mathcal{A}$ is given oracle access to H; Π^H denotes that a concrete scheme is obtained by fixing H. But now this probability is taken over random choice of H as well as the random choices of the parties running Π and those of the adversary $\mathcal{A}$. When using Π in the real world, some (instantiation of) H must be fixed. Unfortunately, security of Π is not guaranteed for any particular choice of H.

Proofs in the random oracle model can exploit the fact that H is chosen at random, and that the only way to evaluate $H(x)$ is to explicitly query x to H (e.g., the adversary is given only oracle access to H, but cannot evaluate H on its own). The reduction can set the value of $H(x)$ (i.e., the response to query x) to a value of its choice, as long as this value is correctly distributed, i.e., uniform, which is known as the programmability feature).

Examples

1. CPA-secure RSA Encryption in the random oracle model in Chapter 9

2. CCA-secure RSA Encryption in the random oracle model in Chapter 9

3. CCA-secure RSA-OAEP in the random oracle model in Chapter 9
4. CMA-secure El Gamal Signature in the random oracle model in Chapter 10
5. CMA-secure FDH-RSA Signature in the random oracle model in Chapter 10
6. CPA-secure BF-IBE in the random oracle model in Chapter 11
7. CCA-secure Delerablee's IBBE in the random oracle model in Chapter 18

2.4   Sequence of Games

A convenient way to structure the reductionist proof is to consider a sequence of games (*aka* Shoup's Modular Proof).

Suppose a cryptographic protocol is built upon several other smaller protocols, which are presumed to be secure. One starts with the assumption that there is an adversary who can break the main protocol with some non-negligible advantage in the given security model. This adversary is then used as a blackbox to construct an algorithm that either solves the underlying hard computational problem X or breaks one of the smaller provably secure protocols with non-negligible probability of success. This contradicts the original hypothesis.

It takes the following form:

> *If (smaller protocols are secure and) some problem X is computationally hard, then the main protocol is secure.*

To prove, for example, the indistinguishability of the encryption of two equal length plaintexts, we construct a sequence of games of the following form.

A Game Sequence
$$G_0,$$
$$G_1,$$
.

.

$$G_k.$$

Let X_i be the event that $\gamma = \gamma'$ in Game G_i. We consider

$$Pr[X_0],$$
$$Pr[X_0] - Pr[X_1],$$

$$\vdots$$

$$Pr[X_{k-1}] - Pr[X_k],$$
$$Pr[X_k].$$

In the above sequence, the following points are to be noted

1. G_0 is the game which defines the security of the protocol and so

$$Adv(\mathcal{A}) = \ | \ Pr[\gamma = \gamma'] - 1/2 \ | \ = \ | \ Pr[X_0] - 1/2 \ |. \qquad (2.3)$$

2. Games G_{i-1} and G_i differ:

   (a) Game G_i is described as being an incrementally modified version of Game G_{i-1}.

   (b) The difference is not too much (that is, G_i is described as being incrementally modified version of G_{i-1}).

   (c) The adversary should not be able to notice whether he is playing Game G_{i-1} or Game G_i.

3. G_k, the last game describing the complete reduction algorithm, is designed such that the bit is statistically hidden from the adversary. So

$$Pr[X_k] = 1/2. \qquad (2.4)$$

4. More precisely, $Pr[X_{i-1}] - Pr[X_i]$ is bounded above by

   (a) either, the advantage of an adversary in breaking one of the smaller protocols,

   (b) or, the advantage of solving the problem P is as
   $$Adv(\mathcal{A}) = \ | \ Pr[X_0] - 1/2 \ | \ = \ | \ Pr[X_0] - Pr[X_k] \ |$$
   $$\leq | \ Pr[X_0] - Pr[X_1] \ |$$
   $$+ | \ Pr[X_1] - Pr[X_2] \ |$$
   $$+ ...$$

   $$+ | \ Pr[X_{k-1}] - Pr[X_k] \ |. \qquad (2.5)$$

If the adversary has a non-negligible advantage then there must be at least two consecutive games, X_{i-1} and X_i such that $| \ Pr[X_{i-1}] - Pr[X_i] \ |$ is non-negligible which contradicts the original hypothesis (that is, small protocols are secure).

This methodology allows us to

1. check proofs more easily (longer proofs are possible).

2. compare different proof strategies.

3. concatenate proofs in a modular way by re-using pre-existing parts.

It enables to build security reductions for cryptographic schemes that use provably secure ingredients.

Examples

1. Waters' IBE in Chapter 13

2. Waters' HIBE in Chapter 14

3. Predicate Encryption in Chapter 21

4. Functional Encryption in Chapter 21

2.4.1   Hybrid Argument

Sequence of games is usually used in hybrid argument (*aka* hybrid proof). The hybrid argument is a proof technique often used in cryptography to show that two distributions are computationally indistinguishable. The name comes from the process of defining several "hybrid" distributions built from the original two distributions.

Proofs that use the hybrid argument follow this basic pattern.

1. Define a sequence of polynomially many (in the security parameter) $\mathcal{D}_0, ..., \mathcal{D}_t$ (called the hybrid distributions, or simply the hybrids) in the following way.

    (a) The extreme distributions $\mathcal{D}_0$ and $\mathcal{D}_t$ are the distributions we wish to show computationally indistinguishable.

    (b) Any adjacent distributions $\mathcal{D}_i$ and $\mathcal{D}_{i+1}$ differ by only one application of a cryptographic primitive. Often we replace a cryptographic primitive by its idealization between adjacent distributions (for example, replace the output of a pseudorandom generator with a truly random string).

2. Since they differ only in one simple aspect, it is (comparatively) easier to prove that adjacent distributions are computationally indistinguishable (in the security parameter).

3. Since computational indistinguishability is transitive across a polynomial number of distributions, we conclude that the endpoints $\mathcal{D}_0$ and $\mathcal{D}_t$ are computationally indistinguishable, as desired.

Often the order in which the hybrids are defined is significant and the proof will not work with a different hybridization of the two distributions.

Example

1. Second proof of CCA-secure encryption scheme using MAC in Chapter 6

2.5 The Generic Group Model

Until now, in order to prove a cryptographic scheme is secure under some well-known hard assumption(s) such as discrete log, factoring, etc., we reduced the scheme to the assumption(s). But how can we prove the security of the scheme under new presumably hard assumption(s)? To do this, we should additionally prove that the new assumptions are hard to solve computationally using the generic group model.

One of the main uses of the generic group model is to analyze computational hardness assumptions. An analysis in the generic group model can answer the question: "What is the fastest generic algorithm for breaking a cryptographic hardness assumption?." This question was answered for the discrete logarithm problem by Victor Shoup using the generic group model [92]. To solve the discrete logarithm and its related problems including the Diffie-Hellman problem, it is known that any generic algorithm must perform at least $p^{1/2}$ group operations, where p is the largest prime dividing the order of the group.

There are two basic requirements when the notion of generic group algorithms is modeled formally.

1. The algorithm which intends to solve a given problem instance must not be able to exploit any property of a given representation of group elements, i.e., the group representation must be hidden.

2. Nevertheless, the algorithm must be able to perform computations on group elements. That is, the algorithm must (at least) be able to perform the group operation and check for equality of elements without knowing a concrete representation of the group elements.

Shoup has modeled a generic group by only a few operations (i.e., performing the group operation) and relations (i.e., checking for equality of elements) but it can be extended by additional operations or relations.

The generic group model is an idealized cryptographic model, where the adversary is denoted by the generic algorithm. A generic algorithm is an algorithm that is allowed to perform group operations by making queries to the group operation oracle and equality test, but no other operations. That is, it does not exploit any special properties of the encodings of group elements (e.g., efficient encodings, such as those used by the finite field or elliptic curve groups used in practice), other than the property that each group element is encoded as a unique random binary string. Note that if special properties of the encodings are available to the adversary, then the adversary can exploit them. If the group should allow for a pairing operation, for example, this operation would be modeled as an additional oracle.

The generic group model is motivated by the fact that the elements of a group must be represented in some way in order to be able to perform computations on group elements. A general way of representing elements, e.g., in a computer, are bit strings. Thus, a representation of a group can be seen as a bijective map from the group to the set of bit strings without loss of generality.

Let $\mathbb{G}$ be a group of order n and S_n be a subset of $\{0,1\}^{log|\mathbb{G}|}$, a set of n different bit strings. Let $\sigma : \mathbb{G} \to S_n$ be a bijective encoding function, chosen at random among all possible functions, which encodes group elements as random, but unique binary strings. The random encoding ensures that the group $\mathbb{G}$ has only the defined properties of an abstract group.

In order to be able to perform computations on randomly encoded group elements, we assume an oracle O that computes operations (i.e., binary functions) or relations (for instance, a query to a decisional Diffie-Hellman oracle can be modeled as a relation) from some operation set on bit strings representing group elements. The equality relation is always included in the relation set implicitly, since the bijectivity of the encoding function allows to check for equality of elements by checking for equality of encodings.

The generic group model suffers from some of the same problems as the random oracle model. Note that the generic group model uses random encoding without planting any input instances, while the random oracle model uses random hashing with planting input instances.

Examples

1. Waters' HIBE in Chapter 14
2. CP-ABE in Chapter 19

Exercise

2.1 Compare the standard model with the random oracle model.

3

Private-Key Encryption (1)

CONTENTS

This chapter discusses private-key encryption schemes. The first part defines a computationally secure private-key encryption as a tuple of probabilistic polynomial-time algorithms for key generation, encryption, and decryption and explains the differences with perfect secure counterparts. The next part of the chapter introduces the notion of pseudo randomness and defines a pseudo random generator. Subsequently, the construction of the private-key encryption scheme based on a pseudo random generator is presented with its security proof.

3.1   Defining Computationally-Secure Encryption

In the previous chapter, we presented a definition of perfect security for private-key encryption, where there is no computational restriction on the adversary. To achieve a practical, but enough security, also called computational security, we need to relax the notion of perfect security: first, security is guaranteed only against efficient (i.e., polynomial-time) adversaries; second, a small (i.e., negligible) probability of success is allowed. To reflect, we introduce a security parameter as 1^n to parameterize a scheme as we usually measure the running time of an algorithm as a function of the length of the input. That is, the syntax of computationally-secure private-key encryption will be the same as that of perfectly secure private-key encryption except for the security parameter as follows.

Definition 1 *A* **private-key encryption scheme** *is a tuple of probabilistic polynomial-time algorithms (Gen, Enc, Dec) such that*

1. The key-generation algorithm *Gen* is a probabilistic (i.e., randomized) algorithm that takes input the security parameter 1^n and outputs a key $k \leftarrow Gen(1^n)$ (that is, chosen uniformly at random).

2. The encryption algorithm *Enc* takes as input a key k and a plaintext message m and outputs a ciphertext $c \leftarrow Enc_k(m)$.

3. The decryption algorithm *Dec* takes as input a key k and a ciphertext c and outputs a plaintext $m = Dec_k(c)$ where Dec is deterministic.

The definition of computationally-secure indistinguishable security will also be syntactically identical to that of perfect security except that we now parameterize the experiment by a security parameter n.

The eavesdropping indistinguishability experiment $PrivK_{\mathcal{A},\Pi}^{eav}(n)$

1. The adversary $\mathcal{A}$ is given input 1^n, and outputs a pair of messages m_0, m_1 of the same length.

2. The challenger generates a random key k by running $Gen(1^n)$, and chooses a random bit $b \leftarrow \{0, 1\}$.
   Then, a ciphertext $c \leftarrow Enc_k(m_b)$ is computed and given to $\mathcal{A}$. We call c the challenge ciphertext.

3. $\mathcal{A}$ outputs a bit b'.

4. The output of the experiment is defined to be 1 if $b = b'$ (In this case, $\mathcal{A}$ was right) and 0 otherwise. We write $PrivK_{\mathcal{A},\Pi}^{eav}(n) = 1$ if the output is 1 and in this case, we say that $\mathcal{A}$ succeeded in breaking the scheme Π.

The above states that an encryption scheme is secure if the success probability of any PPT adversary in the above experiment is at most negligibly greater than $1/2$.

Definition 2 *A private-key encryption scheme Π = (Gen, Enc, Dec) has* **indistinguishable security (exactly speaking, indistinguishable encryptions) in the presence of an eavesdropper** *if for all probabilistic polynomial-time adversaries $\mathcal{A}$, there exists a negligible function negl such that*

$$Pr[PrivK_{\mathcal{A},\Pi}^{eav} = 1] \leq \frac{1}{2} + negl(n), \tag{3.1}$$

where the probability is taken over the random coins used by $\mathcal{A}$ as well as the random coins used in the experiment (that is, the choice of m and the key k, any random coins used in the encryption process).

Note that in the above definition, computational restrictions (e.g., probabilistic polynomial time adversary $\mathcal{A}$) are placed on the adversary.

An equivalent way of formalizing the definition is to state that every adversary *behaves the same way* whether it sees an encryption of m_0 or an encryption of m_1. Since $\mathcal{A}$ outputs a single bit, "behaving the same way" means that it outputs 1 with almost the same probability in each case. The following definition essentially states that $\mathcal{A}$ cannot determine whether it is running experiment $PrivK_{\mathcal{A},\Pi}^{eav}(n,0)$ or experiment $PrivK_{\mathcal{A},\Pi}^{eav}(n,1)$.

Definition 3 *A private-key encryption scheme* $\Pi = (Gen, Enc, Dec)$ *has* **indistinguishable security in the presence of an eavesdropper** *if for all probabilistic polynomial-time adversaries $\mathcal{A}$, there exists a negligible function negl such that*

$$Pr[output(PrivK_{\mathcal{A},\Pi}^{eav}(n,0)) = 1] - Pr[output(PrivK_{\mathcal{A},\Pi}^{eav}(n,1)) = 1] \leq negl(n). \tag{3.2}$$

3.2 Pseudorandomness

We introduce the notion of pseudorandomness and define the basic cryptographic primitive of pseudorandom generator. Pseudorandom functions and permutations are introduced in Chapter 4.

Pseudorandomness refers to a distribution on strings. When $\mathcal{D}$ over strings of length l is indistinguishable from the uniform distribution over strings of length l, $\mathcal{D}$ is called pseudorandom (Strictly speaking, $\mathcal{D} = \{D_n\}$ is a sequence of distribution, where D_n is associated with security parameter n in an asymptotic setting). A string sampled according to the uniform distribution is called a "random string," and a string sampled according to the pseudorandom distribution is called a "pseudorandom string." We can say that a pseudorandom string is a string that looks like a random (that is, uniformly distributed) string to a polynomial-time algorithm.

Usefulness Pseudorandomness is helpful in the construction of secure private-key encryption schemes. It is because if a ciphertext looks random, it is clear that no adversary can learn any information from it about the plaintext. The one-time pad works by computing the XOR of a random string (the key) with the plaintext. If a pseudorandom string were used instead, this should not make any noticeable difference to a polynomial-time observer.

Pseudorandom generator A pseudorandom generator is a deterministic algorithm that receives a short truly random seed of length n and stretches (amplifies) it into a long (e.g., a polynomial function $l(n)$) pseudorandom string in a way that attackers can't tell whether the expanded randomness is amplified from some seed or true randomness. Here, n should be long enough so that it is infeasible to try all possible seeds.

Similarly to the previous indistinguishable security, the definition of pseudorandom can be formalized by requiring that every polynomial-time algorithm outputs (interpreted as the algorithm's "guess") 1 with almost the same probability when given a truly random string and when given a pseudorandom one.

Definition 4 *Let $l(\cdot)$ be a polynomial and let G be a deterministic polynomial time algorithm such that for any input $s \in \{0,1\}^n$, algorithm G outputs a string of length $l(n)$ ($l(n)$ is called the expansion factor of G, i.e., $|G(s)| = l(|s|)$). We say that G is a **pseudorandom generator** if the following two conditions hold.*

1. *(Expansion) For every n, it holds that $l(n) > n$.*

2. *(Pseudorandomness) For all probabilistic polynomial-time distinguishers D, there exists a negligible function negl such that*

$$|Pr[D(r) = 1] - Pr[D(G(s)) = 1]| \leq negl(n), \qquad (3.3)$$

where r is chosen uniformly at random from $\{0,1\}^{l(n)}$, the seed s is chosen uniformly at random from $\{0,1\}^n$, and the probabilities are taken over the random coins used by D and the choice of r and s.

Existence of pseudorandom generators We do not know how to prove the existence of pseudorandom generators. Nevertheless, we believe that pseudorandom generators exist, based on the fact that they can be constructed under the assumption that one-way functions (that is, easy to compute, but hard to invert) exist [57]. Some candidates of one-way functions (e.g., factorization, subset-sum, discrete log, etc.) have been known, but we cannot prove that they are one-way functions. We just believe so.

3.3 A Private-Key Encryption Scheme Based on Pseudorandom Generator

The encryption scheme to construct now is very similar to the one-time pad encryption scheme, except that a pseudorandom string is used as the "pad" rather than a random string. Since a pseudorandom string "looks random" to any polynomial-time adversary, the encryption scheme can be proven to be computationally secure.

Construction 1. A private-key encryption scheme Π from any pseudorandom generator

1. Let G be a pseudorandom generator with expansion factor l.

2. Define a private-key encryption scheme for messages of length $l(n)$ as follows.

   (a) **Gen**: on input the security parameter 1^n, choose $k \leftarrow \{0,1\}^n$ uniformly at random and outputs it as the key.

   (b) **Enc**: on input a key $k \in \{0,1\}^n$ and a message $m \in \{0,1\}^{l(n)}$, output the ciphertext $c = G(k) \oplus m$.

   (c) **Dec**: on input a key $k \in \{0,1\}^n$ and a ciphertext $c \in \{0,1\}^{l(n)}$, output the plaintext message $m = G(k) \oplus c$.

Theorem 1 *If G is a pseudorandom generator, then Construction 1 is a private-key encryption scheme that has indistinguishable security (i.e., indistinguishable encryptions) in the presence of an eavesdropper (i.e., ciphertext only attack).*

Outline of the Proof The proof is based on the "proof by reduction" technique introduced earlier.

1. Define an alternate encryption scheme (e.g., ideal encryption scheme such as one-time pad).

2. Show that any attacker has at most negligible success probability in breaking the original scheme by leading to contradiction with the presumed assumption.

Proof
Intuition We show that if there exists a probabilistic polynomial-time adversary $\mathcal{A}$ for which the indistinguishable security does not hold, then we can construct a probabilistic polynomial-time algorithm that distinguishes the output of G from a truly random string, which contracts the assumption that G is a pseudorandom generator.

Outline 1 We define a modified encryption scheme $\widetilde{\Pi} = (\widetilde{Gen}, \widetilde{Enc}, \widetilde{Dec})$ that is exactly OTP, except that we now incorporate a security parameter that determines the length of the messages to be encrypted. By the perfect security of OTP, we have that

$$Pr[PrivK_{\mathcal{A},\tilde{\Pi}}^{eav} = 1] = \frac{1}{2}. \tag{3.4}$$

Outline 2 We show that any attacker has at most negligible success probability in breaking the original scheme as follows. Let $\mathcal{A}$ be a probabilistic polynomial-time adversary with success probability $\epsilon(n)$ in breaking the original scheme as

$$Pr[PrivK_{\mathcal{A},\Pi}^{eav}(n) = 1] = \frac{1}{2} + \epsilon(n). \tag{3.5}$$

We use $\mathcal{A}$ to construct a distinguisher D for the pseudorandom generator G such that D "succeeds" with probability $\epsilon(n)$. The distinguisher is given a string w as input, and its goal is to determine whether w was a "random string" or "pseudorandom string." D emulates the eavesdropping experiment for $\mathcal{A}$ in the manner described below and guesses that w must be a pseudorandom string if $\mathcal{A}$ succeeds, or a random string otherwise.

Distinguisher D

1. D is given as input a string $w \in \{0,1\}^{l(n)}$.

2. Run $\mathcal{A}(1^n)$ to obtain a pair of messages $m_0, m_1 \in \{0,1\}^{l(n)}$.

3. Choose a random bit $b \leftarrow \{0,1\}$. Set $c = w \oplus m_b$.

4. Give c to $\mathcal{A}$ and obtain output b' from $\mathcal{A}$.

5. Output "1" ("It's a pseudorandom string") if $b' = b$ ($\mathcal{A}$ was right), and output "0" ("It's a random string") otherwise.

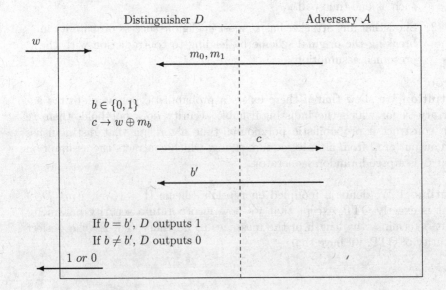

In analyzing D, let us consider the two possibilities for the input string w as follows.

Case I: w is a truly random string.
The view of $\mathcal{A}$ when run as a sub-routine by D is distributed identically to the view of $\mathcal{A}$ in experiment $PrivK_{\mathcal{A},\tilde{\Pi}}^{eav}(n)$. This is because $\mathcal{A}$ is given a ciphertext $c = w \oplus m_b$ where $w \in \{0,1\}^{l(n)}$ is a completely random string. It therefore follows that for $w \in \{0,1\}^{l(n)}$ chosen uniformly at random,

$$Pr[D(w) = 1] = Pr[PrivK_{\mathcal{A},\tilde{\Pi}}^{eav} = 1] = \frac{1}{2}, \qquad (3.6)$$

where the second equality follows from Equation (3.4).

Case II: w is a pseudorandom string.
The view of $\mathcal{A}$ when run as a sub-routine by D is distributed identically to the view of $\mathcal{A}$ in experiment $PrivK_{\mathcal{A},\Pi}^{eav}(n)$. This is because $\mathcal{A}$ is given a ciphertext $c = w \oplus m_b$ where $w = G(k)$ for a uniformly distributed value $k \leftarrow \{0,1\}^n$. Therefore, when $w = G(k)$ for $k \leftarrow \{0,1\}^n$ chosen uniformly at random, we have

$$Pr[D(w) = 1] = Pr[D(G(k)) = 1] = Pr[PrivK_{\mathcal{A},\Pi}^{eav} = 1] = \frac{1}{2} + \epsilon(n), \quad (3.7)$$

where the third equality follows from Equation (3.5).

Finally it remains to show that if we assume that $\epsilon(n)$ is non-negligible, then it leads to a contradiction as follows. By combining Equations (3.6) and (3.7), we get

$$|Pr[D(w) = 1] - Pr[D(G(k)) = 1]| = \epsilon(n). \qquad (3.8)$$

Let's suppose that $\epsilon(n)$ is non-negligible, which contradicts the assumption that G is a pseudorandom generator. Therefore, it must be the case that $\epsilon(n)$ should negligible, which implies that Π has indistinguishable security in the presence of an eavesdropper. $\square$

Exercises

3.1 Why do we introduce alternate schemes in security proof methodologies?

3.2 Why do we simulate? What are we going to model through simulation? Do we always need to simulate?

3.3 Why is perfect or close perfect simulation important? What is the exact meaning of the word "close"?

3.4 Give the attack scenario in the real world corresponding to the attacker abilities as follows: (a) Ciphertext-only attack, (b) Chosen-plaintext attack, and (c) Chosen-ciphertext attack

3.5 If you are modeling the security for a private key encryption scheme used by SSL/TLS, what should the attacker's ability be for the Denial of Service attack on SSL/TLS? Justify your answer.

4

Private-Key Encryption (2)

CONTENTS

The chapter provides further details about the private-key encryption schemes. The first part is about the construction of a stream cipher that generates the stream. In the next part, we consider two stronger security notions, multiple encryption, and chosen plaintext attack. In defining the first security notion, we modify the security goal from single-message encryption distinguishability to multiple-message encryption distinguishability. For the second, we strengthen the attack model from ciphertext only attack to chosen plaintext attack. After defining the security notions, we introduce a construction of CPA secure encryption scheme based on the pseudorandom function. Lastly, as a representative block cipher, we introduce the overall design and detailed components in AES.

4.1 Stream Ciphers

The term "stream cipher" refers to the algorithm that generates the stream (e.g., the pseudorandom generator G_l as shown below) or to the entire encryption scheme (e.g., Construction 1 in Chapter 3) instantiated with a pseudorandom generator. In the first case, a stream cipher is not an encryption scheme per se, but rather a tool for constructing encryption schemes as shown in Algorithm 1.

We view a stream cipher as a pair of deterministic algorithms (Init, GetBits) where,

1. Init takes as input a seed s and an optional *initialization vector IV*, and outputs an initial state st_0.

2. GetBits takes as input state information st_{i-1}, and outputs a bit y and updated state st_i. (In practice, y is a *block* of several bits; we treat y as a single bit here for generality and simplicity.)

Given a stream cipher and any desired expansion factor ℓ, we can define an algorithm G_ℓ mapping inputs of length n to outputs of length $\ell(n)$. The algorithm simply runs Init, and then repeatedly runs GetBits a total of $\ell(n)$ times.

Algorithm G_l

1. Take seed s and optional initialization vector IV as input.

2. $st_0 = \mathsf{Init}(s, IV)$.

3. **for** $i = 1$ to $\ell(n)$
   $(y_i, st_i) = \mathsf{GetBits}(st_{i-1})$.

4. Output $y_1, \ldots, y_{\ell(n)}$.

Stream ciphers are typically extraordinarily fast compared to block ciphers which encrypt a block of data. However, the securities of most stream ciphers including RC4 [3] and LFSR [71] are not yet well established except for one-time pad.

4.2   Stronger Security Notions

Until now we have considered a relatively weak notion of security in which the adversary only passively eavesdrops on a single ciphertext. In this section, we consider two stronger security notions. Recall that a security definition specifies a security goal and an attack model. In defining the first new security notion, we modify the security goal (i.e., from single-message encryption distinguishability to multiple-message encryption distinguishability); for the second we strengthen the attack model (i.e., from ciphertext only attack to chosen-plaintext attack).

4.2.1   Security for Multiple Encryptions

In Chapter 3, we have dealt with the case that the adversary receives a single ciphertext. In the real world, however, we usually use multiple ciphertexts so that we need to extend the security goal from single-message encryption distinguishability to multiple-message encryption distinguishability. The following experiment incorporates this extension by replacing a pair of message and ciphertext with a vector of messages and ciphertexts, respectively.

The multiple-message eavesdropping experiment $PrivK_{\mathcal{A},\Pi}^{mult}(n)$

1. The adversary $\mathcal{A}$ is given input 1^n and outputs a pair of equal-length lists of messages
   $\overrightarrow{M_0}=(m_{0,1},\ldots,m_{0,t})$ and $\overrightarrow{M_1}=(m_{1,1},\ldots,m_{1,t})$, with $|m_{0,i}| = |m_{1,i}|$ for all i.

2. A key k is generated by running $\mathsf{Gen}(1^n)$ and a uniform bit $b \in \{0,1\}$ is chosen. For all i, the ciphertext $c_i \longleftarrow \mathsf{Enc}_k(m_b, i)$ is computed and the list $\overrightarrow{C}=(c_1,\ldots,c_t)$ is given to $\mathcal{A}$.

3. $\mathcal{A}$ outputs a bit b'.

4. The output of the experiment is defined to be 1 if $b' = b$, and 0 otherwise.

The definition of security for multiple messages is the same as before, except that it now refers to the above experiment.

Definition 1 *A private-key encryption scheme* $\Pi =(\mathsf{Gen},\mathsf{Enc},\mathsf{Dec})$ *has* **indistinguishable multiple encryptions in the presence of an eavesdropper** *if for all probabilistic polynomial-time adversaries* $\mathcal{A}$ *there is a negligible function negl such that*

$$P_r[PrivK_{\mathcal{A},\Pi}^{mult}(n) = 1] \leq \frac{1}{2} + negl(n), \qquad (4.1)$$

where the probability is taken over the randomness used by $\mathcal{A}$ *and the randomness used in the experiment.*

Let us recall that Construction 1 in Chapter 3 is secure for a single encryption. However, we can easily presume that the mere knowledge that the same message has been re-sent can provide significant information, which can be useful to cryptanalysts as the following proposition shows. So we can obtain that *any* deterministic scheme including Construction 1 must be insecure for multiple encryptions. Therefore, we need probabilistic encryption rather than deterministic encryption.

Proposition 1 *There is a private-key encryption scheme that has indistinguishable encryptions in the presence of an eavesdropper, but not indistin-*

guishable multiple encryptions in the presence of an eavesdropper.

Theorem 1 *If* Π *is a stateless encryption scheme in which Enc is a deterministic function of the key and the message, then* Π *cannot have indistinguishable multiple encryptions in the presence of an eavesdropper.*

Proof is omitted.

We note that if the encryption scheme is stateful or randomized (which means that each encryption of a message may be different each time), then it is possible to securely encrypt multiple messages even if encryption itself is deterministic. Here *stateful* means that information (a variable such as a counter) stored in the memory is referenced whenever an algorithm is invoked.

4.2.2   Security for Chosen-Plaintext Attack

Until now we have considered a relatively weak adversary who only passively eavesdrops on the communication between two honest parties. Therefore, the previous definition of $PrivK^{eav}$ allows the adversary to choose the plaintexts that are to be encrypted. In this section, we introduce a more powerful type of adversarial attack, called chosen-plaintext attack (CPA), where the adversary is allowed to ask for encryptions of multiple messages chosen *adaptively*.

Example To help understand the concept of chosen-plaintext attack, we start with an example in the real world. In May 1942, US Navy cryptanalysts intercepted an encrypted message from the Japanese which they were able to partially decode. The result indicated that the Japanese were planning an attack on AF, where AF was a ciphertext fragment that the US was unable to decode. For other reasons, the US believed that Midway Island was the target. The Navy cryptanalysts instructed US forces at Midway to send a fake message that their freshwater supplies were low. The Japanese intercepted this message and immediately reported to their superiors that "AF is low on water." The Navy cryptanalysts now had their proof that AF corresponded to Midway.

CPA-security In the formal definition we model chosen-plaintext attacks by giving the adversary $\mathcal{A}$ access to an *encryption oracle*, viewed as a "black box" that encrypts messages of $\mathcal{A}$'s choice using a key k unknown to $\mathcal{A}$. That is, we imagine $\mathcal{A}$ has access to an "oracle" $Enc_k(\cdot)$; when $\mathcal{A}$ queries this oracle by providing it with a message m as input, the oracle returns a ciphertext $c \leftarrow Enc_k(\cdot)$ as the reply. The adversary is allowed to interact with the encryption oracle adaptively as many times as it likes.

The CPA indistinguishability experiment $PrivK_{\mathcal{A},\Pi}^{cpa}(n)$

1. A key k is generated by running $Gen(1^n)$.
2. The adversary $\mathcal{A}$ is given input 1^n and oracle access to $Enc_k(\cdot)$, and outputs a pair of messages m_0, m_1 of the same length.
3. A uniform bit $b \leftarrow \{0,1\}$ is chosen and then a ciphertext $c \leftarrow Enc_k(m_b)$ is computed and given to $\mathcal{A}$.
4. The adversary $\mathcal{A}$ continues to have oracle access to $Enc_k(\cdot)$, and outputs a bit b'.
5. The output of the experiment is defined to be 1 if $b = b'$ (In this case, we say that $\mathcal{A}$ succeeds) and 0 otherwise.

The above experiment can also be described as follows:

1. Challenger runs Gen.
2. (Query Phase) Adversary is given access to an oracle $Enc_k(\cdot)$.
3. (Challenger Phase) Adversary produces two messages m_0 and m_1. The challenger returns the challenge ciphertext $c = Enc_k(m_b)$.
4. Adversary outputs b'.

We define the advantage of an adversary $\mathcal{A}$ in the IND-CPA security game to be $Adv_{\mathcal{A}} = Pr[b' = b] - \frac{1}{2}$. We say that an encryption scheme is IND-CPA secure if for any polynomial time adversary $\mathcal{A}$, $Adv_{\mathcal{A}} = negl(n)$.

Definition 2 *A private-key encryption scheme* Π = *(Gen, Enc, Dec) has* **indistinguishable security (or encryption) under a chosen-plaintext attack,** *or is CPA-secure, if for all probabilistic polynomial-time adversaries* $\mathcal{A}$*, there exists a negligible function negl such that*

$$Pr[PrivK_{\mathcal{A},\Pi}^{cpa} = 1] \leq \frac{1}{2} + negl(n), \tag{4.2}$$

where the probability is taken over the randomness used by $\mathcal{A}$*, as well as the randomness used in the experiment.*

CPA-security for multiple encryptions The above definition can be extended to the case of multiple encryptions by using lists of plaintexts. In this definition, we give the attacker access to a "left-or-right" oracle $LR_{k,b}$ that, on input a pair of equal-length messages m_0, m_1, computes the ciphertext $c \leftarrow Enc_k(\cdot)$ and returns c. That is, if $b = 0$ then the adversary receives an encryption of the "left" plaintext, and if $b = 1$ then the adversary receives an encryption of the "right" plaintext. Here, b is a random bit chosen at the beginning of the experiment, and as in previous definitions the goal of the attacker is to guess b. Now we formally define this experiment, called the LR-oracle experiment.

The LR-oracle experiment $PrivK_{\mathcal{A},\Pi}{}^{LR-cpa}(n)$

1. A key k is generated by running $Gen(1^n)$.
2. A uniform bit $b \leftarrow \{0,1\}$ is chosen.
3. The adversary $\mathcal{A}$ is given input 1^n and oracle access to $LR_{k,b}(\cdot,\cdot)$. as defined above.
4. The adversary $\mathcal{A}$ outputs a bit b'.
5. The output of the experiment is defined to be 1 if $b = b'$ (In this case, we say that $\mathcal{A}$ succeeds) and 0 otherwise.

The L-oracle experiment $PrivK_{\mathcal{A},\Pi}{}^{L-cpa}(n)$

1. A key k is generated by running $Gen(1^n)$.
2. The adversary $\mathcal{A}$ is given input 1^n and oracle access to $LR_{k,0}(\cdot,\cdot)$. as defined above.
3. The adversary $\mathcal{A}$ outputs a bit b'.
4. The output of the experiment is defined to be b'

The R-oracle experiment $PrivK_{\mathcal{A},\Pi}{}^{R-cpa}(n)$

1. A key k is generated by running $Gen(1^n)$.
2. The adversary $\mathcal{A}$ is given input 1^n and oracle access to $LR_{k,1}(\cdot,\cdot)$ as defined above.
3. The adversary $\mathcal{A}$ outputs a bit b'.
4. The output of the experiment is defined to be b'

In the above L-oracle and R-oracle experiments, we define the advantage of an adversary $\mathcal{A}$ in the IND-CPA security game to be $Adv_{\mathcal{A}} = Pr[PrivK_{\mathcal{A},\Pi}^{\mathbf{R}-cpa} = 1] - Pr[PrivK_{\mathcal{A},\Pi}^{\mathbf{L}-cpa} = 1]$. We say that an encryption scheme is IND-CPA secure if for any polynomial time adversary $\mathcal{A}$, $Adv_{\mathcal{A}} = negl(n)$.

Definition 3 *A private-key encryption scheme* $\Pi = $ *(Gen, Enc, Dec) has* **indistinguishable multiple encryptions under a chosen-plaintext attack,** *or is CPA-secure for multiple encryptions, if for all probabilistic polynomial-time adversaries* $\mathcal{A}$, *there exists a negligible function negl such that*

$$Pr[PrivK_{\mathcal{A},\Pi}^{LR-cpa} = 1] \leq \frac{1}{2} + negl(n), \qquad (4.3)$$

where the probability is taken over the randomness used by $\mathcal{A}$, *as well as the randomness used in the experiment.*

In the following, we can find that the advantages of $\mathcal{A}$ in L-oracle and R-oracle experiments are equivalent to those of $\mathcal{A}$ in LR-oracle experiment as
$Adv_{\mathcal{A},\Pi}{}^{ind-cpa}(A)$
$= Pr[PrivK_{\mathcal{A},\Pi}^{\mathbf{R}-cpa} = 1] - Pr[PrivK_{\mathcal{A},\Pi}^{\mathbf{L}-cpa} = 1]$
$= Pr[b' = 1|b = 1] - Pr[b' = 1|b = 0]$
$= 2 \cdot (Pr[b' = 1|b = 1] \cdot \frac{1}{2} + (1 - Pr[b' = 1|b = 0]) \cdot \frac{1}{2}) - 1$
$= 2 \cdot (Pr[b' = 1|b = 1] \cdot \frac{1}{2} + Pr[b' = 0|b = 0] \cdot \frac{1}{2}) - 1$
$= 2 \cdot (Pr[b = b'|b = 1] \cdot \frac{1}{2} + Pr[b = b'|b = 0] \cdot \frac{1}{2}) - 1$
$= 2 \cdot (Pr[b = b'|b = 1] \cdot Pr[b = 1] + Pr[b = b'|b = 0] \cdot Pr[b = 0]) - 1$
$= 2 \cdot Pr[b = b'] - 1$
$= 2 \cdot Pr[PrivK_{\mathcal{A},\Pi}^{LR-cpa} = 1] - 1.$

If a private-key encryption scheme is CPA-secure for multiple encryptions, it is clearly CPA-secure for a single encryption as well. The converse also holds as follows.

Theorem 2 *A private-key encryption scheme that is CPA-secure a single encryption is also CPA-secure for multiple encryptions.*

Proof is omitted.

Fixed-length vs. arbitrary-length messages Given any CPA-secure fixed-length encryption scheme $\Pi = $ (Gen, Enc, Dec), it is possible to construct a CPA-secure encryption scheme $\Pi' = $ (Gen', Enc', Dec') for arbitrary-length messages quite easily, by defining for any message m of length l as $Enc_k'(m) = Enc_k(m_1) \| \cdots \| Enc_k(m_l)$, where m_i denotes the ith bit of m. Decryption is done in the natural way.

4.3   Constructing CPA-Secure Encryption Scheme

A random function can be thought of as a black box (meaning can only feed it inputs and get outputs without looking inside) which given any input returns a random number, except that if you give it the input you already gave before, it returns the same output as previously. Here we should be cautious that the randomness of the function refers to the way it was chosen from the function family, not to an attribute of the selected function itself: it does not talk out the randomness of an individual function.

A keyed function $F : \{0,1\}^* \times \{0,1\}^* \to \{0,1\}^*$ is a two-input function, where the first input is called the key and denoted k (i.e., taking a key as well as an input). If k is chosen and fixed, the single-input function $F : \{0,1\}^* \to \{0,1\}^*$ is defined by $F_k(x) = F(k,x)$.

In the following, we assume that the key, input, and output lengths of F are all the same as n, called *length-preserving* functions. In this case, we also denote F as $Func_n$ meaning the set of all functions mapping n-bit strings to n-bit strings. We want to construct a keyed function F such that F_k ($k \leftarrow \{0,1\}^n$ chosen uniformly at random) is indistinguishable from f ($f \leftarrow Func_n$ chosen uniformly at random). Note that the former is chosen from a distribution over (at most) 2^n distinct functions, whereas the latter is chosen from a distribution over all $2^{2^n \cdot n}$ functions in $Func_n$. Despite this, when the "behaviors" of these functions look the same to any polynomial-time distinguisher, whether it is interacting with F_k or f (Intuitively we can interpret this as follows: since the two spaces have exponential numbers of elements, the selection behavior looks the same to the polynomially bounded adversary), we call F *pseudorandom function*.

Definition 4 *Let $F : \{0,1\}^* \times \{0,1\}^* \to \{0,1\}^*$ be an efficient, length-preserving, keyed function. F is a* **pseudorandom function** *if for all probabilistic polynomial-time distinguishers D, there is a negligible function negl such that*

$$|P_r[D^{F_k(\cdot)}(1^n) = 1] - P_r[D^{f(\cdot)}(1^n) = 1]| \leq negl(n), \qquad (4.4)$$

where the first probability is taken over uniform choice of $k \in \{0,1\}^n$ and the randomness of D, and the second probability is taken over uniform choice of $f \in Func_n$ (the set of all functions mapping n-bit strings to n-bit strings) and the randomness of D.

Note that the distinguisher D is not given the key k. Once k is revealed to D, all claims to the pseudorandomness of F_k no longer hold. The pseudorandom function generator is shown in Figure 4.1.

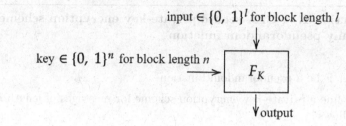

FIGURE 4.1
Pseudorandom function.

It is known that pseudorandom functions exist if and only if pseudorandom generators exist [52]. A pseudorandom function is used to construct CPA-secure encryption which will be shown below and message authentication codes later.

A permutation is a function whose domain and range are the same set D, and the function is a length-preserving (i.e., $|f(x)| = |x|$ for all $x \in D$) bijection (i.e., one-to-one and onto) on the set. Therefore, we can say that a pseudorandom permutation is a kind of pseudorandom function.

If F_k should be used in an encryption scheme, honest parties should be able to compute the inverse F_k^{-1} as well as F_k. Therefore, we need to impose the stronger requirement that F_k should be indistinguishable from a random permutation even if the distinguisher is given oracle access to the inverse of the permutation as shown in the following definition.

Definition 5 *Let $F : \{0,1\}^* \times \{0,1\}^* \to \{0,1\}^*$ be an efficient, length-preserving, keyed function. F is a* **strong pseudorandom permutation** *if for all probabilistic polynomial-time distinguishers D, there exist a negligible function negl such that*

$$|P_r[D^{F_k(\cdot),F_k^{-1}(\cdot)}(1^n) = 1] - P_r[D^{f(\cdot),f^{-1}(\cdot)}(1^n) = 1]| \leq negl(n), \qquad (4.5)$$

where the first probability is taken over uniform choice of $k \in \{0,1\}^n$ and the randomness of D, and the second probability is taken over uniform choice of $f \in \mathrm{Perm}_n$ (the set of all permutations mapping n-bit strings to n-bit strings) and the randomness of D.

As noted earlier, a stream cipher can be modeled as a pseudorandom generator, while a block cipher can be modeled as a strong pseudorandom permutation.

Construction 1. A CPA-secure private-key encryption scheme Π from any pseudorandom function

1. Let F be a pseudorandom function.

2. Define a private-key encryption scheme for messages of length n as follows.

   (a) **Gen:** on input the security parameter 1^n, choose $k \leftarrow \{0,1\}^n$ uniformly at random and outputs it as the key.

   (b) **Enc:** on input a key $k \in \{0,1\}^n$ and a message $m \in \{0,1\}^n$, choose $r \leftarrow \{0,1\}^n$ uniformly at random and output the ciphertext $c = \langle r, F_k(r) \oplus m \rangle$.

   (c) **Dec:** on input a key $k \in \{0,1\}^n$ and a ciphertext $c = \langle r, s \rangle$, output the plaintext message $m = F_k(r) \oplus s$.

Theorem 3 *If F is a pseudorandom function, then Construction 1 is a CPA-secure private-key encryption scheme for messages of length n.*

Proof
Outline of the Proof The proof is based on the "proof by reduction" technique introduced earlier.

1. Define an alternate encryption scheme (e.g., Random Function Encryption)

2. Show that any attacker has at most negligible success probability in breaking the original scheme.

Intuition Security holds because $F_k(r)$ looks completely random to an adversary who observes a ciphertext $\langle r, s \rangle$ and thus the encryption scheme is similar to the one-time pad as long as the value r was not used in some previous encryption. Moreover, this "bad event" (namely, a repeating value of r) occurs with only negligible probability.

Outline 1 We define a modified encryption scheme $\widetilde{\Pi} = (\widetilde{Gen}, \widetilde{Enc}, \widetilde{Dec})$ that is exactly the same as $\Pi = (Gen, Enc, Dec)$, except that a truly random function f is used in place of F_k.

We claim that for every adversary $\mathcal{A}$ that make at most $q(n)$ queries to its encryption oracle, we have

$$Pr[PrivK^{cpa}_{\mathcal{A},\widetilde{\Pi}} = 1] = \frac{1}{2} + \frac{q(n)}{2^n}. \tag{4.6}$$

Let r_* denote the random string used when generating the challenge ciphertext $c^* = (r_*, f(r_*) \oplus m_b)$. There are two interactive phases in the random function game that we consider, the Query Phase and the Challenge Phase.

Query Phase: $r_1, r_2, ..., r_Q$, where $c_i = \langle r_i, f(r_i) \oplus m_i \rangle$
Challenge Phase: $c^* = \langle r_*, f(r_*) \oplus m_b \rangle$

Now we consider two subcases:
Case I (Bad) The value r_* is used by the encryption oracle to answer at least one of $\mathcal{A}$'s queries:
$\mathcal{A}$ may easily determine which of its messages was encrypted because it learns the value of $f(r)$ (since $f(r) = s \oplus m$). Since $\mathcal{A}$ makes at most $q(n)$ queries to its oracle and each oracle query is answered using a value r chosen uniformly at random, the probability of this event is at most $q(n)/2^n$.
Case II (Good) The value r_* is never used by the encryption oracle to answer any of $\mathcal{A}$'s queries:
$\mathcal{A}$ learns nothing about the value of $f(r_c)$ (since f is a truly random function). Since $f(r_*)$ that is XORed with m_b is completely random, the probability that $\mathcal{A}$ outputs $b' = b$ is exactly $1/2$ (as in the case of one-time pad).

$$Pr[PrivK^{cpa}_{\mathcal{A},\tilde{\Pi}} = 1] = Pr[PrivK^{cpa}_{\mathcal{A},\tilde{\Pi}} = 1|CaseI] \cdot Pr[CaseI] +$$
$$Pr[PrivK^{cpa}_{\mathcal{A},\tilde{\Pi}} = 1|CaseII] \cdot Pr[CaseII]$$
$$\leq 1 \cdot \frac{q(n)}{2^n} + \frac{1}{2} \cdot 1 \text{ (in the worst case)}.$$

Outline 2 We show that any attacker has at most negligible success probability in breaking the original scheme as follows. Let $\mathcal{A}$ be a probabilistic polynomial-time adversary with success probability $\epsilon(n)$ in breaking the original scheme as

$$Pr[PrivK^{cpa}_{\mathcal{A},\Pi}(n) = 1] = \frac{1}{2} + \epsilon(n). \tag{4.7}$$

We use $\mathcal{A}$ to construct a distinguisher D for the random function F such that D "succeeds" with probability $\epsilon(n)$. Now it remains to show that $\epsilon(n)$ is negligible.

The distinguisher is given oracle access to some function, and its goal is to determine whether this function is a "random" or "pseudorandom." To do this, D emulates the CPA indistinguishability experiment for $\mathcal{A}$ in the manner described below and observes whether $\mathcal{A}$ succeeds or not. If $\mathcal{A}$ succeeds then D guesses that its oracle must be a pseudorandom function, while if $\mathcal{A}$ does not succeed then D guesses that its oracle must be a random function.

Distinguisher D

1. D has oracle access to $\mathcal{O}$ either a PRF or a RF.

2. D "starts" $\mathcal{A}$.

3. $\mathcal{A}$ asks for the encryption of messages $m_1, m_2, ..., m_{q(n)}$.

4. For each m_i, D chooses $r_i \in \{0,1\}^n$ and set $c_i = \langle r_i, \mathcal{O}(r_i) \oplus m_i \rangle$.

5. $\mathcal{A}$ gives m_0, m_1.

6. D picks a random bit $b \in \{0,1\}$ and $r_* \in \{0,1\}^k$ and sends the challenge ciphertext $c^* = \langle r_*, \mathcal{O}(r_*) \oplus m_b \rangle$ to $\mathcal{A}$.

7. Repeat the query phase from Step 3.

8. D gets guess b' from $\mathcal{A}$.

9. D outputs "1" ("It's a PRF") if $b' = b$ ($\mathcal{A}$ was right), and outputs "0" ("It's a RF") otherwise.

In analyzing D, let us consider the two possibilities for D's oracle as follows:

Case I: D's oracle is a PRF.
The view of $\mathcal{A}$ when run as a sub-routine by D is distributed identically to the view of $\mathcal{A}$ in experiment $PrivK^{cpa}_{\mathcal{A},\Pi}(n)$. This holds because a key k is chosen at random and then every encryption is carried out by choosing a random r, computing $s' = F_k(r)$, and setting the ciphertext equal to $\langle r, s' \oplus m \rangle$, exactly as in Construction 1. Thus

$$Pr[D^{F_k(\cdot)}(1^n) = 1] = Pr[PrivK^{cpa}_{\mathcal{A},\Pi} = 1], \tag{4.8}$$

where $k \leftarrow \{0,1\}^n$ is chosen uniformly at random in the above.

Case II: D's oracle is a RF.
The view of $\mathcal{A}$ when run as a sub-routine by D is distributed identically to the view of $\mathcal{A}$ in experiment $PrivK^{cpa}_{\mathcal{A},\widetilde{\Pi}}(n)$. This can be seen exactly as above, with the only difference being that a random function f is used instead of F_k. Thus,

$$Pr[D^{f(\cdot)}(1^n) = 1] = Pr[PrivK^{cpa}_{\mathcal{A},\widetilde{\Pi}} = 1], \tag{4.9}$$

where $f \leftarrow Func_n$ is chosen uniformly with.

By combining Equations (4.6) and (4.7), we get

$$|Pr[D^{F_k(\cdot),F_k^{-1}(\cdot)}(1^n) = 1] - Pr[D^{f(\cdot),f^{-1}(\cdot)}(1^n) = 1]| \geq \epsilon(n) - \frac{q(n)}{2^n}. \tag{4.10}$$

By the assumption that F is a pseudorandom function, it follows that $\epsilon(n) -$

$\frac{q(n)}{2^n}$ must be negligible. Since q is polynomial, this in turn implies that $\epsilon(n)$ is negligible, and Π is CPA-secure. $\square$

4.4 Advanced Encryption Standard

The Advanced Encryption Standard (AES) is a specification for block cipher standardized by NIST in 2001 [93]. As Figure 4.2 shows, AES processes data blocks of 128 bits using a different key size (128, 192, or 256 bits), which depends on the number of rounds (10, 12, or 14). But the round keys are always 128 bits. The key expansion routine takes the input cipher key and generates a key schedule, e.g., a total of 44 words in the case of 128-bit cipher key.

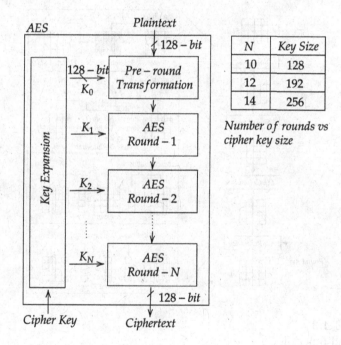

N	Key Size
10	128
12	192
14	256

Number of rounds vs cipher key size

FIGURE 4.2
Design of AES encryption cipher.

As Figure 4.3 shows, all round functions consist of four types of transformations such as SubBytes(), ShiftRows(), MixColumns(), and AddRoundKey(), except for the final round, which does not include the MixColumns() transformation. Individual transformations comprising the round function process on a 4 × 4 array of bytes called the state:

1. SubBytes(): a non-linear substitution step where each byte is re-placed with another using an 8-bit substitution box (S-box) (the substitution value would be determined by the intersection of the row with index of left 4 bits of an input byte and the column with index of right 4 bits of an input byte)

2. ShiftRows(): a permutation step where the last three rows of the state are shifted cyclically depending on the row number of the state matrix

3. MixColumns(): a mixing operation where each column of the state is transformed to a new column by multiplying the column with a constant matrix

4. AddRoundKey(): a key-adding operation where a round key is added to each column of the state using an XOR operation

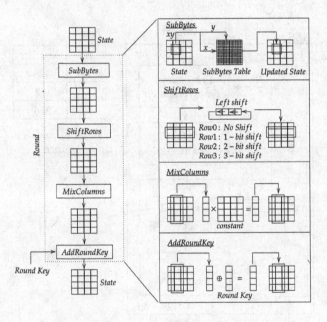

FIGURE 4.3
AES round function.

The round function is parameterized using a key schedule that consists of a one-dimensional array of four-byte words W derived using the key expansion routine. These four-byte words are fed to AddRoundKey. The above transformations can be inverted like InvSubBytes(), InvShiftRows(), InvMix-Columns(), and AddRoundKey(), respectively, and then implemented in reverse order to produce a straightforward decryption algorithm for the AES algorithm as shown in Figure 4.4.

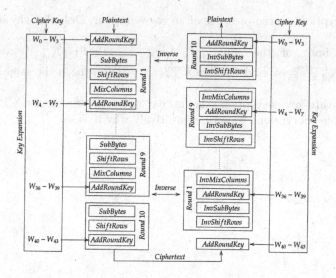

FIGURE 4.4
Overall design of AES.

Exercises

4.1 Why should the success probability of an adversary be half in security experiment? What will happen in case of 1 and 0 probability? Which is better notion of security?

1. A scheme with $\frac{1}{2}$ (random guessing) success probability of adversary.

2. A scheme with 0 success probability of adversary.

4.2 Proposition 2 says that there exists a private-key encryption scheme that is COA (ciphertext-only attack) secure for a single encryption but not COA secure for multiple encryptions. Describe the reason behind it intuitively.

4.3 An encryption scheme that works by just computing $c = F_k(m)$, where F_k is a strong pseudo-random permutation, is not CPA-secure. Why not?

4.4 There is a private-key encryption scheme that has indistinguishable encryptions in the presence of an eavesdropper, but not indistinguishable multiple encryptions in the presence of an eavesdropper. Describe why it is.

4.5 Do both of the equations $Adv_A = Pr[PrivK_{A,\pi}^{R-cpa} = 1] - Pr[PrivK_{A,\pi}^{L-cpa} = 1]$ and $Pr[PrivK_{A,\pi}^{eav}(n) = 1] \leq \frac{1}{2}$ mean the same?

4.6 A private-key encryption scheme that is CPA-secure is also CPA-secure for multiple encryptions. Describe intuitively why it is so.

5

Private-Key Encryption (3)

CONTENTS

The private-key encryption schemes are further illustrated in this chapter. Block ciphers themselves are not secure encryption schemes, but rather building blocks to construct secure private-key encryption schemes. To achieve security, block ciphers are run in certain modes of operations including ECB, CBC, and CTR mode. It concludes that the ECB mode is not IND-CPA secure while CBC and CTR are IND-CPA secure. This is followed by a stronger security notion, i.e., security against a chosen ciphertext attack and some examples which are CPA-secure but not CCA-secure.

5.1   Block Ciphers and Modes of Operation

As with stream ciphers, block ciphers themselves are not secure encryption schemes. Rather, they are building blocks that can be used to construct secure encryption schemes. A block cipher enables partiefs with sharing K to encrypt a 1-block message. Then how do we build an encryption scheme that encrypts arbitrary-length message using a block cipher? The answer is to divide the entire message into multiple blocks and apply the block cipher blockwise. The issue is how to apply the block cipher so that the resulting encryption scheme can be secure. How to apply the block cipher to get an encryption scheme is referred to as modes of operation.

For all of the following modes, we will use the notation.

1. n: keysize
2. m: block length
3. $x[i]$: i-th n-bit block of a string x

As defined earlier, a private-key (*aka* symmetric) encryption scheme $\mathcal{SE} = (\mathcal{K}, \mathcal{E}, \mathcal{D})$ consists of three algorithms:

1. $\mathcal{K}$ is randomized.
2. $\mathcal{E}$ can be randomized (e.g., randomized IV) or stateful (e.g., counter).
3. $\mathcal{D}$ is deterministic.

If $\mathcal{E}$ can be randomized or stateful, then each encryption of a message may be different each time. If $\mathcal{D}$ is deterministic, it returns the same plaintext when the same key and ciphertext are given as input.

5.1.1 Electronic Code Book (ECB) Mode

The is the most naive mode of operation possible. The key generation algorithm simply returns a random key for the block cipher. The ciphertext block is obtained by encrypting each plaintext block separately. Plaintext block is obtained by decrypting each ciphertext block separately. Figure 5.1 shows the ECB mode of operation.

5.1.2 Cipher Block Chaining (CBC) Mode

There are two variants of CBC mode, one random and the other stateful (i.e., counter).

The key generation algorithm simply returns a random key for the block cipher. In the random version, a random initial vector (IV) of length n is first chosen. Then, each of the remaining ciphertext blocks is generated by applying the block cipher to the XOR of the current plaintext block and the

$$\mathcal{SE} = (\mathcal{K}, \mathcal{E}, \mathcal{D}) \text{ where}$$

$Alg \; \mathcal{E}_k(M)$	$Alg \; \mathcal{D}_k(C)$
$for \; i = 1, \ldots m$ do	$for \; i = 1, \ldots m$ do
$\quad C[i] \leftarrow E_k(M[i])$	$\quad M[i] \leftarrow E_k^{-1}(C[i])$
return C	return M

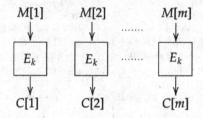

FIGURE 5.1
ECB mode.

previous ciphertext block. Note that the IV is sent in the clear (that is, $C[0]$) as part of the ciphertext. Figure 5.2 shows the CBC with random IV mode.

A drawback of this mode is that encryption and decryption must be carried out sequentially.

The following is CBC with counter mode. The $C[0]$ is IV, which is set to the current value of the counter. The counter is then incremented each time a message is encrypted.

$$\mathcal{SE} = (\mathcal{K}, \mathcal{E}, \mathcal{D}) \text{ where}$$

$Alg \; \mathcal{E}_k(M)$	$Alg \; \mathcal{D}_k(C)$
$C[0] \leftarrow \{0,1\}^n$	$for \; i = 1, \ldots m$ do
$for \; i = 1, \ldots m$ do	$\quad M[i] \leftarrow E_k^{-1}(C[i] \oplus C[i-1])$
$\quad C[i] \leftarrow E_k(M[i] \oplus C[i-1])$	return M
return C	

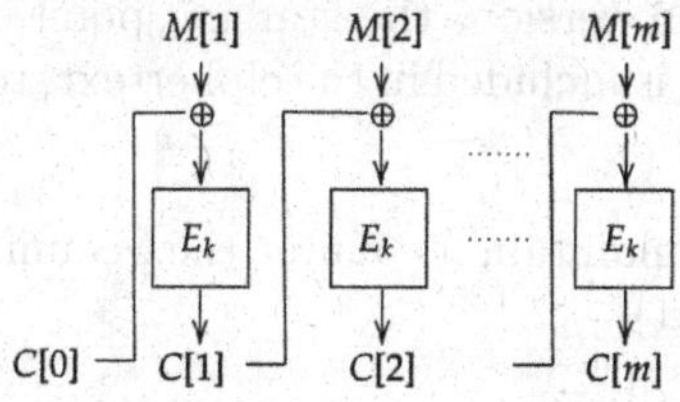

FIGURE 5.2
CBC with random IV mode.

5.1.3   Counter (CTR) Mode

There are two variants of CTR mode, one stateful (i.e., counter) and the other random. Figure 5.3 shows the counter mode.

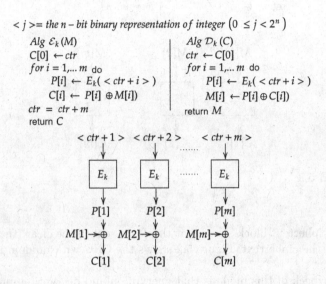

$< j >=$ *the n – bit binary representation of integer* $\left(0 \le j < 2^n\right)$

Alg $\mathcal{E}_k(M)$
$C[0] \leftarrow ctr$
for $i = 1,... m$ do
    $P[i] \leftarrow E_k(< ctr + i >)$
    $C[i] \leftarrow P[i] \oplus M[i])$
$ctr = ctr + m$
return C

Alg $\mathcal{D}_k(C)$
$ctr \leftarrow C[0]$
for $i = 1,... m$ do
    $P[i] \leftarrow E_k(< ctr + i >)$
    $M[i] \leftarrow P[i] \oplus C[i])$
return M

FIGURE 5.3
CTR mode.

The key generation algorithm simply returns a random key for the block cipher. In the stateful version, the encryptor maintains a counter ctr which is initially zero. Position index ctr is not allowed to wrap around: the encryption algorithm returns $\perp$ if this would happen. The position index is included in the ciphertext in order to enable decryption. The encryption algorithm updates the position index upon each invocation, and begins with this updated value the next time it is invoked.

Note that in the random version, the starting point R chosen randomly by the encryption algorithm is included in the ciphertext, to enable decryption.

1. Decryptor does not maintain a counter (i.e., counter is transmitted within the ciphertext).

2. $\mathcal{D}$ does not use E_K^{-1}!

3. Encryption is parallelizable, which can be exploited to speed up the process in the presence of hardware support.

5.2 CPA-Securities of Modes of Operation

How to show a cryptographic scheme is not secure against IND-CPA adversaries? It suffices to design (or construct) an adversary so that the adversary's IND-CPA advantage is close to 1.

5.2.1 IND-CPA Adversary

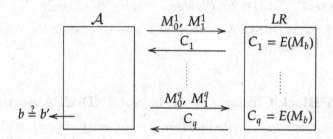

FIGURE 5.4
IND-CPA adversary.

Here we use left-or-right indistinguishability (initially introduced at CPA-Security for Multiple Encryptions in Chapter 3) under a chosen-plaintext attack. In the following, we will describe the CPA indistinguishability experiment and define the adversary's advantage in distinguishing encryptions of two arbitrary messages, as shown in Figure 5.4.

Let $\mathcal{SE} = (\mathcal{K}, \mathcal{E}, \mathcal{D})$ be an encryption scheme. An IND-CPA adversary $\mathcal{A}$ has an oracle LR.

1. It can make a query M_0, M_1 consisting of any two equal-length messages.

2. It can do this many times.

3. Each time it gets back a ciphertext.

4. It eventually outputs a bit.

Note that the adversary chooses the first pair, then receives C_1, then chooses the second pair, then receives C_2, and so on. LR is a kind of encryption oracle.

Now let us formulate the following game between an adversary and LR oracle (i.e., challenger). The adversary must complete the game and output a guess.

1. The LR oracle generates the symmetric key based on some security parameter during the initialization procedure.

2. The adversary performs polynomially bound number of encryptions.

3. The adversary then submits two distinct chosen plaintexts M_0 and M_1 to the LR oracle and repeats for q number of times.

4. The LR oracle sends the encryption result (i.e., the challenge ciphertext) of the message depending on the randomly chosen value $b \in \{0, 1\}$ back to the adversary.

5. The adversary outputs a guess b'. If $b' = b$ then the adversary wins.

The advantage is defined as

$$Adv_{\mathcal{SE}}{}^{ind-cpa}(A) = Pr[Right_{\mathcal{SE}}{}^{\mathcal{A}} = 1] - Pr[Left_{\mathcal{SE}}{}^{\mathcal{A}} = 1]. \qquad (5.1)$$

The scheme is IND-CPA secure if he is able to win the above game with probability $\frac{1}{2} + negl(n)$.

5.2.2   A Block Cipher *Per Se* Is Not IND-CPA Secure

We will construct an experiment where the adversary interacts with the LR oracle, and finally show that the adversary can distinguish encryptions of two arbitrary messages.

Let $\mathcal{SE} = (\mathcal{K}, \mathcal{E}, \mathcal{D})$ be a block cipher, which consists of key generation, encryption, and decryption algorithms, and provides a 128-bit block of the encrypted data. This scheme encrypts only one block of input message at a time. The adversary provides the messages M_0 and M_1 and receives a ciphertext C in each world. Note that two distinct input messages generates two distinct output messages because block ciphers are deterministic. We design the adversary so that if the two ciphertexts are equal, the adversary returns 1 and 0 otherwise. The advantage is calculated. If the two ciphertexts are not equal, then the adversary returns 0 and the probability that the adversary outputs 1 in the left world is 0. If the two ciphertexts are equal, then the adversary returns 1 and the probability that the adversary outputs 1 in the right world is 1. The chances of winning in this case is 1, hence the block cipher is not IND-CPA secure. The reason for this is that block ciphers are deterministic.

5.2.3   ECB Is Not IND-CPA Secure

The encryption process is deterministic and stateless, so that if the same message is encrypted twice, the same ciphertext is returned. We can show that this mode cannot possibly be CPA-secure. Even worse, ECB-mode encryption does not have indistinguishable encryption in the presence of an eavesdropper. ECB mode should therefore never be used.

By generalizing the case of ECB, we can get the following fact.

Proposition 1 *Any deterministic, stateless scheme is not IND-CPA secure.*

Proof is omitted.

5.2.4 CBC Is IND-CPA Secure

Theorem 1 *If E is a pseudorandom permutation, then CBC-mode encryption (random, counter version) is CPA-secure.*

Proof is omitted.

However, note if the *IV* is not random, this mode is not CPA-secure.

5.2.5 CTR Is IND-CPA Secure

Theorem 2 *If F is a pseudorandom permutation, then CTR-mode encryption (random, counter version) is CPA-secure.*

Proof This proof is for the random version of the CTR-mode encryption.
Outline of the Proof The proof is based on the "proof by reduction" technique introduced earlier.

1. Define an alternate encryption scheme (e.g., Random Function Encryption)
2. Show that any attacker has at most negligible success probability in breaking the original scheme.

Outline 1 Let $\Pi = (Gen, Enc, Dec)$ be the CTR mode encryption scheme, we define a modified encryption scheme $\widetilde{\Pi} = (\widetilde{Gen}, \widetilde{Enc}, \widetilde{Dec})$ that is identical to Π except that a truly random function f is used in place of F_k.

Outline 2 We show that any adversary has at most negligible success probability in breaking the original scheme, that is, there is $negl(n)$ such that

$$Pr[PrivK_{\mathcal{A},\Pi}^{cpa} = 1] \leq \frac{1}{2} + negl(n). \tag{5.2}$$

1. At the first step of the *Outline 2*, we claim that there is a negligible function $negl'(n)$ such that

$$Pr[PrivK_{\mathcal{A},\Pi}^{cpa} = 1] - Pr[PrivK_{\mathcal{A},\widetilde{\Pi}}^{cpa} = 1] \leq negl'(n). \tag{5.3}$$

This is proved by reduction in the similar way in the proof of Theorem 3 in Chapter 4.

2. At the second step, we next claim that

$$Pr[PrivK_{\mathcal{A},\widetilde{\Pi}}^{cpa} = 1] < \frac{1}{2} + \frac{2q(n)^2}{2^n}, \qquad (5.4)$$

where $q(n)$ is a polynomial upperbound on the number of encryption-oracle queries made by $\mathcal{A}(1^n)$ as well as the maximum number of blocks in any such query and the maximum number of blocks in m_0 and m_1.

We now prove this equation. Fix some value n for the security parameter.

Let $l^* \leq q(n)$ denote the length (in blocks) of the messages m_0, m_1 output by $\mathcal{A}$ in experiment $PrivK_{\mathcal{A},\widetilde{\Pi}}^{cpa}(n)$, ctr^* denote the initial value used when generating the challenge ciphertext, $l_i \leq q(n)$ be the length (in blocks) of the ith encryption-oracle query made by $\mathcal{A}$, and let ctr_i denote the initial value used when answering this query. When the ith encryption-oracle query is answered, f is applied to the values $\mathsf{ctr}_i + j$ with $(j \leq l_i)$. When the challenge ciphertext is encrypted, f is applied to the values $\mathsf{ctr}^* + j^*$ with $(j^* \leq l^*)$ and the ciphertext $c_i = f(\mathsf{ctr}^* + i) \oplus m_i$. There are two cases:

(a) There do not exist any $i, j, j^* \geq 1$ for which $\mathsf{ctr}_i + j = \mathsf{ctr}^* + j^*$, that is, the values $f(\mathsf{ctr}^* + j^*)$ used when encrypting the challenge ciphertext are uniformly distributed and independent of the rest of the experiment since f was not applied to any of these inputs when encrypting the adversary's oracle queries. In this case, the probability that $\mathcal{A}$ outputs $b' = b$ is exactly $1/2$ (as in the case of the one-time pad).

(b) There exists $i, j, j^* \geq 1$ for which $\mathsf{ctr}_i + j = \mathsf{ctr}^* + j^*$. We denote this event by $\mathsf{Overlap}$. The probability that $\mathsf{Overlap}$ occurs is maximized if $l_i = l^* = q(n)$ for all i. Let $\mathsf{Overlap}_i$ denote the event that the sequence $\mathsf{ctr}_i + j$ overlaps $\mathsf{ctr}^* + j^*$.

Fixing ctr^*, the event $\mathsf{Overlap}_i$ occurs exactly when ctr_i satisfies

$$\mathsf{ctr}^* + 1 - q(n) \leq \mathsf{ctr}_i \leq \mathsf{ctr}^* + q(n) - 1. \qquad (5.5)$$

Since ctr_i is chosen uniformly from $\{0,1\}^n$ and there are $2q(n) - 1$ values for ctr_i, we see that

$$Pr[\mathsf{Overlap}_i] = \frac{2q(n) - 1}{2^n} < \frac{2q(n)}{2^n}. \qquad (5.6)$$

Since there are most $q(n)$ oracle queries, a union bound gives

$$Pr[\text{Overlap}] = \sum_{i=1}^{q(n)} Pr[\text{Overlap}_i] < q(n) \times \frac{2q(n)}{2^n} = \frac{2q(n)^2}{2^n}.$$

(5.7)

Thus, we have the success probability of $\mathcal{A}$ in breaking the scheme $\widetilde{\Pi}$ as Equation 5.4.

3. Finally, by combining Equations 5.3 and 5.4 and , we get

$$Pr[PrivK_{\mathcal{A},\Pi}^{cpa} = 1] < \frac{1}{2} + \frac{2q(n)^2}{2^n} + negl'(n).$$

(5.8)

Since $q(n)$ is polynomial, then $\frac{2q(n)^2}{2^n} + negl'(n)$ is negligible. We conclude that the scheme Π is CPA-secure. $\square$

5.3 Security Against Chosen-Ciphertext Attack (CCA)

Until now we have considered CPA-security in which the adversary is allowed to ask for encryptions of multiple messages chosen adaptively. In this section, we consider a stronger security notion, chosen-ciphertext attack, where the adversary can inject his chosen messages into the communication stream between honest parties and also see how they are decrypted.

Example An ATM card contains a key $K \leftarrow \mathcal{K}$ known also to a bank, where $\mathcal{SE} = (\mathcal{K}, \mathcal{E}, \mathcal{D})$ is a symmetric encryption scheme. Adversary transmits Alice's identity, but how can the adversary answer the challenge (meaning decrypt C) without knowing Alice's key? The adversary tries to learn how to decrypt by creating ciphertexts and getting the card to decrypt them.

The CCA indistinguishability experiment $PrivK_{\mathcal{A},\Pi}^{cca}(n)$

1. A key k is generated by running $Gen(1^n)$.

2. The adversary $\mathcal{A}$ is given input 1^n and oracle access to $Enc_k(\cdot)$ and $Dec_k(\cdot)$. $\mathcal{A}$ outputs a pair of messages m_0, m_1 of the same length.

3. A uniform bit $b \leftarrow \{0,1\}$ is chosen, and then a ciphertext $c \leftarrow Enc_k(m_b)$ (called the *challenge ciphertext*) is computed and given to $\mathcal{A}$.

4. The adversary $\mathcal{A}$ continues to have oracle access to $Enc_k(\cdot)$ and $Dec_k(\cdot)$, but is not allowed to query $Dec_k(\cdot)$ on the challenge ciphertext itself. Eventually $\mathcal{A}$ outputs a bit b'.

5. The output of the experiment is defined to be 1 if $b = b'$ (In this case, we say that $\mathcal{A}$ succeeds.) and 0 otherwise.

The above experiment can also be described as follows.

1. Challenger runs Gen.

2. (Query Phase I) Adversary is given access to two oracles, $Enc_k(\cdot)$ and $Dec_k(\cdot)$.

3. (Challenger Phase) Adversary produces two messages m_0 and m_1. The challenger returns the challenge ciphertext $c^* = Enc_k(m_b)$.

4. (Query Phase II) Same as Query Phase I except that the adversary cannot query the decryption oracle on c^*.

5. Adversary outputs b'.

Definition 1 *A private-key encryption scheme $\Pi = (Gen, Enc, Dec)$ has* **indistinguishable security (or encryption) under a chosen-ciphertext attack**, *or is CCA-secure, if for all probabilistic polynomial-time adversaries $\mathcal{A}$, there exists a negligible function negl such that*

$$Pr[PrivK_{\mathcal{A},\Pi}^{cca} = 1] \leq \frac{1}{2} + negl(n), \tag{5.9}$$

where the probability is taken over the randomness used by $\mathcal{A}$, as well as the randomness used in the experiment.

Note that in the above experiment, the adversary is not allowed to request decryption of the challenge ciphertext itself.

CCA-security Any encryption scheme that allows ciphertexts to be manipulated in any "logical way" cannot be CCA-secure. It means that the ciphertext should be "non-malleable" in the sense that if the adversary tries to modify a given ciphertext, the result is either an invalid ciphertext or one that decrypts to a plaintext having no relation to the original one. An encryption algorithm is malleable if it is possible for an adversary to transform a ciphertext into another ciphertext which decrypts to a related plaintext. That is, given an encryption of a plaintext m, it is possible to generate another ciphertext which decrypts to $f(m)$, for a known function f, without necessarily knowing or learning m.

5.3.1 IND-CCA Adversary

Let $\mathcal{SE} = (\mathcal{K}, \mathcal{E}, \mathcal{D})$ be an encryption scheme. An IND-CCA adversary A has an oracle LR.

1. has access to an LR oracle.
2. has access to a decryption oracle Dec.
3. eventually outputs a bit.

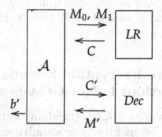

FIGURE 5.5
IND-CCA adversary.

For the IND-CCA scheme, the adversary needs access to the decryption oracle in addition to the encryption oracle (Note that a CPA-adversary is given encryption oracle service only). This is shown in Figure 5.5. The decryption oracle decrypts arbitrary ciphertexts on the request of the adversary except for the challenge ciphertexts, which are the encryption results by the LR oracle. If the output of the adversary is 1, this means that the adversary is in the right world and if the output of the adversary is 0, this means that the adversary is in the left world. The symmetric key is generated during the initialization procedure. The adversary then may request a number of encryptions and decryptions to the oracles (i.e., the adversary submits two distinct chosen plaintexts to the LR oracle; the LR oracle then selects a bit b at random and sends the challenge ciphertexts back to the adversary; the adversary submits the resulting ciphertexts to the decryption oracle; the decryption oracle then sends the decryption results back to the adversary). Finally the adversary outputs a guess for the value of bit b. The scheme is IND-CCA secure if no adversary has a non-negligible advantage in winning the above game.

5.3.2 A CPA-Secure Encryption Scheme from Any Pseudorandom Function Is Not CCA-Secure

Let us consider an IND-CCA experiment, where an adversary $\mathcal{A}$ has access to both the LR oracle and the decryption oracle. $\mathcal{A}$ sends messages $m_0 = 0^n$ and $m_1 = 1^n$ to the LR oracle and gets back $Enc_k(m_b) = (r, F_k(r) \oplus m_b)$. $\mathcal{A}$ has access to the decryption oracle, which will not allow the decryption of the challenged messages (m_0 and m_1). So the idea is to slightly change the ciphertext and query the decryption oracle. That is, $\mathcal{A}$ flip the first bit in the encryption of challenged message m_b and decryption oracle will accept the changed ciphertext ($c \rightarrow c'$), Note that as encryption scheme defined by $s = F_k(r) \oplus m$ is bit wise operation, the change in nth bit of message ($m \rightarrow m'$) will only affect corresponding bit in ciphertext ($c \rightarrow c'$). Therefore, $\mathcal{A}$ can tell whether $m_0 = 0^n$ or $m_1 = 1^n$ was encrypted because $\mathcal{A}$ can expect m_b with the first flipped bit to appear as response from the decryption oracle, where in case of 10^{n-1}, $b = 0$ and in case of 01^{n-1}, $b \overset{.}{=} 1$. Hence, Construction 1 in Chapter 4 is not CCA secure.

5.3.3 A CPA-Secure Encryption Scheme Using CBC Mode (Random Version) Is Not CCA-Secure

In order to analyze the security of CBC (random mode) under the CCA indistinguishably experiment, let us formulate an adversary $\mathcal{A}$ which is provided with the LR oracle access and the decryption oracle. In this experiment, we calculate the advantage of the adversary in succeeding in attacking the scheme and show that the scheme is not CCA-secure.

Let $\mathcal{SE} = (\mathcal{K}, \mathcal{E}, \mathcal{D})$ be a block cipher, which consists of key generation, encryption, and decryption algorithms, and provides a block of the encrypted data using the CBC randomized mode. The adversary provides a message pair (M_0, M_1) and receives a ciphertext C in each world. We design the adversary so that if the retrieved plaintext equals O^n, the adversary returns 0 and 1 otherwise. Note that the query for the challenge ciphertext C is not allowed to the decryption oracle. Before receiving the decryption service, therefore, the adversary needs to slightly modify the challenge ciphertext so that he could finally retrieve the original plaintext from the decrypted result of the modified ciphertext by the decryption oracle.[1] The adversary finally retrieves

---

[1] Let us say the encryption result of M is $C = C[0]C[1]$. The adversary modifies $C = C[0]C[1]$ into $C' = (C[0] \oplus \Delta)C[1] = C'[0]C[1]$ and queries the modified ciphertext C' to the decryption oracle, which returns $M' = M \oplus \Delta$ back to the adversary.

the original plaintext by XORing the decryption of the modified ciphertext with Δ, i.e., $M' \oplus \Delta = M$. Next we show that the adversary wins the game with the advantage of 1.

1. In the Game $\mathsf{Right}_{\mathcal{SE}}$, the LR encryption oracle returns $\langle C[0]C[1] \rangle$ with

$$C[1] = E_K(C[0] \oplus M_1) = E_K(C[0] \oplus 1^n). \qquad (5.10)$$

We have

$$
\begin{aligned}
M' &= \mathsf{Dec}(C'[0]C[1]) \\
   &= E_K^{-1}(C[1]) \oplus C'[0] \\
   &= E_K^{-1}\big(E_K(C[0] \oplus 1^n)\big) \oplus (C[0] \oplus \Delta) \\
   &= (C[0] \oplus 1^n) \oplus (C[0] \oplus 1^n) \\
   &= 0^n.
\end{aligned}
$$

Then, $M = M' \oplus \Delta = 0^n \oplus 1^n = 1^n$. By comparing the retrieved plaintext with 0^n, the adversary will return 1, that is,

$$\Pr[\mathsf{Right}_{\mathcal{SE}}^{\mathcal{A}} \Rightarrow 1] = 1.$$

2. In the Game $\mathsf{Left}_{\mathcal{SE}}$, the LR encryption oracle returns $\langle C[0]C[1] \rangle$ with

$$C[1] = E_K(C[0] \oplus M_0) = E_K(C[0] \oplus 0^n).$$

We have

$$
\begin{aligned}
M' &= \mathsf{Dec}(C'[0]C[1]) \\
   &= E_K^{-1}(C[1]) \oplus C'[0] \\
   &= E_K^{-1}\big(E_K(C[0] \oplus 0^n)\big) \oplus (C[0] \oplus \Delta) \\
   &= (C[0] \oplus 0^n) \oplus (C[0] \oplus 1^n) \\
   &= 1^n.
\end{aligned}
$$

Then, $M = M' \oplus \Delta = 1^n \oplus 1^n = 0^n$. By comparing the retrieved plaintext with 0^n, the adversary will return 0, that is,

$$\Pr[\mathsf{Left}_{\mathcal{SE}}^{\mathcal{A}} \Rightarrow 1] = 0.$$

Exercises

5.1 Explain why Construction 1 in Chapter 4 is not CCA-secure.

5.2 An adversary $\mathcal{A}$ chooses $m_0 = 0^n, m_1 = 1^n$. Upon receiving $c = \langle r, s \rangle$, $\mathcal{A}$ flips the first bit of s, resulting s' and asks for decryption of $c' = \langle r, s' \rangle$. The decryption oracle answers with either 10^{n-1} (in which case it is clear that $b = 0$) or 01^{n-1} (in which case $b = 1$). Why?

Enc: $c = \langle r, F_k(r) \oplus m \rangle = \langle r, s \rangle$
Dec: $m = F_k(r) \oplus s$

5.3 How are garbage messages different from messages chosen by an adversary in the message authentication experiment $Mac - forge_{A,\Pi}(n)$?

6

Message Authentication Code

CONTENTS

This chapter provides an overview of the message authentication code (MAC) starting from the main goal of the message authentication code. Subsequently, the difference between the encryption and the message authentication is analyzed. The next section of the chapter provides the formal definitions of MAC. The construction of fixed length MAC from any pseudorandom function and the construction of a variable length MAC from a fixed length MAC are discussed, respectively. The CBC-MAC construction that is similar to the CBC mode of encryption is widely used in practice, producing fixed length MAC for much longer messages. The final part of the chapter discusses how to guarantee data encryption and authentication at the same time and constructs a CCA-secure private-key encryption scheme using MAC.

6.1   Overview

The goal of message authentication is to ensure that

1. Message M really originates with Alice and not someone else ("data origin").

2. Message M has not been modified in transit by an adversary ("data integrity").

Example In a medical database application as shown in Figure 6.1, we need to ensure that

1. Doctor is authorized to get Alice's file.
2. F_A, F'_A are not modified in transit.
3. F_A is really sent by a database.
4. F'_A is really sent by an authorized doctor.

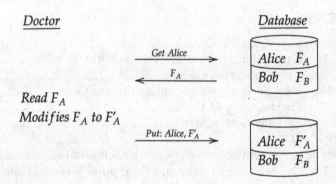

FIGURE 6.1
Message authentication in a medical application.

6.1.1   Encryption vs. Message Authentication

Does encryption provide message authentication? The answer is no.

Encryption using stream ciphers Consider the private-key encryption scheme from any pseudorandom generator G, $c = G(k) \oplus m$. Ciphertexts are very easy to manipulate. Specifically, flipping any bit in the ciphertext c results in the same bit being flipped in the message that is recovered upon decryption - remaining parts are unchanged. The same attack applies to OTP (i.e., the adversary can modify the message by picking Δ), showing that even perfect secrecy is not sufficient to ensure message authentication. Now we explain in detail how OTP does not provide message authentication.

The encryption of the message M is given by $K \oplus M$ while the decryption is given by $K \oplus C$, where K is the key, M is the plaintext message and C is the ciphertext. Here we assume that the adversary knows the message M. Then he can derive the corresponding codes of the pad from the two known elements (M and M'). The adversary then replace the ciphertext with modified ciphertext of the same length. The adversary's knowledge for the OTP is limited and this must be maintained for any other content of the message to remain valid. The decryption of the modified ciphertext provides the modified plaintext from which we can conclude that the OTP does not provide message authentication.

Encryption using block ciphers Single-bit modifications of a ciphertext still cause reasonably predictable changes in the plaintext. When using ECB mode, flipping a bit in the i-th block of the ciphertext affects only the i-th block of the plaintext – all other blocks remain unchanged. When using CBC mode, flipping the j-th bit of the IV changes only the j-th bit of the first message block m_1 (since $m_1 = F_k(c_1) \oplus IV'$, where IV' is the modified IV) – all plaintext blocks other than the first remain unchanged.

From the above, we can presume that if a scheme's ciphertexts are easy to manipulate (i.e., not CCA-secure; CCA-security means that modifying ciphertexts results in garbled or random message), encryption cannot provide message authentication. Later it turns out that our presumption is right.

6.2 Message Authentication Code

Note that the aim of the message authentication code (MAC, interchangeably used with message authentication scheme) is to prevent an adversary from modifying a message sent by one party to another, without the parties detecting that a modification has been made.

Definition 1 *A* **message authentication code** *is a tuple of probabilistic polynomial-time algorithms (Gen, Mac, Vrfy) such that*

1. *The* **key-generation algorithm** *Gen takes as input the security parameter 1^n and outputs a key k with $|k| \geq n$.*

2. *The* **tag-generation algorithm** *Mac takes as input a key k and a message $m \in \{0,1\}^*$, and outputs a message authentication code, also called tag, $t \leftarrow Mac_k(m)$.*

3. *The* **verification algorithm** *Vrfy takes as input a key k, a message m and a tag t. It outputs a bit $b = Vrfy_k(m, t)$, with $b = 1$ meaning valid and $b = 0$ meaning invalid.*

Security of message authentication code The intuitive idea is that no polynomial-time adversary should be able to generate a valid tag on any "new" message that was not previously sent (and authenticated) by one of the communicating parties.

Chosen-message attack in the real world In Figure 6.2, an ATM card contains a key $K \leftarrow \mathcal{K}$ also known to a bank, where $\mathsf{MAC} = (\mathsf{Gen}, \mathsf{Mac}, \mathsf{Vrfy})$ is a message authentication code. An adversary transmits Alice's identity to the bank in order to be accepted under Alice's name. A Trojan horse ATM can mount a chosen-message attack to find the valid tag.

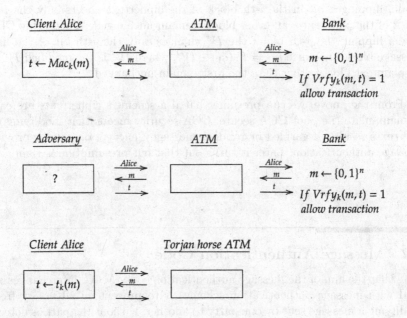

FIGURE 6.2
Authentication in ATM.

The message authentication experiment $Mac - forge_{\mathcal{A},\Pi}(n)$

1. A random key k is generated by running $\mathsf{Gen}(1^n)$.

2. The adversary $\mathcal{A}$ is given input 1^n and oracle access to $\mathsf{Mac}_k(\cdot)$. $\mathcal{A}$ eventually outputs a pair (m,t).
   Let Q denote the set of all queries that $\mathcal{A}$ asked to the its oracle.

3. The output of the experiment is defined to be 1
   if and only if (1) $\mathsf{Vrfy}_k(m,t) = 1$ and (2) $m \notin Q$.

We define a message authentication code to be secure if no efficient adversary can succeed in the above experiment with non-negligible probability.

Definition 2 *A message authentication code* $\Pi = (\text{Gen}, \text{Mac}, \text{Vrfy})$ *is* **existentially unforgeable under an adaptive chosen-message attack,** *or just secure if for all probabilistic polynomial-time adversaries $\mathcal{A}$, there is a negligible function negl such that*

$$Pr[Mac - forge_{\mathcal{A},\Pi}(n) = 1] \leq negl(n). \tag{6.1}$$

A MAC satisfying above is said to be *existentially unforgeable under an adaptive chosen-message attack*. "Existentially unforgeable" refers to the fact that the adversary must not be able to forge a valid tag on *any* message[1] and "adaptive chosen-message attack" refers to the fact that the adversary is able to obtain MAC tags on any messages it likes, where these messages may be chosen adaptively during the attack.

Replay attack Suppose Alice transmits (M_1, T_1) to a bank where $M_1 = $ "Pay USD 100 to Bob." An adversary captures (M_1, T_1) and keeps re-transmitting it to the bank. Then Bob gets USD 100, USD 200, USD 300, ... at each time. Our notion, however, does not protect against such attacks since every time a valid pair (M_1, T_1) is presented to the verification algorithm, it will always output 1. The decision as to whether or not a replayed message should be treated as "valid" is considered to be entirely application-dependent.

Two common techniques for preventing replay attacks are

1. Time stamp

   (a) A sender appends the current time to the message, and a receiver checks whether the included time stamp is within some acceptable window of the current time.

   (b) Both a sender and a receiver need to maintain closely synchronized clocks.

   (c) A replay attack are still possible as long as it is done quickly (i.e., within the acceptable time window).

2. Sequence number

   (a) A sender appends the MAC tag computed over $m \| i$ (i is a sequence number) to the message and a receiver checks the validity of the tag.

   (b) The sender needs to assign a unique sequence number to each message and the receiver keeps track of which sequence numbers it has already seen.

   (c) Both a sender and a receiver need to maintain sequence numbers.

---

[1] It may not be chosen by the adversary. It may be a "garbage" message.

6.3   Constructing Secure Message Authentication Code

We first show a general method for constructing a fixed length MAC from any pseudorandom function. Then, we extend it into a variable length by breaking the message into multiple blocks and including additional information in each block to prevent attacks.

6.3.1   Fixed-Length MAC

Intuition If the MAC tag t is obtained by applying a pseudorandom function to the message m, then forging a tag on a previously unauthenticated message requires the adversary to guess the value of the pseudorandom function at a "new" point (i.e., message). Now, the probability of guessing the value of a *random* function on a new point is 2^{-n} (when the output length of the function is n). It follows that the probability of guessing such a value for a pseudorandom function can be only negligibly greater.

Construction 1. A fixed-length MAC from any pseudorandom function

1. Let F be a pseudorandom function.

2. Define a fixed-length MAC for messages of length n as follows.

   (a) Gen: on input the security parameter 1^n, choose $k \leftarrow \{0,1\}^n$ uniformly at random and outputs it as the key.

   (b) Mac: on input a key $k \in \{0,1\}^n$ and a message $m \in \{0,1\}^n$, output the tag $t = F_k(m)$ (If $|m| \neq |k|$, then output nothing).

   (c) Vrfy: on input a key $k \in \{0,1\}^n$, a message $m \in \{0,1\}^n$ and a tag $t \in \{0,1\}^n$, output 1 if and only if $t = F_k(m)$ (If $|m| \neq |k|$, then output 0).

Theorem 1 *If F is a pseudorandom function, then Construction 1 is a fixed-length MAC for messages of length n that is existentially unforgeable under an adaptive chosen-message attack.*

Proof

Outline of the Proof The proof is based on the "proof by reduction" technique introduced earlier.

1. Define an alternate message authentication code (e.g., by replacing pseudorandom function with random function).

2. Show that any attacker has at most negligible success probability in breaking the original scheme.

Outline 1 We define a modified message authentication code $\widetilde{\Pi} = (\widetilde{Gen}, \widetilde{Mac}, \widetilde{Vrfy})$ that is exactly the same as $\Pi = (Gen, Mac, Vrfy)$, except that a truly random function f is used in place of pseudorandom function F_k.

It is straightforward to see that

$$Pr[Mac - forge_{\mathcal{A}, \widetilde{\Pi}}(n) = 1] \leq 2^{-n} \tag{6.2}$$

because for any message $m \notin Q$, the value $t = f(m)$ is uniformly distributed in $\{0, 1\}^n$ from the $\mathcal{A}$'s viewpoint.

Outline 2 We show that any attacker has at most negligible success probability in breaking the original scheme as follows. Let $\mathcal{A}$ be a probabilistic polynomial-time adversary with success probability $\epsilon(n)$ in breaking the original scheme as

$$\epsilon(n) \stackrel{\text{def}}{=} Pr[Mac - forge_{\mathcal{A}, \Pi}(n) = 1]. \tag{6.3}$$

In order to show that $\epsilon(n)$ is negligible, we use $\mathcal{A}$ to construct a distinguisher D that is given oracle access to some function, whose goal is to determine whether this function is a "random' 'or "pseudorandom." To do this, D emulates the message authentication experiment for $\mathcal{A}$ in the manner described below and observes whether $\mathcal{A}$ succeeds in outputting a valid tag on a "new" message or not. If $\mathcal{A}$ succeeds then D guesses that its oracle must be a pseudorandom function, while if $\mathcal{A}$ does not succeed then D guesses that its oracle must be a random function. D is given input 1^n and accesses to an oracle $\mathcal{O} : \{0, 1\}^n \rightarrow \{0, 1\}^n$ and works as follows.

Distinguisher D

1. D has oracle access to $\mathcal{O}$ either a PRF or a RF.

2. D starts $\mathcal{A}$.

3. **while** Query Phase **do** (repeat up to the number of messages)

4. $\mathcal{A}$ asks for a tag on m_i.

5.   Give $t_i = \mathcal{O}(m_i)$ to $\mathcal{A}$.

6. **end while**

7. $\mathcal{A}$ gives attempted forgery t^* on $m*$.

8. D outputs "1" if and only if (1) $\mathcal{O}(m*) = t^*$ and (2) $\mathcal{A}$ never queried its MAC oracle on m^*.

In analyzing D, let us consider the two possibilities for D's oracle as follows.

Case I: D's oracle is a PRF
The view of $\mathcal{A}$ when run as a sub-routine by D is distributed identically to the view of $\mathcal{A}$ in the experiment $Mac-forge_{\mathcal{A},\Pi}(n)$. Furthermore, D outputs 1 exactly when $Mac-forge_{\mathcal{A},\Pi}(n)=1$. Thus

$$P_r[D^{F_k(\cdot)}(1^n) = 1] = Pr[Mac-forge_{\mathcal{A},\Pi}(n) = 1] = \epsilon(n), \qquad (6.4)$$

where $k \leftarrow \{0,1\}^n$ is chosen uniformly at random in the above.

Case II: D's oracle is a RF
The view of $\mathcal{A}$ when run as a sub-routine by D is distributed identically to the view of $\mathcal{A}$ in the experiment $Mac-forge_{\mathcal{A},\tilde{\Pi}}(n)$. Furthermore, D outputs 1 exactly when $Mac-forge_{\mathcal{A},\tilde{\Pi}}(n)=1$. Thus,

$$P_r[D^{f(\cdot)}(1^n) = 1] = Pr[Mac-forge_{\mathcal{A},\tilde{\Pi}}(n) = 1] \leq \frac{1}{2^n}, \qquad (6.5)$$

where $f \leftarrow Func_n$ is chosen uniformly at random in the above.

By combining Equations (6.4) and (6.5), we get

$$|P_r[D^{F_k(\cdot)}(1^n) = 1] - P_r[D^{f(\cdot)}(1^n) = 1]| \geq \epsilon(n) - \frac{1}{2^n}. \qquad (6.6)$$

By the assumption that F is a pseudorandom function, it follows that $\epsilon(n) - \frac{1}{2^n}$ must be negligible. Since this in turn implies that $\epsilon(n)$ is negligible, Π is existentially unforgeable under an adaptive chosen-message attack. $\square$

6.3.2   Variable-Length MAC

Before constructing a secure variable-length MAC, we consider some examples of insecure MACs and figure out what the problems are.

Some examples of insecure MACs

1. XOR all the blocks together and authenticate the result: Note that E is a block cipher.

    One example of insecure MAC is given. The message is first divided into block of certain bit-length. Each block is then encrypted separately using the block cipher and the result is then XORed to generate the tag. However, this scheme is insecure as the advantage of the adversary can be calculated equal to 1. Let x be a l-bit string and the message is formed by the concatenation of x, i.e.,

$M = x\|x$. Encrypting this will result in the same ciphertext from both the blocks and then performing the xor operation will result an $l - bit$ string of 0. Hence, the adversary created a legitimate tag that can be verified.

2. Authenticate each block separately: Compute $t_i = Mac_k(m_i)$ and output $\langle t_1, ..., t_d \rangle$ as the tag. In this case, without knowledge of the key k, the adversary can compute a valid tag $\langle t_d, ..., t_1 \rangle$ on the message $m_d,...,m_1$ by changing the order of the message blocks.

3. Authenticate each block along with a sequence number: Compute $t_i = Mac_k(i\|m_i)$ and output $\langle t_1, ..., t_d \rangle$ as the tag. This prevents the re-ordering attack described above. However, the adversary can compute a valid tag $\langle t_1, ..., t_{d-1} \rangle$ on the message $m_1,...,m_{d-1}$ by dropping a block from the end of the message.

Construction 2. A variable-length MAC from any fixed-length MAC

Let $\Pi' = (\mathsf{Gen'}, \mathsf{Mac'}, \mathsf{Vrfy'})$ be a fixed-length MAC for messages of length n. Define a MAC as follows.

1. Gen: this is identical to Gen'.

2. Mac: on input a key $k \in \{0,1\}^n$ and a message $m \in \{0,1\}^*$ of length $\ell < 2^{\frac{n}{4}}$, parse m into d blocks $m_1, \ldots, m_d$, each of length $n/4$ (The final block is padded with 0s if necessary). Next, choose a random indentifier $r \leftarrow \{0,1\}^{\frac{n}{4}}$.

   For $i = 1, \ldots, d$, compute $t_i \leftarrow \mathsf{Mac'}_k(r\|\ell\|i\|m_i)$, where i and ℓ are uniquely encoded as strings of length $n/4$. Finally, output the tag $t = \langle r, t_1, \ldots, t_d \rangle$.

3. Vrfy: on input a key $k \in \{0,1\}^n$, a message $m \in \{0,1\}^*$ of length $\ell < 2^{\frac{n}{4}}$ and a tag $t = \langle r, t_1, \ldots, t'_d \rangle$, parse m into d blocks $m_1, \ldots, m_d$, each of length $n/4$ (The final block is padded with 0s if necessary). Output 1 if and only if $d' = d$ and $\mathsf{Vrfy'}_k(r\|\ell\|i\|m_i, t_i) = 1$ for $1 \le i \le d$.

Theorem 2 *If Π' is a secure fixed-length MAC for messages of length n, then Construction 2 is a MAC that is existentially unforgeable under an adaptive chosen-message attack.*

Proof

Let Π denote the MAC in Construction 2. Let $\mathcal{A}$ be a probabilistic polynomial-time adversary. We prove that $Pr[Mac - forge_{\mathcal{A},\Pi}(n) = 1]$ is negligible.

Let Repeat denote the event that the same message identifier in two of the tags is returned by MAC oracles.

Let Forge denote the event that at least one of blocks $r\|\ell\|i\|m_i$ was never previously authenticated by Mac' in the course of answering $\mathcal{A}$'s Mac queries (i.e., Forge is the event that $\mathcal{A}$ tries to output a valid tag on a block that was never authenticated by Mac').

We have

$$
\begin{aligned}
Pr[Mac - forge_{\mathcal{A},\Pi}(n) = 1] = & Pr[Mac - forge_{\mathcal{A},\Pi}(n) = 1 \wedge \text{Repeat}] \\
& + Pr[Mac - forge_{\mathcal{A},\Pi}(n) = 1 \wedge \overline{\text{Repeat}} \wedge \text{Forge}] \\
& + Pr[Mac - forge_{\mathcal{A},\Pi}(n) = 1 \wedge \overline{\text{Repeat}} \wedge \overline{\text{Forge}}].
\end{aligned}
$$

1. Let $q(n)$ be the number of MAC oracle queries made by $\mathcal{A}$. In the i-th query, oracle chooses r_i randomly from a set of size $2^{\frac{n}{4}}$. The probability of event Repeat is the probability that $r_i = r_j$ for some $i \neq j$. By the "birthday bound," we have

$$
Pr[Mac - forge_{\mathcal{A},\Pi}(n) = 1 \wedge \text{Repeat}] \leq \frac{q(n)^2}{2^{\frac{n}{4}}}. \qquad (6.7)
$$

   Since $\mathcal{A}$ makes only polynomially many queries, then this probability is negligible.

2. Next we consider that if $Mac - forge_{\mathcal{A},\Pi}(n) = 1$, but Repeat did not occur, then Forge must have occurred. That is, $Pr[Mac - forge_{\mathcal{A},\Pi}(n) = 1 \wedge \overline{\text{Repeat}} \wedge \overline{\text{Forge}}] = 0$.

   Let (m, t) be the final output of $\mathcal{A}$ (the forged message). Let its length be ℓ and the identifier is r. Parse m into d blocks, each of length $\frac{n}{4}$. Thus, $t = \langle r, t_1, \ldots, t_d \rangle$. We consider two cases as follows.

   (a) Identifier r is different from all the identifiers used by the MAC oracles. That is, $(r\|\ell\|1\|m_1)$ was never previously authenticated by the MAC oracle. So, if $Mac - forge_{\mathcal{A},\Pi}(n) = 1$, then there exists $\text{Vrfy}'_k(r\|\ell\|1\|m_1, t_1) = 1$. Thus, Forge occurs.

   (b) Identifier r was used in exactly one of the tags obtained by $\mathcal{A}$ from the MAC oracles.

   Denote (m', t') be the query-response pair when the identifier r occurs. Since m is not in the queries, then $m \neq m'$. Let ℓ' denote the length of m'. There are two subcases.

   i. Case 1: $\ell \neq \ell'$
      Since all MAC oracles responses used different identifiers, the one oracle using the same identifier has a different length value. This implies that $(r\|\ell\|1\|m_1)$ was never previously authenticated by the MAC oracle. Thus, Forge occurs.

    ii. Case 2: $\ell = \ell'$
In this case, the number of blocks in m and m' are the same. Since $m \neq m'$, there exists i such that $m_i \neq m_i'$. So, $(r\|\ell\|i\|m_i)$ was never previously authenticated by MAC oracle. Thus, Forge occurs.

3. The remainder of the proof is to claim that

$$Pr[Mac - forge_{\mathcal{A},\Pi}(n) = 1 \wedge \overline{\text{Repeat}} \wedge \text{Forge}] \qquad (6.8)$$

is negligible.

We construct the adversary $\mathcal{A}'$ attacking to Π'. $\mathcal{A}'$ runs $\mathcal{A}$ as a subroutine. Whenever $\mathcal{A}$ output (m, t), $\mathcal{A}'$ parses m and checks any m_i which did not occur in its previous oracle queries by Mac'. If so, then $\mathcal{A}'$ outputs $(r\|\ell\|i\|m_i, t_i)$ as a valid tag. If not, $\mathcal{A}'$ outputs nothing. This means that whenever $Mac - forge_{\mathcal{A},\Pi}(n) = 1 \wedge \overline{\text{Repeat}} \wedge \text{Forge}$ occurs, we have $Mac - forge_{\mathcal{A}',\Pi'}(n) = 1$. From the security proof for Construction Π', we have that $Pr[Mac - forge_{\mathcal{A}',\Pi'}(n) = 1]$ is negligible, then $Pr[Mac - forge_{\mathcal{A},\Pi}(n) = 1 \wedge \overline{\text{Repeat}} \wedge \text{Forge}]$ is negligible.

Thus,

$$Pr[Mac - forge_{\mathcal{A},\Pi}(n) = 1] \leq \frac{q(n)^2}{2^{\frac{n}{4}}} + negl(n) \qquad (6.9)$$

is negligible. That is, Construction 2 is existentially unforgeable under an adaptive chosen-message attack. $\square$

6.4 CBC-MAC

The following CBC-MAC construction is similar to the CBC mode of encryption and is widely used in practice, producing fixed-length MAC for much longer messages.

Construction 3. A CBC-MAC from fixed-length messages

Let F be a pseudorandom function and fix a length function ℓ. The basic CBC-MAC construction is as follows.

1. Gen: on input 1^n, choose $k \leftarrow \{0,1\}^n$ uniformly at random.

2. Mac: on input a key $k \in \{0,1\}^n$ and a message m of length $\ell(n) \cdot n$ (i.e., multiple of n), do the following (we set $\ell = \ell(n)$) in what follows.

   (a) Parse m as $m = m_1, \ldots, m_\ell$, where each m_i is of length n and set $t_0 = 0^n$.

   (b) For $i = 1$ to ℓ, set $t_i = F_k(t_{i-1} \oplus m_i)$.

   Output t_ℓ as the tag.

3. Vrfy: on input a key $k \in \{0,1\}^n$, a message m of length $\ell(n) \cdot n$ and a tag t of length n, output 1 if and only if $t_\ell \stackrel{?}{=} \mathsf{Mac}_k(m)$.

Theorem 3 *Let l be a polynomial. If F is a pseudorandom function, then Construction 3 is a fixed-length MAC for messages of length $l(n) \cdot n$ that is existentially unforgeable under an adaptive chosen-message attack.*

Proof is omitted.

Construction 3 is not secure when used to authenticate messages of different lengths

Let us consider CBC-MAC, where the tag of previous block is used to generate a tag for the next block. On the left side of Figure 6.3, we can see that CBC-MAC first generates a tag for message A and then XOR the tag of previous message with message B to finally generate a tag, Tag_{AB}, for message AB. This is how CBC-MAC works with varying length. The right side of Figure 6.3 shows that the adversary can get a tag Tag_{AB} on the modified version, $Tag_A \oplus B$, of the message B, which is a valid forgery. It shows that Construction 3 is insecure if it is used to authenticate messages of varying lengths.

Construction 3 is not secure against splicing attack

When two blocks of messages are injected into a CBC-MAC with the resulting MAC being the same, this is known as the CBC-MAC splicing attack. When used to authenticate messages of different lengths, Construction 3 is not secure because the tag of previous block is used to generate a tag for next block, which allows the adversary to generate another valid tag of various subsequent blocks. The adversary takes a random string x and generates the tag T_1 for it. The adversary then makes another message by concatenating x and T_1 XORed with x, and successfully creates a tag T_1 for the message

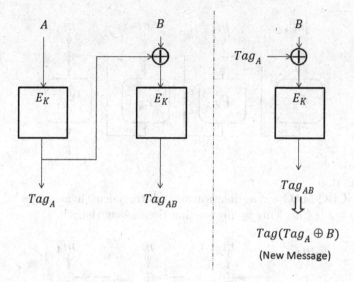

FIGURE 6.3
Construction 3 is not secure for authentication of messages of varying length.

$x \parallel (T_1 \oplus x)$.

Secure CBC-MAC for variable-length messages Three possible options
that can be proven secure are

1. Apply the pseudorandom function (block cipher) to the length l of
   the input message in order to obtain a key k_l (i.e., set $k_l = F_k(l)$).
   Then compute the basic CBC-MAC using the key k_l.

2. Prepend the message with its length $|m|$ (encoded as an n-bit string)
   and then compute the basic CBC-MAC on the resulting message
   (See Figure 6.4).

3. Apply two different keys k_{in}, k_{out} so that it first computes $t = F_{k_{in}}(m)$ of the message m and then outputs the tag $\hat{t} = F_{k_{out}}(t)$
   using CBC-MAC. An example is ECBC-MAC (See Figure 6.5).

6.5 Obtaining Encryption and Message Authentication

Intuition We are interested in how to guarantee data encryption and authentication at the same time.

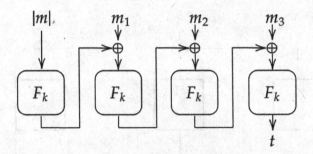

FIGURE 6.4
A secure CBC-MAC for authenticating arbitrary-length messages of three
blocks, $m = m_1 \parallel m_2 \parallel m_3$ by prepending the message length.

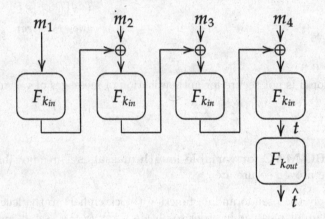

FIGURE 6.5
A secure CBC-MAC for authenticating arbitrary-length messages by applying
two keys.

The unforgeable encryption experiment Enc-Forge$_{\mathcal{A},\Pi(n)}$

1. *Run* Gen(1^n) *to obtain a key* k.

2. *The adversary* $\mathcal{A}$ *is given input* 1^n *and access to encryption oracle* Enc$_k(.)$. *The adversary outputs a ciphertext* c.

3. *Let* $m =$ Dec$_k(c)$ *and let* $\mathcal{Q}$ *denote the set of all queries that* $\mathcal{A}$ *asked its encryption oracle. The output of the experiment is 1 if and only if (1)* $m \neq \bot$ *and (2)* $m \notin \mathcal{Q}$.

Definition 3 *A private-key encryption scheme* Π *is* **unforgeable** *if and only if for all probabilistic polynomial-time adversaries* $\mathcal{A}$, *there is a negligible func-*

tion negl such that

$$Pr[\text{Enc-Forge}_{A,\Pi}(n) = 1] \leq negl(n). \tag{6.10}$$

Definition 4 *A private-key encryption scheme* Π *is an* **authenticated encryption scheme** *if it is CCA-secure and unforgeable.*

Three approaches for combining encryption and authentication are as follows.

1. **Encrypt-and-authenticate:** Encryption and message authentication are computed independently in parallel. This is not IND-CCA secure.

2. **Authenticate-then-encrypt:** Here a MAC tag t is first computed, and then the message and tag are encrypted together. This is not IND-CCA secure.

3. **Encrypt-then-authenticate:** The message m is first encrypted and then a MAC tag is computed over the result.

The following section shows that the combined scheme derived by applying the encrypt-then-authenticate approach is secure.

6.5.1 Constructing CCA-Secure Encryption Schemes Using MAC

Intuition To achieve a CCA-secure encryption scheme, we should not allow an adversary to manipulate a ciphertext. To prevent this type of manipulation of the ciphertext, we can consider deploying a message authentication code to the ciphertext. The followings show that this idea is right.

Construction 4. A CCA-secure private-key encryption scheme

Let $\Pi_E = (\text{Gen}_E, \text{Enc}, \text{Dec})$ be a private-key encryption scheme and let $\Pi_M = (\text{Gen}_E, \text{Mac}, \text{Vrfy})$ be a message authentication code. Define an encryption scheme $\Pi' = (\text{Gen}', \text{Enc}', \text{Dec}')$ as follows

1. Gen': on input 1^n, run $\text{Gen}_E(1^n)$ and $\text{Gen}_M(1^n)$ to obtain keys k_1, k_2, respectively.

2. Enc': on input a key (k_1, k_2) and a plaintext message m, compute $c \leftarrow \text{Enc}_{k_1}(m)$ and $t \leftarrow \text{Mac}_{k_2}(c)$. Output the ciphertext $\langle c, t \rangle$.

3. Dec': on input a key (k_1, k_2) and a ciphertext $\langle c, t \rangle$, first check whether $\text{Vrfy}_{k_2}(c, t) \stackrel{?}{=} 1$. If yes, then output $\text{Dec}_{k_1}(c)$; if no, then output $\perp$.

Theorem 4 *If Π_E is a CPA-secure private-key encryption scheme and Π_M is a secure message authentication code with unique tags, then Construction 4 is an authenticated encryption scheme.*

We provide two different versions of the security proof. The first proves that the scheme is CCA-secure directly by using adversary $\mathcal{A}$ to build two adversaries $\mathcal{A}_{mac}$ (attacking to Π_M) and $\mathcal{A}_{enc}$ (attacking to Π_E). The second proves that the scheme is CCA-secure by using hybrid proof technique (DecryptListGame is built between CCA and CPA).

First Proof
Intuition Since $\Pi_M =(\mathsf{Gen}_M,\mathsf{Mac},\mathsf{Vrfy})$ is a secure message authentication code with unique tags, we can argue that all responses of the decryption oracle are invalid because it simply returns $\bot$ unless the queried ciphertext was previously obtained by the adversary from its encryption oracle. Therefore, the security of the scheme $\Pi' = (\mathsf{Gen}',\mathsf{Enc}',\mathsf{Dec}')$ is reduced to the CPA-security of Π_E because the decryption oracle is useless. So we prove that if the CCA scheme is not secure, then neither is the underlying CPA-scheme Π_E.

Let $\mathcal{A}$ be any probabilistic polynomial-time CCA adversary attacking scheme Π'. Let Valid-Query define the event that $\mathcal{A}$ generates a query (c,t) to the decryption oracle that was not obtained from the encryption oracle and does not result $\bot$ in the experiment $\mathsf{PrivK}^{cca}_{\mathcal{A},\Pi'}(n)$ (that is, $\mathcal{A}$ submits a new query (c,t) to oracle Dec' and $\mathsf{Vrfy}_{k_2}(c,t) = 1$). We have

$$\Pr[\mathsf{PrivK}^{cca}_{\mathcal{A},\Pi'}(n) = 1] \leq \Pr[\mathsf{Valid\text{-}Query}] + \Pr[\mathsf{PrivK}^{cca}_{\mathcal{A},\Pi'}(n) = 1 \wedge \overline{\mathsf{Valid\text{-}Query}}].$$

We need to prove the following claims.

1. $\Pr[\mathsf{Valid\text{-}Query}]$ is at most negligible.
2. $\Pr[\mathsf{PrivK}^{cca}_{\mathcal{A},\Pi'}(n) = 1 \wedge \overline{\mathsf{Valid\text{-}Query}}] \leq \frac{1}{2} + negl(n).$

In the first claim, if oracle does not result $\bot$, then t is a valid MAC tag for c. Thus, if (c,t) was not obtained by querying the encryption oracle, this means that $\mathcal{A}$ must have forged a MAC. Formally, we prove that if the probability that Valid-Query occurs is non-negligible, then we can construct an adversary $\mathcal{A}_{mac}$ that breaks the MAC as follows.

The adversary $\mathcal{A}_{mac}$, interacting in $\mathsf{Mac\text{-}Forge}_{\mathcal{A}_{mac},\Pi_M}(n)$, chooses a random key k_1 for Enc and a random value i from $\{1,\ldots,q(n)\}$. $\mathcal{A}_{mac}$ then simulates the encryption and decryption oracles for $\mathcal{A}$. When $\mathcal{A}$ queries the encryption oracle with m, $\mathcal{A}_{mac}$ computes $c = \mathsf{Enc}_{k_1}(m)$ and requests a tag t for c. Then $\mathcal{A}_{mac}$ returns the pair (c,t) to $\mathcal{A}$ as its oracle reply. In contrast, in every decryption oracle query (c,t) from $\mathcal{A}$ apart from the i-th one, $\mathcal{A}_{mac}$ first checks if (c,t) was ever generated from an encryption query. If yes, $\mathcal{A}_{mac}$ returns the plaintext m that was queried by $\mathcal{A}$ when (c,t) was generated. If not, $\mathcal{A}_{mac}$ returns $\perp$. In contrast, for the i-th decryption oracle query (c, t), $\mathcal{A}_{mac}$ outputs (c, t) as its MAC forgery and stop. Thus, we have Mac-Forge$_{\mathcal{A}_{mac}, \Pi_M}(n) = 1$ occurs if Valid-Query occurs. That is,

$$\Pr[\text{Mac-Forge}_{\mathcal{A}_{mac}, \Pi_M}(n) = 1] =$$
$$\Pr[\text{Mac-Forge}_{\mathcal{A}_{mac}, \Pi_M}(n) = 1 \wedge \text{Valid-Query}] \times \Pr[\text{Valid-Query}].$$

Since $\mathcal{A}$ makes at most $q(n)$ oracle queries, $\Pr[\text{Mac-Forge}_{\mathcal{A}_{mac}, \Pi_M}(n) = 1 | \text{Valid-Query}] \leq 1/q(n)$. Furthermore, $\mathcal{A}_{mac}$ can succeed in Mac-Forge with at most negligible probability, that is $\Pr[\text{Mac-Forge}_{\mathcal{A}_{mac}, \Pi_M}(n) = 1]$ is negligible. Therefore, $\Pr[\text{Valid-Query}]$ is negligible.

In the second claim, we use $\mathcal{A}$ to construct $\mathcal{A}_{enc}$ for the CPA experiment with Π_E. $\mathcal{A}_{enc}$ chooses a key k_2 and invokes the adversary $\mathcal{A}$. Whenever $\mathcal{A}$ asks an encryption query m, $\mathcal{A}_{enc}$ queries its encryption oracle with m and receives back some c. Then $\mathcal{A}_{enc}$ computes $t = \text{Mac}_{k_2}(c)$ and hands $\mathcal{A}$ the pair (c, t). Whenever $\mathcal{A}$ asks for a decryption query (c, t), $\mathcal{A}_{enc}$ checks if (c, t) was generated in a previous encryption query. If yes, $\mathcal{A}_{enc}$ hands $\mathcal{A}$ the value m that was queried when (c, t) was generated. If no, $\mathcal{A}_{enc}$ hands $\mathcal{A}$ the response $\perp$. The success of $\mathcal{A}_{enc}$ in Π_E when Valid-Query does not occur equals the success of $\mathcal{A}$ when Valid-Query does not occur. That is,

$$\Pr[\text{PrivK}_{\mathcal{A}_{enc}, \Pi_E}^{cpa}(n) = 1 \wedge \overline{\text{Valid-Query}}] = \Pr[\text{PrivK}_{\mathcal{A}, \Pi'}^{cca}(n) = 1 \wedge \overline{\text{Valid-Query}}].$$

It implies that

$$\Pr[\text{PrivK}_{\mathcal{A}, \Pi'}^{cca}(n) = 1 \wedge \overline{\text{Valid-Query}}] \leq \Pr[\text{PrivK}_{\mathcal{A}_{enc}, \Pi_E}^{cpa}(n) = 1].$$

Since Π_E is a CPA-secure scheme, therefore, we have

$$\Pr[\text{PrivK}_{\mathcal{A}, \Pi'}^{cca}(n) = 1 \wedge \overline{\text{Valid-Query}}] \leq \tfrac{1}{2} + negl(n).$$

Combining two above claims, we conclude that

$$\Pr[\text{PrivK}_{\mathcal{A}, \Pi'}^{cca}(n) = 1] \leq \tfrac{1}{2} + negl(n) + negl(n),$$

that is, the scheme Π' is CCA-secure. $\square$

Second Proof
Recall that the system was defined as follows.

1. Gen' : Let $K' = K_E, K_M$.
2. $EncMac'(K', M) : C = (c_1 = Enc(K_E, M), c_2 = MAC(K_M, c_1))$.
3. $Vrfy'(K_M, C) : Vrfy(K_M, c_1, c_2)$.
4. $Dec'(K', C)$: If $Vrfy'(K_M, C) = 1$ output $m = Dec(K_E, c_1)$, else $\perp$.

In order to prove the scheme is secure, we will give our proof using a hybrid proof technique.

Intuition To prove the CCA security, we introduce DecryptListGame that consists of both CPA-secure encryption scheme and secure MAC.

First, we show that

$$|Pr[\mathcal{A}_{success}^{CCA}] - Pr[\mathcal{A}_{success}^{DecryptListGame}]| = \epsilon.$$

Next, to show $\epsilon = negl(n)$, we describe the probability of breaking MAC in DecryptListGame by using ϵ. Now, since we assume that MAC is secure, we can say that $\epsilon = negl(n)$. Therefore,

$$|Pr[\mathcal{A}_{success}^{CCA}] - Pr[\mathcal{A}_{success}^{DecryptListGame}]| = negl(n).$$

The detailed explanation is given in the lemma below.

Due to the following reasons, we can say that

$$|Pr[\mathcal{A}_{success}^{DecryptListGame}]| = |Pr[\mathcal{A}_{success}^{CPA}]|.$$

The difference between DecryptListGame and CPA game is the existence of decryption phase and MAC. Since we assume MAC is secure, any difference due to MAC between these two games does not happen. The difference during the decryption phase is removed because DecryptListGame takes a limitation that all ciphertexts must be made by the simulator. In other words, when the simulator makes the ciphertext, it stores the ciphertext and its corresponding message pairs in advance. Therefore, there is no problem at decryption phase to be considered. So, we can conclude that the difference between DecryptListGame and CPA game does not exist. Therefore,

$$|Pr[\mathcal{A}_{success}^{CCA}] - Pr[\mathcal{A}_{success}^{CPA}]|$$

$$= |Pr[\mathcal{A}_{success}^{CCA}] - Pr[\mathcal{A}_{success}^{DecryptListGame}]| + |Pr[\mathcal{A}_{success}^{DecryptListGame}] - Pr[\mathcal{A}_{success}^{CPA}]|$$

$$= negl(n) + 0 = negl(n).$$

DecryptListGame

This game will define a different notion of security that is specific to our encryption scheme and we will show that it is related to IND-CCA security in our proof. The game is defined as follows. The semantic view is shown in Figure 6.6.

1. Challenger runs Gen'.

2. (Query Phase I) For each query M_i to the encryption oracle, return the ciphertext $C_i = (c_{i,1}, c_{i,2})$ and add $(M_i, c_{i,1})$ to a list.

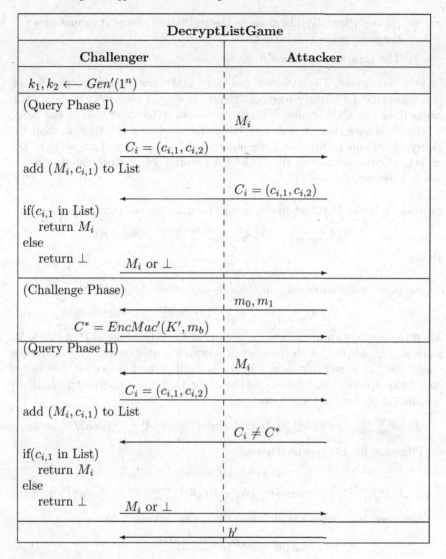

FIGURE 6.6
Semantic view of DecryptListGame.

3. (Query Phase I) For each query $C_i = (c_{i,1}, c_{i,2})$ to the decryption oracle, if $c_{i,1}$ is on the list and C_i is verified, then return the corresponding M_i, else return $\perp$.

4. (Challenge Phase) The attacker produces two messages m_0 and m_1. The challenger returns the challenge ciphertext $C^* = EncMac'(K', m_b)$.

5. (Query Phase II) The same as Query Phase I except it cannot query the decryption oracle on C^*.

6. The attacker outputs b'.

In this new game, the attacker can only make decryption queries for ciphertexts that he already received. Hence, it should be harder to break this game than the CCA game. [2] However, we want to show that if the MAC scheme is secure then it isn't any easier to break the CCA game than the DecryptListGame. Once we have shown this, then we will argue that DecryptListGame is close to the IND-CPA security game since the decryption oracle is essentially useless.

Lemma 1 If the MAC scheme is secure then for any efficient algorithm $\mathcal{A}$,

$$Pr[\mathcal{A}_{success}^{CCA}] - Pr[\mathcal{A}_{success}^{DecrpytListGame}] = negl(n).$$

Proof

Suppose that there exists an efficient algorithm $\mathcal{A}$ such that

$$Pr[\mathcal{A}_{success}^{CCA}] - Pr[\mathcal{A}_{success}^{DecrpytListGame}] = \epsilon.$$

Then there exists an algorithm, $\mathcal{B}$, such that the advantage of $\mathcal{B}$ in the MAC game is ϵ/Q, where Q is the number of decryption queries made by $\mathcal{A}$. Letting "new" be the event that a $c_{i,1}$ query is verified and is not on the list of encryption queries, and "$n\bar{e}w$" be the event that the ciphertext is made by the simulator, for the CCA game,

$$Pr[\mathcal{A}_{success}^{CCA}] = Pr[\mathcal{A}_{success}^{CCA}|new]Pr[new] + Pr[\mathcal{A}_{success}^{CCA}|n\bar{e}w]Pr[n\bar{e}w].$$

Likewise, for DecryptListGame,

$$Pr[\mathcal{A}_{success}^{DecrpytListGame}] =$$
$$Pr[\mathcal{A}_{success}^{DecrpytListGame}|new]Pr[new] + Pr[\mathcal{A}_{success}^{DecrpytListGame}|n\bar{e}w]Pr[n\bar{e}w].$$

However, the games are identical when $n\bar{e}w$ occurs [3], so

$$Pr[\mathcal{A}_{success}^{CCA}|n\bar{e}w] = Pr[\mathcal{A}_{success}^{DecrpytListGame}|n\bar{e}w]$$

and, of course, $Pr[n\bar{e}w]$ does not change. So, when we subtract the two values from each other the second term in each will cancel. So, we get [4]

---

[2]It is because the simulator in DecryptListGame only makes the ciphertext which can be decrypted only by itself. So, there exists no advantage to the attacker by querying the ciphertexts during the decryption phase.

[3]In the case of "$n\bar{e}w$" event, CCA game and DecrpytListGame work the same way that the ciphertext is made by the simulator. Therefore the probabilities of these two games are the same.

[4]Here, $Pr[\mathcal{A}_{success}^{DecrpytListGame}|new]$ is zero because DecrpytListGame does not generate the "new" event. And, $0 \leq Pr[\mathcal{A}_{success}^{CCA}|new] \leq 1$ because the range of probability is from 0 to 1 by definition. Therefore, $(Pr[\mathcal{A}_{success}^{CCA}|new] - Pr[\mathcal{A}_{success}^{DecrpytListGame}|new])$ is less than or equal to 1.

$$\epsilon = (Pr[\mathcal{A}^{CCA}_{success}|new] - Pr[\mathcal{A}^{DecrpytListGame}_{success}|new])Pr[new] \leq 1 \cdot Pr[new].$$

So, $Pr[new] \geq \epsilon$. Now, we will define an algorithm, $\mathcal{B}$ that breaks the MAC scheme with probability ϵ/Q. We define the algorithm as follows.

Algorithm $\mathcal{B}$

1. Given oracle access to MAC and Verify $K_E = Gen_E()$.

2. Runs $\mathcal{A}$.

3. For query $EncMac'(K_E, M)$, responds $C = (c_1 = Enc(K_E, M), c_2 = OracleMAC(c_1))$.

4. For query $Dec'(c_1, c_2)$, use $VerifyOracle(c_1, c_2)$.

5. If at any point a decryption query is verified and is not on the list, return it as a forgery.

6. If $VerifyOracle(c_1, c_2) = $ 'FALSE' then

7.   return $\perp$

8. Else

9.   return $Dec(K_E, c_1)$

10. End if

Now, we must analyze $\mathcal{B}$ to see if it succeeds with non-negligible probability, ϵ/Q.

> **Case 0:** Decryption query is not verified.
> In this case, the adversary does not have any advantage. Because the adversary cannot succeed in attacking the algorithm $\mathcal{B}$. So, the probability of this case is 0.

> **Case 1:** Query is verified but is on the list.
> It means that C was already made from $\mathcal{B}$. Since the adversary cannot make a new valid ciphertext C into a new message, this is not a forgery. So, the probability of this case is also 0.

> **Case 2:** Query is verified and is not on the list (so, we can use it as a forgery).
> It is equal to $Pr[new]$ that it sends the query to the oracle only once. So, the probability of this case is ϵ/Q.

Considering these cases, it is easy to see that $\mathcal{B}$ will succeed with probability ϵ/Q. $\square$

7

Hash Function

CONTENTS

This chapter begins with the introduction of the hash functions that take inputs of arbitrary length and compress them into short, fixed-length outputs. The properties of the hash function, i.e., collision resistance and weaker notions like the second pre-image and the pre-image resistance are discussed along with the candidate solution to these problems. The next section shows how to design a collision resistant hash function that generally takes two steps, a compression function followed by the Merkle-Damgard transform. The security of the hash function along with the security proof based on proof by reduction is presented. Subsequently, the construction of the hash functions that can extend the fixed length input to variable length input are discussed. This can be achieved using the Merkle-Damgard transform. The next section provides the most common attacks on the hash functions. Further the message authentication using the hash function is discussed. The approach "Hash and MAC" is discussed for the message authentication. The final part of the chapter presents the applications of the hash function.

7.1 Definitions

Hash functions are simply functions that take inputs of arbitrary length and compress them into short, fixed-length outputs. The classic use of hash functions is in data structures, where they can be used to build hash tables that enable $O(1)$ lookup time when storing a set of elements.

A "good" hash function H for this purpose is one that yields few collisions, where a *collision* is a pair of distinct items x and x' for which $H(x) = H(x')$; in this case, we also say that x and x' collide.

In the context of data structures, we try to design hash functions to decrease collisions, which results in increasing the lookup time of the hash table. In the context of cryptography, in contrast, we are faced with an adversary who may select elements with the explicit goal of causing collisions. This means that collision-resistant hash functions are pursued to achieve in security aspects rather than performance in cryptography.

7.1.1 Collision Resistance

Informally, a function H is *collision resistant* if it is infeasible for any probabilistic polynomial-time algorithm to find a collision in H. We will only be interested in hash functions whose domain is larger than their range, therefore collisions must exist, but such collisions should be hard to find.

Formally, we consider *keyed hash functions*. That is, H is a two-input function that takes as input a key s (typically generated by Gen rather than chosen uniformly and not kept secret) and a string x, and outputs a string $H^s(x) \overset{\text{def}}{=} H(s, x)$.

Definition 1 *A* **hash function** *(with output length ℓ) is a pair of probabilistic polynomial-time algorithms* (Gen, H) *satisfying the following.*

1. Gen *is a probabilistic algorithm which takes as input a security parameter 1^n and outputs a key s. We assume that 1^n is implicit in s.*

2. H *takes as input a key s and a string $x \in \{0,1\}^*$, and outputs*

a string $H^s(x) \in \{0,1\}^{\ell(n)}$ (where n is the value of the security parameter implicit in s).

If H^s is defined only for inputs $x \in \{0,1\}^{\ell'(n)}$ and $\ell'(n) > \ell(n)$, then we say that (Gen, H) is a fixed-length hash function for inputs of length ℓ'. In this case, we also call H a compression function. Now we proceed to define an experiment for a hash function in order to define its security.

The collision-finding experiment Hash-coll$_{\mathcal{A},\Pi(n)}$

1. A key s is generated by running Gen(1^n).
2. The adversary $\mathcal{A}$ is given s and outputs x, x'. (If Π is a fixed-length hash function for inputs of length $\ell'(n)$, then we require $x, x' \in \{0,1\}^{\ell'(n)}$).
3. The output of the experiment is defined to be 1 if and only if $x \neq x'$ and $H^s(x) = H^s(x')$. In such a case we say that $\mathcal{A}$ has found a collision.

The definition of collision resistance states that no efficient adversary can find a collision in the above experiment except with negligible probability.

Definition 2 A hash function Π = (Gen, H) is **collision resistant** if and only if for all probabilistic polynomial-time adversaries $\mathcal{A}$, there is a negligible function negl such that

$$Pr[\text{Hash-coll}_{\mathcal{A},\Pi(n)} = 1] \leq negl(n). \tag{7.1}$$

Notwithstanding the above, the cryptographic hash functions used in the real world are collision resistant for all practical purposes since colliding pairs are unknown (and computationally difficult to find) even though they must exist.

7.1.2 Weaker Notions of Security

In some applications, it suffices to rely on security requirements weaker than collision resistance. These include

1. *Second preimage* or *target-collision resistance*: Informally, a hash function is second preimage resistant if given s and a uniform x it is infeasible for a PPT adversary to find $x'(\neq x)$ such that $H^s(x') = H^s(x)$.
2. *Preimage resistance* or *one-wayness*: Informally, a hash function is preimage resistant if given s and a uniform $y = H^s(x)$ (note that

x is not given) for a randomly chosen x, it is infeasible for a PPT adversary to find a value x' such that $H^s(x') = y$.

Note that collision resistance is the strongest notion, and second preimage resistance and preimage resistance comes next in order. Any hash function that is collision resistant is also second preimage resistant. Likewise, any hash function that is second preimage resistant is also preimage resistant. The other directions, however, do not hold: second preimage resistance does not imply collision resistance; preimage resistance does not imply second preimage resistance.

7.2   Design of Collision-Resistant Hash Functions

Most hash functions are generally constructed in two steps. First, a compression function (i.e., a fixed-length hash function) h is designed; next, some mechanism (e.g., the Merkle-Damgard transform explained later) is used to extend h so as to handle arbitrary input lengths.

7.2.1   Compression Function Proved Secure Under the Discrete Log Assumption

Now we consider a construction which is less efficient than the hash functions (e.g., MD, SHA family) based on compression functions, but illustrates the feasibility of achieving collision resistance based on standard and well-studied number-theoretic assumptions.

Let $\mathcal{G}$ be a polynomial-time algorithm that, on input 1^n, outputs a (description of a) cyclic group $\mathbb{G}$, its order q (with $\|q\| = n$), and a generator g. Here we also require that q is *prime* except possibly with negligible probability. A fixed-length hash function based on $\mathcal{G}$ is given in Construction 1.

Construction 1. A fixed-length hash function

Let $\mathcal{G}$ be as described above. Define a fixed-length hash function (Gen, H) as follows.

1. Gen: on input 1^n, run $\mathcal{G}(1^n)$ to obtain $(\mathbb{G}, q, g)$ and then select a uniform $h \in \mathbb{G}$.
    Output $s = \langle \mathbb{G}, q, g, h \rangle$ as the key.

2. H: given a key $s = \langle \mathbb{G}, q, g, h \rangle$ and input $(x_1, x_2) \in \mathbb{Z}_q \times \mathbb{Z}_q$, output $H^s(x_1, x_2) = g^{x_1} h^{x_2} \in \mathbb{G}$.

Theorem 1 *If the discrete-logarithm problem is hard, then Construction 1 is a fixed-length collision-resistant hash function.*

Proof

Outline of the Proof The proof is based on the "proof by reduction" technique introduced earlier. That is, we reduce discrete-log problem to collision-finding problem. It means that collision-finding problem is at least harder than discrete-log (DL) problem, which is believed to be hard.

Now we show that $\mathcal{A}$'s existence implies B's existence if we can construct B from any hypothetical $\mathcal{A}$ by converting a DL challenge into a collision-finding challenge, feeding the challenge to $\mathcal{A}$, and converting $\mathcal{A}$'s result into a solution to the DL challenge.

Reduction algorithm B

1. B accepts a DL challenge: (G, p, g, h) with $h = g^a$.

2. B starts $\mathcal{A}$ and gives the key $K = (G, p, g, h)$ to $\mathcal{A}$.

3. B takes $\mathcal{A}$'s output: $m_0 = (x_a, x_b)$ and $m_1 = (y_a, y_b)$ that collide in H_K.

4. If $H_K(m_0) = H_K(m_1), m_0 \neq m_1$ (i.e., $\mathcal{A}$ was successful), continue; else fail and quit.

5. B computes and returns $a = (x_a - y_a)(y_b - x_b)^{-1}$ as the solution to the DL challenge.

---

1. **Correctness** Whenever there is a collision, B returns the correct answer $\log_g h$ as follows.
   Suppose $\mathcal{A}$ output a collision (m_0, m_1) for H. In that case, B does not abort. Since (m_0, m_1) is a collision for H, we know that $H(m_0) = g^{x_a} h^{x_b} = g^{y_a} h^{y_b} = H(m_1)$. Therefore, $g^{x_a - y_a} = h^{y_b - x_b} = g^{a(y_b - x_b)}$. Suppose, for the moment, that $y_b = x_b$, which implies $x_a = y_a$. This is impossible because (m_0, m_1) is a collision. Therefore y_b and x_b should be distinct. Since $y_b \neq x_b$, B can compute $(y_b - x_b)^{-1}$ and then outputs $a = (x_a - y_a)(y_b - x_b)^{-1}$, the correct answer to the DL problem.

2. **Non-negligible advantage** $\mathcal{A}$ succeeds with an ϵ advantage and we just illustrated that B succeeds if and only if $\mathcal{A}$ succeeds, so B's advantage is non-negligible.

3. **Polynomial running time** Steps 1–5 can be done in polynomial time (Steps 1 & 2 take constant time; Step 3 takes polynomial time; Step 4 requires two exponentiations, which can be done in polynomial time; Step 5 requires a couple of additions, an inverse compu-

tation, and a multiplication, all of which can be done in polynomial time).

Here is a schematic diagram of the reduction algorithm B.

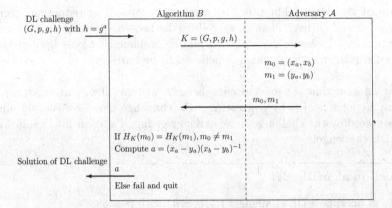

In the above, we showed that using $\mathcal{A}$'s non-negligible advantage, we can construct a polynomial time algorithm that solves the DL problem, which contradicts to the well-known assumption that the discrete log problem is hard. $\square$

Note that the proof technique shown in Theorem 1 is a little bit different from others in the sense that it does not require any alternate scheme, but is based on a supposedly hard problem.

7.2.2 Compression Functions Based on Secure Block Ciphers

One of the most common design is via the Davies-Meyer construction. Let F be a block cipher with n-bit key length and l-bit block length. We can then define the compression function $h : \{0,1\}^{n+l} \to \{0,1\}^l$ by $h(k,x) \stackrel{\text{def}}{=} F^k(x) \oplus x$.

We can prove collision resistance of the resulting compression function based only on the assumption that F is a strong pseudorandom permutation.

Theorem 2 *If F is modeled as an ideal cipher, then the Davies–Meyer construction yields a collision–resistant compression function.*

Proof is omitted.

7.2.3 Proprietary Compression Functions

MD5 [89] is a hash function with a 128-bit output length, designed in 1991. In 2004 a team of Chinese cryptanalysts successfully presented a new method for finding collisions in MD5. It is strongly recommended that MD5 should not be used any more. The Secure Hash Algorithm (SHA) refers to a series of cryptographic hash functions standardized by NIST (National Institute of Standards and Technology). Perhaps the most well known of these is SHA-1 [41] with a 160-bit output length, which was introduced in 1995. An explicit collision has yet to be found in SHA-1. However, collisions in SHA-1 can be found theoretically using significantly fewer than the 280 hash function evaluations that would be necessary using a birthday attack, and it is conjectured that a collision will be found soon. It is therefore recommended to migrate to SHA-2 [51], which does not currently appear to have the same weaknesses. In the aftermath of the theoretical weaknesses found in SHA-1, NIST announced in late 2007 a public competition to design a new cryptographic hash function to be called SHA-3 [40]. In October 2012, NIST announced the selection of *Keccak* as the winner of the competition.

7.3 The Merkle-Damgard Transform

Hash functions are often constructed by first designing a collision-resistant compression function handling fixed-length inputs, and then using *domain extension* to handle arbitrary-length inputs.

The Merkle-Damgard transform is a common approach for extending a compression function to a full-fledged hash function, while maintaining the collision-resistance property of the former. Due to it, when designing collision-resistant hash functions, we can restrict our attention to the fixed-length case. It is extensively used in practice for hash functions including MD5 and the SHA family (See Figure 7.1).

Construction 2. The Merkle-Damgard transform

Let h be a fixed-length hash function for inputs of length $2n$ and with output length n. Construct hash function H as follows.

1. Gen: remains unchanged.

2. H: on input a key s and a string $x \in \{0,1\}^*$ of length $L < 2^n$, do the following:

   (a) Set $B = \lceil \frac{L}{n} \rceil$ (i.e., the number of blocks in x). Pad x with zeros so its length is a multiple of n. Parse the padded result as the sequence of n-bit blocks $x_1, \ldots, x_B$. Set $x_{B+1} = L$, where L is encoded as an n-bit string.

(b) Set $z_0 = 0^n$ (This is also called the IV. Any value can be used instead of 0^n).

(c) For $i = 1, \ldots, B + 1$, compute $z_i = h^s(z_{i-1} \| x_i)$.

(d) Output z_{B+1}.

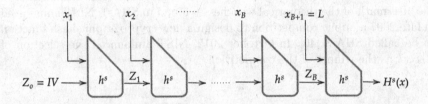

FIGURE 7.1
The Merkle-Damgard transform.

Theorem 3 *If (Gen, h) is collision resistant, then so is (Gen, H).*

Proof
Outline of the Proof Let us prove the contraposition of the theorem, easier to show: If H is not collision-resistant, then h is not collision-resistant. In other words, it suffices to show that we first assume that H_k is not collision-resistant, and then finally reach the statement that h_k is not collision-resistant. There are two cases to consider: The lengths of two blocks is either equal or different. In each case, we will trace the chains backwards to find h-collision.

Case 1: When the blocks are of different lengths:
In case when the blocks are of different lengths, the last step for the computation of $H_k(M_1)$ is $v_1[3] = h_k(v_1[2] \| \langle 2 \rangle)$, which is also termed as x_1. Similarly, the last step for the computation of $H_k(M_2)$ is $v_2[2] = h_k(v_2[1] \| \langle 1 \rangle)$, which is also termed as x_2. Let us suppose that a collision happens with H_k, i.e., $H_k(M_1)$ and $H_k(M_2)$ are equal, but $M_1 \neq M_2$. It follows that $h_k(v_1[2] \| \langle 2 \rangle)$ and $h_k(v_2[1] \| \langle 1 \rangle)$ are equal. However, since $\langle 1 \rangle$ and $\langle 2 \rangle$ are not equal, x_1 and x_2 are two different strings that collide for h_k, which proves that h_k is not collision-resistant.

Case 2: When the blocks are of the same length:
Now we see the case in which the blocks are of equal length. Let $v_1[i]$ and $v_2[i]$ are two intermediate hash values of M_1 and M_2 during the computation of $H_k(M_1)$ and $H_k(M_2)$. Let us suppose that a collision happens with H_k, i.e., $H_k(M_1)$ and $H_k(M_2)$ are equal, but $M_1 \neq M_2$, which means that there must be at least one index i such that $M_1[i] \neq M_2[i]$. Starting from the last, the

procedure calculates $x_1 = \langle 2 \rangle \, || v_1[2]$ and $x_2 = \langle 2 \rangle \, || v_2[2]$. If x_1 and x_2 are not equal, then (x_1, x_2) is returned as a collision for h_k, which proves that h_k is not collision-resistant. Otherwise, it moves down to the next block until it returns $(M_1[i], M_2[i])$ as a collision for h_k, which also proves that h_k is not collision-resistant. $\square$

7.4 Generic Attacks on Hash Functions

The following attacks are *generic* in the sense that they apply to arbitrary hash functions.

7.4.1 Birthday Attacks for Finding Collisions

A birthday attack is a type of cryptographic attack that exploits the mathematics behind the birthday problem in probability theory. Let us assume that we have a class of N students including Alice (Figure 7.2).

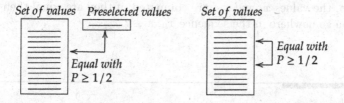

FIGURE 7.2
Birthday attack.

1. What is the minimum value of N where at least one person exists with the same birthday with Alice (that is, how large should N be in order that the probability his/her birthday be the same with Alice is greater than $\frac{1}{2}$)? The probability that any selected person would have different birthday from Alice is $\frac{364}{365}$; the probability that N persons would have different birthdays from Alice's is $(\frac{364}{365})^N$; therefore, the probability that any selected person would have the same birthday with Alice is $1 - (\frac{364}{365})^N$; setting $1 - (\frac{364}{365})^N = \frac{1}{2}$ results in $N = 253$.

2. What is the minimum value of N where at least two persons have the same birthday (that is, how large should N be in order that the probability of existing at least two persons having the same birthday is greater than $\frac{1}{2}$)? Let us first consider that all the persons have different birthdays. The probability the first person will have

a specific birthday would be $\frac{365}{365}$; The probability the second person will have a different birthday from the first person would be $\frac{365}{365} \cdot \frac{364}{365}$; the probability that the last person will have a different birthday from the previous $N-1$ persons would be $\frac{365}{365} \cdot \frac{364}{365} \cdots \frac{365-(N-1)}{365}$; therefore, the probability that at least two persons have the same birthday would be $1 - \frac{365}{365} \cdot \frac{364}{365} \cdots \frac{365-(N-1)}{365}$, which results in $N = 23$ when set to $\frac{1}{2}$.

Note that finding a collision is simply to evaluate a hash function for different input values that may be chosen randomly or pseudorandomly until the same result is found more than once. Because of the birthday problem, this method can be rather efficient as follows.

7.4.2 Small-Space Birthday Attacks

The birthday attacks described above require a large amount of memory. A better birthday attack with drastically reduced memory requirements is known as improved birthday attack. The attack begins by choosing a random value x_0 and then computing $x_i = H(x_{i-1})$ and $x_{2i} = H(H(x_{2(i-1)}))$ for $i > 1$. In each step, the values x_i and x_{2i} are compared; if they are equal then there is a collision somewhere in the sequence $x_0, x_1, ..., x_{2i-1}$.

7.5 Message Authentication Using Hash Functions

In the previous chapter, we presented two constructions of message authentication codes. The first approach was generic, but inefficient. The second was CBC-MAC. Here we see another approach called "Hash-and-MAC" [65] that relies on collision-resistant hashing along with any message authentication code. We then discuss a standardized and widely used construction called HMAC that can be viewed as a specific instantiation of this approach.

7.5.1 Hash-and-MAC

First, an arbitrarily long message m is hashed down to a fixed-length string $H^s(m)$ using a collision-resistant hash function. Then, a (fixed-length) MAC is applied to the result.

Construction 3. The hash-and-MAC paradigm

Let $\Pi = (\mathsf{Gen}, \mathsf{Mac}, \mathsf{Vrfy})$ be a MAC for messages of length $\ell(n)$ and let $\Pi_H = (\mathsf{Gen}_H, H)$ be a hash function with output length $\ell(n)$. Construct a MAC $\Pi' = (\mathsf{Gen}', \mathsf{Mac}', \mathsf{Vrfy}')$ for arbitrary-length messages as follows.

1. Gen': on input 1^n, run Gen to obtain $k \in \{0,1\}^n$ and run $\mathsf{Gen}_H(1^n)$ to obtain s; the key is $k' = \langle k, s \rangle$.

2. Mac': on input a key $\langle k, s \rangle$ and a message $m \in \{0,1\}^*$, output $t \leftarrow \mathsf{Mac}_k(H^s(m))$

3. Vrfy': on input a key $\langle k, s \rangle$, a message $m \in \{0,1\}^*$ and a MAC tag t, output 1 if and only if $\mathsf{Vrfy}_k(H^s(m), t) \overset{?}{=} 1$.

Theorem 4 *If Π is a secure MAC for messages of length l and Π_H is collision resistant, then Construction 3 is a secure MAC for arbitrary-length messages.*

Proof is omitted.

7.5.2 HMAC

Is it possible to construct a secure MAC (for arbitrary-length messages) based directly on a hash function? A first thought might be to define $Mac_k(m) = H(k\|m)$. A MAC designed in this way, however, is completely insecure.

Instead, we can try using two layers of hashing called HMAC.

Construction 4. HMAC

Let (Gen_H, H) be a hash function constructed by applying the Merkle-Damgard transform to a compression function (Gen_H, h) taking inputs of length $n + n'$. Let opad and ipad be fixed constants of length n'. HMAC defines a MAC as follows.

1. Gen: on input 1^n, run $\mathsf{Gen}_H(1^n)$ to obtain a key s. Also choose uniform $k \in \{0,1\}^{n'}$. Output the key $\langle s, k \rangle$.

2. Mac: on input a key $\langle s, k \rangle$ and a message $m \in \{0,1\}^*$, output

$$t = H^s\Big((k \oplus \mathsf{opad})\|H^s\big((k \oplus \mathsf{ipad})\|m\big)\Big).$$

---

3. Vrfy: on input a key $\langle s, k \rangle$, a message $m \in \{0, 1\}^*$, and a tag t,
    output 1 if and only if $t \overset{?}{=} H^s\Big((k \oplus \mathsf{opad})\|H^s\big((k \oplus \mathsf{ipad})\|m\big)\Big)$.

HMAC blocksize is 64 bytes (the same as SHA, MD5); ipad = the byte 0x36 repeated 64 times; opad = the byte 0x5C repeated 64 times:

1. Append zeros to the end of the key k to create a 64 byte string.

2. XOR (bitwise exclusive-OR) the 64 byte string computed in Step (1) with ipad.

3. Append the data stream to the 64 byte string resulting from Step (2).

4. Apply the hash H to the stream generated in Step (3).

5. XOR (bitwise exclusive-OR) the 64 byte string computed in Step (1) with opad.

6. Append the hash result from Step (4) to the 64 byte string resulting from Step (5).

7. Apply the hash H to the stream generated in Step (6) and output the result.

Theorem 5 *If the underlying hash function H meets a certain kind of weak collision-freeness and some limited unpredictability in Construction 4, then HMAC is a secure MAC for arbitrary-length messages.*

Proof is omitted.

HMAC in practice HMAC is an industry standard and widely used in practice (SSL/TLS, SSH, IPSec, FIPS 198, IEEE 802.11, IEEE 802.11b, etc.). It is highly efficient and easy to implement, and is supported by a proof of security based on assumptions that are believed to hold for practical hash functions.

7.6   Applications of Hash Function

Hash functions are one of widely applied cryptographic primitives in computer science and network including computer security and cryptography.

7.6.1 Fingerprinting and Deduplication

When using a collision-resistant hash function H, the hash (or digest) of a file serves as a unique identifier for that file.

1. Virus fingerprinting: Virus scanners identify viruses and block or quarantine them.

2. Deduplication: Data deduplication is used to eliminate duplicate copies of data, especially in the context of cloud storage where multiple users rely on a single cloud service to store their data. Deduplication can be achieved by first having a user upload a hash of the new file they want to store; if a file with this hash is already stored in the cloud, then the cloud-storage provider can simply add a pointer to the existing file to indicate that this specific user has also stored this file, saving both communication and storage.

3. Peer-to-peer (P2P) file sharing: In P2P file-sharing systems, tables are held by servers to provide a file-lookup service. These tables contain the hashes of the available files, once again providing a unique identifier without using much memory.

7.6.2 Merkle Trees

Consider a client who uploads a file x to a server. When the client later retrieves x, how to make sure that the server returns the original, unmodified file x?

A natural solution is to use the "fingerprinting" approach described above: The client can locally store the short digest $h = H(x)$; when the server returns a candidate file x', the client needs only to check that $H(x') \stackrel{?}{=} h$. But when the target consists of many $(x_1, x_2, ..., x_t)$ and/or large sized files, it causes storage (that is, growing linearly in t) and communication problems.

Another solution is to use "Merkle tree" approach. A Merkle tree computed over input values $x_1, ..., x_t$ is simply a binary tree of depth $\log t$ in which the inputs are placed at the leaves, and the value of each internal node is the hash of the values of its two children.

Theorem 6 Let (Gen_H, H) be collision resistant. Then $(Gen_H, \mathcal{MT}_t)$ is also collision resistant for any fixed t.

Proof is omitted.

Merkle tree basically makes it easy for a client to upload a file x to a server. Because it will take less memory to store digest and less number of computation when the client wants to retrieve the file x. Merkle tree is computed over input values $(x_1, x_2, ..., x_t)$ and becomes a simple binary tree of depth $\log t$. Its inputs are placed at leaves. Value of the each node computed using hash function is placed on its two children. Fixing some hash function H, we denote by $\mathcal{MT}_t$ the function that takes t input values $x_1, ..., x_t$, computes the resulting Merkle tree, and outputs the value of the root of the tree.

Let us check how Merkle trees work. Now, let say, a client computes $h_{1...8} = \mathcal{MT}_8(x_1, ..., x_8)$, uploads $x_1, ..., x_8$ to the server, and stores $h_{1...8}$ locally. Now if the client wants to retrieve the x_3, the server sends x_3 along with x_4, $H(x_1, x_2)$, and $h_{5...8} = H(H(x_5, x_6), H(x_7, x_8))$. Then the client using them through the Merkle tree do the following steps.

Small files case
Step 1: It will compute the node $H(x_3, x_4)$ using this node children(x_3, x_4).
Step 2: Then it will compute the node $h'_{1...4} = H(H(x_1, x_2), H(x_3, x_4))$ using this node children $(H(x_1, x_2), H(x_3, x_4))$.
Step 3: Then it will compute the node $h'_{1...8} = H(h'_{1...4}, h_{5...8})$ using this node children$(h'_{1...4}, h_{5...8})$.
Step 4: After getting them, verifies these values with each other $h_{1...8} \stackrel{?}{=} h'_{1...8}$. All the steps are shown in Figure 7.3 (a) with circles for retrieving x_3.

If files are large we may wish to avoid sending any file other than the one the client has requested. That can easily be done if we define the Merkle tree over the hashes of the files rather than the files themselves.

Large files case
Step 1: It will compute the node $H(x_3)$ and $H(x_4)$ using this node children x_3, x_4, respectively.
Step 2: It will compute the node $H(H(x_3), H(x_4))$ using this node children $H(x_3), H(x_4)$.
Step 3: Then it will compute the node $h'_{1...4} = H(H(H(x_1), H(x_2)), H(H(x_3), H(x_4)))$ using this node children $H(H(x_1), H(x_2), H(H(x_3), H(x_4))$.
Step 4: Then it will compute the node $h'_{1...8} = H(h'_{1...4}, h_{5...8})$ using this node children $(h'_{1...4}, h_{5...8})$.
Step 5: After getting them, verifies these values with each other $h_{1...8} \stackrel{?}{=} h'_{1...8}$. All the steps are shown in Figure 7.3 (b) with circles for retrieving x_3. So, we saw that Merkle tree is very efficient and we do not need much computation.

Merkle trees provide an efficient solution to our original problem, since the client's local storage is constant (independent of the number of files t) and the communication from server to client is very small, which is proportional to $\log t$. Note that Merkle trees thus provide an alternative to the Merkle-Damgard transform for achieving domain extension for collision-resistant hash functions (As described, however, Merkle trees are not collision resistant if the number of input values t is allowed to vary).

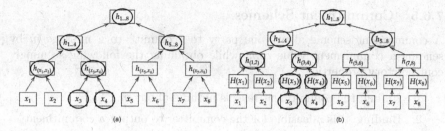

FIGURE 7.3
Merkle tree while computing root for x_3 (a) with small files (b) with large files.

7.6.3 Password Hashing

Important uses of hash functions in computer security is for password protection. Usually the password is not stored at the authenticating server. It stores only the value $hpw = H(pw)$ in a password file; later, when the user enters its password pw, the server checks whether $H(pw) \stackrel{?}{=} hpw$ before granting access.

If we model H as a random oracle, then we can formally prove the security we want, namely, recovering pw from hpw (assuming pw is chosen uniformly from D) requires $|D|/2$ evaluations of H, on average.

One possible way of password cracking is done by preprocessing, which can be used to generate large tables that enable inversion (even of a random function!) faster than exhaustive search. This is a significant concern in practice.

One way to mitigate the threat of password cracking is to introduce a *salt* (a long random value) stored with the hash value of the password in the form, $(s, hpw = H(s, pw))$ in the password file. The best an attacker can do is to obtain the password file and then do a linear-time exhaustive search over the domain D as discussed before.

7.6.4 Key Derivation

All the symmetric-key cryptosystems we have seen require a uniformly distributed bit-string for the secret key. Often, however, it is more convenient for two parties to rely on shared information such as a password or biometric data that is not uniformly distributed, which will be fed into a hash function to result in uniformly distributed string.

7.6.5   Commitment Schemes

A commitment scheme allows one party to "commit" to a message m by sending a commitment value *com*, while obtaining the following seemingly contradictory properties.

1. Hiding: the commitment reveals nothing about m.
2. Binding: it is infeasible for the committer to output a commitment *com* that it can later "open" as two different messages m, m'.

A commitment scheme can be seen as a digital envelope: sealing a message in an envelope and handing it over to another party provides privacy (until the envelope is opened) and binding (since the envelope is sealed).

Exercises

7.1 Second preimage resistance does not imply collision resistance; preimage resistance does not imply second preimage resistance. Why not?

7.2 Explain how the Merkle-Damgard transform works for blocks of the same lengths.

7.3 Explain how the Merkle-Damgard transform works for blocks of different lengths.

7.4 Theorem 3 shows that the Merkle-Damgard transform preserves collision resistance. Explain intuitively why it holds.

7.5 Survey cloud computing applications, find out existing problems, and then fix them by using the original Merkle tree or devising your own variants of the Merkle tree.

8

Introduction to Number Theory

CONTENTS

This chapter serves as a basis to the underlying mathematical concepts, theorems, and algorithms for cryptography including division, prime, modulo, exponentiation, logarithm, and residue. The next section discusses the algebraic structures used in mathematics for cryptography including groups, rings, and fields, followed by Galois Field. Elliptic curves are then defined along with the basic operations like point addition and point multiplication.

8.1   Preliminaries

We review basic mathematical concepts, theorems, and algorithms for cryptography.

8.1.1 Division, Prime, and Modulo

We shall denote the set of integers by $\mathbb{Z}$, the set of positive integers by $\mathbb{Z}^+$, the set of natural numbers by $\mathbb{N}$, and the set of rational numbers by $\mathbb{Q}$, and the set of real numbers by $\mathbb{R}$.

Theorem 1 *For all $a \in \mathbb{Z}$ and $n \in \mathbb{Z}^+$, there exist unique integers q and r such that*

$$a = q \times n + r, \ 0 \leq r < n. \tag{8.1}$$

In this relation, a is called the *dividend*; q, the *quotient*; n, the *divisor*; r, the *remainder*.

Example We have $20 = 3 \times 6 + 2$. We can say that 20 is the dividend, 3 is the quotient, 6 is the divisor, and 2 is the remainder.

In Theorem 1, if a is not zero and we let $r = 0$, we get

$$a = q \times n. \tag{8.2}$$

We then say that n divides a and we write $n \mid a$. If the remainder is not zero, then n does not divide a and we write $n \nmid a$.

Example We have $20 = 4 \times 5$, then we can say that 5 divides 20 and we write $5 \mid 20$. We also have $20 = 3 \times 6 + 2$, then we can say that 6 does not divide 20 and we write $6 \nmid 20$.

Definition 1 (Prime) *A positive integer is a prime if and only if it is exactly divisible by two integers, 1 and itself.*

Definition 2 (Factorization) *Any positive integer n greater than one can be written uniquely in the following prime factorization form, where $p_1, p_2, \ldots, p_k$ are primes and $e_1, e_2, \ldots, e_k$ are positive integers as*

$$n = p_1^{e_1} \times p_2^{e_2} \times \cdots \times p_k^{e_k}. \tag{8.3}$$

No such perfect algorithm has been found to factor large compositive integers efficiently. This is good for cryptography because some modern cryptography relies on this fact.

In Theorem 1, the division relation has two inputs (a and n) and two outputs (q and r). In modular arithmetic, we are interested in only one of the outputs, the remainder r. This binary operator is called the modulo operator and is shown as *mod*. We can write

$$a \ mod \ n = r. \tag{8.4}$$

Example We have $27 \bmod 5 = 2$.
Example Find $5^6 \bmod 7$. The result can be found later by using Fermat's Little Theorem.

8.1.2 Greatest Common Divisor

Definition 3 (Greatest Common Divisor) *The greatest common divisor of two non-negative integers a and b is the largest integer that can divide both a and b, is denoted by gcd(a,b). We say that a and b are relatively prime or coprime if $gcd(a, b) = 1$.*

Example The greatest common divisor of 24 and 36 is 12. We can write gcd(24,36)=12. The greatest common divisor of 24 and 35 is 1, then we say 24 and 35 are relatively prime.

8.1.3 Euclidean Algorithm

The *Euclidean algorithm* is based on the following two facts.
Fact 1. $gcd(a, 0) = a$.
Fact 2. $gcd(a, b) = gcd(b, r)$, where r is the remainder of dividing a by b.

Example $gcd(45, 20) = gcd(20, 5) = gcd(5, 0) = 5$.

8.1.4 Extended Euclidean Algorithm

Given two integers a and b, we often need to find other two integers, s and t, such that

$$s \times a + t \times b = gcd(a, b). \tag{8.5}$$

Example Given $a = 161$ and $b = 28$, we get $gcd(161, 28) = 7$, $s = -1$ and $t = 6$. The answer can be tested because we have $(-1) \times 161 + 6 \times 28 = 7$.

8.1.5 Fermat's Little Theorem

Fermat's little theorem plays a very important role in number theory and cryptography. There are two versions of this theorem.

Theorem 2 *If p is a prime and a is an integer, then $a^p \equiv a \bmod p$.*

Theorem 3 *If p is a prime and a is not divisible by p, then $a^{p-1} \equiv 1 \bmod p$.*

Note that Theorem 2 holding for any integer a, which is equivalent to Theorem 3 holding for a not divisible by p.

Example Find the result of $6^{10} \bmod 11$.

Example Find the result of $3^{12} \bmod 11$.

Theorem 4 *If p is a prime and a is an integer such that p does not divide a, then*

$$a^{-1} \bmod p = a^{p-2} \bmod p. \tag{8.6}$$

We can use the above theorem to find some multiplicative inverse instead of using the extended Euclidean algorithm.

Example Find the multiplicative inverse of 8 with modulus is 17. The result is 15.

8.1.6 Euler's Theorem

Euler's phi function, denoted by $\phi(n)$, which is sometimes also called the Euler's quotient function plays a very important role in cryptography. This function finds the number of integers that are both smaller than n and relatively prime to n. The four following properties helps to find the value of $\phi(n)$:

1. $\phi(0) = 1$.
2. $\phi(p) = p - 1$ if p is a prime.
3. $\phi(m \times n) = \phi(m) \times \phi(n)$ if m and n are relatively prime.
4. $\phi(p^e) = p^e - p^{e-1}$ if p is a prime.

Example What is the value of $\phi(14)$? The result is 6. The number of elements in $Z_{14}{}^*$ is 6. There are 1, 3, 5, 9, 11, and 13.

The modulus in Fermat's Little Theorem is a prime, the modulus in Euler's theorem is an integer. There are two versions of Euler theorem.

Theorem 5 *If a and n are coprime, then $a^{\phi(n)} \equiv 1 \ mod \ n$.*

Example What is the value of 6^{24} mod 35? The result is 1.

Theorem 6 *If $n = p \times q$, $a < n$, and k is an integer, then*

$$a^{k \times \phi(n)+1} \equiv a \ mod \ n. \tag{8.7}$$

Example What is the value of 20^{62} mod 77? The result is 15.

8.1.7 Exponentiation and Logarithm

In cryptography, exponentiation operation is frequently used to calculate

$$y = a^x mod \ n. \tag{8.8}$$

If exponentiation operation is used to encrypt or decrypt, the adversary can use logarithm to attack as

$$x = log_a y \ mod \ n. \tag{8.9}$$

The number x is called the discrete logarithm of y to the base a.
Fast exponentiation is possible using the square-and-multiply method. We can write $y = a^x$ as

$$y = a^{x_{n-1} \times 2^{n-1} + x_{n-2} \times 2^{n-2} + \cdots + x_1 \times 2^1 + x_0 \times 2^0}, \tag{8.10}$$

where x_i is 0 or 1.

Example Compute 5^{41} mod 9. We have two ways to compute as follows.

1. Straightforward approach

   5^{41} mod 9 = 45474735088646411895751953125 mod 9 = 2.

2. Using fast exponentiation

   We write $41 = 101001_{(2)}$, then we have $5^{41} = 5^{32+8+1} = 5^{32} \times 5^8 \times 5^1$.
   We have: 5^1 mod 9 = 5 mod 9 = 5,
   5^2 mod 9 = $(5^1 \times 5^1)$ mod 9 = $(5^1$ mod 9×5^1 mod 9) mod 9 = (5×5) mod 9 = 7,
   5^4 mod 9 = $(5^2 \times 5^2)$ mod 9 = $(5^2$ mod 9×5^2 mod 9) mod 9 = (7×7) mod 9 = 4,
   5^8 mod 9 = $(5^4 \times 5^4)$ mod 9 = $(5^4$ mod 9×5^4 mod 9) mod 9 = (4×4) mod 9 = 7,
   5^{16} mod 9 = $(5^8 \times 5^8)$ mod 9 = $(5^8$ mod 9×5^8 mod 9) mod 9 = (7×7) mod 9 = 4,
   5^{32} mod 9 = $(5^{16} \times 5^{16})$ mod 9 = $(5^{16}$ mod 9×5^{16} mod 9) mod 9 = (4×4) mod 9 = 7,

   then

   5^{41} mod 9 = $(5^{32} \times 5^8 \times 5^1)$ mod 9 = $(5^{32}$ mod 9×5^8 mod 9×5^1 mod 9) mod 9
   $= (7 \times 7 \times 5)$ mod 9 = $((7 \times 7)$ mod 9×5 mod 9) mod 9 = (4×5) mod 9 = 2.

8.1.8 Set of Residues $\mathbb{Z}_n$

Definition 4 (Set of Residues $\mathbb{Z}_n$) *Let n be a positive integer and $\mathbb{Z}_n$ be the set $\{0, 1, 2 \ldots n-1\}$ with the following operations.*

1. $(a+b) \bmod n = [(a \bmod n) + (b \bmod n)] \bmod n$

2. $(a-b) \bmod n = [(a \bmod n) - (b \bmod n)] \bmod n$

3. $(a \times b) \bmod n = [(a \bmod n) \times (b \bmod n)] \bmod n$

The result of modulo operator is always an integer between 0 and $n-1$. We say that the set of all these integers is the set of least residues modulo n or $\mathbb{Z}_n$.

Example We have $\mathbb{Z}_6 = \{0, 1, 2, 3, 4, 5\}$.

Definition 5 (Modulus) *Let $a, b \in \mathbb{Z}$, and $n \in \mathbb{Z}^+$. We say that a is congruent to b modulo n if $n \mid (a - b)$, in which case we can write $a \equiv b$ (mod n). If a is not congruent to b modulo n, then we write $a \not\equiv b$ (mod n). The integer n is called modulus.*

Example We have $2 \equiv 12(\bmod\ 10)$ or $3 \not\equiv 12$ (mod 10).

8.1.9   Inverse Modulo

Definition 6 (Additive Inverse) *In modular arithmetic, each integer has an additive inverse. The sum of an integer and its additive inverse is congruent to 0 modulo n.*

We say that two numbers a and b are additive inverse of each other if $(a+b) \equiv 0$ (mod n).

Example If the modulus is 10, then the additive inverse of 2 is 8. In other words, we have $2 + 8 \equiv 0$ (mod 10).

Definition 7 (Multiplicative Inverse) *Let $a \in \mathbb{Z}$ and $n \in \mathbb{Z}^+$. A multiplicative inverse of a modulo n is an integer b such that $a \times b \equiv 1$ (mod n).*

Example If the modulus is 10, then the multiplicative inverse of 3 is 7. In other words, we have $3 \times 7 \equiv 1$ (mod 10).

Definition 8 ($\mathbb{Z}_n^*$) $\mathbb{Z}_n^*$ *is the set of all elements in $\mathbb{Z}_n$ with a multiplicative inverse, that is,*

$$\mathbb{Z}_n^* = \{a \in \mathbb{Z}_n : gcd(a, n) = 1\}.$$

There are two more sets often used in cryptography: $\mathbb{Z}_p$ and $\mathbb{Z}_p^*$. The modulus in these two sets is a prime number which has only two divisors: 1 and itself. Prime number will be discussed later. $\mathbb{Z}_p$ is the same as $\mathbb{Z}_n$ except that p is a prime. Each member in $\mathbb{Z}_p$ has an additive inverse. $\mathbb{Z}_p^*$ is the same as $\mathbb{Z}_n^*$ except that p is a prime. Each member in $\mathbb{Z}_p^*$ has an additive inverse and a multiplicative inverse.

Note that 1 is relatively prime for all natural numbers.

$\mathbb{Z}_p = \{0, 1, 2, \ldots, p - 1\}$,
$\mathbb{Z}_p^* = \{1, 2, \ldots, p - 1\}$.

Example $\mathbb{Z}_{13} = \{0, 1, 2, 3, 4, 5, 6, 7, 8, 9, 10, 11, 12\}$,
$\mathbb{Z}_{13}^* = \{1, 2, 3, 4, 5, 6, 7, 8, 9, 10, 11, 12\}$.

Properties

1. x has an inverse in $\mathbb{Z}_n$ if x and n are relatively prime.

2. $\mathbb{Z}_n^*$ is the set of invertible elements in $\mathbb{Z}_n$.

3. Let $a, m \in \mathbb{Z}$ and p is a prime. If $p \nmid a$, then $a^m \equiv a^{m \ mod(p-1)}$ (mod p).

> **Proof** Let $q = [m/(p-1)]$ and $r = m \bmod (p-1)$. Recall that $m = q(p-1) + r$ by the division algorithm. If $p \nmid a$, then Fermat's Little Theorem (will be discussed later) implies
>
> $$a^m \equiv a^{q(p-1)+r} \equiv a^{q(p-1)}a^r \equiv (a^{p-1})^q a^r \equiv 1^q a^r \equiv a^r (mod \ p). \tag{8.11}$$

Example Suppose we wish to compute $5^{83315563}$ mod 11. Note that 11 is prime and $11 \nmid 5$, so we can apply the above property. We calculate

$$5^{83315563} \bmod 11 \equiv 5^{83315563 mod 10} \equiv 5^3 \equiv 125 \equiv 4 \ (mod \ 11).$$

Therefore, $5^{83315563} \bmod 11 = 4$. We have another representation of this property as the following.

Fact If p is a prime and g is a generator of $\mathbb{Z}_p^*$, then

$$g^c = g^a g^b \ mod \ p \Leftrightarrow c = (a + b) \ mod \ (p - 1). \tag{8.12}$$

Proof Let $c = q_1(p-1) + r_1$ and $(a+b) = q_2(p-1) + r_2$.

$g^c \bmod p = g^{q_1(p-1)+r_1} \bmod p = (g^{q_1(p-1)} \times g^{r_1}) \bmod p = (g^{q_1(p-1)} \bmod p \times g^{r_1} \bmod p)$

$\qquad = ((g^{p-1})^{q_1} \bmod p \times g^{r_1} \bmod p) \bmod p = 1^{q_1} \bmod p \times g^{r_1} \bmod p = g^{r_1}$ $\bmod p$,

$g^{a+b} \bmod p = g^{q_2(p-1)+r_2} \bmod p = (g^{q_2(p-1)} \times g^{r_2}) \bmod p = (g^{q_2(p-1)} \bmod p \times g^{r_2} \bmod p)$

$\qquad = ((g^{p-1})^{q_2} \bmod p \times g^{r_2} \bmod p) \bmod p = 1^{q_2} \bmod p \times g^{r_2} \bmod p = g^{r_2}$ $\bmod p$.

Thus, we have

$$g^c = g^a g^b \bmod p \Leftrightarrow g^{r_1} \bmod p = g^{r_2} \bmod p \Leftrightarrow c = (a + b) \bmod (p - 1).$$

Theorem 7 *For $x, y \in \mathbb{Z}_p$, y is a square root of x if $y^2 \equiv x \ \ mod \ p$.*

An element has either 0 or 2 square roots in $\mathbb{Z}_p$. If y is a square root of x, so is $-y$.

Definition 9 (QR and QNR) *In the equation* $y^2 \equiv x \mod p$, *for* $x \in \mathbb{Z}_p^*, y \in \mathbb{Z}_p$, y *is called a quadratic residue (QR) if the equation has two square roots in* $\mathbb{Z}_p$, *while* y *is called a quadratic nonresidue (QNR) if the equation has no square root.*

8.1.10   Euler's Criterion

Euler's criterion gives some specific conditions to check if an integer is a QR modulo p.

1. If $y^{(p-1)/2} \equiv 1 \pmod{p}$, y is a quadratic residue modulo p.
2. If $y^{(p-1)/2} \equiv -1 \pmod{p}$, y is a quadratic nonresidue modulo p.

It can be proved that in $\mathbb{Z}_p$, with $p - 1$ elements, exactly $(p - 1)/2$ elements are quadratic residues and $(p - 1)/2$ elements are quadratic nonresidues.

8.2   Algebraic Structure

This section discusses the algebraic structures used in cryptography including groups, rings and fields, Galois field, and elliptic curve.

8.2.1   Group

Definition 10 (Group) *A* $\langle \mathbb{G}, \bullet \rangle$ *is a set of elements with a binary operation* $\bullet$ *that satisfies four properties.*

1. **Closure:** If a and b are elements of $\mathbb{G}$, then $c = a \bullet b$ is also an element of $\mathbb{G}$.
2. **Associativity:** If a, b, and c are elements of $\mathbb{G}$, then $(a \bullet b) \bullet c = a \bullet (b \bullet c)$.
3. **Identity element:** For all a in $\mathbb{G}$, there exists an element e, called the identity element, such that $e \bullet a = a \bullet e = a$.
4. **Existence of inverse:** For each a in $\mathbb{G}$, there exists an element a', called the inverse of a, such that $a \bullet a' = a' \bullet a = e$.

Definition 11 (Abelian Group) *A group* $\langle \mathbb{G}, \bullet \rangle$ *is called abelian or commutative if*

$$a \bullet b = b \bullet a \quad \text{for all a,b in } \mathbb{G}.$$

Theorem 8 *Let* $\langle \mathbb{G}, \bullet, e \rangle$ *be a group. Then*

1. There exists a unique identity element of $\mathbb{G}$ under $\bullet$.
2. For each $a \in \mathbb{G}$, there exists a unique inverse of a under $\bullet$.

Multiplicative and Additive Notation

In multiplicative notation, the group operation is denoted by $\times$, the identity element by 1, the inverse of a by a^{-1}, and m applications of the operation $\times$ to a by a^m.

In additive notation, the group operation is denoted by $+$, the identity element by 0, the inverse of a by $-a$, and m applications of the operation $+$ to a by ma.

Example $\langle \mathbb{Z}_n, + \rangle$, $\langle \mathbb{Z}_n^*, \times \rangle$, $\langle \mathbb{Q} - \{0\}, \times \rangle$ and $\langle \mathbb{R}, + \rangle$ are commutative groups. $\langle \mathbb{Z}_n, + \text{ mod n} \rangle$ and $\langle \mathbb{Z}_n^*, + \text{ mod n} \rangle$ are groups, while $\langle \mathbb{Z}_n, \times \text{ mod n} \rangle$ and $\langle \mathbb{Z}_n^*, \times \text{ mod n} \rangle$ are not groups. $\langle \mathbb{Z}_n, \times \text{ mod n} \rangle$ and $\langle \mathbb{Z}_n^*, \times \text{ mod n} \rangle$ become groups, if n is a prime. Thus, $\langle \mathbb{Z}_p, \times \text{ mod p} \rangle$ and $\langle \mathbb{Z}_p^*, \times \text{ mod p} \rangle$ are groups for a prime p.

Definition 12 (Finite and Infinite Group) *A group is called a finite group if the set has a finite number of elements; otherwise, it is called an infinite group.*

Definition 13 (Order of a Group) *The order of a group, denoted by $|\mathbb{G}|$ or $||\mathbb{G}||$, is the number of elements in the group $\mathbb{G}$. If the group is finite, its order is finite; if the group is infinite, its order is infinite.*

Definition 14 (Subgroup) *Let $\mathbb{G}$ be a group and $\mathbb{H}$ be a subset of $\mathbb{G}$. We say that $\mathbb{H}$ is a subgroup of $\mathbb{G}$ if $\mathbb{H}$ is also a group under the same operation as $\mathbb{G}$.*

Example. Is the group $\mathbb{H} = \langle \mathbb{Z}_{10}, + \rangle$ a subgroup of the group $\mathbb{G} = \langle \mathbb{Z}_{12}, + \rangle$?

Definition 15 (Cyclic Subgroup) *If a subgroup of a group can be generated using the power of an element, the subgroup is called the cyclic subgroup. The term power here is repeatedly applying the group operation to the element a: $a^n = a \bullet a \bullet \cdots \bullet a$ (n times). A cyclic group is a group that has its own cyclic subgroup. The element is referred as a generator.*

Example The group $\mathbb{G} = \langle \mathbb{Z}_6, + \rangle$ is a cyclic group with two generators, $a = 1$ and $a = 5$. The group $\mathbb{G} = \langle \mathbb{Z}_{10}^*, \times \rangle$ is a cyclic group with two generators, $a = 3$ and $a = 7$.

Theorem 9 *For all primes p, the group $\langle \mathbb{Z}_p^*, \times \rangle$ is cyclic with identity element of 1.*

Definition 16 (Order of an Element) *The order of an element a in a group, denoted by ord(a), is the smallest integer n such that $a^n = e$.*

Example In the group $\mathbb{G} = \langle \mathbb{Z}_{10}^*, \times \rangle$, the order of elements are: ord(1)=1, ord(3)=4, ord(7)=4, ord(9)=2.

Primitive root In the group $\mathbb{G} = \langle \mathbb{Z}_n^*, \times \rangle$, when the order of an element is the same as $\phi(n)$, the element is called the primitive root of the group.

The idea of discrete logarithm The group $\mathbb{G} = \langle \mathbb{Z}_p^*, \times \rangle$ has several properties as

1. Its elements include all integers from 1 to $p - 1$.
2. It always has primitive roots.
3. It is a cyclic group. The element can be generated using g^x where x is an integer from 1 to $\phi(n) = p - 1$.
4. If the group has k primitive roots, calculations can be done in k different bases.

8.2.2 Ring

Definition 17 (Ring) *A ring, denoted by $\langle R, \bullet, \circ \rangle$, is an algebraic structure with two operations. The first operation must satisfy all five properties required for an abelian group. The second operation must satisfy only the first two. A commutative ring is a ring in which the commutative property is also satisfied for the second operation.*

Example $\langle \mathbb{Z}, +, \times \rangle$ is a ring. $\langle \mathbb{Z}_n, + \bmod n, \times \bmod n \rangle$ and $\langle \mathbb{Z}_n^*, + \bmod n, \times \bmod n \rangle$ are important rings in cryptography.

8.2.3 Field

Definition 18 (Field) *A field, denoted by $\langle \mathbb{F}, \bullet, \circ \rangle$, is a commutative ring in which the second operation satisfies all five properties defined for the first operation except that the identity of the first operation has no inverse.*

Example $\langle \mathbb{Z}_5, +, \times \rangle$ is a field, but $\langle \mathbb{Z}_6, +, \times \rangle$ is not a field.

Are $\langle \mathbb{Z}_n, + \bmod n, \times \bmod n \rangle$ and $\langle \mathbb{Z}_p, + \bmod p, \times \bmod p \rangle$ fields? Why?

Definition 19 (Finite Field) *A finite field is a field with a finite number of elements (Galois showed that the number of elements should be p^n) and usually called Galois field and denoted by $\mathrm{GF}(p^n)$, where p is a prime and n is a positive integer.*

When $n = 1$, we have $\mathrm{GF}(p)$ as the set $\mathbb{Z}_p$ of integers $\{0, 1, 2 \ldots, p - 1\}$ together with the arithmetic operation modulo p. The operations are defined as: *for all $a, b \in \mathrm{GF}(p)$, we have $a + b = (a + b) \bmod p$ and $a \times b = (a \times b) \bmod p$. The identity element for additive operation is integer 0 and the identity element for multiplicative operation is integer 1.*

8.2.4 $\mathrm{GF}(2^n)$

A polynomial of degree $n-1$ is an expression of the form

$$f(x) = a_{n-1}x^{n-1} + a_{n-2}x^{n-2} + \ldots a_0x^0, \qquad (8.13)$$

where x^i is called the i-th term and a_i is called the coefficient of the i-th term.

When $p = 2$ in Galois field, we have $\mathrm{GF}(2^n)$. An element of $\mathrm{GF}(2^n)$ can be expressed as a bit string of length n. An element of $\mathrm{GF}(2^n)$ is can also be expressed as a polynomial. There is an one-to-one correspondence between n-bit string expression and $(n-1)$ degree polynomial expression. The power of x defines the position of the bit in n-bit word. The coefficients of the terms define the values of the bits.

Example For $n = 5$, we can represent 5-bit word (10111) using a polynomial is $1x^4 + 0x^3 + 1x^2 + 1x^1 + 1x^0$. After simplification, we have $x^4 + x^2 + x + 1$.

Before defining the operations on polynomials, we need to define a modulus polynomial in the set of $\mathrm{GF}(2^n)$ which is referred to as prime polynomial or irreducible polynomial.

Definition 20 (Irreducible or Prime Polynomial) *A irreducible or prime polynomial is a polynomial that no polynomials in the set can divide this polynomial.*

Example For $n = 3$, we have $\mathrm{GF}(2^3)$. There are two irreducible polynomials: $(x^3 + x^2 + 1)$ and $(x^3 + x + 1)$.

We find the result of addition for polynomial, denoted by $\oplus$, by adding the coefficients of the corresponding terms.

Example The result of $(x^7 + x^2 + 1) \oplus (x^5 + x^2 + x)$ in $\mathrm{GF}(2^8)$ is $x^7 + x^5 + x + 1$.

The addition operation for the n-bit string can also be calculated by exclusive-or (XOR). The additive identity in a polynomial is a zero polynomial (a polynomial with all coefficients set to zero). For the n-bit string, we have the identity is $(000\ldots000)$ with length of n bits. The additive inverse of a polynomial with coefficient in $\mathrm{GF}(2)$ is polynomial itself. Note that addition and subtraction operations on polynomials are the same operation.

Multiplication in polynomials, denoted by $\otimes$, is the sum of the multiplication of each term of the first polynomial with each term of the second polynomial, then to be reduced by using a modulus polynomial.

Example The result of $(x^5 + x^2 + x) \otimes (x^7 + x^4 + x^3 + x^2 + x)$ with irreducible polynomial $(x^8 + x^4 + x^3 + x + 1)$ is $x^5 + x^3 + x^2 + x + 1$.

The multiplicative identity in polynomials is always 1. For the n-bit string, we have the identity is $(000\dots001)$ with length of n bits and the first $n-1$ bits set to zero. The multiplicative inverse of a polynomial can be calculated by using the extended Euclidean algorithm.

In the $\mathbb{GF}(2^n)$ with the irreducible polynomial $f(x)$, an element in the field, a must satisfy the relation $f(a) = 0$. If g is a generator of the field, then $f(g) = 0$. The elements of the field can be generated as

$$\{0, g, g^2, g^3, \dots, g^N\}, \text{where } N = 2^n - 2. \tag{8.14}$$

Example Generate the elements of $\mathbb{GF}(2^3)$ using the irreducible polynomial $x^3 + x + 1$.

8.2.5 Elliptic Curve

Definition 21 (Elliptic Curve) *An elliptic curve E is the set of all points over $\mathbb{GF}(p)$ satisfying the Weierstrass equation*

$$y^2 = x^3 + ax + b, \tag{8.15}$$

together with an extra point O (point at infinity or zero point), where the constant a and b must satisfy $4a^3 + 27b^2 \neq 0$.

Operation

Let E be an elliptic curve and $P = (x_1, y_1)$ and $Q = (x_2, y_2)$ be two points on E. There are three cases to find $R = (x_3, y_3) = P + Q$.

1. If P and Q have different x-coordinates and y-coordinates $(x_1 \neq y_1)$ and $(x_2 \neq y_2)$, then calculate λ (the slope of the line) and x_3, y_3 as below.

$$\lambda = (y_2 - y_1)/(x_2 - x_1),$$
$$x_3 = \lambda^2 - x_1 - x_2, \qquad y_3 = \lambda(x_1 - x_3) - y_1.$$

2. If P and Q are two points overlap, $R = P + P$, then

$$\lambda = (3x_1{}^2 + a)/(2y_1),$$
$$x_3 = \lambda^2 - 2x_1, \qquad y_3 = \lambda(x_1 - x_3) - y_1.$$

3. If P and Q are additive inverses of each other, then $R = P + Q = O$, where O is the additive identity of the group.

Theorem 10 *Let P, Q, R be the points on E. The addition operation make the points of the elliptic curve E into an abelian group with the following properties.*

1. *Closure: The addition operation between two points creates another point on the curve.*
2. *Associativity: $(P + Q) + R = P + (Q + R)$.*
3. *Commutiativity: $P + Q = Q + P$.*
4. *Existence of identity: $P + O = O + P = P$.*
5. *Existence of inverse: $P + (-P) = O$.*

Elliptic Curve Over $\mathbb{GF}(2^n)$

The equation $y^2 + xy = x^3 + ax^2 + b$, where $b \neq 0$ is used for $\mathbb{GF}(2^n)$. Note that the values of x, y, a, and b are polynomials representing n-bit words. Addition and multiplication on the elements are the same as addition and multiplication on polynomial.

1. **Finding the inverse** If $P = (x, y)$, then $-P = (x, x + y)$.
2. **Finding the points on the curve** Using generators.
3. **Adding two points** Let $P = (x_1, y_1)$ and $Q = (x_2, y_2)$ be two points on the curve. $R = P + Q = (x_3, y_3)$ can be found as

   (a) If $Q \neq P$ and $Q \neq -P$, then
   $$\lambda = (y_2 + y_1)/(x_2 + x_1),$$
   $$x_3 = \lambda^2 + \lambda + x_1 + x_2 + a, \qquad y_3 = \lambda(x_1 + x_3) + x_3 + y_1.$$
   (b) If $Q = P$, then $R = 2P$ as
   $$\lambda = (x_1 + y_1)/x_1,$$
   $$x_3 = \lambda^2 + \lambda + a, \qquad y_3 = x_1{}^2 + (\lambda + 1)x_3.$$

4. **Multiplying a point by a constant** Multiplication with constant k is defined as k-times repeated addition, $kP = P + P + \cdots + P$.

9

Public-Key Encryption

CONTENTS

This chapter provides an overview of the public-key cryptography. The chapter starts with the discrete logarithm and its related assumptions. The next part of the chapter provides the details about the Diffie-Hellman key exchange protocol since the key exchange is important in the public-key cryptosystems. The public-key encryption scheme is then defined as a triple of probabilistic polynomial-time algorithms for key generation, encryption, and decryption. A comparison of private and public key encryptions is then presented. The next section provides the security of the public key encryption schemes against CPA and CCA. This is followed by the hybrid encryption using the KEM/DEM paradigm. The last part of the chapter introduces several public key encryption schemes that include the El Gamal encryption, the plain (aka textbook) RSA encryption, the padded RSA encryption, the Cramer-Shoup encryption, and the Paillier encryption scheme. The constructions, security proofs, and related examples for each scheme are given as well.

9.1   Discrete Logarithm and Its Related Assumptions

We let $\mathcal{G}$ denote a generic, polynomial-time, *group-generation* algorithm. This is an algorithm that, on input 1^n, outputs a description of a cyclic group $\mathbb{G}$, its order q (with $\|q\| = n$), and a generator $g \in \mathbb{G}$. The description of a cyclic group specifies how elements of the group are represented as bit-strings.

Let p be a prime of the form $p = 2q + 1$, where q is also a prime. Recall that such a prime p is called a *strong prime*. The group $\mathbb{Z}_p^*$ has a subgroup $\mathbb{G}$ of order q. The group $\mathbb{G}$ is known as the group of *quadratic residues modulo* p. Every element of $\mathbb{G}$ except for 1 is a generator of $\mathbb{G}$.

We define the algorithm $\mathcal{G}$ as follows.

Algorithm $\mathcal{G}$

1. Take 1^n as input (where n is a security parameter).

2. Randomly choose an $(n + 1)$-bit prime p of the form $p = 2q + 1$, where q is also a prime.

3. Let $\mathbb{G}$ denote the subgroup of $\mathbb{Z}_p^*$ of order q.

4. Randomly choose a generator g of $\mathbb{G}$.

5. Output (p, g).

Remark: This book considers a more general case in which $\mathcal{G}$ outputs a polynomial-sized description of a cyclic group $\mathbb{G}$ of order $q \geq 2^{n-1}$. For example, suppose $\mathcal{G}$ chooses a prime p of the form $p = 2q + 1$, where q is also a prime, and an element $g \in \mathbb{Z}_p^*$ of order q. Then the pair (p, g) would be a polynomial-sized description of the group $\mathbb{G}$. Since g is already included in (p, g) and q can be derived from p, it suffices for $\mathcal{G}$ to just output (p, g).

If $\mathbb{G}$ is a cyclic group of order q with generator g, then $\mathbb{G} = \{g^0, g^1, ..., g^{q-1}\}$. Equivalently, for every $h \in \mathbb{G}$, there is a unique $x \in \mathbb{Z}_q$ such that $g^x = h$. We call this x the discrete logarithm of h with respect to g and write $x = \log_g h$. The *discrete-logarithm problem* in a cyclic group $\mathbb{G}$ with a generator g is to compute $x = \log_g h$ when given a unique element $h \in \mathbb{G}$.

The discrete-logarithm experiment $\text{DLog}_{\mathcal{A},\mathcal{G}}(n)$

1. Run $\mathcal{G}(1^n)$ to obtain $(\mathbb{G}, q, g)$, where $\mathbb{G}$ is a cyclic group of order q (with $\|q\| = n$), and g is a generator of $\mathbb{G}$.

2. Choose a uniform $h \in \mathbb{G}$.

3. $\mathcal{A}$ is given $\mathbb{G}, q, g, h$ and outputs $x \in \mathbb{Z}_q$.

4. The output of the experiment is defined to be 1 if $g^x = h$, and 0 otherwise.

Definition 1 We say that the **discrete logarithm problem is hard** relative to $\mathcal{G}$ if for all probabilistic polynomial-time algorithms $\mathcal{A}$ there exists a negligible function negl such that

$$\Pr[DLog_{\mathcal{A},\mathcal{G}}(n) = 1] \leq negl(n). \tag{9.1}$$

Fix a cyclic group $\mathbb{G}$ and a generator $g \in \mathbb{G}$. Given elements $h_1, h_2 \in \mathbb{G}$, define $\text{DH}_g(h_1, h_2) \stackrel{\text{def}}{=} g^{log_g h_1 \cdot log_g h_2}$. That is, if $h_1 = g^{x_1}$ and $h_2 = g^{x_2}$ then

$$\text{DH}_g(h_1, h_2) = g^{x_1 \cdot x_2} = h_1^{x_2} = h_2^{x_1}. \tag{9.2}$$

The *CDH (computational Diffie-Hellman) problem* is to compute $\text{DH}_g(h_1, h_2)$ for uniform h_1 and h_2.

The *DDH (decisional Diffie-Hellman) problem*, roughly speaking, is to distinguish $\text{DH}_g(h_1, h_2)$ from a uniform group element when h_1, h_2 are uniform. That is, given uniform h_1, h_2, and a third group element h', the problem is to decide whether $h' = \text{DH}_g(h_1, h_2)$ or whether h' was chosen uniformly from $\mathbb{G}$. It is formally defined as follows.

Definition 2 We say that the **DDH problem is hard** relative to $\mathcal{G}$ if for all probabilistic polynomial-time algorithms $\mathcal{A}$ there exists a negligible function negl such that

$$\left| \Pr[\mathcal{A}(\mathbb{G}, q, g, g^x, g^y, g^z) = 1] - \Pr[\mathcal{A}(\mathbb{G}, q, g, g^x, g^y, g^{xy}) = 1] \right| \leq negl(n), \tag{9.3}$$

where in each case the probabilities are taken over the experiment in which $\mathcal{G}(1^n)$ outputs $(\mathbb{G}, q, g)$ and then uniform $x, y, z \in \mathbb{Z}_q$ are chosen (Note that when z is uniform in $\mathbb{Z}_q$, then g^z is uniformly distributed in $\mathbb{G}$).

9.2   The Diffie-Hellman Key Exchange Protocol

Intuitively, a key-exchange protocol is secure if the key output by two communicating parties, Alice and Bob, is completely unguessable by an eavesdropping adversary. This is formally defined by requiring that an adversary who has eavesdropped on an execution of the protocol should be unable to distinguish the key k generated by that execution from a *uniform* key of length n (This is much stronger than simply requiring that the adversary should be unable to compute k exactly, and this stronger notion is necessary if the parties will subsequently use k for some cryptographic application, e.g., as a key for a private-key encryption scheme). Formalizing the above, let Π be a key-exchange protocol, $\mathcal{A}$ an adversary, and n the security parameter. We have the following experiment.

The key-exchange experiment $\mathsf{KE}_{\mathcal{A},\Pi}^{eav}(n)$

1. *Two parties holding 1^n execute protocol Π. This execution results in a transcript* trans *containing all the messages sent by the parties, and a key k output by each of the parties.*

2. *A uniform bit $b \in \{0,1\}$ is chosen. If $b = 0$, set $\widehat{k} = k$, and if $b = 1$, then choose $\widehat{k} \in \{0,1\}^n$ uniformly at random.*

3. *$\mathcal{A}$ is given* trans *and $\widehat{k}$, and outputs a bit b'.*

4. *The output of the experiment is defined to be 1 if $b = b'$, and 0 otherwise. In case $\mathsf{KE}_{\mathcal{A},\Pi}^{eav}(n) = 1$, we say that $\mathcal{A}$* succeeds.

In the real world, $\mathcal{A}$ would not be given any key; in the experiment the adversary is given $\hat{k}$ only as a means of defining what it means for $\mathcal{A}$ to "break" the security of Π. The adversary succeeds in "breaking" Π if it can correctly determine whether the key $\hat{k}$ is the real key corresponding to the given execution of the protocol, or a uniform key that is independent of the transcript. As expected, we say Π is secure if the adversary succeeds with probability that is at most negligibly greater than $1/2$. That is:

Definition 3 *A key-exchange protocol Π is* **secure in the presence of an eavesdropper** *if for all probabilistic polynomial-time adversaries $\mathcal{A}$ there is a negligible function negl such that*

$$\Pr[\mathsf{KE}_{\mathcal{A},\Pi}^{eav}(n) = 1] \leq \frac{1}{2} + negl(n). \tag{9.4}$$

The Diffie-Hellman key-exchange protocol Let $\mathcal{G}$ be a polynomial-time algorithm that, on input 1^n, outputs a (description of a) cyclic group $\mathbb{G}$, its order q (with $\|q\| = n$), and a generator $g \in \mathbb{G}$. The Diffie-Hellman key-exchange protocol is described formally as Construction 1 and illustrated in Figure 9.1.

Construction 1. The Diffie-Hellman key-exchange protocol

1. **Input** The security parameter 1^n

2. **The protocol**

   (a) Alice runs $\mathcal{G}(1^n)$ to obtain $(\mathbb{G}, q, g)$.

   (b) Alice chooses a uniform $x \in \mathbb{Z}_q$, and computes $h_A = g^x$.

   (c) Alice sends $(\mathbb{G}, q, g, h_A)$ to Bob.

   (d) Bob receives $(\mathbb{G}, q, g, h_A)$. He chooses a uniform $y \in \mathbb{Z}_q$, and computes $h_B = g^y$. Bob sends h_B to Alice and outputs the key $k_B = h_A^y$.

   (e) Alice receives h_B and outputs the key $k_A = h_B^x$.

Let $\widehat{KE}_{\mathcal{A},\Pi}^{eav}(n)$ denote a modified experiment where if $b = 1$ the adversary is given $\widehat{k}$ chosen uniformly from $\mathbb{G}$ instead of a uniform n-bit string.

Theorem 1 *If the decisional Diffie-Hellman problem is hard relative to $\mathcal{G}$, then the Diffie-Hellman key-exchange protocol Π is secure in the presence of an eavesdropper (with respect to the modified experiment $\widehat{KE}_{\mathcal{A},\Pi}^{eav}$).*

Proof is omitted.

Uniform group elements vs. uniform bit-strings The previous theorem shows that the key output by Alice and Bob in the Diffie-Hellman protocol is indistinguishable from a uniform group element. In order to use the key to meet Definition 3, the key output by the parties should instead be indistinguishable from a uniform bit-string of the appropriate length. The Diffie–Hellman protocol can be modified to achieve this by having the parties apply an appropriate *key-derivation function* (cf. hash functions) to the shared group element g^{xy} they each compute.

Active adversaries The Diffie-Hellman protocol is *completely insecure* against man-in-the-middle attacks. In fact, a man-in-the-middle adversary can act in such a way that Alice and Bob terminate the protocol with different keys K_1 and K_2 that are both known to the adversary, yet neither Alice nor Bob can detect that any attack was carried out as shown in Figure 9.2.

The adversary Eve intercepts Alice's public value $R_1 = g^x \bmod p$, generates her own public value $R_2 = g^z \bmod p$ and sends it to Alice and Bob. When Bob sends his public value $R_3 = g^y \bmod p$ to Alice, Eve intercepts it. As a result, Alice and Eve agree on one shared key K_1, and Bob and Eve agree on the other shared key K_2. After that, Eve can decrypt, read and modify the messages communicated between Alice and Bob. This vulnerability occurs because the Diffie-Hellman protocol does not authenticate the participants.

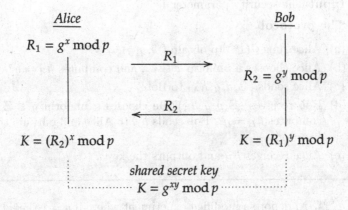

FIGURE 9.1
The Diffie-Hellman key-exchange protocol.

Diffie-Hellman key exchange in practice The Diffie-Hellman protocol serves as the first demonstration that asymmetric techniques could be used to alleviate the problems of key distribution in cryptography. Furthermore, to make the Diffie-Hellman protocol resilient to man-in-the-middle attacks, we adopt the station-to-station protocol which is in wide use today (e.g., SSL). Figure 9.3 describes the station-to-station protocol step by step. First of all, Alice generates her public value $R_1 = g^x \bmod p$ and transmits it to Bob. Bob then generates his public value $R_2 = g^y \bmod p$ and then computes the shared secret key $K = (R_1)^y \bmod p$. Bob now concatenates Alice, R_1 and R_2, signs it with his private key, and encrypts the signature [1] with K, he sends his ciphertext along with R_2 and his certificate to Alice. Alice then computes the secret shared key $K = (R_2)^x \bmod p$ and verifies Bob's signature. Alice then concatenates Bob, R_1 and R_2, signs it with her private key, encrypts the signature using K, and transmits it to Bob. Bob then verifies Alice's signature. Alice and Bob are now mutually authenticated and have a shared secret K.

---

[1] Details of signature will be explained later.

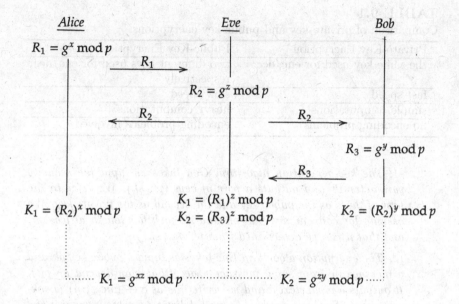

FIGURE 9.2
The man-in-the-middle attack.

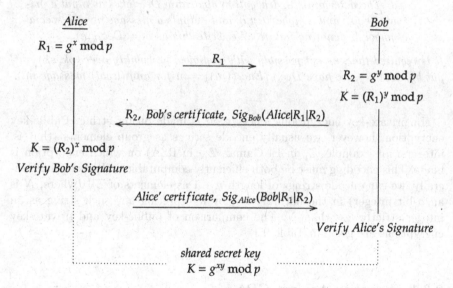

FIGURE 9.3
The station-to-station key agreement protocol.

9.3 Overview of Public-Key Encryption

Definition 4 *A* **public-key encryption scheme** *is a triple of probabilistic polynomial-time algorithms (Gen, Enc, Dec) such that*

TABLE 9.1

Comparison of private-key and public-key encryptions.

Private-Key Encryption	Public-Key Encryption
the same key used for enc/dec	two different keys used for enc/dec, respectively
fast speed	slow speed
simple computations	heavy computations
no encoding problems	encoding problems involved

> 1. *The key-generation algorithm Gen takes as input the security parameter 1^n and outputs a pair of keys (pk, sk). We refer to the first of these as the **public key** and the second as the **private key**. We assume for convenience that pk and sk each has length at least n, and that n can be determined from pk and sk.*

> 2. *The encryption algorithm Enc takes as input a public key pk and a message m from some message space (that may depend on pk). It outputs a ciphertext c and we write this as $c \leftarrow \mathsf{Enc}_{pk}(m)$ (Looking ahead, Enc will need to be probabilistic to achieve meaningful security).*

> 3. *The deterministic decryption algorithm Dec takes as input a private key sk and a ciphertext c, and outputs a message m or a special symbol $\perp$ denoting failure. We write this as $m = \mathsf{Dec}_{sk}(c)$.*

It is required that, except possibly with negligible probability over (pk, sk) output by $Gen(1^n)$, we have $\mathsf{Dec}_{sk}(\mathsf{Enc}_{sk}(m)) = m$ for any (legal) message m.

In private-key encryptions, encryption is made on bit string. Public-key encryption, however, we usually encode strings as group elements (that is, integers; for example, $\mathbb{Z}_p$ in El Gamal, $\mathbb{Z}_N$ in RSA) on which encryption is made. This encoding must be both efficiently computable and reversible. Generally, we can encode strings of length $n - 1$ as elements of $\mathbb{Z}_N$ (where, N is an n-bit integer) in the natural way, by interpreting any such string as an integer strictly less than N. The comparison of public-key and private-key encryptions are given in Table 9.1.

9.3.1   Security Against CPA

Given a public-key encryption scheme $\Pi = (\mathsf{Gen}, \mathsf{Enc}, \mathsf{Dec})$ and an adversary $\mathcal{A}$, consider the following experiment.

The eavesdropping indistinguishability experiment $\mathsf{PubK}^{eav}_{\mathcal{A},\Pi}(n)$

1. $\mathsf{Gen}(1^n)$ *is run to obtain keys* (pk, sk).

2. *Adversary* $\mathcal{A}$ *is given* pk, *and outputs a pair of equal-length messages* m_0, m_1 *in the message space.*

3. *A uniform bit* $b \in \{0, 1\}$ *is chosen, and then a ciphertext* $c \leftarrow \mathsf{Enc}_{pk}(m_b)$ *is computed and given to* $\mathcal{A}$. *We call* c *the* challenge ciphertext.

4. $\mathcal{A}$ *outputs a bit* b'. *The output of the experiment is 1 if* $b' = b$, *and 0 otherwise. If* $b' = b$, *we say that* $\mathcal{A}$ succeeds.

Definition 5 *A public-key encryption scheme* $\Pi = (Gen, Enc, Dec)$ *has* **indistinguishable encryptions in the presence of an eavesdropper** *if for all probabilistic polynomial-time adversaries* $\mathcal{A}$ *there is a negligible function* negl *such that*

$$\Pr[\mathit{PubK}^{eav}_{\mathcal{A},\Pi}(n) = 1] \leq \frac{1}{2} + negl(n). \tag{9.5}$$

The main difference between the public-key and private-key encryptions is that $\mathcal{A}$ in the public-key encryptions is given the public key pk. Furthermore, we allow $\mathcal{A}$ to choose its messages m_0 and m_1 based on this public key.

Proposition 1 *If a public-key encryption scheme has indistinguishable encryptions in the presence of an eavesdropper, it is CPA-secure.*

Proof is omitted.

This is in contrast to the private-key setting, where there exist schemes that have indistinguishable encryptions in the presence of an eavesdropper but are insecure under a chosen-plaintext attack.

Theorem 2 *No deterministic public-key encryption scheme is CPA-secure.*

Proof is omitted.

For encrypting multiple messages, we could formulate security in such a setting by having an adversary output two lists of plaintexts. However, we choose instead to use a definition in which the attacker is given access to an LR oracle ("left-or-right" oracle $\mathsf{LR}_{pk,b}$ on input a pair of equal-length messages m_0, m_1, computes the ciphertext $c \leftarrow \mathsf{Enc}_{pk}(m_b)$ and returns c) because instead of outputting the lists $(m_{0,1}, ..., m_{0,t})$ and $(m_{1,1}, ..., m_{1,t})$, one of whose messages will be encrypted, the attacker can now sequentially query $\mathsf{LR}_{pk,b}(m_{0,1}, m_{1,1})$, $\cdots$, $\mathsf{LR}_{pk,b}(m_{0,t}, m_{1,t})$.

Formally, consider the following experiment defined for a public-key encryption scheme $\Pi = (\mathsf{Gen}, \mathsf{Enc}, \mathsf{Dec})$ and adversary $\mathcal{A}$.

The LR-oracle experiment $\mathsf{PubK}_{\mathcal{A},\Pi}^{LR-cpa}(n)$

1. $\mathsf{Gen}(1^n)$ *is run to obtain keys* (pk, sk).

2. *A uniform bit* $b \in \{0, 1\}$ *is chosen.*

3. *The adversary* $\mathcal{A}$ *is given input* pk *and oracle access to* $\mathsf{LR}_{pk,b}(\cdot, \cdot)$.

4. *The adversary* $\mathcal{A}$ *outputs a bit* b'.

5. *The output of the experiment is 1 if* $b' = b$, *and 0 otherwise. If* $\mathsf{PubK}_{\mathcal{A},\Pi}^{LR-cpa}(n) = 1$, *we say that* $\mathcal{A}$ *succeeds.*

Definition 6 *A public-key encryption scheme* $\Pi = (Gen, Enc, Dec)$ *has* **indistinguishable multiple encryptions** *if for all probabilistic polynomial-time adversaries* $\mathcal{A}$ *there exists a negligible function negl such that*

$$\Pr[\mathit{PubK}_{\mathcal{A},\Pi}^{LR-cpa}(n) = 1] \le \frac{1}{2} + negl(n). \tag{9.6}$$

Theorem 3 *If public-key encryption scheme* Π *is CPA-secure, then it also has indistinguishable multiple encryptions.*

Proof is omitted.

Theorem 4 *If a fixed-length public-key encryption scheme* Π *is CPA-secure, then the arbitrary-length public-key encryption scheme* Π' *constructed as below is also CPA-secure.*

Proof is omitted.

For simplicity, say $\Pi = (Gen, Enc, Dec)$ is an encryption scheme for single-bit messages. We can construct a new scheme $\Pi' = (Gen', Enc', Dec')$ for arbitrary-length messages quite easily, by defining for any message m of length l as $Enc'_k(m) = Enc_k(m_1) \| \cdots \| Enc_k(m_l)$, where m_i denotes the ith bit of m. Decryption is done in the natural way.

9.3.2 Security Against CCA

Assume an eavesdropper $\mathcal{A}$ observes a ciphertext c sent by a sender $\mathcal{S}$ to a receiver $\mathcal{R}$. Broadly speaking, in the public-key setting there are two classes of chosen-ciphertext attacks.

1. $\mathcal{A}$ might send a modified ciphertext c' to $\mathcal{R}$ *on behalf of* $\mathcal{S}$. In this case, although it is unlikely that $\mathcal{A}$ would be able to obtain the entire decryption m' of c', it might be possible for $\mathcal{A}$ to infer some information about m' based on the subsequent behavior of $\mathcal{R}$. Based on this information, $\mathcal{A}$ might be able to learn something about the original message m. (Scenario: Say a user $\mathcal{S}$ logs in to her bank account by sending to her bank an encryption of her password pw concatenated with a timestamp. Assume further that there are two types of error messages the bank sends: it returns "password incorrect" if the encrypted password does not match the stored password of $\mathcal{S}$, and "timestamp incorrect" if the password is correct but the timestamp is not. If an adversary obtains a ciphertext c sent by $\mathcal{S}$ to the bank, the adversary can now mount a chosen-ciphertext attack by sending ciphertexts c' to the bank on behalf of $\mathcal{S}$ and observing the error messages that result.)

2. $\mathcal{A}$ might send a modified ciphertext c' to $\mathcal{R}$ *in its own* name. This class is specific to the context of public-key encryption. In this case, $\mathcal{A}$ might obtain the entire decryption m' of c' if $\mathcal{R}$ responds directly to $\mathcal{A}$ (Scenario: Say $\mathcal{S}$ sends an encrypted email c to $\mathcal{R}$, and this email is observed by $\mathcal{A}$. If $\mathcal{A}$ sends, in its own name, an encrypted email c' to $\mathcal{R}$, then $\mathcal{R}$ might reply to this email and quote the decrypted text m' corresponding to c'. In this case, $\mathcal{R}$ is essentially acting as a decryption oracle for $\mathcal{A}$ and might potentially decrypt any ciphertext that $\mathcal{A}$ sends). Even if $\mathcal{A}$ learns nothing about m', this modified message may have a known relation to the original message m that can be exploited by $\mathcal{A}$ (Scenario: Let an encryption scheme be malleable. For example, suppose that given an encryption of m, it is possible for $\mathcal{A}$ to construct an encryption of $2m$. Now imagine that $\mathcal{R}$ is running an auction, where two parties $\mathcal{S}$ and $\mathcal{A}$ submit their bids by encrypting them using the public key of $\mathcal{R}$. It may be possible for an adversary $\mathcal{A}$ to always place the highest bid (without bidding the maximum) by carrying out the following attack: wait until $\mathcal{S}$ sends a ciphertext c corresponding to its bid m (that is unknown to $\mathcal{A}$); then send a ciphertext c' corresponding to the bid $m' = 2m$. Note that m (and m', for that matter) remains unknown to $\mathcal{A}$ until $\mathcal{R}$ announces the results).

Given a public-key encryption scheme Π and an adversary $\mathcal{A}$, consider the following experiment.

The CCA indistinguishability experiment $\mathsf{PubK}_{\mathcal{A},\Pi}^{cca}(n)$

1. $\mathsf{Gen}(1^n)$ *is run to obtain keys (pk, sk).*

2. *The adversary $\mathcal{A}$ is given pk and access to a decryption oracle $\mathsf{Dec}_{sk}(\cdot)$. It outputs a pair of messages m_0, m_1 of the same length (These messages must be in the message space associated with pk).*

3. *A uniform bit $b \in \{0,1\}$ is chosen, and then a ciphertext $c \leftarrow \mathsf{Enc}_{pk}(m_b)$ is computed and given to $\mathcal{A}$.*

4. *$\mathcal{A}$ continues to interact with the decryption oracle, but may not request a decryption of c itself. Finally, $\mathcal{A}$ outputs a bit b'.*

5. *The output of the experiment is defined to be 1 if $b' = b$, and 0 otherwise.*

Definition 7 *A public-key encryption scheme $\Pi = (Gen, Enc, Dec)$ has* **indistinguishable encryptions under a chosen-ciphertext attack (or is CCA-secure)** *if for all probabilistic polynomial-time adversaries $\mathcal{A}$ there exists a negligible function negl such that*

$$\Pr[PubK_{\mathcal{A},\Pi}^{cca}(n) = 1] \leq \frac{1}{2} + negl(n). \tag{9.7}$$

If a scheme has indistinguishable encryptions under a chosen-ciphertext attack, then it has indistinguishable multiple encryptions under a chosen ciphertext attack. Interestingly, however, the analogue of Theorem 4 does not hold for CCA-security.

9.3.3   Hybrid Encryption and the KEM/DEM Paradigm

It is possible to use private-key encryption in tandem with public-key encryption. This improves efficiency because private-key encryption is significantly faster than public-key encryption, improves bandwidth because private-key schemes have lower ciphertext expansion, and overcomes the limitation of plaintext size a public-key encryption can take in (For instance, RSA's plaintext m can have length $|m| = N$ or m will be corrupted). The resulting combination is called *hybrid encryption* and is used extensively in practice. The basic idea is to use public-key encryption to obtain a shared key k, and then encrypt the message m using a private-key encryption scheme with key k. The receiver uses its long-term (asymmetric) private key to derive k, and then uses private-key decryption with key k to recover the original message.

A more direct approach to hybrid encryption is to use a public-key primitive called a *key-encapsulation mechanism* (KEM) to accomplish both of these "in one shot."

A KEM has three algorithms similar in spirit to those of a public-key encryption scheme. As before, the key-generation algorithm Gen is used to generate a pair of public and private keys. In place of encryption, we now have an encapsulation algorithm Encaps that takes only a public key as input (and no message), and outputs a ciphertext c along with a key k. A corresponding decapsulation algorithm Decaps is run by the receiver to recover k from the ciphertext c using the private key. Formally:

Construction 2. Hybrid encryption using the KEM/DEM paradigm

Let $\Pi = (\text{Gen}, \text{Encaps}, \text{Decaps})$ be a KEM with key length n, and $\Pi' = (\text{Gen}', \text{Enc}', \text{Dec}')$ be a private-key encryption scheme. Construct a public-key encryption scheme $\Pi^{hy} = (\text{Gen}^{hy}, \text{Enc}^{hy}, \text{Dec}^{hy})$ as follows.

1. Gen^{hy}: on input 1^n, run $\text{Gen}(1^n)$ and use the public and private keys (pk, sk) that are output.

2. Enc^{hy}: on input a public key pk and a message $m \in \{0,1\}^*$ do

   (a) Compute $(c, k) \leftarrow \text{Encaps}_{pk}(1^n)$.

   (b) Compute $c' \leftarrow \text{Enc}'_k(m)$.

   (c) Output the ciphertext $\langle c, c' \rangle$.

3. Dec^{hy}: on input a private key sk and a ciphertext $\langle c, c' \rangle$ do

   (a) Compute $k = \text{Decaps}_{sk}(c)$.

   (b) Output the message $m = \text{Dec}'_k(c')$.

9.4 Public-Key Encryption Schemes

The section introduces several public key encryption schemes and discusses their security issues.

9.4.1 The El Gamal Encryption

Let $\mathcal{G}$ be a polynomial-time algorithm that takes as input 1^n and (except possibly with negligible probability) outputs a description of a cyclic group $\mathbb{G}$, its order q (with $\|q\| = n$), and a generator g.

Construction 3. The El Gamal encryption scheme

Let $\mathcal{G}$ be defined as above. Define a public-key encryption scheme as follows.

1. Gen: on input 1^n, run $\mathcal{G}(1^n)$ to obtain $(\mathbb{G}, q, g)$. Then choose a uniform $x \in \mathbb{Z}_q$ and compute $h = g^x$. The public key is $\langle \mathbb{G}, q, g, h \rangle$ and the private key is $\langle \mathbb{G}, q, g, x \rangle$. The message space is $\mathbb{G}$.

2. Enc: on input a public key $pk = \langle \mathbb{G}, q, g, h \rangle$ and a message $m \in \mathbb{G}$, choose a uniform $y \in \mathbb{Z}_q$ and output the ciphertext

$$\langle g^y, h^y \cdot m \rangle.$$

3. Dec: on input a private key $sk = \langle \mathbb{G}, q, g, x \rangle$ and a ciphertext $\langle c_1, c_2 \rangle$, output

$$\widehat{m} = c_2 / c_1^x.$$

Example of El Gamal encryption on a group

1. Public Parameter Creation
   Let $p = 23$, $g = 2$, $\mathbb{Z}_{23}^* = \{0, 1, 2, \ldots, 22\}$.

2. Key Creation
   Let $x = 5$, then $h = 2^5 \bmod 23 = 9$.

3. Encryption
   Let plaintext $m = 7$ and $y = 3$.
   Calculate C_1 and C_2 as $C_1 = 2^3 \bmod 23 = 8$, $C_2 = (7 \times 9^3) \bmod 23 = 20$.
   $(8, 20)$ is sent to Alice.

4. Decryption
   $m = (20 \times (8^5)^{-1}) \bmod 23$. By using multiplicative inverse $a^{-1} \bmod p = a^{p-2} \bmod p$, and then Fast Exponentiation, Alice can get the plaintext $m = (20 \times (8^5)^{21}) \bmod 23 = 7$.

ElGamal encryption on elliptic curve

1. **Public Parameter Creation** Let p be a prime, E be an elliptic curve and be a point $P \in E$.

2. **Key Creation** Alice chooses a private key n_A, then computes and publishes $Q_A = n_A P$.

3. **Encryption** For plaintext M, Bob chooses an ephemeral key k and computes two quantities as

$$C_1 = kP \text{ and } C_2 = M + kQ_A \qquad (9.8)$$

and then sends C_1 and C_2 to Alice.

4. **Decryption** Alice computes the value $P' = C_2 - n_A C_1 = P$.

Note that the operations such as addition and multiplication are over an elliptic curve.

Theorem 5 *If the DDH problem is hard relative to $\mathcal{G}$, then the El Gamal encryption scheme is CPA-secure.*

Proof Assume that the DDH assumption is true for $\mathcal{G}$. Recall that the DDH challenger works as follows: runs $\mathcal{G}(1^n)$ to generate (p, g); chooses $x, y, z \in \mathbb{Z}_q$ uniformly at random, where $q = (\frac{p-1}{2})$; chooses $d \in \{0, 1\}$ uniformly at random; sets $T = g^{xy}$ if $d = 0$ and $T = g^z$ if $d = 1$; and finally, gives (p, g^x, g^y, T) to the attacker.

Let Π (Gen, Enc, Dec) be the El Gamal encryption scheme. Let $\mathcal{A}$ be a polynomial-time algorithm attacking Π. Let ϵ denote the advantage of $\mathcal{A}$ in the IND-CPA security game against Π. We construct an algorithm $\mathcal{B}$ for solving the DDH problem as follows.

Reduction algorithm $\mathcal{B}$

1. Receive (p, g, g^x, g^y, T) from the DDH challenger (Note that $\mathcal{B}$ knows neither x nor y).

2. Let $q = \frac{(p-1)}{2}$ and n be the length of q in bits.

3. Let $pk = (p, g, g^x)$.

4. Give 1^n and pk to $\mathcal{A}$.

5. Receive messages m_0 and m_1 from $\mathcal{A}$.

6. Choose $b \in \{0, 1\}$ uniformly at random.

7. Let $c^* = (g^y, Tm_b)$ and give c^* to $\mathcal{A}$.

8. Let b' denote the guess output by $\mathcal{A}$.

9. If $b = b'$, then set $d' = 0$. If $b \neq b'$, then set $d' = 1$.

10. Output d'.

Algorithm $\mathcal{B}$ runs in polynomial time, because $\mathcal{A}$ runs in polynomial time and because operations in $\mathbb{Z}_p^*$ can be performed in polynomial time. The probability that $\mathcal{B}$ wins the DDH security game is

$$Pr[d = d'] = Pr[d = 0]Pr[d = d'|d = 0] + Pr[d = 1]Pr[d = d'|d = 1]$$
$$= \frac{1}{2}Pr[d' = 0|d = 0] + \frac{1}{2}Pr[d' = 1|d = 1]$$
$$= \frac{1}{2}Pr[b = b'|d = 0] + \frac{1}{2}Pr[b \neq b'|d = 1]. \tag{9.9}$$

When $d = 0$, the DDH challenger sets $T = g^{xy}$, so the view that $\mathcal{B}$ presents to $\mathcal{A}$ is identical to the actual IND-CPA security game against Π. Therefore, the probability that $b = b'$ given $d = 0$ is the same as the probability that $\mathcal{A}$ wins the IND-CPA security game against Π; in other words,

$$Pr[b = b'|d = 0] = \frac{1}{2} + \epsilon. \tag{9.10}$$

When $d = 1$, the DDH challenger sets $T = g^z$. Recall that $\mathbb{G}$ denotes the subgroup of $\mathbb{Z}_p^*$ of order q. Since z is uniformly distributed in $\mathbb{Z}_q$, it follows that $g^z m_b$ is uniformly distributed in the group $\mathbb{G}$, independently of g, m_0, m_1, and b. Moreover, the random variables g, g^x, g^y, $g^z m_b$, and b are jointly independent. Hence, pk and c^* reveal no information about b, so the guess b' output by $\mathcal{A}$ must be independent of b. Since b is either 0 or 1, each with probability $\frac{1}{2}$, it follows that

$$Pr[b \neq b'|d = 1] = \frac{1}{2}. \tag{9.11}$$

It follows from Equations (9.8), (9.9), and (9.10) that

$$Pr[d = d'] = \frac{1}{2}(\frac{1}{2} + \epsilon) + \frac{1}{2} \cdot \frac{1}{2} = \frac{1}{2} + \frac{\epsilon}{2}.$$

Thus, $\mathcal{B}$ wins the DDH security game with advantage $\frac{\epsilon}{2}$. By the DDH assumption, algorithm $\mathcal{B}$ can win the DDH security game with only negligible advantage, so $\frac{\epsilon}{2}$ must be negligible. This implies that ϵ is also negligible. Therefore, the algorithm $\mathcal{A}$ has only negligible advantage ϵ in the IND-CPA game against Π (See Figure 9.4). $\square$

Note that it is not CCA-secure.

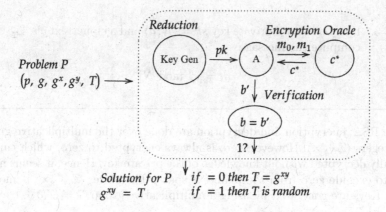

$$\text{Solution for } P \quad \begin{aligned} &if \ = 0 \text{ then } T = g^{xy} \\ &if \ = 1 \text{ then } T \text{ is random} \end{aligned}$$
$$g^{xy} = T$$

FIGURE 9.4
Security proof of El Gamal encryption.

9.4.2 The Plain (*aka* Textbook) RSA Encryption

RSA key generation GenRSA

Input: Security parameter 1^n
Output: N, e, d as described as below
$(N, e, d) \leftarrow \mathsf{GenModulus}(1^n)$
$\phi(N) = (p - 1)(q - 1)$ for two large primes p and q
choose $e > 1$ such that $\gcd(e, \phi(N)) = 1$
compute $d = [e^{-1} \bmod \phi(N)]$
return N, e, d

Construction 4. The plain RSA encryption scheme

Let GenRSA be as in Chapter 8. Define a public-key encryption scheme as follows.

1. Gen: on input 1^n, run $\mathsf{GenRSA}(1^n)$ to obtain N, e, and d. The public key is $\langle N, e \rangle$ and the private key is $\langle N, d \rangle$.

2. Enc: on input a public key $pk = \langle N, e \rangle$ and a message $m \in \mathbb{Z}_N^*$, compute the ciphertext

$$c = [m^e \bmod N].$$

---

3. Dec: on input a private key $sk = \langle N, d \rangle$ and a ciphertext $c \in \mathbb{Z}_N^*$ compute the message

$$m = [c^d \bmod N].$$

In RSA, encryption and decryption are done over the multiplicative group of integers $\langle \mathbb{Z}_N, \times \rangle$. However, zero is always encrypted to zero, which can be trivially decrypted without knowledge of the private key. Hence, it seems more safe to exclude zero from the plaintext space. Therefore, $\langle \mathbb{Z}_N^*, \times \rangle$ is mostly used. Keys are generated by using a multiplicative group $\mathbb{G} = \langle \mathbb{Z}_{\phi(N)}^*, \times \rangle$.

Example

1. Key Generation
   Let $p = 7$ and $q = 11$. Then $N = p \times q = 7 \times 11 = 77$.
   $\phi(n) = (p-1)(q-1) = 60$.
   Select $e = 13$ (e is coprime to $\phi(N)$), and then $d = e^{-1} \bmod \phi(N) = 13^{-1} \bmod 60 = 37$.
   Open $(77, 13)$ to the public.

2. Encryption
   Plaintext $m = 5$
   Calculate $c = 5^{13} \bmod 77 = 26 \bmod 77 = 26$.

3. Decryption
   Calculate $m' = 26^{37} \bmod 77 = 5 \bmod 77 = 5 = m$.

The *RSA problem* is to find x such that $x^e = y \bmod N$ when given (N, e, y), where e is relatively prime to $\phi(N)$, and $y \in \mathbb{Z}_N^*$.

Consider the following experiment for a given algorithm $\mathcal{A}$ and parameter n.

The RSA experiment RSA-inv$_{\mathcal{A}, \mathsf{GenRSA}}(n)$

1. *Run GenRSA to obtain (N, e, d).*

2. *Choose $y \leftarrow \mathbb{Z}_N^*$.*

3. *$\mathcal{A}$ is given N, e, d and outputs $x \in \mathbb{Z}_N^*$.*

4. *The output of the experiment is defined to be 1 if $x^e = y$ mon N, and 0 otherwise.*

Definition 8 *We say that the* **RSA problem is hard** *relative to GenRSA if for all probabilistic polynomial-time algorithms $\mathcal{A}$ there exists a negligible function negl such that*

$$\Pr[RSA\text{-}inv_{\mathcal{A},GenRSA}(n) = 1] \leq negl(n). \qquad (9.12)$$

The RSA assumption means that there exists a *GenRSA* relative to which the RSA problem is hard.

9.4.2.1 RSA Cryptosystem Based on Elliptic Curve

It is well known that the RSA cryptosystem based on elliptic curve has not much benefits compared to the original RSA cryptosystem.

1. Key Generation
   Select an elliptic curve $E_n(a, b)$ with a, b satisfying $4a^3 + 27b^2 \neq 0$.
   Select two primes p and q such that $\gcd(4a^3 + 27b^2, n) = 1$.
   Compute $n = p \times q$ and $\#E_p(a, b)$, $\#E_q(a, b)$, where $\#E_p(a, b)$ denotes the number of points on $E_p(a, b)$.
   Calculate $N_n = \text{lcm}[\#E_p(a, b), \#E_q(a, b)]$, where *lcm* denotes *least common multiple*.
   Select e such that $1 \leq e \leq N_n$ and e is coprime to N_n.
   Compute $d = e^{-1} \pmod{N_n}$ as the private key.
   Publish (n, e) as the public key.

2. Encryption
   Let $P = (x, y)$ is a point on an elliptic curve (which corresponds to a plaintext).
   Calculate $C = e \times P$.

3. Decryption
   Calculate $P' = d \times C = d \times e \times P = P$.

It is well-known that

$$\#E_p(a, b) = p + 1 + t \text{ where } |t| \leq 2\sqrt{p},$$
$$\#E_q(a, b) = q + 1 + t \text{ where } |t| \leq 2\sqrt{q}.$$

Lemma 1 *Let $E_n(a, b)$ be an elliptic curve such that $\gcd(4a^3 + 27b^2, n) = 1$ and $n = pq$ (p, q: prime). Let N_n be $\text{lcm}[\#E_p(a, b), \#E_q(a, b)]$. Then, for any $P \in E_n(a, b)$ and any integer k,*

$$(k.N_n + 1).P = P. \qquad (9.13)$$

Lemma 2 *Let p be an odd prime satisfying $p \equiv 2 \bmod 3$. Then for $0 < b < p$, $E_p(0, b)$ is a cyclic group of order*

$$\#E_p(0, b) = p + 1. \qquad (9.14)$$

Lemma 3 Let p be a prime satisfying $p \equiv 3 \bmod 4$. Then for $0 < a < p$, we have

$$\#E_p(a,0) = p+1. \qquad (9.15)$$

Example

1. Key Generation
   Select $a = 0$, $b = 1$, we have an elliptic curve $y^2 = x^3 + 1$.
   Select two primes $p = 2$ and $q = 5$.
   Compute $n = p \times q = 10$, $\#E_2(0,1) = 2+1 = 3$, and $\#E_5(0,1) = 5+1 = 6$.
   Calculate $N_n = \operatorname{lcm}(3,6) = 6$.
   Select $e = 5$.
   Compute $d = e^{-1} \pmod 6 = 5$ as the private key.
   Publish (n, e) as the public key.

2. Encryption
   Let $P = (2,3)$ is a point on an elliptic curve (which corresponds to a plaintext).
   Calculate $C = e \times P = 5 \times (2,3) = [(2,3) + \cdots + (2,3)]$.
   Return $C = (2,-3)$.

3. Decryption
   Calculate $P' = d \times C = 5 \times (2,-3) = (2,3) = P$.

9.4.3   The Padded RSA Encryption

For the above RSA scheme to be CPA-secure, the mapping from messages to elements of $\mathbb{Z}_N^*$ must be randomized so that encryption is not deterministic.

One simple implementation of the above idea is to randomize the plaintext message before encrypting. That is, to map a message m (viewed as a bit-string) to an element of $\mathbb{Z}_N^*$, the sender chooses a uniform bit-string $r \in \{0,1\}^l$ (for some appropriate l) and sets $\hat{m} = r \| m$; the resulting value can naturally be interpreted as an integer in $\mathbb{Z}_N^*$, and this mapping is clearly reversible. This idea was standardized as The RSA Laboratories Public-Key Cryptography Standard (PKCS) #1 version 1.5 in 1993 [59], which is vulnerable to CCA [17].

Construction 5. The Padded RSA encryption scheme

Let GenRSA be as before, and let ℓ be a function with $\ell(n) \leq 2n - 4$ for all n. Define a public-key encryption scheme as follows.

1. Gen: on input 1^n, run GenRSA(1^n) to obtain (N, e, d). Output the public key $pk = \langle N, e \rangle$ and the private key $sk = \langle N, d \rangle$.

2. Enc: on input a public key $pk = \langle N, e \rangle$ and a message $m \in \{0,1\}^{\|N\|-\ell(n)-2}$, choose a uniform string $r \in \{0,1\}^{\ell(n)}$ and interpret $\widehat{m} = r\|m$ as an element of $\mathbb{Z}_N^*$. Output the ciphertext

$$c = [\widehat{m}^e \bmod N].$$

3. Dec: on input a private key $sk = \langle N, d \rangle$ and a ciphertext $c \in \mathbb{Z}_N^*$, compute

$$\widehat{m} = [c^d \bmod N]$$

and output the $\|N\| - \ell(n) - 2$ least-significant bits of $\widehat{m}$.

Theorem 6 *If the RSA problem is hard relative to GenRSA , then the Padded RSA encryption with $l(n) = \mathcal{O}(\log n)$ is CPA-secure.*

Proof is omitted.

9.4.4 The CPA-Secure RSA Encryption Under the RSA Assumption in the Random Oracle Model

Construction 6. CPA-secure RSA encryption in the random oracle model

Let GenRSA be as before, and let $\ell(n)$ be an arbitrary polynomial. Let H be a function whose domain can be set to $\mathbb{Z}_N^*$ for any N, and whose range can be set to $\{0,1\}^{\ell(n)}$ for any n. Construct a public-key encryption scheme as follows.

1. Gen: on input 1^n, run GenRSA(1^n) to obtain $\langle N, e, d \rangle$. The public key is $\langle N, e \rangle$ and the private key is $\langle N, d \rangle$.

2. Enc: on input a public key $\langle N, e \rangle$ and a message $m \in \{0,1\}^{\ell(n)}$, choose a random $r \leftarrow \mathbb{Z}_N^*$ and output the ciphertext

$$\langle [r^e \bmod N], H(r) \oplus m \rangle.$$

3. Dec: on input a private key $\langle N, d \rangle$ and a ciphertext $\langle c_1, c_2 \rangle$, compute $r = [c_1^d \bmod N]$, and then output the message $H(r) \oplus c_2$.

Theorem 7 *If the RSA problem is hard relative to GenRSA and H is modeled as a random oracle, then Construction 6 is CPA-secure.*

Proof

Outline of the Proof The proof is based on the "proof by reduction" in the random oracle model. Since r is chosen at random, it is infeasible for an eavesdropping adversary to recover r from $c_1 = [r^e \bmod N]$. The adversary will therefore never query r to the random oracle, and so the value $H(r)$ is completely random from the adversary's point of view. But then c_2 is just a "one-time pad"-like encryption of m using the random value $H(r)$, so the adversary gets no information about m.

Let Π denote the above construction. We prove that Π has indistinguishable encryptions in the presence of an eavesdropper, which implies that Π is CPA-secure.

Let $\mathcal{A}$ be a probabilistic polynomial-time adversary and define $\epsilon(n) \overset{\text{def}}{=} Pr[\mathsf{PubK}_{\mathcal{A},\Pi}^{eav}(n) = 1]$. We describe the steps of experiment $\mathsf{PubK}_{\mathcal{A},\Pi}^{eav}(n)$ as follows.

The eavesdropping indistinguishability experiment $\mathsf{PubK}_{\mathcal{A},\Pi}^{eav}(n)$ in the ROM

1. *A random function H is chosen.*

2. *GenRSA(1^n) is run to generate (N, e, d). Adversary $\mathcal{A}$ is given $pk = \langle N, e \rangle$, and may query $H(\cdot)$. Eventually $\mathcal{A}$ outputs two messages $m_0, m_1 \in \{0, 1\}^{l(n)}$.*

3. *A random bit $b \in \{0, 1\}$ and a random $r \leftarrow \mathbb{Z}_N^*$ are chosen. $\mathcal{A}$ is given the ciphertext $\langle [r^e \bmod N], H(r) \oplus m_b \rangle$. The adversary may continue to query $H(\cdot)$.*

4. *$\mathcal{A}$ outputs a bit b'. The output of the experiment is defined to be 1 if $b' = b$ and 0 otherwise.*

Let Query denote that $\mathcal{A}$ queries r to the random oracle H. We also use Success as shorthand for the event that $\mathsf{PubK}_{\mathcal{A},\Pi}^{eav}(n) = 1$. Then

$$Pr[Success] = Pr[\text{Success} \wedge \overline{\text{Query}}] + Pr[\text{Success} \wedge \text{Query}]$$
$$\leq Pr[\text{Success} \wedge \overline{\text{Query}}] + Pr[\text{Query}],$$

where all probabilities are taken over the randomness used in the experiment $\mathsf{PubK}^{eav}_{\mathcal{A},\Pi}(n)$. We show that $Pr[\text{Success} \wedge \overline{\text{Query}}] \leq \frac{1}{2}$ and $Pr[\text{Query}]$ is negligible.

$$Pr[\text{Success} \wedge \overline{\text{Query}}] = Pr[\text{Success}|\overline{\text{Query}}] \cdot Pr[\overline{\text{Query}}]$$
$$\leq Pr[\text{Success}|\overline{\text{Query}}]$$
$$= \frac{1}{2},$$

because, if $\mathcal{A}$ does not explicitly query r to the oracle, then $H(r)$ is completely random from $\mathcal{A}$'s point of view, so $\mathcal{A}$ has no information as to whether m_0 or m_1 was encrypted.

Now it remains to show that if the RSA problem is hard relative to GenRSA and H is modeled as a random oracle, then $Pr[\text{Query}]$ is negligible.

Assume there exists a probabilistic polynomial-time adversary $\mathcal{A}$ in the random oracle model that breaks the IND-EAV security of the scheme. We construct B as follows to defeat the RSA challenge using $\mathcal{A}$.

Reduction algorithm B

1. B accepts a RSA challenge: $(N, e, \hat{c}_1)$.

2. B chooses a random $\hat{k} \leftarrow \{0,1\}^{l(n)}$.   ($B$ implicitly sets $H(\hat{r}) = \hat{k}$, where $\hat{r} \stackrel{\text{def}}{=} [\hat{c}_1^{1/e} \bmod N]$. Note, however, that B does not know $\hat{r}$.)

3. B starts $\mathcal{A}$ on input the public key $pk = \langle N, e \rangle$ and prepares a table, initially empty.

4. When $\mathcal{A}$ makes a query x to the random oracle H, B answers it as follows.

    (a) If there is an entry (x, k) in the table, B returns k to $\mathcal{A}$.

    (b) If $x^e = \hat{c}_1 \bmod N$, B returns $\hat{k}$ and stores $(x, \hat{k})$ in the table. B outputs x as the answer to the RSA challenge and quits.

    (c) Otherwise, B chooses a random $k \leftarrow \{0,1\}^{l(n)}$, returns k and stores (x, k) in the table.

---

5. At some points, $\mathcal{A}$ outputs messages $m_0, m_1 \in \{0,1\}^{l(n)}$.

6. B chooses $b \leftarrow \{0,1\}$, sets $c_2 = \hat{k} \oplus m_b$, and gives $\langle \hat{c}_1, c_2 \rangle$ to $\mathcal{A}$. B goes to Step 4.

Say the input to B is generated by running $\mathsf{GenRSA}(1^n)$ to obtain (N, e, d) and then choosing $\hat{c}_1 \leftarrow \mathbb{Z}_N^*$ at random (See Definition 8). Then the view of $\mathcal{A}$ when run as a subroutine by B is distributed identically to the view of $\mathcal{A}$ in experiment $\mathsf{PubK}_{\mathcal{A},\Pi}^{eav}(n)$ (In each case $\langle N, e \rangle$ is generated the same way; $\hat{c}_1$ is equal to $[r^e \bmod N]$ for a randomly chosen $r \leftarrow \mathbb{Z}_N^*$; and the random oracle queries of $\mathcal{A}$ are answered with random strings). Thus, the probability of event Query remains unchanged. Furthermore, B correctly solves the RSA instance whenever Query occurs. That is,

$$Pr[\text{RSA-inv}_{B,\mathsf{GenRSA}}(n) = 1] = Pr[\text{Query}]. \tag{9.16}$$

Since the RSA problem is hard relative to GenRSA, it must be the case that $Pr[\text{Query}]$ is negligible by Definition 8. $\square$

9.4.5   The CCA-Secure RSA Encryption Under the RSA Assumption in the Random Oracle Model

---

Construction 7. CCA-secure RSA encryption in the random oracle model

Let GenRSA be as usual and let $\ell(n)$ be an arbitrary polynomial. Let $\Pi' = (\mathsf{Gen'}, \mathsf{Enc'}, \mathsf{Dec'})$ be a private-key encryption scheme for messages of length $\ell(n)$. Let H be a function whose domain can be set to $\mathbb{Z}_N^*$ for any N, and whose range can be set to $\{0,1\}^{\ell(n)}$ for any n. Construct a public-key encryption scheme as follows.

1. Gen: on input 1^n, run $\mathsf{GenRSA}(1^n)$ to obtain $\langle N, e, d \rangle$. The public key is $\langle N, e \rangle$ and the private key is $\langle N, d \rangle$.

2. Enc: on input a public key $\langle N, e \rangle$ and a message $m \in \{0,1\}^{\ell(n)}$, choose a random $r \leftarrow \mathbb{Z}_N^*$, compute $k = H(r)$ and output the ciphertext

$$\langle [r^e \bmod N], \mathsf{Enc'}_k(m) \rangle.$$

3. Dec: on input a private key $\langle N, d \rangle$ and a ciphertext $\langle c_1, c_2 \rangle$, compute $r = [c_1^d \bmod N]$ and set $k = H(r)$, and then output the message $\mathsf{Dec'}_k(c_2)$.

Theorem 8 *If the RSA problem is hard relative to GenRSA, the private-key encryption scheme Π' has indistinguishable encryptions under a chosen-ciphertext attack and H is modeled as a random oracle, then Construction 7 is CCA-secure.*

Proof

Let Π denote the above construction. Let $\mathcal{A}$ be a probabilistic polynomial-time adversary and define $\epsilon(n) \stackrel{\text{def}}{=} Pr[\mathsf{PubK}^{cca}_{\mathcal{A},\Pi}(n) = 1]$. We describe the steps of experiment $\mathsf{PubK}^{cca}_{\mathcal{A},\Pi}(n)$ as follows.

The CCA-secure experiment $\mathsf{PubK}^{cca}_{\mathcal{A},\Pi}(n)$ in the ROM

1. *A random function H is chosen.*

2. $\mathsf{GenRSA}(1^n)$ *is run to generate* (N, e, d).
   Adversary $\mathcal{A}$ is given $pk = \langle N, e \rangle$, and may query $H(\cdot)$ and the decryption oracle $\mathsf{Dec}_{\langle N, d \rangle}(\cdot)$.
   Eventually $\mathcal{A}$ outputs two messages $m_0, m_1 \in \{0,1\}^{l(n)}$.

3. *A random bit $b \in \{0,1\}$ and a random $r \leftarrow \mathbb{Z}_N^*$ are chosen. $\mathcal{A}$ is given the ciphertext $\langle [r^e \mod N], \mathsf{Enc}'_{H(r)}(m_b) \rangle$.*
   The adversary may continue to query $H(\cdot)$ and the decryption oracle.

4. *$\mathcal{A}$ outputs a bit b'. The output of the experiment is defined to be 1 if $b' = b$, and 0 otherwise.*

Let Query denote that $\mathcal{A}$ queries r to the random oracle H. We also use Success as shorthand for the event that $\mathsf{PubK}^{cca}_{\mathcal{A},\Pi}(n) = 1$. Then

$$
\begin{aligned}
Pr[Success] =& Pr[\mathsf{Success} \wedge \overline{\mathsf{Query}}] + Pr[\mathsf{Success} \wedge \mathsf{Query}] \\
\leq& \, Pr[\mathsf{Success} \wedge \overline{\mathsf{Query}}] + Pr[\mathsf{Query}],
\end{aligned}
$$

where all probabilities are taken over the randomness used in the experiment $\mathsf{PubK}^{cca}_{\mathcal{A},\Pi}(n)$. We show that $Pr[\mathsf{Success} \wedge \overline{\mathsf{Query}}] \leq \frac{1}{2} + negl(n)$ and $Pr[\mathsf{Query}]$ is negligible.

For the first claim: If the private-key encryption scheme Π' has indistinguishable encryptions under a chosen-ciphertext attack and H is modeled as a random oracle, then there exists a negligible function negl such that

$$
Pr[\mathsf{Success} \wedge \overline{\mathsf{Query}}] \leq \frac{1}{2} + negl(n). \tag{9.17}
$$

Consider the following adversary $\mathcal{A}'$ carrying out a chosen-ciphertext attack on Π'. $\mathcal{A}'$ has access to an encryption oracle $\mathsf{Enc}_k(\cdot)$ and a decryption oracle $\mathsf{Dec}_k(\cdot)$.

1. Run $\mathsf{GenRSA}(1^n)$ to compute (N, e, d). Choose $r \leftarrow \mathbb{Z}_N^*$ and set $c_1 = [r^e \bmod N]$ ($\mathcal{A}'$ is implicitly setting $H(r) = k$).

2. Run $\mathcal{A}$ on input $pk = \langle N, e \rangle$. Pairs of strings $(\cdot; \cdot)$ are stored in a table, initially empty. When $\mathcal{A}$ makes a query $\langle \overline{c_1}, \overline{c_2} \rangle$ to its decryption oracle, answer it as follows.

   (a) If $\overline{c_1} = c_1$, then $\mathcal{A}'$ queries $\overline{c_2}$ to its own decryption oracle and returns the result $\mathsf{Dec}'_{\overline{k}}(\overline{c_2})$ to $\mathcal{A}$.

   (b) If $\overline{c_1} \neq c_1$, then compute $\overline{r} = [\overline{c}_1^d \bmod N]$. Then compute $\overline{k} = H(\overline{r})$ using the procedure discussed below. Return the result $\mathsf{Dec}'_{\overline{k}}(\overline{c_2})$ to $\mathcal{A}$.

   $\overline{k} = H(\overline{r})$ is computed as follows.

   (a) If there is an entry $(\overline{r}, \overline{k})$ in the table, return $\overline{k}$.

   (b) Otherwise, choose a random $\overline{k} \leftarrow \{0, 1\}^n$, return it, and store $(\overline{r}, \overline{k})$ in the table.

3. At some point, $\mathcal{A}$ outputs $m_0, m_1 \in \{0, 1\}^{\ell(n)}$. Adversary $\mathcal{A}'$ outputs these same messages, and is given in return a ciphertext c_2. Then $\mathcal{A}'$ gives the ciphertext $\langle \overline{c_1}, \overline{c_2} \rangle$ to $\mathcal{A}$, and continues to answer the oracle queries of $\mathcal{A}$ as before.

4. When $\mathcal{A}$ outputs its guess b', this value is output by $\mathcal{A}'$.

Let $Pr'[\cdot]$ refer to the probability of an event in the experiment $\mathsf{PrivK}^{cca}_{\mathcal{A}',\Pi'}(n)$. We define Query and Success as above. Then we can intuitively note that as long as $\overline{\mathsf{Query}}$ does not occur, decryption queries by $\mathcal{A}$ of the ciphertext $\langle \overline{c_1}, \overline{c_2} \rangle$ are answered in $\mathsf{PubK}^{cca}_{\mathcal{A},\Pi}(n)$ and $\mathsf{PrivK}^{cca}_{\mathcal{A}',\Pi'}(n)$. Therefore, we have

$$Pr[\mathsf{Success} \wedge \overline{\mathsf{Query}}] + Pr'[\mathsf{Success} \wedge \overline{\mathsf{Query}}] \leq Pr'[\mathsf{Success}]. \qquad (9.18)$$

Since Π' has indistinguishable encryptions under a chosen-ciphertext attack, then

$$Pr'[\mathsf{Success}] \leq \frac{1}{2} + negl(n). \qquad (9.19)$$

Therefore, we claim that

$$Pr[\mathsf{Success} \wedge \overline{\mathsf{Query}}] \leq \frac{1}{2} + negl(n). \qquad (9.20)$$

For the next claim: If the RSA problem is hard relative to GenRSA and H is modeled as a random oracle, then $Pr[\mathsf{Query}]$ is negligible.

Intuitively, $Pr[\mathsf{Query}]$ is negligible for the same reason as in the proof of CPA-secure RSA in Theorem 7. In the formal proof, however, additional difficulties arise due to the fact that the decryption queries of $\mathcal{A}$ must somehow be answered without knowledge of the private (decryption) key. Fortunately, the random oracle model enables a solution: to decrypt a ciphertext $\langle \overline{c_1}, \overline{c_2} \rangle$ (where no prior decryption query was made using the same initial component $\overline{c_1}$), we generate a random key $\overline{k}$ and return the message $\mathsf{Dec}'_{\overline{k}}(\overline{c_2})$. To generate the key $\overline{k} = H(\overline{r})$, we need to query $\overline{r}$ to random oracle. Thus, the reduction must ensure consistency with both prior and later queries of $\mathcal{A}$ to the random oracle (in the case $\overline{r}$ is ever queried to the random oracle in the future).

Actually, a simple data structure handles both cases: maintain a table storing all the random oracle queries and answers as in the proof of Theorem 7 (and as in the proof of the previous claim), except that now the table will contain triples rather than pairs. Two types of entries will appear in the table as follows.

1. The first type of entry has the form $(\overline{r}, \overline{c_1}, \overline{k})$ with $\overline{c_1} = [\overline{r}^e \bmod N]$. This entry means that we have defined $H(\overline{r}) = \overline{k}$.

2. The second type of entry has the form $(\cdot, \overline{c_1}, \overline{k})$, which means that the value $\overline{r} \stackrel{\text{def}}{=} [\overline{c}^{1/e} \bmod N]$ is not yet known. If $\mathcal{A}$ ever asks the random oracle query $H(\overline{r})$, we will return the correct answer $\overline{k}$ because we will check the table for any entry having $[\overline{r}^e \bmod N]$ as its second component.

Now we implement the above ideas as the following algorithm $\mathcal{A}'$ as follows. The algorithm is given (N, e, c_1) as input.

1. Choose random $\overline{k} \leftarrow \{0,1\}^n$. Triple $(\cdot, \cdot, \cdot)$ is stored in a table that initially contains only $(\cdot, \overline{c_1}, \overline{k})$. When $\mathcal{A}$ makes a query $\langle \overline{c_1}, \overline{c_2} \rangle$ to its decryption oracle, answer it as follows.

   (a) If there is an entry in the table whose second component is $\overline{c_1}$ (either $(\overline{r}, \overline{c_1}, \overline{k})$ or $(\cdot, \overline{c_1}, \overline{k})$ is in the table), let $\overline{k}$ be the third component of this entry. Return the result $\mathsf{Dec}'_{\overline{k}}(\overline{c_2})$.

   (b) Otherwise, choose $\overline{k} \leftarrow \{0,1\}^n$, return the result $\mathsf{Dec}'_{\overline{k}}(\overline{c_2})$ to $\mathcal{A}$ and store $(\cdot, \overline{c_1}, \overline{k})$ in the table.

   When $\mathcal{A}$ makes a query $\overline{r}$ to the random oracle, compute $\overline{c_1} = [\overline{r}^e \bmod N]$ and answer the query as follows.

   (a) If there is an entry $(\overline{r}, \overline{c_1}, \overline{k})$ in the table, return $\overline{k}$.

   (b) If there is an entry $(\cdot, \overline{c_1}, \overline{k})$ in the table, return $\overline{k}$, and store $(\overline{r}, \overline{c_1}, \overline{k})$ in the table.

   (c) Otherwise, choose a random $\overline{k} \leftarrow \{0,1\}^n$, return $\overline{k}$, and store $(\overline{r}, \overline{c_1}, \overline{k})$ in the table.

2. At some point, $\mathcal{A}$ outputs $m_0, m_1 \in \{0,1\}^{\ell(n)}$. Choose random $b \in \{0,1\}$ and set ciphertext $c_2 \leftarrow \mathsf{Enc}'_k(m_b)$. Then $\mathcal{A}'$ gives the ciphertext $\langle c_1, c_2 \rangle$ to $\mathcal{A}$, and continues to answer the oracle queries of $\mathcal{A}$ as before.

3. When $\mathcal{A}$ outputs its guess b', this is equivalent to that there exists an entry (r, c_1, k) in the table. That is, $\mathcal{A}'$ successfully outputs r in the RSA problem.

Thus, we have $\mathcal{A}'$ correctly solve the given RSA instance whenever Query occurs. That is,

$$Pr[\text{RSA-inv}_{A',\text{GenRSA}}(n) = 1] = Pr[\text{Query}]. \qquad (9.21)$$

Since the RSA problem is hard relative to GenRSA, it must be the case that $Pr[\text{Query}]$ is negligible by Definition 8.

By combining two claims above, we have Construction 7 is CCA-secure. $\square$

9.4.6 The RSA-OAEP Encryption

We explore a construction of RSA-based CCA-secure encryption using *optimal asymmetric encryption padding* (OAEP). The resulting RSA-OAEP scheme follows the idea of taking a message m, transforming it to an element $\hat{m} \in \mathbb{Z}_N{}^*$, and then letting $c = [\hat{m}^e \mod N]$ be the ciphertext. The transformation here, however, is more complex than before. A version of RSA-OAEP has been standardized as part of RSA PKCS #1, which is widely used in practice.

Construction 8. The RSA-OAEP encryption scheme

Let GenRSA be as usual and let ℓ, k_0, k_1 be as described in the text. Let $G : \{0,1\}^{k_0} \to \{0,1\}^{\ell+k_1}$ and $H : \{0,1\}^{\ell+k_1} \to \{0,1\}^{k_0}$ be functions. Construct a public-key encryption scheme as follows.

1. Gen: on input 1^n, run GenRSA(1^n) to obtain (N, e, d). The public key is $\langle N, e \rangle$ and the private key is $\langle N, d \rangle$.

2. Enc: on input a public key $\langle N, e \rangle$ and a message $m \in \{0,1\}^\ell$, set $m' = m \| 0^{k_1}$ and choose a uniform $r \in \{0,1\}^{k_0}$. Then compute

$$s = m' \oplus G(r), \qquad t = r \oplus H(s)$$

and set $\hat{m} = s \| t$. Output the ciphertext $c = [\hat{m}^e \mod N]$.

3. Dec: on input a private key $\langle N, d \rangle$ and a ciphertext $c \in \mathbb{Z}_N^*$, compute $\hat{m} = [c^d \mod N]$. If $\|\hat{m}\| > \ell + k_0 + k_1$, output $\perp$. Otherwise, parse $\hat{m}$ as $s \| t$ with $s \in \{0,1\}^{\ell+k_1}$ and $t \in \{0,1\}^{k_0}$. Compute $r = H(s) \oplus t$ and $m' = G(r) \oplus s$. If the least-significant k_1 bits of m_0 are not all 0, output $\perp$. Otherwise, output the ℓ most-significant bits of $\hat{m}$.

Theorem 9 *If the RSA problem is hard relative to GenRSA, and G and H are modeled as independent random oracles, then RSA-OAEP can be proven CCA-secure for certain types of public exponents e (including the common case when $e = 3$).*

Proof is omitted.

9.4.7   The Cramer-Shoup Encryption

The Cramer-Shoup encryption scheme [36] is a CCA enhancement of the CPA-secure El Gamal encryption scheme.

The Diffie-Hellman decision problem
Let $\mathbb{G}$ be a group of large prime order q, and consider the following two distributions.

1. the distribution R of random quadruples $(g_1, g_2, u_1, u_2) \in \mathbb{G}^4$;
2. the distribution D of quadruples $(g_1, g_2, u_1, u_2) \in \mathbb{G}^4$, where g_1, g_2 are random, and $u_1 = g_1{}^r$ and $u_2 = g_2{}^r$ for random $r \in \mathbb{Z}_q$.

Given a quadruple coming from one of the two distributions, an algorithm that solves the Diffie-Hellman decision problem is a statistical test that can effectively distinguish these two distributions. It should output 0 or 1, and these should be a non-negligible difference between (a) the probability that it outputs a 1 given an input from R, and (b) the probability that it outputs a 1 given an input from D. We say the Diffie-Hellman decision problem is hard if there is no such polynomial-time statistical test.

Collision-resistant hash functions
A family of hash functions is said to be *collision resistant* if upon drawing a function H at random from the family, it is infeasible for an adversary to find two *different* inputs x and y such that $H(x) = H(y)$.

Construction 9. The Cramer-Shoup public-key scheme

Let $\mathbb{G}$ be a group of prime order q, where q is large.

1. Gen: The key generation algorithm runs as follows.

   (a) Choose $g_1, g_2 \in \mathbb{G}$ randomly.

   (b) Pick random integers $x_1, x_2, y_1, y_2, z \in \mathbb{Z}_q$.

(c) Compute
$$c = g_1{}^{x_1} g_2{}^{x_2}, \; d = g_1{}^{y_1} g_2{}^{y_2}, \; h = g_1{}^z.$$

(d) Choose a hash function H from the family of universal one-way hash functions.

(e) The public key is (g_1, g_2, c, d, h, H).

(f) The private key is (x_1, x_2, y_1, y_2, z).

2. Enc: For given message $m \in \mathbb{G}$ and the public key (g_1, g_2, c, d, h, H), the encryption algorithm runs as follows.

(a) Choose $r \in \mathbb{Z}_q$ randomly.

(b) Compute
$$u_1 = g_1{}^r, \; u_2 = g_2{}^r, \; e = h^r m, \; \alpha = H(u_1, u_2, e), \; v = c^r d^{r\alpha}.$$

(c) The ciphertext is (u_1, u_2, e, v).

3. Dec: For given ciphertext (u_1, u_2, e, v) and the private key (x_1, x_2, y_1, y_2, z), the decryption algorithm runs as follows.

(a) Compute $\alpha = H(u_1, u_2, e)$.

(b) Check $u_1{}^{x_1 + y_1 \alpha} u_2{}^{x_2 + y_2 \alpha} \overset{?}{=} v$.

(c) If yes, output $m = e/u_1{}^z$; otherwise, output $\perp$.

Theorem 10 *Construction 9 is secure against adaptive chosen ciphertext attack assuming that (1) the hash function H is chosen from a universal one-way family, and (2) the Diffie-Hellman decision problem is hard in the group $\mathbb{G}$.*

Proof
Outline of the Proof To prove the theorem, we will assume that there is an adversary that can break the Cramer-Shoup scheme, and that the hash family is universal one-way, and show how to use this adversary to construct a statistical test for the Diffie-Hellman decision problem, that is, reduction from the DDH problem to an attack on the Cramer-Shoup scheme, which shows that if Cramer-Shoup is not IND-CCA secure, then the DDH problem can be solved, or equivalently, if DDH problem is hard to solve, then Cramer-Shoup is IND-CCA secure (i.e., the adversary's advantage is negligible in the IND-CCA game against the Cramer-Shoup scheme).

For the statistical test, we build a simulator $\mathcal{B}$ (as shown in Figure 9.5) which are given (g_1, g_2, u_1, u_2) coming from either the distribution R or D and provides cryptanalysis training to $\mathcal{A}$ so that $\mathcal{A}$ should output 0 or 1, and there should be a negligible difference between the probability that it outputs 1 given an input from R and the probability that it outputs 1 given an input from D. When the input comes from D, $\mathcal{B}$ provides perfect simulation and the success probability of $\mathcal{A}$ in actual construction is identical with the success probability of $\mathcal{A}$ in the simulation (Lemma 1). When the input comes from R, the success probability of $\mathcal{A}$ is negligible (Lemma 2). That is, $\mathcal{A}$ obtains no advantage from the cryptanalysis training courses. Finally, we translate the advantage of $\mathcal{A}$ in guessing hidden bit b to $\mathcal{B}$'s capability in distinguishing between D and R: if $\mathcal{B}$ outputs b and $\mathcal{A}$ outputs b', the distinguisher outputs 1 if $b = b'$, and 0 otherwise.

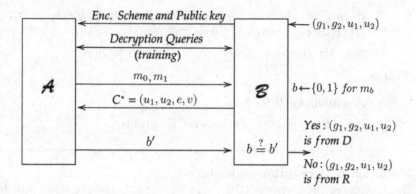

FIGURE 9.5
Reduction from the DDH problem to an attack on Cramer-Shoup scheme.

The simulator $\mathcal{B}$

Setup

$\mathcal{B}$ is given (g_1, g_2, u_1, u_2).

Gen

1. Choose $x_1, x_2, y_1, y_2, z_1, z_2 \in \mathbb{Z}_q$ randomly.
2. Compute $c = g_1^{x_1} g_2^{x_2}$, $d = g_1^{y_1} g_2^{y_2}$, $h = g_1^{z_1} g_2^{z_2}$.
3. Choose a hash function H at random.
4. The public key is (g_1, g_2, c, d, h, H).
5. The private key is $(x_1, x_2, y_1, y_2, z_1, z_2)$.

Decryption Queries
For given ciphertext (u_1, u_2, e, v), $\mathcal{B}$ runs as follows.

1. Compute $\alpha = H(u_1, u_2, e)$.

2. Check $u_1{}^{x_1+y_1\alpha}u_2{}^{x_2+y_2\alpha} \overset{?}{=} v$.

3. If yes, $\mathcal{B}$ outputs $m = e/(u_1{}^{z_1}u_2{}^{z_2})$; otherwise, $\mathcal{B}$ outputs $\perp$.

Challenge Phase

1. $\mathcal{A}$ sends two messages m_0 and m_1 to $\mathcal{B}$.

2. $\mathcal{B}$ chooses a bit $b \in \{0, 1\}$.

3. $\mathcal{B}$ encrypts message m_b as follows: $e = u_1{}^{z_1}u_2{}^{z_2}m_b$, $\alpha = H(u_1, u_2, e)$, $v = u_1{}^{x_1+y_1\alpha}u_2{}^{x_2+y_2\alpha}$.

4. Send the challenge ciphertext (u_1, u_2, e, v) to $\mathcal{A}$.

Guess

1. $\mathcal{A}$ outputs bit b' for b.

2. If $b = b'$, it outputs 1; otherwise, it outputs 0.

Simulation of decryption procedure

When receiving the ciphertext (u_1, u_2, e, v) from $\mathcal{A}$, the simulator will first conduct the check of integrity $u_1{}^{x_1+y_1\alpha}u_2{}^{x_2+y_2\alpha} \overset{?}{=} v$. That is,

$$u_1{}^{x_1+y_1\alpha}u_2{}^{x_2+y_2\alpha} \overset{?}{=} (g_1{}^{x_1}g_2{}^{x_2})^r(g_1{}^{y_1}g_2{}^{y_2})^{r\alpha}.$$

If the check passes, then the ciphertext is valid. In this case, there exists $r \in \mathbb{Z}_q$ such that $u_1{}^{x_1+y_1\alpha}u_2{}^{x_2+y_2\alpha} = (g_1{}^r)^{x_1+y_1\alpha}(g_2{}^r)^{x_2+y_2\alpha}$. Then, the simulator will decrypt as follows.

$$m' = e/(u_1{}^{z_1}u_2{}^{z_2}) = h^r m/(g_1{}^r)^{z_1}(g_2{}^r)^{z_2} = h^r m/h^r = m.$$

Simulation of encryption procedure

In the case (g_1, g_2, u_1, u_2) comes from D, the encrypted simulation is exactly a valid Cramer-Shoup encryption under the given public key (detail is given in Proof of Lemma 1).

In the case (g_1, g_2, u_1, u_2) comes from R, there exist $r_1, r_2 \in \mathbb{Z}_q$ with $r_1 \neq r_2$ such that $u_1 = g_1{}^{r_1}$ and $u_2 = g_2{}^{r_2}$. Since g_1 is a generator of $\mathbb{G}$, there exists $w = log_{g_1} g_2$.

From $h = g_1{}^{z_1}g_2{}^{z_2}$, we have $log_{g_1} h = z_1 + wz_2$.

From $e = u_1{}^{z_1}u_2{}^{z_2}m_b$, we have

$$log_{g_1}(e/m_0) = r_1z_1 + wr_2z_2,$$
$$log_{g_1}(e/m_1) = r_1z_1 + wr_2z_2.$$

Since either m_0 or m_1 is chosen to encrypt by $\mathcal{B}$, we have

$$\begin{cases} z_1 + wz_2 = log_{g_1} h \\ r_1z_1 + wr_2z_2 = log_{g_1}(e/m_0) \end{cases} \tag{9.22}$$

or

$$\begin{cases} z_1 + wz_2 = log_{g_1} h \\ r_1 z_1 + wr_2 z_2 = log_{g_1}(e/m_1). \end{cases} \tag{9.23}$$

There is no way for the adversary $\mathcal{A}$ to verify which one of the messages is encrypted.

Intuition Note that $\mathcal{B}$ cannot determine whether the input distribution comes from D or R because it can decrypt the valid ciphertexts in both cases[2]. Let us suppose $\mathcal{A}$ can break Cramer-Shoup. Then $\mathcal{B}$, given the input distribution, can construct challenge ciphertext C^*, which encrypts one of messages m_0, m_1 given by $\mathcal{A}$ and asks $\mathcal{A}$ to release its attacking advantage. If the distribution comes from D, $\mathcal{A}$ can use its attacking advantage. If not, m_b is encrypted in perfectly secure sense (that is, in Shannon's information theoretically secure sense) and thus cannot be decrypted, and therefore $\mathcal{A}$ cannot have any advantage whatsoever. If $\mathcal{A}$ is about 50% right, the input is probably from R.

Theorem 10 follows from the following two lemmas.

Lemma 1 When the simulator's input comes from D, the joint distribution of the adversary's view and the hidden bit b is statistically indistinguishable from that in the actual attack.

Lemma 1 says that when the simulator's input comes from D, the simulator can provide perfect simulation to the adversary like in the actual system and the adversary's advantage is identical with the simulator's advantage in distinguishing whether the input comes from D.

Proof of Lemma 1 Consider the joint distribution of the adversary's view and the bit b when the input comes from the distribution D. In this case, because there exists $r \in \mathbb{Z}_q$ such that $u_1 = g_1{}^r$ and $u_2 = g_2{}^r$, we have

$$u_1{}^{z_1} u_2{}^{z_2} = g_1{}^{rz_1} g_2{}^{rz_2} = h^r. \tag{9.24}$$

First, we show that the simulated encryption and decryption distributions are appropriately (i.e., indistinguishably) distributed from $\mathcal{A}$'s view. It is clear in this case that the output of the encryption oracle has the right distribution, since $u_1{}^{x_1} u_2{}^{x_2} = c^r$, $u_1{}^{y_1} u_2{}^{y_2} = d^r$, and $u_1{}^{z_1} u_2{}^{z_2} = h^r$; indeed, these equations imply that $e = m_b h^r$ and $v = c^r d^{r\alpha}$, and α itself is already of the right form. We also argue that the output of the decryption oracle has the right distribution. Let us call $(u_1', u_2', e', v') \in \mathbb{G}^4$ a *valid*

---

[2]Since the simulator knows the private key, it can decrypt the valid ciphertexts. If the simulator can decrypt the challenge ciphertext in case D but cannot decrypt the challenge ciphertext in case R, then the simulator can distinguish D and R, itself, which removes the need to use the attacker.

ciphertext if $log_{g_1} u_1' = log_{g_2} u_2'$ [3]. Note that if a ciphertext is valid, then $h^{r'} = (g_1^{z_1} g_2^{z_2})^{r'} = (g_1^{r'})^{z_1}(g_2^{r'})^{z_2} = u_1'^{z_1} u_2'^{z_2}$. Therefore, the decryption oracle outputs $e/h^{r'}$ as in the actual construction.

Next we show the adversary's advantage in simulation is identical with one from the actual construction.

Claim 1 The decryption oracle in both an actual attack against the scheme and in an attack against the simulator rejects all invalid ciphertexts, except with negligible probability.

We now prove this claim by considering the distribution of the point $P = (x_1, x_2, y_1, y_2) \in \mathbb{Z}_q^4$, conditioned on $\mathcal{A}$'s view. Let $log(\cdot)$ denote $log_{g_1}(\cdot)$ and $w = log\ g_2$. From $\mathcal{A}$'s view, P is a random point on the plane $\mathcal{P}$ formed by intersecting the hyperplanes

$$log\ c = x_1 + wx_2 \tag{9.25}$$

and

$$log\ d = y_1 + wy_2. \tag{9.26}$$

These two equations come from the public key [4]. The output from the encryption oracle does not constrain P any further, as the hyperplane defined by

$$log\ v = rx_1 + wrx_2 + \alpha ry_1 + \alpha rwy_2 \tag{9.27}$$

contains $\mathcal{P}$.[5]

Now suppose the adversary submits an invalid ciphertext (u_1', u_2', e', v') to the decryption oracle, where $log\ u_1' = r_1'$ and $log\ u_2' = r_2'$ with $r_1' \neq r_2'$. The decryption oracle will reject, unless P happens to lie on the hyperplane $\mathcal{H}$ defined by

$$log\ v' = r_1' x_1 + wr_2' x_2 + \alpha' r_1' y_1 + \alpha' r_2' wy_2, \tag{9.28}$$

where $\alpha' = H(u_1', u_2', e')$. [6] It clear to see that the Equations (9.25), (9.26), and (9.28) are linearly independent, and so $\mathcal{H}$ intersects the plane $\mathcal{P}$ at a line.[7]

We assume that the adversary queries at most q_D to decryption oracle. For the first invalid ciphertext, the decryption will accept this ciphertext with

---

[3]Because in this case, there exist $r' \in \mathbb{Z}_q$ such that $u_1' = g_1^{r'}$ and $u_2' = g_2^{r'}$.

[4]$c = g_1^{x_1} g_2^{x_2} = g_1^{x_1}(g_1^w)^{x_2}$. Thus, $log\ c = log_{g_1}(g_1^{x_1}) + log_{g_1}(g_1^{wx_2}) = x_1 + wx_2$

$d = g_1^{y_1} g_2^{y_2} = g_1^{y_1}(g_1^w)^{y_2}$. Thus, $log\ d = log_{g_1}(g_1^{y_1}) + log_{g_1}(g_1^{wy_2}) = y_1 + wy_2$

[5]$v = u_1^{x_1 + y_1 \alpha} u_2^{x_2 + y_2 \alpha} = g_1^{rx_1} g_1^{\alpha ry_1} g_2^{rx_2} g_2^{\alpha ry_2} = g_1^{rx_1} g_1^{\alpha ry_1} g_1^{wrx_2} g_1^{\alpha wry_2}$.
Therefore, $log\ v = log_{g_1}(g_1^{rx_1}) + log_{g_1}(g_1^{\alpha ry_1}) + log_{g_1}(g_1^{wrx_2}) + log_{g_1}(g_1^{\alpha wry_2}) = rx_1 + wrx_2 + \alpha ry_1 + \alpha rwy_2$

[6]Equation (9.28) is equivalent with $v' = u_1'^{x_1 + y_1 \alpha} u_2'^{x_2 + y_2 \alpha}$, similar to Equation (9.27).

[7]Since there are 3 independent equations with 4 variables, the solution space is a line.

probability $1/q$. That is, the first invalid ciphertext is rejected with probability $1 - 1/q$. The ith invalid ciphertext submitted by the adversary will be rejected with probability at least $1 - 1/(q - i + 1)$. Therefore, the probability the decryption oracle rejects all invalid ciphertexts is

$$(1 - \frac{1}{q})(1 - \frac{1}{q-1}) \ldots (1 - \frac{1}{q-i+1}) \ldots (1 - \frac{1}{q-q_D+1}) = 1 - \frac{q_D}{q}. \quad (9.29)$$

The probability of the actual attack is also the same. Since q is a large prime, the adversary's advantage both in simulation and in actual attack are negligible ($\frac{q_D}{q}$).

Lemma 2 When the simulator's input comes from R, the distribution of the hidden bit b is (essentially) independent from the adversary's view.

Lemma 2 says that when the input comes from R, the adversary's advantage is negligible. Note that unlike in Lemma 1 in this case the simulator cannot provide perfect simulation to the adversary[8], and therefore the distribution of the adversary's view is not described here.

Proof of Lemma 2
Let $u_1 = g_1{}^{r_1}$ and $u_2 = g_1{}^{wr_2}$. We assume that $r_1 \neq r_2$, since this occurs except with negligible probability. The lemma follows immediately from the following two claims.

Claim 2 If the decryption oracle rejects all invalid ciphertexts during the attack, then the distribution of the hidden bit b is independent of the adversary's view.

Claim 3 The decryption oracle will reject all invalid ciphertexts, except with negligible probability.

Regarding Claim 2, consider the point $Q = (z_1, z_2) \in \mathbb{Z}_q^2$. At the beginning of the attack, this is a random point on the line

$$log\, h = z_1 + wz_2, \quad (9.30)$$

determined by the public key.[9] Moreover, if the decryption oracle only decrypts valid ciphertexts (u_1', u_2', e', v'), then the adversary obtains only linearly dependent relations $r' log\, h = r'z_1 + r'wz_2$ (since $u_1'^{z_1} u_2'^{z_2} = g_1'^{r'z_1} g_2'^{r'wz_2} = h^{r'}$). Thus, no further information about Q is leaked.

---

[8]Since $(g_1, g_2, u_1, u_2) \in R$, there exists $r_1, r_2 \in \mathbb{Z}_q$ with $r_1 \neq r_2$ such that $u_1 = g_1{}^{r_1}$ and $u_2 = g_2{}^{r_2}$. Letting $r_1 = \beta r_2$ ($\beta \neq 1$), we have
$u_1{}^{z_1} u_2{}^{z_2} = (g_1{}^{r_1})^{z_1} (g_2{}^{\beta r_1})^{z_2} = (g_1{}^{z_1})^{r_1} (g_2{}^{z_2})^{\beta r_1} \neq (g_1{}^{z_1})^{r_1} (g_2{}^{z_2})^{r_1} = (g_1{}^{z_1} g_2{}^{z_2})^{r_1} = h^{r_1}$. Thus, $e = u_1{}^{z_1} u_2{}^{z_2} m_b \neq h^{r_1} m_b$. As seen from the above result, the simulated encryption is not the same as in Cramer-Shoup scheme.
[9]Since $h = g_1{}^{z_1} g_2{}^{z_2} = g_1{}^{z_1} g_1{}^{wz_2}$, we have $log\, h = z_1 + wz_2$.

Consider now the output (u_1, u_2, e, v) of the simulator's encryption oracle. We have $e/m_b = u_1{}^{z_1} u_2{}^{z_2}$. That is,

$$log\ (e/m_b) = r_1 z_1 + w r_2 z_2. \tag{9.31}$$

Clearly, (9.30) and (9.31) are linearly independent, so the conditional distribution of e/m_b - conditioning on b and everything in the adversary's view other than e - is uniform. In other words, e/m_b is a perfect one-time pad. There is no way for $\mathcal{A}$ to verify which of the two cases of b is the correct one. It follows that b is independent of the $\mathcal{A}$'s view.

Regarding Claim 3, consider the point $P = (x_1, x_2, y_1, y_2) \in \mathbb{Z}_q^4$. From the $\mathcal{A}$'s view, this is a random point on the line $\mathcal{L}$ formed by intersecting the hyperplanes (9.25), (9.26) and

$$log\ v = r_1 x_1 + w r_2 x_2 + \alpha r_1 y_1 + w \alpha r_2 y_2. \tag{9.32}$$

This equation comes from the output of the encryption oracle.

For any valid ciphertext submitted by $\mathcal{A}$, the returned result of decryption will only confirm $rlog\ h = r_1 z_1 + r_2 w z_2$. Therefore, no information about z_1, z_2 in addition to what has already been shown in the public key can be obtained by $\mathcal{A}$. Therefore, if $\mathcal{A}$ submits valid ciphertexts, then $\mathcal{A}$ learns nothing from these.

Now assume that $\mathcal{A}$ submits an invalid ciphertext $(u_1', u_2', e', v') \neq (u_1, u_2, e, v)$, where $log\ u_1' = r_1'$ and $log\ u_2' = r_2'$ with $r_1' \neq r_2'$. Let $\alpha' = H(u_1', u_2', e')$ ($\mathcal{A}$ is very clever and the returned decryption result of this invalid ciphertext may relate to the challenge ciphertext in some way). There are three cases to consider.

1. $(u_1', u_2', e') = (u_1, u_2, e)$. In this case, $\alpha = \alpha'$, but $v \neq v'$, which implies that the decryption oracle will certainly reject.

2. $(u_1', u_2', e') \neq (u_1, u_2, e)$ and $\alpha \neq \alpha'$. The decryption oracle will reject the invalid ciphertext unless the point P lies on the hyperplane $\mathcal{H}$ defined by (9.28). However, the equations (9.25), (9.26), (9.32), and (9.28) are linearly independent. We can express these equations as

$$
\begin{bmatrix}
1 & w & 0 & 0 \\
0 & 0 & 1 & w \\
r_1 & w r_2 & \alpha r_1 & \alpha w r_2 \\
r_1' & w r_2' & \alpha' r_1' & \alpha' w r_2'
\end{bmatrix}
\cdot
\begin{bmatrix}
x_1 \\
x_2 \\
y_1 \\
y_2
\end{bmatrix}
=
\begin{bmatrix}
log\ c \\
log\ d \\
log\ v \\
log\ v'
\end{bmatrix} .
$$

We have

$$
det \begin{pmatrix} 1 & w & 0 & 0 \\ 0 & 0 & 1 & w \\ r_1 & wr_2 & \alpha r_1 & \alpha wr_2 \\ r_1' & wr_2' & \alpha' r_1' & \alpha wr_2' \end{pmatrix} = det \begin{pmatrix} 1 & 0 & w & 0 \\ 0 & 1 & 0 & w \\ r_1 & \alpha r_1 & wr_2 & \alpha wr_2 \\ r_1 & \alpha' r_1' & wr_2' & \alpha' wr_2' \end{pmatrix}
$$

$$
= det \begin{pmatrix} 1 & 0 & w & 0 \\ 0 & 1 & 0 & w \\ 0 & 0 & w(r_2 - r_1) & w\alpha(r_2 - r_1) \\ 0 & 0 & 0 & w(r_2 - r_1)(r_2' - r_1')(\alpha - \alpha') \end{pmatrix}
$$

$$
= w^2 (r_2' - r_1')(r_2 - r_1)^2 (\alpha - \alpha') \neq 0.
$$

Thus, $\mathcal{H}$ intersects the line $\mathcal{L}$ at a point.[10] It follows that the decryption oracle rejects the invalid ciphertext, except with probability $1/q$.

3. $(u_1', u_2', e') \neq (u_1, u_2, e)$ and $\alpha = \alpha'$. We argue that if this happens with non-negligible probability, then in fact, the family of hash functions is not universal one-way, which is a contradiction to the assumption of H of Theorem 10. We use the adversary to break the universal one-way hash functions as follows. We modify the encryption oracle at Decryption Queries in the simulator, so that it outputs (u_1, u_2, e, v) as before, except that now, $e \in G$ is simply chosen completely at random. Up until such time that a collision occurs, the adversary's view in the modified simulation is statistically indistinguishable from the view in the original simulation. Therefore, the adversary will also find a collision with non-negligible probability in the modified simulation. But the argument (u_1, u_2, e) to H is independent of H, and in particular, we can choose it before choosing H.

The $\mathcal{A}$'s advantage in the case the input comes from R is at most $\dfrac{1}{q}$.

Conclusion of Theorem 10 From the proofs of two lemmas, we can conclude that: $\mathcal{A}$'s capability in guessing hidden bit b, i.e., in attacking the scheme, is identically translated to $\mathcal{B}$'s capability in determining whether given quadruples comes from D or R. Since the Diffie-Helman decision problem is hard, the probabilities of distinguishing between D and R is negligible, then the scheme

---

[10]The determinant of the first matrix (coefficient matrix of (x_1, x_2, y_1, y_2)) is not 0 because $r_1 \neq r_2, r_1' \neq r_2', \alpha \neq \alpha', w \neq 0$. By a simple fact in linear algebra that an inverse matrix exists when its determinant is not 0, for any fixed private key (x_1, x_2, y_1, y_2) and its resulting public key c and d, there exists only one single v', a component of a ciphertext. Therefore, the adversary cannot set v' unambiguously and the probability for constructing invalid ciphertext and escaping rejection is $1/q$.

is secure as shown in detail as follows.

Let ϵ denote the advantage of polynomial time $\mathcal{A}$ in breaking the Cramer-Shoup scheme (denoted by Π). The probability $\mathcal{A}$ can break the IND-CCA game against Π is $\frac{1}{2} + \epsilon$.

In Lemma 1, we only show that when the quadruple comes from D, the probability that $\mathcal{A}$ outputs hidden bit b' correctly is the same as the probability that $\mathcal{B}$ outputs 1. Let ϵ' denote the gap between an attack against the actual construction and an attack against the simulation. Through the proof of Lemma 1, we have

$$|Pr[\mathcal{A}_{outputs}\ b' = b|D] - Pr[\mathcal{B}_{outputs}\ 1|D]| = \epsilon'. \tag{9.33}$$

Thus,

$$Pr[\mathcal{B}_{outputs}\ 1|D] = Pr[\mathcal{A}_{outputs}\ b' = b|D] + \epsilon = \frac{1}{2} + \epsilon + \epsilon'. \tag{9.34}$$

In Lemma 2, we have the probability that $\mathcal{B}$ outputs 1 when the quadruple comes from R is

$$Pr[\mathcal{B}_{outputs}\ 1|R] = \frac{1}{2} + \frac{1}{q}. \tag{9.35}$$

The probability that $\mathcal{B}$ can solve the Diffie-Hellman decision problem is

$$|Pr[\mathcal{B}_{outputs}\ 1|D] - Pr[\mathcal{B}_{outputs}\ 1|R]| = (\frac{1}{2} + \epsilon + \epsilon') - (\frac{1}{2} + \frac{1}{q}) = \epsilon + \epsilon' - \frac{1}{q}, \tag{9.36}$$

with ϵ' and $\frac{1}{q}$ are negligible. Since the Diffie-Hellman Decision Problem is hard, $\mathcal{B}$ cannot solve it except with negligible probability. That implies ϵ is negligible. Therefore, the Cramer-Shoup scheme is secure. $\square$

In the conclusion of Theorem 10, we showed that if the Diffie-Helman decision problem is hard, the probabilities of distinguishing between D and R is negligible, and therefore the scheme is secure. In the following, we give its alternate proof, which makes use of the proof of ElGamal encryption scheme shown before.

Assume that the Diffie-Hellman decision problem is hard for $\mathcal{G}$. Recall that the Diffie-Hellman decision problem challenger works as follows: runs $\mathcal{G}(1^n)$ to generate (p, g); chooses $x, y, z \in \mathbb{Z}_q$ uniformly at random, where $q = (\frac{p-1}{2})$; chooses $d \in \{0, 1\}$ uniformly at random; sets $g_1 = g, g_2 = g^x, u_1 = g^y, u_2 = g^{xy}$ if $d = 0$ and $g_1 = g, g_2 = g^x, u_1 = g^y, u_2 = g^z$ if $d = 1$; and finally, gives (g_1, g_2, u_1, u_2) to the attacker.

Let Π (Gen, Enc, Dec) be the Cramer-Shoup scheme. Let $\mathcal{A}$ be a polynomial-time algorithm attacking Π. Let ϵ denote the advantage of $\mathcal{A}$ in the IND-CCA security game against Π. We construct an algorithm $\mathcal{B}$ for solving the Diffie-Hellman decision problem.

Algorithm $\mathcal{B}$ runs in polynomial time, because $\mathcal{A}$ runs in polynomial time and because operations in $\mathbb{Z}_p^*$ can be performed in polynomial time. The probability that $\mathcal{B}$ wins the security game is

$$Pr[d = d'] = Pr[d = 0]Pr[d = d'|d = 0] + Pr[d = 1]Pr[d = d'|d = 1]$$

$$= \frac{1}{2}Pr[d' = 0|d = 0] + \frac{1}{2}Pr[d' = 1|d = 1]$$

$$= \frac{1}{2}Pr[b = b'|d = 0] + \frac{1}{2}Pr[b \neq b'|d = 1]. \tag{9.37}$$

When $d = 0$, the challenger sets $g_1 = g, g_2 = g^x, u_1 = g^y, u_2 = g^{xy}$, so the view that $\mathcal{B}$ presents to $\mathcal{A}$ is identical to the actual IND-CCA security game against Π except with ϵ' through the proof of Lemma 1, where ϵ' is the gap between an actual attack against the scheme and an attack against the simulator. Therefore, the probability that $b = b'$ given $d = 0$ is the same as the probability that $\mathcal{A}$ wins the IND-CCA security game against Π; in other words,

$$Pr[b = b'|d = 0] = \frac{1}{2} + \epsilon + \epsilon'. \tag{9.38}$$

When $d = 1$, the challenger sets $g_1 = g, g_2 = g^x, u_1 = g^y, u_2 = g^z$. Through the proof of Lemma 2, pk and the challenge ciphertext reveal no information about b except with $\frac{1}{q}$, so the guess b' output by $\mathcal{A}$ is independent of b except with $\frac{1}{q}$. Since b is either 0 or 1, each with probability $\frac{1}{2}$, it follows that

$$Pr[b \neq b'|d = 1] = \frac{1}{2} + \frac{1}{q}. \tag{9.39}$$

It follows from (9.37), (9.38), and (9.39) that

$$Pr[d = d'] = \frac{1}{2}(\frac{1}{2} + \epsilon + \epsilon') + \frac{1}{2} \cdot (\frac{1}{2} + \frac{1}{q}) = \frac{1}{2} + \frac{\epsilon}{2} + \frac{\epsilon'}{2} + \frac{1}{2q}. \tag{9.40}$$

Thus, $\mathcal{B}$ wins the security game with advantage $\frac{\epsilon}{2} - \frac{\epsilon\epsilon'}{2} + \frac{\epsilon'}{2} + \frac{1}{2q}$. By Diffie-Hellman decision assumption, algorithm $\mathcal{B}$ can win the security game with only negligible advantage, so $\frac{\epsilon}{2} - \frac{\epsilon\epsilon'}{2} + \frac{\epsilon'}{2} + \frac{1}{2q}$ must be negligible where ϵ' and $\frac{1}{2q}$ is negligible. This implies that ϵ is also negligible. Therefore, algorithm $\mathcal{A}$ has only negligible advantage ϵ in the IND-CCA game against Π. $\square$

9.4.8 The Paillier Encryption

The Paillier scheme [81] is designed based on the composite residuosity class problem (computing n-th residue classes), which is believed to be computationally difficult. Paillier scheme also exhibits additive homomorphic property, which makes it attractive to many privacy preservation applications. It is currently one of the homomorphic encryption schemes standardized by ISO/IEC 18033-6:2019. The algorithms for key generation, encryption, homomorphic operation, and decryption are briefly described below.

Construction 10. The Paillier encryption scheme

1. Gen: on input 1^n, select two random prime numbers p and q, and compute the value $N = p \times q$. This generates the modulus N which will be shared publicly.

   Compute $\lambda = lcm\ (p-1, q-1) = \dfrac{(p-1)(q-1)}{gcd(p-1, q-1)}$, where lcm stands for "least common multiple" and gcd refers to "greatest common multiple."

   Choose an integer g that lies within the set $\mathbb{Z}_{n^2}^*$ and satisfies the condition $gcd\ (\dfrac{g^\lambda mod\ n^2 - 1}{N}, N) = 1$

   Compute $\mu = (L(g^\lambda\ mod\ N^2))^{-1}\ mod\ n$, where $L(x) = \dfrac{x-1}{N}$.
   Output the public key $pk = \langle N, g \rangle$ and private key $sk = \langle \lambda, \mu \rangle$.

2. Enc: on input public key $pk = \langle N, k \rangle$ and a message $m \in \mathbb{Z}_N^*$, choose a uniform random string $r \in \mathbb{Z}_n^*$. Output the ciphertext

$$c = g^m \times r^n mod N^2.$$

3. Dec: on input private key $sk = \langle \lambda, \mu \rangle$ and a ciphertext $c \in \mathbb{Z}_{N^2}^*$, compute the plaintext $m = \dfrac{L(c^\lambda mod N^2)}{L(g^\lambda mod N^2)} = L(c^\lambda mod N^2) * \mu\ mod\ N$.

The Paillier encryption scheme is a probabilistic cryptosystem. Given the plaintext m, there could be many possible valid ciphertexts c generated through the encryption, due to the introduction of a random string r. In other words, given two known plaintexts m_1 and m_2 together with the ciphertext c generated from either m_1 or m_2, it is hard to determine if c is produced by which plaintexts. Hence, the Paillier scheme is proven to be CPA-secure under the decisional composite residuosity assumption. Unlike the Padded RSA, the introduction of random string r does not destroy its homomorphism. This makes the Paillier scheme an attractive public-key scheme for applications that require privacy preservation.

Homomorphic addition of plaintexts Given two ciphertexts c_1 and c_2 generated through the encryption of two plaintexts m_1 and m_2, the product of c_1 and c_2 will decrypt to the sum of m_1 and m_2 as

$$Dec(Enc(m_1) \times Enc(m_2)) = m_1 + m_2 \bmod N. \qquad (9.41)$$

For additive homomorphic property, the two plaintexts are first encrypted, followed by the homomorphic addition. But for multiplicative property, only one plaintext is encrypted, the other one is in plaintext form (not encrypted).

Homomorphic multiplication of plaintexts A ciphertext c (encryption of plaintext m) raised to the power of a constant k will decrypt to the multiplication of k and c as

$$Dec(Enc(m)^k \bmod N^2) = km \bmod N. \qquad (9.42)$$

Exercises

9.1 Note that the DDH, CDH, DL problems are harder in this order: If the DL problem is easy, so is the CDH problem; If the CDH problem is easy, so is the DDH problem. Why?

9.2 The DDH assumption that the DDH problem is hard to solve is used as a basis to prove the security of many cryptographic protocols, most notably the ElGamal and Cramer–Shoup schemes. However, the DDH assumption does not hold in the multiplicative group $\mathbb{Z}_p^*$, where p is prime (even though DL and CDH are conjectured to be hard). Why not?

9.3 El Gamal Encryption is not CCA-secure. Explain why not.

10

Digital Signature

CONTENTS

An overview of digital signatures has been presented in this chapter. Integrity or authenticity is the main purpose of the digital signatures. In the first part, digital signatures are being compared to the message authentication codes. This is followed by some formal definitions being presented for digital signatures and security of signature schemes. The next part of the chapter gives a detailed discussion about the El Gamal signatures providing its formal construction and security proofs. The final part of the chapter discusses the RSA signature schemes. Among them, the first is the plain RSA signature scheme that is existentially forgeable under arbitrary message attack. The full domain hash RSA is then presented. Subsequently, the probabilistic signature scheme is given that provides the advantage of improved security over full domain hash RSA with the same signature size. The final part of the chapter presents blockchain as an application of hash function and public-key encryption.

TABLE 10.1

Comparison of digital signature and message authentication code.

Message Authentication Code	Digital Signature
private-key (*aka* symmetric) setting	public-key (*aka* asymmetric) setting
complex key distribution and management	easier key distribution and management (good for broadcast, group)
not publicly verifiable	publicly verifiable (a third party verifies it as legitimate)
repudiable	non-repudiable (a signer cannot later deny his signing, goof for legal)
very simple computations	comparatively heavy computations

10.1   Overview

In the public-key settings, public-key encryption can be used to achieve *secrecy*, and integrity (or authenticity) is provided using *digital signature schemes*. Note that message authentication codes provide integrity in the private-key settings. Table 10.1 compares message authentication code with digital signature.

10.2   Definitions

Since digital signatures are the public-key counterpart of message authentication codes, their syntax and security guarantees are analogous. The algorithm that a sender applies to a message is here denoted Sign (rather than Mac), and the output of this algorithm is now called a *signature* (rather than a *tag*). The algorithm that a receiver applies to a message and a signature in order to verify its validity is still denoted Vrfy.

Definition 1 *A* (digital) **signature scheme** *consists of three probabilistic polynomial-time algorithms* (Gen,Sign,Vrfy) *such that*

1. *The* key-generation algorithm Gen *takes as input a security parameter* 1^n *and outputs a pair of keys* (pk, sk). *These are called the* public key *and the* private key, *respectively. We assume that pk and sk each has length at least n, and that n can be determined from pk or sk.*

2. *The* signing algorithm Sign *takes as input a private key sk and a message m from some message space (that may depend on pk). It outputs a signature* σ *and we write this* $\sigma \leftarrow$ Sign$_{sk}(m)$.

3. *The deterministic* verification algorithm Vrfy *takes as input a public key pk, a message m and a signature* σ. *It outputs a bit b, with* $b = 1$ *meaning* valid *and* $b = 0$ *meaning* invalid. *We write this as* $b = \mathsf{Vrfy}_{pk}(m, \sigma)$.

It is required that except with negligible probability over (pk, sk) *output by* $\mathsf{Gen}(1^n)$, *it holds that* $\mathsf{Vrfy}_{pk}(m, \mathsf{Sign}_{sk}(m)) = 1$ *for every (legitimate) message* m.

If there is a function ℓ *such that for every* (pk, sk) *output by* $\mathsf{Gen}(1^n)$ *the message space is* $\{0, 1\}^{\ell(n)}$, *then we say that* (Gen,Sign,Vrfy) *is a signature scheme for messages of length* $\ell(n)$.

We call σ a *valid signature* on a message m (with respect to some public key pk that is understood from the context) if $\mathsf{Vrfy}_{pk}(m, \sigma) = 1$.

Security of signature schemes For a fixed public key pk generated by a signer S, a forgery is a message m along with a valid signature σ, where m was not previously signed by S. Security of a signature scheme means that an adversary should be unable to output a forgery even if he or she obtains signatures on many other messages of his choice.

Let $\Pi = $ (Gen,Sign,Vrfy) be a signature scheme and consider the following experiment for an adversary $\mathcal{A}$ and parameter n.

The signature experiment $\mathsf{Sig}\text{-}\mathsf{forge}_{\mathcal{A},\Pi}(n)$

1. $\mathsf{Gen}(1^n)$ *is run to obtain keys* (pk, sk).

2. *Adversary* $\mathcal{A}$ *is given pk and access to an oracle* $\mathsf{Sign}_{sk}(\cdot)$. *The adversary then outputs* (m, σ). *Let* $\mathcal{Q}$ *denote the set of all queries that* $\mathcal{A}$ *asked to its oracle.*

3. $\mathcal{A}$ succeeds *if and only if (1)* $\mathsf{Vrfy}_{pk}(m, \sigma) = 1$ *and (2)* $m \notin \mathcal{Q}$. *In this case, the output of the experiment is defined to be 1.*

Definition 2 *A signature scheme* $\Pi = $ (Gen,Sign,Vrfy) *is* **existentially unforgeable under an adaptive chosen-message attack,** *or just* secure, *if for all probabilistic polynomial-time adversaries* $\mathcal{A}$, *there is a negligible function* negl *such that*

$$Pr[\mathsf{Sig}\text{-}\mathsf{forge}_{\mathcal{A},\Pi}(n) = 1] \leq negl(n). \tag{10.1}$$

10.3   The El Gamal Signatures

Let $\mathcal{G}$ be a polynomial-time algorithm that takes as input 1^n and (except possibly with negligible probability) outputs a description of a cyclic group $\mathbb{G}$, its order q (with $|q| = n$) and a generator g.

Construction 1. The original El Gamal signature scheme

Let $\mathcal{G}$ be defined as above.

1. Gen: on input 1^n, run $\mathcal{G}(1^n)$ to obtain $(\mathbb{G}, q, g)$. Then choose a uniform $x \in \mathbb{Z}_q$ and compute $h = g^x$. The public key is $\langle \mathbb{G}, q, g, h \rangle$ and the private key is $\langle \mathbb{G}, q, g, x \rangle$. The message space is $\mathbb{G}$.

2. Sign: on input a private key $sk = \langle \mathbb{G}, q, g, x \rangle$ and a message $m \in \mathbb{G}$, choose a uniform $l \in \mathbb{Z}_{q-1}^*$ (i.e., $l < q - 1$, $gcd(l, q - 1) = 1$) and output (r,s) as

$$r = g^l \ (mod \ q),$$
$$s = l^{-1}(m - xr) \ (mod \ q - 1),$$

where l^{-1} can be computed using the extended Euclid's algorithm.

3. Vrfy: on input a public key $pk = \langle \mathbb{G}, q, g, h \rangle$ and a signature (r,s), output 1 if and only if

$$h^r r^s \stackrel{?}{=} g^m \ (mod \ q).$$

Theorem 1 *Construction 1 is existentially forgeable under a known message attack.*

Proof is omitted.

Now we introduce a typical version of the El Gamal-family signature schemes (e.g., Schnorr signature, Digital Signature Algorithm, etc.) which can be provably unforgeable in the random oracle model. It replaces m by the hash value of both the message and random number, and outputs a signature as a triplet (r,e,s).

Construction 2. The triplet El Gamal signature scheme

Let $\mathcal{G}$ be as in the text.

1. Gen: on input 1^n, run $\mathcal{G}(1^n)$ to obtain $(\mathbb{G}, q, g)$. Then choose a uniform $x \in \mathbb{Z}_q$ and compute $h = g^x$. The public key is $\langle \mathbb{G}, q, g, h \rangle$ and the private key is $\langle \mathbb{G}, q, g, x \rangle$. The message space is $\mathbb{G}$.

2. Sign: on input a private key $sk = \langle \mathbb{G}, q, g, x \rangle$ and a message $m \in \mathbb{G}$, choose a uniform $l \in \mathbb{Z}_{q-1}^*$ (i.e., $l < q - 1$ and $gcd(l, q - 1) = 1$) and output a triplet (r, e, s) as

$$r = g^l \ (mod \ q),$$
$$e = H(m, r),$$
$$s = l^{-1}(e - xr) \ (mod \ q - 1),$$

where H is a cryptographic hash functions, $|e| = n$, and l^{-1} can be computed using the extended Euclid's algorithm.

3. Vrfy: on input a public key $pk = \langle \mathbb{G}, q, g, h \rangle$ and a signature (r, e, s), output 1 if and only if

$$e = H(m, r),$$
$$h^r r^s \stackrel{?}{=} g^e \ (mod \ q).$$

Theorem 2 *If the DL problem is hard relative to $\mathcal{G}$, then Construction 2 is existentially unforgeable under a non-adaptive chosen-message attack.*

Proof Assume that the DL assumption is true for $\mathcal{G}$. Let Π (Gen, Enc, Dec) be the triplet El Gamal signature scheme. Let $\mathcal{A}$ be a polynomial-time algorithm attacking Π. We construct an algorithm $\mathcal{B}$ for solving the DL problem relative to $\mathbb{G}$ as follows.

Reduction algorithm $\mathcal{B}$

The algorithm is given $\mathbb{G}, q, g, h$ as input.

1. Run $\mathcal{A}$, answering all its queries as described below: When $\mathcal{A}$ outputs (i.e., queries) (m_i, r_i) (actually, r_i is a random value created by $\mathcal{B}$), choose a random oracle answer e_i and give it to $\mathcal{A}$.

2. Eventually, $\mathcal{A}$ returns (r, e, s).

---

3. Run $\mathcal{A}$ second time, using the same randomness as before except for uniform and independent e_j.

4. Eventually, $\mathcal{A}$ returns (r, e', s').

5. If $h^r r^s = g^e \ (mod\ q)$ and $h^r r^{s'} = g^{e'} \ (mod\ q)$ and $e \neq e'$ then output $\frac{e-ls}{r} \ (mod\ p)$. Otherwise output nothing.

In the above reduction algorithm, why does the simulator run the adversary twice? It is intended to simulate a forgery case, i.e., the adversary successfully generates another message of its choice with the same valid signature, which is originally made by the legitimate signer for a message.

Here is a schematic diagram of the reduction algorithm.

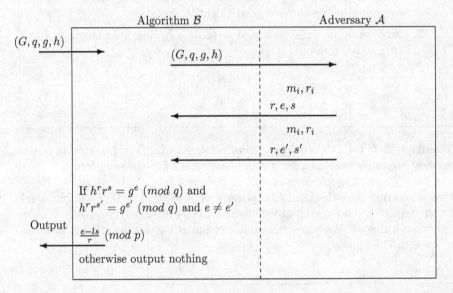

Under the non-adaptive attack scenario, $\mathcal{A}$ does not request a signature to $\mathcal{B}$, who operates as simulated random oracle for H queries. Note that under the adaptive one, $\mathcal{A}$ can adaptively choose messages to be signed, even after observing previous signatures.

Let $\mathcal{A}$'s successful probability for signature forgery be $Adv(n)$ and his spent time on signature forgery be $t(n)$.

First runs of $\mathcal{A}$

Now $\mathcal{B}$ runs $\mathcal{A}$ $\frac{1}{Adv(n)}$ times. Since $\mathcal{A}$ is a successful forger, he will output with probability 1 a valid signature (r,e,s) of message m under the scheme. That is,

$$e = H(m,r),$$

$$h^r r^s \overset{?}{=} g^e \ (mod \ q). \tag{10.2}$$

Under the random oracle model, $\mathcal{A}$ makes random oracle queries to $\mathcal{B}$, whose response is via the simulation of the random oracle: it simulates H by maintaining an H-list of sorted elements $((m_i,r_i),\ e_i)$ (e.g., sorted by m_i), where (m_i,r_i) are queries and e_i are random answers.

Since $\mathcal{A}$ is polynomially bounded, he can only make $k = q_H$ queries where k is polynomially (in n) bounded. Let

$$Q_1 = (m_1, r_1), Q_2 = (m_2, r_2), ..., Q_k = (m_k, r_k) \tag{10.3}$$

be k distinct queries. Let

$$R_1 = e_1, R_2 = e_2, ..., R_k = e_k \tag{10.4}$$

be answers. Since $|H|=n$, $\mathcal{B}$'s answers are uniformly random in the set $\{1,2,3,...,2^n\}$.

The essential intuition is, due to the uniform randomness of $\mathcal{B}$'s answers, when $\mathcal{A}$ outputs a valid forgery (r,e,s) on m, he must have queried (m,r) and obtained the answer $e = H(m,r)$. That is, it must be the case that $(m,r) = (m_i,r_i)$ for some $i \in [1,k]$. The probability for (m,r) not having been queried is 2^{-n} (i.e., $\mathcal{A}$ has guessed $\mathcal{B}$'s uniformly random answer $R_i = e_i$ correctly without making a query to $\mathcal{B}$). Considering the quantity 2^{-n} being negligible, we know that $((m,r),\ e)$ are in $\mathcal{B}$'s H-list.

Note that without making queries to $\mathcal{B}$ and without using $\mathcal{B}$'s answer, $\mathcal{A}$ cannot be successful except for a minute probability value 2^{-n} which is negligible. With this observation, we can imagine as if $\mathcal{A}$ has been "forced" to forge a signature on one of the k messages.

Second runs of $\mathcal{A}$ to achieve a successful forking

Now $\mathcal{B}$ reruns $\mathcal{A}$ $\frac{1}{Adv(n)}$ times under the same condition. However, this time $\mathcal{B}$ resets his k random oracle answers at uniformly random. We must notice that since the reset answers still follow the uniform distribution in the set $\{1,2,3,...,2^n\}$, these answers remain being the correct ones since they have the correct distribution.

After having been fed the second lot of k correct answers, $\mathcal{A}$ must again fully release his forgery capacity and output, with probability 1, a new forgery (r',e',s') on m'. Note again that (m',r') must be a Q_j for some $j \in [1, k]$ except for a minute probability value 2^{-k}.

An event of "successful forking of $\mathcal{A}$'s random oracle queries" occurs when two forged message-signature pairs $(m,(r,e,s))$ and $(m',(r',e',s'))$ satisfy (m,r) $= (m',r')$. Applying the birthday paradox, we know that the probability for this event to occur (i.e., $i = j = b$) is roughly $1/\sqrt{k}$ where i, j are uniformly random and needn't be fixed.

That is, with the non-negligible probability $1/\sqrt{k}$, $\mathcal{B}$ obtains two valid forgeries (r,e,s) and (r',e',s'). Furthermore, because in the second run $\mathcal{B}$ has reset his answers at uniformly random (i.e., erase the previous H-list), we must have with the overwhelming probability $e \neq e' (mod\ p)$, where p is a n-bit prime dividing $q - 1$ and $(q - 1/p)$ has no large prime factors. $\square$

Forking lemma [87] says that if a PPT adversary can forge a signature with non-negligible probability, then there is a non-negligible probability that the same adversary with the same random tape can create a second forgery in an attack with a different random oracle (i.e., by resetting and replaying the random oracle) as shown in Figure 10.1.

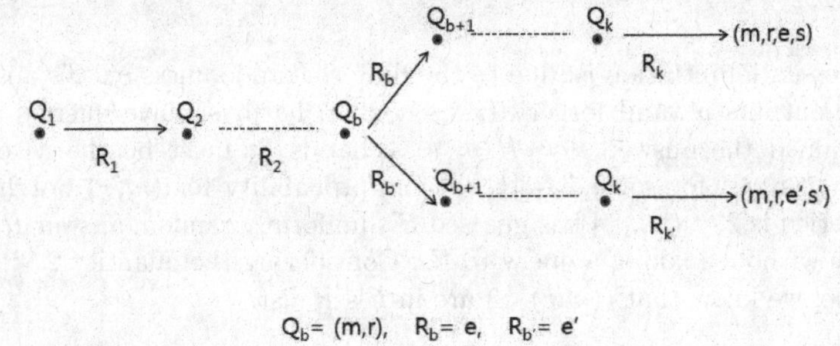

$$Q_b = (m,r), \quad R_b = e, \quad R_{b'} = e'$$

FIGURE 10.1
Forking lemma.

The oracle replay attack:

1. Adversary re-wound to Q_b.
2. Simulate the first run from Q_b using a different random oracle.

Extraction of discrete logarithm

From the two valid forgeries, $\mathcal{B}$ can compute

$$h^r r^s = g^e \ (mod \ q),$$
$$h^r r^{s'} = g^{e'} \ (mod \ q).$$

Since g is a generator element modulo q, we can write $r = g^l \ (mod \ q)$ for some integer $l < q - 1$. Also noticing $h = g^x \ (mod \ q)$, we have

$$xr + ls = e \ (mod \ p),$$
$$xr + ls' = e' \ (mod \ p).$$

Since $e \neq e' (mod \ p)$ implies $s \neq s' (mod \ p)$, we have

$$l = \frac{e - e'}{s - s'} \ (mod \ p).$$

With an overwhelming probability r is relatively prime to p and hence $\mathcal{B}$ can extract $x \ (mod \ p)$ as

$$x = \frac{e - ls}{r} \ (mod \ p).$$

Recall that $(q - 1)/p$ has no large prime factors and $x \ (mod \ q - 1)$ can easily be further extracted.

Since the numbers r, e, and e' are in H's two random oracle lists, and s, s' are $\mathcal{A}$'s output, $\mathcal{B}$ can use the described method to extract the discrete logarithm of h to the base g modulo q.

Reduction result

$\mathcal{B}$'s advantage for extracting discrete logarithm $\approx \frac{Adv(n)}{\sqrt{q_H}}$ is non-negligible. $\mathcal{B}$'s time cost is $\approx \frac{2(t(n) + q_H)}{Adv(n)}$, where t is the adversary's time for forging a signature.

$\square$

Theorem 3 *If the DL problem is hard relative to $\mathcal{G}$, then Construction 1 is existentially unforgeable under an adaptive chosen-message attack.*

Proof The reduction technique will be essentially the same as that in the case of non-adaptive attack. However, now $\mathcal{A}$ is also allowed to make q_S signing queries in addition to random oracle queries. Hence $\mathcal{B}$ must, in addition to responding to random oracle queries, also respond the signing queries with answers which can pass $\mathcal{A}$'s verification steps using Vrfy_{pk}. H must do so even though he does not have possession of the signing key. The signing is the very piece of information he is trying to obtain with $\mathcal{A}$'s help. $\mathcal{B}$'s procedure for signing is done via simulation. Therefore it suffices to show that under the random oracle model, $\mathcal{B}$ can indeed satisfy $\mathcal{A}$'s signing queries with the perfect quality.

Since the signing algorithm uses a hash function which is modeled by a random oracle under the random oracle model, for each signing query m, $\mathcal{B}$ will choose a random element $r < q$ and make the random query (m, r) on behalf of $\mathcal{A}$ and then returns both the random oracle answer and the signing answer to $\mathcal{A}$ as follows.

$\mathcal{B}$ picks random integers u, v less than $q - 1$, and sets

$$r \leftarrow g^u h^v \ (mod \ q),$$
$$s \leftarrow -rv^{-1} \ (mod \ q - 1),$$
$$e \leftarrow -ruv^{-1} \ (mod \ q - 1).$$

Note that the generation of a new r by $\mathcal{B}$ for each signing query follows exactly the signing procedure; $\mathcal{B}$ should never reuse any r which has been used previously.

$\mathcal{B}$ returns e as the random oracle answer and (r,e,s) as the signing answer. Note that the returned signature is indeed valid. Under the random oracle model, this simulated signature has the identical distribution as one issued by the signing algorithm which uses an random oracle in place of the hash function H. Therefore, $\mathcal{A}$'s forgery capacity should be fully released and the same reduction used should also lead to a contradiction as desired.

$\mathcal{B}$'s advantage for extracting discrete logarithm $\approx \frac{1}{\sqrt{q_H}}$ is non-negligible. $\mathcal{B}$'s time cost is $\approx \frac{2(\bar{t}(n)+q_H \cdot \tau)+O_B(q_S \cdot n^3)}{Adv(n)}$, where τ is time for answering an H query and O_B denotes bitwise order notation. $\square$

10.4   The RSA Signatures

The section discusses various RSA signature schemes including plain RSA, full domain hash RSA, and probabilistic signature scheme.

10.4.1 Plain RSA

Construction 3. The plain RSA signature scheme

Let GenRSA be as in the text. Define a signature scheme as follows.

1. Gen on input 1^n, run $\mathsf{GenRSA}(1^n)$ to obtain (N, e, d). The public key is $\langle N, e \rangle$ and the private key is $\langle N, d \rangle$.

2. Sign on input a private key $sk = \langle N, d \rangle$ and a message $m \in \mathbb{Z}_N^*$, compute the signature as

$$\sigma = [m^d \bmod N].$$

3. Vrfy on input a public key $pk = \langle N, e \rangle$, a message $m \in \mathbb{Z}_N^*$ and a signature $\sigma \in \mathbb{Z}_N^*$, output 1 if and only if

$$m \stackrel{?}{=} [\sigma^e \bmod N].$$

Theorem 4 *The plain RSA signature scheme is existentially forgeable under no-message attack.*

Proof is omitted.

Theorem 5 *The plain RSA signature scheme is existentially forgeable under arbitrary message attack.*

Proof is omitted.

10.4.2 Full Domain Hash RSA

Construction 4. The full domain hash RSA signature scheme

Let GenRSA be as in the text.

1. Gen: on input 1^n, run $\mathsf{GenRSA}(1^n)$ to compute (N, e, d). The public key is $\langle N, e \rangle$ and the private key is $\langle N, d \rangle$.
   As part of key generation, a function $H : \{0,1\}^* \to \mathbb{Z}_N^*$ is specified, but we leave this implicit.

---

2. Sign: on input a private key $\langle N, d \rangle$ and a message $m \in \{0, 1\}^*$, compute

$$\sigma = [H(m)^d \bmod N].$$

3. Vrfy: on input a public key $\langle N, e \rangle$, a message m and a signature σ, output 1 if and only if $\sigma^e \stackrel{?}{=} H(m) \bmod N$.

Note that this is called full domain hash because H hashes a message to an image whose size equals the size of the RSA modulus.

Theorem 6 *The full domain hash RSA signature scheme is existentially unforgeable under an adaptive chosen message attack.*

Proof We establish the security of the full domain hash RSA under the random oracle model by giving a describing an algorithm $\mathcal{B}$ that would break the RSA assumption using a black box algorithm $\mathcal{A}$ that breaks the security of FDH with at most $Q = poly(N)$. As usual, the proof establishes $\mathcal{B}$'s efficiency and non-negligible advantage.

Description of $\mathcal{B}$

1. $\mathcal{B}$ gets an RSA challenge N, e, and $h \in \mathbb{Z}_N^*$. $\mathcal{B}$ wins if it produces σ such that $\sigma^e = h$.

2. $\mathcal{B}$ gives N and e to $\mathcal{A}$ as the inputs for an FDH challenge.

3. $\mathcal{B}$ chooses $k \in_u \{1, \ldots, Q\}$ as guess for which random oracle query $\mathcal{A}$ will use to produce a forgery.

4. When $\mathcal{A}$ makes a random oracle query for the hash of m, $\mathcal{B}$ determines an output as follows: If $\mathcal{A}$ has previously queried on m, returns the previous answer. If not, returns $H(m) = h$ if it is the k-th query and $H(m) = x_i^e$ for a random $x_i \in \mathbb{Z}_N^*$ otherwise.

5. When $\mathcal{A}$ makes a signature request for m, $\mathcal{B}$ quits if m was the k-th random oracle query and returns $\sigma_m = x_j$ if m was the query $j \neq k$.

6. If $\mathcal{A}$ forges σ' on m' for m' not the kth oracle query, quits. Otherwise $\mathcal{B}$ outputs $\sigma^* = h^{1/e}$ to the RSA challenger.

Since there is constant time setup, a polynomial number of iterations of constant time steps 4 and 5, and step 6 are bounded by the (polynomial) runtime of $\mathcal{A}$ and $\mathcal{B}$. $\mathcal{B}$ breaks the RSA assumption with non-negligible advantage

ϵ/Q because $\mathcal{B}$ has probability at least $1/Q$ of planting h in the correct random oracle query and $\mathcal{A}$ (independent of $\mathcal{B}$'s construction) has non-negligible advantage ϵ of being successful. $\square$

10.4.3 Probabilistic Signature Scheme (PSS)

PSS [12] [35] has the signature size as FDH-RSA but improved security over FDH-RSA. It has two variants: PSS (with appendix) and PSS-R (with message recovery). With minor modifications, these were standardized in IEEE P1363a and PKCS#1 v2.1, which are widely used in the real world.

Theorem 7 *The probabilistic signature scheme is existentially unforgeable under an adaptive chosen message attack.*

Proof is omitted.

Theorem 8 *The probabilistic signature scheme with message recovery is existentially unforgeable under an adaptive chosen message attack.*

Proof is omitted.

10.5 Blockchain: Application of Hash Function and Public-Key Encryption

This section provides an overview of blockchain by dividing the history of blockchain.

10.5.1 Blockchain 1.0: Early Development of Blockchain Technology

Blockchain had caught the attention of many people since its inception, through the very first concrete example of such technology: bitcoin [77]. There are many motivations to have blockchain, which itself combines several existing technologies: distributed ledgers, public-key encryption, Merkle tree hashing and consensus protocols. The first motivation originates from existing financial transaction mechanism, wherein the financial institutions (a trusted third party (TTP)) charge high fees for financial transactions. There could be problems if this TTP is being compromised by malicious attackers, which creates financial to the involved parties. It can be viewed as a typical "single point of failure." Besides, there is also rising needs in public auditability, in which all the participating nodes are collaborative auditing the transaction to ensure no fraud happens. Another motivation to have blockchain is to enable immutable traceability in transaction. The traceability in blockchain is made possible through the use of cryptographic hash function, wherein each block is linked with the previous block, creating almost irreversible records.

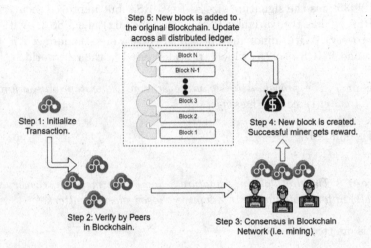

FIGURE 10.2
Simplified data flow in blockchain.

Figure 10.2 shows the simplified data flow in blockchain network. A transaction can be initialized by any node in the blockchain network (Step 1). This transaction is first verified by the peers to ensure that it is coming from the legitimate node within the blockchain network (Step 2). A number of transactions are accumulated over time to form a large transaction block with a fixed size. This transaction block contains the hash of previous transaction block, together with other relevant information (e.g., transaction data, public key of sender, etc.). Based on this information, consensus process is carried out to create a new block in the blockchain network (Step 3). Common consensus algorithms include Proof of Work, Proof of Stake, Practical Byzantine Fault Tolerance, etc. The consensus algorithm is sometimes referred as the "mining" process, which becomes a popular topic due to the widespread of bitcoin. Once the consensus process completes, a new block is created (Step 4) and the successful miner gets reward in terms of cryptocurrency or other incentives. Finally, the new block is added into the blockchain network; all distributed ledger in the peer nodes are then updated with this new information (new block in the blockchain).

The first generation of blockchain is inspired by the seminal work [77] from Satoshi Nakamoto, which demonstrated a cryptocurrency that first solved the double spending problem. In bitcoin, elliptic curve cryptography (e.g.,

ECDSA) is usually used as the signature scheme. The public key in ECDSA is a unique address that serves as an identity for the specific node, while private key is used to sign every transaction. The digital signature is used to allow the nearby nodes to verify that the transaction is originated from a valid and trusted node within the blockchain network. This consensus algorithm used in bitcoin is Proof of Work (PoW), which is used to approve the transaction; only the member who can solve a difficult puzzle can add this block into the blockchain. This consensus process is designed to protect against the Sybil attack, in which the minority can create a lot of pseudonymous identities to seize control of the network. PoW used in bitcoin requires the participating nodes to solve a computationally difficult problem, which is explained briefly in the following paragraphs.

To allow a valid transaction block to be added into the blockchain, PoW consensus requires the participating nodes to compute a hash value that satisfy the relationship provided as

$$Final\ Target\ Hash = SHA-512(PrevBlock + TX + Nonce). \quad (10.5)$$

A hash value is generated using SHA-512 algorithm, which operates on the hash of previous block, current transaction, and a nonce (random number). The final target hash is a long random number with a predetermined trailing 0. With this requirement, it is very difficult for a node to generate the final target hash; it has to keep changing the nonce until the final target hash is found. Bitcoin adjust the difficulty of finding the final target hash by controlling the number of trailing 0. In this way, only the node that has done sufficient work to successfully generate the final target hash can add this new block into the blockchain.

PoW in bitcoin is an expensive operation; it consumes a lot of computational power, which translate into enormous electrical energy consumption. Moreover, special equipment (e.g., Graphics Processing Unit (GPU), Field Programmable Gate Array (FPGA), and Application Specific Integrated Circuits (ASIC) chip) is required to perform PoW due to its complexity, which translate to huge monetary investment. To encourage more participants to contribute to PoW (and maintain the operation of blockchain consensus), bitcoin provide monetary reward (in bitcoin currency) to the first node that successfully generate the final target hash. Table 10.2 shows the evolution of various hardware platforms used to perform PoW mining. It shows that the CPU alone is no longer a viable mining device since 2010, in which GPU gain popularity through its massively parallel architecture. Many mining activities make use of parallel implementation of SHA-512 algorithm on GPU to perform PoW. However, FPGA overtaken GPU within a year, due to its flexibility in designing energy efficient hardware for computing SHA-512. Since 2013, ASIC becomes dominant in mining bitcoin; specialized chips are developed every year with many start-up companies/individuals joining this business.

Although GPU is out of favour in mining bitcoin, it is still popular among the niche communities that mine alternative crypto-currencies.

TABLE 10.2
Evolution of hardware platform for PoW mining in bitcoin [2].

Hardware	Introduction	Hash Rate (h/s)	Energy Efficiency (h/J)
CPU	2009	$10^5 - 10^8$	$10^4 - 10^5$
GPU	Late 2010	$10^6 - 10^9$	$10^5 - 10^6$
FPGA	Mid 2011	$10^8 - 10^{10}$	10^7
ASIC	Early 20013	$10^{10} - 10^{13}$	$10^8 - 10^{10}$

10.5.1.1 The Use of Cryptography in Blockchain

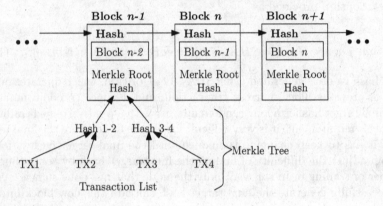

FIGURE 10.3
Blockchain data structure.

Referring to Figure 10.3, each transaction block is linked with the block before it through the use of cryptographic hash function. Moreover, the Merkle root hash is built upon the Merkle Tree which consists of many transactions' information. To modify one of the transaction records in the blockchain, one must generate a lot of valid blocks through PoW and overwrite the subsequent blocks. This is too costly to achieve as the PoW is very time/energy/money consuming. Hence, blockchain can be viewed as an immutable solution to many applications: a clever use of the pre-image resistance property of hash function. On the other hand, public-key cryptography is used as digital signature to authenticate the transactions in blockchain. Each blockchain node (user) is identified through the public key, which served as an address in communication.

10.5.1.2 Other Consensus Algorithms .

Besides PoW, there are other popular consensus algorithms like Proof-of-Stake (PoS) and Proof-of-Storage (PoSt). PoS allows a node to generate a new block with probability proportional to the proof of ownership of digital assets (e.g., digital currencies). When the share of assets that a node within the system grows, it has higher chance to approve the next generated block. This consensus algorithm is developed based on the assumption that users with a more share of the digital assets are more trustworthy during the verification process. On the other hand, PoSt uses the storage space as a proof to gain higher probability in successfully generating a new block. Compared to PoW, these two consensus algorithms do not need to perform a lot of computation, so they are more energy friendly.

The strength of bitcoin as cryptocurrency includes:

1. Cryptographically secure with the use of public-key cryptography (authentication).

2. Publicly verifiable transactions through public distributed ledger. This is a decentralized currency, which contrasts with conventional currency.

3. Resist Sybil attack: we need at least 51% of malicious nodes to break the consensus process.

4. (Almost) Impossible to tamper the public ledger, due to the properties (pre-image and collision resistance) in hash function.

However, bitcoin also comes with a lot of limitations:

1. Slow transaction due to the time taken to organize many transactions into a block, and the time for performing PoW consensus.

2. Huge amount of energy required to store the public distributed ledger.

3. Enormous energy consumed to perform PoW mining: the energy is spent to perform meaningless computation!

4. Bitcoin identify each node (user) through the public key, not the real personal identity. Hence, it is difficult to trace the real identity of a bitcoin user: will this encourage illegal activities like money laundering or ransomware? [96]

Bitcoin is the first version of blockchain that utilize such communication framework to exchange money. Hence, it is also the first cryptocurrency, which is designed to challenge the traditional monetary system. However, is blockchain only good at trading money?

10.5.2   Blockchain 2.0: Smart Contract Beyond Cryptocurrency

Smart contract is a concept introduced after the proliferation of bitcoin, which marks the evolution of blockchain 1.0 into blockchain 2.0. Instead of trading money as in cryptocurrencies, smart contract can be used to trade "computer program." This opens up many innovative applications wherein the blockchain is employed to manage the trading of various data. Ethereum [1] is one of the earliest platforms that provide smart contract services. Smart contract inspired still works under the same blockchain framework wherein the transactions are validated by peer nodes and agreed through the consensus algorithm. The key feature that separate smart contract from the earlier blockchain, is the automation of some agreed work between many parties that do not trust each other. For instance, the smart contract can be in the form of computer scripts or codes that execute some functions when the conditions are met. It can also be contracts that can be partially or fully executed or enforced without human interaction. One example is the use of smart contract in supply chain and logistics industry. Supposed that the supply chain network employs blockchain in their management system. We can use robots with artificial intelligence (AI) to inspect the container and rank the quality of delivered goods, then execute the smart contract based on the outcome of inspection. The payment will be transferred automatically or withheld due to quality issues.

10.5.3   Private, Consortium, and Public Blockchain

In practical applications, blockchain can be implemented in three architectures: private, consortium, and public blockchain [95]. Bitcoin is the most successful example of public blockchain, wherein the transactions are completely decentralized through establishing a distributed P2P network. Direct transactions are allowed between every node within the network. The validation process is also achieved through the decentralized consensus, in which the miner who successfully mined the valid block occurs in a random way. This fully decentralized architecture is generally slower in transaction speed, but it is very flexible as anyone can join the network and transact freely. This also makes it a popular choice for implementing cryptocurrencies. However, such architecture is difficult to scale when the number of users increases. In other words, it may not be suitable for applications that have many users and require fast transaction speed.

On the other hand, private blockchain does not allow public participation; only limited trusted nodes can access it. This would normally be considered a non-properly working design in blockchain, as it is contrast to the principle of blockchain (decentralization). However, it is useful when the applications do not involve many parties. Since all nodes are trusted, lightweight consensus can be employed to improve the communication efficiency. Such architecture also allows the user to preserve privacy (important for enterprises) and at the same time enjoy other features in blockchain (e.g., verifiability and anti-tampering). It is popular among enterprises and organizations that only use blockchain for their own business operations.

Consortium blockchain lies between private and public blockchain: it is fully decentralized (like public blockchain) but the number of participating nodes is limited (like private blockchain). This architecture allows faster transaction speed compared to public blockchain, because the node size is not growing dynamically, so a simpler consensus algorithm can be used. Consortium blockchain may assign different roles to the participating nodes in hierarchical form. For instance, the participating nodes are divided into validating and transaction nodes, in which only validating nodes involved in consensus process. This can effectively govern the transactions, at the same time maintain certain degree of decentralization. It is commonly used for transactions across multiple enterprises and organizations.

Exercises

10.1 Describe intuitively why RSA one-wayness does not guarantee the unforgeability of RSA signature when it uses non-full domain hash.

10.2 Prove Theorem 1.

10.3 Prove Theorem 4.

10.4 Prove Theorem 5.

10.5 Prove Theorem 7.

10.6 Prove Theorem 8.

Part II

Identity-Based Encryption and Its Variants

11

Identity-Based Encryption (1)

CONTENTS

The basics of the identity-based encryption (IBE) is studied in this chapter. The chapter begins with the comparison between the public-key infrastructure and the identity-based encryption. The next part of the chapter defines the preliminaries that include the bilinear map and hardness assumptions. Subsequently, the identity-based encryption is defined. Identity-based encryption is a type of public key encryption in which the public key is based on the unique information of the owner's identity. The construction of Boneh-Franklin IBE scheme is then proceeded in two steps, BasicIdent and FullIdent.

11.1   Overview

Comparison of PKI and IBE   Figure 11.1 and Table 11.1 compares PKI and IBE. Note that the key escrow problem is inherent in IBE because the PKG (Private Key Generator) obtaining a secret key of any user can decrypt any ciphertext.

Comparison of security models between PKI and IBE. Unlike PKIs, the adversary in IBEs is allowed to place an additional key extraction query, with identity as input and receive the corresponding private key as the output as shown in Figure 11.2.

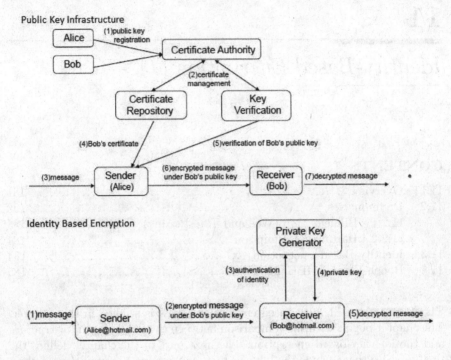

FIGURE 11.1
Comparison of PKI and IBE.

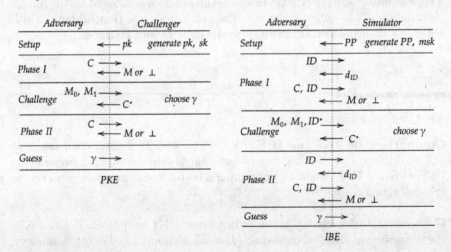

FIGURE 11.2
Comparison of security models.

TABLE 11.1
Comparison of PKI and IBE.

Public-key infrastructure	Identity-based encryption
Public-key is represented by a random string	ID string can serve as a public key
Key pairs are generated by users	IDs can be selected by users
Certificate Authority issues certificates for the public keys	Private Key Generator generates private keys for users

11.2 Preliminaries

This section defines preliminaries that are frequently used in identity-based encryptions.

11.2.1 Bilinear Map (Weil and Tate Pairing)

Let $\mathbb{G}_1$, $\mathbb{G}_1'$, and $\mathbb{G}_2$ be three groups of order q for some large prime q. A bilinear map $\widehat{e}$ is a map $\widehat{e}: \mathbb{G}_1 \times \mathbb{G}_1' \to \mathbb{G}_2$, which satisfies the following properties:

1. Bilinear: For all $P \in \mathbb{G}_1$, $Q \in \mathbb{G}_1'$, and $a, b \in \mathbb{Z}_q^*$, $\widehat{e}(aP, bQ) = \widehat{e}(P, Q)^{ab}$.

2. Non-degeneracy: $\widehat{e}(P, Q) \neq 1$. That is, the map does not send all pairs in $\mathbb{G}_1 \times \mathbb{G}_1'$ to the identity in $\mathbb{G}_2$.

3. Computability: There exists an efficient algorithm to compute $\widehat{e}(P, Q)$, for all $P \in \mathbb{G}_1$ and $Q \in \mathbb{G}_1'$.

There are three types of bilinear maps as follows:

1. Type-1: $\mathbb{G}_1 = \mathbb{G}_1'$.

2. Type-2: $\mathbb{G}_1 \neq \mathbb{G}_1'$ and there is an efficiently computable homomorphic function $\phi : \mathbb{G}_1' \to \mathbb{G}_1$.

3. Type-3: $\mathbb{G}_1 \neq \mathbb{G}_1'$ and there is no efficiently computable homomorphic function.

Decisional Diffie-Hellman problem is easy The decisional Diffie-Hellman problem in $\mathbb{G}_1$ is to distinguish between the distributions $\langle P, aP, bP, abP \rangle$ and $\langle P, aP, bP, cP \rangle$, where a, b, c are random in $\mathbb{Z}_q^*$ and P is random in $\mathbb{G}_1^*$. DDH in $\mathbb{G}_1$ is easy because given $P, aP, bP, cP \in \mathbb{G}_1^*$, we have $c = ab \bmod q \Leftrightarrow \widehat{e}(P, cP) = \widehat{e}(aP, bP)$. Note that $\mathbb{G}_1^* = \mathbb{G} \setminus \{O\}$ where O is the identity element in the group $\mathbb{G}_1$.

11.2.2   Hardness Assumption

Since the DDH problem in $\mathbb{G}_1$ is easy, we cannot use DDH to build cryptosystems in the group $\mathbb{G}_1$. Instead, the security of the Boneh-Franklin IBE scheme is based on a variant of the CDH assumption called the BDH (Bilinear Diffie-Hellman) assumption.

Bilinear Diffie-Hellman problem Let $\mathbb{G}_1$ and $\mathbb{G}_2$ be two groups of large prime order q for some large prime q. Let $\widehat{e}\colon \mathbb{G}_1 \times \mathbb{G}_1 \to \mathbb{G}_2$ be a bilinear map and let P be a generator of $\mathbb{G}_1$. Given $\langle P, aP, bP, cP \rangle$ for some $a, b, c, \in \mathbb{Z}_q^*$, it is hard to compute $W = \widehat{e}(P, P)^{abc} \in \mathbb{G}_2$.

Bilinear Diffie-Hellman assumption Let $\mathcal{G}$ be a BDH parameter generator. We say that an algorithm $\mathcal{A}$ has an advantage $\epsilon(k)$ in solving the BDH problem for $\mathcal{G}$ if for sufficiently large k,

$$Adv_{\mathcal{G},\mathcal{A}}(k) = Pr[\mathcal{A}(q, \mathbb{G}_1, \mathbb{G}_2, \widehat{e}, P, aP, bP, cP)$$
$$= \widehat{e}(P, P)^{abc} | \langle q, \mathbb{G}_1, \mathbb{G}_2, \widehat{e} \rangle \leftarrow \mathcal{G}(1^k), P \leftarrow \mathbb{G}_1^*, a, b, c \leftarrow \mathbb{Z}_q^*] \geq \epsilon(k)$$

We say that $\mathcal{G}$ satisfies the BDH assumption if for any randomized polynomial time (in k) algorithm $\mathcal{A}$ we have that $Adv_{\mathcal{G},\mathcal{A}}(k)$ is a negligible function. When $\mathcal{G}$ satisfies the BDH assumption, we say that BDH is hard in groups generated by $\mathcal{G}$.

11.3   Identity-Based Encryption

Identity based encryption is a type of public key encryption. In this case, the public key is based on unique information about the owner's identity such as name, email address, or employee ID of the user. Identity based encryption uses the central authority to generate the user's private keys that are based on their unique identification. This central authority also generates the master public key and master private key. The master public key is used by all the users to compute another user's public key without requiring them to communicate with each other. In order to setup a new user in identity-based encryption, the new user must contact the central authority to retrieve the master public key. After that the user combines the master public key with their identity value to create their public key. Afterward, the user must simply contact the central authority to generate their private key.

11.4   Boneh-Franklin IBE [24]

Construction of the IBE scheme proceeds in two steps. In the first step a scheme called BasicIdent is developed and shown to be secure in IND-ID-CPA. The security analysis of this scheme showed how to simulate key extraction queries made by an adversary. In the next step, this was further developed to obtain a scheme, called FullIdent, which is secure IND-ID-CCA. In both schemes, certain hash functions are used and the security reduction models these hash functions as random oracles.

Full-ID (*aka* Adaptive-ID) security vs. selective-ID security   In selective-ID model, the adversary commits to a target identity at initialization step before the system is set up. Compared to the security model where the adversary can choose the target identity adaptively, this is a weaker notion of security for identity-based encryption schemes (See Figure 11.3).

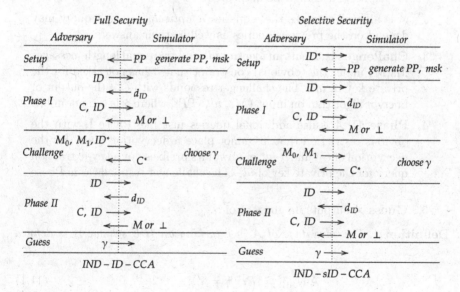

FIGURE 11.3
Comparison of full vs. selective security.

IND-ID-CCA game for a IBE scheme[1]

1. **Setup** Given the security parameter k, the challenger runs the Setup algorithm of the IBE. It provides $\mathcal{A}$ with the public system parameters PP while keeping the master key msk to itself.

2. **Phase I** $\mathcal{A}$ makes a finite number of queries where each query is one of the following two types:

   (a) key-extraction query (id): This query is placed to the key-extraction oracle $\mathcal{O}_k$. Questioned on id, $\mathcal{O}_k$ generates a private key d_{id} of id and returns it to $\mathcal{A}$. The Key-Gen algorithm is probabilistic and so if it is queried more than once on the same identity, then it may provide different (but valid) decryption keys.

   (b) decryption query (id,C): This query is placed to the decryption oracle $\mathcal{O}_d$. It returns the resulting plaintext or $\perp$ if the ciphertext cannot be decrypted.

   $\mathcal{A}$ is allowed to make these queries *adaptively*, i.e., any query may depend on the previous queries as well as their answers.

3. **Challenge** $\mathcal{A}$ outputs an identity id^* and two equal length messages M_0, M_1 under the (obvious) constraint that it has not asked for the private key of id^*. The challenger responds with C^*, the output of Encrypt algorithm on input (M_γ, id^*, PP), where γ is a random bit.

4. **Phase II** $\mathcal{A}$ issues additional queries just like Phase I, with the obvious restriction that it cannot place a decryption query for the decryption of C^* under id^* or any of its prefixes nor a key-extraction query for the private key of id^*. The challenger responds as in Phase I.

5. **Guess** $\mathcal{A}$ outputs its guess γ' of γ.

Definition 1 *The advantage of $\mathcal{A}$ in attacking an IBE scheme Π is defined as*

$$\mathsf{Adv}_{\mathcal{A},\Pi} = |Pr[(\gamma = \gamma')] - 1/2|. \tag{11.1}$$

Definition 2 *An IBE scheme $\Pi = $ (Key-Gen, Encrypt, Decrypt) is said to be $(t, q_{id}, q_C, \epsilon)$-secure against adaptive chosen ciphertext attack if for any t-time adversary $\mathcal{A}$ that makes at most q_{id} private-key queries and at most q_C decryption queries,*

$$\mathsf{Adv}_{\mathcal{A},\Pi} \leq \epsilon. \tag{11.2}$$

---

[1]The description of the IND-ID-CPA game for a IBE scheme is similar to this game, except that the adversary is not allowed access to the decryption oracle $\mathcal{O}_d$. The description of the IND-sID-CCA game for a IBE scheme is similar to this game, except that (1) at additional stage of initialization before the setup stage, the adversary $\mathcal{A}$ outputs a target identity tuple $id^* = (id_1^*, id_2^*, ..., id_u^*)$ on which it will attack before even seeing the systems's public parameters, (2) at challenge stage, the adversary outputs two messages M_0, M_1 only.

Construction 1. BasicIdent

Setup Given a security parameter $k \in \mathbb{Z}^+$

1. Run $\mathcal{G}$ on input k to generate a prime q ($|q| = k$), two groups $\mathbb{G}_1$, $\mathbb{G}_2$ of order q, and $\hat{e} \colon \mathbb{G}_1 \times \mathbb{G}_1 \to \mathbb{G}_2$. Choose a random generator $P \in \mathbb{G}_1$.

2. Pick a random $s \in \mathbb{Z}_q^*$ and set $P_{pub} = sP$.

3. Choose hash functions $H_1 \colon \{0,1\}^* \to \mathbb{G}_1^*$ and $H_2 \colon \mathbb{G}_2 \to \{0,1\}^n$.

4. The system parameters are $\mathsf{params} = (q, \mathbb{G}_1, \mathbb{G}_2, \hat{e}, n, P, P_{pub}, H_1, H_2)$.

5. The master-key is $s \in \mathbb{Z}_q^*$.

Note 1: $\mathbb{G}_1$ is a subgroup of the additive group of points of an elliptic curve $E/\mathbb{F}_p$. $\mathbb{G}_2$ is a subgroup of the multiplicative group of a finite field $\mathbb{F}_{p^2}$.

Extract For a given string $\mathsf{ID} \in \{0,1\}^*$

1. Compute $Q_{\mathsf{ID}} = H_1(\mathsf{ID}) \in \mathbb{G}_1^*$.

2. Set the private key d_{ID} to be $d_{\mathsf{ID}} = sQ_{\mathsf{ID}}$ where s is the master key.

Note 2: H_1 is not a general hash function to map strings to integers, but a map-to-point hash function to map strings to points in $\mathbb{G}_1$.

Encrypt Message $M \in \mathcal{M}$ and public key ID

1. Compute $Q_{\mathsf{ID}} = H_1(\mathsf{ID}) \in \mathbb{G}_1^*$.

2. Choose a random $r \in \mathbb{Z}_q^*$.

3. Set the ciphertext to be

$$C = \langle rP, M \oplus H_2(g_{\mathsf{ID}}^r) \rangle \text{ where } g_{\mathsf{ID}} = \hat{e}(Q_{\mathsf{ID}}, P_{pub}) \in \mathbb{G}_2^*.$$

Decrypt Ciphertext $C = \langle U, V \rangle \in \mathcal{C}$, public key ID and private key $d_{\mathsf{ID}} \in \mathbb{G}_1^*$, compute

$$V \oplus H_2(\hat{e}(d_{\mathsf{ID}}, U)) = M.$$

Theorem 1 (Cascade Reduction) Construction 1 is IND-ID-CPA-secure in the random oracle model. That is, suppose the hash functions H_1, H_2 are random oracles. Then BasicIdent is a semantically secure identity-based encryption scheme (IND-ID-CPA) assuming BDH is hard in groups generated by $\mathcal{G}$. Concretely, suppose there is an IND-ID-CPA adversary $\mathcal{A}$ that has advantage $\epsilon(k)$ against the scheme BasicIdent. Suppose $\mathcal{A}$ makes at most $q_E > 0$ private key extraction queries and $q_{H_2} > 0$ hash queries to H_2. Then there is an algorithm $\mathcal{B}$ that solves BDH in groups generated by $\mathcal{G}$ with advantage at least

$$Adv_{\mathcal{G},\mathcal{B}}(k) \geq \frac{2\epsilon(k)}{e(1+q_E) \cdot q_{H_2}},$$
(11.3)

where $e \approx 2.71$ is the base of the natural logarithm. The running time of $\mathcal{B}$ is $O(\text{time}(\mathcal{A}))$.

Proof

Outline of the Proof IND-ID-CPA security of BasicIdent is proved assuming H_1 and H_2 to be random oracles. The proof uses a public key encryption scheme called BasicPub. Let $\mathcal{A}_1$ be an IND-ID-CPA adversary against BasicIdent and $\mathcal{A}_2$ is an IND-CPA adversary against BasicPub, while $\mathcal{B}$ be an algorithm that solves the given BDH problem. The reduction proceeds in two steps as shown in Figure 11.4. In the first game in Lemma 1, $\mathcal{A}_1$ is used to construct $\mathcal{A}_2$. In the next step in Lemma 2, $\mathcal{A}_2$ is used to construct $\mathcal{B}$. Through this two stage reduction, an advantage of $\mathcal{A}_1$ against BasicIdent can be converted to (roughly) an advantage of $\mathcal{B}$ against the BDH problem. It means that if the advantage of $\mathcal{A}_1$ is non-negligible, then one can solve the BDH problem with non-negligible probability of success. However, the existence of such a $\mathcal{B}$ contradicts the assumption that the BDH problem is computationally hard. So there is no such $\mathcal{B}$ and hence $\mathcal{A}_2$ and $\mathcal{A}_1$.

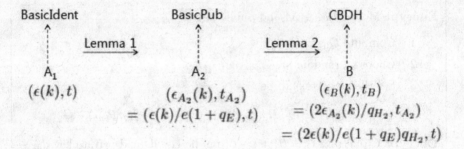

FIGURE 11.4
High-level overview of reductions (1).

Given an instance of the BDH problem, the challenger sets up the IBE scheme and provides the public parameters of the PKG to the adversary. The solution to the BDH problem corresponds to the master secret key of the PKG. But, the challenger does not actually know the master secret key. To make the adversary be forced to output the solution, the challenger should satisfy the adversary's queries with some quality (Note that in this case the quality may not be perfect).

Partitioning the identity space The problem is, how does the challenger answer key extraction queries made by the adversary and also generate a proper challenge ciphertext even without the knowledge of the master secret key of the PKG? This is handled by randomly partitioning the identity space into two disjoint subsets as shown in Figure 11.5. For one part, the challenger generates challenge ciphertexts while for the other part the challenger answers key extraction queries. If the adversary asks for a private key of an identity for which it is not possible to generate the private key, the simulator aborts (i.e., reports failure and terminates). Similarly, if the adversary provides a challenge identity for which the simulator is unable to generate a ciphertext, the simulator aborts.

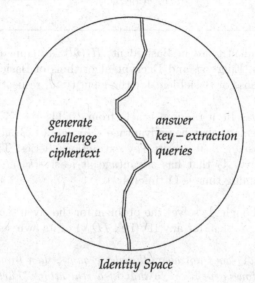

Identity Space

FIGURE 11.5
Implicit partition of the identity space done by the security reduction.

Construction 2. BasicPub

Gen Given a security parameter $k \in \mathbb{Z}^+$

1. Run $\mathcal{G}$ on input k to generate a prime q ($|q| = k$), two groups $\mathbb{G}_1$, $\mathbb{G}_2$ of order q, and a bilinear map $\hat{e}: \mathbb{G}_1 \times \mathbb{G}_1 \to \mathbb{G}_2$. Choose a random generator $P \in \mathbb{G}_1$.

2. Pick a random $s \in \mathbb{Z}_q^*$ and set $P_{pub} = sP$. Pick a random $Q_{\mathsf{ID}} \in \mathbb{G}_1^*$.

3. Choose hash function $H_2 : \mathbb{G}_2 \to \{0,1\}^n$.

4. The public key is $(q,\mathbb{G}_1,\mathbb{G}_2,\widehat{e},n,P,P_{pub},Q_{\mathsf{ID}},H_2)$. The private key is $d_{\mathsf{ID}} = sQ_{\mathsf{ID}} \in \mathbb{G}_1^*$.

Encrypt Message $M \in \{0,1\}^n$ and a random $r \in \mathbb{Z}_q^*$, set the ciphertext to be

$$C = \langle rP, M \oplus H_2(g^r) \rangle \text{ where } g = \widehat{e}(Q_{\mathsf{ID}}, P_{pub}) \in \mathbb{G}_2^*.$$

Decrypt Ciphertext $C = \langle U,V \rangle \in \mathcal{C}$, public key $(q,\mathbb{G}_1,\mathbb{G}_2,\widehat{e},P,P_{pub},Q_{\mathsf{ID}},H_2)$ and private key $d_{\mathsf{ID}} \in \mathbb{G}_1^*$, compute

$$V \oplus H_2(\widehat{e}(d_{\mathsf{ID}}, U)) = M.$$

Note: For some identity id in BasicIdent, $H_1(id)$ is mapped to Q_{id} of BasicPub. The Gen, Encrypt, and Decrypt algorithms of BasicPub essentially corresponds to those of BasicIdent for the identity id, respectively.

Lemma 1 Let H_1 be a random oracle from $\{0,1\}^* \to \mathbb{G}_1^*$. Let $\mathcal{A}_1$ be an IND-ID-CPA adversary that has advantage $\epsilon(k)$ against BasicIdent. Suppose $\mathcal{A}_1$ makes at most $q_E > 0$ private key extraction queries. Then there is an IND-CPA adversary $\mathcal{A}_2$ that has advantage at least $\epsilon(k)/e(1 + q_E)$ against BasicPub. Its running time is $O(\text{time}(\mathcal{A}_1))$.

Note that although $\mathcal{A}_2$ solves the problem for the given (i.e., fixed) ID, $\mathcal{A}_1$ cannot solve the problem for any ID (i.e., ID_{ch}) of its own selection.

Definition 3 *If $\mathcal{A}_2$ does not abort the above game, then from the view point of $\mathcal{A}_1$ the situation is identical to that of a real attack. Furthermore, if $\mathcal{A}_2$ does not abort then we have*

$$|Pr[(\gamma = \gamma')] - 1/2| \geq \epsilon, \tag{11.4}$$

where ϵ is the advantage of $\mathcal{A}_1$ against BasicIdent by Definition 1.

Now it remains to calculate the probability that $\mathcal{A}_2$ does not abort during the simulation. Suppose $\mathcal{A}_1$ makes a total of q_E private key extraction queries. The probability that $\mathcal{A}_2$ does not abort in phases I or II is δ^{q_E}. The probability that $\mathcal{A}_2$ does not abort in challenge step is $1 - \delta$. Therefore, the probability that $\mathcal{A}_2$ does not abort during the simulation is $\delta^{q_E}(1 - \delta)$, which is maximized when setting $\delta_{opt} = 1 - 1/(q_E + 1) = \frac{q_E}{q_E+1}$. Using δ_{opt}, the probability that $\mathcal{A}_2$ does not abort is $\delta^{q_E}(1 - \delta) \overset{\text{when } \delta = \frac{q_E}{q_E+1}}{=} (\frac{q_E}{q_E+1})^{q_E}(\frac{1}{q_E+1}) = (1 + \frac{1}{q_E})^{-q_E}(\frac{1}{q_E+1}) > \frac{1}{e(1+q_E)}$, where e is the base of natural logarithms. This shows that $\mathcal{A}_2$'s advantage is at least $\frac{\epsilon}{e(1+q_E)}$.

Lemma 2 Let H_2 be a random oracle from $\mathbb{G}_2^*$ to $\{0,1\}^n$. Let $\mathcal{A}_2$ be an IND-CPA adversary that has advantage $\epsilon(k)$ against BasicPub. Suppose $\mathcal{A}_2$ makes a total of $q_{H_2} > 0$ queries to H_2. Then there is an algorithm $\mathcal{B}$ that solves the BDH problem for $\mathcal{G}$ with advantage at least $2\epsilon(k)/q_{H_2}$ and a running time $O(\text{time}(\mathcal{A}_2))$.

Algorithm $\mathcal{B}$ is simulating a real attack environment for algorithm $\mathcal{A}_2$ (it simulates the challenger and the oracle for H_2) as shown in Figure 11.6. We show that $\mathcal{B}$ outputs the correct answer D with probability at least $2\epsilon/q_{H_2}$ as required. The proof is based on comparing $\mathcal{A}_2$'s behavior in the simulation to its behavior in a real IND-CPA attack game (against a real challenger and a real random oracle for H_2).

Let $\mathcal{H}$ be the event that algorithm $\mathcal{A}_2$ issues a query for $H_2(D)$ at some point during the simulation above (this implies that at the end of the simulation D appears in some tuple on the H_2^{list}). By Claims 1 and 2 as below, we know that $\Pr[\mathcal{H}] \geq 2\epsilon$ in the simulation above. Hence, at the end of the simulation, D appears in some tuple on the H_2^{list} with probability at least 2ϵ.

Claim 1 *$Pr[\mathcal{H}]$ in the simulation above is equal to $Pr[\mathcal{H}]$ in the real attack.*

Proof Let $\mathcal{H}_\ell$ be the event that $\mathcal{A}_2$ makes a query for $H_2(D)$ in one of its first ℓ queries to the H_2 oracle. We prove by induction on ℓ that $\Pr[\mathcal{H}_\ell]$ in the real attack is equal to $\Pr[\mathcal{H}_\ell]$ in the simulation for all $\ell > 0$. Clearly $\Pr[\mathcal{H}_0] = 0$ in both the simulation and in the real attack. Now suppose that for some $\ell > 0$ we have that $\Pr[\mathcal{H}_{\ell-1}]$ in the simulation is equal to $\Pr[\mathcal{H}_{\ell-1}]$ in the real attack. We show that the same holds for $\Pr[\mathcal{H}_\ell]$. We know that

$$\begin{aligned} Pr[\mathcal{H}_\ell] &= Pr[\mathcal{H}_\ell|\mathcal{H}_{\ell-1}]Pr[\mathcal{H}_{\ell-1}] + Pr[\mathcal{H}_\ell|\neg\mathcal{H}_{\ell-1}]Pr[\neg\mathcal{H}_{\ell-1}] \qquad (11.5) \\ &= Pr[\mathcal{H}_{\ell-1}] + Pr[\mathcal{H}_\ell|\neg\mathcal{H}_{\ell-1}]Pr[\neg\mathcal{H}_{\ell-1}]. \end{aligned}$$

We argue that $\Pr[\mathcal{H}_\ell|\neg\mathcal{H}_{\ell-1}]$ in the simulation is equal to $\Pr[\mathcal{H}_\ell|\neg\mathcal{H}_{\ell-1}]$ in the real attack. To see this observe that as long as $\mathcal{A}_2$ does not issue a query for $H_2(D)$ its view during the simulation is identical to its view in the real attack (against a real challenger and a real random oracle for H_2). Indeed, the public-key and the challenge are distributed as in the real attack. Similarly, all responses to H_2-queries are uniform and independent in $\{0,1\}^n$. Therefore, $\Pr[\mathcal{H}_\ell|\neg\mathcal{H}_{\ell-1}]$ in the simulation is equal to $\Pr[\mathcal{H}_\ell|\neg\mathcal{H}_{\ell-1}]$ in the real attack. It follows by (1) and the inductive hypothesis that $\Pr[\mathcal{H}_\ell]$ in the real attack is equal to $\Pr[\mathcal{H}_\ell]$ in the simulation. By induction on ℓ we obtain that $\Pr[\mathcal{H}]$ in the real attack is equal to $\Pr[\mathcal{H}]$ in the simulation.

Claim 2 *In the real attack we have $Pr[\mathcal{H}] \geq 2\epsilon$.*

Proof In the real attack, if $\mathcal{A}_2$ never issues a query for $H_2(D)$ then the decryption of C is independent of $\mathcal{A}_2$'s view (since $H_2(D)$ is independent of $\mathcal{A}_2$'s view). Therefore, in the real attack $Pr[\gamma = \gamma' | \neg \mathcal{H}] = 1/2$. By definition 3 of $\mathcal{A}_2$, we know that in the real attack $Pr[\gamma = \gamma'] - 1/2 \geq \epsilon$. We show that these two facts imply that $Pr[\mathcal{H}] \geq 2\epsilon$. To do so we first derive simple upper and lower bounds on $Pr[\gamma = \gamma']$:

$$
\begin{aligned}
Pr[\gamma = \gamma'] &= Pr[\gamma = \gamma' | \neg \mathcal{H}]Pr[\neg \mathcal{H}] + Pr[\gamma = \gamma' | \mathcal{H}]Pr[\mathcal{H}] \\
&\leq Pr[\gamma = \gamma' | \neg \mathcal{H}]Pr[\neg \mathcal{H}] + Pr[\mathcal{H}] \\
&= \frac{1}{2}Pr[\neg \mathcal{H}] + Pr[\mathcal{H}] \\
&= \frac{1}{2} + \frac{1}{2}Pr[\mathcal{H}], \\
Pr[\gamma = \gamma'] &\geq Pr[\gamma = \gamma' | \neg \mathcal{H}]Pr[\neg \mathcal{H}] \\
&= \frac{1}{2} - \frac{1}{2}Pr[\mathcal{H}].
\end{aligned}
$$

It follows that $\epsilon \leq |Pr[\gamma = \gamma'] - 1/2| \leq \frac{1}{2}Pr[\mathcal{H}]$. Therefore, in the real attack $Pr[\mathcal{H}] \geq 2\epsilon$.

The probability that $\mathcal{B}$ produces the correct answer $D = \widehat{e}(P,P)^{abc}$ $\geq$ (the probability that $\mathcal{A}_2$ makes a H_2-query of D to $\mathcal{B}$) $\cdot$ (the probability that $\mathcal{B}$ selects D from all the entries of H_2-list) $\geq 2\epsilon \cdot \frac{1}{q_{H_2}}$.

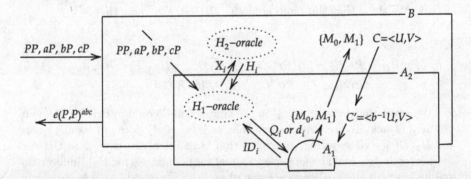

FIGURE 11.6
Simulation of the attacker's environment.

Proof of Theorem 1 The theorem follows directly from Lemma 1 and Lemma 2. Composing both reductions shows that an IND-ID-CPA adversary on BasicIdent with advantage $\epsilon(k)$ gives a BDH algorithm for $\mathcal{G}$ with advantage at least $2\epsilon(k)/e(1 + q_E)q_{H_2}$ as required. $\square$

Why is BasicIdent not CCA-Secure? *BasicIdent*, though secure against a IND-ID-CPA adversary, is not secure against IND-ID-CCA adversary because the value of g_{ID}^r is not a function of the plaintext M. So if adversary wants to decrypt the ciphertext (C_1, C_2) which encrypts the message M, he can do this by issuing to decryption oracle the ciphertext $(C_1, C_2 \oplus \Delta)$ to get the plaintext $M \oplus \Delta$ and then recover M as $M = (M \oplus \Delta) \oplus \Delta$. The Fujisaki-Okamoto transformation can easily eliminate this vulnerability by adding two more hash functions to create a scheme that is secure under chosen-ciphertext attacks.

What is the Fujisaki-Okamoto transformation? Let $E_{pk}(M, r)$ be the encryption of M under the public key pk using random bits r where E is some public key encryption scheme. Let H_1, H_2 be cryptographic hash functions. Fujisaki-Okamoto transformation defines a hybrid scheme as

$$E_{pk}^{hy}(M, r) = \langle E_{pk}(r, H_1(r, M)), H_2(r) \oplus M \rangle. \qquad (11.6)$$

One implication of the Fujisaki-Okamoto transformation is that if E_{pk} is secure against chosen plaintext attack, then E_{pk}^{hy} is secure against chosen ciphertext attack with H_1 and H_2 which are random oracles.

Construction 3. FullIdent

Setup Given a security parameter $k \in \mathbb{Z}^+$

1. Run $\mathcal{G}$ on input k to generate a prime q ($|q| = k$), two groups $\mathbb{G}_1$, $\mathbb{G}_2$ of order q, and a bilinear map $\widehat{e}: \mathbb{G}_1 \times \mathbb{G}_1 \to \mathbb{G}_2$. Choose a random generator $P \in \mathbb{G}_1$.

2. Pick a random $s \in \mathbb{Z}_q^*$ and set $P_{pub} = sP$.

3. Choose hash functions $H_1 : \{0,1\}^* \to \mathbb{G}_1^*$, $H_2 : \mathbb{G}_2 \to \{0,1\}^n$, $H_3 : \{0,1\}^n \times \{0,1\}^n \to \mathbb{Z}_q^*$ and $H_4 : \{0,1\}^n \to \{0,1\}^n$.

4. System parameters: params $= (q, \mathbb{G}_1, \mathbb{G}_2, \widehat{e}, n, P, P_{pub}, H_1, H_2, H_3, H_4)$.

5. The master-key is $s \in \mathbb{Z}_q^*$.

Extract For a given string ID $\in \{0,1\}^*$

1. Compute $Q_{ID} = H_1(ID) \in \mathbb{G}_1^*$.

2. Set the private key d_{ID} to be $d_{ID} = sQ_{ID}$ where s is the master key.

Encrypt Message $M \in \mathcal{M}$ and public key ID

1. Compute $Q_{ID} = H_1(ID) \in \mathbb{G}_1^*$.

2. Choose a random $\sigma \in \{0,1\}^n$.

3. Set $r = H_3(\sigma, M)$.

4. Set the ciphertext to be

$$C = \langle rP, \sigma \oplus H_2(g_{\mathsf{ID}}^r), M \oplus H_4(\sigma) \rangle \text{ where}$$
$$g_{\mathsf{ID}} = \widehat{e}(Q_{\mathsf{ID}}, P_{pub}) \in \mathbb{G}_2.$$

Decrypt Ciphertext $C = \langle U, V.W \rangle$, public key ID and private key $d_{\mathsf{ID}} \in \mathbb{G}_1^*$. If $U \notin \mathbb{G}_1^*$, reject the ciphertext, otherwise

1. Compute $V \oplus H_2(\widehat{e}(d_{\mathsf{ID}}, U)) = \sigma$.

2. Compute $W \oplus H_4(\sigma) = M$.

3. Set $r = H_3(\sigma, M)$. Test that $U = rP$. If not, reject the ciphertext.

4. Output M.

Theorem 2 *Construction 3 is IND-ID-CCA-secure in the random oracle model. That is, suppose the hash functions H_1, H_2, H_3, H_4 are random oracles. Then FullIdent is secure under chosen-ciphertext attacks (IND-ID-CCA) assuming BDH is hard in groups generated by $\mathcal{G}$. Concretely, suppose there is an IND-ID-CCA adversary $\mathcal{A}$ that has advantage $\epsilon(k)$ against the scheme FullIdent and its running time is at most t. Suppose $\mathcal{A}$ makes at most $q_E > 0$ private key extraction queries, $q_D > 0$ decryption queries and $q_{H_1}, q_{H_2}, q_{H_3}, q_{H_4} > 0$ hash queries to H_1, H_2, H_3, H_4, respectively. Then there is an algorithm $\mathcal{B}$ that solves BDH in groups generated by $\mathcal{G}$ with advantage and time where*

$$\epsilon_{\mathcal{B}}(k) \geq 2FO_{adv}\Big(\frac{\epsilon(k)}{q_{H_1}}\big(1 - \frac{q_E}{q_{H_1}}\big), q_{H_3}, q_{H_4}, q_D\Big)/q_{H_2} \approx \frac{\epsilon(k)}{q_H^3},$$
$$t_{\mathcal{B}}(k) \leq FO_{time}(t(k), q_{H_3}, q_{H_4}),$$

where the function FO_{adv} and FO_{time} are defined in Lemma 4.

Proof

Outline of the Proof IND-ID-CCA security of *FullIdent* is proved assuming H_1, H_2, H_3, and H_4 to be random oracles. The proof uses a scheme called $BasicPub^{hy}$ which is the result of applying the Fujisaki-Okamoto transformation to $BasicPub$. Let $\mathcal{A}_1'$ be an IND-ID-CCA adversary against *FullIdent*, $\mathcal{A}_2'$ is an IND-CCA adversary against $BasicPub^{hy}$, $\mathcal{A}_2$ is an IND-CPA adversary against $BasicPub$, while $\mathcal{B}$ be an algorithm that solves the given BDH problem. The reduction proceeds in three steps as shown in Figure 11.7. In the first game in Lemma 3, $\mathcal{A}_1'$ is used to construct $\mathcal{A}_2'$. In the next step in Lemma 4, $\mathcal{A}_2'$ is used to construct $\mathcal{A}_2$. In the last step in Lemma 2, $\mathcal{A}_2$ is used to construct $\mathcal{B}$. Through this three stage reduction, an advantage of $\mathcal{A}'_1$ against *FullIdent* can be converted to (roughly) an advantage of $\mathcal{B}$ against the BDH problem. It means that if the advantage of $\mathcal{A}'_1$ is non-negligible, then one can solve the BDH problem with non-negligible probability of success. However, the existence of such a $\mathcal{B}$ contradicts the assumption that the BDH problem is computationally hard. So there is no such $\mathcal{B}$ and hence $\mathcal{A}_2$, $\mathcal{A}'_2$ and $\mathcal{A}'_1$.

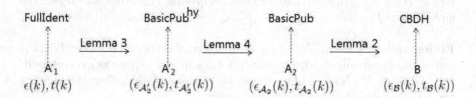

FIGURE 11.7
High-level overview of reductions (2).

Lemma 3 Let $\mathcal{A}'_1$ be an IND-ID-CCA adversary that has advantage $\epsilon(k)$ against *FullIdent*. Suppose $\mathcal{A}'_1$ makes at most $q_E > 0$ private key extraction queries, at most $q_D > 0$ decryption queries and q_{H_1} queries. Then there is an IND-CCA adversary $\mathcal{A}'_2$ that has advantage $\epsilon_{\mathcal{A}'_2}(k) \geq \dfrac{\epsilon(k)}{q_{H_1}}(1 - \dfrac{q_E}{q_{H_1}}) \approx \dfrac{\epsilon(k)}{q_{H_1}}$ against $BasicPub^{hy}$. Its running time is $O(time(\mathcal{A}'_1))$.

Proof

Galindo's Observation [46]

At $Phase I - Decryption\ Queries$, Galindo pointed at a flaw in the original analysis of Boneh-Franklin. Galindo observed that the original argument does not take into account the fact that the decryption algorithm performs a ciphertext integrity check before returning the message. He showed that given the ciphertext $C'_i = \langle b_i U_i, V_i, W_i \rangle$, the $BasicPub^{hy}$ decryption algorithm will reject it with overwhelming probability.

Given $C'_i = \langle b_i U_i, V_i, W_i \rangle$, $BasicPub^{hy}$ decryption algorithm will do as follows:

1. Compute $V_i \oplus H_2(\hat{e}(d_i, b_i U_i)) = \sigma$.
2. Compute $W_i \oplus H_4(\sigma) = M_i$.
3. Set $r = H_3(\sigma, M_i)$. Test that $b_i U_i = rP$. If not, reject the ciphertext.
4. Output M_i.

In the third step, if $b_i U_i \neq rP$, $BasicPub^{hy}$ decryption algorithm will reject the ciphertext C_i'. Recall $U_i = r_i P$, so $b_i U_i = b_i r_i P$. The decryption algorithm is going to check $b_i r_i P \stackrel{?}{=} rP$, that is, $b_i r_i \stackrel{?}{=} H_3(\sigma, M_i)$. Since b_i is uniformly random in $\mathbb{Z}_q^*$ and $r_i = H_3(\sigma, M_i)$ so $b_i r_i$ is uniformly random in $\mathbb{Z}_q^*$. On the other hand, H_3 is a random oracle not controlled by $\mathcal{A}_2'$, then we intuitively have the probability in setting a value $r = H_3(\sigma, M_i)$ in $\mathbb{Z}_q^*$ such that $b_i r_i = H_3(\sigma, M_i)$ is $1/q$. Therefore, the probability of the event $b_i r_i \neq H_3(\sigma, M_i)$, that is, $BasicPub^{hy}$ decryption algorithm will reject the ciphertext is $(1 - 1/q)$.

Fixing the flaw From Galindo's observation, a decryption query $\langle ID_i, C_i \rangle$ can be answered only if it is possible to form a proper private key corresponding to ID_i or $H_1(ID_i) = Q_{ID}$. Based on this observation, Galindo suggests the following modification in the simulation.

If $\mathcal{A}_2'$ does not abort the game, then the view with respect to $\mathcal{A}_1'$ is the same that in a real IND-ID-CCA attack: H_1 behaves as random oracle, and extraction as well as decryption queries are valid. Therefore, $|Pr[(\gamma = \gamma')] - 1/2| \geq \epsilon$, where this probability is over the random bits of $\mathcal{A}_1'$, $\mathcal{A}_2'$ and the challenger for the IND-ID-CCA game.

It remains to bound the probability $Pr[\overline{abort}]$. The algorithm can abort for two reasons: (1) it is asked in Phase I for the private key query corresponding to ID_j , or (2) the challenge identity $ID^* \neq ID_j$. Note that $\mathcal{A}_2'$ cannot abort in Phase II, since in this case $\mathcal{A}_1'$ is not allowed to query the private key for $ID_j = ID^*$. Let E_1 be the event that $\mathcal{A}_2'$ aborts due to (1), and define E_2 in the obvious way. Then

$$Pr[\overline{abort}] = Pr[\overline{E_1} \wedge \overline{E_2}] = Pr[\overline{E_2}|\overline{E_1}]Pr[\overline{E_1}]. \tag{11.7}$$

We can upper bound for $Pr[E_1] \leq q_E/q_{H_1}$, which is the probability that $\mathcal{A}_1'$ makes a extraction query for ID_i in Phase I, since the maximum number of such queries is q_E.

On the other hand, a lower bound for $Pr[\overline{E_2}|\overline{E_1}]$, that is the probability that $\mathcal{A}_1'$ chooses ID_j as the challenge identity, is $1/q_{H_1}$. Therefore,

$$Pr[\overline{abort}] \geq \frac{1}{q_{H_1}} \left(1 - \frac{q_E}{q_{H_1}}\right). \tag{11.8}$$

Since $\mathcal{A}_1'$'s advantage is $\epsilon(k)$, $\mathcal{A}_2'$'s advantage is at least $\dfrac{\epsilon(k)}{q_{H_1}}\left(1 - \dfrac{q_E}{q_{H_1}}\right)$.

Lemma 4 (Fujisaki-Okamoto) Suppose $\mathcal{A}_2'$ is an IND-CCA adversary that achieves advantage $\epsilon(k)$ when attacking $BasicPub^{hy}$. Suppose $\mathcal{A}_2'$ has running time $t(k)$, makes at most q_D decryption queries, and makes at most q_{H_3}, q_{H_4} queries to the hash functions H_3, H_4, respectively. Then there is an IND-CPA adversary $\mathcal{A}_2$ against $BasicPub$ with running time $t_{\mathcal{A}_2}(k)$ and advantage $\epsilon_{\mathcal{A}_2}(k)$, where

$$\epsilon_{\mathcal{A}_2}(k) \geq FO_{adv}(\epsilon(k), q_{H_3}, q_{H_4}, q_D) = \frac{1}{2(q_{H_3} + q_{H_4})}[(\epsilon(k)+1)(1-2/q)^{q_D} - 1],$$
$$t_{\mathcal{A}_2}(k) \geq FO_{time}(t(k), q_{H_3}, q_{H_4}) = t(k) + O((q_{H_4} + q_{H_3}) \cdot n),$$

q is the size of the groups $\mathbb{G}_1$, $\mathbb{G}_2$ and n is the length of σ.

Proof
This result is obtained from Theorem 14 in [44].

Proof of Theorem 2 The theorem follows directly from Lemma 3, Lemma 4, and Lemma 2. By Lemma 3, an IND-ID-CCA adversary on FullIdent implies an IND-CCA adversary on BasicPub^{hy}. By Lemma 4, an IND-CCA adversary on BasicPub^{hy} implies an IND-CCA adversary on BasicPub. By Lemma 2, an IND-CCA adversary on BasicPub implies an algorithm for BDH. Composing all these reductions gives the required bounds. $\square$

12

Identity-Based Encryption (2)

CONTENTS

The concept of identity-based encryption is further enhanced by discussing more about the Gentry's identity based encryption. The chapter starts with the proof of security of IBE scheme using the partitioning approach causing loose reduction. The discussion is further carried out on loose and tight reduction. The preliminaries are then explained that includes the security model for the IBE scheme, hardness assumptions, and the techniques that can be used to achieve the tight reduction. The final part of this chapter is dedicated to the Gentry's IBE that has certain advantages over previous schemes in terms of computational efficiency, shorter public parameters, recipient anonymity, and tight security reduction. The constructions for the chosen plaintext security is explained and then the security proof using the reduction algorithm is given. Similarly, the construction for the chosen ciphertext security for IBE is given along with the security proof using reduction algorithm.

12.1   Overview

Before this Gentry's scheme, in order to prove the security of an IBE scheme, we have used the partitioning approach that divides identity space into two.

But, it has a problem that the resulting reduction is lossy or loose.

What is lossy and tight reduction? Suppose that the adversary $\mathcal{A}$ wins with probability ϵ' in the security game of Π during time t'. Suppose also that the simulator $\mathcal{B}$ solves some problem $\mathcal{P}$ with probability ϵ during time t. $\mathcal{B}$ utilizes $\mathcal{A}$ to solve $\mathcal{P}$. If $\mathcal{B}$ has quite similar success probability and time complexity in comparison with $\mathcal{A}$'s one, i.e., $\epsilon \approx \epsilon'$ and $t \approx t'$, then it is called tight reduction. On the other hand, if $\mathcal{B}$ has much lower success probability and takes much longer time complexity, i.e., $\epsilon \ll \epsilon'$ and $t \gg t'$, then it is called lossy reduction.

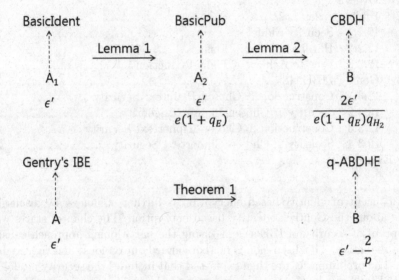

FIGURE 12.1
Comparison of BF-IBE and Gentry's IBE.

Comparison of reductions between CPA-secure BF-IBE and Gentry's IBE The reduction of BF-IBE is lossy reduction as shown in Figure 12.1. Because the simulator $\mathcal{B}$ has much lower success probability (i.e., the security degrades by roughly a factor of $q_E q_{H_2}$) in comparison with adversary $\mathcal{A}_1$'s. On the other hand, the reduction of Gentry's IBE is tight as shown in Figure 12.1. Because the success probability and time complexity of the simulator $\mathcal{B}$ are the same as the adversary $\mathcal{A}$'s, except for additive factors depending on p.

Why is tight reduction important? In general, if a reduction is tight, we commonly say that the security definition of the scheme is meaningful. Because, the scheme whose reduction is not tight is impractical. If a reduction is tight, we know that to break the scheme is as hard as to solve some relevant hard problem. It means that the scheme is secure even if we use the current security parameter.

Why is lossy reduction problematic? In the case of lossy reduction, the security proof implies that the scheme needs higher security parameter than the one used in the scheme. In the time complexity aspect, the time needed for breaking the scheme is less than the time needed for solving the hard problem. Or in the advantage aspect, the lossy reduction shows that the scheme can be broken with lower probability than the probability to solve the hard problem. Due to this two reasons, to achieve a basic security level, the lossy scheme must take much higher security parameter than the original one. Because, if the security parameter is bigger, then the adversary's advantage decreases and the time complexity increases. Using this fact, the advantage and time complexity of adversary can be made similar to those of the simulator. However, having higher security parameter means that the scheme will become inefficient. If the scheme uses the security parameter of the lossy reduction, it may be insecure in practice. Therefore, the security parameter must be increased for security..

12.2 Preliminaries

This section explains the security model for the IBE scheme, hardness assumptions, and techniques that can be used to achieve the tight reduction.

12.2.1 Security Model

ANON-IND-ID-CCA game for an anonymous-IBE scheme[1]

1. **Setup:** Given the security parameter k, the challenger runs the Setup algorithm of the IBE. It provides A with the system parameters params while keeping the master key master-key to itself.

2. **Phase I:** A makes a finite number of queries where each query is one of the following two types:

   (a) key-extraction query (ID): The challenger runs Key-Gen on ID and forwards the resulting private key to A. The Key-Gen algorithm is deterministic and so it does not query more than once on the same identity.

---

[1]The description of the ANON-IND-ID-CPA game for an IBE scheme is similar to this game, except that the adversary is not allowed to ask to the decryption oracle.

(b) decryption query (ID, C): The challenger runs Key-Gen on ID, decrypts C with the resulting private key, and sends the result to the adversary. It returns the resulting plaintext or $\perp$ if the ciphertext cannot be decrypted.

$\mathcal{A}$ is allowed to make these queries *adaptively*, i.e., any query may depend on the previous queries as well as their answers.

3. **Challenge:** $\mathcal{A}$ outputs two identities[2] ID_0, ID_1 and two equal length messages M_0, M_1 must not have appeared in any key generation query in Phase I. The simulator selects a random bit $b, c \in \{0, 1\}$, and responds with C^*, the output of Encrypt algorithm on input $(ID_b, M_c, \text{params})$.

4. **Phase II:** $\mathcal{A}$ issues additional queries just like Phase I, except that $\mathcal{A}$ may not request a private key for ID_0 and ID_1 or the decryption of (ID_0, C^*) and (ID_1, C^*). The challenger responds as in Phase I.

5. **Guess:** $\mathcal{A}$ outputs its guess b' of b and c' of c.

Definition 1 *The advantage of $\mathcal{A}$ in attacking the anonymous-IBE scheme Π is defined as*

$$\text{Adv}_{\mathcal{A},\Pi} = |Pr[[(b = b') \wedge (c = c')] - 1/4|. \tag{12.1}$$

Definition 2 *An IBE scheme $\Pi = (\text{Key-Gen}, \text{Encrypt}, \text{Decrypt})$ is said to be $(t, \epsilon, q_{id}, q_C)$-**secure against adaptive chosen ciphertext attack** if for any t-time adversary $\mathcal{A}$ that makes at most q_{id} private-key queries and at most q_C decryption queries,*

$$\text{Adv}_{\mathcal{A},\Pi} \geq \epsilon. \tag{12.2}$$

12.2.2 Hardness Assumptions

For proving this scheme, Gentry uses a non-static hardness assumption. This is a variant of bilinear Diffie-Hellman exponent problem. For making hardness assumptions, we drive a truncated decision q-augmented bilinear Diffie-Hellman exponent problem from q-bilinear Diffie-Hellman exponent problem. Here q is a parameter of the problem instance ($q = 2^{n+1} - 2$ where $n \in \mathbb{Z}$ and $n > 0$).

q-**Bilinear Diffie-Hellman exponent problem** Let $\mathbb{G}$ and $\mathbb{G}_T$ be two groups of order p for some large prime p. Let $e: \mathbb{G} \times \mathbb{G} \to \mathbb{G}_T$ be a bilinear map and let g, g' be a generator of $\mathbb{G}$.

---

[2]Why does $\mathcal{A}$ output two identities? It is for support of anonymity of identities. In relation to this, $\mathcal{A}$ outputs two values instead of one value in Guess Stage below and the probability that $\mathcal{A}$'s guesses are both correct can be expressed as $\text{Adv}_{\mathcal{A},\Pi} + 1/4$ as shown in Definition 1.

Given $\left(g', g, g^{\alpha}, g^{\alpha^2}, \cdots, g^{\alpha^q}, g^{\alpha^{q+2}}, \cdots, g^{\alpha^{2q}}\right) \in \mathbb{G}^{2q+1}$ for some $\alpha \in \mathbb{Z}_p$, it is hard to compute $Z = e(g, g')^{\alpha^{q+1}} \in \mathbb{G}_T$.

Since the input vector is missing the term $g^{(\alpha^{q+1})}$, the bilinear map does not seem to help compute $e(g, g')^{\alpha^{q+1}}$.

We define the q-ABDHE problem almost identically.

q-augmented bilinear Diffie-Hellman exponent problem Let $\mathbb{G}$ and $\mathbb{G}_T$ be two groups of order p for some large prime p. Let $e \colon \mathbb{G} \times \mathbb{G} \to \mathbb{G}_T$ be a bilinear map and let g, g' be a generator of $\mathbb{G}$.
Given $\left(g', g'^{(\alpha^{q+2})}, g, g^{\alpha}, g^{\alpha^2}, \cdots, g^{\alpha^q}, g^{\alpha^{q+2}}, \cdots, g^{\alpha^{2q}}\right) \in \mathbb{G}^{2q+2}$ for some $\alpha \in \mathbb{Z}_p$, it is hard to compute $Z = e(g, g')^{\alpha^{q+1}} \in \mathbb{G}_T$.

In q-ABDHE problem, even if the additional term $g'^{(\alpha^{q+2})}$ is introduced (i.e., augmented), we still cannot compute $Z = e(g, g')^{\alpha^{q+1}} \in \mathbb{G}_T$ easily.

The q-ABDHE problem is actually more than we need for this IBE system. Instead, we use a truncated version of the q-ABDHE problem, in which the terms $\left(g^{\alpha^{q+2}}, \cdots, g^{\alpha^{2q}}\right)$ are omitted from the input vector.

Truncated decision q-augmented bilinear Diffie-Hellman exponent problem Let $\mathbb{G}$ and $\mathbb{G}_T$ be two groups of order p for some large prime p. Let $e \colon \mathbb{G} \times \mathbb{G} \to \mathbb{G}_T$ be a bilinear map and let g, g' be a generator of $\mathbb{G}$. An algorithm $\mathcal{A}$ has advantage ϵ in solving truncated decision q-ABDHE if

$$|Pr[\mathcal{A}(g', g'_{q+2}, g, g_1, \cdots, g_q) = e(g_{q+1}, g')]| \geq \epsilon, \tag{12.3}$$

where we use g_i and g'_i to denote $g^{(\alpha^i)}$ and $g'^{(\alpha^i)}$, the probability is over the random choice of generators g, g' in $\mathbb{G}$, the random choice of α in $\mathbb{Z}_p$, and the random bits used by $\mathcal{A}$.

The decisional version of truncated q-ABDHE is defined as one would expect.

Truncated decision q-augmented bilinear Diffie-Hellman exponent assumption (truncated decision q-ABDHE) Let $\mathbb{G}$ and $\mathbb{G}_T$ be two groups of order p for some large prime p. Let $e \colon \mathbb{G} \times \mathbb{G} \to \mathbb{G}_T$ be a bilinear map and let g, g' be a generator of $\mathbb{G}$. An algorithm $\mathcal{B}$ that outputs $b \in \{0, 1\}$ has advantage ϵ in solving truncated decision q-ABDHE if

$$|Pr[\mathcal{B}(g', g'_{q+2}, g, g_1, \cdots, g_q, e(g_{q+1}, g')) = 1]$$
$$- Pr[\mathcal{B}(g', g'_{q+2}, g, g_1, \cdots, g_q, Z) = 1]| \geq \epsilon, \tag{12.4}$$

where we use g_i and g_i' to denote $g^{(\alpha^i)}$ and $g'^{(\alpha^i)}$, the probability is over the random choice of generators g, g' in $\mathbb{G}$, the random choice of α in $\mathbb{Z}_p$, the random choice of $Z \in \mathbb{G}_T$, and the random bits consumed by $\mathcal{B}$.

Definition 3 We say that the **truncated decision** (t, ϵ, q)-**ABDHE assumption holds** in $\mathbb{G}$ if no t-time algorithm has advantage at least ϵ in solving the truncated decision q-ABDHE problem in $\mathbb{G}$.

12.2.3   How to Achieve a Tight Reduction?

When the partitioning approach is used for security proof, a simulator has much lower success probability compared with the adversary. The reason why this happen is that the simulator stochastically chooses the space which includes identity. Due to this, as shown in the Boneh-Franklin IBE scheme, the probability of non-abort by the simulator is $\delta^q(1 - \delta) \approx 1/q$ where q is the number of key extraction queries from the adversary. The reduction loses a multiplicative factor of q.

The reason that we divide the identity space is that the simulator cannot generate the private key which can decrypt the challenge ciphertext. For example, in the Boneh-Franklin IBE scheme, the adversary can ask H_1 oracle about the challenge identity before the challenge phase. Computation of H_1 on the challenge identity must be different from the computation of H_1 on the other identities. But, the simulator does not know what the challenge identity is in Phase I. To resolve this problem, the Boneh-Franklin IBE scheme used the partitioning approach.

However, Gentry overcomes this problem. To overcome this problem, Gentry allows the simulator to generate a valid private key for all identities including the challenge identity. And a private key generation process works identically for all identities including the challenge identity. So, unlike the partitioning approach, before a challenge ciphertext is generated, this approach does not need to select the challenge identity stochastically.

Here, we should consider the purpose of the simulator. The purpose of the simulator is to solve the truncated decision q-ABDHE problem, i.e., to distinguish whether Z is $e(g_{q+1}, g')$ or random from the instance of truncated decision q-ABDHE problem, $(g', g_{q+2}', g, g_1, \cdots, g_q, Z)$. On the other hand, the purpose of the adversary is to distinguish which id and message the challenge ciphertext is encrypted from. Since the simulator cannot distinguish, it tries to solve it by using the adversary whose attacking capability against the scheme is presumably improved through the simulation training. Therefore, the simulator makes its own new setup, extract and encrypt algorithms from the setup, extract, and encrypt algorithms of the scheme in order to simulate the public parameters, public keys, private keys from the truncated decision

q-ABDHE problem instances to the adversary. But the issue here is that even if the simulator does not use the adversary's ability, the simulator can distinguish whether Z is $e(g_{q+1}, g')$ or not. It is possible because the challenger can generate a valid private key for the challenge identity, which in turn allows it to distinguish by decrypting the challenge ciphertext itself. In this case, we cannot prove that the scheme is hard to break, which makes the security game invalid. Therefore, we have to make sure that the simulator cannot distinguish whether Z is $e(g_{q+1}, g')$ or not.

To resolve this issue, Gentry sets that (1) if $Z = e(g_{q+1}, g')$, the simulator and the adversary can decrypt the challenge ciphertext; (2) if Z is random, the simulator can decrypt the challenge ciphertext, but the adversary still cannot decrypt the challenge ciphertext except with a trivial (i.e., negligible) probability. The detailed method is as follows.

Since the key extraction algorithm is probabilistic, we can imagine that a space of possible private keys for each identity, S_{key}, exists as shown in Figure 12.2. The key extraction algorithm can be seen to sample from S_{key}. Now, let us suppose that the simulator generates exactly one valid private key for all identities including the challenge identity. Then the space of valid private keys that can be selected by the simulator, S_{sim}, is included in S_{key}. But, $|S_{sim}|$ is much smaller than $|S_{key}|$ that is quite large.

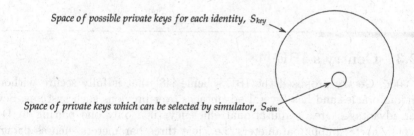

Space of possible private keys for each identity, S_{key}

Space of private keys which can be selected by simulator, S_{sim}

FIGURE 12.2
Comparison of private key spaces in Gentry's IBE.

As above, Gentry limits the range of valid private keys generated by the simulator. In addition, a challenge ciphertext is generated so that that a valid private key which corresponds to the challenge identity generated by the simulator can decrypt it as shown in Figure 12.3. Therefore, even if Z is a random value, the private key generated by the simulator can decrypt the challenge ciphertext. So, the simulator cannot take any advantage from this. And it must use the adversary to solve the underlying hard problem. On the other hand, since the adversary does not know which keys (out of the possible large space of private keys) the simulator can generate, it can generate a valid private key that is not equal to the one made by the simulator with a quite high probability. If Z is random, this adversary cannot decrypt the challenge ciphertext except with trivial probability.

Thus the simulator obtains some non-trivial information from the adversary which it can utilize to attack the underlying hard problem.

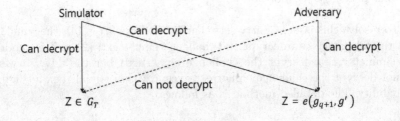

FIGURE 12.3
Different decryption capabilities in Gentry's IBE.

From this, we can distinguish the underlying assumption (truncated decision q-ABDHE) by using the adversary.

12.3 Gentry's IBE [48]

In 2006, Gentry proposed the IBE scheme [48] that is fully secure without random oracles and has several advantages over previous such systems. Several advantages are computational efficiency (i.e., only one pairing in Decrypt), shorter public parameters (i.e., just three parameters such as params $= (g, g_1, h)$), recipient anonymity, and a "tight" security reduction.

12.3.1 Construction 1: Chosen-Plaintext Security

Now present an efficient IBE system that is ANON-IND-ID-CPA secure without random oracles under the truncated decision $(q_{ID} + 1)$-ABDHE assumption.

Construction 1. Chosen-plaintext security

Let $\mathbb{G}$, $\mathbb{G}_T$ be groups of order p and let $e \colon \mathbb{G} \times \mathbb{G} \to \mathbb{G}_T$ be the bilinear map. The IBE system works as follows.

Setup Given a security parameter $k \in \mathbb{Z}^+$, where $k = |p|$:

1. Pick a random generators $g, h \in \mathbb{G}$.
2. Pick a random $\alpha \in \mathbb{Z}_p$.
3. Set $g_1 = g^\alpha \in \mathbb{G}$.
4. The system parameters are params $= (g, g_1, h)$.
5. The master-key is α.

Note: $\mathbb{G}$ is a subgroup of the additive group of points of an elliptic curve $E/\mathbb{F}_p$. $\mathbb{G}_T$ is a subgroup of the multiplicative group of a finite field $\mathbb{F}_{p^2}$.

Extract For a given identity $\mathsf{ID} \in \mathbb{Z}_p$

1. Generate random $r_{\mathsf{ID}} \in \mathbb{Z}_p$.
2. Compute $h_{\mathsf{ID}} = (hg^{-r_{\mathsf{ID}}})^{1/(\alpha - \mathsf{ID})} \in \mathbb{G}$ where α is the master-key.
3. Set the private key $d_{\mathsf{ID}} = (r_{\mathsf{ID}}, h_{\mathsf{ID}})$.

Note: If $\mathsf{ID} = \alpha$, the PKG aborts. We require that the PKG always use the same random value r_{ID} for ID. This can be accomplished, for example, using a PRF to ensure consistency.

Encrypt Message $M \in \mathbb{G}_T$ and identity $\mathsf{ID} \in \mathbb{Z}_p$

1. Generate random $s \in \mathbb{Z}_p$.
2. Compute $u = g_1^s g^{-s \cdot \mathsf{ID}} \in \mathbb{G}$.
3. Compute $v = e(g, g)^s \in \mathbb{G}_T$.
4. Compute $w = M \cdot e(g, h)^{-s} \in \mathbb{G}_T$.
5. Set the ciphertext to be $C = \langle u, v, w \rangle$.

Note: Encryption does not require any pairing computations once $e(g, g)$ and $e(g, h)$ have been pre-computed. Alternatively, $e(g, g)$ and $e(g, h)$ can be included in the system parameters, in which case h can be dropped.

Decrypt Ciphertext $C = \langle u, v, w \rangle$, identity ID and private key d_{ID}, compute

$$w \cdot e(u, h_{\mathsf{ID}}) v^{r_{\mathsf{ID}}} = M.$$

12.3.2   Security 1: Chosen-Plaintext Security

Now prove that the above IBE system is ANON-IND-ID-CPA secure under the truncated decision $(q_{ID} + 1)$-ABDHE assumption.

It uses a stronger assumption that depends on the number of private key generation queries made by the adversary (It means that the number of private key generation queries made by the adversary is already fixed before security game is started).

Theorem 1 Let $q = q_{ID} + 1$. Assume the truncated decision (t, ϵ, q)-ABDHE assumption holds for $(\mathbb{G}, \mathbb{G}_T, e)$. Then, Construction 1 is (t', ϵ', q_{ID})-ANON-IND-ID-CCA secure for $t' = t - O(t_{exp} \cdot q^2)$ and $\epsilon' = \epsilon + 2/p$, where t_{exp} is the time required to exponentiate in $\mathbb{G}$.

Proof Let $\mathcal{A}$ be an adversary that (t', ϵ', q_{ID})-breaks the ANON-IND-ID-CPA security of the IBE system described above. We construct an algorithm, $\mathcal{B}$, that solves the truncated decision q-ABDHE problem, as follows. $\mathcal{B}$ takes as input a random truncated decision q-ABDHE challenge $(g', g'_{q+2}, g, g_1, \cdots, g_q, Z)$, where Z is either $e(g_{q+1}, g')$ or a random element of $\mathbb{G}_T$ (recall that $g_i = g^{(\alpha^i)}$). Algorithm $\mathcal{B}$ proceeds as follows.

Reduction algorithm $\mathcal{B}$

Setup

1. Generate a random polynomial $f(x) \in \mathbb{Z}_p[x]$ of degree q.
2. Set $h = g^{f(\alpha)}$, computing h from $(g, g_1, \cdots, g_q)$.
3. Send the public key (g, g_1, h) to $\mathcal{A}$.

Note: Since $g, \alpha, f(x)$ are chosen uniformly at random, h is uniformly random and this public key has a distribution identical to that in the actual construction.

Phase I

1. $\mathcal{A}$ makes key generation queries.
2. $\mathcal{B}$ responds to a query on $\mathsf{ID} \in \mathbb{Z}_p$ as follows.
   If $\mathsf{ID} = \alpha$, $\mathcal{B}$ uses α to solve truncated decision q-ABDHE immediately.
   Else, let $F_{\mathsf{ID}}(x)$ denote the $(q - 1)$-degree polynomial $\frac{(f(x) - f(\mathsf{ID}))}{(x - \mathsf{ID})}$.
   $\mathcal{B}$ sets the private key $(r_{\mathsf{ID}}, h_{\mathsf{ID}})$ to be $(f(\mathsf{ID}), g^{F_{\mathsf{ID}}(\alpha)})$.

Note: This is a valid private key for ID, since $g^{F_{\text{ID}}(\alpha)} = g^{\frac{(f(\alpha) - f(\text{ID}))}{(\alpha - \text{ID})}} = (hg^{-f(\text{ID})})^{\frac{1}{(\alpha - \text{ID})}}$, as required. We will describe why this private key appears to $\mathcal{A}$ to be correctly distributed below.

Challenge

1. $\mathcal{A}$ outputs identities ID_0, ID_1 and messages M_0, M_1.

2. Again, if $\alpha \in \{\text{ID}_0, \text{ID}_1\}$, $\mathcal{B}$ uses α to solve the truncated decision q-ABDHE immediately.

3. Else, $\mathcal{B}$ generates bits $b, c \in \{0, 1\}$, and computes a private key $(r_{\text{ID}_b}, h_{\text{ID}_b})$ for ID_b as in Phase I.

4. Let $f_2(x) = x^{q+2}$.

5. Let $F_{2,\text{ID}_b}(x) = \frac{(f_2(x) - f_2(\text{ID}_b))}{(x - \text{ID}_b)} = \frac{(x^{q+2} - \text{ID}_b^{q+2})}{(x - \text{ID}_b)} = x^{q+1} + \text{ID}_b x^q + \cdots + \text{ID}_b^q x + \text{ID}_b^{q+1}$, which is a polynomial of degree $q + 1$.

6. $\mathcal{B}$ sets $u = g'^{f_2(\alpha) - f_2(\text{ID}_b)}$, $v = Z \cdot e(g', \prod_{i=0}^{q} g^{F_{2,\text{ID}_b,i} \cdot \alpha^i})$, $w = M_c / e(u, h_{\text{ID}_b}) v^{r_{\text{ID}_b}}$.
   $F_{2,\text{ID}_b,i} = \text{ID}_b^{q+1-i}$ as the coefficient of x^i in $F_{2,\text{ID}_b}(x)$.
   $\prod_{i=0}^{q} g^{F_{2,\text{ID}_b,i} \cdot \alpha^i} = g^{F_{2,\text{ID}_b}(\alpha)} g_{q+1}^{-1} = g^{F_{2,\text{ID}_b}(\alpha) - \alpha^{q+1}}$
   $= g^{\text{ID}_b \alpha^q + \cdots + \text{ID}_b^q \alpha + \text{ID}_b^{q+1}} = g_q^{\text{ID}_b} \times \cdots \times g_1^{\text{ID}_b^q} \times g^{\text{ID}_b^{q+1}}$.

7. Send (u, v, w) to $\mathcal{A}$ as the challenge ciphertext.

Note: Let $s = (\log_g g') F_{2,\text{ID}_b}(\alpha)$. If $Z = e(g_{q+1}, g')$, then $u = g^{s(\alpha - \text{ID}_b)}$, $v = e(g, g)^s$, and $M_c/w = e(u, h_{\text{ID}_b}) v^{r_{\text{ID}_b}} = e(g, h)^s$; thus (u, v, w) is a valid ciphertext for (ID_b, M_c) under randomness s. Since $\log_g g'$ is uniformly random, s is uniformly random, and so (u, v, w) is a valid, appropriately-distributed challenge to $\mathcal{A}$.

Phase II

1. $\mathcal{A}$ makes key generation queries and $\mathcal{B}$ responds as in Phase I.

Guess

1. Finally, the adversary outputs guesses $b', c' \in \{0, 1\}$.

2. If $b = b'$ and $c = c'$, $\mathcal{B}$ outputs 1 (indicating that $Z = e(g_{q+1}, g')$); otherwise, it outputs 0.

Simulation of private key generation

Now, we explain how to generate a valid private key without knowledge of the master-key α. Before explaining, look again a valid private key:

$$d_{\mathsf{ID}} = (r_{\mathsf{ID}}, h_{\mathsf{ID}}) = (r_{\mathsf{ID}}, (hg^{-f(\mathsf{ID})})^{\frac{1}{(\alpha - \mathsf{ID})}}). \tag{12.5}$$

As seen from above, the simulator must know α for generating a valid private key. The difficulty is that the simulator does not know α. But, it can generate a valid private key by using the problem instance only as below. We set h as below in the setup stage

$$h = g^{f(\alpha)}, \tag{12.6}$$

where $f(x) \in \mathbb{Z}_p[x]$ of degree q.

We can generate a valid private key by using h and $f(x)$. As a simple example, we assume $q = 4$, $f(x) = x^4$ and set $h = g^{\alpha^4}$. Also, set $r_{\mathsf{ID}} = \mathsf{ID}^4$. Then we can generate

$$h_{\mathsf{ID}} = (hg^{-f(\mathsf{ID})})^{\frac{1}{(\alpha-\mathsf{ID})}} = (g^{\alpha^4} g^{-\mathsf{ID}^4})^{\frac{1}{(\alpha-\mathsf{ID})}} = g^{\frac{\alpha^4 - \mathsf{ID}^4}{(\alpha-\mathsf{ID})}} =$$

$$g^{(\alpha+\mathsf{ID})(\alpha^2+\mathsf{ID}^2)} = g^{\alpha^3 + \mathsf{ID}\alpha^2 + \mathsf{ID}^2\alpha + \mathsf{ID}^3} = g^{\alpha^3} g^{\mathsf{ID}\alpha^2} g^{\mathsf{ID}^2\alpha} g^{\mathsf{ID}^3} = g_3 g_2^{\mathsf{ID}} g_1^{\mathsf{ID}^2} g^{\mathsf{ID}^3}.$$

Thus the simulator can generate a valid private key without knowledge of α.

The private keys issued by $\mathcal{B}$ are appropriately distributed

We want to show that the keys issued by $\mathcal{B}$ are appropriately distributed from $\mathcal{A}$'s view. It suffices to show that the values $\{f(a) : a \in \mathcal{I}\}$ are uniformly random and independent, where $\mathcal{I}$ is a set consisting of α, ID_b, and the identities queried by $\mathcal{A}$. We can observe that $|\mathcal{I}| \leq q + 1 = q_{ID} + 2$ because of $q = q_{ID} + 1$. This follows from the fact that $f(x)$ is a uniformly random polynomial of degree q whose coefficients are chosen independently and uniformly at random from $\mathbb{Z}_p$. So, r_{ID} and h_{ID} are random, because $r_{\mathsf{ID}} = f(\mathsf{ID})$ and h_{ID} is generated by using $f(x)$. Therefore, the private keys issued by $\mathcal{B}$ are appropriately distributed.

Simulation of challenge ciphertext generation

Now, we explain how to generate a valid challenge ciphertext without knowledge of α. First of all, we must keep in mind that the simulator must generate a valid private key for a challenge identity and decrypt the challenge ciphertext. Before we talk about this issue, we arrange four functions.

1. $f_2(x) = x^{q+2}$.

2. $F_{2,\mathsf{ID}_b}(x) = \frac{(f_2(x) - f_2(\mathsf{ID}_b))}{(x - \mathsf{ID}_b)} = \frac{(x^{q+2} - \mathsf{ID}_b^{q+2})}{(x - \mathsf{ID}_b)} = x^{q+1} + \mathsf{ID}_b x^q + \cdots + \mathsf{ID}_b^q x + \mathsf{ID}_b^{q+1}$, which is a polynomial of degree $q + 1$.

3. $F_{2,\mathsf{ID}_b,i} = \mathsf{ID}_b^{q+1-i}$ is the coefficient of x^i in $F_{2,\mathsf{ID}_b}(x)$.

4. $\prod_{i=0}^q g^{F_{2,\mathsf{ID}_b,i}\cdot\alpha^i} = g^{F_{2,\mathsf{ID}_b}(\alpha)} g_{q+1}^{-1} = g^{F_{2,\mathsf{ID}_b}(\alpha)-\alpha^{q+1}} = g^{\mathsf{ID}_b\alpha^q+\cdots+\mathsf{ID}_b^q\alpha+\mathsf{ID}_b^{q+1}}$
$= g_q^{\mathsf{ID}_b} \times \cdots \times g_1^{\mathsf{ID}_b^q} \times g^{\mathsf{ID}_b^{q+1}}$.

Let $s = (log_g g') F_{2,\mathsf{ID}_b}(\alpha) = (log_g g')\frac{(f_2(\alpha)-f_2(\mathsf{ID}_b))}{(\alpha-\mathsf{ID}_b)}$. Then $g^s = (g')^{\frac{(f_2(\alpha)-f_2(\mathsf{ID}_b))}{(\alpha-\mathsf{ID}_b)}}$.

Now let's see the challenge ciphertext.

$u = g_1^s g^{-s\cdot\mathsf{ID}_b} = g^{s(\alpha-\mathsf{ID}_b)} = g'^{\frac{(f_2(\alpha)-f_2(\mathsf{ID}_b))}{(\alpha-\mathsf{ID}_b)}(\alpha-\mathsf{ID}_b)} = g'^{f_2(\alpha)-f_2(\mathsf{ID}_b)} = g'^{f_2(\alpha)} g'^{f_2(-\mathsf{ID}_b)} = g'^{\alpha^{q+2}} g'^{-(\mathsf{ID}_b)^{q+2}} = g'^{q+2}_{q+2}(g')^{-(\mathsf{ID}_b)^{q+2}}$.

$v = Z \cdot e(g', \prod_{i=0}^q g^{F_{2,\mathsf{ID}_b,i}\cdot\alpha^i}) = Z \cdot e(g', g_q^{\mathsf{ID}_b} \times \cdots \times g_1^{\mathsf{ID}_b^q} \times g^{\mathsf{ID}_b^{q+1}})$.

$w = \dfrac{M_c}{e(u, h_{\mathsf{ID}_b}) v^{r_{\mathsf{ID}_b}}} = \dfrac{M_c}{e(g^{s(\alpha-\mathsf{ID}_b)}, (hg^{-f(\mathsf{ID}_b)})^{\frac{1}{(\alpha-\mathsf{ID}_b)}}) v^{r_{\mathsf{ID}_b}}} = \dfrac{M_c}{e(g^s, (hg^{-f(\mathsf{ID}_b)}) v^{r_{\mathsf{ID}_b}}}$
$= \dfrac{M_c}{e(g^s, h) e(g^s, g^{-f(\mathsf{ID}_b)}) v^{r_{\mathsf{ID}_b}}} = \dfrac{M_c}{e(g, h)^s e(g, g)^{-sf(\mathsf{ID}_b)} v^{r_{\mathsf{ID}_b}}}$.

As shown above, the challenge ciphertext can be made by using the problem instance only[3].

Now check whether it is a valid challenge ciphertext or not in two cases: (1) Z is real and (2) Z is random, respectively. First, in the case that Z is real (i.e., $Z = e(g_{q+1}, g')$), v and w are computed as below.

$v = Z \cdot e(g', \prod_{i=0}^q g^{F_{2,\mathsf{ID}_b,i}\cdot\alpha^i}) = e(g_{q+1}, g') \cdot e(g', g_q^{\mathsf{ID}_b} \times \cdots \times g_1^{\mathsf{ID}_b^q} \times g^{\mathsf{ID}_b^{q+1}}) = e(g', g_{q+1} \times g_q^{\mathsf{ID}_b} \times \cdots \times g_1^{\mathsf{ID}_b^q} \times g^{\mathsf{ID}_b^{q+1}}) = e(g', g^{F_{2,\mathsf{ID}_b}(\alpha)}) = e(g', g^{\frac{(f_2(\alpha)-f_2(\mathsf{ID}_b))}{(\alpha-\mathsf{ID}_b)}}) = e((g')^{\frac{(f_2(\alpha)-f_2(\mathsf{ID}_b))}{(\alpha-\mathsf{ID}_b)}}, g) = e(g^s, g) = e(g, g)^s$.

$w = M_c/e(u, h_{\mathsf{ID}_b}) v^{r_{\mathsf{ID}_b}} = M_c/e(g, h)^s e(g, g)^{-sf(\mathsf{ID}_b)} (e(g, g)^s)^{r_{\mathsf{ID}_b}} = M_c/e(g, h)^s e(g, g)^{s(f(\mathsf{ID}_b)-f(\mathsf{ID}_b))} = M_c \cdot e(g, h)^{-s}$.
As shown above, a valid challenge ciphertext is made. Therefore the simulator can decrypt it by using the appropriate private key.

Next, in the case that Z is random, even if the challenge ciphertext is random, the simulator can decrypt it by using the appropriate private key. Decryption is computed as below.

$M_c = w \cdot e(u, h_{\mathsf{ID}_b}) v^{r_{\mathsf{ID}_b}} = M_c(e(g, h)^s e(g, g)^{-sf(\mathsf{ID}_b)} v^{r_{\mathsf{ID}_b}})^{-1} \cdot e(g'^{f_2(\alpha)-f_2(\mathsf{ID}_b)},$
$g^{\frac{(f(\alpha)-f(\mathsf{ID}_b))}{(\alpha-\mathsf{ID}_b)}}) \cdot v^{r_{\mathsf{ID}_b}}$

---

[3]The simulator can generate u by using the problem instances g'_{q+2}, g' instead of s without knowledge of α. Similarly, v and w can also be generated by using the values generated previously

$$= M_c e(g,h)^{-s} e(g,g)^{sf(\mathsf{ID}_b)} \cdot e(g'^{\frac{f_2(\alpha)-f_2(\mathsf{ID}_b)}{(\alpha-\mathsf{ID}_b)}}, g^{(f(\alpha)-f(\mathsf{ID}_b))})$$

$$= M_c e(g,h)^{-s} e(g,g)^{sf(\mathsf{ID}_b)} \cdot e(g^s, g^{f(\alpha)} g^{-f(\mathsf{ID}_b)})$$

$$= M_c e(g,h)^{-s} e(g,g)^{sf(\mathsf{ID}_b)} \cdot e(g^s, g^{f(\alpha)}) \cdot e(g^s, g^{-f(\mathsf{ID}_b)})$$

$$= M_c e(g,h)^{-s} \cdot e(g,h)^s = M_c.$$

As shown above, even if the challenge ciphertext is random, the simulator can decrypt it by using the appropriate private key. The reason is that v including Z is canceled out in the decryption process. But the adversary cannot decrypt it without negligible probability.

The challenge ciphertext are appropriately distributed

We want to show that the challenge ciphertext are appropriately distributed from $\mathcal{A}$'s view. The challenge ciphertext consists of three elements: u, v and w. Since $log_g g'$ is uniformly random, s is uniformly random. And (u, v, w) is uniformly random because it is made by using s. Therefore the challenge ciphertext are appropriately distributed.

Probability analysis

Remember that all private keys and challenge ciphertext are appropriately distributed.

Before doing analysis, let's define three events:

1. Let X_0 be the event that $\mathcal{A}$'s guesses are correct when Z is real.
2. Let X_1 be the event that $\mathcal{A}$'s guesses are correct when Z is a uniform random element of $\mathbb{G}_T$.
3. Let E be the event that $v = e(u,g)^{1/(\alpha-\mathsf{ID}_0)}$ or $v = e(u,g)^{1/(\alpha-\mathsf{ID}_1)}$. It means that regardless of whether Z is real or random, the challenge ciphertext is valid because

$$v = e(u,g)^{1/(\alpha-\mathsf{ID}_b)} = e((g')^{f_2(\alpha-f_2(\mathsf{ID}_b))}, g)^{1/(\alpha-\mathsf{ID}_b)}$$

$$= e((g')^{(f_2(\alpha-f_2(\mathsf{ID}_b)))/(\alpha-\mathsf{ID}_b)}, g) = e(g^s, g) = e(g,g)^s.$$

When Z is random, since $|v| = p$, and at most two cases are corresponded to this event, $Pr[E] \leq 2/p$. However, when Z is real, $Pr[E] = 1$.

Clearly, we can see that $\mathcal{A}$'s advantage, ϵ', is great than or equal to the gap of two event's probabilities, $\mathcal{B}$'s advantage, ϵ because

$$\epsilon = Pr[X_0] - Pr[X_1] = Pr[\mathcal{B} \text{ outputs } 1|Z \text{ is real}]$$
$$- Pr[\mathcal{B} \text{ outputs } 1|Z \text{ is random}] \leq \epsilon'.$$

First, let us compute $Pr[X_1]$ for computing ϵ. We can show $Pr[X_1]$ as

$$Pr[X_1] = Pr[X_1|E]Pr[E] + Pr[X_1|\overline{E}]Pr[\overline{E}] \leq Pr[E] + Pr[X_1|\overline{E}]$$
$$= 2/p + Pr[X_1|\overline{E}].$$

If E does not occur, then the elements of the challenge ciphertext are uniform random elements of $\mathbb{G}$ and $\mathbb{G}_T$. So, these perfectly hide the bits b and c from $\mathcal{A}$. It means that $Pr[X_1|\overline{E}]$ is the success probability of $\mathcal{A}$ when b and c are randomly chosen from $\mathcal{A}$. Therefore, $Pr[X_1|\overline{E}] = 1/4$. So,

$$Pr[X_1] = 2/p + 1/4.$$

Next, let us compute $Pr[X_0]$ for computing ϵ. If Z is real, $e(g_{q+1}, g')$, then the distribution of the ciphertext is also the same as in the actual scheme. So we can get $Pr[X_0] = \epsilon' + 1/4$ from Definition 1. It means that since $\mathcal{B}$ identically behaves as the actual scheme, $Pr[X_0] = Pr[[(b = b') \wedge (c = c')]$.

Finally, we can get $\mathcal{B}$'s advantage, ϵ, by combining these two probabilities, $Pr[X_0]$ and $Pr[X_1]$ as

$$\epsilon = Pr[X_0] - Pr[X_1] = \epsilon' + 1/4 - (2/p + 1/4) = \epsilon' - 2/p.$$

Time complexity

In the simulation, $\mathcal{B}$'s overhead is dominated by computing $g^{F_{\mathsf{ID}}(\alpha)}$ in response to $\mathcal{A}$'s key generation query on ID, where $F_{\mathsf{ID}}(x)$ is a polynomial of degree $q - 1$. Each such computation requires $O(q)$ exponentiations in $\mathbb{G}$. Since $\mathcal{A}$ makes at most $q - 1$ such queries, $t = t' + O(t_{exp} \cdot q^2)$ where t_{exp} is the time required to exponentiate in $\mathbb{G}$. $\square$

The security of Gentry's scheme is based on the assumption that the truncated decision q-ABDHE problem is hard. This is a *non-static* hardness assumption where the size of an instance depends on some parameter of the scheme (i.e., the number of queries that an adversary is allowed to make).

12.3.3 Construction 2. Chosen-Ciphertext Security

Now we present an efficient IBE system that is ANON-IND-ID-CCA secure without random oracle under the truncated decision $(q_{ID} + 2)$-ABDHE assumption.

Construction 2. Chosen-ciphertext security

Let $\mathbb{G}$, $\mathbb{G}_T$ be groups of order p, and let $e: \mathbb{G} \times \mathbb{G} \to \mathbb{G}_T$ be the bilinear map. The IBE system works as follows.

Setup Given a security parameter $k \in \mathbb{Z}^+$, where $k = |p|$:

---

1. Pick a random generators $g, h_1, h_2, h_3 \in \mathbb{G}$.
2. Pick a random $\alpha \in \mathbb{Z}_p$.
3. Set $g_1 = g^\alpha \in \mathbb{G}$.
4. Choose hash function $H : \mathbb{G} \times \mathbb{G}_T \times \mathbb{G}_T \to \mathbb{Z}_p$.
5. The system parameters are params $= (g, g_1, h_1, h_2, h_3, H)$.
6. The master-key is α.

Note: $\mathbb{G}$ is a subgroup of the additive group of points of an elliptic curve $E/\mathbb{F}_p$. $\mathbb{G}_T$ is a subgroup of the multiplicative group of a finite field $\mathbb{F}_{p^2}$.

Extract For a given identity $\mathsf{ID} \in \mathbb{Z}_p$

1. Generate random $r_{\mathsf{ID},1}, r_{\mathsf{ID},2}, r_{\mathsf{ID},3} \in \mathbb{Z}_p$.
2. Compute $h_{\mathsf{ID},i} = (h_i g^{-r_{\mathsf{ID},i}})^{1/(\alpha - \mathsf{ID})} \in \mathbb{G}$ for $i \in \{1, 2, 3\}$.
3. Set the private key $d_{\mathsf{ID}} = (r_{\mathsf{ID},1}, r_{\mathsf{ID},2}, r_{\mathsf{ID},3}, h_{\mathsf{ID},1}, h_{\mathsf{ID},2}, h_{\mathsf{ID},3})$.

Note: If $\mathsf{ID} = \alpha$, the PKG aborts. We require that the PKG always uses the same random value $r_{\mathsf{ID},i}$ for ID.

Encrypt Message $M \in \mathbb{G}_T$ and identity $\mathsf{ID} \in \mathbb{Z}_p$

1. Generate random $s \in \mathbb{Z}_p$.
2. Compute $u = g_1^s g^{-s \cdot \mathsf{ID}} \in \mathbb{G}$.
3. Compute $v = e(g,g)^s \in \mathbb{G}_T$.
4. Compute $w = M \cdot e(g, h_1)^{-s} \in \mathbb{G}_T$.
5. Compute $y = e(g, h_2)^s e(g, h_3)^{s\beta}$ where $\beta = H(u, v, w)$.
6. Set the ciphertext to be $C = \langle u, v, w, y \rangle$.

Note: Encryption does not require any pairing computations once $e(g,g)$ and $\{e(g, h_i)\}$ have been pre-computed or alternatively included in *params*.

Decrypt Ciphertext $C = \langle u, v, w, y \rangle$, identity ID and private key d_{ID}

1. Set $\beta = H(u, v, w)$.
2. Test $y = e(u, h_{\mathsf{ID},2} h_{\mathsf{ID},3}^\beta) v^{r_{\mathsf{ID},2} + r_{\mathsf{ID},3}\beta}$.
3. If the check fails, the recipient outputs $\bot$.
4. Otherwise, it outputs $M = w \cdot e(u, h_{\mathsf{ID},1}) v^{r_{\mathsf{ID},1}}$.

Correctness of decryption algorithm

After receiving (ID, C) with $C = (u, v, w, y)$, the receiver generates private key for ID, then uses this private key to decrypt C. Since

$$e(u, h_{\mathsf{ID},2} h_{\mathsf{ID},3}{}^\beta) v^{r_{\mathsf{ID},2} + r_{\mathsf{ID},3}\beta} = e(g^{s(\alpha - \mathsf{ID})}, h_2 g^{-r_{\mathsf{ID},2}} h_3 g^{-r_{\mathsf{ID},3}\beta}) v^{r_{\mathsf{ID},2} + r_{\mathsf{ID},3}\beta}$$

$$= e(g^{s(\alpha - \mathsf{ID})}, (h_2 h_3{}^\beta)^{1/(\alpha - \mathsf{ID})} g^{-(r_{\mathsf{ID},2} + r_{\mathsf{ID},3}\beta)/(\alpha - \mathsf{ID})}) e(g, g)^{s(r_{\mathsf{ID},2} + r_{\mathsf{ID},3}\beta)}$$

$$= e(g^{s(\alpha - \mathsf{ID})}, (h_2 h_3{}^\beta))^{1/(\alpha - \mathsf{ID})} = e(g^s, (h_2 h_3{}^\beta)) = e(g, h_2)^s e(g, h_3)^{s\beta};$$

then, if $y = e(u, h_{\mathsf{ID},2} h_{\mathsf{ID},3}{}^\beta) v^{r_{\mathsf{ID},2} + r_{\mathsf{ID},3}\beta}$, the check passes. Moreover,

$$e(u, h_{\mathsf{ID},1}) v^{r_{\mathsf{ID},1}} = e(g^{s(\alpha - \mathsf{ID})}, h_1{}^{1/(\alpha - \mathsf{ID})} g^{-r_{\mathsf{ID},1}/(\alpha - \mathsf{ID})}) e(g, g)^{s r_{\mathsf{ID},1}} = e(g, h_1)^s,$$

as required.

12.3.4   Security 2: Chosen-Ciphertext Security

Now prove that the above IBE system is ANON-IND-ID-CCA secure under the truncated decision $(q_{ID} + 2)$-ABDHE assumption.

Theorem 2 Let $q = q_{ID} + 2$. Assume the truncated decision (t, ϵ, q)-ABDHE assumption holds for $(\mathbb{G}, \mathbb{G}_T, e)$. Then, Construction 2 is $(t', \epsilon', q_{ID}, q_C)$-ANON-IND-ID-CCA secure for $t' = t - O(t_{exp} \cdot q^2)$ and $\epsilon' = \epsilon + 4q_C/p$, where t_{exp} is the time required to exponentiate in $\mathbb{G}$.

Outline of the Proof Since the difference between chosen-ciphertext security and chosen-plaintext security (as in Theorem 1) is querying to decryption oracle, in the security proof of Theorem 2, we only consider decryption queries.

Proof Let $\mathcal{A}$ be an adversary that $(t', \epsilon', q_{\mathsf{ID}}, q_C)$-breaks the ANON-IND-ID-CCA security of the IBE system described above. We construct an algorithm, $\mathcal{B}$, that solves the truncated decision q-ABDHE problem, as follows. $\mathcal{B}$ takes as input a random truncated decision q-ABDHE challenge $(g', g'_{q+2}, g, g_1, \cdots, g_q, Z)$, where Z is either $e(g_{q+1}, g')$ or a random element of $\mathbb{G}_T$ (recall that $g_i = g^{(\alpha^i)}$). Algorithm $\mathcal{B}$ proceeds as follows.

Reduction algorithm $\mathcal{B}$

Setup

1. Generate a random polynomial $f_i(x) \in \mathbb{Z}_p[x]$ of degree q for $i \in \{1, 2, 3\}$.

2. Set $h_i = g^{f_i(\alpha)}$.

3. Send the public key (g, g_1, h_1, h_2, h_3) to $\mathcal{A}$.

Note: Since $g, \alpha, f_i(x)$ are chosen uniformly at random and h_i is uniformly random, this public key has a distribution identical to that in the actual construction.

Phase I (key generation queries)

1. $\mathcal{A}$ makes key generation queries.

2. $\mathcal{B}$ responds to a query on $\mathsf{ID} \in \mathbb{Z}_p$ as follows.

   If $\mathsf{ID} = \alpha$, $\mathcal{B}$ uses α to solve the truncated decision q-ABDHE immediately.

   Else, set $r_{\mathsf{ID},1} = f_1(\mathsf{ID})$ and compute $h_{\mathsf{ID},1} = (h_1 g^{-r_{\mathsf{ID},1}})^{1/(\alpha-\mathsf{ID})}$.

   $\mathcal{B}$ sets the private key pairs $(r_{\mathsf{ID},i}, h_{\mathsf{ID},i})$ to be $(f_i(\mathsf{ID}), g^{F_{\mathsf{ID},i}(\alpha)})$.

Note: These are valid private keys for ID, since $g^{F_{\mathsf{ID},i}(\alpha)} = g^{\frac{(f_i(\alpha)-f_i(\mathsf{ID}))}{(\alpha-\mathsf{ID})}} = (h_i g^{-f_i(\mathsf{ID})})^{\frac{1}{(\alpha-\mathsf{ID})}}$, as required.

Phase I (decryption queries)

1. $\mathcal{A}$ makes decryption queries.

2. $\mathcal{B}$ responds to a query on (ID, C) as follows.
   $\mathcal{B}$ generates private keys for ID.
   Decrypt $C = (u, v, w, y)$ by performing the usual *Decrypt* algorithm with this private key.
   Set $\beta = H(u, v, w)$.
   Test $y = e(u, h_{\mathsf{ID},2} h_{\mathsf{ID},3}{}^\beta) v^{r_{\mathsf{ID},2} + r_{\mathsf{ID},3}\beta}$.
   If the check fails, output $\perp$.
   Otherwise, output $M = w \cdot e(u, h_{\mathsf{ID},1}) v^{r_{\mathsf{ID},1}}$.

Challenge

1. $\mathcal{A}$ outputs identities $\mathsf{ID}_0, \mathsf{ID}_1$, and messages M_0, M_1.

2. Again, if $\alpha \in \{\mathsf{ID}_0, \mathsf{ID}_1\}$, $\mathcal{B}$ uses α to solve the truncated decision q-ABDHE immediately.

3. Else, $\mathcal{B}$ generates bits $b, c \in \{0, 1\}$, and computes a private key $(r_{\mathsf{ID}_b,i}, h_{\mathsf{ID}_b,i})$ for ID_b as in Phase I (key generation queries).

4. Let $f_2'(x) = x^{q+2}$.

5. Let $F_{2,\mathsf{ID}_b}(x) = \frac{(f_2'(x)-f_2'(\mathsf{ID}_b))}{(x-\mathsf{ID}_b)} = \frac{(x^{q+2}-\mathsf{ID}_b^{q+2})}{(x-\mathsf{ID}_b)} = x^{q+1} + \mathsf{ID}_b x^q + \cdots + \mathsf{ID}_b^q x + \mathsf{ID}_b^{q+1}$, which is a polynomial of degree $q + 1$.

6. $\mathcal{B}$ sets $u = g'^{f'_2(\alpha) - f'_2(\mathsf{ID}_b)}$, $v = Z \cdot e(g', \prod_{i=0}^{q} g^{F_{2,\mathsf{ID}_b,i} \cdot \alpha^i})$, $w = M_c / e(u, h_{\mathsf{ID}_b,1}) v^{r_{\mathsf{ID}_b,1}}$. $F_{2,\mathsf{ID}_b,i} = \mathsf{ID}_b^{q+1-i}$ is the coefficient of x^i in $F_{2,\mathsf{ID}_b}(x)$. $\prod_{i=0}^{q} g^{F_{2,\mathsf{ID}_b,i} \cdot \alpha^i} = g^{F_{2,\mathsf{ID}_b}(\alpha)} g_{q+1}^{-1} = g^{F_{2,\mathsf{ID}_b}(\alpha) - \alpha^{q+1}} = g^{\mathsf{ID}_b \alpha^q + \cdots + \mathsf{ID}_b^q \alpha + \mathsf{ID}_b^{q+1}} = g_q^{\mathsf{ID}_b} \times \cdots \times g_1^{\mathsf{ID}_b^q} \times g^{\mathsf{ID}_b^{q+1}}$.
Set $\beta = H(u,v,w)$, compute $y = e(u, h_{\mathsf{ID}_b,2} h_{\mathsf{ID}_b,3}^{\beta}) v^{r_{\mathsf{ID}_b,2} + r_{\mathsf{ID}_b,3}\beta}$.

7. Send (u,v,w,y) to $\mathcal{A}$ as the challenge ciphertext.

Note: Let $s = (log_g g') F_{2,\mathsf{ID}_b}(\alpha)$. If $Z = e(g_{q+1}, g')$, then $u = g^{s(\alpha - \mathsf{ID}_b)}$, $v = e(g,g)^s$, $M_c/w = e(u, h_{\mathsf{ID}_b,1}) v^{r_{\mathsf{ID}_b,1}} = e(g, h_1)^s$ and $y = e(u, h_{\mathsf{ID}_b,2} h_{\mathsf{ID}_b,3}^{\beta}) v^{r_{\mathsf{ID}_b,2} + r_{\mathsf{ID}_b,3}\beta} = e(g, h_2)^s e(g, h_3)^{s\beta}$. Thus (u,v,w,y) is a valid ciphertext for (ID_b, M_c) under randomness s. Since $log_g g'$ is uniformly random, s is uniformly random, and so (u,v,w,y) is a valid, appropriately-distributed challenge to $\mathcal{A}$.

Phase II

1. $\mathcal{A}$ makes key generation queries and $\mathcal{B}$ responds as in Phase I (key generation queries).

2. $\mathcal{A}$ makes decryption queries and $\mathcal{B}$ responds as in Phase I (decryption queries).

Guess

1. Finally, the adversary outputs guesses $b', c' \in \{0, 1\}$.

2. If $b = b'$ and $c = c'$, $\mathcal{B}$ outputs 1 (indicating that $Z = e(g_{q+1}, g')$); otherwise, it outputs 0.

Simulation of private key generation

Now, we explain how to generate a valid private key without knowledge of the master-key α. Before explaining, look again a valid private key

$$d_{\mathsf{ID},i} = (r_{\mathsf{ID},i}, h_{\mathsf{ID},i}) = (f_i(\mathsf{ID}), (h_i g^{-f_i(\mathsf{ID})})^{\frac{1}{(\alpha - \mathsf{ID})}}). \tag{12.7}$$

As seen from above, the simulator must know the α for generating a valid private key. The difficulty is that the simulator does not know α. But, it can generate a valid private key by using the problem instance only as below. We set h_i in the setup stage as

$$h_i = g^{f_i(\alpha)}, \tag{12.8}$$

where $f_i(x) \in \mathbb{Z}_p[x]$ of degree q.

We can generate a valid private key by using h_i and $f_i(x)$. Thus the simulator can generate a valid private key without knowledge of α.

The private keys issued by $\mathcal{B}$ are appropriately distributed

We want to show that the keys issued by $\mathcal{B}$ are appropriately distributed from $\mathcal{A}$'s view. It suffices to show that the values $\{f_i(a) : a \in \mathcal{I}\}$ are uniformly random and independent , where $\mathcal{I}$ is a set consisting of α, ID_b and the identities queried by $\mathcal{A}$. We can observe that $|\mathcal{I}| \leq q = q_{ID} + 2$ because of $q = q_{ID} + 2$. This follows from the fact that $f_i(x)$ is a uniformly random polynomial of degree q whose coefficients are chosen independently and uniformly at random from $\mathbb{Z}_p$. So, $r_{\mathsf{ID},i}$, and $h_{\mathsf{ID},i}$ are random, because $r_{\mathsf{ID},i} = f_i(\mathsf{ID})$ and $h_{\mathsf{ID},i}$ is generated by using $f_i(x)$. Therefore the private keys issued by $\mathcal{B}$ are appropriately distributed.

Simulation of challenge ciphertext generation

Now, we explain how to generate a valid challenge ciphertext without knowledge of α. First of all, we must keep in mind that the simulator must generate a valid private key for a challenge identity and decrypt the challenge ciphertext. Before we talk about this issue, we arrange four functions.

1. $f_2'(x) = x^{q+2}$.

2. $F_{2,\mathsf{ID}_b}(x) = \frac{(f_2'(x) - f_2'(\mathsf{ID}_b))}{(x - \mathsf{ID}_b)} = \frac{(x^{q+2} - \mathsf{ID}_b^{q+2})}{(x - \mathsf{ID}_b)} = x^{q+1} + \mathsf{ID}_b x^q + \cdots + \mathsf{ID}_b^q x + \mathsf{ID}_b^{q+1}$, which is a polynomial of degree $q + 1$.

3. $F_{2,\mathsf{ID}_b,i} = \mathsf{ID}_b^{q+1-i}$ is the coefficient of x^i in $F_{2,\mathsf{ID}_b}(x)$.

4. $\prod_{i=0}^{q} g^{F_{2,\mathsf{ID}_b,i} \cdot \alpha^i} = g^{F_{2,\mathsf{ID}_b}(\alpha)} g_{q+1}^{-1} = g^{F_{2,\mathsf{ID}_b}(\alpha) - \alpha^{q+1}} = g^{\mathsf{ID}_b \alpha^q + \cdots + \mathsf{ID}_b^q \alpha + \mathsf{ID}_b^{q+1}} = g_q^{\mathsf{ID}_b} \times \cdots \times g_1^{\mathsf{ID}_b^q} \times g^{\mathsf{ID}_b^{q+1}}$.

Let $s = (log_g g') F_{2,\mathsf{ID}_b}(\alpha) = (log_g g') \frac{(f_2'(\alpha) - f_2'(\mathsf{ID}_b))}{(\alpha - \mathsf{ID}_b)}$. Then $g^s = (g')^{\frac{(f_2'(\alpha) - f_2'(\mathsf{ID}_b))}{(\alpha - \mathsf{ID}_b)}}$.

Now let us see the challenge ciphertext.

$$u = g_1^s g^{-s \cdot \mathsf{ID}_b} = g^{s(\alpha - \mathsf{ID}_b)} = g'^{\frac{(f_2'(\alpha) - f_2'(\mathsf{ID}_b))}{(\alpha - \mathsf{ID}_b)}(\alpha - \mathsf{ID}_b)} = g'^{f_2'(\alpha) - f_2'(\mathsf{ID}_b)} = g'^{f_2'(\alpha)} g'^{f_2'(-\mathsf{ID}_b)} = g'^{\alpha^{q+2}} g'^{-(\mathsf{ID}_b)^{q+2}} = g_{q+2}'(g')^{-(\mathsf{ID}_b)^{q+2}}.$$

$$v = Z \cdot e(g', \prod_{i=0}^{q} g^{F_{2,\mathsf{ID}_b,i} \cdot \alpha^i}) = Z \cdot e(g', g_q^{\mathsf{ID}_b} \times \cdots \times g_1^{\mathsf{ID}_b^q} \times g^{\mathsf{ID}_b^{q+1}}).$$

$$w = \frac{M_c}{e(u, h_{\mathsf{ID}_b,1}) v^{r_{\mathsf{ID}_b,1}}} = \frac{M_c}{e(g^{s(\alpha - \mathsf{ID}_b)}, (h_1 g^{-f_1(\mathsf{ID}_b)})^{\frac{1}{(\alpha - \mathsf{ID}_b)}}) v^{r_{\mathsf{ID}_b,1}}} = \frac{M_c}{e(g^s, (h_1 g^{-f_1(\mathsf{ID}_b)}) v^{r_{\mathsf{ID}_b,1}}}$$
$$= \frac{M_c}{e(g^s, h_1) e(g^s, g^{-f_1(\mathsf{ID}_b)}) v^{r_{\mathsf{ID}_b,1}}} = \frac{M_c}{e(g, h_1)^s e(g, g)^{-s f_1(\mathsf{ID}_b)} v^{r_{\mathsf{ID}_b,1}}}.$$

$$y = e(u, h_{\mathsf{ID}_b,2} h_{\mathsf{ID}_b,3}^\beta) v^{r_{\mathsf{ID}_b,2} + r_{\mathsf{ID}_b,3}\beta} = e(u, h_2 g^{-f_2(\mathsf{ID}_b)} (h_3 g^{-f_3(\mathsf{ID}_b)})^\beta) v^{r_{\mathsf{ID}_b,2} + r_{\mathsf{ID}_b,3}\beta},$$
where $\beta = H(u, v, w)$.

As shown above, the challenge ciphertext can be made by using the problem instance only.

Now we check whether it is a valid challenge ciphertext or not in two cases: (1)Z is real (2)Z is random, respectively. First, in the case that Z is real (i.e., $Z = e(g_{q+1}, g')$), u, v, w, and y are computed as below.

$u = g_1^s g^{-s \cdot \mathsf{ID}_b} = g^{s(\alpha - \mathsf{ID}_b)}$.

$v = Z \cdot e(g', \prod_{i=0}^{q} g^{F_{2,\mathsf{ID}_b,i} \cdot \alpha^i}) = e(g_{q+1}, g') \cdot e(g', g_q^{\mathsf{ID}_b} \times \cdots \times g_1^{\mathsf{ID}_b^q} \times g^{\mathsf{ID}_b^{q+1}}) = e(g', g_{q+1} \times g_q^{\mathsf{ID}_b} \times \cdots \times g_1^{\mathsf{ID}_b^q} \times g^{\mathsf{ID}_b^{q+1}}) = e(g', g^{F_{2,\mathsf{ID}_b}(\alpha)}) = e(g', g^{\frac{(f_2'(\alpha) - f_2'(\mathsf{ID}_b))}{(\alpha - \mathsf{ID}_b)}}) = e((g')^{\frac{(f_2'(\alpha) - f_2'(\mathsf{ID}_b))}{(\alpha - \mathsf{ID}_b)}}, g) = e(g^s, g) = e(g, g)^s$.

$w = M_c/e(u, h_{\mathsf{ID}_b,1}) v^{r_{\mathsf{ID}_b,1}} = M_c/e(g, h_1)^s e(g, g)^{-sf_1(\mathsf{ID}_b)} (e(g, g)^s)^{r_{\mathsf{ID}_b,1}} = M_c/e(g, h_1)^s e(g, g)^{s(f_1(\mathsf{ID}_b) - f_1(\mathsf{ID}_b,1))} = M_c \cdot e(g, h_1)^{-s}$.

$y = e(u, h_{\mathsf{ID}_b,2} h_{\mathsf{ID}_b,3}^{\beta}) v^{r_{\mathsf{ID}_b,2} + r_{\mathsf{ID}_b,3}\beta} =$
$e(g^{s(\alpha - \mathsf{ID}_b)}, (h_2 g^{-r_{\mathsf{ID}_b,2}})^{1/(\alpha - \mathsf{ID}_b)} (h_3 g^{-r_{\mathsf{ID}_b,3}\beta})^{1/(\alpha - \mathsf{ID}_b)}) v^{r_{\mathsf{ID}_b,2} + r_{\mathsf{ID}_b,3}\beta}$
$= e(g^{s(\alpha - \mathsf{ID}_b)}, (h_2 h_3^{\beta})^{1/(\alpha - \mathsf{ID}_b)}) g^{-(r_{\mathsf{ID}_b,2} + r_{\mathsf{ID}_b,3}\beta)/(\alpha - \mathsf{ID}_b)} e(g, g)^{s(r_{\mathsf{ID}_b,2} + r_{\mathsf{ID}_b,3}\beta)}$
$= e(g^{s(\alpha - \mathsf{ID}_b)}, (h_2 h_3^{\beta})^{1/(\alpha - \mathsf{ID}_b)}) = e(g^s, (h_2 h_3^{\beta})) = e(g, h_2)^s e(g, h_3)^{s\beta}$.

As shown above, a valid challenge ciphertext is made. Therefore the simulator can decrypt it by using the appropriate private key.

Next, in the case that Z is random, even if the challenge ciphertext is random, the simulator can decrypt it by using the appropriate private key. Decryption is computed as below.

$M_c = w \cdot e(u, h_{\mathsf{ID}_b,1}) v^{r_{\mathsf{ID}_b,1}} = M_c/e(g^s, h_1 g^{-f_1(\mathsf{ID}_b)}) v^{r_{\mathsf{ID}_b,1}} \cdot e(g'^{f_2'(\alpha) - f_2'(\mathsf{ID}_b)}, g^{\frac{(f_1(\alpha) - f_1(\mathsf{ID}_b))}{(\alpha - \mathsf{ID}_b)}})$.

$v^{r_{\mathsf{ID}_b,1}} = M_c/e(g, h_1)^s e(g, g)^{-sf_1(\mathsf{ID}_b)} \cdot e(g'^{\frac{f_2'(\alpha) - f_2'(\mathsf{ID}_b)}{(\alpha - \mathsf{ID}_b)}}, g^{(f_1(\alpha) - f_1(\mathsf{ID}_b))}) = M_c/e(g, h_1)^s e(g, g)^{-sf_1(\mathsf{ID}_b)} \cdot e(g^s, g^{f_1(\alpha)} g^{-f_1(\mathsf{ID}_b)})$.
$= M_c/e(g, h_1)^s e(g, g)^{-sf_1(\mathsf{ID}_b)} \cdot e(g^s, g^{f_1(\alpha)}) \cdot e(g^s, g^{-f_1(\mathsf{ID}_b)}) = M_c/e(g, h_1)^s \cdot e(g, h_1)^s = M_c$.

As shown above, even if the challenge ciphertext is random, the simulator can decrypt it by using the appropriate private key. The reason is that v including Z is canceled out in the decryption process. But the adversary cannot decrypt it without negligible probability (We can easily see that in this case the challenge ciphertext is generated by using Encryption algorithm, then y will pass the Decrypt Check).

The challenge ciphertext is appropriately distributed

We want to show that the challenge ciphertext is appropriately distributed from $\mathcal{A}$'s view. The challenge ciphertext consists of three elements u, v, w, and y. Since $\log_g g'$ is uniformly random, s is uniformly random. And (u, v, w, y) is uniformly random because it is made by using s. Therefore the challenge ciphertext is appropriately distributed.

$\mathcal{P}_{ABDHE}$ and $\mathcal{R}_{ABDHE}$ distributions

As mentioned in the security proof of Theorem 1, we have an algorithm $\mathcal{B}$ that outputting (b, c) has advantage ϵ in solving truncated decision q-ABDHE if

$$\epsilon \leq |Pr[\mathcal{B} \text{ outputs } 1|Z \text{ is real}] - Pr[\mathcal{B} \text{ outputs } 1|Z \text{ is random}]|. \quad (12.9)$$

We refer to the distribution on the left as $\mathcal{P}_{ABDHE}$ and the distribution on the right as $\mathcal{R}_{ABDHE}$.

Now, since the time-complexity analysis is as in the proof of Theorem 1, Theorem 2 follows from the following lemmas.

Lemma 1 When $\mathcal{B}$'s input is sampled according to $\mathcal{P}_{ABDHE}$, the joint distribution of $\mathcal{A}$'s view and the bits (b, c) is indistinguishable from that in the actual construction, except with probability $2q_C/p$.

Proof of Lemma 1 When $\mathcal{B}$'s input is sampled according to $\mathcal{P}_{ABDHE}$, $\mathcal{B}$'s simulation appears perfect to $\mathcal{A}$ if $\mathcal{A}$ makes key generation queries only, as in the proof of Theorem 1. $\mathcal{B}$'s simulation still appears perfect if $\mathcal{A}$ makes decryption queries only on identities for which it queries the private key, since $\mathcal{B}$'s responses give $\mathcal{A}$ no additional information. Furthermore, querying well-formed ciphertexts to the decryption oracle does not help $\mathcal{A}$ distinguish between the simulation and the actual construction, since by the correctness of Decrypt, well-formed ciphertexts will be accepted in either case. Finally, querying a non-well-formed ciphertext (u', v', w', y') (unaccepted ciphertexts) for ID will be divided into two cases:

1. $v' = e(u', g)^{1/(\alpha - \text{ID})}$: it does not help $\mathcal{A}$ distinguish, since this ciphertext will fail the *Decrypt* check (w' can be correct for some m, but y' makes the *Decrypt* check fail).

2. $v' \neq e(u', g)^{1/(\alpha - \text{ID})}$: in this case, we say the ciphertext is invalid and accepted with negligible probability as in following claim.

Claim 1 *The decryption oracle, in the simulation and in the actual construction, rejects all invalid ciphertexts under identities not queried by $\mathcal{A}$, except with probability q_C/p.*

Let (u', v', w', y') for ID be "invalid" ciphertext queried by $\mathcal{A}$ for ID, an unqueried identity. Let $\{(r_{\mathsf{ID},i}, h_{\mathsf{ID},i}) : i \in \{1,2,3\}\}$ be $\mathcal{B}$'s private key for ID. Let $a_{u'} = log_g(u')$, $a_{v'} = log_{e(g,g)}(v')$, and $a_{y'} = log_{e(g,g)}(y')$. For (u', v', w', y') to be accepted, we must have

$$y' = e(u', h_{\mathsf{ID},2}h_{\mathsf{ID},3}{}^{\beta'})v'^{r_{\mathsf{ID},2}+r_{\mathsf{ID},3}\beta'} \tag{12.10}$$

with $\beta' = H(u', v', w')$. That is,

$$a_{y'} = a_{u'}(log_g h_{\mathsf{ID},2} + \beta' log_g h_{\mathsf{ID},3}) + a_{v'}(r_{\mathsf{ID},2} + \beta' r_{\mathsf{ID},3}). \tag{12.11}$$

To compute the probability that $\mathcal{A}$ can generate such a y', we must consider the distribution of $\{(r_{\mathsf{ID},i}, h_{\mathsf{ID},i}) : i \in \{2,3\}\}$ from $\mathcal{A}$'s view (since $h_{\mathsf{ID},i}$ is computed from $r_{\mathsf{ID},i}$ and h_i; and $r_{\mathsf{ID},i}$ is set by $\mathcal{B}$).
First, from the followings by construction of the private key $h_{\mathsf{ID},i} = (h_i g^{-r_{\mathsf{ID},i}})^{1/(\alpha-\mathsf{ID})}$, $\mathcal{A}$ knows that

$$log_g h_1 = (\alpha - \mathsf{ID})log_g h_{\mathsf{ID},1} + r_{\mathsf{ID},1}, \tag{12.12}$$

$$log_g h_2 = (\alpha - \mathsf{ID})log_g h_{\mathsf{ID},2} + r_{\mathsf{ID},2}, \tag{12.13}$$

$$log_g h_3 = (\alpha - \mathsf{ID})log_g h_{\mathsf{ID},3} + r_{\mathsf{ID},3}. \tag{12.14}$$

Putting (12.13), (12.14) into (12.11), we get
$a_{y'} = a_{u'}(log_g(h_{\mathsf{ID},2} + \beta' log_g(h_{\mathsf{ID},3})) + a_{v'}(r_{\mathsf{ID},2} + r_{\mathsf{ID},3}\beta') = a_{u'}(\frac{log_g h_2 - r_{\mathsf{ID}_b,2}}{\alpha-\mathsf{ID}} + \frac{log_g h_3 - r_{\mathsf{ID}_b,3}}{\alpha-\mathsf{ID}}\beta') + a_{v'}(r_{\mathsf{ID},2} + r_{\mathsf{ID},3}\beta')$
$= \frac{a_{u'}}{\alpha-\mathsf{ID}}(log_g h_2 + log_g h_3) - \frac{a_{u'}}{\alpha-\mathsf{ID}}(r_{\mathsf{ID},2} + r_{\mathsf{ID},3}\beta') + a_{v'}(r_{\mathsf{ID},2} + r_{\mathsf{ID},3}\beta').$
That is,

$$a_{y'} = (a_{u'}/(\alpha-\mathsf{ID}))(log_g h_2 + \beta' log_g h_3) + (a_{v'} - a_{u'}/(\alpha-\mathsf{ID}))(r_{\mathsf{ID},2} + \beta' r_{\mathsf{ID},3}). \tag{12.15}$$

Note that $a_{v'} - a_{u'}/(\alpha - \mathsf{ID}) \neq 0$ since the ciphertext is invalid (i.e., since $v' \neq e(u', g)^{1/(\alpha-\mathsf{ID})}$, $a_{v'} \neq a_{u'}/(\alpha - \mathsf{ID})$). Let $z' = a_{v'} - a_{u'}/(\alpha - \mathsf{ID})$.

In the actual construction, the values of $r_{\mathsf{ID},i}$ for $i \in \{2,3\}$ are chosen independently for different identities; however, this is not true in the simulation. Since $f_i(\mathsf{ID}) = r_{\mathsf{ID},i}$, $\mathcal{A}$ could conceivably gain information regarding $(r_{\mathsf{ID},2}, r_{\mathsf{ID},3})$ from its information regarding $(f_2(x), f_3(x))$, which includes the evaluations of $(f_2(x), f_3(x))$ at α (from the public key components (h_2, h_3)) and at $q_{\mathsf{ID}} = q - 2$ identities (from its key generation queries). As seen from Equation (5), we can get information from $(r_{\mathsf{ID},2} + \beta' r_{\mathsf{ID},3})$, i.e., $(f_2(x) + \beta' f_3(x))$. Since $f_i(x)$ is a random polynomial of degree q, then we can write as

$$f_2(x_k) = f_{2,0}x_k{}^0 + f_{2,1}x_k{}^1 + \cdots + f_{2,q}x_k{}^q, \tag{12.16}$$

$$f_3(x_k) = f_{3,0}x_k{}^0 + f_{3,1}x_k{}^1 + \cdots + f_{3,q}x_k{}^q. \tag{12.17}$$

Therefore

$$(f_2(x_k) + \beta' f_3(x_k)) = f_{2,0}x_k{}^0 + f_{2,1}x_k{}^1 + \cdots + f_{2,q}x_k{}^q$$
$$+ \beta'(f_{3,0}x_k{}^0 + f_{3,1}x_k{}^1 + \cdots + f_{3,q}x_k{}^q), \qquad (12.18)$$

where $f_{i,j}$ is the coefficient of x^j in $f_i(x)$, x_k is the k-th identity queried by $\mathcal{A}$ to the key generation oracle, and $x_{q-1} = \alpha$. We may represent the knowledge gained from these evaluations as a matrix product as follows.

$$[f_{2,0}, f_{2,1}, \ldots, f_{2,q}, f_{3,0}, f_{3,1}, \ldots, f_{3,q}] \begin{bmatrix} 1 & 1 & \cdots & 1 & 0 & 0 & \cdots & 0 \\ x_1 & x_2 & \cdots & x_{q-1} & 0 & 0 & \cdots & 0 \\ \vdots & \vdots & & \vdots & \vdots & \vdots & & \vdots \\ x_1^q & x_2^q & \cdots & x_{q-1}^q & 0 & 0 & \cdots & 0 \\ 0 & 0 & \cdots & 0 & 1 & 1 & \cdots & 1 \\ 0 & 0 & \cdots & 0 & x_1 & x_2 & \cdots & x_{q-1} \\ \vdots & \vdots & \vdots & \vdots & \vdots & \vdots & \vdots & \vdots \\ 0 & 0 & \cdots & 0 & x_1^q & x_2^q & \cdots & x_{q-1}^q \end{bmatrix}$$

Let $\mathbf{f}$ denote vector on the left and V denote the matrix on the right. Since $f_i(x)$ is a random polynomial of degree q, then the number of values in $\mathbf{f}$ corresponds to the number of rows in V are $2(q+1)$; and if $\mathcal{A}$ makes $q_{\mathsf{ID}} = q - 2$ queries in key generation queries along with α, then we have the number of columns in V is $2(q-1)$. Note that V contains two $(q+1) \times (q-1)$ Vandermonde matrices; its columns are linearly independent. From $\mathcal{A}$'s view, since V has four more rows than columns, the solution space for $\mathbf{f}$ is four-dimensional [4].

Let γ_{ID} denote the vector $(1, ID, \ldots, ID^q)$. When we re-phrase Equation (5) in terms of the simulator's private key vector $\mathbf{f}$, we obtain

$$a_{y'} = public\ terms\ [5] + z'(\mathbf{f} \cdot \gamma_{\mathsf{ID}} || \beta' \gamma_{\mathsf{ID}}), \qquad (12.19)$$

where "$\cdot$" denote the dot product (e.g., $[a, b] \cdot [c, d] = (ac + bd)$) and $\gamma_{\mathsf{ID}} || \beta' \gamma_{\mathsf{ID}}$ denotes the $2q + 2$ - dimensional vector formed by concatenating the coefficients of γ_{ID} and $\beta' \gamma_{\mathsf{ID}}$ (we easily see that $\gamma_{\mathsf{ID}} || \beta' \gamma_{\mathsf{ID}}$ is linearly independent).

We have $\mathcal{A}$ query invalid ciphertexts on the same ID. If the invalid ciphertext C_1 is the first ciphertext queried by $\mathcal{A}$ for ID, then C_1 can be accepted with probability at most $1/p$ (since $\mathsf{ID} \in \mathbb{Z}_p$ and there is only $1/p$ chance that $\mathbf{f}$ is contained in the 3-dimensional solution space (p^3 points) defined by Equation (12.15) and the columns of V, given that $\mathbf{f}$ is contained in the

---

[4] Since we have $2q + 2$ variables while the number of equation is only $2q - 2$, then solution space is four-dimensional.

[5] Since h_2, h_3 are included in system parameters. Although α is secret, but g^α is known.

4-dimensional solution space (p^4 points) defined by the columns of V)[6]. If the invalid ciphertext C_2 is the second ciphertext queried by $\mathcal{A}$ for ID, then C_2 can be accepted with probability at most $1/(p-1)$. So, the i-th invalid ciphertext C_i queried for ID can be accepted with probability at most $1/(p-i+1)$. Therefore $\mathcal{A}$'s i-th is rejected at least $1 - 1/(p-i+1)$. Since $\mathcal{A}$ makes at most q_C queries, we have probability that $\mathcal{A}$'s q_C invalid ciphertexts are all rejected at least

$$(1 - \frac{1}{p})(1 - \frac{1}{p-1}) \ldots (1 - \frac{1}{p - q_c + 1}) = 1 - \frac{q_C}{q}. \qquad (12.20)$$

Thus $\mathcal{A}$'s invalid ciphertexts are all rejected, except with probability at most $\frac{q_C}{q}$. The actual construction is the same. So in this case, we have the probability of the joint distribution $\mathcal{A}$'s invalid ciphertexts are all rejected in the simulation and in the actual construction as

$$(1 - \frac{q_C}{q})(1 - \frac{q_C}{q}) = 1 - \frac{2q_C}{q} + \frac{q_C^2}{q^2} > 1 - \frac{2q_C}{q}. \qquad (12.21)$$

That is, $\mathcal{A}$ cannot distinguish the simulator and the actual construction, except with the probability $\frac{2q_C}{q}$.

Lemma 2 When $\mathcal{B}$'s input is sampled according to $\mathcal{R}_{ABDHE}$, the distribution of the bits (b, c) is independent from the adversary's view, except with probability $2q_C/p$.

Proof of Lemma 2 In the case $\mathcal{B}$'s input is sampled according to $\mathcal{R}_{ABDHE}$, since valid ciphertext is normally decrypted, we should prove all invalid ciphertexts will be rejected, except with negligible probability. Then, in the case the decryption oracle rejects all invalid ciphertexts, guessing (b, c) should be independent from $\mathcal{A}$'s view as in Construction 1. The Lemma 2 follows from the following claims.

Claim 2 *The decryption oracle rejects all invalid ciphertexts, except with probability q_C/p.*

Claim 3 *If the decryption oracle rejects all invalid ciphertexts, then $\mathcal{A}$ has advantage at most q_C/p in guessing the bits (b, c).*

Let $a_u = log_g(u)$, $a_v = log_{e(g,g)}(v)$ and $a_y = log_{e(g,g)}(y)$ for challenge ciphertext $C = (u, v, w, y)$ on (ID_b, M_c). Since (u, v, w, y) is generated by sampling from $\mathcal{R}_{ABDHE}$ in this case, (a_u, a_v) is a uniformly random element of $\mathbb{Z}_p \times \mathbb{Z}_p$ in $\mathcal{A}$'s view. From $M_c = w \cdot e(u, h_{\mathsf{ID}_b, 1})v^{r_{\mathsf{ID}_b, 1}}$ and Equations 12.12–12.14, $\mathcal{A}$ obtains the following equation

---

[6]Since the line (1-dimensional) intersects the plane (2-dimensional) at a point, the plane intersects the 3-dimensional space in a line and the 3-dimensional space intersects the 4-dimensional space in a plane.

$$log_{e(g,g)}(M_c/w) = (a_u/(\alpha - \mathsf{ID}))logh_1 + (a_v - a_u/(\alpha - \mathsf{ID}))r_{\mathsf{ID}_b,1}{}^7. \quad (12.22)$$

Since $y = e(u, h_{\mathsf{ID},2}h_{\mathsf{ID},3}{}^{\beta})v^{r_{\mathsf{ID},2}+r_{\mathsf{ID},3}\beta}$, then

$$a_y = (a_u/(\alpha - \mathsf{ID}))(log_g h_2 + \beta log_g h_3) + (a_v - a_u/(\alpha - \mathsf{ID}))(r_{\mathsf{ID}_b,2} + r_{\mathsf{ID}_b,3}), \quad (12.23)$$

where $\beta = H(u, v, w)$.

Regarding Claim 2, suppose that $\mathcal{A}$ submits an invalid ciphertext (u', v', w', y') for unqueried identity ID, where $(u', v', w', y', \mathsf{ID}) \neq (u, v, w, y, \mathsf{ID}_b)$. Let $\beta' = H(u', v', w')$. There are three cases to consider:

1. $(u', v', w') = (u, v, w)$ and $\beta' = \beta$:
   If $\mathsf{ID} = \mathsf{ID}_b$, but $y \neq y'$, then the ciphertext will certainly rejected. If $\mathsf{ID} \neq \mathsf{ID}_b$, $\mathcal{A}$ must generate a y' that satisfies Equation (7) for the invalid ciphertext to be accepted. However, in this case, the columns of V, $\gamma_{\mathsf{ID}}||\beta\gamma_{\mathsf{ID}}$, $\gamma_{\mathsf{ID}_b}||\beta\gamma_{\mathsf{ID}_b}$, are linearly independent, implying that $\mathcal{A}$ cannot generate solution for y', except with probability at most $1/(p - i + 1)$. Why?[8]. Then, $\mathcal{A}$'s invalid ciphertext are all rejected, except with probability at least q_C/p.

2. $(u', v', w') \neq (u, v, w)$ and $\beta' = \beta$:
   This violates the one-wayness of the hash function H.

3. $(u', v', w') \neq (u, v, w)$ and $\beta' \neq \beta$:
   In this case $\mathcal{A}$ must generate, for some ID, y' that satisfies Equation (7). $\mathcal{A}$ can do this with only negligible probability when $\mathsf{ID} \neq \mathsf{ID}_b$. If $\mathsf{ID} = \mathsf{ID}_b$, then $\gamma_{\mathsf{ID}}||\beta'\gamma_{\mathsf{ID}}$ and $\gamma_{\mathsf{ID}_b}||\beta\gamma_{\mathsf{ID}_b}$ can generate $\gamma_{\mathsf{ID}_b}||0^{q+1}$ and $0^{q+1}||\gamma_{\mathsf{ID}_b}$ since $\beta \neq \beta'$. These vectors are linearly independent to each other and the columns of V. Thus, similar to the first case, $\mathcal{A}$'s invalid ciphertext are all rejected, except with probability at least q_C/p.

Therefore, since these cases cannot happen at the same time, the probability that $\mathcal{A}$ submits an invalid ciphertext and it can be accepted is at least q_C/p.

Regarding Claim 3, if no invalid ciphertexts are accepted, then $\mathcal{B}$'s responses to decryption queries leak no information about $r_{\mathsf{ID}_b,1}$. Thus the distribution of M_c/w – conditioning on (b, c) and everything in $\mathcal{A}$'s view other than w- is uniform. M_c/w serves as a perfect one-time pad; w is uniformly

---

[7] $log_{e(g,g)}(M_c/w) = log_{e(g,g)}[e(u, h_{\mathsf{ID}_b,1})v^{r_{\mathsf{ID}_b,1}}] = (log_g(u)log_g(h_{\mathsf{ID}_b,1})) + log_{e(g,g)}(v^{r_{\mathsf{ID}_b,1}}) = \frac{a_u}{\alpha - \mathsf{ID}}(log_g h_1 - r_{\mathsf{ID}_b,1}) + r_{\mathsf{ID}_b,1}a_v = (a_u/(\alpha - \mathsf{ID}))log h_1 + (a_v - a_u/(\alpha - \mathsf{ID}))r_{\mathsf{ID}_b,1}$

[8] In order to generate y', the adversary can get information from $\mathbf{f}$ which has solution space defined by the columns of V and Equation (12.15) or Equation (12.19). By similar way in Claim 1, we can get the probability is at most $1/(p - i + 1)$.

random and independent, and c is independent of $\mathcal{A}$'s view.

The only part of the ciphertext that can reveal information about b is y, since $\mathcal{A}$ views (u, v, w) as a uniformly random and independent element of $\mathbb{G} \times \mathbb{G}_T \times \mathbb{G}_T$. The $2q - 2$ equations corresponding to the columns of V intersecting Equation (9) is at least three-dimensional solution space. $\mathcal{A}$ views $\mathbf{f}$ as being contained in one of two three-dimensional space, since b has two possible values. Each of $\mathcal{A}$'s invalid ciphertext queries punctures each of these three-dimensional space in a plane, removing each of the two planes from consideration as containing $\mathbf{f}$. Since no valid ciphertext is accepted, each three-dimensional space is left with at least $p^3 - q_C p^2$ (out of p^3) candidates. Thus, $\mathcal{A}$ cannot distinguish b, except with probability at most q_C/p.

Conclusion of Proof of Lemma 2 From Claim 2, we have probability that decryption oracle rejects all invalid ciphertexts is at least $(1 - q_C/p)$. From Claim 3, in the case decryption oracle rejects all invalid ciphertext, $\mathcal{A}$ cannot guess (b, c) with probability $(1 - q_C/p)$. So, when $\mathcal{B}$'s input is sampled according to $\mathcal{R}_{ABDHE}$, the probability $\mathcal{B}$ cannot guess (b, c) is at least

$$(1 - q_C/p)(1 - q_C/p) > 1 - 2q_C/p. \tag{12.24}$$

Therefore, the probability $\mathcal{B}$ can guess (b, c) correctly in this case is at most $2q_C/p$.

Conclusion of Proof of Theorem 2 We have $Pr[X_0] + 2q_C/p = \epsilon' + \frac{1}{4}$ and $Pr[X_1] = 2q_C/p + \frac{1}{4}$. Thus, as in security proof of Theorem 1, $\mathcal{B}$'s advantage is

$$\epsilon = Pr[X_0] - Pr[X_1] = \epsilon' + 1/4 - 2q_C/p - (2q_C/p + 1/4) = \epsilon' - 4q_C/p. \tag{12.25}$$

Time complexity is as in Theorem 1.
This concludes the proof of Theorem 2. $\square$

Exercises

12.1 The columns of $V, \gamma \| \beta \gamma_{ID}, \gamma_{ID_b} \| \beta \gamma_{ID_b}$ are linearly independent, implying that the adversary $\mathcal{A}$ cannot generate solution for y', except with probability at most $\frac{1}{(p-i+1)}$. Why?

12.2 The distribution of M_c/w – conditioning on (b, c) and everything in $\mathcal{A}$'s view other than w – is uniform. Why?

13

Identity-Based Encryption (3)

CONTENTS

This chapter provides the details of the Waters' identity based encryption scheme. The drawbacks from the Gentry's scheme that involves using the non-static assumptions for the security proofs has been replaced by using the static assumptions in the standard model through hybrid games. The problems of the non-static assumptions are stated and then the hybrid proof technique is discussed. The next part of the chapter provides the preliminaries including the security model and hardness assumptions for the Waters' IBE scheme. Waters' scheme uses two static hardness assumptions: Decisional bilinear Diffie-Hellman and decisional linear. The next portion of the chapter gives the dual system encryption followed by the Waters' IBE. The methodology proposed is called dual system encryption allows to prove that an IBE is fully secured based on the static assumptions without random oracle. This is further explained using the formal construction and the security proof using the reduction algorithm.

13.1   Overview

Previously we pointed out the problems of the partitioning paradigm and introduced the Gentry's proof methodology to resolve them. However, since the Gentry's proof methodology is based on non-static assumptions, it also has problems. This time we explain the Waters' proof methodology called *Dual System Encryption* to present fully secure solutions based on static assumptions in the standard model through hybrid games.

Why is a non-static assumption problematic?

The instances of typical standard assumptions like DDH and CDH always have fixed sizes. As a result, when we use proof by reduction, the assumptions are only related to security parameters regardless of some system parameters (e.g., q of q-bilinear Diffie-Hellman exponent problem) or oracle queries (e.g., the number of queries).

On the other hand, non-static assumptions do not have fixed sizes and are related to some system parameters or oracle queries. It means that the instance of the assumption used in the proof is dependent on the number of queries made by an adversary, q, for example. The problem here is, since the instance of non-static assumptions is proportional to q; as a result, non-static assumptions require more instances and stronger assumptions, which is contrary to standard assumptions, where the number of group elements used as public parameters in the real scheme is fixed. Generally, since it means that the strongest assumption should be selected among many assumptions, non-static assumptions are not desirable. Also, it means that group elements as public parameters have to be made by using polynomial f of degree q. This may just cause a substantial overhead.

What is a hybrid argument (or proof, game)?

The natural way of security proof goes as follows. First, assume two oracles or functions, Π_0 and Π_1, and then show that a distinguisher $\mathcal{D}$, probabilistic polynomial time (PPT) algorithm, can distinguish Π_0 and Π_1 with at most negligible probability as

$$\left| Pr\left[\mathcal{D}^{\Pi_0} = 1 \right] - Pr\left[\mathcal{D}^{\Pi_1} = 1 \right] \right| \leq negligible. \qquad (13.1)$$

However, if we cannot reduce a scheme by using only one assumption or theorem, then how can we do? Hybrid argument can help us reduce by using the above procedure multiple times.

The hybrid argument technique is as follows:

1. Define the number of hybrid oracles or functions as polynomial size. In detail, if $q(n)$ is a polynomial function in some security parameter, then we have $q(n) + 1$ hybrid oracles or functions, $(H_0, \cdots, H_{q(n)})$, where $H_0 = \Pi_0$ and $H_{q(n)} = \Pi_1$. Here, hybrid oracles or functions located between Π_0 and Π_1, $(H_1, \cdots, H_{q(n)-1})$, must be indistinguishably selected.

2. Following triangle inequality, specify the following inequality

$$\left|Pr\left[\mathcal{D}^{\Pi_0}=1\right]-Pr\left[\mathcal{D}^{\Pi_1}=1\right]\right|\leq\sum_{i=1}^{q(n)}\left|Pr\left[\mathcal{D}^{H_i}\right]-Pr\left[\mathcal{D}^{H_{i-1}}\right]\right|.$$

(13.2)

This can be shown as in Figure 13.1.

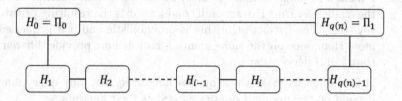

FIGURE 13.1
Hybrid game.

3. For each $i = \{1, 2, \cdots, q(n)\}$, by using reduction or probabilistic argument, show that all PPT distinguishers $\mathcal{D}$ cannot distinguish H_{i-1} and H_i as

$$\left|Pr\left[\mathcal{D}^{H_i}\right]-Pr\left[\mathcal{D}^{H_{i-1}}\right]\right|=negligible.$$

(13.3)

Here, we can proceed the proof by using the same or different arguments at each step.

4. Finally, show that the below holds by using the two steps above as

$$\left|Pr\left[\mathcal{D}^{\Pi_0}=1\right]-Pr\left[\mathcal{D}^{\Pi_1}=1\right]\right|\leq\sum_{i=1}^{q(n)}\left|Pr\left[\mathcal{D}^{H_i}\right]-Pr\left[\mathcal{D}^{H_{i-1}}\right]\right|$$

(13.4)

$$=\sum_{i=1}^{q(n)}negligible=q(n)\times negligible=negligible,$$

where $q(n)$ is a polynomial function in n.

This completes the proof.

13.2 Preliminaries

This section provides preliminaries including the security model and hardness assumptions for the Waters' IBE scheme.

13.2.1   Security Model

IND-ID-CPA game for an IBE scheme

1. **Setup** Given the security parameter k, the challenger runs the Setup algorithm of the IBE. It provides $\mathcal{A}$ with the system parameters params while keeping the master key MSK to itself.

2. **Phase I** $\mathcal{A}$ makes a finite number of key-extraction queries. Then the challenger runs Extract on ID and forwards the resulting private key to $\mathcal{A}$. The Extract algorithm is probabilistic and if it is queried more than once on the same identity, then it may provide different (but valid) decryption keys.

   $\mathcal{A}$ is allowed to make these queries *adaptively*, i.e., any query may depend on the previous queries as well as their answers.

3. **Challenge** $\mathcal{A}$ outputs two equal length messages M_0, M_1, and a challenge identity ID^* must not have appeared in any key generation query in Phase I. The simulator selects a random bit $\beta \in \{0,1\}$, and responds with CT^* on input (ID^*, M_β, params).

4. **Phase II** $\mathcal{A}$ issues additional queries just like Phase I, except that the adversary may not request a private key for ID^*. The challenger responds as in Phase I.

5. **Guess** $\mathcal{A}$ outputs its guess β' of β.

Definition 1 *The advantage of $\mathcal{A}$ in attacking the IBE scheme Π is defined as*

$$\mathsf{Adv}_{\mathcal{A},\Pi} = |Pr[(\beta = \beta')] - 1/2|. \qquad (13.5)$$

Definition 2 *An IBE scheme Π is said to be (t, ϵ, q)-secure against adaptive chosen ciphertext attack if for all polynomial t-time adversaries $\mathcal{A}$ that makes at most q secret-key queries,*

$$\mathsf{Adv}_{\mathcal{A},\Pi} \geq \epsilon. \qquad (13.6)$$

13.2.2   Hardness Assumptions

For proving his scheme, Waters uses two static hardness assumptions.

Decisional bilinear Diffie-Hellman (DBDH) assumption

Let $\mathbb{G}$ and $\mathbb{G}_T$ be two groups of prime order p, where the size of p is a function of the security parameters. Let $e \colon \mathbb{G} \times \mathbb{G} \to \mathbb{G}_T$ be a bilinear map and let g be a generator of $\mathbb{G}$.

Given $(g, g^{c_1}, g^{c_2}, g^{c_3}, T) \in \mathbb{G}^4 \times \mathbb{G}_T$ for some $c_1, c_2, c_3 \in \mathbb{Z}_p$, it must remain hard to distinguish $T = e(g, g)^{c_1 c_2 c_3} \in \mathbb{G}_T$ from a random element in $\mathbb{G}_T$.

An algorithm $\mathcal{B}$ that outputs $z \in \{0, 1\}$ has advantage ϵ_{dbdh} in solving the decisional BDH problem in $\mathbb{G}$ if

$$|Pr\left[\mathcal{B}(g, g^{c_1}, g^{c_2}, g^{c_3}, T = e(g,g)^{c_1 c_2 c_3}) = 0\right] - Pr\left[\mathcal{B}(g, g^{c_1}, g^{c_2}, g^{c_3}, T = R) = 0\right]|$$

$$\geq \epsilon_{dbdh}.$$

Definition 3 *We say that* **the decisional BDH assumption holds** *if no polytime algorithm has a non-negligible advantage in solving the decisional BDH problem.*

Decisional linear (DLin) assumption

Let $\mathbb{G}$ and $\mathbb{G}_T$ be two groups of prime order p, where the size of p is a function of the security parameters. Let $e \colon \mathbb{G} \times \mathbb{G} \to \mathbb{G}_T$ be a bilinear map and let g, f, ν, be random generators of $\mathbb{G}$.

Given $(g, f, \nu, g^{c_1}, f^{c_2}, T) \in \mathbb{G}^6$ for some $c_1, c_2 \in \mathbb{Z}_p$, it must remain hard to distinguish $T = \nu^{c_1 + c_2} \in \mathbb{G}$ from a random element in $\mathbb{G}$.

An algorithm $\mathcal{B}$ that outputs $z \in \{0, 1\}$ has advantage ϵ_{dlin} in solving the decisional linear problem in $\mathbb{G}$ if

$$\left| Pr\left[\mathcal{B}(g, f, \nu, g^{c_1}, f^{c_2}, T = \nu^{c_1 + c_2}) = 0\right] - Pr\left[\mathcal{B}(g, f, \nu, g^{c_1}, f^{c_2}, T = R) = 0\right]\right|$$

$$\geq \epsilon_{dlin}.$$

Definition 4 *We say that* **the decisional linear assumption holds** *if no polytime algorithm has a non-negligible advantage in solving the decisional linear problem.*

13.3 Dual System Encryption

In general, it is not easy to prove that a scheme is fully (or adaptively) secure. The reason behind this is, in the reduction the simulator should be able to create the secret key for all identities, which do not decrypt the challenge ciphertext. However, it is hard to achieve this because the secret key(s) and the challenge ciphertext have some relationship. So, Waters removes the relationship between them by slightly modifying the games at each step using the hybrid argument. Eventually, in the last game, which removes the relationship, even if the challenge ciphertext is changed to random, the simulation still works. Waters proceeds the hybrid argument as in Figure 13.2

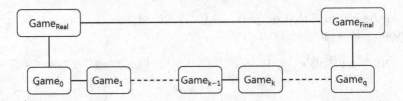

FIGURE 13.2
Waters' hybrid game.

In Figure 13.2, $Game_{Real}$ means a real scheme, and $Game_{Final}$ means an ideal scheme that the adversary's advantage is 0. Also, Waters makes secret key and ciphertext generation algorithms to proceed the proof, where they generate two types (or forms) of secret keys and ciphertexts, respectively. The first type called *normal* is generally used in IBE system. The second type called *semi-functional* is only used in the proof. A normal secret key can decrypt all ciphertexts, normal or semi-functional. A semi-functional secret key can decrypt normal ciphertexts only. A semi-functional secret key cannot decrypt semi-functional ciphertexts. Let us apply these to hybrid argument proof.

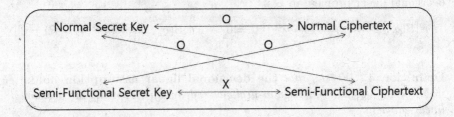

FIGURE 13.3
Comparison of normal and semi-functional forms.

Intuition We define a sequence of games arguing that an attacker cannot distinguish one game from the next. The first game will be the real security game in which the challenge ciphertext and all secret keys are distributed normally. Next we switch our normal challenge ciphertext with a semi-functional one. We argue that no adversary can detect this (under our complexity assumption) since all secret keys given can decrypt the challenge ciphertext regardless of whether it is normal or semi-functional. In the next series of games, we change the secret keys in one game at a time from normal to semi-functional, again arguing indistinguishability. In both the above proof arguments, our reduction algorithm will be able to provide secret keys for any identity and use any identity as a challenge identity – eliminating the need to worry about an abort condition. By repeating the above processes, we change all secret key and the challenge ciphertext to semi-functional. Finally, we end up in a game where the challenge ciphertext is random, and all secret keys are semi-functional. At this point, proving security is straightforward since the challenge ciphertext becomes random.

Let us detail the above intuition in concrete . In $Game_{Real}$, the simulator generates normal secret keys and normal challenge ciphertext. In $Game_0$, the simulator generates normal secret keys and semi-functional challenge ciphertext. And in $Game_i$, the simulator generates semi-functional secret keys for j-th identity, normal secret keys for j'-th identity and semi-functional challenge ciphertext, where $i \in \{0, \cdots, q\}$, $j \in \{0, \cdots, i\}$, and $j' \in \{i+1, \cdots, q\}$. In $Game_q$, the simulator generates semi-functional secret keys and semi-functional challenge ciphertext. Lastly, in $Game_{Final}$, the simulator generates semi-functional secret keys and random challenge ciphertext.

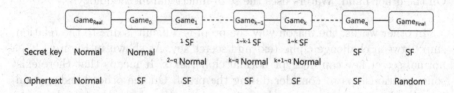

FIGURE 13.4
Change of secret keys and ciphertexts in Waters' hybrid game.

As shown in Figure 13.4, $Game_{Real}$ and $Game_0$ are the same except with a little bit difference internally. It is identically applied among other $Game$s. And the probability distinguishing between $Game_{Real}$ and $Game_0$ is $Game_{Real}Adv_{\mathcal{A}} - Game_0Adv_{\mathcal{A}} = \epsilon_1$. The sum of all games' advantages is as follows.

$$Game_{Real}Adv_{\mathcal{A}} - Game_0Adv_{\mathcal{A}} + \sum_{i=1}^{q}(Game_{i-1}Adv_{\mathcal{A}} - Game_iAdv_{\mathcal{A}})+$$

$$Game_qAdv_{\mathcal{A}} - Game_{Final}Adv_{\mathcal{A}}$$

$$= Game_{Real}Adv_{\mathcal{A}} - Game_{Final}Adv_{\mathcal{A}} = \sum_{i=1}^{q+2} \epsilon_i$$

. The probability that we want to obtain is

$$Game_{Real}Adv_{\mathcal{A}} = \sum_{i=1}^{q+2} \epsilon_i + Game_{Final}Adv_{\mathcal{A}} = \sum_{i=1}^{q+2} \epsilon_i. \qquad (13.7)$$

Now, we have to show that $Game_{Real}Adv_{\mathcal{A}}$ is negligible. To show that each ϵ_i is small than ϵ, we embed T_0 in $Game_{Real}$ and T_1 in $Game_0$. To distinguish the two games, the adversary must solve the aforementioned assumption. Therefore, $|Game_{Real}Adv_{\mathcal{A}} - Game_0 Adv_{\mathcal{A}}|$ becomes the advantage of the assumption. Like this, the same applies to all the subsequent games. In dual system, in the cases from $Game_1$ to $Game_q$, if T_0 is embedded then the secret key is normal, and if T_1 is embedded then the secret key is semi-functional. On the other hand, in the cases of $Game_q$ and $Game_{Final}$, if T_0 is embedded then the challenge ciphertext is semi-functional, and if T_1 is embedded then the challenge ciphertext is random.

Now, we only have to show the proof in $Game_{Final}$. However, when the session key changes to random, a problem occurs because the session key has some relationship with both challenge ciphertext and secret key. Thus, we cannot just change the session key to random. To address this problem, the partitioning methodology in BF-IBE or Gentry's methodology can be used. On the other hand, Waters uses the semi-functional methodology.

In other words, the reason why the proof is difficult is due to the relationship between challenge ciphertext and secret key. As shown in Figure 13.3, a normal secret key can decrypt normal ciphertexts. It means that there exist some relationships to consider during the proof. On the other hand, a semi-functional secret key cannot decrypt semi-functional challenge ciphertexts. Therefore there rarely exists a relationship to consider during the proof. In conclusion, if we can change normal to semi-functional, the proof becomes easier.

So, we must change normal to semi-functional. We change normal challenge ciphertext to semi-functional challenge ciphertext at first. Next, we change normal secret key to semi-functional secret key one by one. As shown in Figure 13.5, there are $Game_{K-1}$ and $Game_K$. Note that the k-th secret key is normal in $Game_{k-1}$ and the k-th secret key is semi-functional in $Game_k$. But, the i-th secret key for $i = \{1, \cdots, k-1\}$ is semi-functional in both games. Here, a contradiction called paradox occurs between $Game_{K-1}$ and $Game_K$: because the simulator in these games can generate normal secret keys, semi-functional secret keys, and semi-functional challenge ciphertext by itself, it can know that the secret key generated by itself is normal or semi-functional. It means that the simulator can distinguish, which is a contradiction.

To overcome this contradiction (i.e., in order *not* to allow the simulator to distinguish), in the proof, we use a tag method to ensure that the normal secret key cannot decrypt semi-functional challenge ciphertext. The method is as follows: We embed tag_k and tag_c in secret keys and challenge ciphertext, respectively. The tags are generated using some function $F()$, which implies

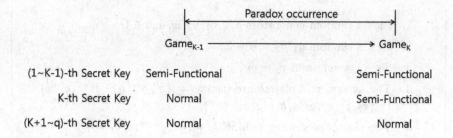

FIGURE 13.5
Paradox between $Game_{K-1}$ and $Game_K$.

that $1/(tag_c - tag_k)$ cannot be computed[1]. Note that if $1/(tag_c - tag_k)$ cannot be computed, the simulator cannot decrypt the challenge ciphertext. For more details, refer to "How to generate tags" in Lemma 2.

Since the contradiction is resolved as above, we have no problem in changing the normal ciphertext and secret key to the semi-functional ciphertext and secret key in the proof from $Game_{Real}$ to $Game_{Final}$.

Therefore, the proof in $Game_{Final}$ can be shown easily and we can get $Game_{Real}Adv_A$.

13.4   Waters' IBE [99]

In 2009, Waters proposed a new methodology called *Dual System Encryption* that allows us to prove that an IBE scheme is fully (adaptively) secure based on static assumptions without random oracle.

Construction 1. IBE

Let $\mathbb{G}$, $\mathbb{G}_T$ be groups of order p, and let $e: \mathbb{G} \times \mathbb{G} \to \mathbb{G}_T$ be the bilinear map. The IBE system works as follows.

Setup Given a security parameter $k \in \mathbb{Z}^+$, where $k = |p|$

---

[1]In this case, $tag_k = tag_c$ because C^* for ID^*, SK^* for ID^*, then $tag_c = F(ID^*)$, $tag_k = F(ID^*)$.

1. Pick a random generators $g, v, v_1, v_2, w, u, h \in \mathbb{G}$.

2. Pick a random $a_1, a_2, b, \alpha \in \mathbb{Z}_p$.

3. Set $\tau_1 = vv_1^{a_1}$ and $\tau_2 = vv_2^{a_2}$.

4. The system parameters are params $= \left(g^b, g^{a_1}, g^{a_2}, g^{b \cdot a_1}, g^{b \cdot a_2} \right)$ $(\tau_1, \tau_2, \tau_1^b, \tau_2^b, w, u, h, e(g, g)^{\alpha \cdot a_1 \cdot b})$.

5. The master secret key is MSK $= (g, g^\alpha, g^{\alpha \cdot a_1}, v, v_1, v_2)$.

The identity space for the described scheme will be $\mathbb{Z}_p$, although we note in practice one can apply a collision resistant hash function to identities of arbitrary lengths.

Extract For a given identity $\mathsf{ID} \in \mathbb{Z}_p$

1. Generate random $r_1, r_2, z_1, z_2, tag_k \in \mathbb{Z}_p$.

2. Let $r = r_1 + r_2$.

3. Compute $D_1 = g^{\alpha \cdot a_1} v^r$, $D_2 = g^{-\alpha} v_1^r g^{z_1}$.

4. Compute $D_3 = (g^b)^{-z_1}$, $D_4 = v_2^r g^{z_2}$.

5. Compute $D_5 = (g^b)^{-z_2}$, $D_6 = g^{r_2 \cdot b}$.

6. Compute $D_7 = g^{r_1}$, $K = (u^{\mathsf{ID}} w^{tag_k} h)^{r_1}$.

7. Set the secret key $SK_{\mathsf{ID}} = (D_1, \cdots D_7, K, tag_k)$.

Encrypt Message $M \in \mathbb{G}_T$ and identity $\mathsf{ID} \in \mathbb{Z}_p$

1. Generate random $s_1, s_2, t, tag_c \in \mathbb{Z}_p$.

2. Let $s = s_1 + s_2$.

3. Compute $C_0 = M \cdot (e(g, g)^{\alpha \cdot a_1 \cdot b})^{s_2}$, $C_1 = (g^b)^s$.

4. Compute $C_2 = (g^{b \cdot a_1})^{s_1}$, $C_3 = (g^{a_1})^{s_1}$, $C_4 = (g^{b \cdot a_2})^{s_2}$.

5. Compute $C_5 = (g^{a_2})^{s_2}$, $C_6 = \tau_1^{s_1} \tau_2^{s_2}$.

6. Compute $C_7 = (\tau_1^b)^{s_1} (\tau_2^b)^{s_2} w^{-t}$.

7. Compute $E_1 = (u^{\mathsf{ID}} w^{tag_c} h)^t$, $E_2 = g^t$.

8. Set the ciphertext to be $CT = \langle C_0, \cdots, C_7, E_1, E_2, tag_c \rangle$.

$(e(g, g)^{\alpha \cdot a_1 \cdot b})^{s_2}$ is called the session key. $C_1, \cdots, C_7, E_1$, and E_2 are called the header information necessary to retrieve the session key.

Decrypt Ciphertext CT and secret key SK_{ID}

1. Compute $A_1 = e(C_1, D_1) \cdot e(C_2, D_2) \cdot e(C_3, D_3) \cdot e(C_4, D_4) \cdot e(C_5, D_5)$.

2. Compute $A_2 = e(C_6, D_6) \cdot e(C_7, D_7)$.

3. Compute $A_3 = A_1/A_2$.

4. Compute $A_4 = (e(E_1, D_7)/e(E_2, K))^{1/(tag_c - tag_k)}$.

5. Compute $M = C_0/(A_3/A_4)$.

The ciphertext tag_c is not equal to the private key tag_k. Since both tags are chosen randomly, decryption will succeed with all but a negligible $1/p$ probability.

Computations between normal ciphertext and normal secret key

1. $A_1 = e(C_1, D_1) \cdot e(C_2, D_2) \cdot e(C_3, D_3) \cdot e(C_4, D_4) \cdot e(C_5, D_5)$

$$= e(g^{b \cdot s}, g^{\alpha \cdot a_1} v^r) \cdot e(g^{b \cdot a_1 \cdot s_1}, g^{-\alpha} v_1^r g^{z_1}) \cdot e(g^{a_1 \cdot s_1}, g^{-b \cdot z_1}) \cdot e(g^{b \cdot a_2 \cdot s_2}, v_2^r g^{z_2}) \cdot e(g^{a_2 \cdot s_2}, g^{-b \cdot z_2})$$

$$= e(g^{b \cdot s}, g^{\alpha \cdot a_1}) \cdot e(g^{b \cdot s}, v^r) \cdot e(g^{b \cdot a_1 \cdot s_1}, g^{-\alpha} g^{z_1}) \cdot e(g^{b \cdot a_1 \cdot s_1}, v_1^r) \cdot e(g^{a_1 \cdot s_1}, g^{-b \cdot z_1}) \cdot e(g^{b \cdot a_2 \cdot s_2}, v_2^r) \cdot e(g^{b \cdot a_2 \cdot s_2}, g^{z_2}) \cdot e(g^{a_2 \cdot s_2}, g^{-b \cdot z_2})$$

$$= e(g, g)^{\alpha \cdot a_1 \cdot b \cdot s} \cdot e(g, v)^{b \cdot s \cdot r} \cdot e(g, g)^{-b \cdot a_1 \cdot s_1 \cdot \alpha + b \cdot a_1 \cdot s_1 \cdot z_1} \cdot e(g, v_1)^{b \cdot a_1 \cdot s_1 \cdot r} \cdot e(g, g)^{-a_1 \cdot s_1 \cdot b \cdot z_1} \cdot e(g, v_2)^{b \cdot a_2 \cdot s_2 \cdot r} \cdot e(g, g)^{b \cdot a_2 \cdot s_2 \cdot z_2} \cdot e(g, g)^{-a_2 \cdot s_2 \cdot b \cdot z_2},$$

where $s = s_1 + s_2$

$$= e(g, g)^{\alpha \cdot a_1 \cdot b \cdot s_1} \cdot e(g, g)^{\alpha \cdot a_1 \cdot b \cdot s_2} \cdot e(g, v)^{b \cdot (s_1 + s_2) \cdot r} \cdot e(g, g)^{-b \cdot a_1 \cdot s_1 \cdot \alpha + b \cdot a_1 \cdot s_1 \cdot z_1} \cdot e(g, v_1)^{b \cdot a_1 \cdot s_1 \cdot r} \cdot e(g, g)^{-a_1 \cdot s_1 \cdot b \cdot z_1} \cdot e(g, v_2)^{b \cdot a_2 \cdot s_2 \cdot r} \cdot e(g, g)^{b \cdot a_2 \cdot s_2 \cdot z_2} \cdot e(g, g)^{-a_2 \cdot s_2 \cdot b \cdot z_2}$$

$$= e(g, g)^{\alpha \cdot a_1 \cdot b \cdot s_2} \cdot e(v, g)^{b(s_1 + s_2)r} \cdot e(v_1, g)^{a_1 \cdot b \cdot s_1 \cdot r} \cdot e(v_2, g)^{a_2 \cdot b \cdot s_2 \cdot r}.$$

2. $A_2 = e(C_6, D_6) \cdot e(C_7, D_7) = e(\tau_1^{s_1} \tau_2^{s_2}, g^{r_2 \cdot b}) \cdot e((\tau_1^b)^{s_1} (\tau_2^b)^{s_2} w^{-t}, g^{r_1})$

$$= e(\tau_1, g)^{s_1 \cdot r_2 \cdot b} \cdot e(\tau_2, g)^{s_2 \cdot r_2 \cdot b} \cdot e(\tau_1, g)^{b \cdot s_1 \cdot r_1} \cdot e(\tau_2, g)^{b \cdot s_2 \cdot r_1} \cdot e(w, g)^{-t \cdot r_1},$$

where $\tau_1 = vv_1^{a_1}$ and $\tau_2 = vv_2^{a_2}$

$$= e(vv_1^{a_1}, g)^{s_1 \cdot r_2 \cdot b} \cdot e(vv_2^{a_2}, g)^{s_2 \cdot r_2 \cdot b} \cdot e(vv_1^{a_1}, g)^{b \cdot s_1 \cdot r_1} \cdot e(vv_2^{a_2}, g)^{b \cdot s_2 \cdot r_1} \cdot e(w, g)^{-t \cdot r_1}$$

$$= e(v,g)^{s_1 \cdot r_2 \cdot b} \cdot e(v_1,g)^{a_1 \cdot s_1 \cdot r_2 \cdot b} \cdot e(v,g)^{s_2 \cdot r_2 \cdot b} \cdot e(v_2,g)^{a_2 \cdot s_2 \cdot r_2 \cdot b} \cdot$$
$$e(v,g)^{b \cdot s_1 \cdot r_1} \cdot e(v_1,g)^{a_1 \cdot b \cdot s_1 \cdot r_1} \cdot e(v,g)^{b \cdot s_2 \cdot r_1} \cdot e(v_2,g)^{a_2 \cdot b \cdot s_2 \cdot r_1} \cdot e(w,g)^{-t \cdot r_1}$$

$$= e(v,g)^{s_1 \cdot r_2 \cdot b} \cdot e(v,g)^{s_2 \cdot r_2 \cdot b} \cdot e(v,g)^{b \cdot s_1 \cdot r_1} \cdot e(v,g)^{b \cdot s_2 \cdot r_1} \cdot e(v_1,g)^{a_1 \cdot s_1 \cdot r_2 \cdot b} \cdot$$
$$e(v_1,g)^{a_1 \cdot b \cdot s_1 \cdot r_1} \cdot e(v_2,g)^{a_2 \cdot s_2 \cdot r_2 \cdot b} \cdot e(v_2,g)^{a_2 \cdot b \cdot s_2 \cdot r_1} \cdot e(w,g)^{-t \cdot r_1},$$

where $r = r_1 + r_2$

$$= e(v,g)^{b(s_1+s_2)r} \cdot e(v_1,g)^{a_1 \cdot b \cdot s_1 \cdot r} \cdot e(v_2,g)^{a_2 \cdot b \cdot s_2 \cdot r} \cdot e(g,w)^{-r_1 \cdot t}.$$

3. $A_3 = A_1/A_2 = e(g,g)^{\alpha \cdot a_1 \cdot b \cdot s_2} \cdot e(g,w)^{r_1 \cdot t}.$

4. $A_4 = (e(E_1,D_7)/e(E_2,K))^{1/(tag_c - tag_k)}$

$$= (e((u^{\mathsf{ID}} w^{tag_c} h)^t, g^{r_1})/e(g^t, (u^{\mathsf{ID}} w^{tag_k} h)^{r_1}))^{1/(tag_c - tag_k)}$$

$$= (e((u^{\mathsf{ID}} w^{tag_c} h)^t, g^{r_1}) \cdot e(g^t, (u^{\mathsf{ID}} w^{tag_k} h)^{r_1})^{-1})^{1/(tag_c - tag_k)}$$

$$= (e(w,g)^{tag_c \cdot t \cdot r_1} \cdot e(g,w)^{-tag_k \cdot t \cdot r_1})^{1/(tag_c - tag_k)}$$

$$= e(g,w)^{r_1 \cdot t}.$$

5. $M = C_0/(A_3/A_4) = M \cdot (e(g,g)^{\alpha \cdot a_1 \cdot b})^{s_2}/(e(g,g)^{\alpha \cdot a_1 \cdot b \cdot s_2} \cdot e(g,w)^{r_1 \cdot t}/e(g,w)^{r_1 \cdot t})$

$$= M \cdot e(g,g)^{\alpha \cdot a_1 \cdot b \cdot s_2} \cdot e(g,g)^{-\alpha \cdot a_1 \cdot b \cdot s_2} \cdot e(g,w)^{-r_1 \cdot t} \cdot e(g,w)^{r_1 \cdot t}$$

Construction 2. Semi-functional algorithms

We will define them as algorithms that are executed with knowledge of the secret exponents. However, in a real system they will not be used. Their main purpose is to define the structures that will be used in the proof. We define both semi-functional ciphertexts and keys in terms of a transformation on a normal ciphertext or key.

Semi-functional ciphertexts The algorithm first runs the encryption algorithm to generate a normal ciphertext $CT = \langle C_0', \cdots, C_7', E_1', E_2', tag_c \rangle$.

1. Pick a random $x \in \mathbb{Z}_p$.

2. Set $C_0 = C_0'$, $C_1 = C_1'$, $C_2 = C_2'$, $C_3 = C_3'$, $E_1 = E_1'$, $E_2 = E_2'$, leaving these elements and the tag_c unchanged.

3. Set $C_4 = C_4' \cdot g^{b \cdot a_2 \cdot x}$, $C_5 = C_5' \cdot g^{a_2 \cdot x}$, $C_6 = C_6' \cdot v_2^{a_2 \cdot x}$, $C_7 = C_7' \cdot v_2^{a_2 \cdot b \cdot x}$.

4. The semi-functional ciphertext is $\langle C_0, \cdots, C_7, E_1, E_2, tag_c \rangle$.

Semi-functional secret keys The algorithm first runs the extract algorithm to generate a normal secret key $SK_{\mathsf{ID}} = (D_1', \cdots D_7', K', tag_k)$.

1. Pick a random $\gamma \in \mathbb{Z}_p$.

2. Set $D_3 = D_3'$, $D_5 = D_5'$, $D_6 = D_6'$, $D_7 = D_7'$, $K = K'$, leaving these elements and the tag_k unchanged.

3. Set $D_1 = D_1' \cdot g^{-a_1 \cdot a_2 \cdot \gamma}$, $D_2 = D_2' \cdot g^{a_2 \cdot \gamma}$, $D_4 = D_4' \cdot g^{a_1 \cdot \gamma}$.

4. The semi-functional secret key is $(D_1, \cdots D_7, K, tag_k)$.

Computations between normal and semi-functional

Here we show the semi-functional ciphertext and secret key work as expected.

1. Decrypt a semi-functional ciphertext with a normal key.

$$e(g^{b \cdot a_2 \cdot x}, D_4) \cdot e(g^{a_2 \cdot x}, D_5) \cdot e(v_2^{a_2 \cdot x}, D_6)^{-1} \cdot e(v_2^{a_2 \cdot b \cdot x}, D_7)^{-1}$$

$$= e(g^{b \cdot a_2 \cdot x}, v_2^r g^{z_2}) \cdot e(g^{a_2 \cdot x}, g^{-b \cdot z_2}) \cdot e(v_2^{a_2 \cdot x}, g^{r_2 \cdot b})^{-1} \cdot e(v_2^{a_2 \cdot b \cdot x}, g^{r_1})^{-1}$$

$$= e(g, v_2)^{b \cdot a_2 \cdot x \cdot r} \cdot e(g, g)^{b \cdot a_2 \cdot x \cdot z_2} \cdot e(g, g)^{-a_2 \cdot x \cdot b \cdot z_2} \cdot e(v_2, g)^{-a_2 \cdot x \cdot r_2 \cdot b} \cdot$$
$$e(v_2, g)^{-a_2 \cdot b \cdot x \cdot r_1} = 1$$

2. Decrypt a normal ciphertext with a semi-functional key.

$$e(C_1, g^{-a_1 \cdot a_2 \cdot \gamma}) \cdot e(C_2, g^{a_2 \cdot \gamma}) \cdot e(C_4, g^{a_1 \cdot \gamma})$$

$$= e(g^{b(s_1 + s_2)}, g^{-a_1 \cdot a_2 \cdot \gamma}) \cdot e(g^{b \cdot a_1 \cdot s_1}, g^{a_2 \cdot \gamma}) \cdot e(g^{b \cdot a_2 \cdot s_2}, g^{a_1 \cdot \gamma})$$

$$= e(g, g)^{-b(s_1 + s_2) \cdot a_1 \cdot a_2 \cdot \gamma} \cdot e(g, g)^{b \cdot a_1 \cdot s_1 \cdot a_2 \cdot \gamma} \cdot e(g, g)^{b \cdot a_2 \cdot s_2 \cdot a_1 \cdot \gamma} = 1$$

3. Decrypt a semi-functional ciphertext with a semi-functional key.

$$e(C_1, g^{-a_1 \cdot a_2 \cdot \gamma}) \cdot e(C_2, g^{a_2 \cdot \gamma}) \cdot e(C_4 \cdot g^{b \cdot a_2 \cdot x}, D_4 \cdot g^{a_1 \cdot \gamma}) \cdot e(g^{a_2 \cdot x}, D_5) \cdot$$
$$e(v_2^{a_2 \cdot x}, D_6)^{-1} \cdot e(v_2^{a_2 \cdot b \cdot x}, D_7)^{-1}$$

$$= e(C_1, g^{-a_1 \cdot a_2 \cdot \gamma}) \cdot e(C_2, g^{a_2 \cdot \gamma}) \cdot e(C_4, D_4) \cdot e(C_4, g^{a_1 \cdot \gamma}) \cdot e(g^{b \cdot a_2 \cdot x}, D_4) \cdot$$
$$e(g^{b \cdot a_2 \cdot x}, g^{a_1 \cdot \gamma}) \cdot e(g^{a_2 \cdot x}, D_5) \cdot e(v_2^{a_2 \cdot x}, D_6)^{-1} \cdot e(v_2^{a_2 \cdot b \cdot x}, D_7)^{-1}$$

By using the above two results in 1 and 2, the computation below is possible.

$$= e(C_4, D_4) \cdot e(g^{b \cdot a_2 \cdot x}, g^{a_1 \cdot \gamma})$$

$$= e(g^{b \cdot a_2 \cdot s_2}, v_2^r g^{z_2}) \cdot e(g^{b \cdot a_2 \cdot x}, g^{a_1 \cdot \gamma}) = e(g^{b \cdot a_2 \cdot s_2}, v_2^r) \cdot e(g^{b \cdot a_2 \cdot s_2}, g^{z_2}) \cdot$$
$$e(g^{b \cdot a_2 \cdot x}, g^{a_1 \cdot \gamma})$$

$$= e(g, v_2)^{b \cdot a_2 \cdot s_2 \cdot r} \cdot e(g, g)^{b \cdot a_2 \cdot s_2 \cdot z_2} \cdot e(g, g)^{b \cdot a_2 \cdot x \cdot a_1 \cdot \gamma} \neq 1$$

As shown above, in the cases of 1 and 2, since the additional parts (i.e., parts added to the normal secret key and normal ciphertext, for example, $g^{b \cdot a_2 x}$) are removed, the computation results of 1 and 2 become 1. Therefore, we can know that the case of 1 and 2 do not affect the decryption computation as expected. However, in the case of 3, since the additional parts are not removed, we can know that the decryption does not work as expected. In conclusion, we know that only the decryption of the semi-functional ciphertext using the semi-functional secret key is not valid.

13.4.1   Proof of IBE Security

As mentioned above, the proof is organized as a sequence of games as shown in Figure 13.6. We define the first game as the real identity-based encryption game and the last one as the ideal encryption game in which the adversary has no advantage unconditionally. Now we show that each game is indistinguishable from the next (under a complexity assumption). As stated before, the crux of Waters' strategy is to move to a security game where both the challenge ciphertext and secret keys are semi-functional. At this point, any keys the challenger gives out are not useful in decrypting the ciphertext. First, let us define the games as:

1. *Game$_{Real}$*: The actual IBE security game defined in Section 13.2.1 Security Model.

2. *Game$_i$*: The real security game with the following two exceptions: (1) The challenge ciphertext will be a semi-functional ciphertext on the challenge identity ID^*; (2) The first i private key queries will return semi-functional private keys. The rest of the keys will be normal. For an adversary that makes at most q queries we will be interested in *Game$_0$*, $\cdots$, *Game$_q$*. We note that in *Game$_0$* the

challenge ciphertext is semi-functional, but all keys are normal and in $Game_q$ all secret keys are semi-functional.

3. $Game_{Final}$: The real security game with the following exceptions: (1) The challenge ciphertext is a semi-functional encryption on a random group element of $\mathbb{G}_T$; (2) All of the secret key queries result in semi-functional keys.

We now prove a set of Lemmas that argue the indistinguishability of these games. For each proof we need to build a reduction simulator that answers private key queries and creates a challenge ciphertext.

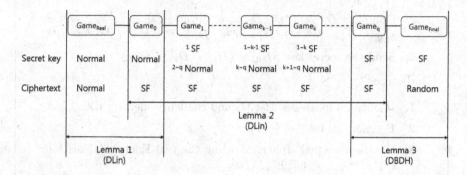

FIGURE 13.6
Proof of IBE security.

Lemma 1 Suppose that there exists an algorithm $\mathcal{A}$ where $Game_{Real}Adv_{\mathcal{A}} - Game_0Adv_{\mathcal{A}} = \epsilon_{dlin}$. Then we can build an algorithm $\mathcal{B}$ that has advantage ϵ_{dlin} in the decision linear game.

Proof The algorithm $\mathcal{B}$ begins by taking in an instance $(\mathbb{G}, g, f, \nu, g^{c_1}, f^{c_2}, T)$ of the decision linear problem. We now describe how it executes the Setup, Key Phase, and Challenge phases of the IBE game with $\mathcal{A}$.

Reduction algorithm $\mathcal{B}$ in Lemma 1

Setup

1. Choose a random exponents $b, \alpha, y_v, y_{v_1}, y_{v_2} \in \mathbb{Z}_p$, and random group elements $w, u, h \in \mathbb{G}$.

2. Set $g = g$, $g^{a_1} = f$, $g^{a_2} = \nu$ where a_1 and a_2 are the exponents that reduction cannot know itself.

3. Set g^b, $g^{b \cdot a_1} = f^b$, $g^{b \cdot a_2} = \nu^b$, $v = g^{y_v}$, $v_1 = g^{y_{v_1}}$, $v_2 = g^{y_{v_2}}$.

4. Compute $\tau_1 = g^{y_v} f^{y_{v_1}}$, $\tau_2 = g^{y_v} \nu^{y_{v_2}}$, $\tau_1^b = g^{b \cdot y_v} f^{b \cdot y_{v_1}}$, $\tau_2^b = g^{b \cdot y_v} \nu^{b \cdot y_{v_2}}$, $e(g,g)^{\alpha \cdot a_1 \cdot b} = e(g,f)^{\alpha \cdot b}$.

5. Send the public parameters params $= (g^b, g^{a_1}, g^{a_2}, g^{b \cdot a_1}, g^{b \cdot a_2})$ $(\tau_1, \tau_2, \tau_1^b, \tau_2^b, w, u, h, e(g,g)^{\alpha \cdot a_1 \cdot b})$.

6. Set the master secret key MSK $= (g, g^\alpha, f^\alpha, v, v_1, v_2)$.

Phase I

1. Choose a random exponents $r_1, r_2, z_1, z_2 \in \mathbb{Z}_p$ and define $r = r_1 + r_2$.

2. Compute $D_1 = f^\alpha v^r$, $D_2 = g^{-\alpha} v_1^r g^{z_1}$, $D_3 = (g^b)^{-z_1}$, $D_4 = v_2^r g^{z_2}$, $D_5 = (g^b)^{-z_2}$, $D_6 = g^{r_2 \cdot b}$, $D_7 = g^{r_1}$, $K = (u^{\mathsf{ID}} w^{tag_k} h)^{r_1}$.

3. Send the secret key $SK_{\mathsf{ID}} = (D_1, \cdots D_7, K, tag_k)$.

Challenge

1. $\mathcal{A}$ outputs messages M_0, M_1 and challenge identity ID^*.

2. $\mathcal{B}$ generates bit $\beta \in \{0, 1\}$.

3. Create a normal ciphertext using the real Encrypt algorithm, $CT = (C_0', \cdots, C_7', E_1', E_2', tag_c)$.

4. Let s_1', s_2', t be the random exponents used in creating the ciphertext.

5. Modify components of the ciphertext as follows.
$C_0 = C_0' \cdot (e(g^{c_1}, f) \cdot e(g, f^{c_2}))^{b \cdot \alpha}$, $C_1 = C_1' \cdot (g^{c_1})^b$, $C_2 = C_2' \cdot (f^{c_2})^{-b}$, $C_3 = C_3' \cdot (f^{c_2})^{-1}$, $C_4 = C_4' \cdot (T)^b$, $C_5 = C_5' \cdot T$, $C_6 = C_6' \cdot (g^{c_1})^{y_v} \cdot (f^{c_2})^{-y_{v_1}} \cdot T^{y_{v_2}}$, $C_7 = C_7' \cdot ((g^{c_1})^{y_v} \cdot (f^{c_2})^{-y_{v_1}} \cdot T^{y_{v_2}})^b$, $E_1 = E_1'$, $E_2 = E_2'$.

6. Send $(C_0, \cdots, C_7, E_1, E_2, tag_c)$ to $\mathcal{A}$ as the challenge ciphertext.

Note: If $T = \nu^{c_1 + c_2}$, then $s_1 = -c_2 + s_1'$, $s_2 = s_2' + c_1 + c_2$, and $s = s_1 + s_2 = c_1 + s_1' + s_2'$ are implicitly set. If $T = \nu^{c_1 + c_2}$, it will have the same distribution as a standard ciphertext; otherwise, it will be distributed identically to a semi-functional ciphertext.

Phase II

1. $\mathcal{A}$ makes key generation queries, and $\mathcal{B}$ responds as in Phase I.

Guess

1. Finally, the adversary outputs guesses $\beta' \in \{0, 1\}$.

2. If $\beta = \beta'$ outputs 0 (indicating that $T = \nu^{c_1+c_2}$); otherwise, it outputs 1.

Simulation of secret key generation in Lemma 1

Extract algorithm in Lemma 1 only generates normal secret keys. The secret key simulation is the same as original one except with $D_1 = f^\alpha v^r = (g^{a_1})^\alpha v^r = g^{\alpha \cdot a_1} v^r$.

Simulation of challenge ciphertext generation in Lemma 1

The difference between $Game_{Real}$ and $Game_0$ is whether the challenge ciphertext is normal or semi-functional. So T must be embedded in the challenge ciphertext because only challenge ciphertext is different. And the challenge ciphertext is normal if T is real, otherwise the challenge ciphertext is semi-functional. Therefore, generation of the challenge ciphertext is complicated compared with secret generation. Here, we demonstrate that the challenge ciphertext is well generated as normal or semi-functional one according to T; if T is real, then it computes the normal ciphertext and if T is random, then it computes the semi-functional ciphertext.

The generated real ciphertext by using s_1', s_2', t is as follows. Since $\mathcal{B}$ knows the public parameters and the master secret key, it can generate the real ciphertext as
$C_0' = M \cdot (e(g,g)^{\alpha \cdot a_1 \cdot b})^{s_2'}, \ C_1' = (g^b)^{s_1'+s_2'}, \ C_2' = (g^{b \cdot a_1})^{s_1'}, \ C_3' = (g^{a_1})^{s_1'}, \ C_4' = (g^{b \cdot a_2})^{s_2'}, \ C_5' = (g^{a_2})^{s_2'}, \ C_6' = \tau_1^{s_1'} \tau_2^{s_2'}. \ C_7' = (\tau_1^b)^{s_1'} (\tau_2^b)^{s_2'} w^{-t}, \ E_1' = (u^{ID} w^{tag_c} h)^t, \ E_2' = g^t.$

In Lemma 1, the ciphertext is generated as
$C_0 = C_0' \cdot (e(g^{c_1}, f) \cdot e(g, f^{c_2}))^{b \cdot \alpha}, \ C_1 = C_1' \cdot (g^{c_1})^b, \ C_2 = C_2' \cdot (f^{c_2})^{-b}, \ C_3 = C_3' \cdot (f^{c_2})^{-1}, \ C_4 = C_4' \cdot (T)^b,$

$C_5 = C_5' \cdot T, \ C_6 = C_6' \cdot (g^{c_1})^{y_v} \cdot (f^{c_2})^{-y_{v_1}} \cdot T^{y_{v_2}}, \ C_7 = C_7' \cdot ((g^{c_1})^{y_v} \cdot (f^{c_2})^{-y_{v_1}} \cdot T^{y_{v_2}})^b, \ E_1 = E_1', \ E_2 = E_2'.$

First, in the case of $T = \nu^{c_1+c_2}$, let us compute the ciphertext.

Do not forget that $s_1 = -c_2 + s_1'$, $s_2 = s_2' + c_1 + c_2$, and $s = s_1 + s_2 = c_1 + s_1' + s_2'$ are implicitly set.

$C_0 = C_0' \cdot (e(g^{c_1}, f) \cdot e(g, f^{c_2}))^{b \cdot \alpha} = M \cdot (e(g,g)^{\alpha \cdot a_1 \cdot b})^{s_2'} \cdot (e(g^{c_1}, g^{a_1}) \cdot e(g, (g^{a_1})^{c_2}))^{b \cdot \alpha} = M \cdot e(g,g)^{\alpha \cdot a_1 \cdot b \cdot s_2'} \cdot (e(g,g)^{c_1 \cdot a_1} \cdot e(g, g^{a_1 \cdot c_2}))^{b \cdot \alpha} = M \cdot e(g,g)^{\alpha \cdot a_1 \cdot b \cdot s_2'} \cdot e(g,g)^{c_1 \cdot a_1 \cdot b \cdot \alpha} \cdot e(g,g)^{a_1 \cdot c_2 \cdot b \cdot \alpha} = M \cdot e(g,g)^{\alpha \cdot a_1 \cdot b \cdot (s_2' + c_1 + c_2)} =$

$M \cdot e(g,g)^{\alpha \cdot a_1 \cdot b \cdot s_2}$,

$C_1 = C_1' \cdot (g^{c_1})^b = (g^b)^{s_1' + s_2'} \cdot (g^{c_1})^b = g^{b(s_1' + s_2')} \cdot g^{c_1 \cdot b} = g^{b(s_1' + s_2') + c_1 \cdot b} = g^{b(s_1' + s_2' + c_1)} = g^{b \cdot s}$,

$C_2 = C_2' \cdot (f^{c_2})^{-b} = (g^{b \cdot a_1})^{s_1'} \cdot ((g^{a_1})^{c_2})^{-b} = g^{b \cdot a_1 \cdot s_1'} \cdot g^{-a_1 \cdot c_2 \cdot b} = g^{b \cdot a_1 \cdot (s_1' - c_2)} = g^{b \cdot a_1 \cdot s_1}$,

$C_3 = C_3' \cdot (f^{c_2})^{-1} = (g^{a_1})^{s_1'} \cdot ((g^{a_1})^{c_2})^{-1} = g^{a_1 \cdot s_1'} \cdot g^{-a_1 \cdot c_2} = g^{a_1 \cdot s_1' - a_1 \cdot c_2} = g^{a_1 \cdot (s_1' - c_2)} = g^{a_1 \cdot s_1}$,

$C_4 = C_4' \cdot (T)^b = (g^{b \cdot a_2})^{s_2'} \cdot (\nu^{c_1 + c_2})^b = g^{b \cdot a_2 \cdot s_2'} \cdot ((g^{a_2})^{c_1 + c_2})^b = g^{b \cdot a_2 \cdot s_2'} \cdot g^{b \cdot a_2 (c_1 + c_2)} = g^{b \cdot a_2 \cdot (s_2' + c_1 + c_2)} = g^{b \cdot a_2 \cdot s_2}$,

$C_5 = C_5' \cdot T = (g^{a_2})^{s_2'} \cdot \nu^{c_1 + c_2} = g^{a_2 \cdot s_2'} \cdot (g^{a_2})^{c_1 + c_2} = g^{a_2 \cdot s_2'} \cdot g^{a_2(c_1 + c_2)} = g^{a_2 \cdot (s_2' + c_1 + c_2)} = g^{a_2 \cdot s_2}$,

$C_6 = C_6' \cdot (g^{c_1})^{y_v} (f^{c_2})^{-y_{v_1}} T^{y_{v_2}} = \tau_1^{s_1'} \tau_2^{s_2'} \cdot (g^{c_1})^{y_v} (f^{c_2})^{-y_{v_1}} (\nu^{c_1 + c_2})^{y_{v_2}} = \tau_1^{s_1'} \tau_2^{s_2'} \cdot g^{c_1 \cdot y_v} f^{-c_2 \cdot y_{v_1}} \nu^{c_1 \cdot y_{v_2} + c_2 \cdot y_{v_2}} = \tau_1^{s_1'} \tau_2^{s_2'} \cdot g^{c_1 \cdot y_v} f^{-c_2 \cdot y_{v_1}} \nu^{c_1 \cdot y_{v_2}} \nu^{c_2 \cdot y_{v_2}} \cdot g^{c_2 \cdot y_v} g^{-c_2 \cdot y_v} = (\tau_1^{s_1'} \cdot g^{-c_2 \cdot y_v} f^{-c_2 \cdot y_{v_1}})(\tau_2^{s_2'} \cdot g^{c_1 \cdot y_v} \nu^{c_1 \cdot y_{v_2}} \nu^{c_2 \cdot y_{v_2}} g^{c_2 \cdot y_v}) = (\tau_1^{s_1'} \cdot \tau_1^{-c_2})(\tau_2^{s_2'} \cdot \tau_2^{c_1 + c_2}) = (\tau_1^{s_1' - c_2})(\tau_2^{s_2' + c_1 + c_2}) = \tau_1^{s_1} \tau_2^{s_2}$,

$C_7 = C_7' \cdot ((g^{c_1})^{y_v} (f^{c_2})^{-y_{v_1}} T^{y_{v_2}})^b = (\tau_1^b)^{s_1'} (\tau_2^b)^{s_2'} w^{-t'} \cdot ((g^{c_1})^{y_v} (f^{c_2})^{-y_{v_1}} (\nu^{c_1 + c_2})^{y_{v_2}})^b = (\tau_1^{s_1'} \tau_2^{s_2'} \cdot (g^{c_1})^{y_v} (f^{c_2})^{-y_{v_1}} (\nu^{c_1 + c_2})^{y_{v_2}})^b \cdot w^{-t'} = (C_6)^b \cdot w^{-t'} = (\tau_1^{s_1} \tau_2^{s_2})^b \cdot w^{-t'} = \tau_1^{s_1 \cdot b} \tau_2^{s_2 \cdot b} w^{-t}$,

$E_1 = E_1' = (u^{\mathsf{ID}} w^{tag_c} h)^t$,

$E_2 = E_2' = g^t$.

As shown above, in the case of $T = \nu^{c_1 + c_2}$, a normal ciphertext is computed.

On the other hand, in the case where T is random, some additional random values are multiplied by C_4, C_5, C_6, and C_7. Let C_4, C_5, C_6, C_7 denote C_4', C_5', C_6', and C_7', respectively. Let an additional random value be $g^{a_2 \cdot x}$. It means that $T = \nu^{c_1 + c_2} \cdot g^{a_2 \cdot x}$. We can compute each value as follows. Here, the reason that an additional random value is $g^{a_2 \cdot x}$ is that x is a randomly chosen value.

$C_4 = C_4' \cdot (g^{a_2 \cdot x})^b = C_4' \cdot g^{b \cdot a_2 \cdot x}$,

$C_5 = C_5' \cdot g^{a_2 \cdot x}$,

$$C_6 = C_6' \cdot (g^{a_2 \cdot x})^{y_{v_2}} = C_6' \cdot (g^{y_{v_2}})^{a_2 \cdot x} = C_6' \cdot v_2^{a_2 \cdot x},$$

$$C_7 = C_7' \cdot ((g^{a_2 \cdot x})^{y_{v_2}})^b = C_7' \cdot (g^{y_{v_2}})^{b \cdot a_2 \cdot x} = C_7' \cdot v_2^{b \cdot a_2 \cdot x}.$$

As shown above, in the case of $T = \nu^{c_1 + c_2} \cdot g^{a_2 \cdot x}$, a semi-functional ciphertext is computed.

Probability analysis in Lemma 1 The probability computation is simple as

$$Game_{Real} Adv_{\mathcal{A}} - Game_0 Adv_{\mathcal{A}} = \epsilon_{dlin}. \qquad (13.8)$$

Lemma 2 Suppose that there exists an algorithm $\mathcal{A}$ that makes at most q queries and $Game_{k-1} Adv_{\mathcal{A}} - Game_k Adv_{\mathcal{A}} = \epsilon_{dlin}$ for some k where $1 \leq k \leq q$. Then we can build an algorithm $\mathcal{B}$ that has advantage ϵ_{dlin} in the decision linear game.

Proof The algorithm $\mathcal{B}$ begins by taking in an instance $(\mathbb{G}, g, f, \nu, g^{c_1}, f^{c_2}, T)$ of the decision linear problem. We now describe how it executes the Setup, Key Phase, and Challenge phases of the IBE game with $\mathcal{A}$.

Reduction algorithm $\mathcal{B}$ in Lemma 2

Setup

1. Choose a random exponents $\alpha, a_1, a_2, y_{v_1}, y_{v_2}, y_w, y_u, y_h, A, B \in \mathbb{Z}_p$.

2. Set $g = g$, $g^b = f$, $g^{b \cdot a_1} = f^{a_1}$, $g^{b \cdot a_2} = f^{a_2}$, $v = \nu^{-a_1 \cdot a_2}$, $v_1 = \nu^{a_2} \cdot g^{y_{v_1}}$, $v_2 = \nu^{a_1} \cdot g^{y_{v_2}}$, $e(g,g)^{\alpha \cdot a_1 \cdot b} = e(f,g)^{\alpha \cdot a_1}$, $w = f g^{y_w}$, $u = f^{-A} g^{y_u}$, $h = f^{-B} g^{y_h}$.

3. Compute $\tau_1 = g^{y_{v_1} \cdot a_1}$, $\tau_2 = g^{y_{v_2} \cdot a_2}$, $\tau_1^b = f^{y_{v_1} \cdot a_1}$, $\tau_2^b = f^{y_{v_2} \cdot a_2}$.

4. Send the public parameters params $= \left(g^b, g^{a_1}, g^{a_2}, g^{b \cdot a_1}, g^{b \cdot a_2} \right)$ $\left(\tau_1, \tau_2, \tau_1^b, \tau_2^b, w, u, h, e(g,g)^{\alpha \cdot a_1 \cdot b} \right)$.

5. Set the master secret key MSK $= (g, g^\alpha, g^{\alpha \cdot a_1}, v, v_1, v_2)$.

Note: For any identity ID, define $tag_c = F(\mathsf{ID}) = A \cdot \mathsf{ID} + B$. $(u^{\mathsf{ID}} w^{tag} h) = f^{tag - A \cdot \mathsf{ID} - B} g^{\mathsf{ID} \cdot y_u + y_h + tag \cdot y_w} = g^{\mathsf{ID} \cdot y_u + y_h + tag \cdot y_w}$. A and B are initially information theoretically hidden from $\mathcal{A}$. This F is a pairwise independent function and so if $\mathcal{A}$ is given $F(\mathsf{ID})$ for some identity ID, then for some $\mathsf{ID} \neq \mathsf{ID}'$, $F(\mathsf{ID}')$ is uniformly distributed over $\mathbb{Z}_p$.

Phase I Break the Key Generation algorithm into three cases. Consider the i-th query made by $\mathcal{A}$.

Case 1: $i > k$
$\mathcal{B}$ generate a normal key for the requested identity ID.
Since it has the master secret key MSK, it can run that algorithm.

Case 2: $i < k$
$\mathcal{B}$ generate a semi-functional key for the requested identity ID. It first creates a normal key using MSK. Then it makes it semi-functional using the procedure from Construction 2.
It can run this procedure since it knows $g^{a_1 \cdot a_2}$, g^{a_1}, g^{a_2}.

Case 3: $i = k$

1. Create a normal secret key using the real Extract algorithm and $tag_k = F(\mathsf{ID})$, $SK_{\mathsf{ID}} = (D'_1, \cdots D'_7, K', tag_k)$.

2. Let $r'_1, r'_2, z'_1, z'_2 \in \mathbb{Z}_p$ be the random exponents used in creating the secret key.

3. Set $D_1 = D'_1 \cdot T^{-a_1 \cdot a_2}$, $D_2 = D'_2 \cdot T^{a_2}(g^{c_1})^{y_{v_1}}$, $D_3 = D'_3 \cdot (f^{c_2})^{y_{v_1}}$, $D_4 = D'_4 \cdot T^{a_1}(g^{c_1})^{y_{v_2}}$, $D_5 = D'_5 \cdot (f^{c_2})^{y_{v_2}}$, $D_6 = D'_6 \cdot f^{c_2}$, $D_7 = D'_7 \cdot (g^{c_1})$, $K = K' \cdot (g^{c_1})^{\mathsf{ID} \cdot y_u + y_h + tag_k \cdot y_w}$.

4. Send the secret key $SK_{\mathsf{ID}} = (D_1, \cdots D_7, K, tag_k)$.

Note: $tag_k = F(\mathsf{ID})$ allows us to create the component K. $z_1 = z'_1 - y_{v_1} \cdot c_2$ and $z_2 = z'_2 - y_{v_2} \cdot c_2$ are implicitly set in order to be able to create D_2 and D_4. If $T = \nu^{c_1 + c_2}$, then the k-th query results in a normal key under randomness $r_1 = r'_1 + c_1$ and $r_2 = r'_2 + c_2$. Otherwise, if T is a random group element, then we can write $T = \nu^{c_1 + c_2} g^{\gamma}$ for random $\gamma \in \mathbb{Z}_p$. This forms a semi-functional key where γ is the added randomness to make it semi-functional.

Challenge

$\mathcal{B}$ does not have the group element v_2^b, so it cannot directly create such a ciphertext. However, in the case where $tag_c^* = F(\mathsf{ID}^*)$ it will have a different method of doing so.

1. $\mathcal{A}$ outputs messages M_0, M_1 and challenge identity ID^*.

2. $\mathcal{B}$ generates a bit $\beta \in \{0, 1\}$.

3. Create a normal ciphertext using the real Encrypt algorithm and $tag_c^* = F(\mathsf{ID}^*)$, $CT = (C_0', \cdots, C_7', E_1', E_2', tag_c^*)$.

4. Choose a random exponents $s_1, s_2, t' \in \mathbb{Z}_p$.

5. Set $C_0 = C_0'$, $C_1 = C_1'$, $C_2 = C_2'$, $C_3 = C_3'$ leaving these elements and tag_c^* unchanged.

6. Modify components of the ciphertext as follows. $C_4 = C_4' \cdot f^{a_2 \cdot x}$, $C_5 = C_5' \cdot g^{a_2 \cdot x}$, $C_6 = C_6' \cdot v_2^{a_2 \cdot x}$, $C_7 = C_7' \cdot f^{y_{v_2} \cdot x \cdot a_2} \nu^{-a_1 \cdot x \cdot y_w \cdot a_2}$, $E_1 = E_1' \cdot (\nu^{\mathsf{ID} \cdot y_u + y_h + tag_c^* \cdot y_w})^{a_1 a_2 x}$, $E_2 = E_2' \cdot \nu^{a_1 \cdot a_2 \cdot x}$.

7. Send $(C_0, \cdots, C_7, E_1, E_2, tag_c)$ to $\mathcal{A}$ as the challenge ciphertext.

Note: This algorithm implicitly sets $g^t = g^{t'} \nu^{a_1 \cdot a_2 \cdot x}$. This allows for the cancellation of the term $v_2^{a_1 \cdot a_2 \cdot b \cdot x}$ by w^{-t} in constructing C_7. The generation of E_1 is problematic. However, since $tag_c^* = F(\mathsf{ID}^*)$, $\mathcal{B}$ is able to create this term. If $T = \nu^{c_1 + c_2}$, then we are in $Game_{k-1}$, otherwise we are in $Game_k$. $\mathcal{A}$ cannot detect any special relationship between tag_c^* and tag_k^* since $F(\mathsf{ID}) = A \cdot \mathsf{ID} + B$ is a pairwise independent function and A, B are hidden from its view.

Phase II

1. $\mathcal{A}$ makes key generation queries and $\mathcal{B}$ responds as in Phase I.

Guess

1. Finally, the adversary outputs guesses $\beta' \in \{0, 1\}$.

2. If $\beta = \beta'$ outputs 0 (indicating that $T = \nu^{c_1 + c_2}$); otherwise, it outputs 1.

Simulation of secret key generation in Lemma 2

The secret key generation proceeds as divided into 3 parts. However, the parts of $i > k$ and $i < k$ only need to generate normal or semi-functional secret key by using its own master secret key, respectively. On the other hand, the case of $i = k$ is different. In the case of $i = k$, the simulator must generate a normal secret key if T is real, and a semi-functional secret key if T is random. Therefore, it is significantly complicated. Here we check whether a normal or semi-functional secret key is generated correctly by embedding T: if T is real, then it computes a normal secret key or if T is random, then it computes a semi-functional secret key.

The generated real secret key by using r_1', r_2', z_1', z_2' is as follows. Since $\mathcal{B}$ knows the public parameters and the master secret key, it can generate the real secret key as

$$D_1' = g^{\alpha \cdot a_1} v_1^{r_1' + r_2'}, \ D_2' = g^{-\alpha} v_1^{r_1' + r_2'} g^{z_1'}, \ D_3' = (g^b)^{-z_1'}, \ D_4' = v_2^{r_1' + r_2'} g^{z_2'},$$
$$D_5' = (g^b)^{-z_2'}, \ D_6' = g^{r_2' \cdot b}, \ D_7' = g^{r_1'}, \ K' = (u^{\mathsf{ID}} w^{tag_k} h)^{r_1'}.$$

In Lemma 2, the secret key is generated as

$$D_1 = D_1' \cdot T^{-a_1 \cdot a_2}, \ D_2 = D_2' \cdot T^{a_2} (g^{c_1})^{y_{v_1}}, \ D_3 = D_3' \cdot (f^{c_2})^{y_{v_1}}, \ D_4 = D_4' \cdot T^{a_1} (g^{c_1})^{y_{v_2}}, \ D_5 = D_5' \cdot (f^{c_2})^{y_{v_2}}, \ D_6 = D_6' \cdot f^{c_2}, \ D_7 = D_7' \cdot (g^{c_1}),$$
$$K = K' \cdot (g^{c_1})^{\mathsf{ID} \cdot y_u + y_h + tag_k \cdot y_w}.$$

First, in the case of $T = \nu^{c_1 + c_2}$, let us compute the secret key.

Do not forget that $z_1 = z_1' - y_{v_1} \cdot c_2$, $z_2 = z_2' - y_{v_2} \cdot c_2$, $r_1 = r_1' + c_1$, and $r_2 = r_2' + c_2$ are implicitly set.

$$D_1 = D_1' \cdot T^{-a_1 \cdot a_2} = g^{\alpha \cdot a_1} v_1^{r_1' + r_2'} \cdot (\nu^{c_1 + c_2})^{-a_1 \cdot a_2} = g^{\alpha \cdot a_1} v_1^{r_1' + r_2'} \cdot (\nu^{-a_1 \cdot a_2})^{c_1 + c_2} =$$
$$g^{\alpha \cdot a_1} v_1^{r_1' + r_2'} \cdot v_1^{c_1 + c_2} = g^{\alpha \cdot a_1} v_1^{r_1' + r_2' + c_1 + c_2} = g^{\alpha \cdot a_1} v_1^{r_1 + r_2},$$

$$D_2 = D_2' \cdot T^{a_2} (g^{c_1})^{y_{v_1}} = g^{-\alpha} v_1^{r_1' + r_2'} g^{z_1'} \cdot (\nu^{c_1 + c_2})^{a_2} (g^{c_1})^{y_{v_1}} = g^{-\alpha} v_1^{r_1' + r_2'} g^{z_1'} \cdot$$
$$\nu^{a_2 (c_1 + c_2)} g^{y_{v_1} \cdot c_1} \cdot g^{y_{v_1} \cdot c_2} g^{-y_{v_1} \cdot c_2} = g^{-\alpha} \cdot v_1^{r_1' + r_2'} \nu^{a_2 (c_1 + c_2)} g^{y_{v_1} \cdot c_1} g^{y_{v_1} \cdot c_2} \cdot$$
$$(g^{z_1'} g^{-y_{v_1} \cdot c_2}) = g^{-\alpha} \cdot v_1^{r_1' + r_2'} (\nu^{a_2 \cdot c_1} g^{y_{v_1} \cdot c_1}) (\nu^{a_2 \cdot c_2} g^{y_{v_1} \cdot c_2}) \cdot g^{z_1} = g^{-\alpha} \cdot$$
$$v_1^{r_1' + r_2'} v_1^{c_1} v_1^{c_2} \cdot g^{z_1} = g^{-\alpha} \cdot v_1^{r_1' + r_2' + c_1 + c_2} \cdot g^{z_1} = g^{-\alpha} v_1^{r_1 + r_2} g^{z_1},$$

$$D_3 = D_3' \cdot (f^{c_2})^{y_{v_1}} = (g^b)^{-z_1'} \cdot ((g^b)^{c_2})^{y_{v_1}} = (g^b)^{-z_1'} \cdot (g^b)^{y_{v_1} \cdot c_2} = (g^b)^{-z_1' + y_{v_1} \cdot c_2} = (g^b)^{-z_1},$$

$$D_4 = D_4' \cdot T^{a_1} (g^{c_1})^{y_{v_2}} = v_2^{r_1' + r_2'} g^{z_2'} \cdot (\nu^{c_1 + c_2})^{a_1} (g^{c_1})^{y_{v_2}} = v_2^{r_1' + r_2'} g^{z_2'} \cdot$$
$$(\nu^{a_1})^{c_1 + c_2} g^{y_{v_2} \cdot c_1} \cdot g^{y_{v_2} \cdot c_2} g^{-y_{v_2} \cdot c_2} = (v_2^{r_1' + r_2'} \nu^{a_1 (c_1 + c_2)} g^{y_{v_2} (c_1 + c_2)}) \cdot (g^{z_2'} g^{-y_{v_2} \cdot c_2}) =$$
$$(v_2^{r_1' + r_2'} v_2^{c_1 + c_2}) \cdot g^{z_2} = v_2^{r_1 + r_2} g^{z_2},$$

$$D_5 = D_5' \cdot (f^{c_2})^{y_{v_2}} = (g^b)^{-z_2'} \cdot ((g^b)^{c_2})^{y_{v_2}} = (g^b)^{-z_2'} \cdot (g^b)^{y_{v_2} \cdot c_2} = (g^b)^{-z_2' + y_{v_2} \cdot c_2} = (g^b)^{-z_2},$$

$$D_6 = D_6' \cdot f^{c_2} = g^{r_2' \cdot b} \cdot (g^b)^{c_2} = g^{r_2' \cdot b} \cdot g^{c_2 \cdot b} = g^{(r_2' + c_2) b} = g^{r_2 \cdot b},$$

$$D_7 = D_7' \cdot (g^{c_1}) = g^{r_1'} \cdot (g^{c_1}) = g^{r_1' + c_1} = g^{r_1},$$

$$K = K' \cdot (g^{c_1})^{\mathsf{ID} \cdot y_u + y_h + tag_k \cdot y_w} = (u^{\mathsf{ID}} w^{tag_k} h)^{r_1'} \cdot (u^{\mathsf{ID}} w^{tag_k} h)^{c_1} = (u^{\mathsf{ID}} w^{tag_k} h)^{r_1' + c_1} = (u^{\mathsf{ID}} w^{tag_k} h)^{r_1}.$$

As shown above, in the case of $T = \nu^{c_1 + c_2}$, a normal secret key is computed.

On the other hand, in the case where T is random, some additional random values are multiplied by D_1, D_2, D_4. Let D_1, D_2, D_4 denote D_1', D_2', D_4' respectively. Let an additional random value be g^γ. It means that $T = \nu^{c_1+c_2} \cdot g^\gamma$. We can compute each value as follows. Here, the reason that an additional random value is g^γ is that γ is randomly chosen value.

$$D_1 = D_1' \cdot (g^\gamma)^{-a_1 \cdot a_2} = D_1' \cdot g^{-a_1 \cdot a_2 \cdot \gamma},$$

$$D_2 = D_2' \cdot (g^\gamma)^{a_2} = D_2' \cdot g^{a_2 \cdot \gamma},$$

$$D_4 = D_4' \cdot (g^\gamma)^{a_1} = D_4' \cdot g^{a_1 \cdot \gamma}.$$

As shown above, in the case of $T = \nu^{c_1+c_2} \cdot g^\gamma$, a semi-functional secret key is computed.

Simulation of challenge ciphertext generation in Lemma 2

The Encrypt algorithm in Lemma 2 only generates semi-functional ciphertexts.

The generated real ciphertext by using s_1, s_2, t' is as follows. Since $\mathcal{B}$ knows the public parameters and master secret key, it can generate the real ciphertext as

$$C_0' = M \cdot (e(g,g)^{\alpha \cdot a_1 \cdot b})^{s_2}, \ C_1' = (g^b)^{s_1+s_2}. \ C_2' = (g^{b \cdot a_1})^{s_1}, \ C_3' = (g^{a_1})^{s_1},$$
$$C_4' = (g^{b \cdot a_2})^{s_2}, \ C_5' = (g^{a_2})^{s_2}, \ C_6' = \tau_1^{s_1} \tau_2^{s_2}. \ C_7' = (\tau_1^b)^{s_1} (\tau_2^b)^{s_2} w^{-t'}, \ E_1' = (u^{\mathsf{ID}} w^{tag_c} h)^{t'}, \ E_2' = g^{t'}.$$

In Lemma 2, the ciphertext is generated as

$$C_0 = C_0', \ C_1 = C_1', \ C_2 = C_2', \ C_3 = C_3', \ C_4 = C_4' \cdot f^{a_2 \cdot x}, \ C_5 = C_5' \cdot g^{a_2 \cdot x}, \ C_6 =$$
$$C_6' \cdot v_2^{a_2 \cdot x}, \ C_7 = C_7' \cdot f^{y_{v_2} \cdot x \cdot a_2} \nu^{-a_1 \cdot x \cdot y_w \cdot a_2}, \ E_1 = E_1' \cdot (\nu^{\mathsf{ID} \cdot y_u + y_h + tag_c^* \cdot y_w})^{a_1 a_2 x},$$
$$E_2 = E_2' \cdot \nu^{a_1 \cdot a_2 \cdot x}.$$

Let's compute the ciphertext.

Do not forget that $g^t = g^{t'} \nu^{a_1 \cdot a_2 \cdot x}$ and $(u^{\mathsf{ID}} w^{tag} h) = g^{\mathsf{ID} \cdot y_u + y_h + tag \cdot y_w}$ are implicitly set.

$$C_0 = C_0', \ C_1 = C_1', \ C_2 = C_2', \ C_3 = C_3',$$

$$C_4 = C_4' \cdot f^{a_2 \cdot x} = C_4' \cdot (g^b)^{a_2 \cdot x} = C_4' \cdot g^{b \cdot a_2 \cdot x},$$

$$C_5 = C_5' \cdot g^{a_2 \cdot x},$$

$$C_6 = C_6' \cdot v_2^{a_2 \cdot x}.$$

Up to this point is a general semi-functional ciphertext.

$$C_7 = C_7' \cdot f^{y_{v_2} \cdot x \cdot a_2} \nu^{-a_1 \cdot x \cdot y_w \cdot a_2} = (\tau_1^b)^{s_1} (\tau_2^b)^{s_2} w^{-t'} \cdot f^{y_{v_2} \cdot x \cdot a_2} \nu^{-a_1 \cdot x \cdot y_w \cdot a_2} =$$
$$(\tau_1^b)^{s_1} (\tau_2^b)^{s_2} w^{-t'} \cdot f^{y_{v_2} \cdot x \cdot a_2} \nu^{-a_1 \cdot x \cdot y_w \cdot a_2} \cdot \nu^{a_1 \cdot a_2 \cdot b \cdot x} \nu^{-a_1 \cdot a_2 \cdot b \cdot x} = (\tau_1^b)^{s_1} (\tau_2^b)^{s_2} w^{-t'} \cdot$$
$$(f^{y_{v_2} \cdot x \cdot a_2} \nu^{a_1 \cdot a_2 \cdot b \cdot x}) \cdot \nu^{-a_1 \cdot x \cdot y_w \cdot a_2} \nu^{-a_1 \cdot a_2 \cdot b \cdot x} = (\tau_1^b)^{s_1} (\tau_2^b)^{s_2} w^{-t'} \cdot ((g^b)^{y_{v_2} \cdot x \cdot a_2}$$
$$\nu^{a_1 \cdot a_2 \cdot b \cdot x}) \cdot \nu^{-a_1 \cdot x \cdot a_2 \cdot (y_w + b)} = (\tau_1^b)^{s_1} (\tau_2^b)^{s_2} w^{-t'} \cdot ((g^{y_{v_2}})^{b \cdot x \cdot a_2} (\nu^{a_1})^{a_2 \cdot b \cdot x}) \cdot$$
$$\nu^{-a_1 \cdot x \cdot a_2 \cdot (y_w + b)} = (\tau_1^b)^{s_1} (\tau_2^b)^{s_2} w^{-t'} \cdot ((g^{y_{v_2}} \nu^{a_1})^{a_2 \cdot b \cdot x}) \cdot \nu^{-a_1 \cdot x \cdot a_2 \cdot (y_w + b)} =$$
$$(\tau_1^b)^{s_1} (\tau_2^b)^{s_2} w^{-t'} \cdot v_2^{a_2 \cdot b \cdot x} \cdot \nu^{-a_1 \cdot x \cdot a_2 \cdot (y_w + b)} = (\tau_1^b)^{s_1} (\tau_2^b)^{s_2} \cdot v_2^{a_2 \cdot b \cdot x} \cdot w^{-t'}$$
$$\nu^{-a_1 \cdot x \cdot a_2 \cdot (y_w + b)},$$

where $w^{-t'} \nu^{-a_1 \cdot x \cdot a_2 \cdot (y_w + b)} = (f g^{y_w})^{-t'} \nu^{-a_1 \cdot x \cdot a_2 \cdot (y_w + b)} = (g^b g^{y_w})^{-t'}$
$\nu^{-a_1 \cdot x \cdot a_2 \cdot (y_w + b)} = g^{-t'(b + y_w)} \nu^{-a_1 \cdot x \cdot a_2 \cdot (y_w + b)} = (g^{t'} \nu^{a_1 \cdot x \cdot a_2})^{-(y_w + b)} =$
$(g^t)^{-(y_w + b)} = (g^{y_w + b})^{-t} = w^{-t}.$

$$C_7 = (\tau_1^b)^{s_1} (\tau_2^b)^{s_2} v_2^{a_2 \cdot b \cdot x} w^{-t} = (\tau_1^b)^{s_1} (\tau_2^b)^{s_2} w^{-t} v_2^{a_2 \cdot b \cdot x},$$

$$E_1 = E_1' \cdot (\nu^{ID \cdot y_u + y_h + tag_c^* \cdot y_w})^{a_1 a_2 x} = (u^{ID} w^{tag_c^*} h)^{t'} \cdot (\nu^{ID \cdot y_u + y_h + tag_c^* \cdot y_w})^{a_1 a_2 x} =$$
$$(g^{ID \cdot y_u + y_h + tag_c^* \cdot y_w})^{t'} \cdot (\nu^{ID \cdot y_u + y_h + tag_c^* \cdot y_w})^{a_1 a_2 x} = (g^{t'} \nu^{a_1 a_2 x})^{ID \cdot y_u + y_h + tag_c^* \cdot y_w} =$$
$$(g^t)^{ID \cdot y_u + y_h + tag_c^* \cdot y_w} = (g^{ID \cdot y_u + y_h + tag_c^* \cdot y_w})^t = (u^{ID} w^{tag_c^*} h)^t,$$

$$E_2 = E_2' \cdot \nu^{a_1 \cdot a_2 \cdot x} = g^{t'} \cdot \nu^{a_1 \cdot a_2 \cdot x} = g^t.$$

As shown above, a semi-functional ciphertext is computed.

How to generate tags?

First, we explain why tags should not be random and draw a conclusion that we should use $F()$ to generate tag.

The simulator sets $F()$ and $(u^{ID} w^{tag} h)$ as follows in Lemma 2:

$$F(x) = A \cdot x + B, \tag{13.9}$$

$$(u^{ID} w^{tag} h) = f^{tag - A \cdot ID - B} g^{ID \cdot y_u + y_h + tag \cdot y_w}. \tag{13.10}$$

If the tag is random, the $f^{tag - A \cdot ID - B}$ part remains, which is added to original semi-functional secret key and challenge ciphertext as below, where we can figure out that the $f^{tag - A \cdot ID - B}$ part works as a hindrance to decryption.

$$E_1 = E_1' \cdot (\nu^{ID \cdot y_u + y_h + tag_c^* \cdot y_w})^{a_1 a_2 x} = (u^{ID} w^{tag_c^*} h)^{t'} \cdot (\nu^{ID \cdot y_u + y_h + tag_c^* \cdot y_w})^{a_1 a_2 x}$$
$$= (g^{ID \cdot y_u + y_h + tag_c^* \cdot y_w} f^{tag_c^* - A \cdot ID - B})^{t'} \cdot (\nu^{ID \cdot y_u + y_h + tag_c^* \cdot y_w})^{a_1 a_2 x} ((\nu^b)^{tag_c^* - A \cdot ID - B}$$
$$(\nu^b)^{-tag_c^* + A \cdot ID + B})^{a_1 a_2 x}$$
$$= (g^{ID \cdot y_u + y_h + tag_c^* \cdot y_w} (g^b)^{tag_c^* - A \cdot ID - B})^{t'} \cdot (\nu^{ID \cdot y_u + y_h + tag_c^* \cdot y_w} (\nu^b)^{tag_c^* - A \cdot ID - B})^{a_1 a_2 x} \cdot$$
$$((\nu^b)^{-tag_c^* + A \cdot ID + B})^{a_1 a_2 x}$$
$$= (g^{ID \cdot y_u + y_h + tag_c^* \cdot y_w} (g^b)^{tag_c^* - A \cdot ID - B})^t \cdot ((\nu^b)^{-tag_c^* + A \cdot ID + B})^{a_1 a_2 x}$$
$$= (u^{ID} w^{tag_c^*} h)^t \cdot ((\nu^b)^{-tag_c^* + A \cdot ID + B})^{a_1 a_2 x}$$

$$= (u^{\mathsf{ID}} w^{tag_c^*} h)^t \cdot ((f^{\log_g \nu})^{-tag_c^* + A \cdot \mathsf{ID} + B})^{a_1 a_2 x}$$
$$= (u^{\mathsf{ID}} w^{tag_c^*} h)^t \cdot (f^{tag_c^* - A \cdot \mathsf{ID} - B})^{-a_1 a_2 x \log_g \nu}.$$

$$K = K' \cdot (g^{c_1})^{\mathsf{ID} \cdot y_u + y_h + tag_k \cdot y_w}$$
$$= K' \cdot (g^{\mathsf{ID} \cdot y_u + y_h + tag_k \cdot y_w})^{c_1} \cdot (f^{tag_k - A \cdot \mathsf{ID} - B} f^{-tag_k + A \cdot \mathsf{ID} + B})^{c_1}$$
$$= (u^{\mathsf{ID}} w^{tag_k} h)^{r_1'} \cdot (g^{\mathsf{ID} \cdot y_u + y_h + tag_k \cdot y_w})^{c_1} (f^{tag_k - A \cdot \mathsf{ID} - B})^{c_1} \cdot (f^{-tag_k + A \cdot \mathsf{ID} + B})^{c_1}$$
$$= (u^{\mathsf{ID}} w^{tag_k} h)^{r_1'} \cdot (u^{\mathsf{ID}} w^{tag_k} h)^{c_1} \cdot (f^{-tag_k + A \cdot \mathsf{ID} + B})^{c_1}$$
$$= (u^{\mathsf{ID}} w^{tag_k} h)^{r_1' + c_1} \cdot (f^{-tag_k + A \cdot \mathsf{ID} + B})^{c_1}$$
$$= (u^{\mathsf{ID}} w^{tag_k} h)^{r_1} \cdot (f^{tag_k - A \cdot \mathsf{ID} - B})^{-c_1}.$$

As shown above, invalid semi-functional secret key and challenge ciphertext are generated. So, we can conclude that we should not use a random tag.

On the other hand, if the tag is $F(\mathsf{ID}) = A \cdot \mathsf{ID} + B$, i.e., not random, then $f^{tag - A \cdot \mathsf{ID} - B} = 1$, $(u^{\mathsf{ID}} w^{tag} h) = f^{tag - A \cdot \mathsf{ID} - B} g^{\mathsf{ID} \cdot y_u + y_h + tag \cdot y_w} = g^{\mathsf{ID} \cdot y_u + y_h + tag \cdot y_w}$, and valid semi-functional secret key and challenge ciphertext are generated. In conclusion, we should use $F()$ to generate tags.

Probability analysis in Lemma 2 The probability computation is simple as

$$Game_{k-1} Adv_{\mathcal{A}} - Game_k Adv_{\mathcal{A}} = \epsilon_{dlin}. \tag{13.11}$$

Lemma 3 Suppose that there exists an algorithm $\mathcal{A}$ that makes at most q queries and $Game_q Adv_{\mathcal{A}} - Game_{Final} Adv_{\mathcal{A}} = \epsilon_{dbdh}$. Then we can build an algorithm $\mathcal{B}$ that has advantage ϵ_{dbdh} in the decision BDH game.

Proof The algorithm $\mathcal{B}$ begins by taking in an instance $(g, g^{c_1}, g^{c_2}, g^{c_3}, T)$ of the decision BDH problem. We now describe how it executes the Setup, Key Phase, and Challenge phases of the IBE game with $\mathcal{A}$.

In both of these games, the challenge ciphertexts and all the private keys are semi-functional. Therefore, $\mathcal{B}$ only needs to be able to generate semi-functional private keys.

Reduction algorithm $\mathcal{B}$ in Lemma 3

Setup

1. Choose a random exponents $a_1, b, y_v, y_{v_1}, y_{v_2}, y_w, y_h, y_u \in \mathbb{Z}_p$.

2. Let $\alpha = c_1 \cdot c_2$ and $a_2 = c_2$, where c_1 and c_2 are the exponents that reduction cannot know itself.

3. Set $g = g$, g^b, g^{a_1}, $g^{a_2} = g^{c_2}$, $g^{b \cdot a_1}$, $g^{b \cdot a_2} = (g^{c_2})^b$, $v = g^{y_v}$, $v_1 =$

$g^{y_{v_1}}$, $v_2 = g^{y_{v_2}}$. $w = g^{y_w}$, $u = g^{y_u}$, $h = g^{y_h}$, $e(g,g)^{a_1 \cdot a \cdot b} = e(g^{c_1}, g^{c_2})^{a_1 \cdot b}$.

4. Compute $\tau_1 = vv_1^{a_1}$, $\tau_2 = v(g^{c_2})^{y_{v_2}}$, $\tau_1^b = v^b v_1^{a_1 \cdot b}$, $\tau_2^b = v^b(g^{c_2})^{y_{v_2} \cdot b}$.

5. Send the public parameters $\mathsf{params} = (g^b, g^{a_1}, g^{a_2}, g^{b \cdot a_1}, g^{b \cdot a_2})$ $(\tau_1, \tau_2, \tau_1^b, \tau_2^b, w, u, h, e(g,g)^{\alpha \cdot a_1 \cdot b})$.

6. $\mathcal{B}$ has partial information of the master secret key MSK, instead of constructing a $\mathsf{MSK} = (g, g^\alpha, g^{\alpha \cdot a_1}, v, v_1, v_2)$, because $g^\alpha, g^{\alpha \cdot a_1}$ cannot be computed.

Phase I

1. Choose a random exponents $r_1, r_2, z_1, z_2, \gamma', tag_k \in \mathbb{Z}_p$ and define $r = r_1 + r_2$.

2. This algorithm implicitly sets $\gamma = c_1 + \gamma'$.

3. Compute $D_1 = (g^{c_2})^{-\gamma' \cdot a_1} v^r$, $D_2 = (g^{c_2})^\gamma v_1^r g^{z_1}$, $D_3 = (g^b)^{-z_1}$, $D_4 = (g^{c_1})^{a_1} g^{a_1 \cdot \gamma'} v_2^r g^{z_2}$, $D_5 = (g^b)^{-z_2}$, $D_6 = g^{r_2 \cdot b}$, $D_7 = g^{r_1}$, $K = (u^{\mathsf{ID}} w^{tag_k} h)^{r_1}$.

4. Send the secret key $SK_{\mathsf{ID}} = (D_1, \cdots D_7, K, tag_k)$.

Challenge $\mathcal{B}$ creates a challenge ciphertext that is a semi-functional ciphertext of either M_β or a random message, depending on T.

1. $\mathcal{A}$ outputs messages M_0, M_1 and challenge identity ID^*.

2. $\mathcal{B}$ generates bit $\beta \in \{0, 1\}$.

3. Choose a random exponents $s_1, t, tag_c, x' \in \mathbb{Z}_p$.

4. This algorithm implicitly sets $s_2 = c_3$ and $x = -c_3 + x'$.

5. Compute $C_0 = M_\beta \cdot T^{a_1 \cdot b}$, $C_1 = g^{s_1 \cdot b}(g^{c_3})^b$, $C_2 = g^{b \cdot a_1 \cdot s_1}$, $C_3 = g^{a_1 \cdot s_1}$, $C_4 = (g^{c_2})^{x' \cdot b}$, $C_5 = (g^{c_2})^{x'}$, $C_6 = \tau_1^{s_1}(g^{c_3})^{y_v}(g^{c_2})^{y_{v_2} \cdot x'}$, $C_7 = (\tau_1^b)^{s_1}(g^{c_3})^{y_v \cdot b}(g^{c_2})^{y_{v_2} \cdot x' \cdot b} w^{-t}$, $E_1 = (u^{\mathsf{ID}} w^{tag_c} h)^t$, $E_2 = g^t$.

6. Send $(C_0, \cdots, C_7, E_1, E_2, tag_c)$ to $\mathcal{A}$ as the challenge ciphertext.

Note If $T = e(g,g)^{c_1 \cdot c_2 \cdot c_3}$, then we are in $Game_q$, otherwise we are in $Game_{Final}$.

Phase II

1. $\mathcal{A}$ makes key generation queries, and $\mathcal{B}$ responds as in Phase I.

Guess

1. Finally, the adversary outputs guesses $\beta' \in \{0, 1\}$.

2. If $\beta = \beta'$ outputs 0 (indicating that $T = \nu^{c_1+c_2}$); otherwise, it outputs 1.

Simulation of secret key generation in Lemma 3

The Extract algorithm in Lemma 3 only generates semi-functional secret keys.

The generated real semi-functional secret key by using $r_1, r_2, z_1, z_2, \gamma', tag_k$ is as follows. Since $\mathcal{B}$ does not know the master secret key, it cannot generate the real secret key unlike previous two lemmas. However, in Lemma 3, a semi-functional secret keys can be generated without knowledge of the master secret key as follows: For convenience, let normal secret keys denote $(D_1', D_2', D_3', D_4', D_5', D_6', D_7', K')$. Do not forget that $\gamma = c_1 + \gamma'$, $\alpha = c_1 \cdot c_2$, $a_2 = c_2$ are implicitly set.

$$
\begin{aligned}
D_1 &= (g^{c_2})^{-\gamma' \cdot a_1} v^r = (g^{c_2})^{-\gamma' \cdot a_1} v^r \cdot g^{\alpha \cdot a_1} g^{-\alpha \cdot a_1} = (g^{\alpha \cdot a_1} v^r) \cdot \\
&(g^{-\alpha \cdot a_1} (g^{c_2})^{-\gamma' \cdot a_1}) = D_1' g^{-\alpha \cdot a_1 - c_2 \cdot \gamma' \cdot a_1} = D_1' g^{-a_1(\alpha + c_2 \cdot \gamma')} \\
&= D_1' g^{-a_1(c_1 \cdot c_2 + c_2 \cdot (\gamma - c_1))} = D_1' g^{-a_1 \cdot c_2 \cdot \gamma} = D_1' g^{-a_1 \cdot a_2 \cdot \gamma},
\end{aligned}
$$

$$
\begin{aligned}
D_2 &= (g^{c_2})^{\gamma'} v_1^r g^{z_1} = (g^{c_2})^{\gamma'} v_1^r g^{z_1} \cdot g^{\alpha} g^{-\alpha} = g^{-\alpha} v_1^r g^{z_1} \cdot g^{\alpha} (g^{c_2})^{\gamma'} = \\
&D_2' g^{\alpha + c_2 \cdot \gamma'} = D_2' g^{c_1 \cdot c_2 + c_2(\gamma - c_1)} = D_2' g^{c_2 \cdot \gamma} = D_2' g^{a_2 \cdot \gamma},
\end{aligned}
$$

$$
D_3 = (g^b)^{-z_1} = D_3',
$$

$$
D_4 = (g^{c_1})^{a_1} g^{a_1 \cdot \gamma'} v_2^r g^{z_2} = v_2^r g^{z_2} \cdot g^{a_1(c_1 + \gamma')} = D_4' g^{a_1(c_1 + \gamma - c_1)} = D_4' g^{a_1 \cdot \gamma},
$$

$$
D_5 = (g^b)^{-z_2} = D_5',
$$

$$
D_6 = g^{r_2 \cdot b} = D_6',
$$

$$
D_7 = g^{r_1} = D_7',
$$

$$
K = (u^{\mathsf{ID}} w^{tag_k} h)^{r_1} = K'.
$$

As shown above, the simulator can generate semi-functional secret key without knowledge of the master secret key.

Simulation of challenge ciphertext generation in Lemma 3

The difference between $Game_q$ and $Game_{Final}$ is whether the challenge ciphertext is semi-functional or random. So T must be embedded in the challenge ciphertext. The challenge ciphertext is semi-functional if T is real, otherwise the challenge ciphertext is random. Here check that if T is real, then it computes the semi-functional ciphertext, or if T is random, then it computes the random ciphertext.

Since $\mathcal{B}$ does not know the master secret key, it cannot generate the real ciphertext unlike previous two lemmas. However, in Lemma 3, a semi-functional ciphertext can be generated without the knowledge of the master secret key as

$$C_0 = M_\beta \cdot T^{a_1 \cdot b}, \; C_1 = g^{s_1 \cdot b}(g^{c_3})^b, \; C_2 = g^{b \cdot a_1 \cdot s_1}, \; C_3 = g^{a_1 \cdot s_1}, \; C_4 = (g^{c_2})^{x' \cdot b},$$
$$C_5 = (g^{c_2})^{x'},$$

$$C_6 = \tau_1^{s_1}(g^{c_3})^{y_v}(g^{c_2})^{y_{v_2} \cdot x'}, \; C_7 = (\tau_1^b)^{s_1}(g^{c_3})^{y_v \cdot b}(g^{c_2})^{y_{v_2} \cdot x' \cdot b}w^{-t}, \; E_1 = (u^{\mathsf{ID}}w^{tag_c}h)^t, \; E_2 = g^t.$$

First, in the case of $T = e(g,g)^{c_1 \cdot c_2 \cdot c_3}$, let us compute the ciphertext by using s_1, t, tag_c as follows.

For convenience, let a normal ciphertext denoted by $(C_0', C_1', C_2', C_3', C_4', C_5', C_6', C_7', E_1', E_2')$. Do not forget that $s_2 = c_3$, $x = -c_3 + x'$, $\alpha = c_1 \cdot c_2$ are implicitly set.

$$C_0 = M_\beta \cdot T^{a_1 \cdot b} = M_\beta \cdot (e(g,g)^{c_1 \cdot c_2 \cdot c_3})^{a_1 \cdot b} = M_\beta \cdot e(g,g)^{c_1 \cdot c_2 \cdot a_1 \cdot b \cdot c_3} = M_\beta \cdot e(g,g)^{\alpha \cdot a_1 \cdot b \cdot s_2} = C_0',$$

$$C_1 = g^{s_1 \cdot b}(g^{c_3})^b = g^{s_1 \cdot b}g^{c_3 \cdot b} = g^{b(s_1 + c_3)} = g^{b(s_1 + s_2)} = C_1',$$

$$C_2 = g^{b \cdot a_1 \cdot s_1} = C_2',$$

$$C_3 = g^{a_1 \cdot s_1} = C_3',$$

$$C_4 = (g^{c_2})^{x' \cdot b} = (g^{a_2})^{x' \cdot b} = g^{a_2 \cdot x' \cdot b} = g^{a_2 \cdot (c_3 + x) \cdot b} = g^{a_2 \cdot (s_2 + x) \cdot b} = g^{a_2 \cdot s_2 \cdot b}g^{a_2 \cdot x \cdot b} = C_4'g^{b \cdot a_2 \cdot x},$$

$$C_5 = (g^{c_2})^{x'} = (g^{a_2})^{x'} = g^{a_2 \cdot x'} = g^{a_2 \cdot (c_3 + x)} = g^{a_2 \cdot (s_2 + x)} = g^{a_2 \cdot s_2}g^{a_2 \cdot x} = C_5'g^{a_2 \cdot x} = C_5'g^{a_2 \cdot x},$$

$$C_6 = \tau_1^{s_1}(g^{c_3})^{y_v}(g^{c_2})^{y_{v_2} \cdot x'} = \tau_1^{s_1}g^{c_3 \cdot y_v}g^{c_2 \cdot y_{v_2} \cdot (x + c_3)} = \tau_1^{s_1}g^{c_3 \cdot y_v}g^{c_2 \cdot y_{v_2} \cdot x}g^{c_2 \cdot y_{v_2} \cdot c_3} = \tau_1^{s_1}(g^{c_3 \cdot y_v}g^{c_2 \cdot y_{v_2} \cdot c_3})g^{c_2 \cdot y_{v_2} \cdot x}$$

$$= \tau_1^{s_1}g^{c_3(y_v + c_2 \cdot y_{v_2})}(g^{c_2})^{y_{v_2} \cdot x} = \tau_1^{s_1}g^{s_2(y_v + c_2 \cdot y_{v_2})}(g^{a_2})^{y_{v_2} \cdot x} = \tau_1^{s_1}(g^{y_v + c_2 \cdot y_{v_2}})^{s_2}(g^{y_{v_2}})^{a_2 \cdot x} = \tau_1^{s_1}(\tau_2)^{s_2}(v_2)^{a_2 \cdot x} = C_6'v_2^{a_2 \cdot x},$$

$$C_7 = (\tau_1^b)^{s_1}(g^{c_3})^{y_v \cdot b}(g^{c_2})^{y_{v_2} \cdot x' \cdot b}w^{-t} = (C_6)^bw^{-t} = (\tau_1^{s_1}\tau_2^{s_2}v_2^{a_2 \cdot x})^bw^{-t} = \tau_1^{s_1 \cdot b}\tau_2^{s_2 \cdot b}w^{-t}v_2^{a_2 \cdot x \cdot b} = C_7'v_2^{a_2 \cdot b \cdot x},$$

$$E_1 = (u^{\mathsf{ID}} w^{tag_c} h)^t = E_1',$$

$$E_2 = g^t = E_2'.$$

As shown above, in the case of $T = e(g, g)^{c_1 \cdot c_2 \cdot c_3}$, a semi-functional ciphertext is computed as expected.

On the other hand, in the case that T is random, some additional random values are multiplied by the computed value C_0. Therefore, we know that random ciphertext is computed in the case that T is random.

Probability analysis in Lemma 3 The probability computation is simple as

$$|Game_q Adv_{\mathcal{A}} - Game_{Final} Adv_{\mathcal{A}}| = \epsilon_{dbdh}. \tag{13.12}$$

Probability analysis of Waters' IBE scheme

Theorem 1 If the decisional Linear and decisional BDH assumptions hold, then no polynomial-time algorithm can break Waters' IBE system.

Proof The proof proceeds through a total of $(q + 3)$ games. The initial game $Game_{Real}$ is the actual security game used in defining CPA-security of IBE. Then there are $(q + 1)$ security games from $Game_0$ to $Game_q$ followed by $Game_{Final}$. Suppose $Game_{Real} Adv_{\mathcal{A}}$, $Game_0 Adv_{\mathcal{A}}$, $\cdots, Game_q Adv_{\mathcal{A}}$, $Game_{Final} Adv_{\mathcal{A}}$ be the events that the adversary's guesses in games $Game_{Real}$, $Game_0$ to $Game_q$, and $Game_{Final}$ respectively are correct.

A sequence of lemmas below shows the following results.

1. $Game_{Real} Adv_{\mathcal{A}} - Game_0 Adv_{\mathcal{A}} = \epsilon_{dlin}.$
2. $Game_{k-1} Adv_{\mathcal{A}} - Game_k Adv_{\mathcal{A}} = \epsilon_{dlin}$ for $k = 1, \cdots, q.$
3. $Game_q Adv_{\mathcal{A}} - Game_{Final} Adv_{\mathcal{A}} = \epsilon_{dbdh}.$

The probability of $Game_{Final} Adv_{\mathcal{A}}$ is 0 and so

$$|Game_{Real} Adv_{\mathcal{A}} - Game_{Final} Adv_{\mathcal{A}}|$$

$$= |Game_{Real} Adv_{\mathcal{A}} - Game_0 Adv_{\mathcal{A}}| + \sum_{k=1}^{q} |Game_{k-1} Adv_{\mathcal{A}} - Game_k Adv_{\mathcal{A}}|$$

$$+ |Game_q Adv_{\mathcal{A}} - Game_{Final} Adv_{\mathcal{A}}|$$

$$= (q+1)\epsilon_{dlin} + \epsilon_{dbdh}.$$

$\square$

Exercises

13.1 Why is static assumption preferred compared to non-static assumption?

13.2 In Setup Phase of Waters' IBE scheme, describe why we cannot use identity space $\mathbb{Z}_p$ for arbitrary length strings.

14

Hierarchical Identity-Based Encryption

CONTENTS

This chapter provides the details of the hierarchical identity based encryption (HIBE). The overview section introduces the existing problems with the IBE schemes and provides the solutions that can be obtained using HIBE. Certain advantages and differences of HIBE over the IBE are discussed. The next portion of the chapter presents the preliminaries starting from the general construction of HIBE. This is followed by the security model of the HIBE. HIBE has three static hardness assumptions that are discussed in detail in the chapter. The master theorem for hardness in composite order bilinear groups is presented. The concept of normally semi-functional keys are then discussed in the Waters' realization. Subsequently, the Waters' HIBE with composite order is presented along with the formal construction. The proof of HIBE security is then given as a hybrid argument over a sequence of games in detail. The final part of this chapter discusses the generic group model. In order to understand this, the decisional linear Diffie-Hellman assumption and linear problem in generic bilinear groups are discussed.

14.1   Overview

In IBE schemes, there is a common property: they use a single PKG to generate all private keys. This has some disadvantages. The first is that the PKG knows Bob's private key, i.e., key escrow is inherent in IBE systems. Clearly, escrow may be a serious problem for some applications. Moreover, having a single PKG is undesirable for a large network because the PKG has as much management overhead as the size increases. Not only is private key generation computationally expensive, but also the PKG must verify proofs of identities and must establish secure channels to transmit private keys to users.

Hierarchical Identity-Based Encryption (HIBE) allows a root PKG to distribute the workload by delegating private key generation and identity authentication to lower-level PKGs. In a HIBE scheme, a root PKG generates private keys for domain-level PKGs only, who in turn generate private keys for users in their domains at the next level. Authentication and private key transmission can be done locally. To encrypt a message to Bob, Alice obtains only the public parameters of Bob's root PKG (and Bob's identifying information); there are no "lower-level parameters." That is, public parameters are shared throughout the entire level. Another advantage of HIBE schemes is damage control: disclosure of a domain PKG's secret does not compromise the secrets of higher-level PKGs. Thus, recovering from a compromise is also easier, because it only needs to recreate the affected parts of the hierarchy instead of the entire system. The difference between IBE and HIBE is shown in Figure 14.1.

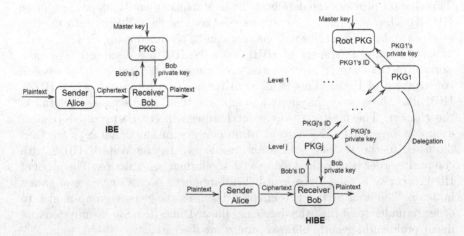

FIGURE 14.1
Difference between IBE and HIBE.

In an HIBE scheme, a single user can have different identities for each level of the HIBE, so that for an HIBE scheme with a maximum of j levels, an identity can have the form $\overrightarrow{\mathsf{ID}} = (\mathsf{ID}_1, \mathsf{ID}_2, \ldots, \mathsf{ID}_j)$, where each of the ID_i are potentially different.

A user at level i can delegate secret keys to descendant identities at lower levels, but cannot decrypt messages intended for a recipient that is not among its descendants. For example, a user with the identity "Gachon University: Department of Computer Engineering" can delegate a key for the identity "Gachon University: Department of Computer Engineering: undergraduate student," but cannot delegate keys for identities that do not begin with "Gachon University: Department of Computer Engineering." A more formal definition of an HIBE system is given later.

14.2 Preliminaries

This section presents preliminaries including general construction and security model of HIBE, composite order bilinear groups and hardness assumptions.

14.2.1 General Construction of HIBE

A Hierarchical Identity Based Encryption scheme has five algorithms: Setup, Encrypt, Gen, Decrypt, and Delegate which are described as follows.

Setup The setup algorithm takes a security parameter k as input and outputs the public parameters params and a master secret key MSK.

Gen The key generation algorithm takes the master secret key and an identity vector $\overrightarrow{\mathsf{ID}}$ as input and outputs a private key $SK_{\overrightarrow{\mathsf{ID}}}$.

Delegate The delegation algorithm takes a secret key for the identity vector $\overrightarrow{\mathsf{ID}}$ of depth d and an identity I as input and outputs a secret key for the depth $d+1$ identity vector $\overrightarrow{\mathsf{ID}} : I$ formed by concatenating I onto the end of $\overrightarrow{\mathsf{ID}}$.

Encrypt The encryption algorithm takes the public parameters *parmas*, a message M and an identity vector $\overrightarrow{\mathsf{ID}}$ as input, and outputs a ciphertext CT.

Decrypt The decryption algorithm takes the public parameters params, a ciphertext CT and a secret key $SK_{\overrightarrow{\mathsf{ID}}}$ as input, and outputs the message M,

if the ciphertext was an encryption to an identity vector $\overrightarrow{\text{ID}}$ and the secret key
is for the same identity vector.

Notice that the decryption algorithm works only when the identity vector
of the ciphertext matches the secret key exactly. However, someone who has
a secret key for a prefix of the identity vector can delegate it for generating
the required secret key and also decrypt the ciphertext by themselves.

14.2.2 Security Model for HIBE

In HIBE, the intermediate user can generate the private keys of users at lower
level. Therefore, it needs to be applied in secure games.

IND-ID-CPA game for an HIBE scheme

1. **Setup** The challenger runs the Setup algorithm to generate public
   parameters *params* which it gives to the adversary. We let S denote
   the set of private keys that the challenger has created but not yet
   given to the adversary. At this point, $S = \emptyset$.

2. **Phase I** The adversary makes repeated queries of one of three
   types[1]:

   (a) **Create** To make a Create query, the attacker specifies an iden-
       tity vector $\overrightarrow{\text{ID}}$. In response, the challenger creates a key for this
       vector by calling the Key Generation algorithm, and places this
       key in the set S. It only gives the attacker a reference to this
       key, not the key itself.

   (b) **Delegate** To make a Delegate query, the attacker specifies a
       key $SK_{\overrightarrow{\text{ID}}}$ in the set S and specifies an identity I'. In response,
       the challenger appends I' to $\overrightarrow{\text{ID}}$ and makes a key for this new
       identity by running the Delegation algorithm on $SK_{\overrightarrow{\text{ID}}}$ and I'.
       It adds this key to the set S and again gives the attacker only
       a reference to it, not the actual key.

---

[1] Why the challenger gives the attacker a reference to the key, not the key itself during
Create and Delegate queries?

In a real scheme, for generating the private key, PKG that is not root must run the
Delegate algorithm. On the other hand, in the security game, for generating the private
key, not only root PKG, but also PKG that is not root runs the Gen algorithm instead
of the Delegate algorithm. However, even if the Delegate algorithm is included, it should
show that the scheme is secure. The problem occurs in the process that the simulator
simulates both the Gen and the Delegate algorithms as follows. If the simulator performs
the Gen algorithm rather than the Delegate algorithm and gives the private key, then the
scheme would be different from the original scheme. Therefore, the reveal query is made. The
attacker must use the Reveal query to get the private key, and we should take the limitation
that the attacker cannot request the Delegate query to get the private key anymore.

    (c) **Reveal** To make a Reveal query, the attacker specifies an element of the set S. The challenger gives this key to the attacker and removes it from the set S. We note that the attacker no longer need to make a delegation query for this key because it can run the Delegation algorithm on the revealed key for itself.

3. **Challenge** The adversary gives the challenger two messages M_0 and M_1, and a challenge identity vector $\overrightarrow{\mathsf{ID}}^*$. This identity vector must satisfy the property that no revealed identity in Phase I was a prefix of it. The challenger sets $\beta \in \{0, 1\}$ randomly and encrypts M_β under $\overrightarrow{\mathsf{ID}}^*$. It sends the ciphertext to the adversary.

4. **Phase II** This is the same as Phase I, with the added restriction that any revealed identity vector must not be a prefix of $\overrightarrow{\mathsf{ID}}^*$.

5. **Guess** The adversary must output a guess β' for β.
   The advantage of an adversary $\mathcal{A}$ is defined to be $Pr[\beta' = \beta] - \frac{1}{2}$.

Definition 1 *A hierarchical identity-based encryption scheme is secure if all polynomial time adversaries achieve at most a negligible advantage in the security game.*

14.2.3 Composite Order Bilinear Groups

Let $\mathbb{G}$ and $\mathbb{G}_T$ be cyclic groups of order $N = p_1 p_2 p_3$, where p_1, p_2, p_3 are distinct primes. A bilinear map e is a map: $\mathbb{G} \times \mathbb{G} \to \mathbb{G}_T$, which satisfies the following properties:

1. Bilinear: For all $g, h \in \mathbb{G}$, and $a, b \in \mathbb{Z}_N$, $e(g^a, h^b) = e(g, h)^{ab}$.

2. Non-degenerate: There exists $g \in \mathbb{G}$ such that $e(g, g)$ has order N in $\mathbb{G}_T$.

3. Computation in groups: Let $\mathbb{G}_{p_1}, \mathbb{G}_{p_2}$ and $\mathbb{G}_{p_3}$ denote the subgroups of order p_1, p_2 and p_3 in $\mathbb{G}$, respectively. We note that when $h_i \in \mathbb{G}_{p_i}$ and $h_j \in \mathbb{G}_{p_j}$ for $i \neq j$, $e(h_i, h_j)$ is the identity in $\mathbb{G}_T$. To see this, suppose $h_1 \in \mathbb{G}_{p_1}$ and $h_2 \in \mathbb{G}_{p_2}$. Let g denote a generator of $\mathbb{G}$. Then, $g^{p_1 p_2}$ generates $\mathbb{G}_{p_3}$, $g^{p_1 p_3}$ generates $\mathbb{G}_{p_2}$, and $g^{p_2 p_3}$ generates $\mathbb{G}_{p_1}$. Hence, for some α_1, α_2, $h_1 = (g^{p_2 p_3})^{\alpha_1}$ and $h_2 = (g^{p_1 p_3})^{\alpha_2}$. We note that

$$e(h_1, h_2) = e(g^{p_2 p_3 \alpha_1}, g^{p_1 p_3 \alpha_2}) = e(g^{\alpha_1}, g^{p_3 \alpha_2})^{p_1 p_2 p_3} = 1. \quad (14.1)$$

This property will be used in security proof of HIBE with composite order in Section 14.2.7 (The final result of computation will be given after applying this property).

14.2.4   Hardness Assumptions

Let $\mathbb{G}$ and $\mathbb{G}_T$ be cyclic groups of order $N = p_1 p_2 p_3$, where p_1, p_2, p_3 are distinct primes. Let e is a bilinear map: $\mathbb{G} \times \mathbb{G} \to \mathbb{G}_T$. Let $\mathbb{G}_{p_1 p_2}$ denote the subgroup of order $p_1 p_2$ in $\mathbb{G}$. We have three assumptions below. Note that they are static (for example, not dependent on the depth of the hierarchy or the number of queries made by an attacker).

Assumption 1 (Subgroup decision problem for 3 primes)

Given $g \in \mathbb{G}_{p_1}$, $X_3 \in \mathbb{G}_{p_3}$, an algorithm $\mathcal{A}$ has advantage ϵ in solving extended subgroup decision problem in a composite group $\mathbb{G}$ if

$$|Pr[\mathcal{A}(\mathbb{G}, g, X_3, T \in \mathbb{G}_{p_1 p_2}) = 0] - Pr[\mathcal{A}(\mathbb{G}, g, X_3, T \in \mathbb{G}_{p_1}) = 0]| \geq \epsilon. \quad (14.2)$$

The problem basically states that if we are given generators in the p_1, p_3 but not p_2 subgroup then we cannot distinguish a random element in the $\mathbb{G}_{p_1 p_2}$ subgroup from the $\mathbb{G}_{p_1}$ subgroup. (We note that $T \in \mathbb{G}_{p_1 p_2}$ can be written (uniquely) as the product of an element of $\mathbb{G}_{p_1}$ and an element of $\mathbb{G}_{p_2}$.)

Definition 2 *We say that Assumption 1 holds if no polynomial time algorithm $\mathcal{A}$ has a non-negligible advantage in solving Assumption 1.*

Assumption 2

Given $g, X_1 \in \mathbb{G}_{p_1}$, $X_2, Y_2 \in \mathbb{G}_{p_2}$, $X_3, Y_3 \in \mathbb{G}_{p_3}$, an algorithm $\mathcal{A}$ has advantage ϵ in solving the extended subgroup decision problem in a composite group $\mathbb{G}$ if

$$|Pr[\mathcal{A}(\mathbb{G}, g, X_1 X_2, X_3, Y_2 Y_3, T \in \mathbb{G}) = 0] - Pr[\mathcal{A}(\mathbb{G}, g, X_1 X_2, X_3, Y_2 Y_3, T \in \mathbb{G}_{p_1 p_3}) = 0]| \geq \epsilon.$$

The problem basically states that if we are given generators in the p_1, p_2, p_3, $p_1 p_2$, $p_2 p_3$ subgroups but not $p_1 p_3$ subgroup, then we cannot distinguish a random element in the $\mathbb{G}$ from the $\mathbb{G}_{p_1 p_3}$ subgroup. (We note that $T \in \mathbb{G}_{p_1 p_3}$ can be written (uniquely) as the product of an element of $\mathbb{G}_{p_1}$ and an element of $\mathbb{G}_{p_3}$.)

Definition 3 *We say that Assumption 2 holds if no polynomial time algorithm $\mathcal{A}$ has a non-negligible advantage in solving Assumption 2.*

Assumption 3

Given $g \in \mathbb{G}_{p_1}$, $X_2, Y_2, Z_2 \in \mathbb{G}_{p_2}$, $X_3 \in \mathbb{G}_{p_3}$, $\alpha, s \in \mathbb{Z}_N$, an algorithm $\mathcal{A}$ has advantage ϵ in solving the extended subgroup decision problem in a composite group $\mathbb{G}$ if

$$|Pr[\mathcal{A}(\mathbb{G}, g, g^\alpha X_2, X_3, g^s Y_2, Z_2, T = e(g,g)^{\alpha s}) =$$
$$0] - Pr[\mathcal{A}(\mathbb{G}, g, g^\alpha X_2, X_3, g^s Y_2, Z_2, T \in \mathbb{G}_T) = 0]| \geq \epsilon.$$

In Assumption 3, it must remain hard to distinguish $T = e(g,g)^{\alpha s}$ from a random element in $\mathbb{G}_T$.

Definition 4 *We say that Assumption 3 holds if no polynomial time algorithm $\mathcal{A}$ has a non-negligible advantage in solving Assumption 3.*

14.2.5 A "Master Theorem" for Hardness in Composite Order Bilinear Groups [60]

Before stating the theorems that shows the above assumptions are hard, we introduce some notation. We will consider cyclic bilinear groups of order N, where $N = \prod_{i=1}^{m} p_i$ is the product of m distinct primes, each larger than 2^n. Let $\mathbb{G}$ denote the "base group" and let $\mathbb{G}_T$ denote the "target group;" i.e., the bilinear map e is from $\mathbb{G} \times \mathbb{G}$ to $\mathbb{G}_T$. Each element $g \in \mathbb{G}$ can be written as $g = g_{p_1}^{a_1} g_{p_2}^{a_2} \cdots g_{p_m}^{a_m}$, where $a_i \in \mathbb{Z}_{p_i}$ and g_{p_i} denotes some fixed generator of the subgroup of order p_i. We can therefore represent each element $g \in \mathbb{G}$ as an m-tuple $(a_1, \cdots, a_m)$. We can do the same with elements in $\mathbb{G}_T$ (with respect to the generators $e(p_i, p_i)$), and will represent elements in $\mathbb{G}_T$ as bracketed tuples $[a_1, \cdots, a_m]$.

Using the notation above, the product of $(a_1, \cdots, a_m)$ and $(b_1, \cdots, b_m)$ is the element $(a_1 + b_1, \cdots, a_m + b_m)$, where addition in component i is done modulo $\mathbb{Z}_{p_i}$. Similarly $(a_1, \cdots, a_m)$ raised to the power $\gamma \in \mathbb{Z}$ is the element $(\gamma a_1, \cdots, \gamma a_m)$ (Analogous results hold for elements of $\mathbb{G}_T$). Therefore, it will be convenient to treat these tuples as "vectors" where vector addition corresponds to multiplication in the group and vector multiplication by a scalar corresponds to group exponentiation. The pairing of $(a_1, \cdots, a_m), (b_1, \cdots, b_m) \in \mathbb{G}$ gives the element $[a_1 b_1, \cdots, a_m b_m] \in \mathbb{G}_T$.

In an experiment involving the generic group, we will present an algorithm with a set of elements generated at random according to some distributions. We will describe these random variables using formal variables (written using capital letters) that are each chosen independently and uniformly at random from the appropriate domain. For example, a random element A of $\mathbb{G}$ would be described as $(X_1, \cdots, X_m)$, where each X_i is chosen uniformly from $\mathbb{Z}_{p_i}$. We say a random variable expressed in this way has degree t if the maximum degree of any variable is t.

Dependencies are made explicit by re-using the same formal variable; for example, a random "Diffie-Hellman-like" tuple (with $m = 2$) would be described by the three elements (X_1, X_2), (Y_1, Y_2), and $(X_1 Y_1, X_2 Y_2)$. Random variables taking values in $\mathbb{G}_T$ are expressed in the same way, but using the bracket notation.

Given random variables $X, B_1, \cdots, B_l$ (expressed as above) over the same group, we say that X is dependent on $\{B_i\}$ if there exist $\gamma_i \in \mathbb{Z}_N^*$ such that $X = \sum_i \gamma_i B_i$, where equality refers to equality in terms of the underlying formal variables. If no such $\{\gamma_i\}$ exist, then X is said to be independent of $\{B_i\}$.

Given a random variable $A = (X_1, \cdots, X_m)$, when we say that an algorithm is given A, we mean that random $x_1, \cdots, x_m$ are chosen appropriately and the adversary is given (the handle for) the element $(x_1, \cdots, x_m)$.

We may now state our theorems.

Theorem 1 Let $N = \prod_{i=1}^{m} p_i$ be a product of distinct primes, each greater than 2^n. Let $\{A_i\}$ be random variables over $\mathbb{G}$, and let $\{B_i\}, T_0, T_1$ be random variables over $\mathbb{G}_T$, where all random variables have degree at most t. Consider the following experiment in the generic group model:

An algorithm is given N, $\{A_i\}$ and $\{B_i\}$. A random bit b is chosen, and the adversary is given T_b. The algorithm outputs bit b' and succeeds if $b' = b$. The algorithm's advantage is the value of the difference between its success probability and $\frac{1}{2}$.

Say each of T_0 and T_1 is independent of $\{B_i\} \cup \{e(A_i, A_i)\}$. Then given any algorithm $\mathcal{A}$ issuing at most q instructions and having advantage δ in the above experiment, $\mathcal{A}$ can be used to find a non-trivial factor of N (in time polynomial in k and the running time of $\mathcal{A}$) with probability at least $\delta - O(q^2 t/2^n)$, where t and q are polynomial-time.

Thus, if N is generated in such a way that it is hard to find a non-trivial factor of N, the advantage of any polynomial-time algorithm $\mathcal{A}$ is negligible in n.

Proof
Game 1 In the original game, each of the random variables $\{A_i\}, \{B_i\}, T_0, T_1$ are instantiated by choosing random values for each of the formal variables and giving the handles of $\{A_i\}, \{B_i\}$, and T_b to the algorithm $\mathcal{A}$.

The algorithm then issues a sequence of multiplication, exponentiation, and pairing instructions, and is given in return the appropriate handles. Finally, the algorithm outputs a bit b' and its advantage is measured as defined above.

Game 2 We next define a second game in which the formal variables are never concretely instantiated, but instead the game only keeps track of the formal polynomials themselves.

Furthermore the game now uses identical handles for two elements only if these elements are equivalent to the formal polynomials in each of their components (So, in the original game the random variables $X = (X_1, \cdots, X_m)$ and $Y = (Y_1, \cdots, Y_m)$ could be assigned the same handle if it happened to be the case that $X_i = Y_i$ for all i. In this game, however, these two tuples of formal polynomials are always treated as different). This only introduces a difference in case it happens during the course of the experiment that two different formal polynomials would take on the same value.

For any particular pair of elements, the probability that this occurs is bounded by $2t/2^n$ (since the maximum degree of any polynomial constructed during the course of the experiment is $2t$).[2]

Summing over all pairs of elements produced during the course of the experiment shows that the statistical difference between these experiments is $O(q^2 \cdot t/2^n)$.

Game 3 In the third game, we record the formal polynomials as before except that now all computation, in each of the m components, is done modulo N rather than modulo the appropriate p_i. That is, until second game, each of the m components is computed by modulo p_i, but, from third game, each of the m components is computed modulo by N.

Now, two elements are assigned identical handles only if they are equivalent as (tuples of) formal polynomials over $\mathbb{Z}_N$. This only introduces a difference in case two polynomials are generated during the course of the experiment that are different modulo N but would have been identical modulo one of the p_i. But whenever this occurs, a non-trivial factor of N can be recovered from the coefficients of any two such polynomials.

Finally, we observe that in the third game the only possible way in which the algorithm can distinguish whether it is given T_0 or T_1 is if the algorithm is able to generate a formal polynomial that would be symbolically equivalent to some previously-generated polynomial for one value of b but not the other.

But in this case, we can write (for some b)

$$\gamma \cdot T_b = \sum_{i,j} \gamma_{i,j} \cdot e(A_i, A_j) + \sum_i \gamma_i \cdot B_i, \qquad (14.3)$$

---

[2]The reason that the maximum degree of any polynomial is $2t$ is that during the course of the experiment, the algorithm issues some instructions, one of which occurs $2t$ degree (e.g., the pairing operation of two polynomials).

where $\gamma \neq 0$ and equality denotes symbolic equality in terms of the formal variables constituting the different random variables. By assuming independence of T_0 and T_1, it must be the case that one of the coefficients of the above equation is not in $\mathbb{Z}_N^*$.

But then a non-trivial factor of N can be recovered. $\square$

Theorem 2 Let $N = \prod_{i=1}^m p_i$ be a product of distinct primes, each greater than 2^n. Let $\{A_i\}$, T_0, T_1 be random variables over $\mathbb{G}$, and let $\{B_i\}$ be random variables over $\mathbb{G}_T$, where all random variables have degree at most t. Consider the same experiment as in the theorem above.

Let $S \stackrel{def}{=} \{i \mid e(T_0, A_i) \neq e(T_1, A_i)\}$ (where inequality refers to inequality as formal polynomial). Say each of T_0 and T_1 is independent of $\{A_i\}$, and furthermore that for all $k \in S$ it holds that $e(T_0, A_k)$ is independent of $\{B_i\} \cup \{e(A_i, A_j)\} \cup \{e(T_0, A_i)\}_{i \neq k}$, and $e(T_1, A_k)$ is independent of $\{B_i\} \cup \{e(A_i, A_j)\} \cup \{e(T_1, A_i)\}_{i \neq k}$. Then given any algorithm $\mathcal{A}$ issuing at most q instructions and having advantage δ, the algorithm can be used to find a non-trivial factor of N (in time polynomial in k and the running time of $\mathcal{A}$) with probability at least $\delta - O(q^2 t/2^n)$.

Thus, if N is generated in such a way that it is hard to find a non-trivial factor of N, the advantage of any polynomial-time algorithm $\mathcal{A}$ is negligible in n.

Proof
The proof is identical to the proof of the theorem above except for the analysis of the third game. As in the earlier proof, in the third game the only possible way in which the algorithm can distinguish whether it is given T_0 or T_1 is if the algorithm is able to generate a formal polynomial that would be symbolically equivalent to some previously generated polynomial for one value of b but not the other. But then we either have (for some b)

$$\gamma \cdot T_b = \sum_i \gamma_i A_i \tag{14.4}$$

(with $\gamma \neq 0$), or else we have

$$\sum_{i \in S} \alpha_i \cdot e(T_b, A_i) + \sum_{i \notin S} \beta_i \cdot e(T_b, A_i) = \sum_i \gamma_i \cdot B_i + \sum_{i,j} \gamma_{i,j} \cdot e(A_i, A_j), \tag{14.5}$$

where $\alpha_i \neq 0$ for at least one $i \in S$ (otherwise, symbolic equality would hold for both values of b). By the independence assumptions, this implies that a non-trivial factor of N can be recovered.

We apply these theorems to prove the security of three assumptions in the generic group model.

Assumption 1 By applying Theorem 2, we can express this assumption as

$$A_1 = (1, 0, 0), \ A_2 = (0, 0, 1),$$
$$T_0 = (X_1, X_2, 0), \ T_1 = (X_1, 0, 0).$$

We note that $S = \emptyset$ in this case. It is clear to see that T_0 and T_1 are both independent of $\{A_1, A_2\}$ because X_1 does not appear in A_1 and A_2. Thus, Assumption 1 is generically secure, assuming it is hard to find a non-trivial factor of N.

Assumption 2 By applying Theorem 2, we can express this assumption as

$$A_1 = (1, 0, 0), \ A_2 = (X_1, 1, 0), \ A_3 = (0, 0, Y_3), \ A_4 = (0, X_2, 1),$$
$$T_0 = (Z_1, Z_2, Z_3), \ T_1 = (Z_1, 0, Z_3).$$

We note that $S = \{2, 4\}$ in this case. It is clear to see that T_0 and T_1 are both independent of $\{A_i\}$ because Z_1 does not appear in A_i's, for example.

$e(T_0, A_2)$ is independent of $\{e(A_i, A_j)\} \cup \{e(T_0, A_i)\}_{i \neq 2}$ because it is impossible to obtain $X_1 Z_1$ in the first coordinate of a combination of elements of $\{e(A_i, A_j)\} \cup \{e(T_0, A_i)\}_{i \neq 2}$.

$e(T_1, A_2)$ is independent of $\{e(A_i, A_j)\} \cup \{e(T_1, A_i)\}_{i \neq 2}$ because it is impossible to obtain $X_1 Z_1$ in the first coordinate of a combination of elements of $\{e(A_i, A_j)\} \cup \{e(T_1, A_i)\}_{i \neq 2}$.

$e(T_0, A_4)$ is independent of $\{e(A_i, A_j)\} \cup \{e(T_0, A_i)\}_{i \neq 4}$ and $e(T_1, A_4)$ is independent of $\{e(A_i, A_j)\} \cup \{e(T_1, A_i)\}_{i \neq 4}$ because it is impossible to obtain Z_3 in the third coordinate.

Thus, Assumption 2 is generically secure, assuming it is hard to find a non-trivial factor of N.

Assumption 3 By applying Theorem 1, we can express this assumption as

$$A_1 = (1, 0, 0), \ A_2 = (B, 1, 0), \ A_3 = (0, 0, 1), \ A_4 = (S, X_2, 0), \ A_5 = (0, Y_2, 0),$$
$$T_0 = [BS, 0, 0], \ T_1 = [Z_1, Z_2, Z_3].$$

We have T_1 independent of $\{e(A_i, A_j)\}$ because Z_1, Z_2, Z_3 do not appear in A_i. T_0 is independent of $\{e(A_i, A_j)\}$ because the only way to obtain BS in the first coordinate is to take $e(A_2, A_4)$, but then we are left with an X_2 in the second coordinate that cannot be canceled. Thus, Assumption 3 is generically secure, assuming it is hard to find a non-trivial factor of N. $\square$

14.3   Waters' Realization

As in Chapter 13, there exists a paradox problem between $Game_{k-1}$ and $Game_k$, and the tag method is used to resolve this problem. Decryption works only when the tag values of the ciphertext and decrypting key are unequal. If the simulator attempted to test semi-functionality of key k for itself by creating a semi-functional ciphertext for the same identity, it would only be able to create one with an equal tag, and hence decryption would *unconditionally fail*. This correlation of tags is hidden from an attacker who cannot request a key with the same identity as the challenge ciphertext, so the tags look randomly distributed from the attacker's point of view.

In the new technique, instead of using tag method, that is, having decryption *unconditionally fail* when the simulator attempts to test semi-functionality of the kth key, the system is designed so that decryption will *unconditionally succeed*. A variant of semi-functional keys introduced is called *nominally semi-functional keys*. These keys are semi-functional in name only, meaning that they are distributed like semi-functional keys, but are actually correlated with semi-functional ciphertexts. In such case, when a nominally semi-functional key is used to decrypt a semi-functional ciphertext, the interaction of the two semifunctional components results in cancelation and decryption is successful.

For given k_{th} identity $\overrightarrow{\mathsf{ID}} = (\mathsf{ID}_1, \ldots, \mathsf{ID}_j)$ in Gen queries,

set $z_k = a_1 \mathsf{ID}_1 + \cdots + a_j \mathsf{ID}_j + b$ for $a_i, b \in \mathbb{Z}_N$.

The identity in Challenge phase is $\overrightarrow{\mathsf{ID}^*} = (\mathsf{ID}_1^*, \ldots, \mathsf{ID}_j^*)$.

Set $z_c = a_1 \mathsf{ID}_1^* + \cdots + a_j \mathsf{ID}_j^* + b$.

In the case the simulator tries to test itself whether the key k is semi-functional by creating a semi-functional ciphertext for $\overrightarrow{\mathsf{ID}}$ and trying to decrypt, the decryption algorithm will work, regardless of whether the key k is semi-functional or not, because $z_k = z_c$ (the key is nominally semi-functional). This nominally semi-functional key will appear to be distributed like a regular semi-functional key to the attacker, who cannot request a key that can decrypt the challenge ciphertext. That is, the simulator cannot distinguish between the semi-functional keys and the normal keys.

14.4 Waters' HIBE with Composite Order

HIBE construction will use composite order groups of order $N = p_1p_2p_3$ and identities in $\mathbb{Z}_N$. We note that the subgroup $\mathbb{G}_{p_2}$ is not used in our actual scheme, instead it serves as semi-functional space. Keys and ciphertexts will be semi-functional when they include terms in $\mathbb{G}_{p_2}$ and decryption will proceed by pairing key elements with ciphertext elements. When we pair a normal key with a semi-functional ciphertext or a normal ciphertext with a semi-functional key, the terms in $\mathbb{G}_{p_2}$ are orthogonal to terms in $\mathbb{G}_{p_1}$ and $\mathbb{G}_{p_3}$ under the pairing and will cancel out. When we pair a semi-functional key with a semi-functional ciphertext, we will get an additional term arising from the pairing of the terms in $\mathbb{G}_{p_2}$.

Construction 1. HIBE

Let $\mathbb{G}$, $\mathbb{G}_T$ be groups of order N, and let $e\colon \mathbb{G} \times \mathbb{G} \to \mathbb{G}_T$ be the bilinear map. The HIBE system works as follows.

Setup Choose a bilinear group of order $N = p_1p_2p_3$ and let ℓ denote the maximum depth of the HIBE.

1. Choose $g, h, u_1, \ldots, u_\ell \in \mathbb{G}_{p_1}$.
2. Choose $X_3 \in \mathbb{G}_{p_3}$.
3. Choose $\alpha \in \mathbb{Z}_N$.
4. The system parameters are params $= (N, g, h, u_1, \ldots, u_\ell, X_3, e(g,g)^\alpha)$.
5. The master secret key is α.

Extract For a given identity $\overrightarrow{\mathsf{ID}} = (\mathsf{ID}_1, \ldots, \mathsf{ID}_j)$ and master key $\alpha \in \mathbb{Z}_N$

1. Choose $r \in \mathbb{Z}_N$ randomly.
2. Choose random elements $R_3, R_3', R_{j+1}, \ldots, R_\ell$ of $\mathbb{G}_{p_3}$.
3. Set $K_1 = g^r R_3$.
4. Set $K_2 = g^\alpha \big(u_1^{\mathsf{ID}_1} \cdots u_j^{\mathsf{ID}_j} h\big)^r R_3'$.
5. Set $E_{j+1} = u_{j+1}^r R_{j+1}, \ldots, E_\ell = u_\ell^r R_\ell$.
6. Set the secret key $SK_{\overrightarrow{\mathsf{ID}}} = (K_1, K_2, E_{j+1}, \ldots, E_\ell)$.

Encrypt For a message $M \in \mathbb{G}_T$ and an identity $\overrightarrow{\mathsf{ID}} = \mathsf{ID}_1, \ldots, \mathsf{ID}_j$

1. Choose $s \in \mathbb{Z}_N$ randomly.

2. Compute $C_0 = M \cdot e(g,g)^{\alpha s}$.

3. Compute $C_1 = \left(u_1^{\mathsf{ID}_1} \cdots u_j^{\mathsf{ID}_j} h\right)^s$.

4. Compute $C_2 = g^s$.

5. Set the ciphertext to be $CT = \langle C_0, C_1, C_2 \rangle$.

Delegate For given secret key $SK_{\overrightarrow{\mathsf{ID}}} = (K_1', K_2', E_{j+1}', \ldots, E_\ell')$, the delegation algorithm creates a key for $\overrightarrow{\mathsf{ID}'} = (\mathsf{ID}_1, \ldots, \mathsf{ID}_j, \mathsf{ID}_{j+1})$ as follows.

1. Choose $r' \in \mathbb{Z}_N$ randomly.

2. Choose random elements $\widetilde{R_3}, \widetilde{R_3'}, \widetilde{R}_{j+1}$ of $\mathbb{G}_{p_3}$.

3. Set $K_1 = K_1' g^{r'} \widetilde{R_3}$.

4. Set $K_2 = K_2' (u_1^{\mathsf{ID}_1} \cdots u_j^{\mathsf{ID}_j} h)^{r'} (E_{j+1}')^{\mathsf{ID}_{j+1}} u_{j+1}^{r'\mathsf{ID}_{j+1}} \widetilde{R_3'}$.

5. Set $E_{j+2} = E_{j+2}' u_{j+2}^{r'} \widetilde{R}_{j+2}, \ldots, E_\ell = E_\ell' u_\ell^{r'} \widetilde{R}_\ell$.

6. Set the secret key $SK_{\overrightarrow{\mathsf{ID}'}} = (K_1, K_2, E_{j+2}, \ldots, E_\ell)$.

Note that this new key is fully re-randomized: it is only tie to the previous key in the values $(\mathsf{ID}_1, \ldots, \mathsf{ID}_j)$.

Decrypt The decryption algorithm assumes that the key and ciphertext CT both correspond to the same identity $(\mathsf{ID}_1, \ldots, \mathsf{ID}_j)$. If the key identity is a prefix of this instead, then the decryption algorithm starts by running the key delegation algorithm to create a key with identity matching the ciphertext identity exactly. The decryption algorithm is computed as follows:

1. Compute $KEM = \dfrac{e(K_2, C_2)}{e(K_1, C_1)} = e(g,g)^{\alpha s}$.

2. Compute $M = C_0 / KEM$.

Note that even though a PKG comes under the attacker's control and generates a different secret key to a user by using different random values, the ciphertext before the attack can be decrypted using the newly generated secret key.

Computation between normal ciphertext and normal secret key

$$\frac{e(K_2, C_2)}{e(K_1, C_1)} = \frac{e(g^\alpha (u_1^{\mathsf{ID}_1} \cdots u_j^{\mathsf{ID}_j} h)^r R_3', g^s)}{e(g^r R_3, (u_1^{\mathsf{ID}_1} \cdots u_j^{\mathsf{ID}_j} h)^s)} =$$

$$\frac{e(g,g)^{\alpha s} e(u_1^{\mathsf{ID}_1} \cdots u_j^{\mathsf{ID}_j} h, g)^{rs} e(R_3', g)^s}{e(u_1^{\mathsf{ID}_1} \cdots u_j^{\mathsf{ID}_j} h, g)^{rs} e(R_3', u_1^{\mathsf{ID}_1} \cdots u_j^{\mathsf{ID}_j} h)^s} = e(g,g)^{\alpha s}.$$

Computation between level j and level $j+1$

1. The delegation algorithm is used when the identity $\overrightarrow{\mathsf{ID}} = (\mathsf{ID}_1, \ldots, \mathsf{ID}_j)$ is a prefix of $(\mathsf{ID}_1, \ldots, \mathsf{ID}_{j+1})$, that is, the user level j wants to delegate the identity level $j+1$ to decrypt the ciphertext of lower level $j+1$. In this case, we have the ciphertext of level $j+1$ is formed as
$$C_0 = M \cdot e(g,g)^{\alpha s},$$
$$C_1 = \left(u_1^{\mathsf{ID}_1} \cdots u_{j+1}^{\mathsf{ID}_{j+1}} h\right)^s,$$
$$C_2 = g^s.$$

The components K_1, K_2 in the secret key created by the delegation algorithm is as
$$K_1 = K_1' g^{r'} \widetilde{R_3} = g^r R_3 g^{r'} \widetilde{R_3},$$
$$K_2 = K_2' \left(u_1^{\mathsf{ID}_1} \cdots u_j^{\mathsf{ID}_j} h\right)^{r'} (E_{j+1}')^{\mathsf{ID}_{j+1}} u_{j+1}^{r'\mathsf{ID}_{j+1}} \widetilde{R_3'} = g^\alpha \left(u_1^{\mathsf{ID}_1} \cdots u_j^{\mathsf{ID}_j} h\right)^r,$$
$$R_3' \left(u_1^{\mathsf{ID}_1} \cdots u_j^{\mathsf{ID}_j} h\right)^{r'} \left(u_{j+1}^r R_{j+1}\right)^{\mathsf{ID}_{j+1}} u_{j+1}^{r'\mathsf{ID}_{j+1}} \widetilde{R_3'}.$$

We have

$$\frac{e(K_2, C_2)}{e(K_1, C_1)} = \frac{e\left(g^\alpha \left(u_1^{\mathsf{ID}_1} \cdots u_j^{\mathsf{ID}_j} h\right)^r R_3' \left(u_1^{\mathsf{ID}_1} \cdots u_j^{\mathsf{ID}_j} h\right)^{r'} \left(u_{j+1}^r R_{j+1}\right)^{\mathsf{ID}_{j+1}} u_{j+1}^{r'\mathsf{ID}_{j+1}} \widetilde{R_3}, g^s\right)}{e\left(g^r R_3 g^{r'} \widetilde{R_3}, \left(u_1^{\mathsf{ID}_1} \cdots u_{j+1}^{\mathsf{ID}_{j+1}} h\right)^s\right)}$$

$$= \frac{e(g^\alpha, g^s) e\left(\left(u_1^{\mathsf{ID}_1} \cdots u_j^{\mathsf{ID}_j} h\right)^r, g^s\right) e(R_3', g^s) e\left(\left(u_1^{\mathsf{ID}_1} \cdots u_j^{\mathsf{ID}_j} h\right)^{r'}, g^s\right) e\left(u_{j+1}^{r\mathsf{ID}_{j+1}}, g^s\right)}{e\left(g^r, \left(u_1^{\mathsf{ID}_1} \cdots u_{j+1}^{\mathsf{ID}_{j+1}} h\right)^s\right) e\left(R_3, \left(u_1^{\mathsf{ID}_1} \cdots u_{j+1}^{\mathsf{ID}_{j+1}} h\right)^s\right) e\left(g^{r'}, \left(u_1^{\mathsf{ID}_1} \cdots u_{j+1}^{\mathsf{ID}_{j+1}} h\right)^s\right)}$$
$$\cdot \frac{e(R_{j+1}, g^s) e\left(u_{j+1}^{r'\mathsf{ID}_{j+1}}, g^s\right) e(\widetilde{R_3'}, g^s)}{e\left(\widetilde{R_3}, \left(u_1^{\mathsf{ID}_1} \cdots u_{j+1}^{\mathsf{ID}_{j+1}} h\right)^s\right)}$$

$$= \frac{e(g,g)^{\alpha s} e\left(u_1^{\mathsf{ID}_1} \cdots u_j^{\mathsf{ID}_j} h, g\right)^{rs} e(R_3', g)^s e\left(u_1^{\mathsf{ID}_1} \cdots u_j^{\mathsf{ID}_j} h, g\right)^{r's} e(u_{j+1}, g)^{rs\mathsf{ID}_{j+1}}}{e\left(u_1^{\mathsf{ID}_1} \cdots u_{j+1}^{\mathsf{ID}_{j+1}} h, g\right)^{rs} e\left(R_3, u_1^{\mathsf{ID}_1} \cdots u_{j+1}^{\mathsf{ID}_{j+1}} h\right)^s e\left(g, u_1^{\mathsf{ID}_1} \cdots u_{j+1}^{\mathsf{ID}_{j+1}} h\right)^{r's}}$$
$$\cdot \frac{e(R_{j+1}, g)^{s\mathsf{ID}_{j+1}} e(u_{j+1}, g)^{r's\mathsf{ID}_{j+1}} e(\widetilde{R_3'}, g^s)}{e\left(\widetilde{R_3}, u_1^{\mathsf{ID}_1} \cdots u_{j+1}^{\mathsf{ID}_{j+1}} h\right)^s}$$

$$= \frac{e(g,g)^{\alpha s} e\left(u_1^{\mathsf{ID}_1} \cdots u_j^{\mathsf{ID}_j} h, g\right)^{rs} e\left(u_1^{\mathsf{ID}_1} \cdots u_j^{\mathsf{ID}_j} h, g\right)^{r's} e(u_{j+1}, g)^{r'sID_{j+1}} e(u_{j+1}, g)^{rs\mathsf{ID}_{j+1}}}{e\left(u_1^{\mathsf{ID}_1} \cdots u_{j+1}^{\mathsf{ID}_{j+1}} h, g\right)^{rs} e(g, u_1^{\mathsf{ID}_1} \cdots u_{j+1}^{\mathsf{ID}_{j+1}} h)^{r's}}$$

$$= \frac{e(g,g)^{\alpha s} e\left(u_1^{\mathsf{ID}_1} \cdots u_j^{\mathsf{ID}_j} h, g\right)^{rs} e\left(u_1^{\mathsf{ID}_1} \cdots u_j^{\mathsf{ID}_j} h, g\right)^{r's} e(u_{j+1}, g)^{r'sID_{j+1}}}{e\left(u_1^{\mathsf{ID}_1} \cdots u_j^{\mathsf{ID}_j} h, g\right)^{rs} e(u_{j+1}, g)^{r's\mathsf{ID}_{j+1}} e\left(u_1^{\mathsf{ID}_1} \cdots u_j^{\mathsf{ID}_j} h, g\right)^{r's}}$$
$$\cdot \frac{e(u_{j+1}, g)^{rs\mathsf{ID}_{j+1}}}{e(u_{j+1}, g)^{rs\mathsf{ID}_{j+1}}} = e(g,g)^{\alpha s}$$

Thus, the user at level j can decrypt the ciphertext at level $j+1$.

2. However, the user at lower level $j + 1$ cannot use the secret key at level j to decrypt the ciphertext at higher level j. We can see this fact by computing as follows:

The ciphertext at level j:

$C_0 = M \cdot e(g, g)^{\alpha s}$,

$C_1 = \left(u_1^{ID_1} \cdots u_j^{ID_j} h\right)^s$,

$C_2 = g^s$.

The components K_1, K_2 of secret key at level $j + 1$:

$K_1 = K_1' g^{r'} \widetilde{R_3} = g^r R_3 g^{r'} \widetilde{R_3}$.

$$K_2 = K_2' \left(u_1^{ID_1} \cdots u_j^{ID_j} h\right)^{r'} \left(E_{j+1}'\right)^{ID_{j+1}} u_{j+1}^{r' ID_{j+1}} \widetilde{R_3'}$$
$$= g^\alpha \left(u_1^{ID_1} \cdots u_j^{ID_j} h\right)^r R_3' \left(u_1^{ID_1} \cdots u_j^{ID_j} h\right)^{r'} \left(u_{j+1}^r R_{j+1}\right)^{ID_{j+1}} u_{j+1}^{r' ID_{j+1}} \widetilde{R_3'}.$$

We have

$$\frac{e(K_2, C_2)}{e(K_1, C_1)} = \frac{e\left(g^\alpha \left(u_1^{ID_1} \cdots u_j^{ID_j} h\right)^r R_3' \left(u_1^{ID_1} \cdots u_j^{ID_j} h\right)^{r'} \left(u_{j+1}^r R_{j+1}\right)^{ID_{j+1}} u_{j+1}^{r' ID_{j+1}} \widetilde{R_3'}, g^s\right)}{e\left(g^r R_3 g^{r'} \widetilde{R_3}, \left(u_1^{ID_1} \cdots u_j^{ID_j} h\right)^s\right)}$$

$$= \frac{e(g^\alpha, g^s) e\left(\left(u_1^{ID_1} \cdots u_j^{ID_j} h\right)^r, g^s\right) e(R_3', g^s) e\left(\left(u_1^{ID_1} \cdots u_j^{ID_j} h\right)^{r'}, g^s\right) e(u_{j+1}^{r ID_{j+1}}, g^s)}{e\left(g^r, \left(u_1^{ID_1} \cdots u_j^{ID_j} h\right)^s\right) e\left(R_3, \left(u_1^{ID_1} \cdots u_j^{ID_j} h\right)^s\right) e\left(g^{r'}, \left(u_1^{ID_1} \cdots u_j^{ID_j} h\right)^s\right)}$$

$$\cdot \frac{e(R_{j+1}, g^s) e(u_{j+1}^{r' ID_{j+1}}, g^s) e(\widetilde{R_3'}, g^s)}{e\left(\widetilde{R_3}, \left(u_1^{ID_1} \cdots u_j^{ID_j} h\right)^s\right)}$$

$$= \frac{e(g, g)^{\alpha s} e\left(u_1^{ID_1} \cdots u_j^{ID_j} h, g\right)^{rs} e(R_3', g)^s e\left(u_1^{ID_1} \cdots u_j^{ID_j} h, g\right)^{r's} e(u_{j+1}, g)^{rs ID_{j+1}}}{e\left(u_1^{ID_1} \cdots u_j^{ID_j} h, g\right)^{rs} e\left(R_3, u_1^{ID_1} \cdots u_j^{ID_j} h\right)^s e\left(g, u_1^{ID_1} \cdots u_j^{ID_j} h\right)^{r's}}$$

$$\cdot \frac{e(R_{j+1}, g)^{s ID_{j+1}} e(u_{j+1}, g)^{r's ID_{j+1}} e(\widetilde{R_3'}, g)^s}{e\left(\widetilde{R_3}, u_1^{ID_1} \cdots u_j^{ID_j} h\right)^s}$$

$$= \frac{e(g, g)^{\alpha s} e\left(u_1^{ID_1} \cdots u_j^{ID_j} h, g\right)^{rs} e\left(u_1^{ID_1} \cdots u_j^{ID_j} h, g\right)^{r's} e(u_{j+1}, g)^{r's ID_{j+1}} e(u_{j+1}, g)^{rs ID_{j+1}}}{e\left(u_1^{ID_1} \cdots u_j^{ID_j} h, g\right)^{rs} e\left(g, u_1^{ID_1} \cdots u_j^{ID_j} h\right)^{r's}}$$

$$= e(g, g)^{\alpha s} e(u_{j+1}, g)^{r's ID_{j+1}} e(u_{j+1}, g)^{rs ID_{j+1}} = e(g, g)^{\alpha s} e(u_{j+1}, g)^{(r+r')s ID_{j+1}} \neq e(g, g)^{\alpha s}.$$

3. In the case $\overrightarrow{ID} = (ID_1, \ldots, ID_j)$ is not the prefix of $\overrightarrow{ID'} = (ID_1, \ldots, ID_{j'}, ID_{j'+1})$, the delegation algorithm is not used, that is, it cannot use $SK_{\overrightarrow{ID}}$ at level j to create the secret key for a user at level $j' + 1$.

Construction 2. Semi-functional algorithms

To prove the security of our HIBE system, we again rely on the static Assumptions 1, 2, and 3. We first define two additional structures: semi-functional ciphertexts and semi-functional keys. These will not be used in the real system, but will be used in our proof. We define both semi-functional ciphertexts and semi-functional keys in terms of a transformation on a normal ciphertext or key.

Semi-functional ciphertexts Let g_2 denote a generator of $\mathbb{G}_{p_2}$. The algorithm first runs the encryption algorithm to generate a normal ciphertext $CT = (C_0', C_1', C_2')$.

1. Choose random exponents $x, z_c \in \mathbb{Z}_N$.
2. Set $C_0 = C_0'$.
3. Set $C_1 = C_1' g_2^{xz_c}$.
4. Set $C_2 = C_2' g_2^{x}$.
5. The semi-functional ciphertext is (C_0, C_1, C_2).

Semi-functional secret keys The algorithm first runs the extract algorithm to generate a normal secret key $(K_1', K_2', E_{j+1}', \ldots, E_\ell')$.

1. Choose random exponents $\gamma, z_k, z_{j+1}, \ldots, z_\ell \in \mathbb{Z}_N$.
2. Set $K_1 = K_1' g_2^{\gamma}$.
3. Set $K_2 = K_2' g_2^{\gamma z_k}$.
4. Set $E_{j+1} = E_{j+1}' g_2^{\gamma z_{j+1}}, \ldots, E_\ell = E_\ell' g_2^{\gamma z_\ell}$.
5. The semi-functional secret key is $(K_1, K_2, E_{j+1}, \ldots, E_\ell)$.

Computation between semi-functional ciphertext and normal secret key

$$\frac{e(K_2', g_2^{x})}{e(K_1', g_2^{xz_c})} = \frac{e(g^\alpha (u_1^{\mathsf{ID}_1} \cdots u_j^{\mathsf{ID}_j} h)^r R_3', g_2^{x})}{e(g^r R_3, g_2^{xz_c})}$$

$$= \frac{e(g, g_2)^{\alpha x} e(u_1^{\mathsf{ID}_1} \cdots u_j^{\mathsf{ID}_j} h, g_2)^{rx} e(R_3', g_2)^{x}}{e(g, g_2)^{rxz_c} e(R_3, g_2)^{xz_c}} = 1$$

Computation between normal ciphertext and semi-functional secret key

$$\frac{e(g_2^{\gamma z_k}, C_2')}{e(g_2^{\gamma}, C_1')} = \frac{e(g_2^{\gamma z_k}, g^s)}{e(g_2^{\gamma}, (u_1^{\mathsf{ID}_1} \cdots u_j^{\mathsf{ID}_j} h)^s)} = \frac{e(g_2, g)^{s\gamma z_k}}{e(g_2, u_1^{\mathsf{ID}_1} \cdots u_j^{\mathsf{ID}_j} h)^{\gamma s}} = 1$$

**Computation between semi-functional ciphertext and
semi-functional secret key**

$$\frac{e(K_2', g_2^x)e(g_2^{\gamma z_k}, C_2')e(g_2^{\gamma z_k}, g_2^x)}{e(K_1', g_2^{xz_c})e(g_2^\gamma, C_1')e(g_2^\gamma, g_2^{xz_c})} = \frac{e(K_2', g_2^x)}{e(K_1', g_2^{xz_c})} \cdot \frac{e(g_2^{\gamma z_k}, C_2')}{e(g_2^\gamma, C_1')} \cdot \frac{e(g_2^{\gamma z_k}, g_2^x)}{e(g_2^\gamma, g_2^{xz_c})}$$

Applying two results above, we have the computation as

$$= \frac{e(g_2^{\gamma z_k}, g_2^x)}{e(g_2^\gamma, g_2^{xz_c})} = \frac{e(g_2, g_2)^{x\gamma z_k}}{e(g_2, g_2)^{x\gamma z_c}} = e(g_2, g_2)^{x\gamma(z_k - z_c)}.$$

If $z_k = z_c$, the decryption algorithm still works. In this case, the key is *nominally semi-functional*: it has terms in $\mathbb{G}_{p_2}$, which do not hinder decryption.

14.4.1   Proof of HIBE Security

The proof of security will again be structured as a hybrid argument over a sequence of games as shown in Figure 14.2. Let q denote the number of key queries the attacker makes. Let us define the games as:

1. Game_{Real}: is the real HIBE security game.

2. $\text{Game}_{Real'}$: is the same as Game_{Real} except that all key queries will be answered by fresh calls to the key generation algorithm (the challenger will not be asked to delegate keys in a particular way).

3. $\text{Game}_{Restricted}$: is the same as $\text{Game}_{Real'}$ except that the attacker cannot ask for keys for identities which are prefixes of the challenge identity modulo p_2.

4. Game_k (for k from 0 to q): This is like $\text{Game}_{Restricted}$, except that the ciphertext given to the attacker is semi-functional and the first k keys are semi-functional. The rest of the keys are normal.
    In Game_0, only the challenge ciphertext is semi-functional.
    In Game_q, the challenge ciphertext and all of the keys are semi-functional.

5. Game_{Final}: is the same as Game_q except that the challenge ciphertext is a semi-functional encryption of a random message, not one of the messages provided by the attacker.

We will show these games are indistinguishable in the following five lemmas.

Lemma 1 For any algorithm $\mathcal{A}$, $\text{Game}_{Real} Adv_\mathcal{A} = \text{Game}_{Real'} Adv_\mathcal{A}$.

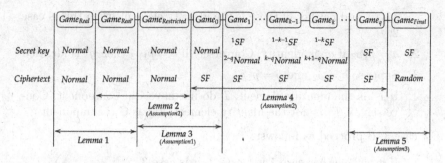

FIGURE 14.2
Proof of HIBE security.

Proof of Lemma 1

We note that keys are identically distributed whether they are produced by the key delegation algorithm from a previous key or from a fresh call to the key generation algorithm. Thus, in the attacker's view, there is no difference between these games.

Lemma 2 Suppose there exists an algorithm $\mathcal{A}$ such that $\text{Game}_{Real'}Adv_{\mathcal{A}}$ - $\text{Game}_{Restricted}Adv_{\mathcal{A}} = \epsilon$. Then we can build an algorithm $\mathcal{B}$ with advantage $\geq \frac{\epsilon}{2}$ in breaking Assumption 2.

The algorithm begins by taking in an instance $(\mathbb{G}, g, X_1X_2, X_3, Y_2Y_3)$. Now algorithm $\mathcal{B}$ can use algorithm $\mathcal{A}$ to simulate $Game_{Real}$. $\mathcal{A}$ has probability ϵ in producing ID and ID* given $\text{ID} - \text{ID}^* \, mod \, N \neq 0$ and $\text{ID} - \text{ID}^* \, mod \, p_2 = 0$. Using ID and ID*, $\mathcal{B}$ can produce the non-trivial factors of N by computing $a = gcd(\text{ID} - \text{ID}^*, N)$ and $b = N/a$. Now we have three cases.

1. a is p_1 and b is p_2p_3 or conversely b is p_1 and a is p_2p_3
2. a is p_2 and b is p_1p_3 or conversely b is p_2 and a is p_1p_3
3. a is p_3 and b is p_1p_2 or conversely b is p_3 and a is p_1p_2

For case 1, $\mathcal{B}$ proceed as follows:

1. It is case 1 if either $(Y_2Y_3)^a$ or $(Y_2Y_3)^b$ is the identity element.
2. Suppose $a = p_1$ and $b = p_2p_3$.
3. If $e(T^a, X_1X_2)$ is identity element, T do not have $\mathbb{G}_{p_2}$ component. Conversely, if $e(T^a, X_1X_2)$ is not identity element, T has $\mathbb{G}_{p_2}$ component.

For case 2, $\mathcal{B}$ proceed as follows:

1. Check if $(X_1X_2)^a$ or $(X_1X_2)^b$ is the identity element. If it was not

case 1 and neither of these is the identity element, then this is case 2.

2. $a = p_1 p_3$ if g^a is identity. Conversely if $b = p_1 p_3$ then g^b is identity.

3. Suppose $a = p_2$ and $b = p_1 p_3$.

4. If T^b is the identity element, T do not have $\mathbb{G}_{p_2}$ component. Conversely, if T^b is not the identity element, T has $\mathbb{G}_{p_2}$ component.

For case 3, $\mathcal{B}$ proceed as follows:

1. If it was neither case 1 nor case 2, it is case 3.

2. $a = p_3$ if X_3^b is not identity. Conversely $b = p_3$ if X_3^a is identity.

3. Suppose $a = p_3$.

4. If $e(T^a, Y_2 Y_3)$ is the identity element, T does not have $\mathbb{G}_{p_2}$ component. Conversely, if $e(T^a, Y_2 Y_3)$ is not the identity element, T has $\mathbb{G}_{p_2}$ component.

Lemma 3 Suppose there exists an algorithm $\mathcal{A}$ such that $\text{Game}_{Restricted} Adv_{\mathcal{A}}$ - $\text{Game}_0 Adv_{\mathcal{A}} = \epsilon$. Then we can build an algorithm $\mathcal{B}$ with advantage ϵ in breaking Assumption 1.

Proof of Lemma 3
The algorithm $\mathcal{B}$ begins by taking in an instance $(\mathbb{G}, g, X_3, T)$ of Assumption 1. It simulates Game_{Real} or Game_0 with $\mathcal{A}$.

Reduction algorithm $\mathcal{B}$ in Lemma 3

Setup

1. Choose random exponents $\alpha, a_1, \ldots, a_\ell, b \in \mathbb{Z}_N$.

2. Set $g = g$, $u_i = g^{a_i}$ for $i \in \{1, \ldots, \ell\}$ and $h = g^b$.

3. Send the public parameters params $=$ $(N, g, u_1, \ldots, u_\ell, h, e(g, g)^\alpha)$ to $\mathcal{A}$.

4. Set the master secret key MSK is α.

Phase I For an identity $(\mathsf{ID}_1, \ldots, \mathsf{ID}_j)$

1. Choose a random exponents $r, t, w, v_{j+1}, \ldots, v_\ell \in \mathbb{Z}_N$.

2. Compute $K_1 = g^r X_3^t$.

3. Compute $K_2 = g^\alpha (u_1^{\mathsf{ID}_1} \cdots u_j^{\mathsf{ID}_j} h)^r X_3^w$.

4. Compute $E_{j+1} = u_{j+1}^r X_3^{v_{j+1}}, \ldots, E_\ell = u_\ell^r X_3^{v_\ell}$.

5. Send the secret key $SK_{\mathsf{ID}} = (K_1, K_2, E_{j+1}, \ldots, E_\ell)$.

Challenge

1. $\mathcal{A}$ outputs messages M_0, M_1 and challenge identity $(\mathsf{ID}_1^*, \ldots, \mathsf{ID}_j^*)$.

2. $\mathcal{B}$ generates bit $\beta \in \{0, 1\}$.

3. The ciphertext (C_0, C_1, C_2) is formed as follows:
$C_0 = M_\beta e(T, g)^\alpha$,
$C_1 = T^{(a_1 \mathsf{ID}_1^* + \cdots + a_j \mathsf{ID}_j^* + b)}$,
$C_2 = T$.

Note: This implicitly sets g^s equal to the $\mathbb{G}_{p_1}$ part of T. If $T \in \mathbb{G}_{p_1 p_2}$, then this is a semi-functional ciphertext with $z_c = a_1 \mathsf{ID}_1^* + \cdots + a_j \mathsf{ID}_j^* + b$. If $T \in \mathbb{G}_{p_1}$, then this is a normal ciphertext.

Phase II

1. $\mathcal{A}$ makes key generation queries, and $\mathcal{B}$ responds as in Phase I.

Guess

1. Finally, the adversary outputs guesses $\beta' \in \{0, 1\}$.

2. If $\beta = \beta'$, it outputs 0 (indicating that $T \in \mathbb{G}_{p_1 p_2}$); otherwise, it outputs 1.

Simulation of secret key generation in Lemma 3
Key generation algorithm in Lemma 3 generates normal secret keys.

Simulation of challenge ciphertext generation in Lemma 3
The difference between Game$_{Real}$ and Game$_0$ is whether the challenge ciphertext is normal or semi-functional.

In the case $T \in \mathbb{G}_{p_1}$, there exists $s, x \in \mathbb{Z}_N$ such that $T = g^s$. The normal ciphertext is computed as follows:

$$C_0 = M_\beta e(T, g)^\alpha = M_\beta e(g^s, g)^\alpha = M_\beta e(g, g)^{\alpha s} = C_0',$$

$$C_1 = T^{(a_1 \mathsf{ID}_1^* + \cdots + a_j \mathsf{ID}_j^* + b)} = (g^s)^{(a_1 \mathsf{ID}_1^* + b + \cdots + a_j \mathsf{ID}_j^* + b)} = (g^{a_1 \mathsf{ID}_1^*} \cdots g^{a_j \mathsf{ID}_j^*})^s = (u_1{}^{\mathsf{ID}_1^*} \cdots u_j{}^{\mathsf{ID}_j^*})^s = C_1',$$

$$C_2 = T = g^s = C_2'.$$

In the case $T \in \mathbb{G}_{p_1 p_2}$, there exists $s, x \in \mathbb{Z}_N$ such that $T = g^s g_2^x$. First, run the encryption algorithm to generate a normal ciphertext (C_0', C_1', C_2').

The semi-functional ciphertext is computed as follows:

$$C_0 = M_\beta e(T, g)^\alpha = M_\beta e(g^s g_2{}^x, g)^\alpha = M_\beta e(g, g)^{\alpha s} e(g_2, g)^{\alpha x} = M_\beta e(g, g)^{\alpha s} = C_0',$$

$$C_1 = T^{(a_1 \mathsf{ID}_1^* + \cdots + a_j \mathsf{ID}_j^* + b)} = (g^s g_2{}^x)^{(a_1 \mathsf{ID}_1^* + b + \cdots + a_j \mathsf{ID}_j^* + b)}$$

$$= C_1'(g_2{}^x)^{(a_1 \mathsf{ID}_1^* + \cdots + a_j \mathsf{ID}_j^* + b)} = C_1' g_2{}^{x z_c},$$

$$C_2 = T = g^s g_2{}^x = C_2' g_2{}^x.$$

Since the normal keys can decrypt both normal and semi-functional ciphertext, $\mathcal{B}$ can use the output of $\mathcal{A}$ to distinguish if T is from $\mathbb{G}_{p_1 p_2}$ subgroup or $\mathbb{G}_{p_1}$ subgroup.

Probability analysis in Lemma 3 The probability computation is simple as

$$Game_{Restricted} Adv_{\mathcal{A}} - Game_0 Adv_{\mathcal{A}} = \epsilon. \tag{14.6}$$

Lemma 4 Suppose there exists an algorithm $\mathcal{A}$ such that $Game_{k-1} Adv_{\mathcal{A}}$ - $Game_k Adv_{\mathcal{A}} = \epsilon$. Then we can build an algorithm $\mathcal{B}$ with advantage ϵ in breaking Assumption 2.

Proof of Lemma 4

The algorithm $\mathcal{B}$ begins by taking in an instance $(\mathbb{G}, g, X_1 X_2, X_3, Y_2 Y_3, T)$ of Assumption 2. It simulates $Game_{k-1}$ or $Game_k$ with $\mathcal{A}$.

Reduction algorithm $\mathcal{B}$ in Lemma 4

Setup

1. Pick random exponents $a_1, \ldots, a_\ell, b \in \mathbb{Z}_N$.
2. Set $g = g$, $u_i = g^{a_i}$ for $i \in \{1, \ldots, \ell\}$ and $h = g^b$.
3. Send the public parameters params $= (g, u_1, \ldots, u_\ell, h, e(g, g)^\alpha)$ to $\mathcal{A}$.
4. Set the master secret key MSK is α.

Phase I

1. When $\mathcal{A}$ requests the ith ($i < k$) identity $(\mathsf{ID}_1, \ldots, \mathsf{ID}_j)$, $\mathcal{B}$ creates a semi-functional key as follows.

   (a) Choose a random exponents $r, z, t, z_{j+1}, \ldots, z_\ell \in \mathbb{Z}_N$.

(b) Compute $K_1 = g^r (Y_2 Y_3)^t$.

(c) Compute $K_2 = g^\alpha (u_1^{\mathsf{ID}_1} \cdots u_j^{\mathsf{ID}_j} h)^r (Y_2 Y_3)^z$.

(d) Compute $E_{j+1} = u_{j+1}{}^r (Y_2 Y_3)^{z_{j+1}}, \ldots, E_\ell = u_\ell{}^r (Y_2 Y_3)^{z_\ell}$.

(e) Send the secret key $SK_{\mathsf{ID}} = (K_1, K_2, E_{j+1}, \ldots, E_\ell)$. This is a properly distributed semi-functional key with $g_2{}^\gamma = Y_2{}^t$.

2. When $\mathcal{A}$ requests the ith $(i > k)$ identity $(\mathsf{ID}_1, \ldots, \mathsf{ID}_j)$, $\mathcal{B}$ creates a normal key by using the key generation algorithm.

3. When $\mathcal{A}$ requests the kth for $(\mathsf{ID}_1, \ldots, \mathsf{ID}_j)$:

   (a) Let $z_k = a_1 \mathsf{ID}_1 + \cdots + a_j \mathsf{ID}_j + b$.

   (b) Choose a random exponents $w_k, w_{j+1}, \ldots, w_\ell \in \mathbb{Z}_N$.

   (c) Compute $K_1 = T$.

   (d) Compute $K_2 = g^\alpha T^{z_k} X_3{}^{w_k}$.

   (e) Compute $E_{j+1} = T^{a_{j+1}} X_3{}^{w_{j+1}}, \ldots, E_\ell = T^{a_\ell} X_3{}^{w_\ell}$.

   (f) Send the secret key $SK_{\mathsf{ID}} = (K_1, K_2, E_{j+1}, \ldots, E_\ell)$.

Note: If $T \in \mathbb{G}_{p_1 p_3}$, then this is a normal key with g^r equal to the $\mathbb{G}_{p_1}$ part of T. If $T \in \mathbb{G}$, then this is a semi-functional key.

Challenge

1. $\mathcal{A}$ outputs messages M_0, M_1 and challenge identity $(\mathsf{ID}_1^*, \ldots, \mathsf{ID}_j^*)$.

2. $\mathcal{B}$ generates a bit $\beta \in \{0, 1\}$.

3. The ciphertext (C_0, C_1, C_2) is formed as
$C_0 = M_\beta e(X_1 X_2, g)^\alpha$,
$C_1 = (X_1 X_2)^{(a_1 \mathsf{ID}_1^* + \cdots + a_j \mathsf{ID}_j^* + b)}$,
$C_2 = X_1 X_2$.

Note: This implicitly sets $g^s = X_1$ and $z_c = a_1 \mathsf{ID}_1^* + \cdots + a_j \mathsf{ID}_j^* + b$.

Phase II

1. $\mathcal{A}$ makes key generation queries and $\mathcal{B}$ responds as in Phase I.

Guess

1. Finally, the adversary outputs guesses $\beta' \in \{0, 1\}$.

2. If $\beta = \beta'$, it outputs 0 (indicating that $T \in \mathbb{G}_{p_1 p_3}$); otherwise, it outputs 1.

Simulation of secret key generation in Lemma 4

The secret key generation process is divided into 3 parts. However, the parts of $i > k$ and $i < k$ only need to generate normal or semi-functional secret key by using its own master secret key, respectively. On the other hand, the case of $i = k$ is different. Letting $(K_1', K_2', E_{j+1}', \ldots, E_\ell')$ denote the normal key generated by using the key generation algorithm, the key generated in the case $i = k$ is computed as follows.

If $T \in \mathbb{G}_{p_1 p_3}$, there exists $R_3 \in \mathbb{G}_{p_3}$ such that $T = g^r R_3$. The a normal key is computed as follows:

$$K_1 = T = g^r R_3.$$

$$K_2 = g^\alpha T^{z_k} X_3{}_k^w = g^\alpha (g^r R_3)^{z_k} X_3{}^{w_k} = g^\alpha (g^{z_k})^r R_3{}^{z_k} X_3{}^{w_k}$$
$$= g^\alpha (g^{a_1 \mathsf{ID}_1 + \cdots + a_j \mathsf{ID}_j + b})^r R_3{}^{z_k} X_3{}^{w_k} = g^\alpha (u_1^{\mathsf{ID}_1} \cdots u_j^{\mathsf{ID}_j} h)^r R_3{}^{z_k} X_3{}^{w_k};$$
since $R_3, X_3 \in \mathbb{G}_{p_3}$, there exists $R_3' = R_3{}^{z_k} X_3{}^{w_k} \in \mathbb{G}_{p_3}$. Therefore, we have
$$K_2 = g^\alpha (u_1^{\mathsf{ID}_1} \cdots u_j^{\mathsf{ID}_j} h)^r R_3'.$$

$$E_{j+1} = T^{a_{j+1}} X_3{}^{w_{j+1}} = (g^r R_3)^{a_{j+1}} X_3{}^{w_{j+1}} = (g^{a_{j+1}})^r R_3{}^{a_{j+1}} X_3{}^{w_{j+1}} = u_{j+1}{}^r R_3{}^{a_{j+1}} X_3{}^{w_{j+1}};$$
since $R_3, X_3 \in \mathbb{G}_{p_3}$, then there exists $\widetilde{R'}_{j+1} = R_3{}^{a_{j+1}} X_3{}^{w_{j+1}} \in \mathbb{G}_{p_3}$. Therefore, we have $E_{j+1} = u_{j+1}{}^r \widetilde{R'}_{j+1}$.

$$\ldots$$

$$E_\ell = T^{a_\ell} X_3{}^{w_\ell} = (g^r R_3)^{a_\ell} X_3{}^{w_\ell} = (g^{a_\ell})^r R_3{}^{a_\ell} X_3{}^{w_\ell} = u_\ell{}^r R_3{}^{a_\ell} X_3{}^{w_\ell};$$ since $R_3, X_3 \in \mathbb{G}_{p_3}$, there exists $\widetilde{R'}_\ell = R_3{}^{a_\ell} X_3{}^{w_\ell} \in \mathbb{G}_{p_3}$. Therefore, we have $E_\ell = u_\ell{}^r \widetilde{R'}_\ell$.

If $T \in \mathbb{G}$, then there exists $g_2{}^\gamma \in \mathbb{G}_{p_2}$ such that $T = g^r R_3 g_2{}^\gamma$. The semi-functional key is computed as follows:

$$K_1 = T = g^r R_3 g_2{}^\gamma = K_1' g_2{}^\gamma.$$

$$K_2 = g^\alpha T^{z_k} X_3{}_k^w = g^\alpha (g^r R_3 g_2{}^\gamma)^{z_k} X_3{}_k^w = g^\alpha (g^{z_k})^r R_3{}^{z_k} X_3{}^{w_k} g_2{}^{\gamma z_k} = K_2' g_2{}^{\gamma z_k}.$$

$$E_{j+1} = T^{a_{j+1}} X_3{}^{w_{j+1}} = (g^r R_3 g_2{}^\gamma)^{a_{j+1}} X_3{}^{w_{j+1}} = (g^{a_{j+1}})^r R_3{}^{a_{j+1}} X_3{}^{w_{j+1}} g_2{}^{\gamma a_{j+1}} = K_2' g_2{}^{\gamma a_{j+1}}.$$

$$\ldots$$

$$E_\ell = T^{a_\ell} X_3{}^{w_\ell} = (g^r R_3 g_2{}^\gamma)^{a_\ell} X_3{}^{w_\ell} = (g^{a_\ell})^r R_3{}^{a_\ell} X_3{}^{w_\ell} g_2{}^{\gamma a_\ell} = K_2' g_2{}^{\gamma a_\ell}.$$

Simulation of challenge ciphertext generation in Lemma 4

The encryption algorithm in Lemma 4 only generates semi-functional ciphertext. Letting (C_0', C_1', C_2') denote the normal ciphertext generated by using the encryption algorithm, the ciphertext in Lemma 4 is computed as follows in both cases: T from $\mathbb{G}_{p_1 p_3}$ and T from $\mathbb{G}$. Since $X_2 \in \mathbb{G}_{p_2}$, there exists $x \in \mathbb{Z}_N$ such that $X_2 = g_2{}^x$.

$$C_0 = M_\beta e(X_1 X_2, g)^\alpha = M_\beta e(g^s X_2, g)^\alpha = M_\beta e(g^s, g)^\alpha = M_\beta e(X_2, g)^\alpha = M_\beta e(g, g)^{\alpha s}.$$

$$C_1 = (X_1 X_2)^{(a_1 \mathsf{ID}_1^* + \cdots + a_j \mathsf{ID}_j^* + b)} = (g^s g_2{}^x)^{(a_1 \mathsf{ID}_1^* + \cdots + a_j \mathsf{ID}_j^* + b)}$$
$$= (g^s)^{(a_1 \mathsf{ID}_1^* + \cdots + a_j \mathsf{ID}_j^* + b)} (g_2{}^x)^{(a_1 \mathsf{ID}_1^* + \cdots + a_j \mathsf{ID}_j^* + b)}$$

$$= \left(u_1^{\mathsf{ID}_1^*} \cdots u_j^{\mathsf{ID}_j^*} h\right)^s g_2{}^{x z_c} = C_1' g_2{}^{x z_c};$$

$$C_2 = X_1 X_2 = g^s g_2{}^x = C_2' g_2{}^x.$$

For $i = k$, z_k and z_c are randomly distributed to $\mathcal{A}$. Though it is hidden from $\mathcal{A}$, in the case the simulator attempts to test itself whether key k is semi-functional by creating a semi-functional ciphertext for this identity and trying to decrypt, then the decryption will work regardless of whether key k is semi-functional or not (because $z_k = z_c$, the simulator can only create a nominally semi-functional key k). That is, the attacker cannot request a key that can decrypt the challenge ciphertext.

In the case $T \in \mathbb{G}_{p_1 p_3}$, the normal key is used to decrypt the semi-functional ciphertext. Then $\mathcal{B}$ has properly simulated Game_{k-1}. In the case $T \in \mathbb{G}$, $\mathcal{B}$ has properly simulated Game_k. Hence, $\mathcal{B}$ can use the output of $\mathcal{A}$ to distinguish between these possibilities for T.

Probability analysis in Lemma 4 The probability computation is simple as

$$\text{Game}_{k-1} Adv_{\mathcal{A}} - \text{Game}_k Adv_{\mathcal{A}} = \epsilon. \tag{14.7}$$

Lemma 5

Suppose there exists an algorithm $\mathcal{A}$ such that $\text{Game}_q Adv_{\mathcal{A}} - \text{Game}_{Final} Adv_{\mathcal{A}} = \epsilon$. Then we can build an algorithm $\mathcal{B}$ with advantage ϵ in breaking Assumption 3.

Proof of Lemma 5

The algorithm $\mathcal{B}$ begins by taking in an instance $(\mathbb{G}, g, g^\alpha X_2, X_3, g^s Y_2, Z_2, T)$ of Assumption 3. It simulates Game_q or Game_{Final} with $\mathcal{A}$.

Reduction algorithm $\mathcal{B}$ in Lemma 5

Setup

1. Pick random exponents $a_1, \ldots, a_\ell, b \in \mathbb{Z}_N$.

2. Set $g = g$, $u_i = g^{a_i}$ for $i \in \{1, \ldots, \ell\}$, $h = g^b$ and $e(g,g)^\alpha = e(g^\alpha X_2, g)$.

3. Send the public parameters params $= (g, u_1, \ldots, u_\ell, h, e(g,g)^\alpha)$ to $\mathcal{A}$.

4. Set the master secret key MSK is α.

Phase I When $\mathcal{A}$ requests a key for identity $(\mathsf{ID}_1, \ldots, \mathsf{ID}_j)$, $\mathcal{B}$ creates a semi-functional key as follows.

1. Choose a random exponents $c, r, t, w, z, z_{j+1}, \ldots, z_\ell, w_{j+1}, \ldots, w_\ell \in \mathbb{Z}_N$.

2. Compute $K_1 = g^r Z_2 X_3{}^t$.

3. Compute $K_2 = g^\alpha X_2 Z_2{}^c (u_1^{\mathsf{ID}_1} \cdots u_j^{\mathsf{ID}_j} h)^r X_3{}^w$.

4. Compute $E_{j+1} = u_{j+1}{}^r Z_2{}^{z_{j+1}} X_3{}^{w_{j+1}}, \ldots, E_\ell = u_\ell{}^r Z_2{}^{z_\ell} X_3{}^{w_\ell}$.

5. Send the secret key $SK_{\mathsf{ID}} = (K_1, K_2, E_{j+1}, \ldots, E_\ell)$.

Challenge

1. $\mathcal{A}$ outputs messages M_0, M_1 and challenge identity $(\mathsf{ID}_1^*, \ldots, \mathsf{ID}_j^*)$.

2. $\mathcal{B}$ generates bit $\beta \in \{0, 1\}$.

3. The ciphertext (C_0, C_1, C_2) is formed as
$$C_0 = M_\beta T, \qquad C_1 = (g^s Y_2)^{(a_1 \mathsf{ID}_1^* + \cdots + a_j \mathsf{ID}_j^* + b)}, \qquad C_2 = g^s Y_2.$$

Note: This implicitly sets $z_c = a_1 \mathsf{ID}_1^* + \cdots + a_j \mathsf{ID}_j^* + b$. We note that the value of z_c only matters modulo p_2, whereas $u_1 = g^{a_1}, \ldots, u_\ell = g^{a_\ell}$, and $h = g^b$ are elements of $\mathbb{G}_{p_1}$, so when $a_1, \ldots, a_\ell$ and b are chosen randomly modulo N, there is no correlation between the values of $a_1, \ldots, a_\ell, b$ modulo p_1 and the value $z_c = a_1 \mathsf{ID}_1^* + \cdots + a_j \mathsf{ID}_j^* + b$ modulo p_2.

Phase II

1. $\mathcal{A}$ makes key generation queries, and $\mathcal{B}$ responds as in Phase I.

Guess

1. Finally, the adversary outputs guesses $\beta' \in \{0, 1\}$.

2. If $\beta = \beta'$, it outputs 0 (indicating that $T = e(g,g)^{\alpha s}$); otherwise, it outputs 1.

Simulation of secret key generation in Lemma 5

The key generation algorithm in Lemma 5 generates only semi-functional keys. Since $\mathcal{B}$ does not know the master secret key, it cannot generate the real secret key as in previous Lemmas. However, in Lemma 5, the semi-functional keys can be generated without knowledge of the master secret key. For convenience, let $(K_1', K_2', E_{j+1}', \ldots, E_\ell')$ denote the normal key generated by using the key generation algorithm. There exist $\gamma \in \mathbb{Z}_N$ and $R_3, R_3', R_{j+1} \in \mathbb{G}_{p_3}$ such that $Z_2 = g_2{}^\gamma$, $R_3 = X_3{}^t$, $R_3' = X_3{}^w$, $X_3{}^{w_{j+1}} = R_{j+1}$, $X_2 Z_2{}^c = g_2{}^{\gamma z_k}$, $Y_2{}^{z_c} = g_2{}^{\gamma z_k}$. We have the semi-functional key as follows:

$$K_1 = g^r Z_2 X_3{}^t = g^r g_2{}^\gamma R_3.$$

$$K_2 = g^\alpha X_2 Z_2{}^c (u_1^{\mathsf{ID}_1} \cdots u_j^{\mathsf{ID}_j} h)^r X_3{}^w = g^\alpha (u_1^{\mathsf{ID}_1} \cdots u_j^{\mathsf{ID}_j} h)^r R_3' g_2{}^{\gamma z_k} = K_2' g_2{}^{\gamma z_k}.$$

$$E_{j+1} = u_{j+1}{}^r Z_2{}^{z_{j+1}} X_3{}^{w_{j+1}} = u_{j+1}{}^r g_2{}^{\gamma z_{j+1}} R_{j+1} = E_{j+1}' g_2{}^{\gamma z_{j+1}}.$$

$$\ldots$$

$$E_\ell = u_\ell{}^r Z_2{}^{z_\ell} X_3{}^{w_\ell} = u_\ell{}^r g_2{}^{\gamma z_\ell} R_\ell = E_\ell' g_2{}^{\gamma z_\ell}.$$

Simulation of challenge ciphertext generation in Lemma 5

The difference between Game_q and Game_{Final} is whether the challenge ciphertext is semi-functional or random. So, T must be embedded in the challenge ciphertext. The challenge ciphertext is semi-functional if T is real; otherwise, the challenge ciphertext is random. Here check that if T is real, then it computes the semi-functional ciphertext, or if T is random, it computes the random ciphertext. Since $\mathcal{B}$ does not know the master secret key, it cannot generate the real ciphertext as in previous Lemmas. However, in Lemma 5, the semi-functional ciphertext can be generated without knowledge of the master secret key. For convenience, let (C_0', C_1', C_2') denote the normal ciphertext generated by using the encryption algorithm. Since $Y_2 \in \mathbb{G}_{p_2}$, there exist $x \in \mathbb{Z}_N$ such that $Y_2 = g_2{}^x$.

In the case $T = e(g, g)^{\alpha s}$, the ciphertext is computed as follows:

$$C_0 = M_\beta e(g, g)^{\alpha s} = C_0'.$$

$$C_1 = (g^s Y_2)^{(a_1 \mathsf{ID}_1^* + \cdots + a_j \mathsf{ID}_j^* + b)} = (g^s g_2{}^x)^{(a_1 \mathsf{ID}_1^* + \cdots + a_j \mathsf{ID}_j^* + b)} = (g^s)^{(a_1 \mathsf{ID}_1^* + \cdots + a_j \mathsf{ID}_j^* + b)} (g_2{}^x)^{(a_1 \mathsf{ID}_1^* + \cdots + a_j \mathsf{ID}_j^* + b)} = C_1' g_2{}^{x z_c}.$$

$$C_2 = g^s Y_2 = g^s g_2{}^x = C_2' g_2{}^x.$$

In the case T is a random element from $\mathbb{G}_T$, then some additional random values are multiplied by the computed value of C_0. Therefore, we know that the ciphertext computed in this case is random.

Probability analysis in Lemma 5 The probability computation is simple as

$$Game_q Adv_\mathcal{A} - Game_{Final} Adv_\mathcal{A} = \epsilon. \tag{14.8}$$

Theorem 3 If Assumptions 1, 2, and 3 hold, then our HIBE system is secure.

Proof of Theorem 3

If Assumptions 1, 2, and 3 hold, then we have shown by the previous lemmas that the real security game is indistinguishable from $Game_{Final}$, in which the value of $\mathcal{B}$ is information theoretically hidden from the attacker. Hence the attacker can attain no advantage in breaking the HIBE system. $\square$

14.5   The Generic Group Model

To understand the generic group model more easily, we introduce [22].

14.5.1   The Decision Linear Diffie-Hellman Assumption

With $g_1 \in \mathbb{G}_1$, along with arbitrary generators u, v, and h of $\mathbb{G}_1$, consider the following problem.

Decision linear problem in $\mathbb{G}_1$. Given $u, v, h, u^a, v^b, h^c \in \mathbb{G}_1$ as input, output yes if $a + b = c$ and no otherwise.

One can easily show that an algorithm for solving the decision linear problem in $\mathbb{G}_1$ gives an algorithm for solving DDH in $\mathbb{G}_1$. The converse is believed to be false. That is, it is believed that decision linear is a hard problem even in bilinear groups where DDH is easy (e.g., when $\mathbb{G}_1 = \mathbb{G}_2$). More precisely, we define the advantage of an algorithm $\mathcal{A}$ in deciding the decision linear problem in $\mathbb{G}_1$ as

$$\text{Adv Linear}_\mathcal{A} \stackrel{def}{=} \left| \begin{array}{l} Pr[\mathcal{A}(u, v, h, u^a, v^b, h^{a+b}) = \text{yes} : u, v, h \stackrel{R}{\leftarrow} \mathbb{G}_1, a, b \stackrel{R}{\leftarrow} \mathbb{Z}_p] \\ -Pr[\mathcal{A}(u, v, h, u^a, v^b, \eta) = \text{yes} : u, v, h, \eta \stackrel{R}{\leftarrow} \mathbb{G}_1, a, b \stackrel{R}{\leftarrow} \mathbb{Z}_p] \end{array} \right|.$$

The probability is over the uniform random choice of the parameters to $\mathcal{A}$, and over the coin tosses of $\mathcal{A}$. We say that an algorithm $\mathcal{A}$ (t, ϵ)-decides decision linear in $\mathbb{G}_1$ if $\mathcal{A}$ runs in time at most t, and Adv Linear$_\mathcal{A}$ is at least ϵ.

Definition 5 We say that the (t, ϵ)-**decision linear assumption holds** in $\mathbb{G}_1$ if no t-time algorithm has advantage at least ϵ in solving the decision linear problem in $\mathbb{G}_1$. In the next section, we show that the decision linear assumption holds in generic bilinear groups [92].

14.5.2 The Linear Problem in Generic Bilinear Groups

To provide more confidence in the decision linear assumption, we prove a lower bound on the computational complexity of the decision linear problem for generic groups in the sense of Shoup [92]. In this model, elements of $\mathbb{G}_1$, $\mathbb{G}_2$, and $\mathbb{G}_T$ appear to be encoded as unique random strings, so that no property other than equality can be directly tested by the adversary.

Five oracles are assumed to perform operations between group elements, such as computing the group action in each of the three groups $\mathbb{G}_1$, $\mathbb{G}_2$, $\mathbb{G}_T$, as well as the isomorphism $\psi : \mathbb{G}_2 \to \mathbb{G}_1$, and the bilinear pairing $e : \mathbb{G}_1 \times \mathbb{G}_2 \to \mathbb{G}_T$ (where possibly $\mathbb{G}_1 = \mathbb{G}_2$).

The opaque encoding of the elements of $\mathbb{G}_1$ is modeled as an injective function $\xi_1 : \mathbb{Z}_p \to \Xi_1$, where $\Xi_1 \subset \{0, 1\}^*$, which maps all $a \in \mathbb{Z}_p$ to the string representation $\xi_1(a)$ of $g^a \in \mathbb{G}_1$. Analogous maps $\xi_2 : \mathbb{Z}_p \to \Xi_2$ for $\mathbb{G}_2$ and $\xi_T : \mathbb{Z}_p \to \Xi_T$ for $\mathbb{G}_T$ are also defined. The attacker $\mathcal{A}$ communicates with the oracles using the ξ-representations of the group elements only.

Let $x, y, z, a, b, c \xleftarrow{R} \mathbb{Z}_p^*$, $T_0 \leftarrow g^{z(a+b)}$, $T_1 \leftarrow g^c$, and $d \xleftarrow{R} \{0, 1\}$. We show that no generic algorithm $\mathcal{A}$ that is given the encodings of $g^x, g^y, g^z, g^{xa}, g^{yb}, T_d, T_{1-d}$ and makes up to q oracle queries can guess the value of d with probability greater than $\frac{1}{2} + O(q^2/p)$. Note that here g^x, g^y, and g^z play the role of the generators u, v, and h in the decision linear problem definition.

Theorem 4 Let $\mathcal{A}$ be an algorithm that solves the decision linear problem in the generic group model. Assume that ξ_1, ξ_2, ξ_T are random encoding functions for $\mathbb{G}_1$, $\mathbb{G}_2$, $\mathbb{G}_T$. If $\mathcal{A}$ makes a total of at most q queries to the oracles computing the group action in $\mathbb{G}_1$, $\mathbb{G}_2$, $\mathbb{G}_T$, the isomorphism ψ, and the bilinear pairing e, then

$$\left| Pr \left[\mathcal{A} \left(\begin{array}{c} p, \xi_1(1), \xi_1(x), \xi_1(y), \xi_1(z), \\ \xi_1(xa), \xi_1(yb), \xi_1(t_0), \xi_1(t_1), \xi_2(1) \end{array} \right) = d : \\ x, y, z, a, b, c \xleftarrow{R} \mathbb{Z}_p^*, d \xleftarrow{R} \{0, 1\}, \\ t_d \leftarrow z(a+b), t_{1-d} \leftarrow c \right] - \frac{1}{2} \right| \leq \frac{8(q+9)^2}{p}.$$

Proof Consider an algorithm $\mathcal{B}$ that plays the following game with $\mathcal{A}$.

$\mathcal{B}$ maintains three lists of pairs, $L_1 = \{(F_{1,i}, \xi_{1,i}) : i = 0, ..., \tau_1 - 1\}$, $L_2 = \{(F_{2,i}, \xi_{2,i}) : i = 0, ..., \tau_2 - 1\}$, $L_T = \{(F_{T,i}, \xi_{T,i}) : i = 0, ..., \tau_T - 1\}$, under the invariant that, at step τ in the game, $\tau_1 + \tau_2 + \tau_T = \tau + 9$. Here, the $F_{\star,\star} \in \mathbb{Z}_p[X, Y, Z, A, B, T_0, T_1]$ are polynomials in the indeterminates X, Y, Z, A, B, T_0, T_1 with coefficients in $\mathbb{Z}_p$. The $\xi_{\star,\star} \in \{0, 1\}^*$ are arbitrary distinct strings.

The lists are initialized at step $\tau = 0$ by initializing $\tau_1 \leftarrow 8$, $\tau_2 \leftarrow 1$, $\tau_T \leftarrow 0$, and setting $F_{1,0} = 1$, $F_{1,1} = X$, $F_{1,2} = Y$, $F_{1,3} = Z$, $F_{1,4} = XA$, $F_{1,5} = YB$, $F_{1,6} = T_0$, $F_{1,7} = T_1$, and $F_{2,0} = 1$, where the degrees of $F_{1,1}$, $F_{1,2}$, $F_{1,3}$, $F_{1,6}$, $F_{1,7}$ are 1, and the degrees of $F_{1,4}$ and $F_{1,5}$ are 2. The corresponding strings are set to arbitrary distinct strings in $\{0, 1\}^*$.

We may assume that $\mathcal{A}$ only makes oracle queries on strings previously obtained from $\mathcal{B}$, since $\mathcal{B}$ can make them arbitrarily hard to guess. We note that $\mathcal{B}$ can determine the index i of any given string $\xi_{1,i}$ in L_1 (resp. $\xi_{2,i}$ in L_2, or $\xi_{T,i}$ in L_T), where ties between multiple matches are broken arbitrarily.

$\mathcal{B}$ starts the game by providing $\mathcal{A}$ with the encodings $\xi_{1,0}, \xi_{1,1}, \xi_{1,2}, \xi_{1,3}, \xi_{1,4}, \xi_{1,5}, \xi_{1,6}, \xi_{1,7}$, and $\xi_{2,0}$. The simulator $\mathcal{B}$ responds to algorithm $\mathcal{A}$'s queries as follows.

Group action Given a multiply/divide selection bit and two operands $\xi_{1,i}$ and $\xi_{1,j}$ with $0 \leq i, j < \tau_1$, compute $F_{1,\tau_1} \leftarrow F_{1,i} \pm F_{1,j}$ depending on whether a multiplication or a division is requested. If $F_{1,\tau_1} = F_{1,l}$ for some $l < \tau_1$, set $\xi_{1,\tau_1} \leftarrow \xi_{1,l}$; otherwise, set ξ_{1,τ_1} to a string in $\{0, 1\}^*$ distinct from $\xi_{1,0}, \cdots, \xi_{1,\tau_1-1}$. Add $(F_{1,\tau_1}, \xi_{1,\tau_1})$ to the list L_1 and give ξ_{1,τ_1} to $\mathcal{A}$, then increment τ_1 by one. Group action queries in $\mathbb{G}_2$ and $\mathbb{G}_T$ are treated similarly.

Isomorphism Given a string $\xi_{2,i}$ with $0 \leq i < \tau_2$, set $F_{1,\tau_1} \leftarrow F_{2,i}$. If $F_{1,\tau_1} = F_{1,l}$ for some $l < \tau_1$, set $\xi_{1,\tau_1} \leftarrow \xi_{1,l}$; otherwise, set ξ_{1,τ_1} to a string in $\{0, 1\}^* \setminus \{\xi_{1,0}, \cdots, \xi_{1,\tau_1-1}\}$. Add $(F_{1,\tau_1}, \xi_{1,\tau_1})$ to the list L_1, and give ξ_{1,τ_1} to $\mathcal{A}$, then increment τ_1 by one.

Pairing Given two operands $\xi_{1,i}$ and $\xi_{2,j}$ with $0 \leq i < \tau_1$ and $0 \leq j < \tau_2$, compute the product $F_{T,\tau_T} \leftarrow F_{1,i} F_{2,j}$. If $F_{T,\tau_T} = F_{T,l}$ for some $l < \tau_T$, set $\xi_{T,\tau_T} \leftarrow \xi_{T,l}$; otherwise, set ξ_{T,τ_T} to a string in $\{0, 1\}^* \setminus \{\xi_{T,0}, \cdots, \xi_{T,\tau_1-1}\}$. Add $(F_{T,\tau_T}, \xi_{T,\tau_T})$ to the list L_T, and give ξ_{T,τ_T} to $\mathcal{A}$, then increment τ_T by one.

Observe that at any time in the game, the total degree of any polynomial in each of the three lists is bounded as follows: $\deg(F_{1,i}) \leq 2$, $\deg(F_{2,i}) = 0$ (or $\deg(F_{2,i}) \leq 2$ if $\mathbb{G}_1 = \mathbb{G}_2$), and $\deg(F_{T,i}) \leq 2$ (or $\deg(F_{T,i}) \leq 4$ if $\mathbb{G}_1 = \mathbb{G}_2$).

After at most q queries, $\mathcal{A}$ terminates and returns a guess $\hat{d} \in \{0, 1\}$. At this point $\mathcal{B}$ chooses random $x, y, z, a, b, c \stackrel{R}{\leftarrow} \mathbb{Z}_p$. Consider $t_d \leftarrow z(a + b)$ and $t_{1-d} \leftarrow c$ for both choices of $d \in \{0, 1\}$. The simulation provided by $\mathcal{B}$ is perfect and reveals nothing to $\mathcal{A}$ about d unless the chosen random values for the indeterminates give rise to a non-trivial equality relation between the simulated group elements that was not revealed to $\mathcal{A}$, i.e., when we assign $X \leftarrow x, Y \leftarrow y, Z \leftarrow z, A \leftarrow a, B \leftarrow b$, and either $T_0 \leftarrow z(a + b), T_1 \leftarrow c$ or the converse $T_0 \leftarrow c, T_1 \leftarrow z(a + b)$.

This happens only if for some i, j one of the following holds:

1. $F_{1,i}(x, y, z, a, b, z(a + b), c) - F_{1,j}(x, y, z, a, b, z(a + b), c) = 0$, yet $F_{1,i} \neq F_{1,j}$,

2. $F_{2,i}(x, y, z, a, b, z(a + b), c) - F_{2,j}(x, y, z, a, b, z(a + b), c) = 0$, yet $F_{2,i} \neq F_{2,j}$,

3. $F_{T,i}(x, y, z, a, b, z(a + b), c) - F_{T,j}(x, y, z, a, b, z(a + b), c) = 0$, yet $F_{T,i} \neq F_{T,j}$,

4. any relation similar to the above in which $z(a + b)$ and c have been exchanged.

We first need to argue that the adversary is unable to engineer any of the above equalities, so that they can only occur due to an unfortunate random choice of x, y, z, a, b, c. First, observe that the adversary can only manipulate the polynomials on the three lists through additions and subtractions (disguised as multiplications and divisions in the groups $\mathbb{G}_1$, $\mathbb{G}_2$, and $\mathbb{G}_T$) as well as multiplications between polynomials which are not the result of a previous multiplication (disguised as pairings between elements of $\mathbb{G}_1$ and $\mathbb{G}_2$).

Now, notice that in the initial population of the lists, the only occurrence of the variable A is within the monomial XA, the only occurrence of the variable B is within the monomial YB, and the only occurrence of the variable Z is by itself.

Given the available operations, it is easy to see that, in the three group representations:

1. The adversary is unable to generate any polynomial that contains at least one of the monomials mZA and mZB for any integer $m \neq 0$, which is a prerequisite to synthesize a multiple of $Z(A + B)$ in $\mathbb{G}_1$ or $\mathbb{G}_2$ (recall that the maximum degree in those groups is 2);

2. The adversary is unable to simultaneously generate the terms FZA and FZB for any non-zero monomial F of degree at most 2, which is a prerequisite to synthesize a multiple of the polynomial $Z(A+B)$ in $\mathbb{G}_T$ (the maximum degree in this group being 4).

Since in the above polynomial differences all arguments to the polynomials are independent except for $z(a+b)$, it is easy to see that the adversary will not be able to cause any of them to cancel identically and non-trivially without knowledge of a multiple of $Z(A+B)$. The adversary is thus reduced to find a numeric cancellation for random assignments of the variables.

We now determine the probability of a random occurrence of a non-trivial numeric cancellation. Since $F_{1,i} - F_{1,j}$ for fixed i and j is a polynomial of degree at most 2, it vanishes for random assignment of the indeterminates in $\mathbb{Z}_p$ with probability at most $2/p$. Similarly, for fixed i and j, the second case occurs with probability 0 (or $\leq 2/p$ when $\mathbb{G}_1 = \mathbb{G}_2$), and the third with probability $\leq 2/p$ (or $\leq 4/p$ when $\mathbb{G}_1 = \mathbb{G}_2$)[3]. The same probabilities are found in the analogous cases where $z(a+b)$ and c have been exchanged.

Now, absent any of the above events, the distribution of the bit d in $\mathcal{A}$'s view is independent, and $\mathcal{A}$'s probability of making a correct guess is exactly $\frac{1}{2}$. Thus, by summing over all valid pairs i, j in each case, we find that $\mathcal{A}$ makes a correct guess with advantage $\epsilon \leq 2 \cdot \left(\binom{\tau_1}{2} \frac{2}{p} + \binom{\tau_2}{2} \frac{2}{p} + \binom{\tau_T}{2} \frac{4}{p} \right)$. Since $\tau_1 + \tau_2 + \tau_T \leq q + 9$, we have $\epsilon \leq 8(q+9)^2/p$, as required. $\square$

Exercises

14.1 Explain the random variables, formal variables, and handles of the random variables with concrete examples.

14.2 Show concrete examples about the differences between Game 1 and 2.

14.3 Give a concrete example of formal polynomials.

---

[3]To understand this, refer to the Schwartz–Zippel lemma.

15

Identity-Based Encryption (4)

CONTENTS

This chapter introduces the concept of Boneh and Boyen's identity based encryption scheme. Although the Waters' proof methodology of dual system encryption is able to resolve the issue of the non-static assumptions to provide fully secure proof, it also raises a problem of efficiency degradation, which is not a problem in a selectively secure model. The Boneh and Boyen's scheme is presented to give a selectively secure solution based on static assumption in the standard model. The differences between selectively secure and fully secure models are then discussed. The next part of the chapter introduces the preliminaries starting from the security model for selective identity IBE. A static hardness assumption for the Boneh and Boyen scheme is then discussed called decisional bilinear Diffie-Hellman (DBDH) assumption. The final part of this chapter introduces the formal construction of the Boneh and Boyen scheme. This version is an efficient IBE system that is selective identity and CPA-secure IBE based on DBDH without random oracles.

15.1   Overview

Previously, we pointed out the problems of the non-static assumption in Gentry's scheme and introduced the Waters' proof methodology of *Dual System Encryption* to resolve them. Waters' scheme presents fully (adaptively) secure solutions based on static assumptions in the standard model through hybrid games. On the other hand, the Waters' proof methodology allows us to easily provide fully secure proof, it also raises a problem of efficiency degradation. On the other hand, the selectively secure model is easy to prove with greater efficiency, but it's security is lower than the fully secure model. In this chapter, we explain the Boneh and Boyen's scheme to present selectively secure solution based on static assumption in the standard model.

What are differences between selectively secure and fully (adaptively) secure models?

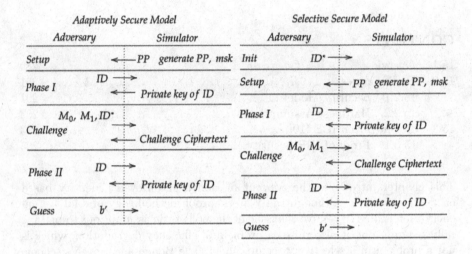

FIGURE 15.1
Comparison of the selectively secure and the fully secure models.

In the selectively secure model, an adversary must commit ahead of time to the identity, called *challenge identity* that it intends to attack, whereas in the fully secure model the adversary is allowed to choose this identity adaptively during the game. So, the biggest difference is whether the adversary publishes the challenge identity or not before starting the game. This seemingly minor difference decides the complexity level (i.e., level of difficulty) of a proof as a result. Figure 15.1 shows the comparison of selectively secure and fully secure models.

Before explaining why this difference in complexity level happens when proving, we have to consider once more: a simulator should not solve a hard problem by itself, but use an adversary to solve it instead. If the simulator solves it by itself, the proof fails because the security game is not valid (i.e., does not establish). Normally, the simulator solves it by embedding the instances of the hard problem into the challenge ciphertext as well as the private keys, and then by reducing the adversary's decryption of the challenge ciphertext to solving the hard problem.

To proceed a valid proof, therefore, the simulator should not decrypt the challenge ciphertext by itself. For example, if the underlying hard problem is to distinguish whether the input instance is random or not, we should make sure that the simulator cannot distinguish them by itself. This can be achieved by allowing the simulator to either decrypt in both cases or not to decrypt in both cases, where the input instance comes from random or non-random distribution.

If the simulator knows the challenge identity in advance, we only have to make sure that the simulator cannot generate the corresponding private key for the challenge identity (and in turn cannot decrypt the challenge ciphertext). Instead, if the simulator does not know the challenge identity in advance, all possible identities can be candidates to be challenged, which makes the simulation very complex. This renders a proof in fully secure model difficult or degrades the efficiency of the scheme.

Note that in [48] and [99], the simulator can decrypt the challenge ciphertext by itself, whereas [19] and [24] construct reduction algorithms so that simulators cannot generate the corresponding private key for the challenge identity and cannot decrypt the challenge ciphertext accordingly.

15.2 Preliminaries

This section provides a security model and hardness assumption for identity-based encryption.

15.2.1 Security Model

The selective identity IBE security is defined using the following game.

IND-sID-CCA game for an IBE scheme

1. **Init** The adversary outputs an identity ID^* where it wishes to be challenged.

2. **Setup** The challenger runs the Setup algorithm. It gives the adversary the resulting system parameters params. It keeps the master-key to itself.

3. **Phase I** The adversary issues queries $q_1, \cdots, q_m$ where query q_i is one of:

    (a) Private key query (ID_i) where $ID_i \neq ID^*$. The challenger responds by running the Gen algorithm to generate the private key d_i corresponding to the public key (ID_i). It sends d_i to the adversary.

(b) Decryption query (C_i) where $\mathsf{ID}_i \neq \mathsf{ID}^*$. The challenger responds by running the Gen algorithm to generate the private key d_i corresponding to ID_i (or the relevant prefix thereof as requested). It then runs the Decrypt algorithm to decrypt the ciphertext C_i using the private key d_i. It sends the resulting plaintext to the adversary.

These queries may be asked adaptively, that is, each query q_i may depend on the replies to $q_1, \cdots, q_{i-1}$.

4. **Challenge** Once the adversary decides that Phase I is over it outputs two equal length plaintexts $M_0, M_1 \in \mathcal{M}$ on which it wishes to be challenged. The challenger picks a random bit $b \in \{0, 1\}$ and sets the challenge ciphertext to $C = \mathsf{Encrypt}(\mathsf{params}, \mathsf{ID}^*, M_b)$. It sends C as the challenge to the adversary.

5. **Phase II** The adversary issues additional queries $q_{m+1}, \cdots, q_n$ where q_i is one of:

(a) Private key query (ID_i) where $\mathsf{ID}_i \neq \mathsf{ID}^*$. The challenger responds as in Phase I.

(b) Decryption query (C_i) for identity ID_i where $\mathsf{ID}_i \neq \mathsf{ID}^*$. The challenger responds as in Phase I.

These queries may be asked adaptively as in Phase I.

6. **Guess** Finally, the adversary outputs a guess $b' \in \{0, 1\}$. The adversary wins if $b = b'$.

We refer to such an adversary $\mathcal{A}$ as an IND-sID-CCA adversary. We define the advantage of the adversary $\mathcal{A}$ in attacking the scheme Π as

$$\mathsf{Adv}_{\Pi,\mathcal{A}} = |Pr[(b = b')] - 1/2|. \tag{15.1}$$

The probability is over the random bits used by the challenger and the adversary.

Definition 1 *We say that an IBE system Π is $(t, q_{ID}, q_C, \epsilon)$-**selective identity, adaptive chosen ciphertext secure** if for any t-time IND-sID-CCA adversary A that makes at most q_{ID} chosen private key queries and at most q_C chosen decryption queries we have that $\mathsf{Adv}_{\Pi,\mathcal{A}} < \epsilon$. As shorthand, we say that Π is $(t, q_{ID}, q_C, \epsilon)$-IND-sID-CCA secure.*

Definition 2 *We say that an IBE system Π is (t, q_{ID}, ϵ)-**selective identity, chosen plaintext secure** if Π is (t, q_{ID}, ϵ)-selective identity, chosen ciphertext secure. As shorthand, we say that Π is (t, q_{ID}, ϵ)-IND-sID-CPA secure.*

15.2.2 Hardness Assumption

For proving their scheme, Boneh and Boyen use a static hardness assumption.

Decisional bilinear Diffie-Hellman (DBDH) assumption

Let $\mathbb{G}$ and $\mathbb{G}_1$ be two groups of prime order p, where the size of p is a function of the security parameters. Let $e\colon \mathbb{G} \times \mathbb{G} \to \mathbb{G}_1$ be a bilinear map and let g be a generator of $\mathbb{G}$.

Given $(g, g^a, g^b, g^c, T) \in \mathbb{G}^4 \times \mathbb{G}_1$ for some $a, b, c \in \mathbb{Z}_p$, it must remain hard to distinguish $T = e(g,g)^{abc} \in \mathbb{G}_1$ from a random choice (i.e., element) $R \in \mathbb{G}_1$.

An algorithm $\mathcal{B}$ that outputs $b \in \{0,1\}$ has advantage ϵ in solving the DBDH problem in $\mathbb{G}$ if

$$\left| Pr\left[\mathcal{B}(g, g^a, g^b, g^c, T = e(g,g)^{abc}) = 0\right] - Pr\left[\mathcal{B}(g, g^a, g^b, g^c, T = R) = 0\right] \right| \geq \epsilon.$$
(15.2)

We refer to the distribution on the left as $\mathcal{P}_{BDH}$ and the distribution on the right as $\mathcal{R}_{BDH}$.

Definition 3 *We say that* **the (t, ϵ)-DBDH assumption holds** *in $\mathbb{G}$ if no t-time algorithm has an advantage at least ϵ in solving the DBDH problem in $\mathbb{G}$.*

Occasionally we drop the t and ϵ when referring to the BDH and DBDH assumptions in $\mathbb{G}$.

15.3 Boneh-Boyen IBE [19]

In 2004, Boneh and Boyen proposed an efficient HIBE system that is selective identity secure without random oracles based on the DBDH assumption. In particular, this implies an efficient selective identity, chosen ciphertext secure IBE based on DBDH without random oracles.

Construction 1. Boneh-Boyen IBE

Let $\mathbb{G}$ and $\mathbb{G}_1$ be groups of order p and let $e\colon \mathbb{G} \times \mathbb{G} \to \mathbb{G}_1$ be the bilinear map. The IBE system works as follows.

Setup Given a security parameter $k \in \mathbb{Z}^+$, where $k = |p|$:

1. Pick a random generators $g, h_1 \in \mathbb{G}$, and $g_2 \in \mathbb{G}^*$.
2. Pick a random $\alpha \in \mathbb{Z}_p^*$.
3. Set $g_1 = g^\alpha$.
4. The public parameters are $\mathsf{params} = (g, g_1, g_2, h_1)$.
5. The master secret key is $\mathsf{master\text{-}key} = (g_2^\alpha)$.

We define $F_1 : \mathbb{Z}_p \to \mathbb{G}$ to be the function: $F_1(x) = g_1^x h_1$.

Extract For a given identity $\mathsf{ID} \in \mathbb{Z}_p$

1. Pick a random $r_1 \in \mathbb{Z}_p$.
2. Compute $d_0 = g_2^\alpha \cdot F_1(\mathsf{ID})^{r_1}$.
3. Compute $d_1 = g^{r_1}$.
4. Set the secret key $d_{\mathsf{ID}} = (d_0, d_1)$.

Encrypt Message $M \in \mathbb{G}_1$

1. Pick a random $s \in \mathbb{Z}_p$.
2. Compute $A = e(g_1, g_2)^s \cdot M$.
3. Compute $B = g^s$.
4. Compute $C_1 = F_1(\mathsf{ID})^s$.
5. Set the ciphertext to be: $C = \langle A, B, C_1 \rangle$.

Note that $e(g_1, g_2)$ can be precomputed once and for all so that the encryption does not require any pairing computations. Alternatively, $e(g_1, g_2)$ can be included in the system parameters.

Decrypt Ciphertext C and secret key d_{ID}

1. Compute $M = A \cdot \frac{e(C_1, d_1)}{e(B, d_0)}$.

Correctness:

$$A \cdot \frac{e(C_1, d_1)}{e(B, d_0)} = e(g_1, g_2)^s \cdot M \cdot \frac{e(F_1(\mathsf{ID})^s, g^{r_1})}{e(g^s, g_2^\alpha \cdot F_1(\mathsf{ID})^{r_1})}$$

$$= e(g_1, g_2)^s \cdot M \cdot \frac{e(F_1(\mathsf{ID}), g)^{s \cdot r_1}}{e(g^s, g_2^\alpha) e(g^s, F_1(\mathsf{ID})^{r_1})}$$

$$= e(g_1, g_2)^s \cdot M \cdot \frac{e(F_1(\mathsf{ID}), g)^{s \cdot r_1}}{e(g, g_2)^{s \cdot \alpha} e(g, F_1(\mathsf{ID}))^{s \cdot r_1}}$$

$$= e(g_1, g_2)^s \cdot M \cdot \frac{1}{e(g^\alpha, g_2)^s}$$

$$= e(g_1, g_2)^s \cdot M \cdot \frac{1}{e(g_1, g_2)^s} = M$$

TABLE 15.1

Computational cost of Boneh-Boyen IBE [19].

Public Parameters	$4|\mathbb{G}| + |\mathbb{G}_1|$
Secret Key	$2|\mathbb{G}|$
Communication	$2|\mathbb{G}| + |\mathbb{G}_1|$
Gen	$2M + 3E$
Encrypt	$1M + 3E + M_1 + E_1$
Decrypt	$2M_1 + 2P$

The computational cost of Boneh-Boyen IBE [19] is shown in Table 15.1. Note that this is the most efficient identity-based encryption scheme published until now.

15.3.1   Proof of IBE Security

Theorem 1 *Suppose the (t, ϵ)-DBDH assumption holds in $\mathbb{G}$. Then the previously defined IBE system is (t', q_S, ϵ)-selective identity, chosen plaintext (IND-sID-CPA) secure for arbitrary q_S and any $t' < t - O(t)$.*

Intuition of the Proof As mentioned earlier, the advantage of a selectively secure proof is to obtain the target identity (also called *challenge identity*) to be attacked by the adversary, which is the central pillar of the proof. In short, we only have to make sure that the simulator cannot generate the corresponding private keys for the challenge identity, but can generate challenge ciphertext for the challenge identity instead. This will be enabled by a function $F_1(x)$ and a generator h_1 as follows.

$F_1(x)$ is defined as $F_1(x) = g_1^x h_1$. h_1 is defined as $h_1 = g_1^{-\mathsf{ID}^*} g^{\alpha_1}$. From the above, $F_1(x)$ can be defined as

$$F_1(x) = g_1^x g_1^{-\mathsf{ID}^*} g^{\alpha_1} = g_1^{x-\mathsf{ID}^*} g^{\alpha_1}. \qquad (15.3)$$

When x is ID^*,

$$F_1(\mathsf{ID}^*) = g_1^{\mathsf{ID}^* - \mathsf{ID}^*} g^{\alpha_1} = g^{\alpha_1}. \qquad (15.4)$$

By making use of these, we make sure that when $F_1(x)$ is calculated to be g^{α_1}, a private key cannot be generated but a challenge ciphertext can be generated, which resolves the issue that the simulator can solve the problem by itself. Therefore, the security game becomes valid.

Proof Suppose $\mathcal{A}$ has advantage ϵ in attacking the IBE system. We build an algorithm $\mathcal{B}$ that solves the DBDH problem in $\mathbb{G}$. On input (g, g^a, g^b, g^c, T), $\mathcal{B}$'s goal is to output 1 if $T = e(g, g)^{abc}$ and 0 otherwise. Let $g_1 = g^a, g_2 = g^b, g_3 = g^c$. Algorithm $\mathcal{B}$ works by interacting with $\mathcal{A}$ in a selective identity game as follows.

Reduction algorithm $\mathcal{B}$

Initialization

1. Choose a random exponent $\alpha_1 \in \mathbb{Z}_p$.

2. Set $g = g$, $g_1 = g^a$, $g_2 = g^b$ where a and b are the exponents which are unknown to $\mathcal{B}$.

3. Define $h_1 = g_1^{-\mathsf{ID}^*} g^{\alpha_1}$.

4. Send the public parameters params $= (g, g_1, g_2, h_1)$.

5. Set the master key master-key $= (g_2^a = g^{ab})$ which is unknown to $\mathcal{B}$.

6. Define $F_1 : \mathbb{Z}_p \to \mathbb{G}$ to be the function $F_1(x) = g_1^x h_1 = g_1^{x-\mathsf{ID}^*} g^{\alpha_1}$.

Phase I

1. Choose a random exponent $r_1 \in \mathbb{Z}_p$.

2. Set $d_0 = g_2^{\frac{-\alpha_1}{\mathsf{ID}-\mathsf{ID}^*}} F_1(\mathsf{ID})^{r_1}$ and $d_1 = g_2^{\frac{-1}{\mathsf{ID}-\mathsf{ID}^*}} g^{r_1}$.

3. Send the private key $d_{\mathsf{ID}} = (d_0, d_1)$.

Challenge

1. $\mathcal{A}$ outputs messages M_0, M_1.

2. $\mathcal{B}$ generates a bit $b \in \{0, 1\}$.

3. Set $A = M_b \cdot T$, $B = g^c$, $C_1 = (g^c)^{\alpha_1}$.

4. Send the challenge ciphertext $C = (A, B, C_1)$.

Note: If $T = e(g, g)^{abc}$, then the challenge ciphertext is valid. If T is random, then the challenge ciphertext is invalid.

Phase II

1. $\mathcal{A}$ issues its complement of private key queries not issued in Phase I.

Guess

1. Finally, the adversary outputs guesses $b' \in \{0, 1\}$.

2. If $b = b'$, it outputs 1 (indicating that $T = e(g, g)^{abc}$); otherwise, it outputs 0 (indicating that $T \neq e(g, g)^{abc}$).

Simulation of secret key generation in Theorem 1

The original private key is set as follows.

$$d_0 = g_2^\alpha \cdot F_1(\mathsf{ID})^{r_1}, \qquad d_1 = g^{r_1}.$$

In the above reduction algorithm, the private key is set as follows.

$$d_0 = g_2^{\frac{-\alpha_1}{\mathsf{ID}-\mathsf{ID}^*}} F_1(\mathsf{ID})^{r_1}, \qquad d_1 = g_2^{\frac{-1}{\mathsf{ID}-\mathsf{ID}^*}} g^{r_1}.$$

The private key must be generated in the case of $\mathsf{ID} \neq \mathsf{ID}^*$.
If $\mathsf{ID} \neq \mathsf{ID}^*$ and $r_1' = r_1 - \frac{b}{\mathsf{ID}-\mathsf{ID}^*}$, then d_0 and d_1 are valid and computed as follows.

$$
\begin{aligned}
d_0 &= g_2^{\frac{-\alpha_1}{\mathsf{ID}-\mathsf{ID}^*}} F_1(\mathsf{ID})^{r_1} = g^{b\frac{-\alpha_1}{\mathsf{ID}-\mathsf{ID}^*}} g^{a(\mathsf{ID}-\mathsf{ID}^*)r_1} g^{\alpha_1 r_1} = g^{a(\mathsf{ID}-\mathsf{ID}^*)r_1} g^{\alpha_1 r_1} g^{b\frac{-\alpha_1}{\mathsf{ID}-\mathsf{ID}^*}} \\
&= g^{a(\mathsf{ID}-\mathsf{ID}^*)b\frac{1}{\mathsf{ID}-\mathsf{ID}^*}} g^{-a(\mathsf{ID}-\mathsf{ID}^*)b\frac{1}{\mathsf{ID}-\mathsf{ID}^*}} g^{a(\mathsf{ID}-\mathsf{ID}^*)r_1} g^{\alpha_1 r_1} g^{b\frac{-\alpha_1}{\mathsf{ID}-\mathsf{ID}^*}} \\
&= g^{a(\mathsf{ID}-\mathsf{ID}^*)b\frac{1}{\mathsf{ID}-\mathsf{ID}^*}} g^{-a(\mathsf{ID}-\mathsf{ID}^*)b\frac{1}{\mathsf{ID}-\mathsf{ID}^*}} g^{a(\mathsf{ID}-\mathsf{ID}^*)r_1} g^{\alpha_1(r_1 - \frac{b}{\mathsf{ID}-\mathsf{ID}^*})} \\
&= g^{ab} g^{-a(\mathsf{ID}-\mathsf{ID}^*)b\frac{1}{\mathsf{ID}-\mathsf{ID}^*}} g^{a(\mathsf{ID}-\mathsf{ID}^*)r_1} g^{\alpha_1(r_1 - \frac{b}{\mathsf{ID}-\mathsf{ID}^*})} \\
&= g^{ab} g^{a(\mathsf{ID}-\mathsf{ID}^*)(r_1 - \frac{b}{\mathsf{ID}-\mathsf{ID}^*})} g^{\alpha_1(r_1 - \frac{b}{\mathsf{ID}-\mathsf{ID}^*})} = (g^b)^a g^{a(\mathsf{ID}-\mathsf{ID}^*)r_1'} g^{\alpha_1 r_1'} = g_2^a F_1(\mathsf{ID})^{r_1'}
\end{aligned}
$$

$$d_1 = g_2^{\frac{-1}{\mathsf{ID}-\mathsf{ID}^*}} g^{r_1} = g^{b\frac{-1}{\mathsf{ID}-\mathsf{ID}^*}} g^{r_1} = g^{r_1 - \frac{b}{\mathsf{ID}-\mathsf{ID}^*}} = g^{r_1'}.$$

If $\mathsf{ID} = \mathsf{ID}^*$ and $r_1' = r_1 - \frac{b}{\mathsf{ID}-\mathsf{ID}^*}$, then d_0 and d_1 cannot be computed, because $\mathsf{ID}^* - \mathsf{ID}^* = 0$ and $\frac{1}{0}$ cannot be computed. So, the private key for the challenge identity ID^* cannot be generated.

Simulation of challenge ciphertext generation in Theorem 1

The original ciphertext is set as follows.

$$A = e(g_1, g_2)^s \cdot M, \qquad B = g^s, \qquad C_1 = F_1(\mathsf{ID}^*)^s.$$

In the above reduction algorithm, the challenge ciphertext is set as follows.

$$A = T \cdot M, \qquad B = g^c, \qquad C_1 = F_1(\mathsf{ID}^*)^c, \text{ where } c = s.$$

If $T = e(g, g)^{abc}$, then A is valid, because $T = e(g, g)^{abc} = e(g^a, g^b)^c = e(g_1, g_2)^s$, and can set A by using the instance of the problem, T. On the other hand, if T is random, then naturally A is invalid.

Since $c = s$, B is valid ($B = g^c = g^s$) and can set B by using the instance of the problem, g^c.

Since $F_1(\mathsf{ID}^*)^c = g_1^{(\mathsf{ID}^* - \mathsf{ID}^*)c} g^{\alpha_1 c} = g^{\alpha_1 c}$, C_1 is also valid and can set $C_1 = (g^c)^{\alpha_1}$ by using the instance of the problem, g^c.

Even though $\mathcal{B}$ tries to generate the challenge ciphertext of other identity ID, it cannot generate it. It is because in order to generate the challenge ciphertext of other identity ID, $\mathcal{B}$ has to know g^{ac} as follows: $F_1(\mathsf{ID})^c = g_1^{(\mathsf{ID} - \mathsf{ID}^*)c} g^{\alpha_1 c} = (g^{ac})^{(\mathsf{ID} - \mathsf{ID}^*)} (g^c)^{\alpha_1}$. But, $\mathcal{B}$ does not know g^{ac}. So, the challenge ciphertext of other identity ID cannot be generated.

In conclusion, we can say that:

1. If $T = e(g, g)^{abc})$, then the challenge ciphertext is a valid encryption of M_b under ID^* (In this case, $\mathcal{B}$ can make use of A's capability).

2. If T is random, then the challenge ciphertext is independent of M_b under ID^* (In this case, $\mathcal{B}$ cannot make use of A's capability).

Probability analysis in Theorem 1

When the input 5-tuple is sampled from $\mathcal{P}_{BDH}$ (where $T = e(g, g)^{abc}$), then $\mathcal{A}$'s view is identical to its view in a real attack game and therefore $\mathcal{A}$ must satisfy $|Pr[b = b'] - \frac{1}{2}| > \epsilon$, which means $Pr[b = b'] \geq |\frac{1}{2} \pm \epsilon|^1$. On the other hand, when the input 5-tuple is sampled from $\mathcal{R}_{BDH}$ (where T is uniform in $\mathbb{G}_1$), then $Pr[b = b'] = \frac{1}{2}$ (i.e., no distinguishing capability). Therefore, with g uniform in $\mathbb{G}^*$, a, b, c uniform in $\mathbb{Z}_p^*$ and T is uniform in $\mathbb{G}_1^*$, we have that

$$|Pr[\mathcal{B}(g, g^a, g^b, g^c, e(g, g)^{abc}) = 0] - Pr[\mathcal{B}(g, g^a, g^b, g^c, T) = 0]| \geq |(\frac{1}{2} \pm \epsilon) - \frac{1}{2}| = \epsilon.$$
(15.5)

$\square$

---

[1]Because $Pr[b = b'] - \frac{1}{2} < -\epsilon$ and $Pr[b = b'] - \frac{1}{2} > \epsilon$. It holds that $Pr[b = b'] < \frac{1}{2} - \epsilon$ and $Pr[b = b'] > \frac{1}{2} + \epsilon$. Therefore $Pr[b = b'] \geq |\frac{1}{2} \pm \epsilon|$.

16

Tight Reduction

CONTENTS

This chapter provides an overview of reduction algorithms that shows us how an attack on the crypto systems by a polynomial-time adversary can be employed to solve some underlying hard computational problem in polynomial time. The crypto system studied in this chapter is an IBE system. The importance of tight reduction is explained in the next section. There are several obstacles in achieving the tight reduction that involves an all-and-any strategy, in which the reduction algorithm must be able to answer private key queries for all identities as the challenge identity. The next is the relationship between the security models and the strategies followed by the need for a searching method and solving a self-decryption paradox. The final part of this chapter discusses two all-and-any strategy techniques in the random oracle model. The first is Katz-Wang technique that requires cryptographic hash function that maps a string to a group element. The second is Park-Lee technique that makes use of two cryptographic hash functions that are modeled as random oracles, in order to generate a group element.

16.1 Overview

We will study a reduction algorithm that demonstrates how an attack by a polynomial-time adversary can be employed to solve some underlying hard computational problems. Because the security proof for a crypto system is given by describing a reduction algorithm, it is important to research the reduction algorithms in cryptography. Here, we instantiate the case of an identity-based encryption (IBE) system as one of the crypto systems.

16.2 Why Is Tight Reduction Important?

Typically, security proofs for IBE systems [24, 91] are given by describing a reduction algorithm. The existence of such a reduction algorithm shows that if some underlying problem is assumed to be difficult to solve, the IBE system is secure under some appropriately defined security model. The results of such a reduction can be measured by time and advantage functions that are determined by some security parameter. Here, the advantage can be roughly interpreted as the maximum possible bound on the probability of either breaking the IBE system or solving some hard computational problem.

For a security parameter, let (t, ϵ) be an assumed time and advantage for breaking an IBE system, and similarly let (t', ϵ') be an assumed time and advantage for solving an instance of a particular problem. The ideal case for a security reduction is that $t \approx t'$ and $\epsilon \approx \epsilon'$ simultaneously. This means that the IBE system is as secure as the underlying hard computational problem. Therefore, to achieve a certain level of security, the IBE system can be designed on the basis of algebraic groups (or other settings) in which a certain instance of the hard computational problem is justified at the same level of security. Such an ideal security reduction is said to be *tight*.

When designing an IBE system, a tight security reduction is an accepted goal as described in [10]. If a security reduction is not tight, the IBE system must be based on algebraic groups in which an instance of the hard computational problem is justified at a higher security level. In most cases, a larger security parameter results in inefficiency and costlier operations. For instance, assume that a security reduction is given by $\epsilon \approx c \cdot \epsilon'$ for a large reduction coefficient c. If $c = 2^{60}$, then aiming for $\epsilon = 2^{-80}$ as the desired security level (by expending some amount of time) implies that a security parameter on which an IBE system is constructed must, in reality, be chosen for a particular instance of a hard computational problem that satisfies $\epsilon' = 2^{-140}$.

The bilinear Diffie–Hellman (BDH) problem [24] is considered to be the standard underlying hard computational problem for IBE systems, and has been well studied. Therefore, building an IBE system with a tight security reduction to the BDH problem is a significant concern.

16.3   Obstacles and Solutions in Tight Reduction

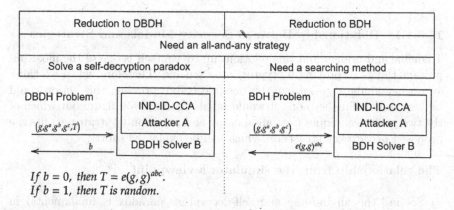

If $b = 0$, then $T = e(g, g)^{abc}$.
If $b = 1$, then T is random.

FIGURE 16.1
Necessary conditions for tight security reduction to the (D)BDH problem. In the reduction to DBDH, b outputted from a solver is a bit that an attacker guessed.

To obtain such a tight security reduction, several obstacles must be overcome. Figure 16.1 summarizes the conditions necessary for a tight security reduction to the DBDH or BDH problem when designing an IBE system.

16.3.1   All-and-Any Strategy

The first is to provide what is known as an all-and-any strategy in security analysis. According to this strategy, a reduction algorithm must be able to answer private key queries for all identities and handle any identity ID^* (not queried for a private key) as the challenge identity. Indeed, the all-and-any strategy truly reflects the security model [24] for an IBE system, where a challenger interacting with an adversary behaves in the same manner as the reduction algorithm. Implementing an all-and-any strategy becomes the first step toward removing a large reduction coefficient c (explained above), even though an additional strategy is required. This is contrary to the previous partitioning strategy[1] used for proving adaptive [24, 33, 98] or selective security [19, 20], where the identity space is partitioned into two parts beforehand. One part is used for key generation and the other part is used for generating the challenge ciphertext. If any identity chosen by the adversary does not fall favorably in the partition, the reduction algorithm should abort; this causes significant security degradations[2] (i.e., large reduction coefficients). When using the all-and-any strategy, it is important to note that the reduction algorithm can create a private key for all identities, including any challenge identity ID^*. As a result, the reduction algorithm can easily manage decryption queries made by an adversary when proving chosen-ciphertext security.

16.3.1.1   Relationship Between Security Models and Strategies

To define and understand this relationship by yourself is one of the most important things in proving a cryptography scheme. Therefore, when we think over what kinds of proof may be possible before proving, this action could be very useful. Furthermore, it would be also good if you figure out which of the two proof techniques (i.e., all-and-any and partitioning strategies) fits the proposed private key structures which will be explained shortly.

The relationship from the simulator's viewpoint

Solving the all-and-any and self-decryption paradox is fundamental in proving the selectively secure as well as fully secure models based on the decisional assumption. It is because that in order to solve the issue (i.e., self-decryption paradox) that the simulator can make a challenge private key by itself, when the scheme is proved by using an all-and-any strategy, those two secure models devise an equipment that keeps the simulator from generating a challenge private key. We can see that this equipment solves the self-decryption paradox. The only difference between selectively and fully secure models is that, before starting the security game, whether the challenge identity becomes known to the simulator or not.

The partitioning strategy does not solve the self-decryption paradox but only depends on luck. Therefore it does not achieve a tight reduction because the probability to abort is high. In other words, the partitioning strategy can be defined as the opposite of what can resolve the self-decryption paradox.

---

[1]The term partitioning was first introduced in [99].

[2]Hereinafter, a reduction coefficient c such that $\epsilon \approx c \cdot \epsilon'$ is considered a security degradation.

The relationship from the prover's viewpoint

The partitioning strategy can be defined as a generic term of the proof techniques that allocate the challenge identity space and the other space before starting the security game. It can be used to prove in fully secure as well as selectively secure models. When it is used to prove in a selectively secure model, we can achieve a tight reduction by reducing the probability of abort event. However, when it is used to prove in a fully secure model, we cannot achieve a tight reduction because we cannot reduce the abort probability. In addition, because selectively secure model sets the challenge identity space in advance, it is more suitable to use the partitioning strategy in order to achieve a tight reduction.

On the other hand, the all-and-any strategy can be defined as a generic term of the proof techniques that decide the challenge identity space during the security game. Therefore, it is more suitable to prove a scheme in a fully secure model for achieving a tight reduction because in the case using the all-and-any strategy, the probability of abort event is low.

16.3.2 Searching Method

One of the obstacles to overcome is to search for the solution to a single instance of the BDH problem. In order to analyze a security of a scheme by proving under the BDH problem, a reduction algorithm must obtain the correct answer based on certain values issued by an adversary. However, searching the correct answer is not easy because the reduction algorithm does not know the correct answer in advance. Thus, a search method should be provided to the reduction algorithm; otherwise, it has no option but to choose among the entire set of candidate values. If the number of values is small, a tight reduction can still hold. However, in the most pessimistic cases, the adversary issues a large number of values, which means that a tight reduction can no longer be guaranteed. For instance, during a security analysis in which the correct answer is randomly chosen from q random oracle queries made by an adversary, the reduction coefficient becomes (at least) $c = q$ for q queried values. If $q = 2^{50}$ is the accepted number [11] of random oracle queries, then the reduction at least causes a 50 bit security loss. Note that a search strategy is not relevant to an all-and-any strategy; this means that even if private keys are known for all identities, it will not help the reduction algorithm to solve the BDH problem. If private keys created by the reduction algorithm can be used to obtain the correct answer, then the decisional BDH (DBDH) problem[3] is easily solved by using private keys to test whether a target value of the DBDH problem is the solution to the BDH problem.

---

[3]Informally, the DBDH problem is defined as follows: given $(g, g^a, g^b, g^c, T) \in \mathbb{G}^4 \times \mathbb{G}_T$ as input, determine whether $T = e(g, g)^{abc}$.

TABLE 16.1

IBE systems with tight security reduction to the (D)BDH problem.

	To the DBDH Problem	To the BDH Problem
Based on Katz–Wang technique[61]	ACF^+-IBE [6]	Nishioka-FO_{ID} IBE [64], [79]
Based on Park–Lee technique	PL-IBE [82]	PLL-IBE [83]

16.3.3   Self-Decryption Paradox

When attempting to achieve a tight security reduction to the DBDH problem, a distinct obstacle known as a self-decryption paradox must be overcame. This arises from the fact that (1) a target value of the DBDH problem is embedded in the challenge ciphertext CT^* corresponding to ID^*, and (2) a reduction algorithm can generate a private key for the same identity ID^*. The self-decryption paradox occurs because the reduction algorithm can generate a private key for the challenge identity ID^*, simply decrypt CT^* itself by using the key for ID^*, and solve the DBDH problem without adversary's help. To solve the self-decryption paradox, some reasonable technique must be devised, either prevents the decryption from being performed normally or allows decryption that is not relevant to the target value of the DBDH problem. Nevertheless, decrypting ciphertexts other than CT^* must normally be performed with the private key for ID^*. Several techniques have been suggested [6],[48],[82], each of which works differently according to its underlying all-and-any strategy. The ideas behind each technique will be explained when analyzing each all-and-any strategy.

16.4   All-and-Any Strategy Techniques in the Random Oracle Model

Table 16.1 shows that there exist two techniques for the all-and-any strategy in the random oracle model, and five IBE systems that have been suggested to achieve tight security reductions to the (D)BDH problem. FO_{ID} [64] is another tight variant of the Fujisaki–Okamoto transform [33] that can be applied to some chosen-plaintext secure IBE system.

Table 16.2 briefly shows the difference between these techniques. We describe the ideas behind these techniques, and then we discuss how each IBE system can solve the self-decryption paradox or provide a search method.

TABLE 16.2

Difference between Katz–Wang and Park–Lee techniques.

	Katz–Wang Technique	Park–Lee Technique
Mandatory requirement	full domain hash, two public keys	two equation technique
Private key structure	$H(\mathsf{ID}, b_{\mathsf{ID}})^s$, b_{ID}	$g^\alpha u^s$, g^s, $(H(\mathsf{ID})u^{h(g^\alpha u^s\|g^s)})^s$
Ciphertext structure	two ciphertext elements $Enc_K(m)$, g^r, $G(e(g^\alpha, H(\mathsf{ID}, 0))^r, \mathsf{ID}, 0)$, $G(e(g^\alpha, H(\mathsf{ID}, 1))^r, \mathsf{ID}, 1)$,	a parallel private key $e(g, g^\alpha)^r m$, g^r $(H(\mathsf{ID})u^{h(e(g,g^\alpha)^r m\|g^r)})^r$

(Note: H is map-to-point hash, G is hash, $b_{\mathsf{ID}} \in \{0, 1\}$, $\alpha, s, r \in \mathbb{Z}_p$, $g, u \in \mathbb{G}$)

16.4.1 Katz-Wang Technique

The Katz–Wang technique [61] is based on the BF-IBE scheme. It requires a cryptographic hash function H that maps a string to a group element; the function is modeled as a random oracle for security analysis. However, the difference is that the BF-IBE scheme uses one public key, $H(ID)$, and one private key corresponding to the public key. On the other hand, the Katz–Wang technique uses two public keys, $H(ID, 0)$ and $H(ID, 1)$, when encrypting a message for one identity ID. However, its private key paired to one of the two public keys is given and known to a user with ID. In security analysis, one public key $H(ID, b)$ chosen according to a randomly chosen $b \in \{0, 1\}$ is controlled under the simulator in order to be able to answer to extract queries for all ID except for an challenge identity ID^*. On the other hand, $H(ID^*, 1\text{-}b)$ is used to simulate the challenge ciphertext for the challenge identity ID^* in the challenge phase. Therefore, even if a reduction algorithm can only use $H(ID, b)$ for computing a private key, it is sufficient to respond a private key query for all non-challenge identities ID. In addition, for the challenge identity ID^*, $H(ID^*, 1\text{-}b)$ will be used to calculate a computational Diffie–Hellman (CDH) value. This shows that the reduction algorithm can answer private key queries for all identities and use any identity as the challenge ID^*.

Compared to the BF-IBE scheme, the Katz-Wang technique causes inefficiency in terms of encryption cost and ciphertext size. Moreover, the encryption in the Nishioka-FO_{ID} IBE system becomes increasingly expensive, because it requires the dual form. Furthermore, when obtaining IND-ID-CCA security, the decryption algorithm in FO_{ID} requires re-encryption to determine whether a ciphertext is well formed. This is because each user is assigned a private key for one $H(ID, b)$ for a random $b \in \{0, 1\}$. Thus, ciphertext elements for $H(ID, b)$ cannot be decrypted directly. Instead, decrypting ciphertext elements for $H(ID, b)$ can yield a random value (and message) that is the same as that used in encryption. By using the random value to re-encrypt the message, a user can determine whether the other ciphertext part corresponding to $H(ID, b)$ is also well formed. Such a re-encryption doubles the running time of the security reduction when relying on FO_{ID}; however, this is not overly costly and still allows for a relatively tight reduction.

16.4.2   Park-Lee Technique

The main idea behind the Park-Lee technique [82] is to make use of two cryptographic hash functions H and h that are modeled as random oracles, in order to generate an element in the form of $(H(ID)u^{h(A)})^r$. Here, u is a public parameter, A refers to other key elements, and r is a randomly chosen exponent. Let (g, g^a, g^b, g^c) be an instance of the BDH problem given to the reduction algorithm. In security analysis, $H(ID)$ is programmed to embed an information-theoretically hidden exponent γ in the element g^a for some unknown a; that is, $H(ID) = (g^a)^\gamma g^\tau$ for a randomly chosen τ. When generating a private key for any ID, the random exponent r of $(H(ID)u^{h(A)})^r$ should include an unknown exponent b that entails computing the CDH value g^{ab}. However, when $u = (g^a)^{-1} g^\delta$ for a random δ, programming $h(A) = \gamma$ can make it possible to avoid computing the CDH value g^{ab} and thus the reduction algorithm can generate the crucial element $(H(ID)u^{h(A)})^r$. Using this technique, the reduction algorithm can create a private key for all identities. A similar method is applied to construct a challenge ciphertext element $(H(ID^*)u^{h(B)})^c$ for any identity ID^*, where B refers to other ciphertext elements and c comes from g^c. In that case, $h(B)$ is programmed to be γ^* when $H(ID^*) = (g^a)^{\gamma^*} g^{\tau^*}$ for randomly chosen γ^* and τ^*, and thus the reduction algorithm can avoid computing the CDH value g^{ac}.

Park and Lee [82] proved that their IBE system is tightly IND-ID-CCA secure under the DBDH assumption. The manner in which the self-decryption paradox is resolved comes from the idea that, when generating the private key for the challenge identity ID^*, the reduction algorithm should set $h(A)$ to be γ^* and therefore $h(A) = \gamma^* = h(B)$. That is, the same information-theoretically hidden exponent γ^* should be used twice for generating both the private key for ID^* as $h(A)$ and the challenge ciphertext as $h(B)$. In that case, decrypting the challenge ciphertext using the private key for ID^* is impossible, because the decryption algorithm in the Park-Lee IBE system must calculate a value $\frac{1}{h(A)-h(B)}$ using the values $h(A)$ and $h(B)$.

A primary advantage of the Park-Lee technique is that it provides an easy and efficient scheme to obtain chosen-ciphertext security. This can be achieved by simply hashing other ciphertext elements B (including the message encryption portion) into $h(B)$ and embedding the result in $(H(ID)u^{h(B)})^s$ for a randomly chosen exponent s. Specifically, this can be performed without the assistance of conversions such as FO_{ID} or the Encrypt-then-authenticate paradigm. Hence, the decryption algorithm does not require an additional computation, such as the re-encryption that is necessary with the Katz-Wang technique.

Exercises

16.1 Why is the all-and-any strategy required for supporting tight reduction?

16.2 Can a proof technique using the partitioning strategy achieve tight reduction?

17

Transformation Technique

CONTENTS

The chapter begins with the introduction of the Canetti-Halevi-Katz (CHK) transformation. CHK transformation puts forward an efficient construction for a CCA-secure public-key encryption scheme from any CPA-secure identity based encryption scheme. The construction is extended from CPA-secure binary tree encryption (BTE) scheme to CCA-secure one. A BTE scheme is a variant of HIBE scheme. The next part of the chapter gives some basic definitions. A BTE is defined as a 4-tuple of PPT algorithms such as setup, key derivation, encryption, and decryption. Then one-time signature is defined. The next part of the chapter discusses how to generate CCA-secure PKE from the CPA-secure IBE and CCA-secure BTE from CPA-secure BTE. Both of these transformations are given along with the formal construction and security proof using the reduction algorithms.

17.1 Canetti-Halevi-Katz Transformation [32]

Canetti-Halevi-Katz [32] proposed a simple and efficient construction of a CCA-secure public-key encryption scheme from any CPA-secure identity-based encryption (IBE) scheme. In the paper, they prove the construction satisfies only a relatively "weak" notion, which is "selective-ID" in standard model where the adversary needs to provide the challenge identity in advance. The transformation in this paper can be used to construct any CPA-secure (H)IBE scheme to CCA-secure (H)IBE scheme in standard model.

    Making a CPA-secure IBE scheme is considered to be easier than CCA-secure one. The construction is quite efficient so that it allows cryptographers to focus on making CPA-secure schemes and then transform it to CCA-secure schemes easily.

In this chapter, we show how to achieve a CCA-secure PKE scheme from a CPA-secure IBE one. The construction is extended from CPA-secure (BTE-secure) binary tree encryption (BTE) scheme to CCA-secure one. The BTE scheme [31] is known as a variant of HIBE scheme. The difference between BTE and HIBE is:

1. In BTE each node has only two children, whereas in HIBE each node has arbitrarily-many children.

2. In BTE the children is labeled as "0" and "1," whereas in HIBE the children have arbitrary strings.

As a result, there is an important application of this transformation: We derive a CCA-secure HIBE scheme from a CPA-secure HIBE scheme. Here we only mention about the CCA-secure BTE but the result also implies CCA-secure HIBE.

17.1.1 Definitions

This section defines binary tree encryption and one-time signature.

17.1.1.1 Binary Tree Encryption

Definition 1 *A* **binary tree encryption scheme** *(BTE) is a 4-tuple of PPT algorithms* $(Setup, Der, \mathcal{E}, \mathcal{D})$ *such that:*

1. *The randomized setup algorithm Setup takes as input a security parameter* 1^k *and a value* l *representing the maximum tree depth. It outputs some system-wide parameters PK along with a master (root) secret key* SK_ϵ *(we assume that* k *and* l *are implicit in PK and all secret keys).*

2. *The (possibly randomized) key derivation algorithm Der takes as input the name of a node* $w \in \{0,1\}^{\leq l}$ *and its associated secret key* SK_w. *It returns secret keys* SK_{w0}, SK_{w1} *for the two children of* w.

3. *The randomized encryption algorithm* $\mathcal{E}$ *takes as input PK, the name of a node* $w \in \{0,1\}^{\leq l}$, *and a message* m, *and returns a ciphertext* C. *We write* $C \leftarrow \mathcal{E}_{PK}(w, m)$.

4. *The decryption algorithm* $\mathcal{D}$ *takes as input the name of a node* $w \in \{0,1\}^{\leq l}$, *its associated secret key* SK_w, *and a ciphertext* C. *It returns a message* m *or the distinguished symbol* $\bot$. *We write* $m \leftarrow \mathcal{D}_{SK_w}(w, C)$.

We require that for all (PK, SK_ϵ) output by *Setup*, any $w \in \{0,1\}^{\leq l}$, and any correctly-generated secret key SK_w for this node, any message m, and all C output by $\mathcal{E}_{PK}(w, m)$, we have $\mathcal{D}_{SK_w}(w, C) = m$.

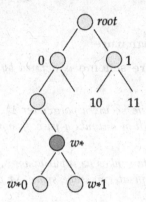

FIGURE 17.1
Binary tree encryption.

Definition 2 *A binary tree encryption scheme (BTE) is* **secure against selective-node, chosen-plaintext attacks** *if for all polynomially-bounded functions $l(\cdot)$, the advantage of any PPT adversary $\mathcal{A}$ in the following game is negligible in the security parameter k:*

1. *$\mathcal{A}(1^k, l(k))$ outputs a node label $w^* \in \{0,1\}^{\leq l(k)}$.*

2. *$Setup(1^k, l(k))$ outputs (PK, SK_ϵ). In addition, algorithm Der is used to generate the secret keys of all the nodes on the path P from the root to w^*, and also the secret keys for the two children of w^* (if $|w^*| < l$). The adversary is given PK and the secret keys SK_w for all nodes w of the following form as shown in Figure 17.1.*

   (a) *$w = w'\bar{b}$, where $w'b$ is a prefix of w^* and $b \in \{0,1\}$ (i.e., w is a sibling of prefix nodes of the challenge node in P)[1]; or*

   (b) *$w = w^*0$ or $w = w^*1$ (i.e., w is a child of w^*; this assumes $|w^*| < l$)[2].*

   Note that this allows the adversary to compute $SK_{w'}$ for any node $w' \in \{0,1\}^{\leq l(k)}$ that is not a prefix of w^*.

3. *At some point, $\mathcal{A}$ outputs two messages m_0, m_1 with $|m_0| = |m_1|$. A bit b is randomly chosen and the adversary is given a "challenge ciphertext" $C^* \leftarrow \mathcal{E}_{PK}(w^*, m_b)$.*

---

[1] It means that query of prefixes of the challenge node is not allowed.
[2] It means that query of secret keys of two children of the challenge node is allowed.

4.   *Finally, $\mathcal{A}$ outputs a guess b'.*

We say that $\mathcal{A}$ succeeds if $b' = b$, and denote the probability of this event by $Pr_{\mathcal{A},BTE}[Succ]$. The adversary's advantage is defined as $\mid Pr_{\mathcal{A},BTE}[Succ] - 1/2 \mid$.

17.1.1.2   One-Time Signature

Definition 3 *A **signature scheme** is defined by three PPT algorithms as follows:*

1. $G(1^k)$: *On input the security parameter 1^k, this probabilistic polynomial time algorithm outputs a pair of signing key (sk) and verification key (vk).*

2.   *Sign: This algorithm takes as input a signing key sk and a message M from the appropriate message space $\mathcal{M}$ and outputs a signature σ .*

3.   *Vrfy: This is a deterministic algorithm which on input a verification key vk, a message M and a signature σ on M outputs accept or reject ($\perp$ symbol), depending on whether σ is a valid signature on M or not.*

Definition 4 *A signature scheme (G, Sign, Vrfy) is a **strong, one-time signature scheme** if the success probability of any PPT adversary $\mathcal{A}$ is negligible in the following game.*

1. $G(1^k)$ *outputs (vk, sk). The adversary $\mathcal{A}$ is given vk.*

2. $\mathcal{A}(1^k, vk)$ *may take one of the following actions:*

   (a) $\mathcal{A}$ *outputs a message M and in return is given a signature of M under the signing key sk, i.e., $\sigma \leftarrow Sign_{sk}(M)$. Then $\mathcal{A}$ outputs a pair (M^*, σ^*).*

   (b) $\mathcal{A}$ *outputs a pair (M^*, σ^*) and halts. In this case (M, σ) is undefined, i.e., the adversary outputs a possible forgery without even seeing a single valid message-signature pair.*

$\mathcal{A}$ succeeds in the game if σ^* is a proper signature of M^* under the verification key vk, i.e., $\text{Vrfy}_{vk}(M^*, \sigma^*) = 1$ but $(M^*, \sigma^*) \neq (M, \sigma)$. Note that, $\mathcal{A}$ may succeed even if $M^* = M$, which is the reason to call the scheme a strong one-time signature.

17.1.2   Chosen-Ciphertext Security from IBE

Given:

1.   ID-based encryption scheme $\Pi' = (Setup, Der, \mathcal{E}', \mathcal{D}')$ secure against selective-identity chosen-plaintext attacks.

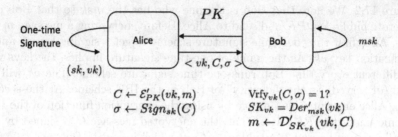

FIGURE 17.2
CCA-secure PKE from CPA-secure IBE.

2. One-time signature scheme $Sig = (G, Sign, \text{Vrfy})$ in which the verification key output by $G(1^k)$ has length $l_s(k)$.

We construct a (standard) public-key encryption scheme $\Pi = (Gen, \mathcal{E}, \mathcal{D})$ secure against chosen-ciphertext attacks.

Construction 1. CCA-secure PKE

Construction of CCA-secure PKE from CPA-secure IBE

Setup $Gen(1^k)$ runs $Setup(1^k, l_s(k))$ to obtain (PK, msk). The public key is PK and the secret key is msk.

Encrypt $\mathcal{E}_{PK}(m)$ encrypts message m using public key PK.

1. Sender first runs $G(1^k)$ to obtain verification key vk and signing key sk (with $|vk| = l_s(k)$).

2. Compute $C \leftarrow \mathcal{E}'_{PK}(vk, m)$ (i.e., the sender encrypts m with respect to "identity" vk).

3. Compute $\sigma \leftarrow Sign_{sk}(C)$.

4. Output ciphertext $CT = \langle vk, C, \sigma \rangle$.

Decrypt $\mathcal{D}_{msk}(CT)$ decrypts ciphertext CT.

1. Check whether $\text{Vrfy}_{vk}(C, \sigma) = 1$. If not, output $\bot$.

2. Compute $SK_{vk} = Der'_{msk}(vk)$.

3. Output $m \leftarrow \mathcal{D}'_{SK_{vk}}(vk, C)$.

Let us suppose that Alice securely sends a message m to Bob as shown Figure 17.2. We note that Bob is the one who has the msk so that Bob can generate public key PK and send to Alice. Before encrypting a message m for Bob, Alice first runs one-time signature scheme to get a signing key sk and a verification key vk. As the name of one-time signature implies, the keys will be different every time Bob runs one-time signature scheme. The vk will be used (or served) as the "identity" of Bob in the IBE scheme. At the second step, Alice encrypts the message by using the encryption function of the IBE scheme under the PK. After that, the encrypted message C is signed by sk. Finally, the ciphertext is a tuble $\langle vk, C, \sigma \rangle$ which is sent to Bob.

At the receiver's side, receiving the ciphertext, Bob first verifies whether the ciphertext is valid or not. If the ciphertext is not valid, then he rejects this one. Otherwise, he moves to the next step, where he runs the Der' algorithm under msk to derive the decryption key SK_{vk}, which will be used to decrypt C together with vk.

What is the role of the signature? If we do not use the signature, the adversary can get some information from decryption query; or it can modify the challenge ciphertext and then submit the modified ciphertext to the decryption oracle to get the correct answer of the bit b. The signature is the key point to make the scheme to be CCA-secure.

Why do we use one-time signature instead of normal signatures? If we use a normal signature, the vk will be the same in every ciphertext. In general, one-time signature is stronger notion than normal signatures, i.e., the adversary will win even if it can forge a signature of message m where m is the previously submitted query to the $Sign$ oracle[3]. That is, in this case, the adversary will win if he can forge vk^* such that $\text{Vrfy}_{vk^*}(C, \sigma) = 1$. As we will see in the security proof, the one-time signature will be the key point to make the scheme to be CCA-secure (If it is not "one-time," then the scheme is only CPA-secure, i.e., in the reduction below. If we always have $vk = vk^*$ then the adversary cannot have the result for decryption query)[4].

Theorem 1 *If Π' is an IBE scheme which is secure against selective-identity, chosen-plaintext attacks and Sig is a strongly unforgeable one-time signature scheme, then Π is a PKE scheme which is secure against adaptive chosen-ciphertext attacks.*

---

[3]This is called *strong unforgeability*. *Unforgeability* requires the adversary to be unable to forge a signature for "new" message. On the other hand, *strong unforgeability* requires the adversary to be unable to forge "new" signature even for an "old" message as well as unable to forge a signature for an "new" message. Note that if a scheme is not *strong unforgeability*-secure, then it may be vulnerable to replay attack.

[4]In [32], they construct a CCA-secure public-key encryption from a CPA-secure IBE using a digital signature. This is very similar to Chapter 6, where they construct a CCA-secure private-key encryption from a CPA-secure private-key encryption using MAC in the symmetric key setting.

Proof Given any PPT adversary $\mathcal{A}$ attacking Π in an adaptive chosen-ciphertext attack, we construct a PPT adversary $\mathcal{A}'$ attacking Π' in a selective-identity, chosen-plaintext attack. We denote the challenge ciphertext received by $\mathcal{A}$ by $\langle vk^*, C^*, \sigma^* \rangle$.

Forge event

1. $\mathcal{A}$ submits a ciphertext $\langle vk^*, C, \sigma \rangle$ with $\text{Vrfy}_{vk}(C, \sigma) = 1$ to its decryption oracle before receiving the challenge ciphertext.

2. $\mathcal{A}$ submits to its decryption oracle a ciphertext $\langle vk^*, C, \sigma \rangle$ with $(C, \sigma) \neq (C^*, \sigma^*)$ and $\text{Vrfy}_{vk}(C, \sigma) = 1$ after receiving the challenge ciphertext.

We will use $\mathcal{A}$ to break the underlying one-time signature scheme Sig with probability $Pr_{\mathcal{A}}[Forge]$; since Sig is a strongly unforgeable one-time signature scheme, we have $Pr_{\mathcal{A}}[Forge]$ is negligible.

Reduction

Initialization $\mathcal{A}'(1^k, l_s(k))$ runs $G(1^k)$ to generate (vk^*, sk^*). It then outputs the "target identity" $ID^* = vk^*$.

Setup $Setup(1^k, l_s(k))$ outputs (PK, msk) and $\mathcal{A}'$ is given PK. $\mathcal{A}'$, in turn, runs $\mathcal{A}$ on input 1^k and PK.

Phase I When $\mathcal{A}$ makes decryption oracle query $\mathcal{D}(vk, C, \sigma)$, $\mathcal{A}'$ proceeds as follows.

1. If $\text{Vrfy}_{vk}(C, \sigma) \neq 1$, then $\mathcal{A}'$ simply returns $\perp$.

2. If $\text{Vrfy}_{vk}(C, \sigma) = 1$ and $vk = vk^*$ (i.e., event Forge occurs), then $\mathcal{A}'$ terminates and outputs a random bit.

3. If $\text{Vrfy}_{vk}(C, \sigma) = 1$ and $vk \neq vk^*$, then $\mathcal{A}'$ makes the oracle query $Der_{msk}(vk)$ to obtain SK_{vk}. It then computes $m \leftarrow \mathcal{D}'_{SK_{vk}}(vk, C)$ and returns m.

Challenge $\mathcal{A}$ outputs two equal-length messages m_0, m_1. These messages are output by $\mathcal{A}'$. In return, $\mathcal{A}'$ is given a challenge ciphertext C^*. $\mathcal{A}'$ then computes $\sigma^* \leftarrow Sign_{vk^*}(C^*)$ and returns $\langle vk^*, C^*, \sigma^* \rangle$ to $\mathcal{A}$.

Phase II $\mathcal{A}$ may continue to make decryption oracle queries, and these are answered as before (Recall that $\mathcal{A}$ may not query the decryption oracle on the challenge ciphertext itself).

Guess $\mathcal{A}$ outputs a guess b'; this same guess is output by $\mathcal{A}'$.

We have:

1. $\mathcal{A}'$ represents a legal adversarial strategy for attacking Π' in a selective-identity, chosen-plaintext attack.

2. $\mathcal{A}'$ never requests the secret key corresponding to "target identity" vk^*.

We can claim that $\mathcal{A}'$ provides a perfect simulation for $\mathcal{A}$ (and thus $\mathcal{A}'$ succeeds whenever $\mathcal{A}$ succeeds) unless event $Forge$ occurs. Therefore

$$Pr_{\mathcal{A}',\Pi'}[Succ] \geq Pr_{\mathcal{A},\Pi}[Succ] - 1/2 \cdot Pr_{\mathcal{A}}[Forge]$$
$$\Leftrightarrow Pr_{\mathcal{A},\Pi}[Succ] - Pr_{\mathcal{A}',\Pi'}[Succ] \leq 1/2 \cdot Pr_{\mathcal{A}}[Forge]$$

Note that in the case of $Forge$ the adversary will output a random bit so that the probability that $\mathcal{A}$ guesses correctly bit b' in this case is $1/2 \cdot Pr_{\mathcal{A}}[Forge]$.

Since $| Pr_{\mathcal{A}',\Pi'}[Succ] - 1/2 |$ is negligible (or we can say that $Pr_{\mathcal{A}',\Pi'}[Succ]$ is negligibly close to $1/2$) and $Pr_{\mathcal{A}}[Forge]$ is negligible, we have

$$| Pr_{\mathcal{A},\Pi}[Succ] - 1/2 | \leq negl. \tag{17.1}$$

$\square$

17.1.3   Chosen-Ciphertext Security for BTE Schemes

Given:

1. BTE scheme $\Pi' = (Setup, Der', \mathcal{E}', \mathcal{D}')$ secure against selective-identity chosen-plaintext attacks.

2. One-time signature scheme $Sig = (G, Sign, \text{Vrfy})$ in which the verification key output by $G(1^k)$ has length $l_s(k)$.

3. Encode function as

$$Encode(w) = \begin{cases} \epsilon, & \text{if } w = \epsilon \\ 1w_1 1w_2...1w_t, & \text{if } w = w_1...w_t (w_i \in \{0,1\}). \end{cases}$$

We construct a BTE scheme $\Pi = (Gen, Der, \mathcal{E}, \mathcal{D})$ secure against chosen-ciphertext attacks.

Construction 2. CCA-secure BTE

Construction of CCA-secure BTE from CPA-secure BTE

Setup $Setup(1^k, l)$ runs $Setup'(1^k, 2l + l_s(k) + 1)$ to obtain (PK, SK_ϵ). The system-wide public key is PK and the root secret key is SK_ϵ.

Derivation $Der(w, SK_w)$ proceeds as follows.

1. Set $w' = Encode(w)$.
2. Compute $SK'_{w'1}$ using $Der'_{SK_w}(w')$, $(SK'_{w'10}, SK'_{w'11}) \leftarrow Der'_{SK'_{w'1}}(w'1)$.
3. Set $SK_{w0} = SK'_{w'10}$ and $SK_{w1} = SK'_{w'11}$.

Encrypt $\mathcal{E}_{PK}(w, m)$ encrypts message m for a node $w \in \{0,1\} \le l$ using public parameters PK.

1. First run $G(1^k)$ to obtain verification key vk and signing key sk (with $|vk| = l_s(k)$).
2. Set $w' = Encode(w)$.
3. Compute $C \leftarrow \mathcal{E}'_{PK}(w' \mid 0 \mid vk, m)$ (i.e., the sender encrypts m with respect to "identity" vk).
4. Compute $\sigma \leftarrow Sign_{sk}(C)$.
5. Output ciphertext $CT = \langle vk, C, \sigma \rangle$.

Decrypt $\mathcal{D}_{SK_w}(w, CT)$ decrypts ciphertext CT at node w with secret key SK_w.

1. Check whether $\mathrm{Vrfy}_{vk}(C, \sigma) = 1$. If not, output $\bot$. Else, do the following steps.
2. Derive the secret key $SK'_{w'|0|vk}$.
3. Output $m \leftarrow \mathcal{D}'_{SK'_{w'|0|vk}}(w' \mid 0 \mid vk, C)$.

In order to understand the Derivation please refer to Figure 17.3, where the secret key of grandchildren of node w' in CPA-secure BTE will be set for the secret key of children of node w in CCA-secure BTE.

Theorem 2 *If Π' is a BTE scheme which is secure in the sense of selective node, chosen-ciphertext attack and Sig is a strongly unforgeable one-time signature scheme, then Π is a BTE scheme which is secure in the sense of selective node, chosen-ciphertext attack.*

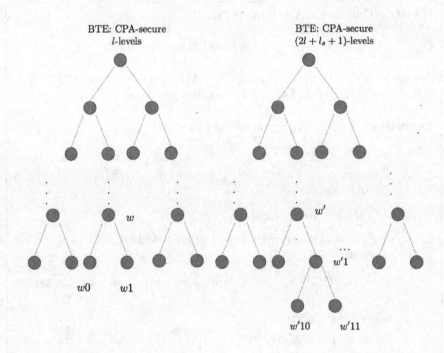

FIGURE 17.3
Grandchildren's secret keys of w' will be children's secret keys of w.

Proof Given any PPT adversary $\mathcal{A}$ attacking Π in a selective node, chosen-ciphertext attack, we construct a PPT adversary $\mathcal{A}'$ attacking Π' in a selective node, chosen-plaintext attack.

We denote the node initially output by $\mathcal{A}$ by w^* and the challenge ciphertext received by $\mathcal{A}$ by $\langle vk^*, C^*, \sigma^* \rangle$.

Forge event

1. $\mathcal{A}$ submits a ciphertext $(\langle w^*, < vk^*, C, \sigma \rangle)$ with $\mathrm{Vrfy}_{vk}(C, \sigma) = 1$ to its decryption oracle before receiving the challenge ciphertext.

2. $\mathcal{A}$ submits to its decryption oracle a ciphertext $(w^*, \langle vk^*, C, \sigma \rangle)$ with $(C, \sigma) \neq (C^*, \sigma^*)$ and $\mathrm{Vrfy}_{vk}(C, \sigma) = 1$ after receiving the challenge ciphertext.

We will use $\mathcal{A}$ to break the underlying one-time signature scheme Sig with probability $Pr_{\mathcal{A}}[Forge]$; since Sig is a strongly unforgeable one-time signature scheme, we have $Pr_{\mathcal{A}}[Forge]$ is negligible.

Reduction

Initialization $\mathcal{A}'(1^k, l')$ sets $l = (l' - l_s(k) - 1)/2$ and runs $\mathcal{A}(1^k, l)$ who, in turn, outputs a node $w^* \in \{0, 1\}^{\leq l}$.
$\mathcal{A}'$ sets $w' = Encode(w^*)$, runs $G(1^k)$ to generate (vk^*, sk^*), and outputs the node $w^{*'} = w' \mid 0 \mid vk^*$.

Setup $Setup(1^k, l)$ outputs (PK, msk) and $\mathcal{A}'$ is given PK. $\mathcal{A}'$, in turn, runs $\mathcal{A}$ on input 1^k and PK.

Phase I $\mathcal{A}'$ is given secret keys $SK_{w'}$ for all nodes w of the following form.

1. $w = v\bar{b}$, where vb is a prefix of $w^{*'}$ and $b \in \{0, 1\}$.
2. $w = w^{*'}0$ or $w = w^{*'}1$ (in case $\mid w^{*'} \mid < l'$).

Using these, $\mathcal{A}'$ can compute and give to $\mathcal{A}$ all the relevant secret keys that $\mathcal{A}$ expects. When $\mathcal{A}$ makes decryption oracle query $\mathcal{D}(w, \langle vk, C, \sigma \rangle)$, $\mathcal{A}'$ proceeds as follows.

1. If $\mathrm{Vrfy}_{vk}(C, \sigma) \neq 1$, then $\mathcal{A}'$ simply returns $\perp$.
2. If $\mathrm{Vrfy}_{vk}(C, \sigma) = 1$ and $vk = vk^*$ (i.e., event *Forge* occurs), then $\mathcal{A}'$ terminates and outputs a random bit.
3. If $\mathrm{Vrfy}_{vk}(C, \sigma) = 1$ and $vk \neq vk^*$, set $\tilde{w} = Encode(w)$, then $\mathcal{A}'$ makes the oracle query $Der(\tilde{w} \mid 0 \mid vk)$ to obtain $SK_{\tilde{w}|0|vk}$. It then computes $m \leftarrow \mathcal{D}'_{SK_{\tilde{w}|0|vk}}(\tilde{w} \mid 0 \mid vk, C)$ and returns m.

Challenge $\mathcal{A}$ outputs two equal-length messages m_0, m_1. These messages are output by $\mathcal{A}'$.
In return, $\mathcal{A}'$ is given a challenge ciphertext C^*.
$\mathcal{A}'$ then computes $\sigma^* \leftarrow Sign_{vk^*}(C^*)$ and returns $\langle vk^*, C^*, \sigma^* \rangle$ to $\mathcal{A}$.

Phase II $\mathcal{A}$ may continue to make decryption oracle queries, and these are answered as before (Recall that $\mathcal{A}$ may not query the decryption oracle on the challenge ciphertext itself).

Guess $\mathcal{A}$ outputs a guess b'; this same guess is output by $\mathcal{A}'$

We have:

1. $\mathcal{A}'$ represents a legal adversarial strategy for attacking Π' in a selective-node, chosen-plaintext attack.
2. $\mathcal{A}'$ never requests the secret key corresponding to "target node" $w^{*'} = w' \mid 0 \mid vk^*$.

We can claim that $\mathcal{A}'$ provides a perfect simulation for $\mathcal{A}$ (and thus $\mathcal{A}'$ succeeds whenever $\mathcal{A}$ succeeds) unless event Forge occurs. Therefore

$$Pr_{\mathcal{A}',\Pi'}[Succ] \geq Pr_{\mathcal{A},\Pi}[Succ] - 1/2 \cdot Pr_{\mathcal{A}}[Forge]$$
$$\Leftrightarrow Pr_{\mathcal{A},\Pi}[Succ] - Pr_{\mathcal{A}',\Pi'}[Succ] \leq 1/2 \cdot Pr_{\mathcal{A}}[Forge]$$

Note that in the case of Forge the adversary will output a random bit so that the probability that $\mathcal{A}$ guesses correctly bit b' in this case is $1/2 \cdot Pr_{\mathcal{A}}[Forge]$.

Since $| \Pr_{\mathcal{A}',\Pi'}[Succ] - 1/2 |$ is negligible (or we can say that $\Pr_{\mathcal{A}',\Pi'}[Succ]$ is negligibly close to $1/2$) and $Pr_{\mathcal{A}}[Forge]$ is negligible, we have

$$| Pr_{\mathcal{A},\Pi}[Succ] - 1/2 | \leq negl. \tag{17.2}$$

□

From the theorem above, we have:

Theorem 3 *If there exists a BTE scheme secure in the sense of selective node, chosen-plaintext attack, then there exists a BTE scheme secure in the sense of selective node, chosen-ciphertext attack.*

Proof is omitted.

18

Broadcast Encryption

CONTENTS

This chapter presents broadcast encryption (BE). BE is a type of encryption in which the encrypted content is delivered over a broadcast channel in such a way that only the authorized users can decrypt the content. It can be considered as a revocation scheme where the revoked users find insufficient information to recover the key. The subset-cover algorithms to find the efficient revocation scheme are discussed in detail. The next part of the chapter presents the identity-based broadcast encryption, where a broadcasting sender typically encrypts a message by combining public identities of receivers and system parameters. Dynamic BE is then discussed in which the total number of users are not fixed. The preliminaries and the security model of the identity-based BE is then discussed. One important scheme regarding the identity based BE is the Delerablée's scheme. The formal construction and the security analysis using the reduction algorithm are then discussed in detail at the end of the chapter.

18.1   Introduction

In any large scale public key infrastructure (PKI), there will be users whose private keys will be compromised. In order to mitigate the damage that a compromised key can cause, any certificates associated with a compromised key should be revoked. The purpose of revocation is to inform relevant parties that certain certificates should no longer be accepted as valid even though they have not yet expired.

Broadcast Encryption In Broadcast Encryption (BE), we consider a scenario where there is a center and a set of users. The center provides the users with prearranged keys when they join. BE deals with methods to efficiently broadcast information to a dynamically changing group of users who are allowed to receive the data. It is often convenient to think of it as a revocation scheme, which enables some subset of the users (non-members) to be excluded from receiving the information. Naturally, the non-members are curious about the contents of the message that is being broadcasted, and may try to learn it.

One special case in BE is when the receivers are stateless. In such a scenario, a (legitimate) receiver is not capable of recording the past history of transmissions and change its state accordingly. Instead, its operation must be based on the current transmission and its initial configuration. Stateless receivers are important for the case where the receiver is a device that is not constantly on-line, such as a media player (e.g., a CD or DVD player where the "transmission" is the current disc), a satellite receiver (GPS), and so on.

Therefore, one of the goals in BE is to find efficient revocation schemes which are suitable for stateless receivers.

Issues with broadcast encryption

1. **Tracing mechanism** It is a mechanism which enables the efficient tracing of leakage, specially, the source of keys used by illegal devices such as pirate decoders or clones.

2. **Preventing leakage of keys** The idea is to provide a user with personal keys that contain some sensitive information about the user which the user will be reluctant to disclose.

3. **Content tracing** In addition to tracing leakers who give away their private keys, there are methods that attempt to detect illegal users who redistribute the content after it is decoded.

4. **Integration of tracing and revocation** Broadcast encryption can be combined with tracing schemes to yield trace-and-revoke schemes. The "Trace-and-revoke" approach is to design a method

that can trace the identity of the user whose key was leaked; in turn, this user's key is revoked from the system for future uses.

Classification of broadcast encryption Broadcast encryption started from *Secret Key Broadcast Encryption* [78]. Later *Public Key Broadcast Encryption* [25] was constructed following the hierarchical identity-based encryption scheme [21]. *Identity-Based Broadcast Encryption* was proposed in [37] and [50], respectively.

18.2 Subset-Cover Revocation Framework [78]

In order to find an efficient revocation scheme, the framework of such algorithms is defined, called the *Subset-Cover algorithms* which are based on the principle of covering all non-revoked users by disjoint subsets from a predefined collection, together with a method for assigning (long-lived) keys to subsets in the collection.

18.2.1 Problem Definition

Let $\mathcal{N}$ be the set of all users, $|\mathcal{N}| = N$, and $\mathcal{R} \subset \mathcal{N}$ be a group of $|\mathcal{R}| = r$ users whose decryption privileges should be revoked. The goal of a revocation algorithm is to allow a center to transmit a message M to all users such that any user $u \in \mathcal{N} \setminus \mathcal{R}$ can decrypt the message correctly, while even a coalition consisting of all members of $\mathcal{R}$ cannot decrypt it.

The system consists of three parts.

1. An initiation scheme assigns the receivers secret information that will allow them to decrypt.

2. A broadcast algorithm, given a message M and the set $\mathcal{R}$ of users that should be revoked, outputs a ciphertext message M' that is broadcast to all receivers.

3. A decryption algorithm allows a (non-revoked) user that receives ciphertext M' to retrieve the original message M using his or her secret information .

18.2.2 The Framework

In the framework for the Subset-Cover algorithm, let $\mathcal{S}_1, \ldots, \mathcal{S}_w$ be a collection of subsets with $\mathcal{S}_j \subseteq \mathcal{N}$. Each subset $\mathcal{S}_j$ is assigned a long-lived key L_j; each member u of $\mathcal{S}_j$ should be able to deduce L_j from its secret information. Given a revoked set $\mathcal{R}$, the remaining users $\mathcal{N} \setminus \mathcal{R}$ are partitioned into disjoint subsets $\mathcal{S}_{i_1}, \ldots, \mathcal{S}_{i_m}$[1] so that

$$\mathcal{N} \setminus \mathcal{R} = \cup_{j=1}^m \mathcal{S}_{i_j} \qquad (18.1)$$

and a session key K is encrypted m times with $L_{i_1}, \ldots, L_{i_m}$.
Specifically, an algorithm in the framework uses two encryption schemes.

1. A method $F_K : \{0,1\}^* \to \{0,1\}^*$ to encrypt the message itself. The key K used will be chosen fresh for each message M as a random bit string. F_K should be a fast method and should not expand the plaintext. The simplest implementation is to XOR the message M with a stream cipher generated by K.

2. A method E_L to deliver the session key to the receivers, for which we will employ for an encryption scheme. The key L here is long-lived. The simplest implementation is to make $E_L : \{0,1\}^\ell \to \{0,1\}^\ell$ a block cipher.

The system consists of three components as mentioned above.

1. **Scheme initiation**
    Every receiver u is assigned private information I_u. For all $1 \leq i \leq w$ such that $u \in \mathcal{S}_i$, I_u allows u to deduce the key L_i corresponding to the set $\mathcal{S}_i$. Note that the keys L_i can be chosen either

    (a) uniformly at random and independently from each other (which we call the *information-theoretic* case) or

    (b) as a function of other (secret) information (which we call the *computational* case), and thus may not be independent of each other.

2. **Broadcast algorithm** at the center:

    (a) Choose a session encryption key K.

    (b) Given a set $\mathcal{R}$ of revoked receivers, the center finds a partition of the users in $\mathcal{N} \setminus \mathcal{R}$ into disjoint subsets $\mathcal{S}_{i_1}, \ldots, \mathcal{S}_{i_m}$. Let $L_{i_1}, \ldots, L_{i_m}$ be the keys associated with the above subsets.

    (c) The center encrypts K with keys $L_{i_1}, \ldots, L_{i_m}$ and sends the ciphertext
    $$\langle [i_1, i_2, \ldots, i_m, E_{L_{i_1}}(K), E_{L_{i_2}}(K), \ldots, E_{L_{i_m}}(K)], F_K(M) \rangle$$
    The portion in square brackets preceding $F_K(M)$ is called the *header* and $F_K(M)$ is called the *body*.

3. **Decryption algorithm** at the receiver u, upon receiving a broadcast message

---

[1] $i_1, i_2, \ldots, i_m$ are indices. Refer to Figure 18.5 for example.

$$\langle [i_1, i_2, \ldots, i_m, C_{i_1}, C_{i_2}, \ldots, C_{i_m}], M' \rangle:$$

  (a) Find i_j such that $u \in S_{i_j}$ (in case, $u \in \mathcal{R}$ the result is *null*).

  (b) Extract the corresponding key L_{i_j} from I_u.

  (c) Compute $D_{L_{i_j}}(C_{i_j})$ to obtain K.

  (d) Compute $D_K(M')$ to obtain and output M.

We can see that BE is symmetric since both the encryption at the center and the decryption at the receiver u use the same key(s).

A particular implementation of such scheme is specified by

1. the collection of subsets $S_1, \ldots, S_w$,

2. the key assignment to each subset in the collection,

3. a method to cover the non-revoked receivers $\mathcal{N} \setminus \mathcal{R}$ by disjoint subsets from this collection,

4. a method that allows each user u to find its cover S_j and compute its key L_{i_j} from I_u.

Such scheme is evaluated based upon three parameters.

1. Message length - the length of the header that is attached to $F_K(M)$, which is proportional to m, and the number of sets in the partition covering $\mathcal{N} \setminus \mathcal{R}$.

2. Storage size at the receiver - how much private information (typically, keys) a receiver needs to store. For instance, I_u can simply consists of all the keys S_i such that $u \in S_i$, or if the key assignment is more sophisticated it should allow the computation of all such keys.

3. Message processing time at the receiver. We often distinguish between decryption and other types of operations.

It is important to characterize the dependence of the above three parameters in both N and r. Specifically, we say that a revocation scheme is *flexible with respect to r* if the storage at the receiver is not a function of r. Note that the efficiency of setting up the scheme and computing the partition (given $\mathcal{R}$) is not taken into account in the scheme's analysis.

18.2.3   Two Subset-Cover Algorithms

Two different methods in the *Subset-Cover algorithm* are defined with different performance trade-off as in Table 18.1.

Each method is defined over a different collection of subsets. Both methods are r-flexible, namely they work with any number of revocations. In the

TABLE 18.1

Performance trade-off for the Complete Subtree (CS) method and the Subset Difference (SD) method (N is the number of all users and r is the number of revocations).

Method	Message Length	Storage at Receiver	Processing Time
Complete Subtree	$r \, log \, (N/r)$	$log \, N$	$O(log \, log \, N)$
Subset Difference	$2r - 1$	$\frac{1}{2} log^2 N + \frac{1}{2} log N + 1$	$O(log \, N)$

Note: In the CS method, the message length is $r \, log \, (N/r)$ on average and grows too rapidly in r. Each receiver needs to store $log \, N$ keys, wherein number grows with N. Therefore, when N is big, a receiver's storage cost increases. In the SD method, the message length also grows in r, but it is substantially improved compared to CS: $2r - 1$ in the worst case and $1.38r$ in the average case. This improvement is (provably) due to the fact that the key assignment is computational and not information theoretic. A receiver's storage cost, however, is greater than that in CS.

first method, the key assignment is information-theoretic whereas in the other method the key assignment is computational. While the first method is relatively simple, the second method is more complex.

In both schemes, the subsets and the partitions are obtained by imagining the receivers as the leaves in a rooted full binary tree with N leaves (assume that N is a power of 2). Such a tree contains $2N-1$ nodes (leaves plus internal nodes) and for any $1 \leq i \leq 2N - 1$, assume that v_i is a node in the tree. Let $ST(\mathcal{R})$ denote for the Steiner Tree induced by the set $\mathcal{R}$ of vertices and the root, i.e., the minimal subtree of the full binary tree that connects all the leaves in $\mathcal{R}$ ($ST(\mathcal{R})$ is unique) as shown in Figure 18.1.

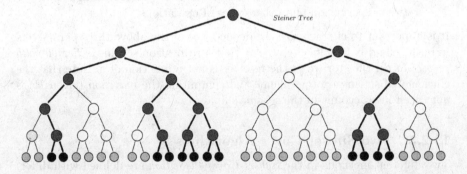

FIGURE 18.1
Steiner tree.

18.2.3.1 Complete Subtree (CS) Method

The collection of subsets $S_1, \ldots, S_w$ corresponds to all complete subtrees in the full binary tree with N leaves. For any node v_i in the full binary tree (either an internal node or a leaf, $2N - 1$ altogether) let the subset S_i be the collection of receivers u that correspond to the leaves of the subtree rooted at node v_i as in Figure 18.2. In other words, $u \in S_i$ iff v_i is an ancestor of u.

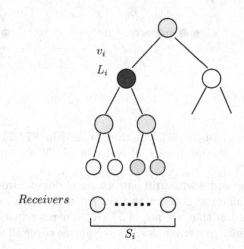

FIGURE 18.2
Subset S_i at node v_i in CS.

Key assignment

The key assignment method in CS is simple; it is shown in Figure 18.3.

1. Assign an independent and random key L_i to every node v_i in the complete tree.

2. Provide every receiver u with the $log\ N + 1$ keys[2] associated with the nodes along the path from the root to leaf u.

Subset-Cover of non-revoked devices
For a given set $\mathcal{R}$ of revoked receivers, let $u_1, \ldots, u_r$ be the leaves corresponding to the elements in $\mathcal{R}$. The method to partition $\mathcal{N} \setminus \mathcal{R}$ into disjoint subsets is as follows:

Let $S_{i_1}, \ldots, S_{i_m}$ be all the subtrees whose roots $v_1, \ldots, v_m$ are adjacent to

---

[2]Here we assume that N is a power of 2. If $N = 2^k$, then the binary tree has k levels. Therefore, the receiver u is given $k + 1$ keys, that is, $log\ N + 1$ keys.

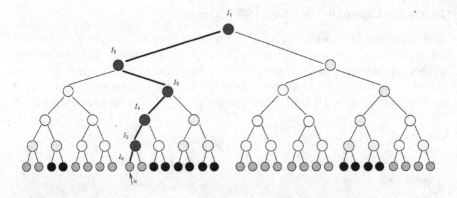

FIGURE 18.3
Key assignment in CS.

nodes of outdegree 1 in $ST(\mathcal{R})$, but they are not in $ST(\mathcal{R})$. It follows immediately that this collection covers all nodes in $\mathcal{N} \setminus \mathcal{R}$ and only them.

In Figure 18.4, the nodes with grid pattern are nodes of outdegree 1 in $ST(\mathcal{R})$.
So we can determine the nodes with lines pattern, which are adjacent to the
grid pattern ones, but they are not in $ST(\mathcal{R})$. Therefore, we can induce 5 subtrees from these lines pattern nodes. These subtree cover all non-revoked users.

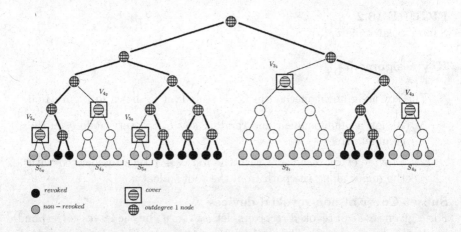

FIGURE 18.4
Subset cover of non-revoked devices in CS.

Cover size

The Steiner tree $ST(\mathcal{R})$ has r leaves. An internal node is in $ST(\mathcal{R})$ iff it
is on some path to a point in $\mathcal{R}$, therefore there are at most $r \ log \ N$ nodes in
$ST(\mathcal{R})$.

However, there could be double counting when the nodes are closer to the root and a node of outdegree 2 in $ST(\mathcal{R})$ does not produce a subset. Therefore, the number of subsets is at most $r \log (N/r)$.

Decryption step

Given a ciphertext

$$\langle [i_1, i_2, \ldots, i_m, E_{L_{i_1}}(K), E_{L_{i_2}}(K), \ldots, E_{L_{i_m}}(K)], F_K(M) \rangle,$$

a receiver u needs to find if any of its ancestors is among $i_1, i_2, \ldots, i_m$. Note that there can be only one such ancestor, so u may belong to at most one subset. Then, the receiver can decrypt to obtain key K and finally obtain plaintext M.

Example

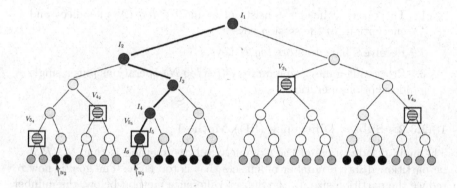

FIGURE 18.5
Example in CS.

By using the CS method as in Figure 18.4, subsets of non-revoked users can be covered as in Figure 18.5. In this example, there are 5 subsets $(S_{3_1}, S_{4_2}, S_{4_3}, S_{5_4}, S_{5_5})$.

Non-revoked users receive private information from a center, while revoked users are not given this information. Here u_1 is a non-revoked user while u_2 is a revoked user. Therefore, user u_1 will be given the corresponding private information as

$$I_{u_1} = \{I_1, I_2, I_3, I_4, I_5, I_6\}.^3$$

---

[3] $I_1, I_2, I_3, I_4, I_5, I_6$ are parts of the private information sent from the center to receiver u_1.

This private information will allow user u_1 to deduce the key L_{5_5}.
Upon receiving the ciphertext

$$\langle [3_1, 4_2, 4_3, 5_4, 5_5, C_{3_1}, C_{4_2}, C_{4_3}, C_{5_4}, C_{5_5}], M' \rangle,$$

u_1 uses the key L_{5_5} to decrypt the corresponding part $D_{L_{5_5}}(C_{5_5})$ [4] to obtain
session key K. Finally, it uses key K in decrypting $D_K(M')$ to obtain the
original message M.

The receiver u_2 is also receiving the ciphertext $\langle [3_1, 4_2, 4_3, 5_4, 5_5, C_{3_1}, C_{4_2},$
$C_{4_3}, C_{5_4}, C_{5_5}], M' \rangle$. However, since it is in revocation list, it is not given the
private information. Thus, it cannot extract the long-lived key to obtain K
and decrypt the ciphertext.

Summary
In the Complete Subtree method, the result can be obtained from [78] as
follows.

1. The message header consists of at most $r \, log \, (N/r)$ indices and
   encryptions of the session key.

2. Receivers have to store $log \, N$ keys.

3. Processing a message requires $O(log \, log \, N)$ operations plus a single
   decryption operation.

18.2.3.2   Subset Difference (SD) Method

The main disadvantage of the Complete Subtree method is that $\mathcal{N} \setminus \mathcal{R}$ may
be partitioned into a number of subsets that is too large. The goal is now to
reduce the partition size. In the Subset-Difference method below, the number
of subsets is improved into $2r - 1$, thus got rid of a $log \, N$ factor and effectively
reduced the message length. The number of keys stored by each receiver increases by a factor of $\frac{1}{2} \, log \, N$.

Subset description

As in the previous method, the receivers are viewed as leaves in a complete
binary tree. The collection of subsets $\mathcal{S}_1, \ldots, \mathcal{S}_w$ corresponds to subsets of the
form "a group of receivers G_1 minus another group G_2" where $G_2 \subset G_1$. The
two groups G_1 and G_2 correspond to leaves in two full binary subtrees. Therefore a valid subset S is represented by two nodes in the tree (v_i, v_j) such that
v_i is an ancestor of v_j. We denote such subset as $\mathcal{S}_{i,j}$. A leaf u is in $\mathcal{S}_{i,j}$ iff
it is in the subtree rooted at v_i but not in the subtree rooted at v_j. In other
words $u \in \mathcal{S}_{i,j}$ iff v_i is an ancestor of u but v_j is not as shown in Figure 18.6.

---

[4] $D_{L_{5_5}}(C_{5_5}) = D_{L_{5_5}}(E_{L_{5_5}}(K)) = K$

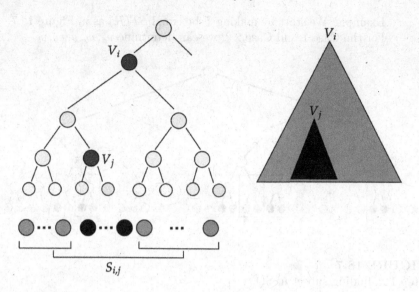

FIGURE 18.6
Subsets in CS.

Finding the cover

For a given set $\mathcal{R}$ of revoked receivers, let $u_1, \ldots, u_r$ be the leaves corresponding to the elements in $\mathcal{R}$. A cover is a collection of disjoint subsets $S_{i_1,j_1}, \ldots, S_{i_m,j_m}$ which partitions $\mathcal{N} \setminus \mathcal{R}$. Below is an algorithm for finding the cover, and an analysis of its size (number of subsets).

The method partitions $\mathcal{N} \setminus \mathcal{R}$ into disjoint subsets $S_{i_1,j_1}, \ldots, S_{i_m,j_m}$ as follows.
Let $ST(\mathcal{R})$ be the (directed) Steiner Tree induced by $\mathcal{R}$ and the root. We build the subsets collection iteratively, maintaining a tree T which is a subtree of $ST(\mathcal{R})$ with the property that any $u \in \mathcal{N} \setminus \mathcal{R}$ that is below a leaf of T has been covered. We start by making T be equal to $ST(\mathcal{R})$ and then iteratively remove nodes from T (while adding subsets to the collection) until T consists of just a single node.

1. Find two leaves v_a and v_b in T such that the least-common-ancestor v of v_a and v_b does not contain any other leaf of T in its subtree. Let v_l and v_k be the two children of v such that v_a a descendant of v_l and v_b a descendant of v_k. (If there is only one leaf left, make $v_a = v_b$ to the leaf, v to be the root of T and $v_l = v_k = v$).

Example: We start by making T be equal $ST(\mathcal{R})$ as in Figure 18.7. For the Case 1 and Case 2 [5], we can determine v_a, v_b, v, v_k, v_l.

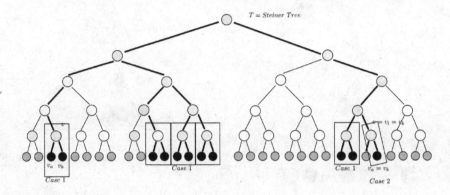

FIGURE 18.7
Step 1 in finding subset in SD.

2. If $v_l \neq v_a$, then add the subset $\mathcal{S}_{l,a}$ to the collection; likewise, if $v_k \neq v_b$, add the subset $\mathcal{S}_{k,b}$ to the collection.

    Example: After Step 1, we can see that for the Case 1, we cannot find v_l and v_k which are two children of v such that v_a a descendant of v_l and v_b a descendant of v_k. Therefore, Step 2 shown in Figure 18.8 is omitted for Case 1.
    In Case 2, we can see that $v_l \neq v_a$ and if $v_k \neq v_b$, so we add $\mathcal{S}_{l,a}$ (equivalent with $\mathcal{S}_{k,b}$) to the collection of subsets.

3. Remove from T all the descendants of v and make it a leaf.

    Example: After Step 2, by removing from T all the descendants of v and by making it a leaf, we have a new subtree T as in Figure 18.9.

We continue to perform Step 1 to Step 3 for the new subtree T as above. Finally we have the result of finding the cover as in Figure 18.10.

From the proof of lemmas in [78], we have the number of disjoint subsets of at most $2r - 1$.

---

[5]Case 1: There are two leaves. Case 2: There is only one leaf left.

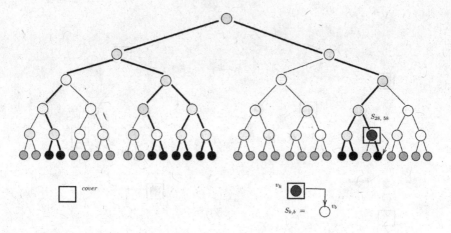

FIGURE 18.8
Step 2 in finding subset in SD.

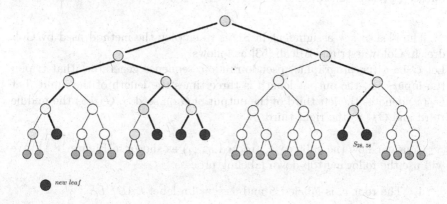

FIGURE 18.9
Step 3 in finding subset in SD.

Key assignment

If we apply the information theoretic approach of the previous method, then it is impractical in this method. If every pair (v_i, v_j) is assigned a key $L_{i,j}$, then each receiver must store $O(N)$ keys. Therefore, we need to devise a key assignment method that requires a receiver to store only $O(log\ N)$ keys per subtree, for a total of $O(log^2 N)$ keys [6].

---

[6]Note that a receiver u has $log\ N$ subtrees because the subtrees contain the receiver can be formed up to the number of the level of the tree. Every subtree has $log\ N$ keys. Therefore, the total number of keys of u is $log^2 N$.

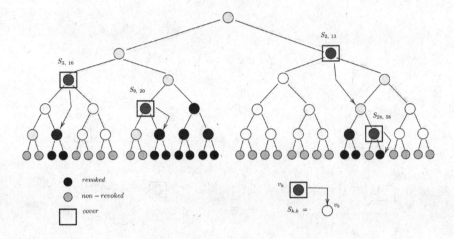

FIGURE 18.10
Subset Cover of non-revoked devices in SD.

The idea of key assignment in SD is to employ the method used by Goldreich, Goldwasser and Micali [53] as follows.

Let G be a (cryptographic) pseudo-random sequence generator[7] that triples the input, i.e., the output length is three times the length of the input. Let $G_L(S)$ denotes the left third of the output of G on seed S, $G_M(S)$ the middle third and $G_R(S)$ the right third.

Consider now the subtree T_i (rooted at v_i) as shown in Figure 18.11. We will use the following top-down labeling process.

1. The root v_i is labeled S and assigned a label $LABEL_i$.

2. S's two children are labeled $G_L(S)$ and $G_R(S)$, respectively.

3. Let $LABEL_{i,j}$ be the label of node v_j derived in the subtree T_i from $LABEL_i$.

4. The key $L_{i,j}$ assigned to set $S_{i,j}$ is G_M of $LABEL_{i,j}$.

Note that each label induces three parts: G_L - the label for the left child, G_R - the label for the right child and G_M the key at the node. For such a labeling process, given the label of a node it is possible to compute the labels (and keys) of all its descendants. On the other hand, without receiving the label of an ancestor of a node, its label is pseudo-random and for a node j, given the labels of all its descendants (but not including itself) the key $L_{i,j}$ is pseudo-random ($LABEL_{i,j}$, the label of v_j , is not pseudo-random given

---

[7]We say that $G: \{0,1\}^n \rightarrow \{0,1\}^{3n}$ is a pseudo-random sequence generator if no polynomial-time adversary can distinguish the output of G on a randomly chosen seed from a truly random string of similar length.

this information simply because one can check for consistency of the labels). It is important to note that given $LABEL_i$, computing $L_{i,j}$ requires at most $log\ N$ invocations of G.

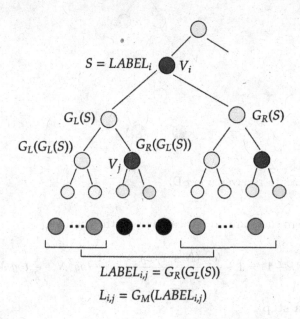

$$LABEL_{i,j} = G_R(G_L(S))$$

$$L_{i,j} = G_M(LABEL_{i,j})$$

FIGURE 18.11
Key assignment in SD.

Providing keys to receivers

We now describe the information I_u that each receiver u gets in order to derive key assignment described above.

For each subtree T_i such that u is a leaf of T_i, the receiver u should be able to compute $L_{i,j}$ iff j is not an ancestor of u [8]. Consider the path from v_i to u and let $v_{i1}, v_{i2}, \ldots, v_{ik}$ be the nodes which are adjacent to the path but not ancestors of u as in Figure 18.12. Each j in T_i that is not an ancestor of u is a descendant of one of these nodes. Therefore, if u receives the labels of $v_{i1}, v_{i2}, \ldots, v_{ik}$ as part of I_u, then invoking G at most $log\ N$ times suffices to compute $L_{i,j}$ for any j that is not an ancestor of u.

As for the total number of keys (in fact, labels) stored by receiver u, each tree T_i of depth k that contains u will contribute $k - 1$ keys (plus one key for

---

[8]Since the receiver u in this case is non-revoked, it can use its private information to deduce $L_{i,j}$.

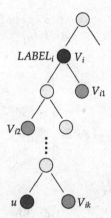

FIGURE 18.12
Providing keys to receiver u in SD.

the case where there are no revocations), so the total is

$$1 + \sum_{k=1}^{log\ N+1} (k-1) = 1 + \frac{log\ (N+1)log\ N}{2} = \frac{1}{2}\ log^2 N + \frac{1}{2}\ log\ N + 1. \quad (18.2)$$

Decryption step

Upon receiving the ciphertext, a receiver u first finds the subset $\mathcal{S}_{i,j}$ such that $u \in \mathcal{S}_{i,j}$, computes the key corresponding to $L_{i,j}$, then using this key obtains the session key and decrypts the ciphertext to obtain the original message.

Summary

In the Subset Difference method, the result can be obtained from [78] as follows.

1. The message header consists of at most $2r - 1$ indices and encryptions of the session key.

2. Receivers have to store $\frac{1}{2}\ log^2 N + \frac{1}{2}\ log\ N + 1$ keys.

3. Processing a message requires $O(log\ N)$ operations plus a single decryption operation.

18.3 Identity-Based Broadcast Encryption

This section describes the first identity-based broadcast encryption scheme (IBBE) with constant size ciphertexts and private keys [37]. In this scheme, the public key is of size linear in the maximal size m of the set of receivers, which is smaller than the number of possible users (identities) in the system. Compared with a broadcast encryption system introduced by Boneh, Gentry and Waters [25], this system has a better efficiency: the public key is shorter than in [25]. Moreover, the total number of possible users in the system does not have to be fixed in the setup. We called this property "Dynamic Broadcast Encryption." Since it is also a Key Encapsulation Mechanism (KEM), long messages can be encrypted under a short symmetric key.

Dynamic broadcast encryption[9] The concept of dynamic broadcast encryption (DBE) was introduced by Delerablée, Paillier, and Pointcheval in [38]. A DBE scheme is a BE in which the total number of users is not fixed in the setup, with the property that any new user can decrypt all previously distributed messages.

18.3.1 Preliminaries

This section provides a formal definition of identity-based broadcast encryption and its security models.

18.3.1.1 Definition

Setup(λ, m) Takes as input the security parameter λ, the maximal size m of the set of receivers for one encryption, and outputs a master secret key MSK and a public key PK. The PKG is given MSK and makes PK public.

Extract(MSK, ID_i) Takes as input the master secret key MSK and a user identity ID_i. Extract generates a user private key sk_{ID_i}.

Encrypt$(\mathcal{S}, PK)$ Takes as input the public key PK and a set of included identities $\mathcal{S} = \{ID_1, \cdots, ID_s\}$ with $s \leq m$ and outputs a pair (Hdr, K), where Hdr is called the header and $K \in \mathcal{K}$, where $\mathcal{K}$ is a set of keys for the symmetric encryption scheme.

When a message $M \in \{0,1\}^*$ is to be broadcasted to users in $\mathcal{S}$, the broad-

---

[9]In [78], the total number of possible users N is fixed. However, the scheme in [37] does not depend on N, but only depends on the maximal size of the set of receivers m as can be checked in the Setup stage.

caster generates $(Hdr, K) \leftarrow Encrypt(\mathcal{S}, PK)$, computes the encryption C_M of M under the symmetric key $K \in \mathcal{K}$ and broadcasts $(Hdr, \mathcal{S}, C_M)$. We refer Hdr as the header or broadcast ciphertext, $(Hdr, \mathcal{S})$ as the full header, K as the message encryption key and C_M as the broadcast body.

Decrypt$(\mathcal{S}, ID, sk_{ID}, Hdr, PK)$ Takes as input a subset $\mathcal{S} = \{ID_1, \cdots, ID_s\}$ (with $s \leq m$), an identity ID, the corresponding private key sk_{ID}, a header Hdr, and the public key PK. If $ID \in \mathcal{S}$, the algorithm outputs the message encryption key K which is then used to decrypt the broadcast body C_M and recover M.

18.3.1.2   Security Model

We define IND-sID-CCA security of an IBBE system. Security is defined using the following game between an adversary $\mathcal{A}$ and a challenger. Both the adversary and the challenger are given as input m, the maximal size of a set of receivers $\mathcal{S}$. The only difference with normal IBE systems is that the challenge identity here is not an identity but a set of identities.

Init The adversary $\mathcal{A}$ first outputs a set $\mathcal{S}^* = \{ID_1^*, \cdots, ID_s^*\}$ of identities that he wants to attack (with $s \leq m$).

Setup The challenger runs $Setup(\lambda, m)$ to obtain a public key PK. He gives $\mathcal{A}$ the public key PK.

Phase I The adversary $\mathcal{A}$ adaptively issues queries $q_1, \cdots, q_{s_0}$, where q_i is one of the following.

(a) Extraction query (ID_i) with the constraint that $ID_i \notin \mathcal{S}^*$: The challenger runs $Extract$ on ID_i and forwards the resulting private key to the adversary.

(b) Decryption query, which consists of a triple $(ID_i, \mathcal{S}, Hdr)$ with $\mathcal{S} \subseteq \mathcal{S}^*$ and $ID_i \in \mathcal{S}$. The challenger responds with $Decrypt(\mathcal{S}, ID_i, sk_{ID_i}, Hdr, PK)$.

Challenge When $\mathcal{A}$ decides that Phase I is over, the challenger runs the $Encrypt$ algorithm to obtain $(Hdr^*, K) = Encrypt(\mathcal{S}^*, PK)$, where $K \in \mathcal{K}$. The challenger then randomly selects $b \leftarrow \{0, 1\}$, sets $K_b = K$ and sets K_{1-b} to a random value in $\mathcal{K}$. The challenger returns (Hdr^*, K_0, K_1) to $\mathcal{A}$.

Phase II The adversary continues to issue queries $q_{s_0+1}, \cdots, q_s$, where q_i is one of the following.

(a) Extraction query (ID_i), as in Phase I.

(b) Decryption query, as in phase 1, but with the constraint that $Hdr \neq Hdr^*$. The challenger responds as in Phase I.

Guess Finally, the adversary $\mathcal{A}$ outputs a guess $b' \in \{0, 1\}$ and wins the game if $b = b'$.

We denote by q_D the total number of decryption queries and by t the total number of extraction queries that can be issued by the adversary during the game. Viewing t, m, q_D as attack parameters, we denote by $Adv_{IBBE}^{ind}(t, m, q_D, \mathcal{A})$ the advantage of $\mathcal{A}$ in winning the game as

$$Adv_{IBBE}^{ind}(t, m, q_D, \mathcal{A}) = |2 \times Pr[b' = b] - 1| = |Pr[b' = 1 | b = 1] - Pr[b' = 1 | b = 0]|,$$

where the probability is taken over the random coins of $\mathcal{A}$ and all probabilistic algorithms are run by the challenger. Here we can know that $Pr[b' = 1 | b = 1] = Pr[b' = b]$ and $Pr[b' = 1 | b = 0] = 1 - Pr[b' = b]$.

Definition 1 *Let $Adv_{IBBE}^{ind}(t, m, q_D) = max_{\mathcal{A}} Adv_{IBBE}^{ind}(t, m, q_D, \mathcal{A})$, where the maximum is taken over all probabilistic algorithms $\mathcal{A}$ running in time $poly(\lambda)$. An identity-based broadcast encryption scheme IBBE is said to be (t, m, q_D)-IND-sID-CCA secure if $Adv_{IBBE}^{ind}(t, m, q_D) = negl(\lambda)$.*

Definition 2 *We say that an identity-based broadcast encryption system is (t, m)-IND-sID-CPA secure if it is $(t, m, 0)$-IND-sID-CCA secure.*

Remark. In [25], the choice of $\mathcal{S}^*$ implies a choice of corrupted users, because the total number of users is fixed in the setup. In the model we described before, the corrupted users are not chosen at the beginning but adaptively. We describe below a modification of the model which does not allow adaptive corruptions, as in [25].

Definition 3 *(t, m, q_D)-IND-na-sID-CCA security (non-adaptive sID): at initialization time, the attacker outputs a set $\mathcal{S}^* = \{ID_1^*, \cdots, ID_s^*\}$ of identities that he wants to attack, and a set $\mathcal{C} = \{I\bar{D}_1, \cdots, I\bar{D}_t\}$ of identities that he wants to corrupt (i.e., to obtain the corresponding private key). Thus the attacker issues t extraction queries only at the beginning of the game.*

Definition 4 *We say that an identity-based broadcast encryption system is (t, m)-IND-na-sID-CPA secure if it is $(t, m, 0)$-IND-na-sID-CCA secure.*

18.3.1.3 Hardness Assumptions

For proving this scheme, Delerablée [38] makes use of the generalization of the Diffie-Hellman exponent assumption due to Boneh, Boyen, and Goh [21]. They introduced a class of assumptions which includes, for example, DDH (in $\mathbb{G}_T$), BDH, q-BDHI, and q-BDHE assumptions. We give an overview in the symmetric case.

Let $\mathcal{B} = (p, \mathbb{G}_1, \mathbb{G}_2, \mathbb{G}_T, e(\cdot, \cdot))$ be a bilinear map group system such that $\mathbb{G}_1 = \mathbb{G}_2 = \mathbb{G}$. Let $g_0 \in \mathbb{G}$ be a generator of $\mathbb{G}$ and set $g = e(g_0, g_0) \in \mathbb{G}_T$.

Let s, n be positive integers and $P, Q \in \mathbb{F}_p[X_1, \cdots, X_n]^s$ be two s-tuples of n-variate polynomials over $\mathbb{F}_p$. Thus, P and Q are just two lists containing s multivariate polynomials each. It means that $|P| = |Q| = s$ and $\mathbb{F}_p[X_1, \cdots, X_n] = c_{x,1,i}X_1 + c_{x,2,i}X_2 + \cdots + c_{x,n,i}X_n$, where $c_{x,j,i} \in \mathbb{F}_p$ for $1 \leq i \leq s$, $1 \leq j \leq n$ and $x \in \{p, q\}$. We write $P = (p_1, p_2, \cdots, p_s)$, $Q = (q_1, q_2, \cdots, q_s)$ and impose that $p_1 = q_1 = 1$. It means that $p_i = (c_{p,1,i}X_1 + c_{p,2,i}X_2 + \cdots + c_{p,n,i}X_n)$. For a set Ω, any function $h : \mathbb{F}_p \to \Omega$, and vector $(x_1, \cdots, x_n) \in \mathbb{F}_p^n$, $h(P(x_1, \cdots, x_n))$ stands for $(h(p_1(x_1, \cdots, x_n)), ..., h(p_s(x_1, \cdots, x_n))) \in \Omega^s$. We use a similar notation for the s-tuple Q. Let $f \in \mathbb{F}_p[X_1, \cdots, X_n]$. It is said that f depends on (P, Q), which we denote by $f \in \langle P, Q \rangle$, when there exists a linear decomposition

$$f = \sum_{1 \leq i,j \leq s} a_{i,j} \cdot p_i \cdot p_j + \sum_{1 \leq i \leq s} b_i \cdot q_i, \qquad a_{i,j}, b_i \in \mathbb{Z}_p.$$

Let P, Q be as above and $f \in \mathbb{F}_p[X_1, \cdots, X_n]$. The (P, Q, f)-General Diffie-Hellman Exponent problems are defined as follows.

Definition 5 $((P, Q, f)$-**GDHE**$)$ *Given the tuple*

$$H(x_1, \cdots, x_n) = \left(g_0^{P(x_1, \cdots, x_n)}, g^{Q(x_1, \cdots, x_n)} \right) \in \mathbb{G}^s \times \mathbb{G}_T^s,$$

compute $g^{f(x_1, \cdots, x_n)}$.

Definition 6 $((P, Q, f)$-**GDDHE**$)$ *Given the tuple* $H(x_1, \cdots, x_n) \in \mathbb{G}^s \times \mathbb{G}_T^s$ *as above and* $T \in \mathbb{G}_T$, *decide whether* $T = g^{f(x_1, \cdots, x_n)}$.

Delerablée refers to [21] for a proof that (P, Q, f)-$GDHE$ and (P, Q, f)-$GDDHE$ have generic security when $f \notin \langle P, Q \rangle$. We will prove that these constructions are secure based on the assumption that (P, Q, f)-$GDDHE$ is intractable for any $f \notin \langle P, Q \rangle$ and polynomial parameters $s, n = poly(\lambda)$. We just have to determine P, Q, and f, such that we can perform this simulation, and then proving the condition on the polynomials will prove the intractability of this problem (because as seen before, the (P, Q, f)-$GDDHE$ problem is hard for any choice of P, Q, and f which satisfy the aforementioned condition).

18.3.2 Delerablée's Scheme [37]

Construction 1. Delerablée's scheme with random oracle

Setup Given the security parameter $\lambda \in \mathbb{Z}^+$, where $\lambda = |p|$

1. Pick two random generators $g \in \mathbb{G}_1$ and $h \in \mathbb{G}_2$.
2. Pick a random $\gamma \in \mathbb{Z}_p^*$.
3. Choose a cryptographic hash function $\mathcal{H} : \{0,1\}^* \to \mathbb{Z}_p^*$.
4. Set $w = g^\gamma \in \mathbb{G}_1$ and $v = e(g,h) \in \mathbb{G}_T$.
5. The public key is $\mathsf{PK} = (w, v, h, h^\gamma, \cdots, h^{\gamma^m})$.
6. The master secret key is $\mathsf{MSK} = (g, \gamma)$.

Extract For a given identity ID

1. Set the private key as

$$\mathsf{sk_{ID}} = g^{\frac{1}{\gamma + \mathcal{H}(\mathsf{ID})}}.$$

Encrypt Given the list of receivers $\mathcal{S}$ and PK, assume for notational simplicity that $\mathcal{S} = \{\mathsf{ID}_j\}_{j=1}^s$ with $s \leq m$.

1. Pick a random $k \in \mathbb{Z}_p$.
2. Compute $C_1 = w^{-k} \in \mathbb{G}_1$.
3. Compute $C_2 = h^{k \cdot \prod_{i=1}^s (\gamma + \mathcal{H}(\mathsf{ID}_i))} \in \mathbb{G}_2$.
4. Compute $K = v^k \in \mathbb{G}_T$.
5. Set the Hdr as (C_1, C_2).

It outputs (Hdr, K) (Then K is used to encrypt the message).

Decrypt In order to retrieve the message encryption key K encapsulated in the header $\mathsf{Hdr} = (C_1, C_2)$, a user with identity ID_i and the corresponding private key $\mathsf{sk_{ID}}_i$ (with $\mathsf{ID}_i \in \mathcal{S}$), computes

$$K = \left(e(C_1, h^{p_{i,\mathcal{S}}(\gamma)}) \cdot e(\mathsf{sk_{ID}}_i, C_2) \right)^{\frac{1}{H(s,\mathsf{ID}_j)}}$$

with

$$p_{i,\mathcal{S}}(\gamma) = \tfrac{1}{\gamma} \cdot \left(\prod_{j=1, j \neq i}^s (\gamma + \mathcal{H}(\mathsf{ID}_j)) - H(s, \mathsf{ID}_j) \right)$$

and

$$H(s, \mathsf{ID}_j) = \prod_{j=1, j \neq i}^s \mathcal{H}(\mathsf{ID}_j).$$

Correctness:

$K' = e(C_1, h^{p_i, s(\gamma)}) \cdot e(\text{sk}_{\text{ID}_i}, C_2)$

$= e(g^{-k \cdot \gamma}, h^{p_i, s(\gamma)}) \cdot e(g^{\frac{1}{\gamma + \mathcal{H}(\text{ID})}}, h^{k \cdot \prod_{i=1}^{s}(\gamma + \mathcal{H}(\text{ID}_i))})$

$= e(g, h)^{-k \cdot (\prod_{j=1, j \neq i}^{s}(\gamma + \mathcal{H}(\text{ID}_j)) - \prod_{j=1, j \neq i}^{s} \mathcal{H}(\text{ID}_j))} \cdot e(g, h)^{k \cdot \prod_{j=1, j \neq i}^{s}(\gamma + \mathcal{H}(\text{ID}_j))}$

$= e(g, h)^{k \cdot \prod_{j=1, j \neq i}^{s} \mathcal{H}(\text{ID}_j)}$

$= K^{\prod_{j=1, j \neq i}^{s} \mathcal{H}(\text{ID}_j)}.$

Thus $(K')^{\frac{1}{\prod_{j=1, j \neq i}^{s} \mathcal{H}(\text{ID}_j)}} = K.$

Note In case the maximal size of the set of receivers m is increased, we don't need to set up the scheme again. For example, when we increase m to $m + 1$, we have to broadcast only the public key $\text{PK} = (w, v, h, h^{\gamma}, \cdots, h^{\gamma^m}, h^{\gamma^{m+1}})$.

Efficiency This construction achieves $O(1)$-size ciphertexts, $O(m)$-size public keys and constant size private keys. Note that the public key is linear in the maximal size of $\mathcal{S}$, but not in the number of decryption keys that can be distributed. Note also that as we said before, the broadcaster has to send the set $\mathcal{S}$ of identities that are included in the ciphertext. This set needs to be decrypted, as in previous schemes, thus it is counted in the full header, but not in the header.

18.3.3   Security Analysis of Delerablée's Scheme

Now we prove the IND-sID-CPA security of this system by using the GDDHE framework of [21]. We start by defining the following intermediate decisional problem.

Definition 7 (f, g, F)-*GDDHE. Let* $\mathcal{B} = (p, \mathbb{G}_1, \mathbb{G}_2, \mathbb{G}_T, e(\cdot, \cdot))$ *be a bilinear map group system and let* f *and* g *be two coprime polynomials with pairwise distinct roots of respective orders* t *and* n. *Let* g_0 *be a generator of* $\mathbb{G}_1$ *and* h_0 *a generator of* $\mathbb{G}_2$. *Solving the* (f, g, F)-*GDDHE problem consists, given*

$$g_0, g_0^{\gamma}, \cdots, g_0^{\gamma^{t-1}}, g_0^{\gamma \cdot f(\gamma)}, g_0^{k \cdot \gamma \cdot f(\gamma)}, h_0, h_0^{\gamma}, \cdots, h_0^{\gamma^{2n}}, h_0^{k \cdot g(\gamma)},$$

and $T \in \mathbb{G}_T$, *in deciding whether* T *is equal to* $e(g_0, h_0)^{k \cdot f(\gamma)}$ *or to some random element of* $\mathbb{G}_T$.

   We denote by $Adv^{gddhe}(f, g, F, \mathcal{A})$ the advantage of an algorithm $\mathcal{A}$ in distinguishing the two distributions and set $Adv^{gddhe}(f, g, F) = max_{\mathcal{A}} Adv^{gddhe}(f, g, F, \mathcal{A})$ over $poly(|p|)$-time $\mathcal{A}$'s.

Corollary 1 (Generic security of (f, g, F)**-GDDHE).** For any probabilistic algorithm $\mathcal{A}$ that totalizes of at most q queries to the oracles performing the group operations in $\mathbb{G}_1$, $\mathbb{G}_2$, $\mathbb{G}_T$ and the bilinear map $e(\cdot, \cdot)$,

$$Adv^{gddhe}(f, g, F, \mathcal{A}) \leq \frac{(q + 2(n + t + 4) + 2)^2 \cdot d}{2p} \qquad (18.3)$$

with $d = 2 \cdot max(n, t + 1)$.

Theorem 1 *For any n, t, we have $Adv^{ind}_{IBBE}(t, n) \leq 2 \cdot Adv^{gddhe}(f, g, F)$.*

Proof To establish the semantic security of $IBBE$ against static adversaries, we assume an adversary $\mathcal{A}$ breaking it under a (t, n)-collusion is given and we build a reduction algorithm $\mathcal{R}$ that distinguishes the two distributions of the (f, g, F)-$GDDHE$ problem.

Both the adversary and the challenger are given as input n, the maximal size of a set of included users $\mathcal{S}$, and t, the total number of extraction queries and random oracle queries that can be issued by the adversary.

Algorithm $\mathcal{R}$ is given as input a group system $\mathcal{B} = (p, \mathbb{G}_1, \mathbb{G}_2, \mathbb{G}_T, e(\cdot, \cdot))$, and a (f, g, F)-$GDDHE$ instance in $\mathcal{B}$ (as described in Definition 7). We thus have f and g, two coprime polynomials with pairwise distinct roots, of respective orders t and n, and $\mathcal{R}$ is given

$$g_0, g_0^{\gamma}, \cdots, g_0^{\gamma^{t-1}}, g_0^{\gamma \cdot f(\gamma)}, g_0^{k \cdot \gamma \cdot f(\gamma)}, h_0, h_0^{\gamma}, \cdots, h_0^{\gamma^{2n}}, h_0^{k \cdot g(\gamma)}, \qquad (18.4)$$

and $T \in \mathbb{G}_T$, in deciding whether T is equal to $e(g_0, h_0)^{k \cdot f(\gamma)}$ or to some random element of $\mathbb{G}_T$.

For simplicity, we state that f and g are unitary polynomials, but this is not a mandatory requirement.

Notations

1. $f(X) = \prod_{i=1}^{t}(X + x_i)$.

2. $g(X) = \prod_{i=t+1}^{t+n}(X + x_i)$.

3. $f_i(x) = \frac{f(x)}{x + x_i}$ for $i \in [1, t]$, which is a polynomial of degree $t - 1$.

4. $g_i(x) = \frac{g(x)}{x + x_i}$ for $i \in [t + 1, t + n]$, which is a polynomial of degree $n - 1$.

Reduction algorithm $\mathcal{R}$

Init The adversary $\mathcal{A}$ outputs a set $\mathcal{S}^* = \{ID_1^*, \cdots, ID_{s^*}^*\}$ of identities that he wants to attack (with $s^* \leq n$).

Setup

1. Set $g = g_0^{f(\gamma)}$ (No actual calculations are made).

2. Compute $h = h_0^{\prod_{i=t+s^*+1}^{t+n}(\gamma + x_i)}$.

3. Compute $w = g_0^{\gamma \cdot f(\gamma)} = g^{\gamma}$.

4. Compute $v = e(g_0, h_0)^{f(\gamma) \cdot \prod_{i=t+s^*+1}^{t+n}(\gamma + x_i)} = e(g, h)$.
5. Set the public key as $PK = (w, v, h, h^\gamma, \cdots, h^{\gamma^n})$.

Hash Queries At any time the adversary $\mathcal{A}$ can query the random oracle on any identity ID_i (at most $t - q_E$ times, with q_E the number of extraction queries). To respond to these queries, $\mathcal{R}$ maintains a list $\mathcal{L}_H$ of tuples (ID_i, x_i, sk_{ID_i}) that contains at the beginning

$$\{(*, x_i, *)\}_{i=1}^t, \qquad (ID_i, x_i, *)_{i=t+1}^{t+s^*}$$

(we choose to note "*" an empty entry in $\mathcal{L}_H$). When the adversary issues a hash query on identity ID_i,

1. If ID_i already appears in the list $\mathcal{L}_H$, $\mathcal{R}$ responds with the corresponding x_i.
2. Otherwise, $\mathcal{R}$ sets $\mathcal{H}(ID_i) = x_i$ and completes the list with $(ID_i, x_i, *)$.

Phase I The adversary $\mathcal{A}$ adaptively issues queries $q_1, \cdots, q_m$, where q_i is an extraction query (ID_i). The challenger runs Extract on $ID_i \notin \mathcal{S}^*$ and forwards the resulting private key to the adversary. To generate the keys,

1. If $\mathcal{A}$ has already issued an extraction query on ID_i, $\mathcal{R}$ responds with the corresponding sk_{ID_i} in the list $\mathcal{L}_H$.
2. Else, if $\mathcal{A}$ has already issued a hash query on ID_i, then $\mathcal{R}$ uses the corresponding x_i to compute

$$\mathsf{sk_{ID}} = g_0^{f_i(\gamma)} = g^{\frac{1}{\gamma + \mathcal{H}(\mathsf{ID})}}.$$

    $\mathcal{R}$ then completes the list $\mathcal{L}_H$ with sk_{ID_i} for ID_i.
3. Otherwise, $\mathcal{R}$ sets $\mathcal{H}(ID_i) = x_i$, computes the corresponding sk_{ID_i} exactly as above, and completes the list $\mathcal{L}_H$ for ID_i.

Challenge When $\mathcal{A}$ decides that Phase I is over, algorithm $\mathcal{R}$ computes Encrypt to obtain $(Hdr^*, K) = Encrypt(\mathcal{S}^*, PK)$ as

$$C_1 = g_0^{-k \cdot \gamma \cdot f(\gamma)}, \quad C_2 = h_0^{k \cdot g(\gamma)}, \quad K = T^{\prod_{i=t+s^*+1}^{t+n} x_i} \cdot e\left(g_0^{k \cdot \gamma \cdot f(\gamma)}, h_0^{q(\gamma)}\right)$$

with $q(\gamma) = \frac{1}{\gamma} \cdot \left(\prod_{i=t+s^*+1}^{t+n}(\gamma + x_i) - \prod_{i=t+s^*+1}^{t+n} x_i\right)$.

The challenger then randomly selects $b \leftarrow \{0, 1\}$, sets $K_b = K$ and sets K_{1-b} to a random value in K. The challenger returns (Hdr^*, K_0, K_1) to $\mathcal{A}$.

Phase II The adversary continues to issue queries $q_{m+1}, \cdots, q_E$, where q_i is an extraction query (ID_i) with the constraint that $ID_i \notin S^*$ (identical to Phase I).

Guess Finally, the adversary $\mathcal{A}$ outputs a guess $b' \in \{0,1\}$ and wins the game if $b = b'$.

Simulation of private key generation

Now, we explain how to generate a valid private key without knowledge of the master secret key γ. Before explaining, look again a valid private key

$$\mathsf{sk}_{\mathsf{ID}} = g^{\frac{1}{\gamma + \mathcal{H}(\mathsf{ID})}}. \tag{18.5}$$

As seen from above, the simulator must know the γ for generating a valid private key. The difficulty is that the simulator does not know γ. But, it can generate a valid private key by using the problem instance only as below. We set g as below in the setup stage as

$$g = g_0^{f(\gamma)}, \tag{18.6}$$

where $f(x) \in \mathbb{Z}_p[x]$ of degree t.

We can generate a valid private key by using g, the instance $g_0, g_0^{\gamma}, \cdots, g_0^{\gamma^{t-1}}$, and the hash values $(x_1, \cdots, x_t)$ as

$$\mathsf{sk}_{\mathsf{ID}} = g^{\frac{1}{\gamma + \mathcal{H}(\mathsf{ID})}} = g_0^{\frac{f(\gamma)}{\gamma + \mathcal{H}(\mathsf{ID})}} = g_0^{\frac{\prod_{i=1}^{t}(\gamma + x_i)}{\gamma + \mathcal{H}(\mathsf{ID})}}. \tag{18.7}$$

If $\mathcal{H}(\mathsf{ID}) = x_1$,

$$\mathsf{sk}_{\mathsf{ID}} = g_0^{\frac{\prod_{i=1}^{t}(\gamma + x_i)}{\gamma + x_1}} = g_0^{\prod_{i=2}^{t}(\gamma + x_i)} = g_0^{\gamma^{t-1}} g_0^{(\sum_{i=2}^{t} x_i)\gamma^{t-2}} \cdots g_0^{\prod_{i=2}^{t} x_i}. \tag{18.8}$$

Thus the simulator can generate a valid private key without knowledge of γ.

Simulation of challenge ciphertext generation

We explain how to generate a valid challenge ciphertext without knowledge of γ. First of all, we must keep in mind that the simulator cannot generate a valid private key for a challenge identities and decrypt the challenge ciphertext. Now let us see the challenge ciphertext.

$$C_1 = g_0^{-k \cdot \gamma \cdot f(\gamma)} = (g_0^{f(\gamma)})^{-k \cdot \gamma} = (g^{\gamma})^{-k} = w^{-k},$$

$$C_2 = h_0^{k \cdot g(\gamma)} = h_0^{k \cdot \prod_{i=t+1}^{t+n}(\gamma + x_i)} = (h_0^{\prod_{i=t+s^*+1}^{t+n}(\gamma + x_i)})^{k \cdot \prod_{i=t+1}^{t+s^*}(\gamma + x_i)}$$

$$= (h)^{k \cdot \prod_{i=t+1}^{t+s^*}(\gamma + x_i)} = (h)^{k \cdot \prod_{i=t+1}^{t+s^*}(\gamma + \mathcal{H}(ID_i^*))},$$

$$K = T^{\prod_{i=t+s^*+1}^{t+n} x_i} \cdot e\left(g_0^{k \cdot \gamma \cdot f(\gamma)}, h_0^{\frac{1}{\gamma} \cdot (\prod_{i=t+s^*+1}^{t+n}(\gamma + x_i) - \prod_{i=t+s^*+1}^{t+n} x_i)}\right)$$

$$= T^{\prod_{i=t+s^*+1}^{t+n} x_i} \cdot e(g_0, h_0)^{k \cdot \gamma \cdot f(\gamma) \cdot \frac{1}{\gamma} \cdot (\prod_{i=t+s^*+1}^{t+n}(\gamma + x_i) - \prod_{i=t+s^*+1}^{t+n} x_i)},$$

$$= T^{\prod_{i=t+s^*+1}^{t+n} x_i} \cdot e(g_0, h_0)^{k \cdot f(\gamma) \cdot \prod_{i=t+s^*+1}^{t+n}(\gamma + x_i)} \cdot e(g_0, h_0)^{-k \cdot f(\gamma) \cdot \prod_{i=t+s^*+1}^{t+n} x_i},$$

$$= T^{\prod_{i=t+s^*+1}^{t+n} x_i} \cdot v^k \cdot e(g_0, h_0)^{-k \cdot f(\gamma) \cdot \prod_{i=t+s^*+1}^{t+n} x_i}.$$

As shown above, the challenge ciphertext can be made by using the problem instance only.

Now check whether it is a valid challenge ciphertext or not in two cases: (1)T is real (2)T is random, respectively. First, in the case that T is real (i.e., $T = e(g_0, h_0)^{k \cdot f(\gamma)}$), K is computed as

$$K = T^{\prod_{i=t+s^*+1}^{t+n} x_i} \cdot v^k \cdot e(g_0, h_0)^{-k \cdot f(\gamma) \cdot \prod_{i=t+s^*+1}^{t+n} x_i}$$

$$= e(g_0, h_0)^{k \cdot f(\gamma) \cdot \prod_{i=t+s^*+1}^{t+n} x_i} \cdot v^k \cdot e(g_0, h_0)^{-k \cdot f(\gamma) \cdot \prod_{i=t+s^*+1}^{t+n} x_i}$$

$$= v^k.$$

As shown above, a valid challenge ciphertext is made. Therefore the simulator can decrypt it by using the appropriate private key.

But, in the case that T is random, the simulator cannot make any valid challenge ciphertext.

Probability analysis

$$Adv^{gddhe}(f, g, F, \mathcal{R})$$

$$= Pr[b' = b|real] - Pr[b' = b|rand]$$

$$= \frac{1}{2} \times (Pr[b' = 1|b = 1 \wedge real] - Pr[b' = 1|b = 0 \wedge real])$$

$$- \frac{1}{2} \times (Pr[b' = 1|b = 1 \wedge rand] - Pr[b' = 1|b = 0 \wedge rand]).$$

Now in the random case, the distribution of b is independent from the adversary's view, where

$$Pr[b' = 1|b = 1 \wedge rand] = Pr[b' = 1|b = 0 \wedge rand]. \qquad (18.9)$$

In the real case, however, the distributions of all variables defined by $\mathcal{R}$ perfectly comply with the semantic security game since all simulations are perfect. Therefore

$$Adv_{IBBE}^{ind}(t, n, \mathcal{A}) = Pr[b' = 1|b = 1 \wedge real] - Pr[b' = 1|b = 0 \wedge real]. \qquad (18.10)$$

Putting it altogether, we get that

$$Adv^{gddhe}(f, g, F, \mathcal{R}) = \frac{1}{2} \cdot Adv_{IBBE}^{ind}(t, n, \mathcal{A}). \qquad (18.11)$$

□

About chosen-ciphertext attacks The Cannetti, Halevi, and Katz [32] result applies here by just making one of the identities that we broadcast to derive from a verification key of a strong signature scheme. Then it can be used to sign the ciphertext.

Removing the random oracle model One way to remove the random oracle model could be to randomize the private key extraction as follows: For an identity ID_i, $sk_{ID_i} = g^{\frac{1}{\gamma + ID_i}}$ could be replaced by $A_i = g^{\frac{1}{\gamma + ID_i + r_i \cdot \alpha}}$, with α, an element of MSK, and r_i chosen by the PKG. Note that this randomization has already been employed in [19].

Note also that we could easily obtain $IND\text{-}na\text{-}sID\text{-}CPA$ without random oracles by using an assumption which is not fully non-interactive. Indeed, during the setup, if the algorithm is given a $(f, g, F)\text{-}GDDHE$ instance with g that corresponds to the target set and f to the corrupted set (chosen by the attacker at initialization), then the rest of the proof can be done without any oracle.

Exercises

18.1 Explain why a simulator cannot generate a valid private key for challenge identities.

18.2 Explain $Adv^{gddhe}(f, g, F, \mathcal{R})$ in detail.

19

Attribute-Based Encryption

CONTENTS

The attribute-based encryption (ABE) is presented in this chapter. It is a type of public-key encryption in which the secret key of a user and a ciphertext are dependent upon the attributes of the user. This scheme involves two additional components: access tree, and set of attributes. The comparison of ABE and IBE is then given. There are two types of ABE: KP-ABE and CP-ABE. The next part of the chapter describes the structures of access tree. Satisfying the access trees can only result in the decryption of the messages. The preliminaries related to ABE are then discussed. The next part of the chapter discusses the KP-ABE approach. In KP-ABE, a ciphertext is constructed such that part containing the set of attributes and a private key along with access structure is generated by a trusted party. Similarly, the CP-ABE scheme is discussed. In CP-ABE, a part of a user's private key is composed of attribute set, and the ciphertext contains the structure specifying the access policy defined over the universe of attributes in the system. Decryption happens only if his or her attributes satisfy the access structure.

19.1   Overview

When multiple parties need same data, that may contain sensitive information including personal, financial, or medical details. It requires some additional measures to hide specific details of the user, compared to conventional public key cryptography, where private key (i.e., decryption key) is different for each user. In order to provide fine grained access to the user based on his attributes, attribute based encryption was first presented in [55]. Working of this scheme involves two additional components. One is access structure, and the other is set of attributes. If user is successful in satisfying the access structure, the user can decrypt ciphertext.

Comparison between IBE and ABE In IBE, a public key is bit string and secret key corresponding to the public key is generated by KGC. Public and private key act as pair, ciphertext created through the public key can be decrypted through its paired private key. Whereas the concept of ABE is similar to Fuzzy-IBE, but ABE provides more fine-grained access[1] than Fuzzy-IBE encryption. In ABE, the private keys and users are associated through access structure. While Fuzzy-IBE allows a private key for an identity ω to decrypt to a ciphertext encrypted with an identity ω', if and only if the identities ω and ω' are close to each other as measured by the "set overlap"[2] distance metric. Thus, Fuzzy-IBE achieves error tolerance, but it has limited applicability to access control of data. Due to error tolerance in Fuzzy-IBE, supported access structure is a threshold gate. Its value is fixed as specified at the setup time. Similar to Fuzzy-IBE, ABE scheme is also based on attributes instead of a single identity. User's keys and ciphertexts are labeled with sets of descriptive attributes and a particular key can decrypt a particular ciphertext only if there is a match between the attributes of the ciphertext and the attributes of the user's key.

Comparison between KP-ABE and CP-ABE There are two kinds of ABE: KP-ABE and CP-ABE.
In KP-ABE, ciphertext is associated with the attributes and user key is associated with access structure. In the other hand, in CP-ABE, ciphertext is associated with the access structure and user key is associated with attributes.

---

[1] Refined in terms of attribute-based key generation. In Fuzzy-IBE, user is considered valid for decryption if his attribute set look like the attribute set defined by the encryption party, that is, it will allow some margin of error. This error margin is based on statistical distance between the attribute set of the user requesting for the decryption and attribute set defined at the time of encryption.

[2] It is defined as the similarities between the attribute set of the user requesting for the decryption and attribute set defined at the time of encryption.

19.2 Access Structure

Definition 1 *For set $\mathbb{Z}_n$ and a threshold value $0 < k \leq n$, the* **threshold function** $\amalg_k : \mathbb{Z}_n \to \{0, 1\}$ *is defined as*

$$\amalg_k(x) = \begin{cases} 0, & \text{if } x < k \\ 1, & \text{if } x \geq k. \end{cases} \tag{19.1}$$

19.2.1 Secret Sharing Scheme

Secret Sharing Schemes (SSS) are used to divide a secret s among multiple parties. The information of a single party i is called share λ_i of that party. Every SSS is paired with an access structure, which defines the set of parties that should be able to reconstruct the secret using their shares.

The access structure can be seen as the threshold function, i.e., at least k number of parties must use their share to construct the secret. Furthermore access structure can be represented as a tree such that there is a threshold function associated with each node of the tree. Each non-leaf node x with num_x children in such access tree is "AND" or "OR" gate, with threshold 1 and num_x respectively. For each leaf node x, $att(x)$ is defined as the attribute associated with the leaf node x. In access tree, the leaf node is analogous to the share of a party. Therefore, any set of parties that satisfy the access structure can combine their share to reconstruct the secret.

Definition 2 *For a finite field $\mathbb{F}$ and set of random variables $\{\varrho_1, \cdots, \varrho_l\}$,* **secret sharing scheme is linear** *if:*

1. *Share of each party is vector over $\mathbb{F}$.*

2. *The generation of shares of each parties is carried out such that, each coordinate of the share λ_i of every party i is linear combination of $\{\varrho_1, \cdots, \varrho_l\}$ and the secret s.*

19.2.2 Access Trees

Definition 3 *The* **Lagrange coefficient** $\Delta_{i,S}$ *for $i \in \mathbb{Z}_p$ and a set S, of the elements in $\mathbb{Z}_p : \Delta_{i,S}(x) = \prod_{j \in S, j \neq i} \frac{x-j}{i-j}$.*

Let $\mathcal{T}$ be a structure representing an access tree with root r, the $\mathcal{T}_x$ denotes the access tree rooted at node x, i.e., $\mathcal{T}_r$ is same as $\mathcal{T}$. For a non-leaf node x, let num_x be the count of its children nodes, we also define threshold value k_x, $0 < k_x \leq num_x$. We can think of each node as a threshold gate, when

$k_x = 1$ the gate is an OR gate and when $k_x = num_x$, it is an AND gate. For each leaf node x of the tree, threshold value is 1, i.e., $k_x|_{x=leaf} = 1$.

Let for node x, $parent(x)$ be its parent, the function $index(x)$ defines the index to the children nodes of x, uniquely assigned to the nodes in an access structure in arbitrary manner. For each leaf node, function $att(x)$ is defined corresponding to the attribute associated with the leaf node x.

Definition 4 *Let $\{P_1, P_2, \ldots, P_n\}$ be set of parties. A collection $\mathbb{A} \subset 2^{\{P_1, P_2, \ldots, P_n\}}$, is monotone if $\forall B, C$: if $B \in \mathbb{A}$ and $B \in C$ then $C \in \mathbb{A}$. An* **access structure** $\mathbb{A}$ *is a collection of non-empty subsets of $\{P_1, P_2, \ldots P_n\}$, i.e., $\mathbb{A} \subset 2^{\{P_1, P_2, \ldots P_n\}} \backslash \{\phi\}$. Sets in $\mathbb{A}$ are called authorized sets while others are unauthorized sets.*

19.2.3   Satisfying the Access Tree

Definition 5 *If attribute set γ satisfies the access tree $\mathcal{T}_x$, we say $\mathcal{T}_x(\gamma) = 1$. $\mathcal{T}_x(\gamma)$ is computed recursively. For all children x' of a non-leaf node x, evaluate $\mathcal{T}_{x'}(\gamma)$. If minimum k_x number of children of x return 1, $\mathcal{T}_x(\gamma) = 1$. For each leaf node x, $\mathcal{T}_x(\gamma) = 1$ if and only if $att(x) \in \gamma$.*

To relate an example for access tree, please refer to Figure 19.1. For access tree $\mathcal{T}_x$ rooted at node x, and universe of attributes $\mathcal{U} = \{A\,hospital, B\,hospital, C\,hospital, Pediatric\,dept, Surgical\,dept, Doctor\}$, threshold function $(A\,hospital \mid B\,hospital \mid C\,hospital) \wedge ((Pediatric\,dept \mid Surgical\,dept) \wedge Doctor)$ is satisfied for the node x and set of attributes $\gamma = \{C\,hospital, Surgical\,dept, Doctor\}$. In this access tree, on each node, threshold gate is indicated inside circle and index number is written outside of the circle. Table 19.1 demonstrates conceptual working of tree using threshold function.

Let us compute polynomial for root node x of Figure 19.1 access tree. Note that d_x is degree of every non-leaf node polynomial, which we compute in this way, $d_x = k_x - 1$. Note that in this example, if a node is an AND gate, then the number of its child nodes must be 2. Therefore, d_x must be 0 or 1. If we ignore $d_x = k_x - 1$ and assume that if a node is an AND gate, then its d_x is 1 and if a node is an OR gate, then its d_x is 0, we can remove the limitation that child nodes must be 2. Now, in our case, the root node $x = 1$ has an AND gate so this node has $num_1 = 2, k_1 = 2, d_1 = 1$. Because the degree of polynomial, $d_1 = 1$ so we will take $q_1(0) = y$ (where y is a uniformly random value $y \in \mathbb{Z}_p$) and add it with a random number $a \in \mathbb{F}_p$ to complete polynomial $q_1(x) = ax + y$. Next, we compute each polynomials for nodes that its parent is root node. First, put index in the polynomial of root node. Second, compute d_x, then, according to d_x, add random number.

TABLE 19.1
Flow of satisfying an access tree.

(index,threshold)→ $\mathcal{T}_r(\gamma) = \mathrm{II}_k(k')$	(index,threshold)→ $\vee$ ← $\mathcal{T}_x(\gamma) = \mathrm{II}_k(k')$	(index,threshold)→ $\vee$ ← $\mathcal{T}_x(\gamma) = \mathrm{II}_k(k')$ $\vee$ ← $\mathcal{T}_x(\gamma) = (att(x) \in \gamma)$	← $\mathcal{T}_x(\gamma) = (att(x) \in \gamma)$
(1,2) →			
	(2,2) →		
		← $\mathcal{T}_5(\gamma) = 1\ (att(5) \in \gamma)$	
		(4,1) →	
			← $\mathcal{T}_6(\gamma) = 0$ $(att(6) \in \gamma)$
			← $\mathcal{T}_7(\gamma) = 1$ $(att(7) \in \gamma)$
		← $\mathcal{T}_4(\gamma) = \mathrm{II}_1(1) = 1$	
	← $\mathcal{T}_2(\gamma) = \mathrm{II}_2(2) = 1$		
	(3,1) →		
		← $\mathcal{T}_8(\gamma) = 0\ (att(8) \in \gamma)$	
		← $\mathcal{T}_9(\gamma) = 0\ (att(9) \in \gamma)$	
		← $\mathcal{T}_{10}(\gamma) = 1\ (att(10) \in \gamma)$	
	← $\mathcal{T}_3(\gamma) = \mathrm{II}_1(1) = 1$		
$\mathcal{T}_1(\gamma) = \mathrm{II}_2(2) = 1$			

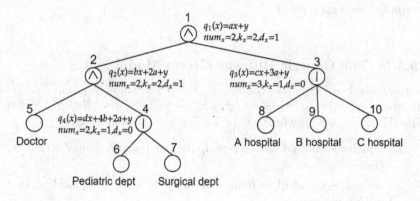

FIGURE 19.1
Satisfying an access tree.

In case of node with index 2, $d_2 = 1$. Therefore, its polynomial is set to $q_2(x) = bx + 2a + y$, where b is random number. In case of node with index 3, $d_3 = 0$. Therefore, its polynomial is set to $q_3(x) = 3a + y$. In the same way, we make polynomial equation for each non-leaf node. Furthermore, polynomials of all non-leaf nodes (including root node) of above tree are given below:

1. Root Node: $q_1(x) = ax + y$.

2. Child with index=2: $q_2(x) = bx + 2a + y$.

3. Child with index=3: $q_3(x) = 3a + y$.

4. Child with index=4: $q_4(x) = 4b + 2a + y$.

In case of leaf node, it is dealt with OR gate. In such a way as non-leaf node, polynomials of all leaf nodes of above tree are computed as follows:

1. Leaf Node with index=5: $q_5(0) = q_2(5) = 5b + 2a + y$.

2. Leaf Node with index=6: $q_6(0) = q_4(6) = 4b + 2a + y$.

3. Leaf Node with index=7: $q_7(0) = q_4(7) = 4b + 2a + y$.

4. Leaf Node with index=8: $q_8(0) = q_3(8) = 3a + y$.

5. Leaf Node with index=9: $q_9(0) = q_3(9) = 3a + y$.

6. Leaf Node with index=10: $q_{10}(0) = q_3(10) = 3a + y$.

19.3   Preliminaries

This section provides some hardness assumptions and security models for attribute-based encryption.

19.3.1   The Generic Bilinear Group Model

Suppose for two random encodings ψ_0, ψ_1 of the additive group $\mathbb{F}_p$. These encodings are injective maps, $\psi_0, \psi_1 : \mathbb{F}_p \to \{0, 1\}^m$, $m > 3log(p)$ [3]. That is $\mathbb{G}_i = \{\psi_i(x) : x \in \mathbb{F}_p\}$, where $i \in \{0, 1\}$. We have the following:

1. Oracles such that we can compute the induced group action on $\mathbb{G}_0, \mathbb{G}_1$.

2. An oracle to calculate bilinear map $e : \mathbb{G}_0 \times \mathbb{G}_0 \to \mathbb{G}_1$ as described in Bilinear map.

3. A random oracle to represent the hash function H.

In the generic group model, we will refer g^x and $e(g, g)^x$ as $\psi_0(x)$ and $\psi_1(x)$ respectively.

---

[3] This is because of the fact we have three oracles $\mathbb{G}_0, \mathbb{G}_1, H$. Range of each oracle is of order p. Therefore, to generate a unique string from the response of each oracle size of the string must be greater than $3log(p)$.

19.3.2 The Decisional Bilinear Diffie-Hellman (DBDH) Assumption

Let $a, b, c, z \in \mathbb{Z}_p$ be chosen at random and g be a generator of $\mathbb{G}_0$. The decisional BDH assumption is that no probabilistic polynomial-time algorithm $\mathcal{B}$ can distinguish the tuple $(A = g^a, B = g^b, C = g^c, e(g,g)^{abc})$ from the tuple $(A = g^a, B = g^b, C = g^c, e(g,g)^z)$ with more than a negligible advantage. The advantage of $\mathcal{B}$ is

$$|Pr[\mathcal{B}(A,B,C,e(g,g)^{abc}) = 0] - Pr[\mathcal{B}(A,B,C,e(g,g)^z)] = 0| \leq \epsilon. \quad (19.2)$$

19.3.3 Selective-Set Model for KP-ABE

The game model for selective-set model is defined as below.

1. **Init** The adversary declares the set of attributes γ, that he wishes to be challenged upon.

2. **Setup** The challenger runs the Setup algorithm of ABE and gives the public parameters to the adversary.

3. **Phase I** The adversary is allowed to issue queries for private keys for many access structures $\mathbb{A}_j$, where $\gamma \notin \mathbb{A}_j$ for all j.

4. **Challenge** The adversary submits two equal length messages m_0 and m_1. The challenger flips a random coin v, and encrypts m_v with γ. The ciphertext is passed to the adversary.

5. **Phase II** The same as in Phase I.

6. **Guess** The adversary outputs the guess v'.

The advantage of the adversary $\mathcal{A}$ in this game is defined as $Pr|b' = b| - \frac{1}{2}$.

Definition 6 *The **KP-ABE scheme is secure in the Selective-Set Model** if all polynomial time adversaries have at most a negligible advantage in the above security game.*

19.3.4 Security Model for CP-ABE

The adoptive security model game is described as below.

1. **Setup** The challenger runs the *Setup* algorithm and gives the public parameters PK to the adversary.

2. **Phase I** The adversary makes repeated private keys corresponding to sets of attributes $S_1, \ldots, S_{q_1}$.

3. **Challenge** The adversary submits two equal length messages M_0 and M_1 and challenge access structure $\mathbb{A}^*$ such that "attribute sets" from Phase 1 (i.e., $S_1, \ldots, S_{q_1}$) do not satisfy the $\mathbb{A}^*$. $\mathcal{A}$ receives CT^* as a response of the query.

4. **Phase II** Phase I is repeated with the restriction that none of the sets of attributes, $S_{q_1+1}, \ldots, S_q$, satisfy access structure $\mathbb{A}^*$ corresponding to the challenge.

5. **Guess** The adversary guesses b' of b.

The advantage of adversary $\mathcal{A}$ in this game is defined as $Pr|b' = b| - \frac{1}{2}$.

Definition 7 *The* **CP-ABE scheme is secure in the security model** *if all polynomial time adversaries have at most a negligible advantage in the above security game.*

19.4   KP-ABE [55]

KP-ABE is an approach in public-key cryptography where identity is defined as a set of attributes. The person authorized to decrypt the ciphertext holds a key for matching attributes. Such private keys are generated by trusted parties. In KP-ABE, structure maintains the access policy, which is encoded into the secret key. In this case, monotonic tree is the access structure $\mathcal{T}$. In KP-ABE, ciphertext is constructed such that part of it contains the set of attributes γ. In addition, the private key along with access structure is generated by trusted party.

Construction 1. KP-ABE

Setup

1. On input of security parameter κ, determine groups $\mathbb{G}_0, \mathbb{G}_1$, a bilinear map $e : \mathbb{G}_0 \times \mathbb{G}_0 \to \mathbb{G}_1$, and associate each attribute with a unique element in $\mathbb{Z}_p^*$.

2. Define a universe of attributes, $\mathcal{U} = \{1, 2, \ldots, n\}$.

3. Choose uniformly random values $t_i \in \mathbb{Z}_p$ for each $i \in \mathcal{U}$.

4. Choose uniformly random value $y \in \mathbb{Z}_p$.

5. The public parameters PK are $(T_1 = g^{t_1}, \cdots, T_n = g^{t_n}, Y = e(g,g)^y)$ and the master key MK is $t_1, \cdots, t_n, y$.

Key Generation This algorithm outputs the key which enables the user to decrypt a message encrypted under set of attributes γ only if $\mathcal{T}(\gamma) = 1$.

1. Choose polynomial q_x for each non-leaf node x, in the tree $\mathcal{T}$.

2. Polynomials are chosen in a top-down manner, starting from root node r.

3. For node x set degree of polynomial q_x, such that $d_x = k_x - 1$, where k_x is threshold value for the node.

4. For any root node r, set $q_r(0) = y$, d_r, and other points randomly.

5. For other nodes x, set $q_x(0) = q_{parent(x)}(index(x))$, d_x, and other point randomly.

6. After polynomials have been decided, for each leaf node x, give these values to the user as

$$D_x = g^{\frac{q_x(0)}{t_i}}, \ where \ i = att(x).$$

7. The set of above secret values is decryption key D.

Encryption For message $m \in \mathbb{G}_1$ under the set of attributes γ, and random $s \in \mathbb{Z}_p$.

1. Publish

$$E = (\gamma, E', \{E_i\}_{i \in \gamma}),$$
$$E' = MY^s,$$
$$E_i = T_i^s.$$

Decryption If the node x is a leaf node,
$DecryptNode(E, D, x) = e(D_x, E_i),$

1. If $i \in \gamma$

$$e(D_x, E_i)$$
$$= e(g_2^{\frac{q_x(0)}{t_i}}, g^{s.t_i})$$
$$= e(g,g)^{s.q_x(0)}.$$

2. Else

$$return \perp .$$

If the node x is a non-leaf node, $DecryptNode$ algorithm is recursively worked.

Let $i = att(x)$, if the node x is a leaf node then it simply proceeds as mentioned in the Decryption process described above. Now consider the recursive case when x is a non-leaf node, in this case algorithm $DecryptNode(E, D, x)$ [4] proceeds as

For all nodes z that are children of x, it calls $DecryptNode(E, D, z)$ and compute the output as F_z, as shown below. Let S_x be an arbitrary k_x-sized set of child nodes z such that $F_z \neq \perp$. If no such set exists, then node was not satisfied and function returns $\perp$. Otherwise, function return the result after computing as

$$F_x = \prod_{z \in S_x} F_z^{\Delta_{i, S_x'}(0)}, \quad Where \quad \begin{array}{l} i = index(z) \\ S_x' = \{index(z) : z \in S_x\} \end{array}$$

$$= \prod_{z \in S_x} (e(g, g)^{s \cdot q_z(0)})^{\Delta_{i, S_x'}(0)}$$

$$= \prod_{z \in S_x} (e(g, g)^{s \cdot q_{parent(z)}(index(z))})^{\Delta_{i, S_x'}(0)}$$

$$= \prod_{z \in S_x} e(g, g)^{s \cdot q_x(i) \cdot \Delta_{i, S_x'}(0)} = e(g, g)^{s \cdot q_x(0)}.$$

Here $\Delta_{i, S_x'}(0)$ is the Lagrange coefficient. We started calling function from the root of access tree, we can observe that $DecryptNode(CT, SK, r) = e(g, g)^{ys} = Y^s$ (Here using r because it is for root node) if and only if ciphertext satisfies the tree $\mathcal{T}$. Since $E' = MY^s$ the decryption algorithm simply divides out Y^s and recovers the message M.

For an example, a user has the private key for the access tree as in Figure 19.1. So, the private key is comprised as follows:

$$D_5 = g^{\frac{q_5(0)}{s_1}} = g^{\frac{5b + 2a + y}{s_1}}, \quad D_6 = g^{\frac{q_6(0)}{s_2}} = g^{\frac{6d + 4b + 2a + y}{s_2}}, \quad D_7 = g^{\frac{q_7(0)}{s_3}} = g^{\frac{7d + 4b + 2a + y}{s_3}},$$

$$D_8 = g^{\frac{q_8(0)}{s_4}} = g^{\frac{3a + y}{s_4}}, \quad D_9 = g^{\frac{q_9(0)}{s_5}} = g^{\frac{3a + y}{s_5}}, \quad D_{10} = g^{\frac{q_{10}(0)}{s_6}} = g^{\frac{3a + y}{s_5}}.$$

The set of attributes γ of the ciphertext is $\{Doctor, Surgical\ dept, B\ hospital\}$. So, the ciphertext is computed as follows:

$$E' = MY^s, \quad E_1 = T_1^s = g^{\frac{s}{s_1}}, \quad E_3 = T_3^s = g^{\frac{s}{s_3}}, \quad E_5 = T_5^s = g^{\frac{s}{s_5}}.$$

To compute F_1, i.e., F_r, we compute as follows:

1. $F_9 = e(D_9, E_5) = e(g^{\frac{3a + y}{s_5}}, g^{\frac{s}{s_5}}) = e(g, g)^{s(3a + y)}.$

---

[4] Here if we consider Figure 19.1, then for the node which have index 2, we know $q_2(x) = b \cdot x + 2a + y$; therefore the secret value for this node will be: $D_2 = \frac{q_2(0)}{t_i} = \frac{2a + y}{t_i}$.

2. $F_7 = e(D_7, E_3) = e(g^{\frac{4b+2a+y}{s_3}}, g^{\frac{s}{s_3}}) = e(g,g)^{s(4b+2a+y)}$.

3. $F_5 = e(D_5, E_1) = e(g^{\frac{5b+2a+y}{s_1}}, g^{\frac{s}{s_1}}) = e(g,g)^{s(5b+2a+y)}$.

4. $F_4 = F_7^{\Delta_{4,\{4\}}(0)} = e(g,g)^{s(4b+2a+y)}$, where $\Delta_{4,\{4\}}(0) = 1$.

5. $F_3 = F_9^{\Delta_{3,\{3\}}(0)} = e(g,g)^{s(3a+y)}$, where $\Delta_{3,\{3\}}(0) = 1$.

6. $F_2 = \prod_{z \in \{4,5\}} F_z^{\Delta_{z,\{4,5\}}(0)} = F_4^{\Delta_{4,\{4,5\}}(0)} \times F_5^{\Delta_{5,\{4,5\}}(0)} = F_4^{\frac{0-5}{4-5}} \times$
   $F_5^{\frac{0-4}{5-4}} = F_4^5 \times F_5^{-4}$
   $= (e(g,g)^{s(4b+2a+y)})^5 \times (e(g,g)^{s(5b+2a+y)})^{-4} = e(g,g)^{s(20b+10a+5y)} \times$
   $e(g,g)^{s(-20b-8a-4y)}$
   $= e(g,g)^{s(20b+10a+5y-20b-8a-4y)} = e(g,g)^{s(2a+y)}$.

7. $F_1 = \prod_{z \in \{2,3\}} F_z^{\Delta_{z,\{2,3\}}(0)} = F_2^{\Delta_{2,\{2,3\}}(0)} \times F_3^{\Delta_{3,\{2,3\}}(0)} = F_2^{\frac{0-3}{2-3}} \times$
   $F_3^{\frac{0-2}{3-2}} = F_2^3 \times F_3^{-2}$
   $= (e(g,g)^{s(2a+y)})^3 \times (e(g,g)^{s(3a+y)})^{-2} = (e(g,g)^{s(6a+3y)}) \times$
   $(e(g,g)^{s(-6a-2y)})$
   $= (e(g,g)^{s(6a+3y-6a-2y)}) = (e(g,g)^{sy}) = Y$.

19.4.1 Security Analysis of KP-ABE

Theorem 1 *If an adversary can break Construction 1 in the Selective-Set model, then a simulator can be constructed to play the Decisional BDH game with a non-negligible advantage ϵ.*

Proof Suppose there exists a polynomial time adversary $\mathcal{A}$, capable of breaking Construction 1 in Selective-Set model with advantage ϵ, then we can build a simulator $\mathcal{B}$ that can solve Decisional BDH problem with advantage $\epsilon/2$.

The challenger first sets two groups $\mathbb{G}_0$ and $\mathbb{G}_1$ with an efficient bilinear map e and generator g. The challenger defines universe $\mathcal{U}$ and selects uniformly random bit μ out of $\mathcal{B}$'s view. For $\mu = 0$, the challenger sets $(A, B, C, Z) = (g^a, g^b, g^c, e(g,g)^{abc})$, otherwise, $(A, B, C, Z) = (g^a, g^b, g^c, e(g,g)^z)$ for random a, b, c, z.

Init The simulator $\mathcal{B}$ runs adversary $\mathcal{A}$ that chooses set of attributes γ to be challenged upon.

Setup The simulator sets the parameter $Y = e(A, B) = e(g,g)^{ab}$. $\forall i \in \mathcal{U}$, if $i \in \gamma$, $\mathcal{B}$ chooses a random $r_i \in \mathbb{Z}_p$ and sets $t_i = r_i$ (i.e., $T_i = g^{r_i}$). Otherwise, if $i \notin \gamma$, $\mathcal{B}$ sets $t_i = b\beta_i$, for random value $\beta_i \in \mathbb{Z}_p$ (i.e., $T_i = g^{b\beta_i} = B^{\beta_i}$). $\mathcal{B}$ gives the public parameters to $\mathcal{A}$. Here note that $\mathcal{B}$ does not know the master key. If $\mathcal{B}$ knows the master key, then $\mathcal{B}$ does not need to run this process, because $\mathcal{B}$ can differentiate himself on the basis of given instance.

Phase I $\mathcal{A}$ adaptively makes requests for the keys corresponding to any access structure $\mathcal{T}$, such that the challenge set γ does not satisfy $\mathcal{T}$, i.e., $\mathcal{T}(\gamma) = 0$. To generate a secret key, $\mathcal{B}$ needs to assign a polynomial Q_x of degree d_x for each non-leaf node x in $\mathcal{T}$. Furthermore, to simulate key generation for each node x in access tree based on attributes, the computation is carried out through two procedures PolySat($\mathcal{T}_x$, γ, λ_x) and PolyUnsat($\mathcal{T}_x$, γ, g^{λ_x}). The details are in the below box:

PolySat($\mathcal{T}_x$, γ, λ_x)

This procedure sets up the polynomials for nodes of an access sub-tree $\mathcal{T}_x$ with satisfied root node, i.e., $\mathcal{T}_x(\gamma) = 1$. Input parameters for this procedure are tree rooted at $\mathcal{T}_x$, set of attributes γ, challenge set, and an integer $\lambda_x \in \mathbb{Z}_p$. The algorithm proceeds as follows:

1. To set up a polynomial q_x of degree d_x for root node x, set $q_x(0) = \lambda_x$ and the rest of the points randomly to completely fix q_x.

2. Set polynomials for each child node x' of node x by calling procedure PolySat($\mathcal{T}_{x'}$, γ, $q_x(index(x'))$). Notice that in this way, $q_{x'}(0) = q_x(index(x'))$ for each node x' of x.

PolyUnsat($\mathcal{T}_x$, γ, g^{λ_x})

This procedure sets up the polynomials for the nodes of an access tree with unsatisfied root node, i.e., $\mathcal{T}_x(\gamma) = 0$. For unsatisfied child node x' of node x, the polynomial is set such that $q_{x'}(0) \neq q_x(index(x'))$. Input parameters for this procedure are tree rooted at $\mathcal{T}_x$, set of attributes γ, challenge set, and an element $g^{\lambda_x} \in \mathbb{G}_0$, where $\lambda_x \in \mathbb{Z}_p$:

1. Define a polynomial q_x of degree d_x for the root node x such that $q_x(0) = \lambda_x$. As $\mathcal{T}_x(\gamma) = 0$, no more than d_x children of x are satisfied. Remember that $d_x = k_x - 1$ and k_x is threshold value. Let $h_x \leq d_x$ be the number of satisfied children of x.

2. For each satisfied children x' of x, the procedure chooses a random point $\lambda_{x'} \in \mathbb{Z}_p$ and sets $q_x(index(x')) = \lambda_{x'}$. Remember that even if the access trees of two users are same, the polynomials of each nodes in private keys of two users are different. So, the relationship between the private keys of two users do not exist, except for $q_r(0) = y$. Therefore, to randomly select $\lambda_{x'}$ is not effected to simulate the private keys of the others.

3. It than fixes the remaining $d_x - h_x$ points of q_x randomly to completely define q_x.

---

4. For each node x' of x, the algorithm calls:

   (a) PolySat($\mathcal{T}_{x'}$, γ, $q_x(index(x'))$), if x' is a satisfied node ($q_x(index(x'))$ is known).

   (b) PolyUnsat($\mathcal{T}_{x'}$, γ, $g^{q_x(index(x'))}$), if x' is not a satisfied node (For $g^{q_x(index(x'))}$, only $g^{q_x(0)}$ is known, and the rest points are set randomly to complete its definition).

   Why PolyUnsat algorithm takes $g^{q_x(index(x'))}$ as input? When x is root, PolySat algorithm cannot run. Because $q_x(0) = ab$, where a, b are exponents of instances of assumption, the simulator cannot know these values. However, PolyUnsat can run without knowing the exponents of instances of assumption, because even if $g^{q_x(0)} = g^{ab}$, according to the setting of T_i, D_x is using only g^a.

We need to make sure that the private key created through this process works properly.

We completely know q_x if $\mathcal{T}_x$ is satisfied with the challenge attribute set γ, because it is randomly set. In other case, at least $g^{q_x(0)}$ is known, and we may or may not know q_x completely. The simulator defines the final polynomial, $Q_x(\cdot) = b \cdot q_x(\cdot)$ for each node x of $\mathcal{T}$. Now as $q_r(0) = a$ (q_r presents root node polynomial), procedure sets $y = Q_r(0) = ab$. Simulator defines the polynomial $Q_x(\cdot)$ and returns private key as follow:
if $att(x) \in \gamma$

$$D_x = g^{\frac{Q_x(0)}{t_i}} = g^{\frac{b \cdot q_x(0)}{t_i}} = B^{\frac{q_x(0)}{r_i}}, \tag{19.3}$$

else

$$D_x = g^{\frac{Q_x(0)}{t_i}} = g^{\frac{b \cdot q_x(0)}{b \cdot \beta_i}} = g^{\frac{q_x(0)}{\beta_i}}. \tag{19.4}$$

The distribution of the private key for $\mathcal{T}$ is identical to that in the original scheme.

Challenge The adversary $\mathcal{A}$ will submit two messages m_0, m_1 to the simulator. The simulator chooses a uniform random bit v and returns an encryption of m_v as

$$E = (\gamma, E' = m_v Z, \{E_i = C^{r_i}\}_{i \in \gamma}). \tag{19.5}$$

Now if $\mu = 0$ then $Z = e(g, g)^{abc}$. If $s = c$, then $Y^s = (e(g, g)^{ab})^c = e(g, g)^{abc}$ and $E_i = (g^{r_i})^c = C^{r_i}$. Therefore, the ciphertext is a valid random encryption of message m_v.

Otherwise, if $\mu = 1$ then $Z = e(g,g)^z$, $E' = m_v e(g,g)^z$, as z is random, E' will be random element in $\mathbb{G}_1$. Therefore, the ciphertext contains no information about m_v, in $\mathcal{A}$'s point of view.

Phase II The challenger $\mathcal{B}$ responds to the queries of $\mathcal{A}$, similar as in Phase I.

Guess $\mathcal{A}$ will submit a guess v' of v. If $v' = v$, $\mathcal{B}$ will output $\mu' = 0$ to indicate that it was given a valid BDH-tuple. Otherwise $\mathcal{B}$ will output $\mu' = 1$ to indicate that it was given a random tuple.

19.4.2 Probability Analysis

In this section, we will perform probability analysis of KP-ABE. Now for the case $\mu = 1$, the adversary gains no information about v. Therefore when $v \neq v'$, the simulator guesses $\mu' = 1$ with the following probability

$$Pr[\mu' = \mu | \mu = 1] = \frac{1}{2}.$$

Now if $\mu = 0$, $\mathcal{A}$ can decrypt an encryption of m_v. So, its advantage is ϵ as per definition. Therefore the simulator guesses $\mu' = 0$ when $v \neq v'$ as

$$Pr[\mu' = \mu | \mu = 0] = \frac{1}{2} + \epsilon.$$

The overall advantage of the simulator in Decisional BDH game is

$$Pr[\mu' = \mu | \mu = 0]Pr[\mu = 0] + Pr[\mu' = \mu | \mu = 1]Pr[\mu = 1] - \frac{1}{2}$$

$$(Note: \ Pr[\mu = 1] = Pr[\mu = 0] = \frac{1}{2})$$

$$= \frac{1}{2}Pr[\mu' = \mu | \mu = 0] + \frac{1}{2}Pr[\mu' = \mu | \mu = 1] - \frac{1}{2}$$

$$= \frac{1}{2}(\frac{1}{2} + \epsilon) + \frac{1}{2}\frac{1}{2} - \frac{1}{2} = \frac{1}{2}\epsilon.$$

$\square$

19.5 CP-ABE [14]

In CP-ABE, part of user's private key is composed of attribute set, and ciphertext contains the structure specifying access policy defined over the universe of attributes in the system. A user will be able to decrypt a ciphertext, if and only if his attributes satisfy the access structure associated with ciphertext. In CP-ABE, authorization is included into the encrypted data, and the user who satisfies this policy can decrypt data. In addition, the user encrypts the message and defines the access structure by defining attributes of legitimate users for decryption. Therefore, key generation authority assigns private key based on the attributes of the user.

Construction 2. CP-ABE

Setup

1. Choose a bilinear group $\mathbb{G}_0$ of prime order p with generator g.

2. Choose two random exponents $\alpha, \beta \in \mathbb{Z}_p$.

3. Choose a hash function $H : \{0,1\}^* \to \mathbb{G}_0$.

4. The public key PK is $(\mathbb{G}_0, g, h = g^\beta, f = g^{\frac{1}{\beta}}, e(g,g)^\alpha$ and master key MK is (β, g^α), where f is only used for delegation.

Key Generation For a set of attributes S, choose a random value $r \in \mathbb{Z}_p$ and $\forall j \in S, r^j \in \mathbb{Z}_p$, and output

$$SK = (D = g^{(\alpha+r)/\beta}, \forall j \in S : D_j = g^r \cdot H(j)^{r_j}, D'_j = g^{r_j}).$$

Delegate

1. Take as input the secret key SK, for a set of attributes S and set $\tilde{S} \subset S$
$$SK = (D, \forall j \in S : D_j, D'_j).$$

2. Output a secret key $\tilde{SK}$ for the set of attributes $\tilde{S}$ as

$$\tilde{SK} = (\tilde{D} = Df^{\tilde{r}}, \forall k \in \tilde{S} : \tilde{D}_k, \tilde{D}'_k),$$

$$\tilde{D}_k = D_k g^{\tilde{r}} H(k)^{\tilde{r}_k}, \tilde{D}'_k =, D'_k g^{\tilde{r}_k}.$$

Encryption

1. Choose polynomial q_x for each node (including the leaf) x, in the tree $\mathcal{T}$.

2. These polynomials are chosen in a top-down manner, starting from root node r.

3. For each node x, set degree d_x of polynomial q_x, such that $d_x = k_x - 1$, where k_x is its threshold value.

4. Choose random $s \in \mathbb{Z}_p$, for root node r, set $q_r(0) = s$, d_r and other points set randomly.

5. For other nodes x, set $q_x(0) = q_{parent(x)}(index(x))$, and other points are set randomly.

6. Let, Y be the set of leaf nodes in $\mathcal{T}$. The ciphertext is constructed as:

$$CT = (\mathcal{T}, \tilde{C} = M \cdot e(g,g)^{\alpha s}, C, \forall y \in Y : C_y, C_y'),$$

$$C = h^s, C_y = g^{q_y(0)}, C_y' = H(att(y))^{q_y(0)}.$$

Decryption It uses DecryptNode(CT, SK, x) to get polynomial interpolation.

1. If $\mathcal{T}$ is satisfied by S, and $A = $ DecryptNode$(CT, SK, r) = e(g,g)^{rs}$, we have

$$M = \frac{\tilde{C}}{e(C,D)/A} = \frac{M \cdot e(g,g)^{\alpha s}}{e(h^s, g^{(\alpha+r)/\beta})/e(g,g)^{rs}}.$$

2. Else, return $\perp$

DecryptNode On input ciphertext CT, secret key SK and node x, if x is leaf node, let $i = att(x)$:

1. If $i \notin S$, return $\perp$.

2. Else, return $\dfrac{e(D_i, C_x)}{e(D_i', C_x')} = \dfrac{e(g^r H(i)^{r_i}, g^{q_x(0)})}{e(g^{r_i}, H(i)^{q_x(0)})} = e(g,g)^{r q_x(0)}.$

If x is non-leaf node, for all children nodes z, evaluate $F_z = $ DecryptNode(CT, SK, z). For set of children $S_x = \{z | F_z \neq \perp\}$:

1. If its size $|S_x| < k_x$, return $\perp$.

2. Else, let $i = index(z), S_x' = \{index(z), z \in S_x\}$:

$$\text{return } F_x = \prod_{z \in S_x} F_z^{\Delta_{i, S_x'}(0)} = e(g,g)^{r q_x(0)}.$$

Correctness of F_z:

$$F_x = \prod_{z \in S_x} F_z^{\Delta_{i, S_x'}(0)} = \prod_{z \in S_x} \left(e(g,g)^{r \cdot q_z(0)} \right)^{\Delta_{i, S_x'}(0)}$$

$$= \prod_{z \in S_x} \left(e(g,g)^{r \cdot q_{parent(z)}(index(z))} \right)^{\Delta_{i, S_x'}(0)}$$

$$= \prod_{z \in S_x} e(g,g)^{r \cdot q_x(i) \cdot \Delta_{i, S'_x}(0)} = e(g,g)^{r \cdot q_x(0)}$$

As in the case of KP-ABE, it also has to show the full process.

Theorem 2 *Given $\psi_0, \psi_1, \mathbb{G}_0, \mathbb{G}_1$ for an adversary $\mathcal{A}$. If $\mathcal{A}$ is bounded in q number of query responses to oracles for the hash function, groups $\mathbb{G}_0, \mathbb{G}_1$ of order p and bilinear map e, the adversary can break Construction 2 in CP-ABE security model with at most advantage $O(q^2/p)$.*

Intuition of the Proof It can be observed that in the security game of CP-ABE, $\tilde{C}$, a component of the challenge ciphertext, is $M_b \cdot e(g,g)^{\alpha s}$ ($= M_b \cdot \psi_1(\alpha s)$), where b is chosen randomly from $\{0,1\}$. Suppose there is another game in which $\tilde{C}$ is either $e(g,g)^{\alpha s}$ ($= \psi_1(\alpha s)$) or $e(g,g)^{\theta}$ ($= \psi_1(\theta)$), where θ is selected uniformly at random from $\mathbb{F}_p$, and the adversary has to guess between two cases. Furthermore, the adversary that has an advantage ϵ in CP-ABE game can be modified into an adversary that has the advantage $\epsilon/2$ in the another game. It may be seen as two hybrid games, i.e., in one game, the adversary has to distinguish between $M_0 \cdot e(g,g)^{\alpha s}$ ($= M_0 \cdot \psi_1(\alpha s)$) and $e(g,g)^{\theta}$ ($= \psi_1(\theta)$) and in other game, the adversary has to distinguish between $e(g,g)^{\theta}$ ($= \psi_1(\theta)$) and $M_1 \cdot e(g,g)^{\alpha s}$ ($= M_1 \cdot \psi_1(\alpha s)$). The combination of these two games is equivalent to CP-ABE security game.

Proof For the proof of security in the generic bilinear group model, details of response of the simulator to the adversary $\mathcal{A}$ are described below:

Setup The simulator chooses α, β randomly from $\mathbb{F}_p$. If $\beta = 0$, i.e., $1/p$ of the times, setup is aborted. Same is the case in actual scheme. The public parameters $h = g^{\beta}$ ($= \psi_0(\beta)$), $f = g^{1/\beta}$ ($= \psi_0(1/\beta)$) and $e(g,g)^{\alpha}$ ($= \psi_1(\alpha)$) are sent to the adversary.

Phase I The simulator has to respond two types of queries. For different queries, the simulator proceeds as follows:

1. **Hash Query** On query for the evaluation of $H(i)$, where i is any string, $t_i \in \mathbb{F}_p$ is chosen uniformly at random such that value was not chosen before. Finally the value g^{t_i} ($= \psi_0(t_i)$) are passed to the adversary.

2. **Key Generation Query** On the jth key generation query, for attribute set S_j, the new random value $r^{(j)}$ is chosen from $\mathbb{F}_p$. The simulator then computes $D = g^{(\alpha + r^{(j)})/\beta}$ ($= \psi_0((\alpha + r^{(j)})/\beta)$) and $\forall i \in S_j$, we have $D_i = g^{r^{(j)} + t_i r_i^{(j)}}$ ($= \psi_0(r^{(j)} + t_i r_i^{(j)})$) and $D'_i = g^{r_i^{(j)}}$ ($= \psi_0(r_i^{(j)})$) and the values are passed to the adversary.

Challenge In this phase, the adversary sends two messages M_0, M_1 and access tree $\mathbb{A}$ to the challenger $\mathcal{B}$. $\mathcal{B}$ chooses $s \in \mathbb{F}_p$. Then it constructs the shares λ_i, of s for all relevant attributes i, by using linear secret sharing scheme associated with $\mathbb{A}$. That is, for attribute i to satisfy access tree $\mathbb{A}$, λ_i must include s. λ_i are chosen uniformly at random from the $\mathbb{F}_p$ which depends on the correctness imposed on them (λ_i) by access structure. The choice of λ_i is simulated by choosing l random values $\varrho_1, \ldots, \varrho_l$ chosen uniformly at random form $\mathbb{F}_p$, for some value l, and then letting the λ_i be the fixed public linear combinations of ϱ_k and s. The simulator chooses a random $\theta \in \mathbb{F}_p$ and constructs the encryption as $\tilde{C} = e(g,g)^\theta \ (= \psi_1(\theta))$ and $C = h^s \ (= \psi_0(\beta s))$. For each attribute i, we have $C_i = g^{\lambda_i} \ (= \psi_0(\lambda_i))$, and $C_i' = g^{t_i \lambda_i} \ (= \psi_0(t_i \lambda_i))$, and these values are sent back to the adversary.

In the proof, it will be shown that if the simulator can choose the variable values[5] randomly with the probability $1 - O(q^2/p)$, then the adversary will see the same distribution of ciphertext as the $\tilde{C} = e(g,g)^{\alpha s}$. It will be concluded that for stated conditions, the adversary's advantage would be at most $O(q^2/p)$.

Reduction algorithm $\mathcal{R}$

Setup

1. Choose two random values α, β.

2. Compute $h = g^\beta$.

3. Compute $f = g^{1/\beta}$.

4. Compute $v = e(g,g)^\alpha$.

5. Set the public key as $PK = (g, h, f, v)$.

Hash Queries To respond queries for the evaluation of hash on any attribute string i, $\mathcal{R}$ maintains a list, $(i, H(i), t_i)$ where $i \in \{0,1\}^*$, and proceed as follows.

1. If i already appears in the list, respond with the corresponding $H(i)$.

2. Else, choose a random value $t_i \in \mathbb{F}_p$, set $H(i) = g^{t_i}$, respond with $H(i)$, and complete the list with $(i, H(i), t_i)$.

Phase I To respond key generation queries $S_1, S_2, \ldots, S_{q1}$ requested by the adversary $\mathcal{A}$, where S_i is a set of attributes in i^{th} query, the challenger runs *Gen* on S_i and forwards corresponding key to $\mathcal{A}$. Proceedings are as follows.

---

[5]This includes all values chosen uniformly from $\mathbb{F}_p$ i.e., $\alpha, \beta, t_i, r^{(j)}, s, \lambda_i, \varrho_1, \ldots, \varrho_l, \theta$.

1. Choose a random value $r^{(i)}$ and calculate $D^{(i)} = g^{(\alpha + r^{(i)})/\beta}$.

2. For each attribute $j \in S_i$, choose a random value $r_j^{(i)}$, and request $H(j)$ from hash oracle.

3. Calculate $D_j^{(i)} = g^{r^{(i)}} \cdot H(j)^{r_j^{(i)}}$ and $D_j^{(i)\prime} = g^{r_j^{(i)}}$.

4. Return $(D^{(i)}, D_j^{(i)}, D_j^{(i)\prime})$ as response of query.

Challenge

1. $\mathcal{A}$ outputs messages M_0, M_1, and challenge access structure $\mathbb{A}^*$, such that none of the sets in Phase I satisfy $\mathbb{A}^*$.

2. $\mathcal{B}$ chooses a bit $b \in \{0, 1\}$.

3. $\mathcal{B}$ chooses a random value $s \in \mathbb{Z}_p$, which is a constant value of polynomial for root node R, i.e., the $q_R(0) = s$.

4. $\mathcal{B}$ generates values $\lambda_i = q_y(0)$ where i is attribute corresponding to each leaf node $y \in Y$, where Y is set of all leave nodes in $\mathbb{A}^*$.

5. $\mathcal{B}$ calculates random $\theta = \alpha \cdot s$, $\tilde{C} = M_b \cdot e(g, g)^\theta$, and $C = h^s$.

6. $\mathcal{B}$ calculates $\forall y \in Y$, $C_y = g^{\lambda_i}, C_y' = g^{t_i \cdot \lambda_i}$.

7. Send $(\tilde{C}, C, C_y, C_y')$ to $\mathcal{A}$.

Phase II In this phase, $\mathcal{A}$ requests for keys of attribute sets $S_{q_1+1}, S_{q_1+2}, \ldots, S_q$. This phase is the same as Query Phase I, except for none of the requested set of the attribute is appeared in Phase I and they do not satisfy $\mathbb{A}^*$.

Guess Finally, $\mathcal{A}$ outputs $b' \in \{0, 1\}$.

Adversary can make valid queries on group oracles with the probability $1 - O(1/p)$, if the following conditions are imposed on queries:

1. The legitimate input from the adversary is either received from the simulation, or intermediate values it already received from the oracles.

2. There are p distinct values in the ranges of responses in both oracles ψ_0 and ψ_1.

As such, we may keep track of the algebraic expressions being called for from the oracles, as long as no "unexpected collisions" happen. More precisely, we can think of an oracle query as the response from a rational function[6] $\nu = \eta/\xi$.

---

[6]In actual scheme, it is exponential function in these independent variables but in generic

Independent variables of Oracle (ν) are $\theta, \alpha, \beta, t_i, r^{(j)}, r_i^{(j)}, s$ and ϱ_k[7]. We define an unexpected collision when two distinct functions $\eta/\xi \neq \eta'/\xi'$ collide for a specific query (Say x_1), i.e., $\eta/\xi(x_1) = \eta'/\xi'(x_1)$[8]. We now condition on the event that no such unexpected collision occur in either group $\mathbb{G}_0$ or $\mathbb{G}_1$. For any pair of queries (within a group) corresponding to distinct rational functions η/ξ and η'/ξ', a collision occurs only if the non-zero polynomial $\eta\xi' - \eta'\xi$ evaluates to zero. Note that the total degree of $\eta\xi' - \eta'\xi$ is in this case at most 5. By Schwartz-Zippel lemma[9], the probability of this event is $O(1/p)$. By a union bound, the probability that any of such collision happen is at most $O(q^2/p)$ [10]. Therefore under these conditions, the probability that there is no collision is still $1 - O(q^2/p)$.

Remember that it is working in the generic group model where each group element's representation is chosen uniformly. The only way that the adversary's view can differ in the case of $\theta = \alpha s$ is the case there are two queries ν and ν' into $\mathbb{G}_1$ such that there is an unexpected collision in ν and ν' when $\theta = \alpha s$, i.e., $\nu \neq \nu'$, but $\nu|_{\theta=\alpha s} = \nu'|_{\theta=\alpha s}$. θ only occurs as $e(g,g)^\theta$ or $(\psi_1(\theta)) \in \mathbb{G}_1$. The only dependence that ν or ν' can have on θ is by having some additive terms of the form $\gamma'\theta$, for constant γ'. Therefore, we have $\nu - \nu' = \gamma\alpha s - \gamma\theta$, for some constant $\gamma \neq 0$. We can artificially add the query $\nu - \nu' + \gamma\theta = \gamma\alpha s$ to the adversary's queries. In the following part, it is shown that an adversary can never construct a query for $e(g,g)^{\gamma\alpha s}$ $(= \psi_1(\gamma\alpha s))$.

Table 19.2 enumerates all possible rational queries into $\mathbb{G}_1$ by means of the bilinear maps and the group elements given to an adversary by simulation, except queries described as follows.

1. Every monomial involves the variable β, since β will not be relevant to constructing the query involving αs.

2. The variables i and i'. These are the possible attribute strings which appear in terms of λ_i. And these expressions do not contain the terms of ϱ_k. (As defined in Linear Secret Sharing Scheme, λ_i is linear combination of $\varrho_1, \ldots, \varrho_l$ and s. However, without information of

---

group model, we define $e(g,g)^x = \psi_1(x)$. Therefore it is rational function in generic group model, where both η and ξ are polynomials.

[7]The query contains either λ_i and $\lambda_{i'}$, these are linear combinations of s and ϱ_k. That is why subscript k of ϱ_k is different from subscript of other variables, i.e., i, i'.

[8]To understand this case, we can think of two rational function as curve in a space, and at certain point, there is point of intersection of these curves.

[9]Let $\mathbb{F}$ be a field. Let $f(x_1, \ldots, x_n)$ be a multivariate polynomial of total degree d, and suppose that f is not the zero polynomial. Let S be a finite subset of $\mathbb{F}$. Let $r_1, r_2, \ldots, r_n$ are the variables chosen at random uniformly and independently from S. Then the probability that $f(r_1, r_2, \ldots, r_n) = 0$ is $\leq \frac{d}{|S|}$.

[10]Union bond is calculated as $O(q_0 \times q_1 \times p_0)$, where q_0 is the number of $\mathbb{G}_0$ queries, q_1 is the number of $\mathbb{G}_1$ queries, and p_0 is the probability that a polynomial evaluates to 0, which is $O(q \times q \times \frac{1}{p})$.

TABLE 19.2

Possible query types from the adversary.

$t_i t_{i'}$	$\lambda_i t_{i'}$	$t_i t_{i'} \lambda_{i'}$	$t_i r^{(j)} + t_i t_{i'} r_{i'}^{(j)}$
$t_{i'} r_{i'}^{(j)}$	t_i	$\alpha + r^{(j)}$	$\alpha s + sr^{(j)}$
$\lambda_i \lambda_{i'}$	$t_i \lambda_i \lambda_{i'}$	$\lambda_{i'} r^{(j)} + \lambda_{i'} t_i r_i^{(j)}$	$\lambda_i r_i^{(j)}$
λ_i	$t_i t_{i'} \lambda_i \lambda_{i'}$	$t_i \lambda_i r_i^{(j)} + t_i t_{i'} \lambda_i r_i^{(j)}$	$t_i \lambda_i r_{i'}^{(j)}$
$t_i \lambda_i$	$(r^{(j)} + t_i r_i^{(j)})(r^{(j)} + t_{i'} r_{i'}^{(j)})$	$(r^{(j)} + t_i r_i^{(j)}) r_{i'}^{(j')}$	$r^{(j)} + t_i r_i^{(j)}$
$r_i^{(j)} r_{i'}^{(j)}$	$r_i^{(j)}$	s	

ϱ_k, the adversary cannot find the value of s, we can say that these expressions do not contain the terms of ϱ_k.)

3. The variables j and j'. These are the indices of secret key queries which appear in terms of λ_i. And these expressions do not contain the terms of ϱ_k.

In addition to polynomials in Table 19.2, the adversary also has access to 1 and α [11]. The adversary can query arbitrary linear combinations of these. Therefore, we must show that none of these polynomials can be equal to a polynomial of the form $\gamma \alpha s$ where γ is non-zero constant[12]. From the discussion above, it is clear that the only way that the adversary can create term containing αs is by pairing $s\beta$ with $(\alpha + r^{(j)})/\beta$ to get the term $\alpha s + sr^{(j)}$. In this way, the adversary could create a query polynomial containing $\gamma \alpha s + \Sigma_{j \in T} \gamma_j sr^{(j)}$, for set T and constants $\gamma, \gamma_j \neq 0$, where T means that the set of private keys made by the simulator. Now if the adversary wants to obtain polynomial of the form $\gamma \alpha s$, the adversary must add other linear combinations in order to cancel the term $\Sigma_{j \in T} \gamma_j sr^{(j)}$. By referring to Table 19.2, we can say that the only other term that the adversary has access to that could involve monomials of the form $sr^{(j)}$ are obtained by pairing $r^{(j)} + t_i r_i^{(j)}$ with some $\lambda_{i'}$, where $\lambda_{i'}$ are linear combinations of s and ϱ_k's.[13] Considering all these things for sets T'_j and constants $\gamma_{(i,j,i')} \neq 0$, the adversary can construct a query polynomial of the form:

$$\gamma \alpha s + \sum_{j \in T} \left(\gamma_j sr^{(j)} + \sum_{i,i' \in T'_j} \gamma_{(i,j,j')} \left(\lambda_{i'} r^{(j)} + \lambda_{i'} t_i r_i^{(j)} \right) \right) + other\ terms \quad (19.6)$$

The following case analysis completes the proof:

---

[11]$e(g, g)^1$ and $e(g, g)^\alpha$ are in public parameters.

[12]These are queries to oracle ψ_1 in generic group model.

[13]In the proof, the secret key j is function of attribute strings i, and the proof concludes by computing the probability of collision in the secret keys caused by the random selection of attribute strings, so in order to differentiate two different keys (j, j') that may collide on the basis of two different attribute strings (i, i'). We have simple and $\prime$ notation to differentiate one from another.

1. There exists some $j \in T$ such that the set of secret shares $L_j = \{\lambda_{i'} : \exists i : (i, i') \in T_j'\}$ [14] does not allow for the reconstruction of the secret s.

   If this is true, then the term $sr^{(j)}$ will not be canceled, and so the adversary's query polynomial cannot be of the form $\gamma \alpha s$.

2. For all $j \in T$, the set of secret shares $L_j = \{\lambda_{i'} : \exists i : (i, i') \in T_j'\}$ allow for the reconstruction of the secret s.

   Fix any $j \in T$. Consider an attribute set S_j, the set of attributes belonging to the jth adversary key request. From the assumption that no requested key should pass the challenge access structure, and the properties of the secret sharing scheme, we know that the set $L_j' = \{\lambda_i : i \in S_j\}$ cannot allow for the reconstruction of s, where i is an attribute. It is because that (1) the secret sharing scheme guarantees that unless a sufficient number of shares are gathered, the secret value s is not known and (2) the assumption guarantees that a sufficient number of shares cannot gather.

   Thus, there must exist at least one share $\lambda_{i'}$ in L_j such that $\lambda_{i'}$ is linearly independent of L_j' when written in terms of s and the ϱ_k's. By the case analysis, this means that in the adversary's query (Equation 19.6), there is a term of the form $\lambda_{i'} t_i r_i^{(j)}$ for some $i \in S_j$, because at least one share $\lambda_{i'}$ including the term $\lambda_{i'} t_i r_i^{(j)}$ must be included in the set of secret shares L_j for all $j \in T$.

   However, (examining the table above), there is no term that the adversary has access to that can cancel this term. Therefore, any adversary query polynomial of this form cannot be of the form $\gamma \alpha s$.

   $\square$

---

[14] Here the attribute strings for two different shares are from the set of valid attribute strings.

20

Secret Sharing

CONTENTS

This chapter discusses secret sharing methods. Secret sharing or secret splitting are methods for the distribution of a secret among the group participants, each of whom is given a chunk of the secret. Reconstruction is only possible when sufficient shares are combined. The next part of the chapter discusses efficient secret sharing techniques that involve Shamir's and Blakley's secret sharing schemes. The schemes are discussed in detail by providing overviews, mathematical definitions, constructions, and examples. The final part of the chapter shows an application of secret sharing.

20.1   Overview

Encryptions have been traditionally used to keep information confidential. But some critital information such as missile launch code requires reliability as well as confidentiality. It could be disastrous if it is lost. Traditional encryption methods are not suitable for achieving high levels of reliability because keeping multiple copies of the same information encrypted in different locations may lead to additional attacks. To address this problem, secret sharing was proposed independently by Adi Shamir [90] and George Blakley [16] in 1979.

Secret sharing (also called secret splitting) is a method for distributing a secret among a group of participants, where each of them is allocated a share of the secret and the secret can be reconstructed only when a sufficient number of shares are combined together. Let us suppose that there is one dealer and n players. The dealer sets the specific conditions (e.g., t: threshold) and gives a share of the secret to the players, so that the players are able to reconstruct the secret when more than t different shares are gathered; otherwise they cannot reconstruct the secret. Such a system is called a (t, n)-threshold scheme (sometimes also written as an (n, t)-threshold scheme interchangeably).

20.2   Efficient Secret Sharing

Trivial $t = n$ schemes can be used to reveal a secret to any desired subsets of the players simply by applying the scheme for each subset. For example, to reveal a secret s to any two of the three players Alice, Bob, and Carol, we create three different $(2, 2)$ secret shares for s (e.g., $a_1 = r_1$, $a_2 = s - r_1$, $b_1 = r_2$, $b_2 = s - r_2$, $c_1 = r_3$, $c_2 = s - r_3$), giving the three sets of two shares to Alice and Bob, Alice and Carol, and Bob and Carol (e.g., Alice has $a_1 = r_1$ and $b_2 = s - r_2$, Bob has $b_1 = r_2$ and $c_2 = s - r_3$, and Carol has $c_1 = r_3$ and $a_2 = s - r_1$).

However, the trivial approach raises space efficiency problem because as n increases, the players are required to maintain a larger number of subsets. For example, when revealing a secret to any 30 of 50 players, it requires $\binom{50}{30} \approx 4.7 \times 10^{13}$ schemes to be created and each player to maintain $\binom{49}{29} \approx 2.8 \times 10^{13}$ distinct sets of shares for each scheme. To solve this problem, schemes that allow secrets to be shared efficiently with a threshold of players have been developed.

20.2.1   Shamir's Secret Sharing [90]

In this scheme, any t out of n shares can be used to recover the secret. The system bases on the idea that a unique polynomial of degree $(t - 1)$ can be obtained from any set of t points that lie on the polynomial. It takes two points to define a straight line, three points to fully define a quadratic, four points to define a cubic curve, and so on. That is, it takes t points to define a polynomial of degree $t - 1$. The method is to create a polynomial of degree $t - 1$ with the secret as the first coefficient and the remaining coefficients picked at random. Next find n points on the curve and give one to each of the players. When at least t out of the n players reveal their points, there is sufficient information to get a $(t-1)$-th degree polynomial to them, the first coefficient being the secret.

20.2.1.1 Mathematical Definition

The goal is to divide secret S (that is, a safe combination) into n pieces of data $S_1, \ldots, S_n$ in such a way that

1. Knowledge of any t or more S_i pieces makes S easily computable. That is, the complete secret S can be reconstructed from any combination of t pieces of data.

2. Knowledge of any $t - 1$ or fewer S_i pieces leaves S completely undetermined. That is, the secret S cannot be reconstructed with fewer than t pieces.

20.2.1.2 The Construction

As mentioned above, the essential idea of Adi Shamir's threshold scheme is that it takes t points to define a polynomial of degree $t - 1$.

Suppose we want to use a (t, n) threshold scheme to share our secret S, which are without loss of generality assumed to be an element in a finite field $\mathbb{F}$ of size P where $0 < t \leq n < P$, $S < P$, and P is a prime number.

Choose at random $t - 1$ positive integers $a_1, \cdots, a_{t-1}$ with $a_i < P$ and let $a_0 = S$. Build the polynomial $f(x) = a_0 + a_1 x + a_2 x^2 + a_3 x^3 + \cdot + a_{t-1} x^{t-1}$. Let us construct any n points out of it, for instance set $i = 1, \cdots, n$ to retrieve $(i, f(i))$. Every participant is given a point (a non-zero integer input to the polynomial, and the corresponding integer output) along with the prime which defines the finite field to use. Given any subset of t of these pairs, we can find the coefficients of the polynomial using interpolation. The secret is the constant term a_0.

20.2.1.3 Example

The following example illustrates the basic idea. Note that calculations in the example are done using integer arithmetic rather than using finite field arithmetic. Therefore the example below does not provide perfect secrecy and is not a true example of Shamir's scheme. So we will explain this problem and show the right way to implement it using finite field arithmetic.

1. Suppose that our secret is 2357 ($S = 2357$).

2. We wish to divide the secret into 7 parts ($n = 7$), where any subset of 5 parts ($k = 5$) is sufficient to reconstruct the secret. It means that it is $(5, 7)$ secret-sharing scheme. At random we obtain four

$(t-1)$ numbers: 904, 282, 710, and 21. ($a_0 = 2357, a_1 = 904, a_2 = 282, a_3 = 710, a_4 = 21$).

3. We construct 7 points $D_{x-1} = (x, f(x) = a_0 + a_1 x + a_2 x^2 + a_3 x^3 + a_4 x^4)$ from the polynomial as
$D_0 = (1, 4274), D_1 = (2, 11309), D_2 = (3, 28478), D_3 = (4, 61301), D_4 = (5, 115802), D_5 = (6, 198509), D_6 = (7, 316454)$.

We give each participant a different single point (both x and $f(x)$). Since we use D_{x-1} instead of D_x, the points start from $(1, f(1))$, not from $(0, f(0))$. This is necessary because $f(0)$ is the secret.

Reconstruction

In order to reconstruct the secret, any 5 points will be enough.

Let us consider $(x_0, y_0) = (1, 4274)$, $(x_1, y_1) = (3, 28478)$, $(x_2, y_2) = (5, 115802)$, $(x_3, y_3) = (6, 198509)$, $(x_4, y_4) = (7, 316454)$.

We can drive the secret $f(0)$ in the following way.

$$l_0 = \frac{x_1}{x_1 - x_0} \cdot \frac{x_2}{x_2 - x_0} \cdot \frac{x_3}{x_3 - x_0} \cdot \frac{x_4}{x_4 - x_0} = \frac{3}{3-1} \cdot \frac{5}{5-1} \cdot \frac{6}{6-1} \cdot \frac{7}{7-1} = \frac{630}{240},$$

$$l_1 = \frac{x_0}{x_0 - x_1} \cdot \frac{x_2}{x_2 - x_1} \cdot \frac{x_3}{x_3 - x_1} \cdot \frac{x_4}{x_4 - x_1} = \frac{1}{1-3} \cdot \frac{5}{5-3} \cdot \frac{6}{6-3} \cdot \frac{7}{7-3} = \frac{210}{-48},$$

$$l_2 = \frac{x_0}{x_0 - x_2} \cdot \frac{x_1}{x_1 - x_2} \cdot \frac{x_3}{x_3 - x_2} \cdot \frac{x_4}{x_4 - x_2} = \frac{1}{1-5} \cdot \frac{3}{3-5} \cdot \frac{6}{6-5} \cdot \frac{7}{7-5} = \frac{126}{16},$$

$$l_3 = \frac{x_0}{x_0 - x_3} \cdot \frac{x_1}{x_1 - x_3} \cdot \frac{x_2}{x_2 - x_3} \cdot \frac{x_4}{x_4 - x_3} = \frac{1}{1-6} \cdot \frac{3}{3-6} \cdot \frac{5}{5-6} \cdot \frac{7}{7-6} = \frac{105}{-15},$$

$$l_4 = \frac{x_0}{x_0 - x_4} \cdot \frac{x_1}{x_1 - x_4} \cdot \frac{x_2}{x_2 - x_4} \cdot \frac{x_3}{x_3 - x_4} = \frac{1}{1-7} \cdot \frac{3}{3-7} \cdot \frac{5}{5-7} \cdot \frac{6}{6-7} = \frac{90}{48}.$$

Finally,

$$f(0) = \sum_{j=1}^{k} f(j) l_{j-1} = 4274 \frac{630}{240} + 28478 \frac{210}{-48} +$$

$$115802 \frac{126}{16} + 198509 \frac{105}{-15} + 316454 \frac{90}{48} = 2357.$$

Problem and solution

Although the above method works fine, there is a security problem that an adversary gains a lot of information about S with every D_i that it finds, because the method uses integer arithmetic. By using finite field arithmetic, this problem can be solved without a big change.

20.2.2 Blakley's Secret Sharing [16]

Two nonparallel lines in the same plane intersect at exactly one point. Three nonparallel planes in space intersect at exactly one point. More generally, any n nonparallel $(n-1)$-dimensional hyperplanes intersect at a specific point. The secret may be encoded as any single coordinate of the point of intersection. If the secret is encoded using all the coordinates, even if they are random, then an insider (someone in possession of one or more of the $(n-1)$-dimensional hyperplanes) gains information about the secret since he knows it must lie on his plane. If an insider can gain any more knowledge about the secret than an outsider can, then the system no longer has information theoretic security. If only one of the n coordinates is used, then the insider knows no more than an outsider (i.e., the secret must lie on the x-axis for a two-dimensional system). If each player is given enough information to define a hyperplane, the secret is recovered by calculating the planes' point of intersection and then taking a specified coordinate of that intersection.

Blakley's scheme is less space-efficient than Shamir's; while Shamir's shares are each only as large as the original secret, Blakley's shares are t times larger, where t is the threshold number of players. Blakley's scheme can be tightened by adding restrictions on which planes are usable as shares. The resulting scheme is equivalent to Shamir's polynomial system.

20.2.2.1 The Construction

Preparation

1. Pick a prime p.
2. If we wish to divide the secret, where any subset of 4 parts ($k = 4$) is sufficient to reconstruct the secret, create a point $Q(w, x, y, z)$ such that
   (a) Let w be the secret.
   (b) Choose $x, y, z \in \mathbb{Z}_p$ randomly.
3. Construct a share for each participant.
   (a) Pick $a, b, c \in \mathbb{Z}_p$ randomly, then set $d = z - aw - bx - cy \pmod{p}$.
   (b) Plane is $z = aw + bx + cy + d$.
   (c) Give each participant a different plane (a, b, c, d).

Reconstruction

1. We know that $a_i w + b_i x + c_i y - z = -d_i \pmod{p}$, $1 \le i \le 4$.

2. Yield a matrix equation

$$\begin{pmatrix} a_1 & b_1 & c_1 & -1 \\ a_2 & b_2 & c_2 & -1 \\ a_3 & b_3 & c_3 & -1 \\ a_4 & b_4 & c_4 & -1 \end{pmatrix} \begin{pmatrix} w_0 \\ x_0 \\ y_0 \\ z_0 \end{pmatrix} = \begin{pmatrix} -c_1 \\ -c_2 \\ -c_3 \\ -c_4 \end{pmatrix}.$$

3. As long as determinant of matrix is nonzero mod p, the matrix can be inverted and the secret can be found.

4. Row operations work as well.

20.2.2.2 Example

1. Let $p = 103$.

2. Suppose the share $A, ..., F$ are as follows.

   (a) $A : z = 88w + 51x + 26y + 99$

   (b) $B : z = 9w + 98x + 22y + 40$

   (c) $C : z = 100w + 70x + 35y + 26$

   (d) $D : z = 62w + 96x + 81y + 76$

   (e) $E : z = 43w + 11x + 71y + 2$

   (f) $F : z = 94w + 13x + 84y + 55$

3. To retrieve a secret, we need to use only 4 shares (e.g., A, B, C, D).

   (a) Convert A, B, C, D to:
   $$\begin{pmatrix} 88 & 51 & 26 & -1 \\ 9 & 98 & 22 & -1 \\ 100 & 70 & 35 & -1 \\ 62 & 96 & 81 & -1 \end{pmatrix} \begin{pmatrix} w \\ x \\ y \\ z \end{pmatrix} = \begin{pmatrix} -99 \\ -40 \\ -26 \\ -76 \end{pmatrix}.$$

   (b) Compute the inverse matrix of $\begin{pmatrix} 88 & 51 & 26 & -1 \\ 9 & 98 & 22 & -1 \\ 100 & 70 & 35 & -1 \\ 62 & 96 & 81 & -1 \end{pmatrix}$:

   $$\begin{pmatrix} 27 & 76 & 74 & 29 \\ 15 & 11 & 62 & 15 \\ 81 & 70 & 91 & 67 \\ 96 & 5 & 92 & 12 \end{pmatrix}.$$

   (c) Compute (w, x, y, z):
   $$\begin{pmatrix} 27 & 76 & 74 & 29 \\ 15 & 11 & 62 & 15 \\ 81 & 70 & 91 & 67 \\ 96 & 5 & 92 & 12 \end{pmatrix} \begin{pmatrix} -99 \\ -40 \\ -26 \\ -76 \end{pmatrix} = \begin{pmatrix} w \\ x \\ y \\ z \end{pmatrix} = \begin{pmatrix} 47 \\ 61 \\ 57 \\ 73 \end{pmatrix}.$$

4. The secret is 47.

Exercise

20.1 What if we remove the restriction like choosing a large prime in the above secret sharing schemes?

21

Predicate Encryption and Functional Encryption

CONTENTS

This chapter explains predicate encryption (PE) and functional encryption (FE). The first part of the chapter defines PE and provides the comparison of PE and ABE followed by the definition of FE. The next part of the chapter provides preliminaries required starting from the discussion of bilinear map and hardness assumptions. The first hardness assumption is the asymmetric decisional bilinear Diffie-Hellman. Subsequently, the external Diffie-Hellman assumption is defined. Next, the formal definitions of PE and the security notions are then discussed. Similarly, definitions of FE along with the algorithms are discussed. The next section presents the predicate-only encryption that is based on anonymous HIBE. The extension of this scheme is the PE scheme which is given in detail in the next section. The constructions and security proofs of a predicate-only encryption and a PE scheme are also given. Similarly, the final section presents the constructions and security proofs of a FE scheme. The applications of FE are then discussed including distance measurement, exact threshold, and weighted average.

21.1   Overview

In this chapter, we explain the basic concepts behind the construction of predicate encryption (PE) and functional encryption (FE).

21.1.1   Predicate Encryption

PE in [60] and [80] is a kind of public-key encryption (PKE) such as RSA, attribute-based encryption (ABE), and identity-based encryption (IBE). In PE schemes, the secret keys of users are associated with predicates $f \in \mathcal{F}$ and ciphertexts are bound to attributes $x \in \sum$. The decryption procedure is successful if and only if $f(x) = 1$. If this relation is not satisfied, decryption fails and no information about the message is leaked. Informally, an attribute is expressed as vector $\vec{x}$ and predicate $f_{\vec{v}}$ is associated with vector $\vec{v}$, where $f_{\vec{v}}(\vec{x}) = 1$ iff $\langle \vec{v}, \vec{x} \rangle = 0$. In contrast to traditional PKE schemes supporting the payload-hiding property only, PE schemes support the attribute-hiding property. While payload-hiding means that users cannot decrypt the ciphertext without the corresponding key, the attribute-hiding property makes sure that no information about attribute x is leaked during the decryption process. Also, PE schemes enable constructions in which the predicates correspond to the evaluations of disjunctions, conjunctions, polynomials, CNF formula, DNF formula, and threshold. As a result, such schemes can achieve high flexibility in terms of access control. In addition, a PE supporting "inner product" can be used as a primitive to construct additional schemes such as anonymous identity-based encryption and hidden-vector encryption.

Comparison of ABE and PE

Note that the attribute exposure problem is inherent in ABE because the attributes are stored in each user's storage (e.g., CP-ABE) or transmitted with ciphertext to receivers without any encoding (e.g., KP-ABE). However, because PE schemes basically support the attribute-hiding property, it does not have the attribute exposure problem.

Why is attribute-hiding important?

The decryptor can collect information using direct decryption, then infer important meanings from them through indirect methods such as big data processing technologies.

For example, a credit card company commonly uses attributes such as the identity of the owner and date/amount/place of purchase. This information may then be used to create a profile of the user's purchase style. For a military application, attributes could include position, number of participants, and area/period of operation. Analyzing the surrounding situations from encrypted communications and the ensuing operation may allow an attacker to obtain hints about the future troop movements and encrypted communications. In the medical field, we can also see the importance of ensuring privacy in data transmissions. Although medical data usually require a high degree of privacy, they are referenced by many entities such as the patient himself/herself or staff (e.g., doctors, nurses, technicians) from various departments or belonging to different medical institutions. Even partial exposure of those attributes could hurt the patient's privacy.

21.1.2   Functional Encryption

FE in [69] and [26] is a new paradigm of PKE used to calculate a particular function using the encrypted data without retrieving the original data. Also, it can overcome the all-or-nothing approach which inherently allows a user to either access a full message or obtain nothing depending on whether or not a proper secret key is presented in the traditional PKE. Over the last few decades, a number of primitives such as IBE, ABE, and PE have been introduced for providing more fine-grained access control which is highly desirable for modern applications. Recently, such studies have been generalized to FE.

In FE, the owner of the MSK (master secret key) can generate a secret key SK_f for a function f. Given the ciphertext $C(x)$ of a message x, the result of $f(x)$ is available to a user by decrypting $C(x)$ with SK_f. In this case, only the information about $f(x)$, that is, the result of the function f, is exposed, but no information about x can be published.

Why do we focus on inner product functionality?

To design an efficient FE scheme that can provide a sufficient expressiveness applicable to the real world, numerous studies have focused on applicable inner product functionality. By extending the ciphertext to any monomials that appear in the desired family of polynomials, an inner product can be made sufficient to calculate arbitrary polynomial evaluations. As a result, inner product encryption has been established as a useful tool in building FE associated with both secret key and ciphertext vectors.

Figures 21.1, 21.2, and 21.3 show the difference of ABE, PE, and FE.

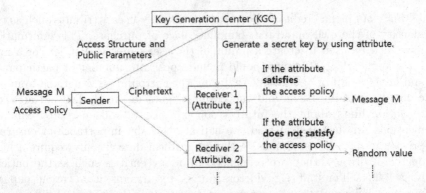

FIGURE 21.1
Attribute-based encryption.

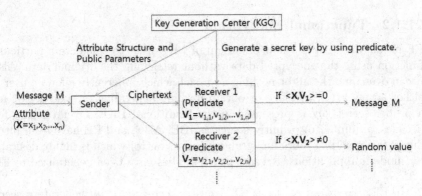

FIGURE 21.2
Predicate encryption.

In ABE (e.g., CP-ABE), a sender encrypts a message according to access policy he chooses and broadcasts the resulting ciphertext. When a receiver gets the ciphertext, he tries to decrypt it. If the receiver's attribute satisfies the access policy of the ciphertext, he can retrieve the message from the ciphertext. On the other hand, if the receiver's attribute does not satisfy the access policy of the ciphertext, he cannot retrieve the message from the ciphertext.

In PE (supporting inner product), a sender encrypts a message according to attribute vector he chooses and broadcasts the resulting ciphertext. When a receiver gets the ciphertext, he tries to decrypt it. If the result of inner product of both the receiver's predicate vector and the attribute vector of the ciphertext is 0, he can retrieve the message from the ciphertext. On the other hand, if the result of inner product of both the receiver's predicate vector and

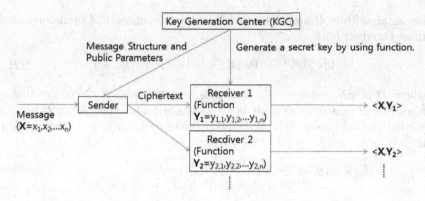

FIGURE 21.3
Functional encryption.

the attribute vector of the ciphertext is not 0, he cannot retrieve the message from the ciphertext.

In FE (for inner products evaluations), a sender encrypts a message vector and broadcasts the resulting ciphertext. When a receiver gets the ciphertext, he tries to decrypt it for getting the result of inner product of both the receiver's function vector and the message vector of the ciphertext. Unlike other schemes (e.g., ABE and PE), since FE basically outputs the function result instead of the message itself, all receivers which have a valid secret key can get the function result.

21.2 Preliminaries

This section provides fundamentals and definitions of PE and FE.

21.2.1 Hardness Assumptions

Asymmetric Decisional Bilinear Diffie-Hellman (DBDH)

Consider the following two distributions: For $g \in \mathbb{G}_1$, $h \in \mathbb{G}_2$, $a, b, c \in \mathbb{Z}_p^*$, and $T \in \mathbb{G}_T$ chosen uniformly at random, we define

1. $\mathcal{P}_A = \left(g, g^a, g^c, h, h^a, h^b, e(g,h)^{abc}\right) \in \mathbb{G}_1^3 \times \mathbb{G}_2^3 \times \mathbb{G}_T$,
2. $\mathcal{R}_A = \left(g, g^a, g^c, h, h^a, h^b, T\right) \in \mathbb{G}_1^3 \times \mathbb{G}_2^3 \times \mathbb{G}_T$.

For an algorithm $\mathcal{A}$, we let $Adv_{\mathcal{A}}^{DBDH}$ be the advantage of $\mathcal{A}$ in distinguishing these two distributions as

$$Adv_{\mathcal{A}}^{DBDH} = |Pr[\mathcal{A}(D) = 1] - Pr[\mathcal{A}(R) = 1]|, \qquad (21.1)$$

where D is sampled from $\mathcal{P}_A$ and R is sampled from $\mathcal{R}_A$. We say that an algorithm $\mathcal{B}$ that outputs a bit in $\{0, 1\}$ has the advantage $Adv_{\mathcal{A}}^{DBDH} = \epsilon$ in solving the Decisional Bilinear Diffie-Hellman problem in asymmetric paring if

$$|Pr[\mathcal{B}(g, g^a, g^c, h, h^a, h^b, e(g, h)^{abc}) = 0] - $$
$$Pr[\mathcal{B}(g, g^a, g^c, h, h^a, h^b, T) = 0]| \geq \epsilon,$$

where the probability is over the random choice of generator $g \in \mathbb{G}_1$ and $h \in \mathbb{G}_2$, exponents $a, b, c \in \mathbb{Z}_p^*$, $T \in \mathbb{G}_T$ and the random bits used by $\mathcal{B}$.

As usual, to state the assumption asymptotically, we rely on a bilinear group generator $\mathcal{G}$ that takes a security parameter λ as input and outputs the description of a bilinear group.

Definition 1 *Let $\mathcal{G}$ be a bilinear group generator. We say that* **DBDH** *holds for $\mathcal{G}$ if, for all probabilistic polynomial-time (PPT) algorithms $\mathcal{A}$, the function $Adv_{\mathcal{A}}^{DBDH}(\lambda)$ is a negligible function of λ.*

$\mathcal{P}$-Asymmetric Decisional Bilinear Diffie-Hellman ($\mathcal{P}$-DBDH)

Consider the following two distributions: For $g \in \mathbb{G}_1$, $h \in \mathbb{G}_2$, $a, b, c \in \mathbb{Z}_p^*$ and $T \in \mathbb{G}_1$ chosen uniformly at random, we define

1. $\mathcal{D}_N = \left(g, g^a, g^{ab}, g^c, h, h^a, h^b, g^{abc}\right) \in \mathbb{G}_1^4 \times \mathbb{G}_2^3 \times \mathbb{G}_1$,
2. $\mathcal{D}_R = \left(g, g^a, g^{ab}, g^c, h, h^a, h^b, T\right) \in \mathbb{G}_1^4 \times \mathbb{G}_2^3 \times \mathbb{G}_1$.

For an algorithm $\mathcal{A}$, we let $Adv_{\mathcal{A}}^{\mathcal{P}\text{-}DBDH}$ be the advantage of $\mathcal{A}$ in distinguishing these two distributions

$$Adv_{\mathcal{A}}^{\mathcal{P}\text{-}DBDH} = |Pr[\mathcal{A}(N) = 1] - Pr[\mathcal{A}(P) = 1]|, \qquad (21.2)$$

where N is sampled from $\mathcal{D}_N$ and P is sampled from $\mathcal{D}_R$. We say that an algorithm $\mathcal{B}$ that outputs a bit in $\{0, 1\}$ has the advantage $Adv_{\mathcal{A}}^{\mathcal{P}\text{-}DBDH} = \epsilon_{\mathcal{P}}$ in solving the $\mathcal{P}$-DBDH problem in asymmetric paring if

$$|Pr[\mathcal{B}(g, g^a, g^{ab}, g^c, h, h^a, h^b, g^{abc}) = 0] - $$
$$Pr[\mathcal{B}(g, g^a, g^{ab}, g^c, h, h^a, h^b, T) = 0]| \geq \epsilon_{\mathcal{P}},$$

where the probability is over the random choice of generator $g \in \mathbb{G}_1$ and $h \in \mathbb{G}_2$, exponents $a, b, c \in \mathbb{Z}_p^*$, $T \in \mathbb{G}_1$, and the random bits used by $\mathcal{B}$.

Definition 2 *Let $\mathcal{G}$ be a bilinear group generator. We say that* **$\mathcal{P}$-DBDH** *holds for $\mathcal{G}$ if, for all PPT algorithms $\mathcal{A}$, the function $Adv_{\mathcal{A}}^{\mathcal{P}\text{-}DBDH}(\lambda)$ is a negligible function of λ.*

External Diffie-Hellman (XDH)

Consider the following two distributions: For $g \in \mathbb{G}_1$, $h \in \mathbb{G}_2$, $a, b \in \mathbb{Z}_p^*$ and $T \in \mathbb{G}_1$ chosen uniformly at random, we define

1. $\mathcal{D}_N = \left(g, g^a, g^b, h, g^{ab}\right) \in \mathbb{G}_1^3 \times \mathbb{G}_2 \times \mathbb{G}_1$,
2. $\mathcal{D}_R = \left(g, g^a, g^b, h, T\right) \in \mathbb{G}_1^3 \times \mathbb{G}_2 \times \mathbb{G}_1$.

For an algorithm $\mathcal{A}$, we let $Adv_{\mathcal{A}}^{XDH}$ be the advantage of $\mathcal{A}$ in distinguishing these two distributions

$$Adv_{\mathcal{A}}^{XDH} = |Pr[\mathcal{A}(N) = 1] - Pr[\mathcal{A}(P) = 1]|, \qquad (21.3)$$

where N is sampled from $\mathcal{D}_N$ and P is sampled from $\mathcal{D}_R$. We say that an algorithm $\mathcal{B}$ that outputs a bit in $\{0, 1\}$ has the advantage $Adv_{\mathcal{A}}^{XDH} = \epsilon$ in solving the XDH problem in asymmetric pairing if

$$|Pr[\mathcal{B}(g, g^a, g^b, h, g^{ab}) = 0] - Pr[\mathcal{B}(g, g^a, g^b, h, T) = 0]| \geq \epsilon,$$

where the probability is over the random choice of generator $g \in \mathbb{G}_1$ and $h \in \mathbb{G}_2$, exponents $a, b \in \mathbb{Z}_p^*$, $T \in \mathbb{G}_1$ and the random bits used by $\mathcal{B}$.

Definition 3 *Let $\mathcal{G}$ be a bilinear group generator. We say that* **XDH** *holds for $\mathcal{G}$ if, for all PPT algorithms $\mathcal{A}$, the function $Adv_{\mathcal{A}}^{XDH}(\lambda)$ is a negligible function of λ.*

21.2.2 Definition of Predicate Encryption

Below are the formal definitions and security notion of predicate encryption.

Definition 4 *A* **predicate encryption scheme** *for the class of predicates $\mathcal{F}$ over the set of attributes $\sum$ consists of PPT algorithms Setup, Gen, Encrypt, and Decrypt. They are given as follows.*

1. **Setup**(λ) *takes as input the security parameter λ. It outputs the public parameters PP and the master secret key MSK.*

2. **Gen**$(PP, MSK, \vec{v})$ *takes as input the public parameters PP, the master secret key MSK and the predicate vector $\vec{v} \neq \vec{0}$. It outputs a corresponding secret key $sk_{\vec{v}}$.*

3. **Encrypt**$(PP, M, \vec{x})$ *takes as input the public parameters PP, the message M and the attribute vector $\vec{x}$. It outputs the ciphertext C.*

4. **Decrypt**$(sk_{\vec{v}}, C)$ takes as input the secret key $sk_{\vec{v}}$ and the ciphertext C. It outputs the message M or a random value.

For correctness, we require that for all (PP, MSK) generated by Setup(λ), all $\vec{v} \in \mathcal{F}$, any key $sk_{\vec{v}} \leftarrow Gen(PP, MSK, \vec{v})$ and all attribute vector $\vec{x} \in \sum$

1. If $\langle \vec{x}, \vec{v} \rangle = 0$,
   then **Decrypt**$(sk_{\vec{v}}, \textbf{Encrypt}(PP, M, \vec{x})) = M$.

2. If $\langle \vec{x}, \vec{v} \rangle \neq 0$,
   then **Decrypt**$(sk_{\vec{v}}, \textbf{Encrypt}(PP, M, \vec{x})) = \perp$ with all but negligible probability.

We further consider a variant of the above, called a predicate-only encryption scheme. Compared with a predicate encryption scheme, the difference is that in a predicate-only encryption scheme, an encryption algorithm takes as input only a vector $\vec{x}$, and its corresponding decryption algorithm **Decrypt**$(sk_{\vec{v}}, \textbf{Encrypt}(PP, \vec{x}))$ outputs 1 if $\langle \vec{x}, \vec{v} \rangle = 0$ and $\perp$ with all but negligible probability otherwise.

Definition 5 *An inner-product predicate encryption scheme for predicate $\mathcal{F}$ over attributes $\sum$ is* **selective attribute-secure against chosen-plaintext attacks** *if for all PPT adversary $\mathcal{A}$, the advantage of $\mathcal{A}$ in the following security game Γ_w is negligible in the security parameter.*

1. **Initialization** $\mathcal{A}$ outputs challenge attribute vectors $\vec{x}_0$ and $\vec{x}_1 \in \sum$.

2. **Setup** The challenger $\mathcal{B}$ runs **Setup**(λ) for generating the public parameters PP and the master secret key MSK and sends PP to $\mathcal{A}$.

3. **Phase I** $\mathcal{A}$ may adaptively make a polynomial number of queries to create a secret key for a predicate $\vec{v} \in \mathcal{F}$ subject to the restrictions that $\langle \vec{x}_0, \vec{v} \rangle \neq 0$ and $\langle \vec{x}_1, \vec{v} \rangle \neq 0$. $\mathcal{B}$ creates a secret key and sends it to $\mathcal{A}$.

4. **Challenge** $\mathcal{A}$ outputs challenge messages M_0 and M_1. $\mathcal{B}$ chooses a random bit w. $\mathcal{A}$ is given $C \leftarrow \textbf{Encrypt}(PP, M_w, \vec{x}_w)$.

5. **Phase II** $\mathcal{A}$ may continue to request secret keys for additional predicate vectors subject to the restrictions given in Phase I.

6. **Guess** $\mathcal{A}$ outputs a bit w', and succeeds if $w' = w$.

For $w \in \{0, 1\}$, let W_w be the event for $w = w'$ in Game Γ_w and define $\mathcal{A}$'s advantage as

$$Adv^{IND\text{-}sAH\text{-}CPA}(\lambda) = |Pr[W_0] - Pr[W_1]|. \tag{21.4}$$

The above game can be used to define the attribute-hiding property for the predicate-only encryption scheme if the adversary does not output messages in the challenge phase. Naturally, the challenge ciphertext is given to $\mathcal{A}$ as $C \leftarrow$ **Encrypt**$(PP, \vec{x}_w)$. Under this slight modification with a similar $Adv^{IND\text{-}sAH\text{-}CPA}(\lambda)$ as the one above, we say that a predicate-only encryption scheme is attribute-hiding if for all PPT adversary $\mathcal{A}$, $Adv^{IND\text{-}sAH\text{-}CPA}(\lambda)$ is negligible.

21.2.3 Definition of Functional Encryption

Below are formal definition and security notion of functional encryption.

Definition 6 *A* **functionality** *F defined over $(\mathcal{Y}, \mathcal{X})$ is a function $F :$ $\mathcal{Y} \times \mathcal{X} \to \sum$, where $\mathcal{Y}$ is the key space, $\mathcal{X}$ is the message space, and $\sum$ is the output space.*

Definition 7 *A* **functional encryption scheme** *for functionality F consists of PPT algorithms Setup, Gen, Encrypt, and Decrypt. They are given as follows.*

1. **Setup**(λ, n) takes as input the security parameter λ and the vector length parameter n. It outputs the public parameters PP and the master secret key MSK.

2. **Gen**$(PP, MSK, \vec{y})$ takes as input the public parameters PP, the master secret key MSK, and the key vector $\vec{y} \in \mathcal{Y} \setminus \{\vec{0}\}$. It outputs a corresponding secret key $SK_{\vec{y}}$.

3. **Encrypt**$(PP, \vec{x})$ takes as input the public parameters PP and the message vector $\vec{x} \in \mathcal{X}$. It outputs the ciphertext C.

4. **Decrypt**$(SK_{\vec{y}}, C)$ takes as input the secret key $SK_{\vec{y}}$ and the ciphertext C. It outputs $\langle \vec{x}, \vec{y} \rangle$.

For correctness, we require that for all (PP, MSK) generated by **Setup**(λ), all $\vec{y} \in \mathcal{Y} \setminus \{\vec{0}\}$, any key $SK_{\vec{y}} \leftarrow$ **Gen**$(PP, MSK, \vec{y})$, and all message vector $\vec{x} \in \mathcal{X}$, we have **Decrypt**$(SK_{\vec{y}},$ **Encrypt**$(PP, \vec{x})) = \langle \vec{x}, \vec{y} \rangle$ with all but negligible probability.

Definition 8 *A functional encryption scheme for functionality F is* **selectively secure against chosen-plaintext attacks** *if for all PPT adversary $\mathcal{A}$, the advantage of $\mathcal{A}$ in the following security game Γ_w is negligible in the security parameter.*

1. **Initialization** $\mathcal{A}$ outputs challenge message vectors $\vec{x}_0$ and $\vec{x}_1 \in \mathcal{X}$.

2. **Setup** The challenger $\mathcal{B}$ runs **Setup**(λ, n) for generating the public parameters PP, the master secret key MSK, and sends PP to $\mathcal{A}$.

3. **Phase I** $\mathcal{A}$ may adaptively make a polynomial number of queries to create a secret key for a key vector $\vec{y} \in \mathcal{Y} \setminus \{\vec{0}\}$ subject to the restrictions that $\langle \vec{x}_0, \vec{y} \rangle = \langle \vec{x}_1, \vec{y} \rangle$. $\mathcal{B}$ creates a secret key $SK_{\vec{y}}$ and sends it to $\mathcal{A}$.

4. **Challenge** $\mathcal{B}$ chooses a random bit w. $\mathcal{A}$ is given $C \leftarrow$ **Encrypt**$(PP, \vec{x}_w)$.

5. **Phase II** $\mathcal{A}$ may continue to request secret keys for additional key vectors subject to the restrictions given in Phase I.

6. **Guess** $\mathcal{A}$ outputs a bit w' and succeeds if $w' = w$.

For $w \in \{0, 1\}$, let W_w be the event for $w = w'$ in Game Γ_w and define $\mathcal{A}$'s advantage as

$$Adv^{IND\text{-}sCPA}(\lambda) = |Pr[W_0] - Pr[W_1]|. \qquad (21.5)$$

21.3   Predicate-Only Encryption [62]

In this section, we present a predicate-only encryption scheme under the $\mathcal{P}$-DBDH assumption. In the next section, we describe how to extend the present scheme to obtain a predicate encryption scheme.

Construction 1. Predicate-only encryption

Setup (λ) Given a security parameter $\lambda \in \mathbb{Z}^+$

1. Run $\mathcal{G}$ on input λ to generate a prime q ($|q| = \lambda$), three groups $\mathbb{G}_1$, $\mathbb{G}_2$ and $\mathbb{G}_T$ of order q, and $\hat{e}: \mathbb{G}_1 \times \mathbb{G}_2 \rightarrow \mathbb{G}_T$. Choose two random generators $g \in \mathbb{G}_1$ and $h \in \mathbb{G}_2$.

2. Select random $(\gamma, a_1, \cdots, a_n, z) \in (\mathbb{Z}_p^*)^{n+2}$.

3. Compute as follows.

   (a) $g_1 = g^{\gamma}, g_{2,1} = g^{a_1}, \cdots, g_{2,n} = g^{a_n}, g_0 = g^z \in \mathbb{G}_1$,
   (b) $h_1 = h^{\gamma}, h_{2,1} = h^{a_1}, \cdots, h_{2,n} = h^{a_n} \in \mathbb{G}_2$.

4. The public parameters are $PP = (g, g_0, g_1, g_{2,1}, \cdots, g_{2,n}) \in \mathbb{G}_1^{n+3}$.

5. The master secret key is $MSK = (h, h_1, h_{2,1}, \cdots, h_{2,n}) \in \mathbb{G}_2^{n+2}$.

Note that n is the dimension of the attribute/predicate vectors.

Gen$(PP, MSK, \vec{v})$ For the predicates $\vec{v} \in \mathcal{F}$

1. Pick random $r, R \in \mathbb{Z}_p^*$.
2. Compute as follows.
   - (a) $k_1 = \prod_{i=1}^{n} (h_{2,i})^{v_i r} h_1^R$,
   - (b) $k_2 = h^r$,
   - (c) $k_3 = h^R$.
3. The secret key is $sk_{\vec{v}} = (k_1, k_2, k_3, \vec{v}) \in \mathbb{G}_2^3 \times (\mathbb{Z}_p^*)^n$.

Encrypt$(PP, \vec{x})$ For the attribute set $\vec{x} \in \sum$

1. Pick a random $s \in \mathbb{Z}_p^*$.
2. Compute as follows.
   - (a) $c_1 = g^s$,
   - (b) $c_{2,i} = g_0^{x_i s} (g_{2,i})^s$ for $1 \le i \le n$,
   - (c) $c_3 = g_1^s$.
3. The ciphertext is $C = (c_1, c_{2,1}, \cdots, c_{2,n}, c_3) \in \mathbb{G}_1^{n+2}$.

Decrypt$(sk_{\vec{v}}, C)$ To decrypt a given ciphertext $C = (c_1, c_{2,1}, \cdots, c_{2,n}, c_3) \in \mathbb{G}_1^{n+2}$ using the secret key $sk_{\vec{v}} = (k_1, k_2, k_3, \vec{v}) \in \mathbb{G}_2^3 \times (\mathbb{Z}_p^*)^n$, compute

$$\frac{e\left(\prod_{i=1}^{n} (c_{2,i})^{v_i}, k_2\right) \cdot e(c_3, k_3)}{e(c_1, k_1)} \in \mathbb{G}_T.$$

Correctness To see that correctness holds, let C and $sk_{\vec{v}}$ be as above. Then

$$e\left(\prod_{i=1}^{n} (c_{2,i})^{v_i}, k_2\right) \cdot e(c_3, k_3) \cdot e(c_1, k_1)^{-1}$$
$$= e\left(\prod_{i=1}^{n} (g_0^{x_i s} (g_{2,i})^s)^{v_i}, h^r\right) \cdot e\left(g_1^s, h^R\right) \cdot e\left(g^s, \prod_{i=1}^{n} (h_{2,i})^{v_i r} h_1^R\right)^{-1}$$
$$= e\left(\prod_{i=1}^{n} (g^{z x_i v_i s} g^{a_i v_i s}), h^r\right) \cdot e\left(g^{\gamma s}, h^R\right) \cdot e\left(g^s, \prod_{i=1}^{n} h^{a_i v_i r} h^{\gamma R}\right)^{-1}$$
$$= e\left(g^{zs\langle \vec{x}, \vec{v} \rangle} g^{\langle \vec{a}, \vec{v} \rangle s}, h^r\right) \cdot e\left(g^{\gamma s}, h^R\right) \cdot e\left(g^s, h^{\langle \vec{a}, \vec{v} \rangle r} h^{\gamma R}\right)^{-1}$$
$$= e\left(g^{zs\langle \vec{x}, \vec{v} \rangle}, h^r\right) \cdot e\left(g^{\langle \vec{a}, \vec{v} \rangle s}, h^r\right) \cdot e\left(g^{\gamma s}, h^R\right) \cdot e\left(g^s, h^{\langle \vec{a}, \vec{v} \rangle r}\right)^{-1} \cdot e\left(g^s, h^{\gamma R}\right)^{-1}$$
$$= e(g, h)^{zsr\langle \vec{x}, \vec{v} \rangle} \cdot e(g, h)^{\langle \vec{a}, \vec{v} \rangle sr} \cdot e(g, h)^{\gamma sR} \cdot e(g, h)^{-\langle \vec{a}, \vec{v} \rangle sr} \cdot e(g, h)^{-s\gamma R}$$
$$= e(g, h)^{zsr\langle \vec{x}, \vec{v} \rangle} \in \mathbb{G}_T.$$

If $\langle \vec{x}, \vec{v} \rangle = 0$, then we can get 1.

21.3.1   Proof of Predicate-Only Encryption Security

The following theorem proves the security of this scheme under the $\mathcal{P}$-DBDH assumption.

Theorem 1 The predicate-only encryption scheme is selectively attribute-hiding secure against chosen plaintext attacks in the standard model under the $\mathcal{P}$-DBDH assumption. For all PPT algorithms $\mathcal{B}$, the function $Adv_{\mathcal{B}}^{IND-sAH-CPA}(\lambda)$ is a negligible function of λ.

Proof The proof proceeds by a hybrid argument across a number of games. Let $C = (B, C_1, \cdots, C_n, D) \in \mathbb{G}_1^{n+2}$ denote the challenge ciphertext given to the adversary during two real attacks (Γ_0 and Γ_1). Additionally, let $R_1, \cdots, R_n$ and R' be random elements of $\mathbb{G}_1$. We define the following hybrid experiments, which differ in how the challenge ciphertext is generated as follows.

1. Game $\Gamma_{0,1}$: This game is the original security game, where the challenge attribute is $\vec{x}_0$ and the challenge ciphertext is $C = (B, C_1, \cdots, C_n, D)$.

2. Game $\Gamma_{0,2}$: In this game, element D of the ciphertext is changed to a random element R' of $\mathbb{G}_1$. The challenge attribute is the same as for $\Gamma_{0,1}$, but the challenge ciphertext is $C = (B, C_1, \cdots, C_n, R')$.

3. Game $\Gamma_{0,3}$: In this game, elements $C_1, \cdots, C_n$ of the ciphertext are changed to the random elements $R_1, \cdots, R_n$ of $\mathbb{G}_1$. The element R' and challenge attribute are the same as for $\Gamma_{0,2}$, but the challenge ciphertext is $C = (B, R_1, \cdots, R_n, R')$.
    For the security proof, we additionally define a sequence of games $\Gamma_{0,2,1}, \Gamma_{0,2,2}, \cdots, \Gamma_{0,2,n}$, where $\Gamma_{0,2} = \Gamma_{0,2,0}$ and $\Gamma_{0,3} = \Gamma_{0,2,n} = \Gamma_{1,3}$. In the game $\Gamma_{0,2,j}$ for $1 \leq j \leq n$, the first j-th attribute elements are random numbers in $\mathbb{Z}_p^*$, and the remaining attribute elements are the elements in the challenge attribute with the challenge ciphertext $C = (B, R_1, \cdots, R_j, C_{j+1}, \cdots, C_n, R')$.

4. Game $\Gamma_{1,3}$: This game is almost the same as $\Gamma_{0,3}$ except that the challenge attribute is $\vec{x}_1$ and the challenge ciphertext is $C = (B, R_1, \cdots, R_n, R')$.

5. Game $\Gamma_{1,2}$: This game is almost the same as $\Gamma_{0,2}$ except that the challenge attribute is $\vec{x}_1$ and the challenge ciphertext is $C = (B, C_1, \cdots, C_n, R')$.

6. Game $\Gamma_{1,1}$: This game is almost the same as $\Gamma_{0,1}$ except that the challenge attribute is $\vec{x}_1$ and the challenge ciphertext is $C = (B, C_1, \cdots, C_n, D)$.

$\Gamma_{0,1}$ and $\Gamma_{1,1}$ are the same as games Γ_0 and Γ_1 in Definition 5, respectively. Therefore,

$$Adv_{\mathcal{B}}^{IND\text{-}sAH\text{-}CPA}(\lambda) \leq \left| Pr[\mathcal{A}^{\Gamma_{0,1}} = 0] - Pr[\mathcal{A}^{\Gamma_{1,1}} = 0] \right|. \tag{21.6}$$

To prove that $\Gamma_{0,1}$ is indistinguishable from $\Gamma_{1,1}$, we prove that each step of the hybrid argument is indistinguishable from the next.

Lemma 1 Let $\mathcal{A}$ be an adversary playing the $IND\text{-}sAH\text{-}CPA$ attack game. Then, there exists an algorithm $\mathcal{B}$ solving the $\mathcal{P}$-DBDH problem such that

$$\left| Pr[\mathcal{A}^{\Gamma_{w,1}} = 0] - Pr[\mathcal{A}^{\Gamma_{w,2}} = 0] \right| \leq Adv_{\mathcal{B}}^{\mathcal{P}\text{-}DBDH}.$$

Lemma 2 Let $\mathcal{A}$ be an adversary playing the $IND\text{-}sAH\text{-}CPA$ attack game. Then, there exists an algorithm $\mathcal{B}$ solving the $\mathcal{P}$-DBDH problem such that

$$\left| Pr[\mathcal{A}^{\Gamma_{w,2,j-1}} = 0] - Pr[\mathcal{A}^{\Gamma_{w,2,j}} = 0] \right| \leq Adv_{\mathcal{B}}^{\mathcal{P}\text{-}DBDH}. \tag{21.7}$$

In Lemma 1 and 2, $w \in \{0, 1\}$.

Thus, if there is no algorithm $\mathcal{B}$ that solves the $\mathcal{P}$-DBDH problem with an advantage better than $\epsilon_{\mathcal{P}}$, for all adversary $\mathcal{A}$,
$|Pr[\mathcal{A}^{\Gamma_{0,1}} = 0] - Pr[\mathcal{A}^{\Gamma_{1,1}} = 0]| \leq$
$|Pr[\mathcal{A}^{\Gamma_{0,1}} = 0] - Pr[\mathcal{A}^{\Gamma_{0,2}} = 0]| +$
$|Pr[\mathcal{A}^{\Gamma_{0,2}} = 0] - Pr[\mathcal{A}^{\Gamma_{0,2,1}} = 0]| + \cdots +$
$|Pr[\mathcal{A}^{\Gamma_{0,2,j-1}} = 0] - Pr[\mathcal{A}^{\Gamma_{0,2,j}} = 0]| + \cdots +$
$|Pr[\mathcal{A}^{\Gamma_{0,2,n-1}} = 0] - Pr[\mathcal{A}^{\Gamma_{0,2,n}} = 0]| +$
$|Pr[\mathcal{A}^{\Gamma_{1,2,n}} = 0] - Pr[\mathcal{A}^{\Gamma_{1,2,n-1}} = 0]| + \cdots +$
$|Pr[\mathcal{A}^{\Gamma_{1,2,j}} = 0] - Pr[\mathcal{A}^{\Gamma_{1,2,j-1}} = 0]| + \cdots +$
$|Pr[\mathcal{A}^{\Gamma_{1,2,1}} = 0] - Pr[\mathcal{A}^{\Gamma_{1,2}} = 0]| +$
$|Pr[\mathcal{A}^{\Gamma_{1,2}} = 0] - Pr[\mathcal{A}^{\Gamma_{1,1}} = 0]| \leq 2(n+1)\epsilon_{\mathcal{P}}.$

Consequently, under the $\mathcal{P}$-DBDH assumption, Game $\Gamma_{0,1}$ is indistinguishable from $\Gamma_{1,1}$.

In the following, we prove Lemma 1 and 2 under the $\mathcal{P}$-DBDH assumption.

Proof of Lemma 1 Suppose $\mathcal{A}$ has an advantage $\epsilon_{\mathcal{P}}$ in distinguishing Game $\Gamma_{w,1}$ from Game $\Gamma_{w,2}$. We build an algorithm $\mathcal{B}$ that solves the $\mathcal{P}$-DBDH problem in asymmetric pairing. $\mathcal{B}$ is given as input a random 8-tuple $(g, g^a, g^{ab}, g^c, h, h^a, h^b, T)$ that is either sampled from $\mathcal{D}_N$ (where $T = g^{abc}$) or from $\mathcal{D}_R$ (where T is uniform and independent in $\mathbb{G}_1$). Algorithm $\mathcal{B}$'s goal is to output 1 if $T = g^{abc}$ and 0 otherwise. Algorithm $\mathcal{B}$ works by interacting with $\mathcal{A}$ in a selective attribute game as follows.

Reduction algorithm

Initialization The selective attribute game begins with $\mathcal{A}$ by outputting the attribute vectors $\vec{x}_0$ and $\vec{x}_1 \in \sum$ that it intends to attack.

Setup

1. Pick random exponents $z', a'_1, \cdots, a'_n \in \mathbb{Z}_p^*$.

2. Define as follows: $\vec{x} = \vec{x}_w, g_0 = g^{z'}g^a, g_1 = g^{ab}$,
   $g_{2,1} = g^{-ax_1}g^{a'_1}, \cdots, g_{2,n} = g^{-ax_n}g^{a'_n}$,
   $h_1 = h^{ab}, h_{2,1} = h^{-ax_1}h^{a'_1}, \cdots, h_{2,n} = h^{-ax_n}h^{a'_n}$.
   where a and b are the exponents which are unknown to $\mathcal{B}$,

3. Simulate the system for the following parameters
   $\gamma = ab, a_1 = -ax_1 + a'_1, \cdots, a_n = -ax_n + a'_n, z = z' + a$.

4. Send the public parameters
   $PP = (g, g_0 = g^z, g_1 = g^\gamma, g_{2,1} = g^{a_1}, \cdots, g_{2,n} = g^{a_n})$.

5. Set the master secret key
   $MSK = (h, h_1 = h^\gamma, h_{2,1} = h^{a_1}, \cdots, h_{2,n} = h^{a_n})$, where h_1 is unknown to $\mathcal{B}$.

Phase I Consider a query for the secret key corresponding to the predicate vector $\vec{v} \in \mathcal{F}$, which satisfies $\langle \vec{x}_0, \vec{v} \rangle \neq 0$ and $\langle \vec{x}_1, \vec{v} \rangle \neq 0$.

1. Pick random exponents $r', R \in \mathbb{Z}_p^*$.

2. Set $k_1 = \prod_{i=1}^n (h^{-ax_i}h^{a'_i})^{v_i r'} h^{\frac{a'_i v_i bR}{I}}, k_2 = h^{r'}h^{b\frac{R}{I}}, k_3 = h^R$,
   where $I = \langle \vec{x}, \vec{v} \rangle$.

3. Send the secret key $sk_{\vec{v}} = (k_1, k_2, k_3, \vec{v})$.

Challenge $\mathcal{A}$ decides that Phase I is over.

1. Set the challenge ciphertext as
   $C = (g^c, (g^c)^{z'x_1+a'_1}, \cdots, (g^c)^{z'x_n+a'_n}, T)$,
   where c is an exponent which is unknown to $\mathcal{B}$.

2. Send the challenge ciphertext $C = (B, C_1, \cdots, C_n, D)$.

Phase II $\mathcal{A}$ continues to adaptively make a polynomial number of queries not issued in Phase I. $\mathcal{B}$ responds as before.

Guess

1. Finally, $\mathcal{A}$ outputs guesses $w' \in \{0, 1\}$.

2. If $w = w'$, it outputs 1 (indicating that $T = g^{abc}$);
   otherwise, it outputs 0 (indicating that $T \neq g^{abc}$).

Simulation of secret key generation in Lemma 1

The original secret key is set as follows.
$$k_1 = \prod_{i=1}^{n}(h_{2,i})^{v_i r} h_1^R, \qquad k_2 = h^r, \qquad k_3 = h^R.$$

In the above reduction algorithm, the secret key is set as follows.
$$k_1 = \prod_{i=1}^{n}(h^{-ax_i}h^{a'_i})^{v_i r'} h^{\frac{a'_i v_i bR}{I}}, \qquad k_2 = h^{r'} h^{b\frac{R}{I}}, \qquad k_3 = h^R.$$

The secret key must be generated in the cases of $\langle \vec{x}_0, \vec{v}\rangle \neq 0$ and $\langle \vec{x}_1, \vec{v}\rangle \neq 0$. If $\langle \vec{x}_0, \vec{v}\rangle \neq 0$, $\langle \vec{x}_1, \vec{v}\rangle \neq 0$, and $r = r' + b\frac{R}{I}$, then k_1 and k_2 are valid and computed as follows.

$$
\begin{aligned}
k_1 &= \prod_{i=1}^{n}(h^{-ax_i}h^{a'_i})^{v_i r'} h^{\frac{a'_i v_i bR}{I}} \\
&= \prod_{i=1}^{n} h^{-ax_i v_i r'} h^{a'_i v_i r'} h^{\frac{a'_i v_i bR}{I}} \\
&= \prod_{i=1}^{n} h^{-ax_i v_i r'} h^{-abx_i v_i \frac{R}{I}} h^{abx_i v_i \frac{R}{I}} h^{a'_i v_i r'} h^{\frac{a'_i v_i bR}{I}} \\
&= \prod_{i=1}^{n}(h^{-ax_i v_i r'} h^{-abx_i v_i \frac{R}{I}} h^{a'_i v_i r'} h^{\frac{a'_i v_i bR}{I}}) \prod_{i=1}^{n} h^{abx_i v_i \frac{R}{I}} \\
&= \prod_{i=1}^{n}(h^{-ax_i v_i r'} h^{-abx_i v_i \frac{R}{I}} h^{a'_i v_i r'} h^{\frac{a'_i v_i bR}{I}}) h^{abI \frac{R}{I}} \\
&= \prod_{i=1}^{n}(h^{-ax_i}h^{a'_i})^{v_i(r' + b\frac{R}{I})} h^{abR} \\
&= \prod_{i=1}^{n}(h_{2,i})^{v_i r} h_1^R,
\end{aligned}
$$

$$k_2 = h^{r'} h^{b\frac{R}{I}} = h^r.$$

If $\langle \vec{x}_0, \vec{v}\rangle = \langle \vec{x}_1, \vec{v}\rangle = 0$, then k_1 and k_2 cannot be computed, because $\frac{1}{0}$ cannot be computed. So, it cannot generate the secret key for using to decrypt the challenge ciphertext.

Simulation of challenge ciphertext generation in Lemma 1

The original ciphertext is set as follows.
$$B = g^s, \ C_1 = g_0^{x_1 s}(g_{2,1})^s, \cdots, C_n = g_0^{x_n s}(g_{2,n})^s, \ D = g_1^s.$$
In the above reduction algorithm, the challenge ciphertext is set as follows.
$$B = g^c, \ C_1 = (g^c)^{z' x_1 + a'_1}, \cdots, C_n = (g^c)^{z' x_n + a'_n}, \ D = T, \text{ where } c = s.$$

If $T = g^{abc}$, then D is valid, because $T = g^{abc} = (g^{ab})^c = (g_1)^s$, and can set D by using the instance of the problem, T. On the other hand, if T is random, then naturally D is invalid.

Since $c = s$, B is valid ($B = g^c = g^s$) and can set $B = g^s$ by using the instance of the problem, g^c.

Since $(g^c)^{z' x_i + a'_i} = (g^c)^{z' x_i + ax_i - ax_i + a'_i} = (g^c)^{z' x_i + ax_i}(g^c)^{-ax_i + a'_i} = g_0^{x_i s}(g_{2,i})^s$ for $1 \leq i \leq n$, C_i is also valid and can set $C_i = g_0^{x_i s}(g_{2,i})^s$ by using the instance of the problem, g^c.

If $\mathcal{B}$ tries to generate the challenge ciphertext of other attribute vectors $\vec{y}$, then it cannot generate it. This is because in order to generate the challenge ciphertext of other attribute vectors $\vec{y}$, $\mathcal{B}$ has to know g^{ac} as follows: $C_i = (g^c)^{z'y_i}(g^{ac})^{(y_i-x_i)}(g^c)^{a'_i} = g_0^{y_i s}(g_{2,i})^s$ for $1 \leq i \leq n$. But, $\mathcal{B}$ does not know g^{ac}. So, the challenge ciphertext of other attribute vectors $\vec{y}$ cannot be generated.

In conclusion, we can say that

1. When $T = g^{abc} = g_3^c$, i.e., when $\mathcal{B}$'s 8-tuple input is sampled from $\mathcal{D}_N$, then $C = (B, C_1, \cdots, C_n, D)$: Thus, $\mathcal{A}$ is playing Game $\Gamma_{w,1}$.

2. When T is uniform and independent in $\mathbb{G}_1$, i.e., when $\mathcal{B}$'s 8-tuple input is sampled from $\mathcal{D}_R$, then $C = (B, C_1, \cdots, C_n, R')$ for a random R': Thus, $\mathcal{A}$ is playing Game $\Gamma_{w,2}$.

So, if $\mathcal{A}$ has an advantage $\epsilon_{\mathcal{P}}$ in distinguishing Game $\Gamma_{w,1}$ from Game $\Gamma_{w,2}$, then $\mathcal{B}$ has the same advantage $\epsilon_{\mathcal{P}}$ against $\mathcal{P}$-DBDH.

Proof of Lemma 2

Suppose $\mathcal{A}$ has an advantage $\epsilon_{\mathcal{P}}$ in distinguishing Game $\Gamma_{w,2,j-1}$ from Game $\Gamma_{w,2,j}$. We build an algorithm $\mathcal{B}$ that solves the $\mathcal{P}$-DBDH problem in asymmetric pairing. $\mathcal{B}$ is given as input a random 8-tuple $(g, g^a, g^{ab}, g^c, h, h^a, h^b, T)$ that is either sampled from $\mathcal{D}_N$ (where $T = g^{abc}$) or from $\mathcal{D}_R$ (where T is uniform and independent in $\mathbb{G}_1$). Algorithm $\mathcal{B}$'s goal is to output 1 if $T = g^{abc}$ and 0 otherwise. Algorithm $\mathcal{B}$ works by interacting with $\mathcal{A}$ in a selective attribute game as follows.

Reduction algorithm

Initialization The selective attribute game begins with $\mathcal{A}$ by outputting the attribute vectors $\vec{x}_0$ and $\vec{x}_1 \in \sum$ that it intends to attack.
Setup

1. Pick random exponents $z', a'_1, \cdots, a'_n \in \mathbb{Z}_p^*$.

2. Define as follows: $\vec{x} = \vec{x}_w, g_0 = g^{z'}g^{-a}, g_1 = g^a$,
    $g_{2,j} = g^{-ab}g^{ax_j}g^{-a'_j}, \{g_{2,i} = g^{ax_i}g^{-a'_i}\}_{i=1, i \neq j}^n$,
    $h_1 = h^a, h_{2,j} = h^{-ab}h^{ax_j}h^{-a'_j}, \{h_{2,i} = h^{ax_i}h^{-a'_i}\}_{i=1, i \neq j}^n$,
    where a and b are the exponents which are unknown to $\mathcal{B}$.

3. Simulate the system for the following parameters
    $z = z' - a, \gamma = a, a_j = -ab + ax_j - a'_j, \{a_i = ax_i - a'_i\}_{i=1, i \neq j}^n$.

4. Send the public parameters
    $PP = (g, g_0 = g^z, g_1 = g^\gamma, g_{2,1} = g^{a_1}, \cdots, g_{2,n} = g^{a_n})$.

---

5. Set the master secret key
   $MSK = (h, h_1 = h^\gamma, h_{2,1} = h^{a_1}, \cdots, h_{2,n} = h^{a_n})$,
   where $h_{2,j}$ is unknown to $\mathcal{B}$.

Phase I Consider a query for the secret key corresponding to the predicate vector $\vec{v} \in \mathcal{F}$, which satisfies $\langle \vec{x}_0, \vec{v} \rangle \neq 0$ and $\langle \vec{x}_1, \vec{v} \rangle \neq 0$.

1. Pick random exponents $r', R' \in \mathbb{Z}_p^*$.

2. Set $k_1 = \prod_{i=1}^n (h^{ax_i v_i \frac{r'}{I}} h^{-a_i' v_i \frac{r'}{I}}) h^{aR'}$, $k_2 = h^{\frac{r'}{I}}$, $k_3 = h^{R'} h^{bv_j \frac{r'}{I}}$,
   where $I = \langle \vec{x}, \vec{v} \rangle$.

3. Send the secret key $sk_{\vec{v}} = (k_1, k_2, k_3, \vec{v})$.

Challenge $\mathcal{A}$ decides that Phase I is over.

1. Set the challenge ciphertext as follows:
   $B = g^c$, $C_1 = R_1, \cdots, C_{j-1} = R_{j-1}$, $C_j = (T)^{-1} g^{z' x_j c} g^{-a_j' c}$,
   $C_{j+1} = g^{z' x_{j+1} c} g^{-a_{j+1}' c}, \cdots, C_n = g^{z' x_n c} g^{-a_n' c}$, $D = R'$,
   where $R_1, \cdots, R_{j-1}, R'$ are uniformly and independently chosen from $\mathbb{G}_1$.

2. Send the challenge ciphertext $C = (B, C_1, \cdots, C_n, D)$.

Phase II $\mathcal{A}$ continues to adaptively make a polynomial number of queries not issued in Phase I. $\mathcal{B}$ responds as before.

Guess

1. Finally, $\mathcal{A}$ outputs guesses $w' \in \{0, 1\}$.

2. If $w = w'$, it outputs 1 (indicating that $T = g^{abc}$);
   otherwise, it outputs 0 (indicating that $T \neq g^{abc}$).

Simulation of secret key generation in Lemma 2

The original secret key is set as follows.
$$k_1 = \prod_{i=1}^n (h_{2,i})^{v_i r} h_1^R, \qquad k_2 = h^r, \qquad k_3 = h^R.$$

In the above reduction algorithm, the secret key is set as follows.
$$k_1 = \prod_{i=1}^n (h^{ax_i v_i \frac{r'}{I}} h^{-a_i' v_i \frac{r'}{I}}) h^{aR'}, \qquad k_2 = h^{\frac{r'}{I}}, \qquad k_3 = h^{R'} h^{bv_j \frac{r'}{I}}.$$

The secret key must be generated in the cases of $\langle \vec{x}_0, \vec{v} \rangle \neq 0$ and $\langle \vec{x}_1, \vec{v} \rangle \neq 0$. If $\langle \vec{x}_0, \vec{v} \rangle \neq 0$, $\langle \vec{x}_1, \vec{v} \rangle \neq 0$, $r = \frac{r'}{I}$ and $R = R' + bv_j \frac{r'}{I} \in \mathbb{Z}_p^*$, then k_1, k_2 and k_3 are valid and computed as follows.

$$k_1 = \prod_{i=1}^{n}(h^{ax_iv_i\frac{r'}{T}}h^{-a'_iv_i\frac{r'}{T}})h^{aR'}$$
$$= \prod_{i=1}^{n}(h^{ax_iv_i\frac{r'}{T}}h^{-a'_iv_i\frac{r'}{T}})h^{-abv_j\frac{r'}{T}}h^{aR'}h^{abv_j\frac{r'}{T}}$$
$$= \prod_{i=1,i\neq j}^{n}(h^{ax_iv_i\frac{r'}{T}}h^{-a'_iv_i\frac{r'}{T}})(h^{-abv_j\frac{r'}{T}}h^{ax_jv_j\frac{r'}{T}}h^{-a'_jv_j\frac{r}{T}})h^{a(R'+bv_j\frac{r'}{T})}$$
$$= \prod_{i=1,i\neq j}^{n}(h^{ax_i}h^{-a'_i})^{v_i\frac{r'}{T}}(h^{-ab}h^{ax_j}h^{-a'_j})^{v_i\frac{r'}{T}}h_1^{R}$$
$$= \prod_{i=1,i\neq j}^{n}((h_{2,i})^{v_ir})(h_{2,j})^{v_jr}h_1^{R}$$
$$= \prod_{i=1}^{n}((h_{2,i})^{v_ir})h_1^{R},$$

$$k_2 = h^{\frac{r'}{T}} = h^r,$$

$$k_3 = h^{R'}h^{bv_j\frac{r'}{T}} = h^R.$$

If $\langle\vec{x}_0,\vec{v}\rangle = \langle\vec{x}_1,\vec{v}\rangle = 0$, then k_1 and k_2 cannot be computed, because $\frac{1}{0}$ cannot be computed. So, it cannot generate the secret key for using to decrypt the challenge ciphertext.

Simulation of challenge ciphertext generation in Lemma 2

The original ciphertext is set as follows.
$B = g^s$, $C_1 = g_0^{x_1s}(g_{2,1})^s, \cdots, C_n = g_0^{x_ns}(g_{2,n})^s$, $D = g_1^s$.

In the above reduction algorithm, the challenge ciphertext is set as follows.
$B = g^c$, $C_1 = R_1, \cdots, C_{j-1} = R_{j-1}$, $C_j = (T)^{-1}g^{z'x_jc}g^{-a'_jc}$,
$C_{j+1} = g^{z'x_{j+1}c}g^{-a'_{j+1}c}, \cdots, C_n = g^{z'x_nc}g^{-a'_nc}$, $D = R'$, where $c = s$.

If $T = g^{abc}$, then C_j is valid, because $C_j = (T)^{-1}g^{z'x_jc}g^{-a'_jc} = (g^{abc})^{-1}g^{z'x_jc}g^{-a'_jc} = (g^{-ab})^{c}g^{z'x_jc}g^{-a'_jc} = (g^{-ab+z'x_j-a'_j})^c = g_{2,j}^{c}$ and can set C_j by using the instance of the problem, T. On the other hand, if T is random, then naturally C_j is invalid.
Since $c = s$, B is valid ($B = g^c = g^s$) and can set $B = g^s$ by using the instance of the problem, g^c.
Since $g^{z'x_ic}g^{-a'_ic} = g^{z'x_ic-ax_ic}g^{ax_ic-a'_ic} = g^{(z'-a)x_ic}g^{(ax_i-a'_i)c} = g_0^{x_is}(g_{2,i})^s$ for $j+1 \le i \le n$, C_i is also valid and can set $C_i = g_0^{x_is}(g_{2,i})^s$ by using the instance of the problem, g^c.
If $\mathcal{B}$ tries to generate the challenge ciphertext of other attribute vectors $\vec{y}$, it cannot generate it. It is because in order to generate the challenge ciphertext of other attribute vectors $\vec{y}$, $\mathcal{B}$ has to know g^{ac} as follows: $C_j = g^{z'y_jc}g^{-a(y_j-x_j)c}g^{-a'_jc} = g_0^{y_js}(g_{2,j})^s$. But, $\mathcal{B}$ does not know g^{ac}. Therefore, the challenge ciphertext of other attribute vectors $\vec{y}$ cannot be generated.

In conclusion, we can say that

1. When $T = g^{abc} = g_3^c$, i.e., when $\mathcal{B}$'s 8-tuple input is sampled from $\mathcal{D}_N$, then $C = (B, R_1, \cdots, R_{j-1}, C_j, \cdots, C_n, R')$ for a random R', $R_1, \cdots, R_{j-1}$: Thus, $\mathcal{A}$ is playing Game $\Gamma_{w,2,j-1}$.

2. When T is uniform and independent in $\mathbb{G}_1$, i.e., when $\mathcal{B}$'s 8-tuple input is sampled from $\mathcal{D}_R$, then $C = (B, R_1, \cdots, R_j, C_{j+1}, \cdots, C_n, R')$ for a random R', $R_1, \cdots, R_j$: Thus, $\mathcal{A}$ is playing Game $\Gamma_{w,2,j}$.

So, if $\mathcal{A}$ has an advantage $\epsilon_{\mathcal{P}}$ in distinguishing Game $\Gamma_{w,2,j-1}$ from Game $\Gamma_{w,2,j}$, then $\mathcal{B}$ has the same advantage $\epsilon_{\mathcal{P}}$ against $\mathcal{P}$-DBDH. $\square$

21.4 Predicate Encryption [62]

We now describe the predicate encryption scheme which is attribute-hiding under the DBDH and $\mathcal{P}$-DBDH assumptions by slightly modifying the predicate-only encryption scheme. The main difference is that the present predicate encryption scheme should be allowed to encrypt a message M as well as the attributes $\vec{x} \in \sum$, where we assume that $\sum = (\mathbb{Z}_p^*)^n$ and $M \in \mathbb{G}_T$.

Construction 2. Predicate encryption

Setup (λ) Given a security parameter $\lambda \in \mathbb{Z}^+$

1. Run $\mathcal{G}$ on input λ to generate a prime q $(|q| = \lambda)$, three groups $\mathbb{G}_1$, $\mathbb{G}_2$, and $\mathbb{G}_T$ of order q, and $\hat{e}$: $\mathbb{G}_1 \times \mathbb{G}_2 \to \mathbb{G}_T$. Choose two random generators $g \in \mathbb{G}_1$ and $h \in \mathbb{G}_2$.

2. Select random $(\alpha, \beta, \gamma, a_1, \cdots, a_n, z) \in (\mathbb{Z}_p^*)^{n+4}$.

3. Compute as follows.

    (a) $g_1 = g^\gamma, g_{2,1} = g^{a_1}, \cdots, g_{2,n} = g^{a_n}, g_0 = g^z \in \mathbb{G}_1$,

    (b) $h_1 = h^\gamma, h_{2,1} = h^{a_1}, \cdots, h_{2,n} = h^{a_n} \in \mathbb{G}_2$,

    (c) $Y = e(g, h^{\alpha\beta}) \in \mathbb{G}_T$.

4. The public parameters are
    $PP = (g, g_0, g_1, g_{2,1}, \cdots, g_{2,n}, Y) \in \mathbb{G}_1^{n+3} \times \mathbb{G}_T$.

5. The master secret key is
    $MSK = (h^{\alpha\beta}, h, h_1, h_{2,1}, \cdots, h_{2,n}) \in \mathbb{G}_2^{n+3}$.

Note that n is the dimension of the attribute/predicate vectors.

Gen$(PP, MSK, \vec{v})$ For the predicates $\vec{v} \in \mathcal{F}$

1. Pick random $r, R \in \mathbb{Z}_p^*$.

2. Compute as follows.

    (a) $k_1 = h^{\alpha\beta} \prod_{i=1}^n (h_{2,i})^{v_i r} h_1^R$,

(b) $k_2 = h^r$,

(c) $k_3 = h^R$.

3. The secret key is $sk_{\vec{v}} = (k_1, k_2, k_3, \vec{v}) \in \mathbb{G}_2^3 \times (\mathbb{Z}_p^*)^n$.

Encrypt $(PP, M, \vec{x})$ To encrypt a message $M \in \mathbb{G}_T$ under the attributes $\vec{x} \in \sum$

1. Pick a random $s \in \mathbb{Z}_p^*$.

2. Compute as follows.

(a) $c_0 = M \cdot Y^s$,

(b) $c_1 = g^s$,

(c) $c_{2,i} = g_0^{x_i s} (g_{2,i})^s$ for $1 \le i \le n$,

(d) $c_3 = g_1^s$.

3. The ciphertext is $C = (c_0, c_1, c_{2,1}, \cdots, c_{2,n}, c_3) \in \mathbb{G}_T \times \mathbb{G}_1^{n+2}$.

Decrypt $(sk_{\vec{v}}, C)$ To decrypt a given ciphertext
$C = (c_0, c_1, c_{2,1}, \cdots, c_{2,n}, c_3) \in \mathbb{G}_T \times \mathbb{G}_1^{n+2}$ using the secret key $sk_{\vec{v}} = (k_1, k_2, k_3, \vec{v}) \in \mathbb{G}_2^3 \times (\mathbb{Z}_p^*)^n$, compute

$$c_0 \cdot \frac{e\left(\prod_{i=1}^n (c_{2,i})^{v_i}, k_2\right) \cdot e(c_3, k_3)}{e(c_1, k_1)} \in \mathbb{G}_T.$$

Correctness To see that the correctness holds, let C and $sk_{\vec{v}}$ be as above. Then

$$c_0 \cdot e\left(\prod_{i=1}^n (c_{2,i})^{v_i}, k_2\right) \cdot e(c_3, k_3) \cdot e(c_1, k_1)^{-1}$$
$$= M \cdot e(g,h)^{\alpha \beta s} \cdot e\left(\prod_{i=1}^n (g_0^{x_i s} (g_{2,i})^s)^{v_i}, h^r\right) \cdot e\left(g_1^s, h^R\right)$$
$$\cdot e\left(g^s, h^{\alpha \beta} \prod_{i=1}^n (h_{2,i})^{v_i r} h_1^R\right)^{-1}$$
$$= M \cdot e(g,h)^{\alpha \beta s} \cdot e\left(\prod_{i=1}^n (g^{z x_i v_i s} g^{a_i v_i s}), h^r\right) \cdot e\left(g^{\gamma s}, h^R\right)$$
$$\cdot e\left(g^s, h^{\alpha \beta} \prod_{i=1}^n h^{a_i v_i r} h^{\gamma R}\right)^{-1}$$
$$= M \cdot e(g,h)^{\alpha \beta s} \cdot e\left(g^{zs\langle \vec{x}, \vec{v} \rangle} g^{\langle \vec{a}, \vec{v} \rangle s}, h^r\right) \cdot e\left(g^{\gamma s}, h^R\right)$$
$$\cdot e\left(g^s, h^{\alpha \beta} h^{\langle \vec{a}, \vec{v} \rangle r} h^{\gamma R}\right)^{-1}$$
$$= M \cdot e(g,h)^{\alpha \beta s} \cdot e\left(g^{zs\langle \vec{x}, \vec{v} \rangle}, h^r\right) \cdot e\left(g^{\langle \vec{a}, \vec{v} \rangle s}, h^r\right) \cdot e\left(g^{\gamma s}, h^R\right) \cdot e\left(g^s, h^{\alpha \beta}\right)^{-1} \cdot$$
$$e\left(g^s, h^{\langle \vec{a}, \vec{v} \rangle r}\right)^{-1} \cdot e\left(g^s, h^{\gamma R}\right)^{-1}$$
$$= M \cdot e(g,h)^{\alpha \beta s} \cdot e(g,h)^{zsr\langle \vec{x}, \vec{v} \rangle} \cdot e(g,h)^{\langle \vec{a}, \vec{v} \rangle sr} \cdot e(g,h)^{\gamma sR} \cdot e(g,h)^{-\alpha \beta s} \cdot$$
$$e(g,h)^{-\langle \vec{a}, \vec{v} \rangle sr} \cdot e(g,h)^{-s\gamma R}$$
$$= e(g,h)^{zsr\langle \vec{x}, \vec{v} \rangle} \in \mathbb{G}_T.$$

If $\langle \vec{x}, \vec{v} \rangle = 0$, we can get M.

21.4.1   Proof of Predicate Encryption Security

The following theorem proves the security of this scheme under the DBDH and $\mathcal{P}$-DBDH assumptions.

Theorem 2 The predicate encryption scheme is selectively attribute-hiding secure against chosen plaintext attacks in the standard model under the DBDH and $\mathcal{P}$-DBDH assumptions. For all PPT algorithms $\mathcal{B}$, the function $Adv_{\mathcal{B}}^{IND\text{-}sAH\text{-}CPA}(\lambda)$ is a negligible function of λ.

Proof The proof proceeds by a hybrid argument across a number of games. Let $C = (A, B, C_1, \cdots, C_n, D) \in \mathbb{G}_T \times \mathbb{G}_1^{n+2}$ denote the challenge ciphertext given to the adversary during two real attacks (Γ_0 and Γ_1). Additionally, let R be a random element of $\mathbb{G}_T$ and $R_1, \cdots, R_n$, and R' be random elements of $\mathbb{G}_1$. We define the following hybrid experiments, which differ in how the challenge ciphertext is generated as

1. Game $\Gamma_{0,0}$: This game is the original security game, where the challenge attribute, message, and ciphertext are $\vec{x}_0$, M_0, and $C = (A, B, C_1, \cdots, C_n, D)$, respectively.

2. Game $\Gamma_{0,1}$: In this game, the element A of the ciphertext is changed to a random element R of $\mathbb{G}_T$. But the challenge attribute and message are the same as for $\Gamma_{0,0}$. The challenge ciphertext is $C = (R, B, C_1, \cdots, C_n, D)$.

3. Game $\Gamma_{0,2}$: In this game, the element D of the ciphertext is changed to a random element R' of $\mathbb{G}_1$. However, the element R of the ciphertext, the challenge attribute, and the message are the same as for $\Gamma_{0,1}$. The challenge ciphertext is $C = (R, B, C_1, \cdots, C_n, R')$.

4. Game $\Gamma_{0,3}$: In this game, the elements $C_1, \cdots, C_n$ of the ciphertext are changed to the random elements $R_1, \cdots, R_n$ of $\mathbb{G}_1$. However, elements R' and R of the ciphertext, the challenge attribute, and the message are the same as for $\Gamma_{0,2}$. The challenge ciphertext is $C = (R, B, R_1, \cdots, R_n, R')$.

   For the security proof, we additionally define a sequence of games $\Gamma_{0,2,1}, \Gamma_{0,2,2}, \cdots, \Gamma_{0,2,n}$, where $\Gamma_{0,2} = \Gamma_{0,2,0}$ and $\Gamma_{0,3} = \Gamma_{0,2,n} = \Gamma_{1,3}$. In the game $\Gamma_{0,2,j}$ for $1 \leq j \leq n$, the first j-th attribute elements are random numbers in $\mathbb{Z}_p^*$ and the remaining attribute elements are the elements in the challenge attribute. The challenge ciphertext is $C = (R, B, R_1, \cdots, R_j, C_{j+1}, \cdots, C_n, R')$.

5. Game $\Gamma_{1,3}$: This game is almost the same as $\Gamma_{0,3}$ except that the challenge attribute and the message are $\vec{x}_1$ and M_1, respectively. The challenge ciphertext is $C = (R, B, R_1, \cdots, R_n, R')$.

6. Game $\Gamma_{1,2}$: This game is almost the same as $\Gamma_{0,2}$ except that the

challenge attribute and the message are $\vec{x}_1$ and M_1, respectively. The challenge ciphertext is $C = (R, B, C_1, \cdots, C_n, R')$.

7. Game $\Gamma_{1,1}$: This game is almost the same as $\Gamma_{0,1}$ except that the challenge attribute and the message are $\vec{x}_1$ and M_1, respectively. The challenge ciphertext is $C = (R, B, C_1, \cdots, C_n, D)$.

8. Game $\Gamma_{1,0}$: This game is almost the same as $\Gamma_{0,0}$ except that the challenge attribute and the message are $\vec{x}_1$ and M_1, respectively. The challenge ciphertext is $C = (A, B, C_1, \cdots, C_n, D)$.

$\Gamma_{0,0}$ and $\Gamma_{1,0}$ are the same as games Γ_0 and Γ_1 in Definition 5, respectively. Therefore,

$$Adv_{\mathcal{B}}^{IND\text{-}sAH\text{-}CPA}(\lambda) \leq \left| Pr[\mathcal{A}^{\Gamma_{0,0}} = 0] - Pr[\mathcal{A}^{\Gamma_{1,0}} = 0] \right|. \qquad (21.8)$$

To prove that $\Gamma_{0,0}$ is indistinguishable from $\Gamma_{1,0}$, we prove that each step of the hybrid argument is indistinguishable from the next.

Lemma 3 Let $\mathcal{A}$ be an adversary playing the $IND\text{-}sAH\text{-}CPA$ attack game. Then, there exists an algorithm $\mathcal{B}$ solving the DBDH problem such that

$$\left| Pr[\mathcal{A}^{\Gamma_{w,0}} = 0] - Pr[\mathcal{A}^{\Gamma_{w,1}} = 0] \right| \leq Adv_{\mathcal{B}}^{DBDH}. \qquad (21.9)$$

Lemma 4 Let $\mathcal{A}$ be an adversary playing the $IND\text{-}sAH\text{-}CPA$ attack game. Then, there exists an algorithm $\mathcal{B}$ solving the $\mathcal{P}$-DBDH problem such that

$$\left| Pr[\mathcal{A}^{\Gamma_{w,1}} = 0] - Pr[\mathcal{A}^{\Gamma_{w,2}} = 0] \right| \leq Adv_{\mathcal{B}}^{\mathcal{P}\text{-}DBDH}. \qquad (21.10)$$

Lemma 5 Let $\mathcal{A}$ be an adversary playing the $IND\text{-}sAH\text{-}CPA$ attack game. Then, there exists an algorithm $\mathcal{B}$ solving the $\mathcal{P}$-DBDH problem such that

$$\left| Pr[\mathcal{A}^{\Gamma_{w,2,j-1}} = 0] - Pr[\mathcal{A}^{\Gamma_{w,2,j}} = 0] \right| \leq Adv_{\mathcal{B}}^{\mathcal{P}\text{-}DBDH}. \qquad (21.11)$$

In Lemma 3, 4, and 5, $w \in \{0, 1\}$.

Thus, if there is no algorithm $\mathcal{B}$ that solves DBDH and $\mathcal{P}$-DBDH problems with an advantage better than ϵ and $\epsilon_{\mathcal{P}}$, respectively, then, for all adversary $\mathcal{A}$,

$|Pr[\mathcal{A}^{\Gamma_{0,0}} = 0] - Pr[\mathcal{A}^{\Gamma_{1,0}} = 0]|$
$\leq \left| Pr[\mathcal{A}^{\Gamma_{0,0}} = 0] - Pr[\mathcal{A}^{\Gamma_{0,1}} = 0] \right|$
$+ \left| Pr[\mathcal{A}^{\Gamma_{0,1}} = 0] - Pr[\mathcal{A}^{\Gamma_{0,2}} = 0] \right|$
$+ \left| Pr[\mathcal{A}^{\Gamma_{0,2}} = 0] - Pr[\mathcal{A}^{\Gamma_{0,2,1}} = 0] \right| + \cdots$
$+ \left| Pr[\mathcal{A}^{\Gamma_{0,2,j-1}} = 0] - Pr[\mathcal{A}^{\Gamma_{0,2,j}} = 0] \right|$
$+ \cdots + \left| Pr[\mathcal{A}^{\Gamma_{0,2,n-1}} = 0] - Pr[\mathcal{A}^{\Gamma_{0,2,n}} = 0] \right|$
$+ \left| Pr[\mathcal{A}^{\Gamma_{1,2,n}} = 0] - Pr[\mathcal{A}^{\Gamma_{1,2,n-1}} = 0] \right| + \cdots$
$+ \left| Pr[\mathcal{A}^{\Gamma_{1,2,j}} = 0] - Pr[\mathcal{A}^{\Gamma_{1,2,j-1}} = 0] \right|$

$$+ \cdots + \left| Pr[\mathcal{A}^{\Gamma_{1,2,1}} = 0] - Pr[\mathcal{A}^{\Gamma_{1,2}} = 0] \right|$$
$$+ \left| Pr[\mathcal{A}^{\Gamma_{1,2}} = 0] - Pr[\mathcal{A}^{\Gamma_{1,1}} = 0] \right|$$
$$+ \left| Pr[\mathcal{A}^{\Gamma_{1,1}} = 0] - Pr[\mathcal{A}^{\Gamma_{1,0}} = 0] \right|$$
$$\leq 2(\epsilon + (n+1)\epsilon_{\mathcal{P}}).$$

Consequently, under the DBDH and $\mathcal{P}$-DBDH assumptions, Game $\Gamma_{0,0}$ is indistinguishable from $\Gamma_{1,0}$.

Proof of Lemma 3 Suppose $\mathcal{A}$ has the advantage ϵ in distinguishing Game $\Gamma_{w,0}$ from Game $\Gamma_{w,1}$. We build an algorithm $\mathcal{B}$ that solves the DBDH problem in asymmetric pairing. $\mathcal{B}$ is given as input a random 7-tuple $(g, g^a, g^c, h, h^a, h^b, T)$ that is either sampled from $\mathcal{P}_{\mathcal{A}}$ (where $T = e(g, h)^{abc}$) or from $\mathcal{R}_{\mathcal{A}}$ (where T is uniform and independent in $\mathbb{G}_T$). Algorithm $\mathcal{B}$'s goal is to output 1 if $T = e(g, h)^{abc}$ and 0 otherwise. Algorithm $\mathcal{B}$ works by interacting with $\mathcal{A}$ in a selective attribute game as follows.

Reduction algorithm

Initialization The selective attribute game begins with $\mathcal{A}$ by outputting the attribute vectors $\vec{x}_0$ and $\vec{x}_1 \in \sum$ that it intends to attack.

Setup

1. Pick random exponents $z', \gamma', \delta, a'_1, \cdots, a'_n \in \mathbb{Z}_p^*$.

2. Define as follows:
    $\vec{x} = \vec{x}_w, h^{\alpha\beta} = h^{ab}, g_0 = g^{z'} g^{a\delta}, Y = e(g^a, h^b),$
    $g_1 = g^{\gamma'}, g_{2,1} = g^{-a\delta x_1} g^{a'_1}, \cdots, g_{2,n} = g^{-a\delta x_n} g^{a'_n},$
    $h_1 = h^{\gamma'}, h_{2,1} = h^{-ax_1} h^{a'_1}, \cdots, h_{2,n} = h^{-ax_n} h^{a'_n},$
    where a and b are the exponents which are unknown to $\mathcal{B}$.

3. Simulate the system for the following parameters
    $\alpha = a, \beta = b, \gamma = \gamma', z = z' + a\delta, a_1 = -a\delta x_1 + a'_1, \cdots, a_n = -a\delta x_n + a'_n$.

4. Send the public parameters
    $PP = (g, g_0 = g^z, g_1 = g^\gamma, g_{2,1} = g^{a_1}, \cdots, g_{2,n} = g^{a_n}, Y)$.

5. Set the master secret key
    $MSK = (h, h^{\alpha\beta}, h_1 = h^\gamma, h_{2,1} = h^{a_1}, \cdots, h_{2,n} = h^{a_n}),$
    where $h^{\alpha\beta}$ is unknown to $\mathcal{B}$.

Phase I Consider a query for the secret key corresponding to the predicate vector $\vec{v} \in \mathcal{F}$, which satisfies $\langle \vec{x}_0, \vec{v} \rangle \neq 0$ and $\langle \vec{x}_1, \vec{v} \rangle \neq 0$.

1. Pick random exponents $r', R \in \mathbb{Z}_p^*$.

2. Set $k_1 = \prod_{i=1}^{n}(h^{-a\delta x_i}h^{a'_i})^{v_i r'}h^{\frac{a'_i v_i b}{\delta I}}h^{\gamma' R}$, $k_2 = h^{r'}h^{b\frac{1}{\delta I}}$, $k_3 = h^R$, where $I = \langle \vec{x}, \vec{v} \rangle$.

3. Send the secret key $sk_{\vec{v}} = (k_1, k_2, k_3, \vec{v})$.

Challenge When $\mathcal{A}$ decides that Phase I is over, it outputs two messages M_0 and $M_1 \in \mathbb{G}_T$ on which it wishes to be challenged.

1. Select a message M_w according to the game and set it to M.

2. Set the challenge ciphertext
$C = (M \cdot T, g^c, (g^c)^{z'x_1 + a'_1}, \cdots, (g^c)^{z'x_n + a'_n}, (g^c)^{\gamma'})$,
where c is an exponent which is unknown to $\mathcal{B}$.

3. Send the challenge ciphertext $C = (A, B, C_1, \cdots, C_n, D)$.

Phase II $\mathcal{A}$ continues to adaptively make a polynomial number of queries not issued in Phase I. $\mathcal{B}$ responds as before.

Guess

1. Finally, $\mathcal{A}$ outputs guesses $w' \in \{0, 1\}$.

2. If $w = w'$, it outputs 1 (indicating that $T = e(g, h)^{abc}$); otherwise, it outputs 0 (indicating that $T \neq e(g, h)^{abc}$).

Simulation of secret key generation in Lemma 3

The original secret key is set as follows.
$k_1 = \prod_{i=1}^{n}(h_{2,i})^{v_i r}h_1^R$, $\qquad k_2 = h^r$, $\qquad k_3 = h^R$.

In the above reduction algorithm, the secret key is set as follows.
$k_1 = \prod_{i=1}^{n}(h^{-a\delta x_i}h^{a'_i})^{v_i r'}h^{\frac{a'_i v_i b}{\delta I}}h^{\gamma' R}$, $\qquad k_2 = h^{r'}h^{b\frac{1}{\delta I}}$, $\qquad k_3 = h^R$.
The secret key must be generated in the cases of $\langle \vec{x}_0, \vec{v} \rangle \neq 0$ and $\langle \vec{x}_1, \vec{v} \rangle \neq 0$.

If $\langle \vec{x}_0, \vec{v} \rangle \neq 0$, $\langle \vec{x}_1, \vec{v} \rangle \neq 0$ and $r = r' + \frac{b}{\delta I} \in \mathbb{Z}_p^*$, then k_1 and k_2 are valid and computed as follows.

$$k_1 = \prod_{i=1}^{n}(h^{-a\delta x_i}h^{a'_i})^{v_i r'}h^{\frac{a'_i v_i b}{\delta I}}h^{\gamma' R} = \prod_{i=1}^{n}(h^{-a\delta x_i v_i r'}h^{a'_i v_i r'})h^{\frac{a'_i v_i b}{\delta I}}h^{\gamma' R}$$
$$= \prod_{i=1}^{n}(h^{-a\delta x_i v_i r'}h^{ab\delta x_i v_i \frac{1}{\delta I}}h^{-ab\delta x_i v_i \frac{1}{\delta I}}h^{a'_i v_i r'})h^{\frac{a'_i v_i b}{\delta I}}h^{\gamma' R}$$
$$= h^{ab\delta I \frac{1}{\delta I}}\prod_{i=1}^{n}(h^{-a\delta x_i v_i r'}h^{-ab\delta x_i v_i \frac{1}{\delta I}}h^{a'_i v_i r'})h^{\frac{a'_i v_i b}{\delta I}}h^{\gamma' R}$$
$$= h^{ab}\prod_{i=1}^{n}((h^{-a\delta x_i})^{v_i r'}(h^{-a\delta x_i})^{v_i b\frac{1}{\delta I}}(h^{a'_i})^{v_i r'}(h^{a'_i})^{v_i b\frac{1}{\delta I}})h^{\gamma' R}$$
$$= h^{ab}\prod_{i=1}^{n}((h^{-a\delta x_i})^{v_i(r'+b\frac{1}{\delta I})}(h^{a'_i})^{v_i(r'+b\frac{1}{\delta I})})h^{\gamma' R}$$
$$= h^{ab}\prod_{i=1}^{n}((h^{-a\delta x_i}h^{a'_i})^{v_i(r'+b\frac{1}{\delta I})})h^{\gamma' R} = h^{ab}\prod_{i=1}^{n}(h_{2,i})^{v_i r}h_1^R,$$

$$k_2 = h^{r'}h^{b\frac{1}{\delta I}} = h^r.$$

If $\langle \vec{x}_0, \vec{v} \rangle = \langle \vec{x}_1, \vec{v} \rangle = 0$, then k_1 and k_2 cannot be computed, because $\frac{1}{0}$ cannot be computed. So, it cannot generate the secret key for using to decrypt the challenge ciphertext.

Simulation of challenge ciphertext generation in Lemma 3

The original ciphertext is set as follows.
$$A = M \cdot Y^s, \ B = g^s, \ C_1 = g_0^{x_1 s}(g_{2,1})^s, \cdots, C_n = g_0^{x_n s}(g_{2,n})^s, \ D = g_1^s.$$

In the above reduction algorithm, the challenge ciphertext is set as follows.
$$A = M \cdot T, B = g^c, C_1 = (g^c)^{z'x_1 + a_1'}, \cdots, C_n = (g^c)^{z'x_n + a_n'}, D = (g^c)^{\gamma'},$$
where $c = s$.

If $T = e(g,h)^{abc}$, then A is valid, because $T = e(g,h)^{abc} = (e(g,h)^{ab})^c = (Y)^s$, and can set A by using the instance of the problem, T. On the other hand, if T is random, then naturally A is invalid.

Since $c = s$, B is valid ($B = g^c = g^s$) and can set $B = g^s$ by using the instance of the problem, g^c.

Since $(g^c)^{z'x_i + a_i'} = (g^c)^{z'x_i + a\delta x_i - a\delta x_i + a_i'} = (g^c)^{z'x_i + a\delta x_i}(g^c)^{-a\delta x_i + a_i'} = g_0^{x_i s}(g_{2,i})^s$ for $1 \le i \le n$, C_i is also valid and can set $C_i = g_0^{x_i s}(g_{2,i})^s$ by using the instance of the problem, g^c.

If $\mathcal{B}$ tries to generate the challenge ciphertext of the other attribute vectors $\vec{y}$, then it cannot generate it. It is because in order to generate the challenge ciphertext of other attribute vectors $\vec{y}$, $\mathcal{B}$ has to know g^{ac} as follows: $C_i = (g^c)^{z'y_i}(g^{ac})^{\delta(y_i - x_i)}(g^c)^{a_i'} = g_0^{y_i s}(g_{2,i})^s$ for $1 \le i \le n$. But, $\mathcal{B}$ does not know g^{ac}. So, the challenge ciphertext of other attribute vectors $\vec{y}$ cannot be generated.

In conclusion, we can say that

1. When $T = e(g,h)^{abc} = e(g,h^{ab})^c$, i.e., when $\mathcal{B}$'s 7-tuple input is sampled from $\mathcal{P}_{\mathcal{A}}$, then C is a valid encryption of M under the attribute $\vec{x}$ initially chosen by the adversary: Thus, $\mathcal{A}$ is playing Game $\Gamma_{w,0}$.

• 2. When T is uniform and independent in $\mathbb{G}_T$, i.e., when $\mathcal{B}$'s 7-tuple input is sampled from $\mathcal{R}_{\mathcal{A}}$, then $C = (R, B, C_1, \cdots, C_n, D)$ for a random R: Thus, $\mathcal{A}$ is playing Game $\Gamma_{w,1}$.

So, if $\mathcal{A}$ has an advantage ϵ in distinguishing Game $\Gamma_{w,0}$ from Game $\Gamma_{w,1}$, then $\mathcal{B}$ has the same advantage ϵ against DBDH. $\square$

At this point, we have achieved confidentiality by using the DBDH assumptions. By slightly modifying the proofs of Lemma 1 and 2, the remaining proofs of Lemma 4 and 5 for attribute-hiding can be achieved.

21.5   Functional Encryption

In this section, we present a pairing-based public key FE scheme for inner products evaluations under the XDH assumption. This scheme is based on the predicate-only encryption scheme [62]. So, by finding the gap between FE and [62] in the scheme and proof, we can understand how to make FE from [62].

Construction 3. Functional encryption

Setup(λ) Given a security parameter $\lambda \in \mathbb{Z}^+$

1. Run $\mathcal{G}$ on input λ to generate a prime q ($|q| = \lambda$), three groups $\mathbb{G}_1$, $\mathbb{G}_2$ and $\mathbb{G}_T$ of order q, and $\widehat{e} \colon \mathbb{G}_1 \times \mathbb{G}_2 \to \mathbb{G}_T$. Choose two random generators $g \in \mathbb{G}_1$ and $h \in \mathbb{G}_2$.

2. Select random $(a_1, \cdots, a_n) \in (\mathbb{Z}_p^*)^n$.

3. Compute as follows.

    (a) $g_1 = g^{a_1}, \cdots, g_n = g^{a_n} \in \mathbb{G}_1$,
    (b) $h_1 = h^{a_1}, \cdots, h_n = h^{a_n} \in \mathbb{G}_2$,
    (c) $Y = e(g, h) \in \mathbb{G}_T$.

4. The public parameters are $PP = (g, g_1, \cdots, g_n) \in \mathbb{G}_1^{n+1}$.

5. The master secret key is $MSK = (h, h_1, h_1, \cdots, h_n, Y) \in \mathbb{G}_2^{n+1} \times \mathbb{G}_T$.

Note that n is the dimension of the key(function)/message vectors.

Gen$(PP, MSK, \vec{y})$ For the key vector $\vec{y} \in \mathcal{Y} \setminus \{\vec{0}\}$

1. Pick a random $R \in \mathbb{Z}_p^*$.

2. Compute as follows.

    (a) $k_1 = \prod_{i=1}^n (h_i)^{y_i R}$,
    (b) $k_2 = h^R$,
    (c) $k_3 = e(g, h)^R$.

3. The secret key is $SK_{\vec{y}} = (k_1, k_2, k_3, \vec{y}) \in \mathbb{G}_2^2 \times \mathbb{G}_T \times (\mathbb{Z}_p^*)^n$.

Encrypt $(PP, \vec{x})$ To encrypt the message vector $\vec{x} \in \mathcal{X}$

1. Pick a random $s \in \mathbb{Z}_p^*$.

2. Compute as follows.

---

3. (a) $c_1 = g^s$,

    (b) $c_{2,i} = g^{x_i} (g_i)^s$ for $1 \le i \le n$.

  3. The ciphertext is $C = (c_1, c_{2,1}, \cdots, c_{2,n}) \in \mathbb{G}_1^{n+1}$.

Decrypt $(SK_{\vec{y}}, C)$ To decrypt a given ciphertext $C = (c_1, c_{2,1}, \cdots, c_{2,n}) \in \mathbb{G}_1^{n+1}$ using the secret key $SK_{\vec{y}} = (k_1, k_2, k_3, \vec{y}) \in \mathbb{G}_2^2 \times \mathbb{G}_T \times (\mathbb{Z}_p^*)^n$, compute as follows.

1. $D = e(c_1, k_1)^{-1} e\left(\prod_{i=1}^n (c_{2,i})^{y_i}, k_2\right) \in \mathbb{G}_T$,

2. $\langle \vec{x}, \vec{y} \rangle = log_{k_3} D$.

Correctness To see that the correctness holds, let C and $SK_{\vec{y}}$ be as above. Then

$$
\begin{aligned}
D &= e(c_1, k_1)^{-1} \cdot e\left(\prod_{i=1}^n (c_{2,i})^{y_i}, k_2\right) \\
&= e\left(g^s, \prod_{i=1}^n (h_i)^{y_i R}\right)^{-1} \cdot e\left(\prod_{i=1}^n (g^{x_i} (g_i)^s)^{y_i}, h^R\right) \\
&= e\left(g^s, \prod_{i=1}^n (h^{a_i})^{y_i R}\right)^{-1} \cdot e\left(\prod_{i=1}^n (g^{x_i} (g^{a_i})^s)^{y_i}, h^R\right) \\
&= e\left(g^s, \prod_{i=1}^n (h^{a_i})^{y_i R}\right)^{-1} \cdot e\left(\prod_{i=1}^n (g^{x_i y_i}), h^R\right) \cdot e\left(\prod_{i=1}^n (g^{a_i s y_i}), h^R\right) \\
&= e(g, h)^{-Rs \sum_{i=1}^n a_i y_i} \cdot e(g, h)^{R \sum_{i=1}^n x_i y_i} \cdot e(g, h)^{Rs \sum_{i=1}^n a_i y_i} = e(g, h)^{R \langle \vec{x}, \vec{y} \rangle}.
\end{aligned}
$$

If $\langle \vec{x}, \vec{y} \rangle$ has a small magnitude, then we can get the actual value of the inner product by using a discrete logarithm computation. In order to ensure correctness of this construction, it assumes that the target inner products are contained within a range of polynomial-size.

21.5.1 Proof of Functional Encryption Security

To prove the security of this pairing-based public key FE scheme, we organize hybrid games that change the encryption of $\vec{x}_0$ to the encryption of $\vec{x}_1$. The following theorem proves the security of this scheme under the XDH assumption.

Theorem 3 This scheme is selectively secure against chosen-plaintext attacks in the standard model under the XDH assumption. For all PPT algorithms $\mathcal{B}$, the function $Adv_{\mathcal{B}}^{IND-sCPA}(\lambda)$ is a negligible function of λ.

Proof The proof proceeds by a hybrid argument across a number of games. Let $C = (A, B_1, \cdots, B_n) \in \mathbb{G}_1^{n+1}$ denote the challenge ciphertext given to the adversary during two real attacks (Γ_0 and Γ_1). Additionally, let $R_1, \cdots, R_n$ be random elements of $\mathbb{G}_1$. We define the following hybrid experiments, which differ in how the challenge ciphertext is generated as

1. Game $\Gamma_{0,0}$ This game is the original security game, where the challenge message is $\vec{x}_0$ and the challenge ciphertext is $C = (A, B_1, \cdots, B_n)$.

2. Game $\Gamma_{0,1}$ In this game, the elements $B_1, \cdots, B_n$ of the ciphertext are changed to the random elements $R_1, \cdots, R_n$ of $\mathbb{G}_1$, because the challenge ciphertext is generated for $\vec{x}_0 + r(\vec{x}_1 - \vec{x}_0)$, where $r \in \mathbb{Z}_p^*$ is a hidden random value and $C = (A, R_1, \cdots, R_n)$.

3. Game $\Gamma_{1,1}$ This game is almost the same as $\Gamma_{0,1}$ except that the challenge ciphertext is generated for $\vec{x}_1 + r'(\vec{x}_1 - \vec{x}_0)$, where $r' \in \mathbb{Z}_p^*$ is a hidden random value and $C = (A, R_1, \cdots, R_n)$.

4. Game $\Gamma_{1,0}$ This game is almost the same as $\Gamma_{0,0}$ except that the challenge message is $\vec{x}_1$. The challenge ciphertext is $C = (A, B_1, \cdots, B_n)$.

$\Gamma_{0,0}$ and $\Gamma_{1,0}$ are the same as games Γ_0 and Γ_1 in Definition 4, respectively. Therefore,

$$Adv_{\mathcal{B}}^{IND\text{-}sCPA}(\lambda) = \left| Pr[\mathcal{A}^{\Gamma_{0,0}} = 0] - Pr[\mathcal{A}^{\Gamma_{1,0}} = 0] \right|. \qquad (21.12)$$

To prove that $\Gamma_{0,0}$ is indistinguishable from $\Gamma_{1,0}$, we prove that each step of the hybrid argument is indistinguishable from the next.

Lemma 6 Let $\mathcal{A}$ be an adversary playing the $IND\text{-}sCPA$ attack game. Then, there exists an algorithm $\mathcal{B}$ solving the XDH problem such that

$$\left| Pr[\mathcal{A}^{\Gamma_{w,0}} = 0] - Pr[\mathcal{A}^{\Gamma_{w,1}} = 0] \right| \le Adv_{\mathcal{B}}^{XDH}, \qquad (21.13)$$

where $w \in \{0, 1\}$.

In the following, we prove Lemma 6 under the XDH assumption.

Proof of Lemma 6 Suppose $\mathcal{A}$ has an advantage ϵ in distinguishing Game $\Gamma_{w,1}$ from Game $\Gamma_{w,0}$. We build an algorithm $\mathcal{B}$ that solves the XDH problem in asymmetric pairing. $\mathcal{B}$ is given as input a random 5-tuple (g, g^a, g^b, h, T) that is sampled either from $\mathcal{D}_N$ (where $T = g^{ab}$) or from $\mathcal{D}_R$ (where T is uniform and independent in $\mathbb{G}_1$). Algorithm $\mathcal{B}$'s goal is to output 0 if $T = g^{ab}$ and 1 otherwise. Algorithm $\mathcal{B}$ works by interacting with $\mathcal{A}$ in a selective message game as follows.

Reduction algorithm

Initialization The selective game begins with $\mathcal{A}$ by outputting message vectors $\vec{x}_0$ and $\vec{x}_1 \in \mathcal{X}$ that it intends to attack.

Setup

1. Pick random exponents $a'_1, \cdots, a'_n \in \mathbb{Z}_p^*$.

2. Define as follows: $\vec{x} = \vec{x}_w, g_1 = g^{ax_{1,1}} g^{-ax_{0,1}} g^{a'_1}, \cdots, g_n = g^{ax_{1,n}} g^{-ax_{0,n}} g^{a'_n}, h_1 = h^{ax_{1,1}} h^{-ax_{0,1}} h^{a'_1}, \cdots, h_n = h^{ax_{1,n}} h^{-ax_{0,n}} h^{a'_n}$. where a is the exponent which is unknown to $\mathcal{B}$.

3. Simulate the system for the following parameters $a_1 = ax_{1,1} - ax_{0,1} + a'_1, \cdots, a_n = ax_{1,n} - ax_{0,n} + a'_n$.

4. Send the public parameters $PP = (g_1 = g^{a_1}, \cdots, g_n = g^{a_n})$.

5. Set the master secret key $MSK = (h, h_1 = h^{a_1}, \cdots, h_n = h^{a_n})$, where $\{h_i\}_{i=1}^n$ are unknown to $\mathcal{B}$.

Phase I Consider a query for the secret key corresponding to the key vector $\vec{y} \in \mathcal{Y} \setminus \{\vec{0}\}$, which satisfies $\langle \vec{x}_0, \vec{y} \rangle = \langle \vec{x}_1, \vec{y} \rangle$.

1. Pick a random exponent $R \in \mathbb{Z}_p^*$.

2. Set $k_1 = \prod_{i=1}^n (h^{a_i y_i R})$, $\quad k_2 = h^R$, $\quad k_3 = e(g, h)^R$.

3. Send the secret key $SK_{\vec{y}} = (k_1, k_2, k_3, \vec{y})$.

Challenge $\mathcal{A}$ decides that Phase I is over.

1. Set the challenge ciphertext
$c_1 = g^b$, $\quad \{c_{2,i} = g^{x_i} T^{x_{1,i} - x_{0,i}} g^{a'_i b}\}_{i=1}^n$,
where b is an exponent which is unknown to $\mathcal{B}$.

2. Send the challenge ciphertext $C = (A, B_1, \cdots, B_n)$.

Phase II $\mathcal{A}$ continues to adaptively make a polynomial number of queries not issued in Phase I. $\mathcal{B}$ responds as before.

Guess

1. Finally, $\mathcal{A}$ outputs guesses $w' \in \{0, 1\}$.

2. If $w = w'$, it outputs 1 (indicating that $T = g^{ab}$); otherwise, it outputs 0 (indicating that $T \neq g^{ab}$).

Simulation of secret key generation in Lemma 6

The original secret key is set as follows.
$$k_1 = \prod_{i=1}^n (h_i)^{y_i R}, \qquad k_2 = h^R, \qquad k_3 = e(g, h)^R.$$

In the above reduction algorithm, the secret key is set as follows.
$$k_1 = \prod_{i=1}^{n} (h^{a'_i y_i R}), \qquad k_2 = h^R, \qquad k_3 = e(g,h)^R.$$

The secret key must be generated in the cases of $\langle \vec{x}_0, \vec{y} \rangle = \langle \vec{x}_1, \vec{y} \rangle$.
If $\langle \vec{x}_0, \vec{y} \rangle - \langle \vec{x}_1, \vec{y} \rangle = 0$, k_1 is valid and computed as follows.

$$k_1 = \prod_{i=1}^{n} (h^{a'_i y_i R}) = h^{a(\langle \vec{x}_0, \vec{y} \rangle - \langle \vec{x}_1, \vec{y} \rangle)R} \prod_{i=1}^{n} h^{a'_i y_i R}$$
$$= h^{a \sum_{i=1}^{n} (x_{1,i} y_i - x_{0,i} y_i)R} \prod_{i=1}^{n} h^{a'_i y_i R} = \prod_{i=1}^{n} h^{a(x_{1,i} y_i - x_{0,i} y_i)R} \prod_{i=1}^{n} h^{a'_i y_i R}$$
$$= \prod_{i=1}^{n} h^{a x_{1,i} y_i R} \prod_{i=1}^{n} h^{-a x_{0,i} y_i R} \prod_{i=1}^{n} h^{a'_i y_i R} = \prod_{i=1}^{n} (h^{a x_{1,i}} h^{-a x_{0,i}} h^{a'_i})^{y_i R}$$
$$= \prod_{i=1}^{n} (h^{a_i})^{y_i R} = \prod_{i=1}^{n} (h_i)^{y_i R}.$$

If $\langle \vec{x}_0, \vec{y} \rangle \neq \langle \vec{x}_1, \vec{y} \rangle$, k_1 cannot be computed, because we do not know h^a. So, it cannot generate the secret keys needed for distinguishing the two games.

Simulation of challenge ciphertext generation in Lemma 6

The original ciphertext is set as follows.
$$A = g^s, B_1 = g^{x_1} (g_1)^s, \cdots, B_n = g^{x_n} (g_n)^s.$$

In the above reduction algorithm, the challenge ciphertext is set as
$$A = g^b, B_1 = g^{x_1} T^{x_{1,1} - x_{0,1}} g^{a'_1 b}, \cdots, B_n = g^{x_n} T^{x_{1,n} - x_{0,n}} g^{a'_n b},$$
where $c = s$.

If $T = g^{ab}$, then $B_1, \cdots, B_n$ are valid, because for $1 \leq i \leq n$, $T^{x_{1,i} - x_{0,i}} g^{a'_i b} = (g^{ab})^{x_{1,i} - x_{0,i}} g^{a'_i b} = (g^{a(x_{1,i} - x_{0,i})})^b g^{a'_i b} = (g^{a x_{1,i} - a x_{0,i} + a'_i})^b = (g_i)^b$, and can set $B_1, \cdots, B_n$ by using the instance of the problem, T. On the other hand, if T is random, then naturally $B_1, \cdots, B_n$ are invalid.

Since $c = s$, B is valid ($B = g^c = g^s$) and can set $B = g^s$ by using the instance of the problem, g^c.

Unlike the proof of the predicate encryption, $\mathcal{B}$ does not try to generate the challenge ciphertext of other message vectors, because changing the challenge message vector does not give any advantage to $\mathcal{B}$ in this game.

In conclusion, we can say that

1. When $T = g^{ab}$, i.e., when $\mathcal{B}$'s 5-tuple input is sampled from $\mathcal{D}_N$, $C = (c_1, c_{2,1}, \cdots, c_{2,n})$. Thus, $\mathcal{A}$ is playing Game $\Gamma_{w,0}$.

2. When T is uniform and independent in $\mathbb{G}_1$, i.e., when $\mathcal{B}$'s 5-tuple input is sampled from $\mathcal{D}_R$, $C = (c_1, r_{2,1}, \cdots, r_{2,n})$ for a random $r_{2,1}, \cdots, r_{2,n}$. Thus, $\mathcal{A}$ is playing Game $\Gamma_{w,1}$.

So, if $\mathcal{A}$ has an advantage ϵ in distinguishing Game $\Gamma_{w,1}$ from Game $\Gamma_{w,0}$, then $\mathcal{B}$ has the same advantage ϵ against XDH.

Lemma 7 Adversary $\mathcal{A}$ cannot distinguish $\Gamma_{1,1}$ from $\Gamma_{0,1}$, that is,

$$\left| Pr[\mathcal{A}^{\Gamma_{0,1}} = 0] - Pr[\mathcal{A}^{\Gamma_{1,1}} = 0] \right| = 0. \tag{21.14}$$

In the following, we prove Lemma 7.

Proof of Lemma 7

To prove Lemma 7, we show that the challenge ciphertext C that is the encryption of $\vec{x}_0 + r(\vec{x}_1 - \vec{x}_0)$ can be restated as the encryption of $\vec{x}_1 + r'(\vec{x}_1 - \vec{x}_0)$, where r and r' are hidden to the adversary. By simply setting $r = r' + 1$, we obtain the following equation

$$\vec{x}_0 + r(\vec{x}_1 - \vec{x}_0) = \vec{x}_0 + (r' + 1)(\vec{x}_1 - \vec{x}_0) = \vec{x}_1 + r'(\vec{x}_1 - \vec{x}_0). \tag{21.15}$$

Note that the secret key $SK_{\vec{y}}$ cannot be used to distinguish the change since $\langle \vec{x}_0, \vec{y} \rangle = \langle \vec{x}_1, \vec{y} \rangle$ by the restriction of the security model.

This completes the proof of Lemma 7.

Thus, if there is no algorithm $\mathcal{B}$ that solves the XDH problem with an advantage better than ϵ, then, for all adversary $\mathcal{A}$,

$$\left| Pr[\mathcal{A}^{\Gamma_{0,0}} = 0] - Pr[\mathcal{A}^{\Gamma_{1,0}} = 0] \right|$$
$$= \left| Pr[\mathcal{A}^{\Gamma_{0,0}} = 0] - Pr[\mathcal{A}^{\Gamma_{0,1}} = 0] \right| + \left| Pr[\mathcal{A}^{\Gamma_{0,1}} = 0] - Pr[\mathcal{A}^{\Gamma_{1,1}} = 0] \right| $$
$$+ \left| Pr[\mathcal{A}^{\Gamma_{1,1}} = 0] - Pr[\mathcal{A}^{\Gamma_{1,0}} = 0] \right| \leq 2\epsilon.$$

Consequently, under the XDH assumption, Game $\Gamma_{0,0}$ is indistinguishable from $\Gamma_{1,0}$. $\square$

21.5.2 Applications of Functional Encryption

FE has a lot of new applications in contrast with previous PKE schemes (e.g., IBE, ABE, PE). It is because the purpose of previous PKE schemes is to output a message included in a ciphertext according to access policy. On the other hand, since FE schemes output function results, they can be used to support additional purposes. For details on applications of FE, readers are referred to [63].

21.5.2.1 Distance Measurement

In an online random chatting environment, when each element of a vector reflects a personal preference, one can know who has the similar preference with him by computing the inner products. Note that one cannot see the personal information of others directly. After figuring out whether a specific user has the similar preference, one can start chatting with him or her accordingly.

21.5.2.2 Exact Threshold

Recently, biometric-based authentication is gaining popularity since it is more convenient than traditional password-based one. In contrast to password-based authentication, biometric-based authentication involves certain noises when measuring biometric information. A viable method to address this problem is to check whether the user's secret key matches the measured biometric information within an approximate value by computing the inner products.

21.5.2.3 Weighted Average

Weighted average computed from the inner products can be used to gather information without exposing personal information. Let us suppose a recruitment system where a job seeker's own data is $\vec{x} = \{x_1, \cdots, x_n\}$ and a job provider sets up a function using an assessment indicator $\vec{y} = \{y_1, \cdots, y_n\}$. Here, the elements of $\vec{x}$ might include licenses and practical experience, while the elements of $\vec{y}$ do the weighted values of licenses and practical experience displayed. A job seeker uploads the ciphertext $C(\vec{x})$ and a job provider receives the corresponding secret key $SK_{\vec{y}}$. In this case, the job provider can get various results from different job seekers according to the decrypted data generated from $C(\vec{x})$s by using corresponding $SK_{\vec{y}}$s, respectively. Note that job seekers do not need to worry about their personal information being revealed during this recruitment process because the job providers can only access the evaluated results but not the job seekers' plain data.

Part III

Post-Quantum Cryptography

22

Introduction to Lattice

CONTENTS

The first part of the chapter is dedicated to the introduction of lattices and dual lattices. Determinant is then explained with the Gram-Schmidt orthogonalization process as it is an important numerical invariant attached to the lattice. The next section describes representative lattice problems. The final part of the chapter describes the NRTU cryptosystem which is closely related to lattice problems for a certain class of lattices.

22.1   Preliminaries

This chapter is written with the intention to provide the theoretical foundation for lattice-based cryptography. For further details on lattice, readers refer to [68].

Definition 1 (Lattice) *Any Euclidean vector space E is a metric space with distance function $d : E \times E \to \mathbb{R}$ defined by $d(x, y) = ||x - y||$. A subset L of a vector space E is a lattice if and only if there are linearly independent vectors $b_1, \cdots, b_n \in E$ such that*

$$L = \sum_{i=1}^{n} \mathbb{Z}b_i = \{\sum_{i=1}^{n} c_i b_i : c_i \in \mathbb{Z}, 1 < i \leq n\}. \tag{22.1}$$

Definition 2 (Rank and Lattice Basis) *The integer n is called the rank of the lattice, and the sequence of vectors $b_1, \cdots, b_n$ is called a lattice basis . The dimension of E determines the dimension of the lattice.*

An n-dimensional lattice L is an additive subgroup of E such that L is discrete, which means there is a real number $\epsilon > 0$ such that any two distinct points $x \neq y \in L$ are at distance at least $||x - y|| \geq \epsilon$. Equivalently, an n-dimensional lattice L is an additive subgroup of $\mathbb{R}^n$. The value of ϵ depends on the difference between successive points in vector space E. For example, $\mathbb{Q}^n$ is a subgroup of $\mathbb{R}^n$, but not a lattice, because it is not discrete. $\mathbb{Z}^n$ is a lattice because it is an additive subgroup of $\mathbb{R}^n$ and the distance between any two points in $\mathbb{Z}^n$ is at least 1.

Example A simple example of n-dimensional lattice is given by the set $\mathbb{Z}^n$ of all vectors with integral coordinates. When the number of basis vectors equals the number of coordinates, we say that the lattice is *full rank* or *full dimensional*. A lattice L is full rank if and only if the basis vectors of L linearly span across the entire space E.

Definition 3 (Dual Lattice) *Suppose that L is a lattice of full rank in a vector space E. The dual lattice of L, denoted $L^\dagger$, is the lattice of vectors having integral inner products with all vectors in L: $L^\dagger = \{x \in E : \langle x, L \rangle \in \mathbb{Z}\}$. $L^\dagger$ is also a lattice of full rank in E.*

Definition 4 (Determinant of a Lattice) *The determinant of a lattice L, denoted $d(L)$ or $det(L)$, is the signed volume of the fundamental parallelepiped spanned by the basis vectors. The determinant is independent of the choice of the basis.*

A way to compute the determinant is given by the **Gram-Schmidt orthogonalization** process. For any basis vectors $b_1, \cdots, b_n$ for L, the process computes the orthogonalized vectors $b_1{}^*, \cdots, b_n{}^*$ iteratively by

$$b_i^* = b_i - \Sigma_{j<i} \; \mu_{ij} b_j^*, \tag{22.2}$$

where $\mu_{ij} = \frac{\langle b_i, b_j^* \rangle}{\langle b_j^*, b_j^* \rangle}$ and $b_1^* = b_1$. That is, $b_i{}^*$ is the component of $b_i{}^*$ orthogonal to $b_1, \cdots, b_{i-1}$. The determinant of the lattice equals the product of the lengths of the orthogonalized vectors

$$det(L) = \Pi_{i=1}^n ||b_i{}^*||. \tag{22.3}$$

22.2   Lattice Problems

This section provides definitions of representative lattice problems.

Definition 5 (Shortest Vector Problem (SVP)) *Given a lattice L, the shortest vector problem is to find a non-zero vector $v \in L$ for any non-zero $u \in L$ such that $||v|| \leq ||u||$.*

Definition 6 (Approximate Shortest Vector Problem (γ-SVP)) *Given a lattice L, the shortest vector problem is to find a non-zero vector $v \in L$ for any non-zero $u \in L$ such that $||v|| \leq \gamma||u||$, where γ is a real number.* Observe that taking $\gamma = 1$ corresponds to the exact versions of the problems, and also that the problems become easier as γ increases.

Definition 7 (Closest Vector Problem (CVP)) *Given a lattice L and a target vector $w \in L$, the approximate closest vector problem is to find a vector $u \in L$ closest to the target w, i.e., for any $v \in L$ such that $||u-w|| \leq ||v-w||$.*

Definition 8 (Approximate Closest Vector Problem (γ-CVP)) *Given a lattice L and a target vector $w \in L$, the approximate closest vector problem is to find a vector $u \in L$ closest to the target w, i.e., for any $v \in L$ such that $||u - w|| \leq \gamma||v - w||$, where γ is a real number.* Note that the closest vector problem is a generalization of the shortest vector problem.

To date, we do not know any polynomial time algorithm to solve SVP. Goldreich et al. showed that any hardness of SVP implies the same hardness for CVP [54]. Therefore, no algorithm can solve CVP in polynomial time.

The shortest vector problem can be described as follows: given a lattice L of positive rank, find a non-zero element $x \in L$ with $q(x)$ smallest possible. If we are given short basis vectors, we can easily solve this problem. Thus, the key to the problem is to get short basis vectors from given random long basis vectors. The so-called LLL algorithm [15] turns out to approximately solve SVP by generating reduced basis.

When we construct a cryptographic scheme based on lattices, we can design one-way functions based on the fact that it is hard to get short basis vectors from given long basis vectors. For example, in the public key encryption such as the following NTRU cryptosystem, the short basis vectors constitute a private key and the corresponding long basis vectors are open as the corresponding public key.

22.3 NTRU Cryptosystem

The original NTRU [58] was proposed by Hoffstein, Pipher, and Silverman which was based on rings. Micciancio and Regev presented the lattice NTRU version. The lattices used in NTRU belongs to a special class such as convolutional modular lattices with even dimensions [74]. Its security is closely related to the hardness of CVP, but it is rarely known whether lattices used in NTRU are as hard as the general case. NTRU has a number of performance benefits such as fast encryption, decryption, and key generation along with comparatively short public key size.

The NTRU cryptosystem proceeds as follows.

1. **Setup**

   The NTRU cryptosystem parameters include a prime dimension n, an integer modulus q, a smaller integer p, and an integer weight bound b_f.

2. **Gen**

   Private Key: The private key is set to be a short vector (f, g) with the following restrictions.

   (a) The matrix $[T * f]$ should be invertible modulo q, where

   $$T = \begin{bmatrix} 0 & 0 & \cdots & 0 & 1 \\ 1 & 0 & \cdots & 0 & 0 \\ 0 & 1 & \cdots & 0 & 0 \\ \vdots & \vdots & \ddots & \vdots & \vdots \\ 0 & 0 & \cdots & 1 & 0 \end{bmatrix}.$$

   (b) $f \in e_1 + pu$ and $g \in pv$, where $u, v \in \{-1, 0, 1\}$ and f, g are random polynomials, and e_1 is defined such that $f - e_1$ and g have exactly $d_f + 1$ positive entries and d_f negative entries.

   Public Key: The public key is the Hermite Normal Form (HNF) of the convolutional modular lattice $L_q((T * x, T * g)^t)$ such that

   $$H = \begin{bmatrix} I & O \\ T * h & q \cdot I \end{bmatrix}, where \ h = [T * f]^{-1} g \ mod \ q.$$

3. **Encryption**

   Given the message $m \in \{-1, 0, 1\}^n$ with $d_f + 1$ positive and d_f negative entities, a random vector r is chosen with the same conditions that the message has. The ciphertext is $c = f(-r, m) \ mod \ H$ shown as

   $$c = (0, (m + [T * h]r) \ mod \ q). \tag{22.4}$$

4. **Decryption**

   The decryption process is divided into two stages. In the first stage, ciphertext c is multiplied with the matrix $[T * f]$ mod q such that

$$[T*f]c \, mod \, q = [T*f][m]+[T*f][T*h]r \, mod \, q = [T*f]m+[T*g]r \, mod \, q, \tag{22.5}$$

where $[T * f][T * h] = [T * ([T * f]h)]$, $[T * f] = I \, mod \, p$, $[T * g] = O \, mod \, p$, I is identity and O is zero matrix. Therefore, message m can be obtained by reducing it to mod p as

$$[T * f]m + [T * g]r \, modp = I \cdot m + O \cdot r = m. \tag{22.6}$$

Exercises

22.1 Answer the following questions:

1. Given a $m \times n$ integer matrix A, show that $\{b \in \mathbb{Z}^m : bA = 0\}$ is a lattice of rank $m - rk(A)$.

2. Given a $m \times n$ integer matrix A and an integer N, show that $\{b \in \mathbb{Z}^m : bA = 0 \, mod \, N\}$ is a lattice of rank m.

22.2 Let A be a basis matrix of a full rank lattice L.

1. Show that $(A^T)^{-1}$ is a basis matrix for the dual lattice.

2. Show that the determinant of the dual lattice is $d(L)^{-1}$.

22.3 Give an example of a lattice L of rank 1 in $\mathbb{Z}^2$ whose determinant $d(L)$ is not an integer.

22.4 Let L be a rank 2 lattice in $\mathbb{R}^2$ and let $\{b_1, b_2\}$ be a basis for L. Show that $d(L) = ||b_1|| \cdot ||b_2|||sin(\theta)|$ where θ is the angle between b_1, b_2.

22.5 Given a lattice L with the basis matrix $A = \begin{bmatrix} 1001 & 0 \\ 1 & 2008 \end{bmatrix}$:

1. What are the two shortest non-zero vectors?

2. What is the closest vector to (5005, 6024)?

3. Why is it easy to find the closest vector in this lattice?

22.6 Given two bases for $\mathbb{Z}^2$ as $(24, 25)$ and $(23, 24)$, find the Gram-Schmidt vectors b_1, b_2, and their corresponding lengths.

22.7 Give a working encryption and decryption example on message $m = -x^5 + x^3 + x^2 - x + 1$ for NTRU encryption scheme with the parameters $n = 7, p = 3, q = 41$.

22.8 Give a working encryption and decryption example on message $m = x^{10} + x^9 - x^8 - x^4 + x^3 - 1$ for NTRU encryption scheme with the parameters $n = 11, p = 3, q = 32$.

23

Lattice-Based Cryptography

CONTENTS

An overview of lattice-based post-quantum cryptography is provided in this chapter. Post-quantum cryptography refers to the cryptographic algorithms that are thought to be secure against an attack by a quantum computer. The first section introduces post-quantum cryptography. The next section describes the preliminaries that must be mastered in order to understand the post-quantum cryptography. The remaining sections describe lattice-based cryptographic constructions of post-quantum cryptography. Learning with errors (LWE), learning with rounding (LWR), and ring variants of LWE and LWR are then discussed.

23.1   Overview

Post-quantum cryptography are the cryptographic algorithms (usually public-key algorithms) thought to be secure against an attack by a quantum computer. However, this is not true for the most existing popular public-key algorithms, which can be efficiently broken by a sufficiently large quantum computer. The problem with the currently popular algorithms is that their security relies on one of these hard mathematical problems: (1) the integer factorization problem, (2) the discrete logarithm problem, or (3) the elliptic-curve discrete logarithm problem. All of these problems can be easily solved on a sufficiently powerful quantum computer running the Shor's algorithm [66].

In contrast to the threat which quantum computing poses to current public-key algorithms, most current symmetric cryptographic algorithms, and hash functions are considered to be relatively secure against attacks by quantum computers. Although the Grover's algorithm [102] does speed up attacks against symmetric ciphers, doubling the key size can effectively thwart these attacks. Thus post-quantum symmetric cryptography does not need to differ significantly from the current symmetric cryptography.

23.2   Preliminaries

All logarithms in this chapter are base 2 (e.g., $\log a = \log_2 a$) unless otherwise indicated. For a positive integer q, we use $\mathbb{Z} \cap (-q/2, q/2]$ as a representative of $\mathbb{Z}_q$. For a real number r, $\lfloor r \rceil$ denotes the nearest integer to r, rounding upwards in case of a tie, e.g., $\lfloor 4.5 \rceil = 5$ and $\lfloor 4.4 \rceil = 4$. We denote vectors in bold, e.g., $\mathbf{a}$, and every vector in this chapter is a column vector ($\mathbf{a}^T = [a_1, a_2, \ldots, a_n]$), where n is the dimension of vector. The norm $||\cdot||$ is always 2-norm in this chapter (2-norm= $||\vec{x}||_2 = \sqrt{\prod_{i=1}^{n} |x_i|^2}$). We denote by $\langle \cdot, \cdot \rangle$ the usual dot product of two vectors. We use $x \leftarrow \mathcal{D}$ to denote the sampling x according to the distribution $\mathcal{D}$. It denotes the uniform sampling when $\mathcal{D}$ is a finite set. For an integer $n \geq 1$, $\mathcal{D}^n$ denotes the product of i.i.d.(independent and identically distributed) random variables $\mathcal{D}_i \sim \mathcal{D}$ ('$\sim$' can mean "similar to," including "of the same order of magnitude as" such as $x \sim y$ meaning that x and y are of the same order of magnitude). We let λ denote the security parameter: all known valid attacks against the cryptographic scheme under scope should take $\Omega(2^\lambda)$ bit operations. A function $negl : \mathbb{N} \to \mathbb{R}^+$ ($\mathbb{N}$: natural number, $\mathbb{R}^+$: positive real number) is negligible if for every positive polynomial $p(\lambda)$ there exists $\lambda_0 \in \mathbb{N}$ such that $negl(\lambda) < 1/p(\lambda)$ for all $\lambda > \lambda_0$. For two matrices A and B with the same number of rows, $(A||B)$ denotes their row concatenation, i.e., for $A \in \mathbb{Z}^{m \times n_1}$ and $B \in \mathbb{Z}^{m \times n_2}$, the $m \times (n_1 + n_2)$ matrix $C = (A||B)$ is defined as

$$C_{ij} = \begin{cases} a_{i,j} & 1 \leq j \leq n_1 \\ b_{i,(j-n_1)} & n_1 \leq j \leq n_1 + n_2. \end{cases}$$

23.2.1 Distributions

For a positive integer q, we define $\mathcal{U}_q$ by the uniform distribution over $\mathbb{Z}_q$. For a real $\sigma > 0$, the discrete Gaussian distribution of parameter σ, denoted by $\mathcal{DG}_\sigma$, is a probability distribution with support $\mathbb{Z}$ that assigns a probability proportional to $exp(-(\pi x^2)/\sigma^2)$ to each $x \in \mathbb{Z}$. Note that the variance of $\mathcal{DG}_\sigma$ is very close to $\sigma^2/2\pi$ unless σ is very small. [34] will apply the following simple lemmas for tail bounds (bound probabilities of extreme events) to discrete Gaussian distributions.

1. $\mathcal{HWT}_n(h)$: For an integer $0 \leq h \leq n$, the distribution uniformly samples vector from $\{0, \pm 1\}^n$ under the condition to have exactly h non-zero elements.

2. $\mathcal{ZO}_n(\rho)$: For a real number $0 \leq \rho \leq 1$, the distribution samples vector $\mathbf{v}$ from $\{0, \pm 1\}^n$, where each element of vector $\mathbf{v}$ is chosen satisfying $Pr[v_i = 0] = 1 - \rho$ and $Pr[v_i = 1] = \rho/2 = Pr[v_i = -1]$. That is, the probability of that the element becomes to 0 is $1 - \rho$, and the probability of that the element becomes to 1 or -1 is $\rho/2$.

23.3 Lattice-Based Cryptography

Lattice-based cryptographic constructions are one of candidates of post-quantum cryptography, which are believed to be secure against quantum computers. It has the following unique advantages.

1. Very strong security proofs based on worst-case hardness[1]

---

[1] Worst-case hardness of lattice problems means that breaking the lattice based cryptographic construction (even with some small non-negligible probability) is provably at least as hard as solving several lattice problems (approximately, within polynomial factors) in the worst case. In other words, breaking the lattice based cryptographic construction implies that there is an efficient algorithm that can solve for every instance of the underlying lattice problem.

In most of the cases, the underlying problem is to approximate lattice problems such as SVP to polynomial elements. It is thought to be a difficult problem. This strong security guarantee is one of the characteristics of lattice-based cryptography.

The worst-case security guarantee is important because of the following two reasons.

(a) It is sure that the attacks on cryptographic construction are only effective when the range of to selection parameters is restricted and not asymptotically effective. In other words, it ensures that there is no fundamental defect in the design of the cryptographic construction.

(b) In principle, a worst-case security guarantee can help to select specific parameters for the cryptographic system. However, in practice the parameter estimates are selected conservatively (either too few or too many). Therefore, it is often the case that parameters are set according to the best known attack.

2. Relatively efficient implementations

3. Simplicity

4. Applicable in various applications

23.3.1   Learning with Errors (LWE)

LWE is one of the most promising primitives in many usages (especially post-quantum cryptography) due to its lightweight operation and rigorous security reduction against the worst-case of the lattice problems that are considered to be hard to solve even after the advance of quantum computers.

In 2005, LWE was first introduced by Regev[88] to construct a public key encryption. After that, many cryptographic systems based on LWE have been proposed depending on its versatility. However, some variants [49], [86] of the Regev's technique requiring somewhat larger parameters are not practical. Lindner and Peikert [70] had improved the LWE based scheme to use the method to insert the noise into a combination of LWE samples in the encryption phase. However, it is still impractical, because the noise sampling from the discrete Gaussian distribution requires inefficient floating point operations of high bit precision [42]. From 2012 through 2016, some post-quantum key exchanges [4], [28], [27], [39], [85], and more efficient Public-Key Encryption (PKE) [100], [23] were proposed, where they use sparse small secrets based on the hardness assumptions of LWE and its ring variant. Although they are practical and support quantum-resistant security, they are still inefficient due to Gaussian sampling. There have been some attempts [27], [85] to improve it, which are not yet satisfactory. Recently, Lizard [34] was proposed to improve the performance.

LWE

For an n-dimensional vector $\mathbf{s} \in \mathbb{Z}^n$ and an error distribution $\mathcal{X}$ over $\mathbb{Z}$, LWE distribution $A_{n,q,\mathcal{X}}^{LWE}(\mathbf{s})$ over $\mathbb{Z}_q^n \times \mathbb{Z}_q$ is obtained by choosing a vector $\mathbf{a}$ uniformly and randomly from $\mathbb{Z}_q^n$ and error e from $\mathcal{X}$, and outputting $(\mathbf{a}, b = \langle \mathbf{a}, \mathbf{s} \rangle + e) \in \mathbb{Z}_q^n \times \mathbb{Z}_q$.

The search LWE problem

Find $\mathbf{s} \in \mathbb{Z}_q$ for given arbitrarily many independent samples $(\mathbf{a}_i, \mathbf{b}_i)$ from $A_{n,q,\mathcal{X}}^{LWE}(\mathbf{s})$.

The decision LWE problem

The decision LWE denoted by $LWE_{n,q,\mathcal{X}}(\mathcal{D})$ aims to distinguish the distribution $A_{n,q,\mathcal{X}}^{LWE}(\mathbf{s})$ from the uniform distribution over $\mathbb{Z}_q^n \times \mathbb{Z}_q$ with non-negligible advantage, for a fixed $\mathbf{s} \leftarrow \mathcal{D}$. When the number of samples are limited by m, we denote the problem by $LWE_{n,m,q,\mathcal{X}}(\mathcal{D})$.

Jung Hee Cheon et al. [34] only consider the discrete Gaussian $\mathcal{X} = \mathcal{D}G_{\alpha q}$ as an error distribution where α is the error rate in $(0, 1)$, so α will substitute the distribution $\mathcal{X}$ in description of LWE problem, say $LWE_{n,m,q,\alpha}(\mathcal{D})$. The LWE problem is self-reducible[2] so we usually omit the key distribution $\mathcal{D}$ (For example, $LWE_{n,m,q,\mathcal{X}}$, $LWE_{n,m,q,\alpha}$) when it is a uniform distribution over $\mathbb{Z}_q^n$.

Its hardness is guaranteed by the decision version of the shortest vector problem (GapSVP), and the shortest independent vectors problem (SIVP) which are the worst case hardness of the standard lattice problems. After Regev [88] presented the quantum reduction from those lattice problems to the LWE problem, Peikert et al. [30], [84] improved the reduction to a classical version for significantly worse parameter (the dimension should be the size of $n\log_q$). In this case, the reduction holds only for GapSVP, not SIVP.

The decision LWE problem with sparse binary secret

After the research about the connection between the LWE problem and some lattice problems, some variants of LWE, of which the secret distributions are modified from the uniform distribution, were proposed. Zvika Brakerski et al. [30] proved that the LWE problem with binary secret is at least as hard as the original LWE problem. Following the approach of Zvika Brakerski et al. [30], Cheon et al. [34] proved the hardness of the LWE problem with sparse secret(the number of non-zero components of the secret vector is a constant).

The hardness of the LWE problem with signed-binary secret of Hamming weight h, $LWE_{n,m,q,\beta}(\mathcal{H}WT_n(h))$ is guaranteed by the following theorem.

Theorem 1 (Informal) If $log(_nC_h) + h > klog_q$ and $\beta > \alpha(10h)^{1/2}$, the $LWE_{n,m,q,\beta}(\mathcal{H}WT_n(h))$ problem is at least as hard as the $LWE_{n,m,q,\alpha}$, where $_nC_k = \frac{_nP_k}{k!} = \frac{n!}{k!(n-k)!}$ is the number of k-combinations from a given set S of n elements.

Proof is omitted.

The multiple secret LWE

In [29], [85], [86], to encrypt a string, not a bit, LWE with single secret

---

[2]Problem of deciding language sometimes called "decision problem:" given input x, solution = yes/no answer. But many problems are more naturally "search problems:" given input x, find solution y.

Many languages come from natural search problems. Clearly, efficient solution to search problem would give efficient solution to corresponding decision problem. So proof that decision problem is NP-hard implies that search problem is "hard" as well, and does not have any efficient solution.

But exactly how much more difficult are search problems? Perhaps surprisingly, many (but not all) are only polynomially more difficult than corresponding decision problem, in the following sense: any efficient solution to the decision problem can be used to solve the search problem efficiently. This is called "self-reducibility."

was generalized to LWE with multiple secrets. An instance of multi-secret LWE is $(\mathbf{a}, \langle \mathbf{a}, \mathbf{s}_1 \rangle + \mathbf{e}_1, ..., \langle \mathbf{a}, \mathbf{s}_n \rangle + \mathbf{e}_n)$, where $\mathbf{s}_1, ..., \mathbf{s}_k$ are secret vectors and $\mathbf{e}_1, ..., \mathbf{e}_k$ are independently chosen error vectors. Using the hybrid argument, multi-secret LWE is proved to be at least as hard as LWE with single secret. Based on this hardness guarantee, [34] uses the LWE instances with a number of sparse signed-binary secrets to construct an encryption scheme.

The conclusion of this section is that in the case of $log(_nC_h) + h > k \, log_q$ and $\beta > \alpha(10h)^{1/2}$, the LWE problem with signed-binary secret of Hamming weight h is difficult, and the scheme using LWE instances with a number of sparse signed-binary secrets applying multi-secret LWE can be easily proved. So, a secure and efficient scheme can be developed by using these.

23.3.2   Learning with Rounding (LWR)

The LWR problem which was introduced from [7] is the variant of LWE problem. Instead of adding auxiliary errors, the instance of the LWR problem is generated through the deterministic rounding process into a smaller modulus. Because the error generated in above process is deterministic, the LWR problem is called "derandomized" version of the LWE problem. More precisely, to hide the secret information, the LWR problem uses the rounding to modulus p instead of adding errors; the deterministic error is generated by scaling down from $\mathbb{Z}_q$ to $\mathbb{Z}_p$, where $q > p$. When modulus is somewhat large, [5] and [7] show that the LWR problem is not easier than the LWE problem. However, due to the constraint which modulus must be large, the LWR problem has been used only for special applications such as pseudorandom generator (PRG) [7]. In [18], when the number of samples are limited, it is proven that the LWR problem is difficult under the hardness assumption of the LWE problem.

LWR

For an n-dimensional vector $\mathbf{s}$ over $\mathbb{Z}_q$, the LWR distribution $A_{n,q,p}^{LWR}(\mathbf{s})$ over $\mathbb{Z}_q^n \times \mathbb{Z}_p$ is obtained by choosing a vector $\mathbf{a}$ from $\mathbb{Z}_q^n$ uniform randomly, and returning $(\mathbf{a}, \lfloor p/q \cdot \mathbf{a} \cdot \mathbf{s} \rceil) \in \mathbb{Z}_q^n \times \mathbb{Z}_p$.

Like the LWE problem, $A_{n,m,q,p}^{LWR}(\mathbf{s})$ indicates the distribution of m samples from $A_{n,q,p}^{LWR}(\mathbf{s})$; that is contained in $\mathbb{Z}_q^{m \times n} \times \mathbb{Z}_p^m$.

The search LWR problem

It is defined to find secret $\mathbf{s}$ as the search version of the LWE problem

The decision LWR problem($LWR_{n,m,q,p}(\mathcal{D})$)

It's purpose is to distinguish the distribution $A_{n,q,p}^{LWR}(\mathbf{s})$ from the uniform distribution over $\mathbb{Z}_q^n \times \mathbb{Z}_p$ with m instances for a fixed $\mathbf{s} \leftarrow \mathcal{D}$.

23.3.3 Ring Variants of LWE and LWR

In [73], Lyubashevsky et al. deal with the LWE problem over rings, namely ring-LWE. For positive integers n and q, and an irreducible polynomial $g(x) \in \mathbb{Z}[x]$ of degree n, we define the ring $R = \mathbb{Z}[x]/(g(x))$ and its quotient ring modulo q, $R_q = \mathbb{Z}_q[x]/(g(x))$. The ring-LWE problem is to distinguish between the uniform distribution and the distribution of $(a, a \cdot s + e) \in R_q^2$ where a is uniform randomly chosen polynomial, e is chosen from an error distribution and s is a secret polynomial.

Due to the efficiency and compactness of ring-LWE, many lattice-based cryptosystems are constructed as ring-LWE based, rather than LWE-based. Similarly to LWE, the ring-LWE problem over the ring R is at least as hard as approximate version of SVP over the ideal lattices of R in the sense of quantum reduction.

The ring variant of LWR is introduced in [7], [18] as an analogue of LWR. In the ring-LWR problem, the vectors chosen from $\mathbb{Z}_q^n$ are substituted by polynomials in R_q, i.e., the ring-LWR instance for a secret polynomial $s \in R_q$ is $(a, \lfloor p/q \cdot a \cdot s \rceil) \in R_q \times R_p$ where $\lfloor p/q \cdot a \cdot s \rceil$ is obtained by applying the rounding function to each coefficient of $p/q \cdot a \cdot s$. The search and decision ring-LWR problems are defined in the same way as the LWR problem, but over rings.

Abhishek Banerjee et al. [7] proved that decision ring-LWR is at least as hard as decision ring-LWE for sufficiently large modulus. Later, reduction from search ring-LWE to search ring-LWR was constructed in overall scope of the modulus [7] when the number of samples is bounded.

23.4 (LWE+LWR)-Based Public-Key Encryption [34]

The PKE schemes based on LWE problem have a simple and fast decryption, but encryption is rather slow due to large parameter size for leftover hash lemma [8] or expensive Gaussian samplings [43]. Jung Hee Cheon et al. [34] proposed a novel PKE scheme called Lizard based on LWE and LWR problems with provable security. Based on [9] that the LWR assumption is hard under the hardness assumption of LWE; when the number of samples is limited, the LWR assumption can be securely used in the encryption phase. To make a ciphertext by using the LWR instances instead of the LWE instances not only reduces the parameters and the ciphertext size, but also substitutes the expensive discrete Gaussian sampling by deterministic and efficient rounding.

Lizard has a conceptually simple encryption procedure consisting of subset sum and rounding operations without Gaussian samplings and leftover hash lemma. Also, by taking some advantages of sparse binary secrets, Lizard becomes very practical in the sense that it could compress the ciphertext size by scaling it down from $\mathbb{Z}_q$ to $\mathbb{Z}_p$ where p is the rounding modulus, and the other is that it speed up the encryption algorithm by eliminating the Gaussian sampling process.

23.4.1   The Construction

We now describe the public-key encryption scheme based on both the LWE and LWR problems. The public key consists of m number of n dimensional LWE instances, and encryptions of zero form $(n+l)$ samples of m dimensional LWR, where l is the dimension of plaintext vectors. The scheme is described as follows.

1. *Lizard.Setup*(1^λ): Choose positive integers m, n, q, p, t, and l. Choose private key distribution $\mathcal{D}_s$ over $\mathbb{Z}^n$, ephemeral secret distribution $\mathcal{D}_r$ over $\mathbb{Z}^m$, and parameter σ for discrete Gaussian distribution $\mathcal{DG}_\sigma$. Output *params* $\leftarrow (m, n, q, p, t, l, \mathcal{D}_s, \mathcal{D}_r, \sigma)$.

2. *Lizard.Gen*(*params*): Generate a random matrix $A \leftarrow \mathbb{Z}_q^{(m \times n)}$. Choose a secret matrix $S = (\mathbf{s}_1 || \cdots || \mathbf{s}_l)$ by sampling column vectors $\mathbf{s}_i \in \mathbb{Z}^n$ independently from the distribution $\mathcal{D}_s$. Generate an error matrix $E = (\mathbf{e}_1 || \cdots || \mathbf{e}_l)$ from $\mathcal{DG}_\sigma^{(m \times l)}$ and let $B \leftarrow AS + E \in \mathbb{Z}_q^{(m \times l)}$ where the operations are held in modular q. Output the public key $pk \leftarrow (A || B) \in \mathbb{Z}_q^{(m \times (n+l))}$ and the secret key $sk \leftarrow S \in \mathbb{Z}^{(n \times l)}$.

3. *Lizard.Enc*$_{pk}(\mathbf{m})$: For a plaintext $\mathbf{m} = (m_i)_{1 \leq i \leq l} \in \mathbb{Z}_t^l$, choose an m dimensional vector $\mathbf{r} \in \mathbb{Z}^m$ from the distribution $\mathcal{D}_r$. Compute the vectors $\mathbf{c}_1' \leftarrow A^T \mathbf{r}$ and $\mathbf{c}_2' \leftarrow B^T \mathbf{r}$ over $\mathbb{Z}_q$, and output the vector $\mathbf{c} \leftarrow (\mathbf{c}_1, \mathbf{c}_2) \in \mathbb{Z}_p^{(n+l)}$ where $\mathbf{c}_1 \leftarrow \lfloor (p/q) \cdot \mathbf{c}_1' \rceil \in \mathbb{Z}_p^n$ and $\mathbf{c}_2 \leftarrow \lfloor (p/t) \cdot \mathbf{m} + (p/q) \cdot \mathbf{c}_2' \rceil \in \mathbb{Z}_p^l$.

4. *Lizard.Dec*$_{sk}(\mathbf{c})$: For a ciphertext $c \leftarrow (\mathbf{c}_1, \mathbf{c}_2) \in \mathbb{Z}_p^{(n+l)}$, compute and output the vector $\mathbf{m}' \leftarrow \lfloor t/p \cdot (\mathbf{c}_2 - S^T \mathbf{c}_1) \rceil \pmod{t}$.

Here, we assume $t|p|q$ (t can divide p, and p can divide q) in the rest of paper. However, this scheme still works correctly for parameters that do not satisfy $t|p|q$.

23.4.2 Correctness

Lemma 1 The cryptosystem described above works correctly as long as the following inequality holds for the security parameter λ:

$$Pr\left[|\langle \mathbf{e}, \mathbf{r} \rangle + \langle \mathbf{s}, \mathbf{f} \rangle| < q/2t - q/2p : \mathbf{e} \leftarrow \mathcal{D}G_\rho^m, \mathbf{r} \leftarrow \mathcal{D}_r, \mathbf{s} \leftarrow \mathcal{D}_s, \mathbf{f} \leftarrow \mathbb{Z}_{q/p}^n \right]$$
$$< negl(\lambda).$$

Proof. Let $\mathbf{r} \in \mathbb{Z}^m$ be a vector sampled from $\mathcal{D}_r$ in this encryption procedure, and let $\mathbf{c}' = (\mathbf{c}_1', \mathbf{c}_2') \leftarrow (A^T \mathbf{r}, B^T \mathbf{r}) \in \mathbb{Z}_q^{n+l}$. The output ciphertext is $\mathbf{c} \leftarrow (\mathbf{c}_1 = \lfloor (p/q) \cdot \mathbf{c}_1' \rceil, \mathbf{c}_2 = \lfloor (p/t) \cdot \mathbf{m} + (p/q) \cdot \mathbf{c}_2' \rceil)$.

Let $\mathbf{f}_1 \leftarrow \mathbf{c}_1' \pmod{q/p} \in \mathbb{Z}_{q/p}^n$ and $\mathbf{f}_2 \leftarrow \mathbf{c}_2' \pmod{q/p} \in \mathbb{Z}_{q/p}^l$ be the vectors satisfying $(p/q) \cdot \mathbf{c}_1 = \mathbf{c}_1' - \mathbf{f}_1$ and $(p/q) \cdot (\mathbf{c}_2 - (p/t) \cdot \mathbf{m}) = \mathbf{c}_2' - \mathbf{f}_2$. (where $\mathbf{f}_1$ and $\mathbf{f}_2$ can be thought of as the error of $\mathbf{c}_1'$ and $\mathbf{c}_2'$, respectively). Note that $\mathbf{f}_1 = A^T \mathbf{r} \pmod{q/p}$ is uniformly and randomly distributed over $\mathbb{Z}_{q/p}^n$ independently from the choice of $\mathbf{r}$, $\mathbf{e}$, and $\mathbf{s}$. Then for any $1 \leq i \leq l$, the i-th component of $\mathbf{c}_2 - S^T \mathbf{c}_1 \in \mathbb{Z}_q^l$ is

$$(\mathbf{c}_2 - S^T \mathbf{c}_1)[i] = (p/t) \cdot m_i + (p/q) \cdot (\mathbf{c}_2' - S^T \mathbf{c}_1')[i] - (p/q) \cdot (\mathbf{f}_2[i] - \langle \mathbf{s}_i, \mathbf{f}_1 \rangle)$$

$$= (p/t) \cdot m_i + (p/q) \cdot (B^T \mathbf{r} - S^T A^T \mathbf{r})[i] - (p/q) \cdot (\mathbf{f}_2[i] - \langle \mathbf{s}_i, \mathbf{f}_1 \rangle)$$

$$= (p/t) \cdot m_i + (p/q) \cdot ((AS + E)^T \mathbf{r} - S^T A^T \mathbf{r})[i] - (p/q) \cdot (\mathbf{f}_2[i] - \langle \mathbf{s}_i, \mathbf{f}_1 \rangle)$$

$$= (p/t) \cdot m_i + (p/q) \cdot ((S^T A^T + E^T) \mathbf{r} - S^T A^T \mathbf{r})[i] - (p/q) \cdot (\mathbf{f}_2[i] - \langle \mathbf{s}_i, \mathbf{f}_1 \rangle)$$

$$= (p/t) \cdot m_i + (p/q) \cdot (S^T A^T \mathbf{r}[i] + \langle \mathbf{e}_i, \mathbf{r} \rangle - S^T A^T \mathbf{r}[i]) - (p/q) \cdot (\mathbf{f}_2[i] - \langle \mathbf{s}_i, \mathbf{f}_1 \rangle)$$

$$= (p/t) \cdot m_i + (p/q) \cdot (\langle \mathbf{e}_i, \mathbf{r} \rangle + \langle \mathbf{s}_i, \mathbf{f}_1 \rangle) - (p/q) \cdot \mathbf{f}_2[i]$$

$$= (p/t) \cdot m_i + \lfloor (p/q) \cdot (\langle \mathbf{e}_i, \mathbf{r} \rangle + \langle \mathbf{s}_i, \mathbf{f}_1 \rangle) \rceil,$$

since $\mathbf{f}_2 = (AS + E)^T \mathbf{r} = S^T \mathbf{f}_1 + E^T \mathbf{r} \pmod{q/p}$. Therefore, the correctness of this scheme is guaranteed if the encryption error is bounded by $p/2t$, or equivalently, $|\langle \mathbf{e}_i, \mathbf{r} \rangle + \langle \mathbf{s}_i, \mathbf{f}_1 \rangle| < (q/2t) - (q/2p)$ with an overwhelming probability.

23.4.3 Security

[34] argues that the proposed encryption scheme is IND-CPA secure under the hardness assumptions of the LWE problem and the LWR problem. The following theorem gives an explicit proof of this argument on security.

Lemma 2 The PKE scheme Lizard is IND-CPA secure under the hardness assumption of $LWE_{n,m,q,\mathcal{D}G_\sigma}(\mathcal{D}_s)$ and $LWR_{m,n+l,q,p}(\mathcal{D}_r)$.

Proof. An encryption of **m** can be generated by adding $(p/t) \cdot \mathbf{m}$ to an encryption of zero. Hence it is enough to show that the pair of public information $pk = (A\|B) \leftarrow Lizard.Gen(params)$ and encryption of zero $\mathbf{c} \leftarrow Lizard.Enc_{pk}(\mathbf{0})$ is computationally indistinguishable from the uniform distribution over $\mathbb{Z}_q^{m \times (n+l)} \times \mathbb{Z}_q^{(n+l)}$ for a parameter set $params \leftarrow Lizard.Setup(1^{\lambda})$.

1. $\mathcal{D}_0 = \{(pk, \mathbf{c}) : pk \leftarrow Lizard.Gen(params), \mathbf{c} \leftarrow Lizard.Enc_{pk}(\mathbf{0})\}$.

2. $\mathcal{D}_1 = \{(pk, \mathbf{c}) : pk \leftarrow \mathbb{Z}_q^{m \times (n+l)}, \mathbf{c} \leftarrow Lizard.Enc_{pk}(\mathbf{0})\}$.

3. $\mathcal{D}_2 = \{(pk, \mathbf{c}) : pk \leftarrow \mathbb{Z}_q^{m \times (n+l)}, \mathbf{c} \leftarrow \mathbb{Z}_q^{(n+l)}\}$.

The public key $pk = (A\|B) \leftarrow Lizard.Gen(params)$ is generated by sampling m instances of LWE problem with l independent secret vectors $\mathbf{s}_1, \cdots, \mathbf{s}_l \leftarrow \mathcal{D}_s$. In addition, the multi-secret LWE problem is no easier than ordinary LWE problem. Hence, distributions $\mathcal{D}_0$ and $\mathcal{D}_1$ are computationally indistinguishable under the $LWE_{n,m,q,\mathcal{D}G_{\sigma}}(\mathcal{D}_s)$ assumption.

Now assume that pk is uniformly random over $\mathbb{Z}_q^{m(n+l)}$. Then pk and $\mathbf{c} \leftarrow Lizard.Enc_{pk}(\mathbf{0})$ together form $(n + l)$ instances of the m dimensional LWR problem with secret $\mathbf{r} \leftarrow \mathcal{D}_r$. Therefore, distributions $\mathcal{D}_1$ and $\mathcal{D}_2$ are computationally indistinguishable under the $LWR_{m,n+l,q,p}(\mathcal{D}_r)$ assumption.

As a result, distributions $\mathcal{D}_0$ and $\mathcal{D}_2$ are computationally indistinguishable under the hardness assumption of $LWE_{n,m,q,\mathcal{D}G_{\sigma}}(\mathcal{D}_s)$ and $LWR_{m,n+l,q,p}(\mathcal{D}_r)$, which denotes the IND-CPA security of the PKE scheme.

Remark 1. Lizard can be naturally converted into two IND-CCA versions: one in the random oracle model using the Fujisaki-Okamoto conversion [45], and the other in the quantum random oracle model using the Targhi-Unruh conversion [94]. We denote the CCA version of Lizard by CCALizard. The scheme description of CCALizard is in Appendix A of [34].

23.5   Ring Variant of Lizard

In this section, we introduce a ring variant of Lizard scheme, called RLizard [67], IND-CCA secure encryption scheme.

We bring some notations for the description of this ring-based encryption scheme. For an integer d, let $\Phi_d(X)$ be the d-th cyclotomic polynomial of degree $n = \phi(d)$, where $\phi(d)$ is called "Euler's phi-function." $\phi(d)$ means that (1) the number of the integers is less than d and (2) $\phi(d)$ and d are relative prime. We write the cyclotomic ring and its residue ring modulo an integer q

by $R = \mathbb{Z}[X]/(\Phi_d(X))$ and $R_q = \mathbb{Z}_q[X]/(\Phi_d(X))$. [3] We identify the vectors of $\mathbb{Z}_q^n$ with the elements of R_q by $(a_0, \cdots, a_{n-1}) \mapsto \sum_{i=0}^{n-1} a_i X^i$. For any distribution $\mathcal{D}$ over $\mathbb{Z}_q$, sampling a polynomial $\sum_{i=0}^{n-1} a_i X^i \in R_q$ from $\mathcal{D}^n$ denotes sampling the coefficient vector $(a_0, \cdots, a_{n-1})$ from the distribution $\mathcal{D}^n$. For the simplicity of ring operations, we choose a power-of-two degree in the following description.

The cyclotomic polynomial In mathematics, more specifically in algebra, the n-th cyclotomic polynomial for any positive integer n is the unique irreducible polynomial with integer coefficients, which is a divisor of $x^n - 1$ and is not a divisor of $x^k - 1$ for any $k < n$. Its roots[4] are all n-th primitive roots of unity[5] $e^{2\sqrt{-1}\pi \frac{k}{n}}$, where k runs over the positive integers not greater than n and coprime to n. In other words, the n-th cyclotomic polynomial is equal to

$$\Phi_n(x) = \prod_{\substack{1 \le k \le n \\ \gcd(k,n)=1}} \left(x - e^{2\sqrt{-1}\pi \frac{k}{n}} \right). \tag{23.1}$$

It may also be defined as the monic polynomial[6] with integer coefficients, which is the minimal polynomial over the field of the rational numbers of any primitive n-th-root of unity ($e^{2\sqrt{-1}\pi/n}$ is an example of such a root). An important relation linking cyclotomic polynomials and primitive roots of unity is

$$\prod_{b|n} \Phi_b(x) = x^n - 1, \tag{23.2}$$

showing that every root of $x^n - 1$ is a b-th primitive root of unity for some b that divides n.

---

[3] e.g., If $\Phi_d(X) = X^{1024} - 1$ then $R = a_{1023}X^{1023} + \cdots + a_0$, where $\{a_i\}_{i=0}^{1023} \in \mathbb{Z}$, and $R_q = a_{1023}X^{1023} + \cdots + a_0$, where $\{a_i\}_{i=0}^{1023} \in \mathbb{Z}_q$.

[4] In mathematics, a zero, also sometimes called a root, of a real-, complex-, or generally vector-valued function f is a member x of the domain of f such that $f(x)$ vanishes at x; that is, x is a solution of the equation $f(x) = 0$.

In other words, a "zero" of a function is an input value that produces an output of zero (0).

A root of a polynomial is a zero of the corresponding polynomial function. The fundamental theorem of algebra shows that any non-zero polynomial has a number of roots at most equal to its degree and that the number of roots and the degree are equal when one considers the complex roots (or more generally the roots in an algebraically closed extension) counted with their multiplicities. For example, the polynomial f of degree two, defined by $f(x) = x^2 - 5x + 6$ has two roots 2 and 3, since $f(2) = 2^2 - 5 \cdot 2 + 6 = 0$ and $f(3) = 3^2 - 5 \cdot 3 + 6 = 0$.

[5] n-th roots of unity: the number x satisfy $x^n = 1$.

[6] In algebra, a monic polynomial is a univariate polynomial in which the leading coefficient (the nonzero coefficient of highest degree) is equal to 1. Therefore, a monic polynomial has the form

$$x^n + c_{n-1}x^{n-1} + \cdots + c_2x^2 + c_1x + c_0.$$

A polynomial in one indeterminate is called a univariate polynomial, and a polynomial in more than one indeterminate is called a multivariate polynomial.

In particular, if $n = p^m$ is a prime power (where p is prime), then

$$\Phi_n(x) = \Phi_p(x^{p^{m-1}}) = \prod_{i=0}^{p-1} \left(x^{ip^{m-1}} \right). \tag{23.3}$$

For example, if $n = 2 \cdot 2^{10} = 2^{11}$ then $\Phi_n(x) = \prod_{i=0}^{2-1} \left(x^{i2^{11-1}} \right) = \left(x^{2^{10}} + 1 \right) = \left(x^{1024} + 1 \right)$.

The cyclotomic ring Let $f(x) = x^n + 1 \in \mathbb{Z}[x]$, where the security parameter n is a power of 2, making $f(x)$ irreducible over the rationals. Let $R = \mathbb{Z}[x]/\langle f(x) \rangle$ be the ring of integer polynomials modulo $f(x)$. Elements of R (i.e., residues modulo $f(x)$) can be represented by integer polynomials of degree less than n. Let $q = 1 \bmod 2n$ be a sufficiently large public prime modulus (bounded by a polynomial in n), and let $R_q = \mathbb{Z}[x]/\langle q \rangle = \mathbb{Z}_q[x]/\langle f(x) \rangle$ be the ring of integer polynomials modulo both $f(x)$ and q. The q^n elements of R_q may be represented by polynomials of degree less than n whose coefficients are from some set of canonical representatives of $\mathbb{Z}_q$, for example, $\{0, \cdots, q-1\}$.[7]

23.5.1   The Construction

RLizard has a natural analogue based on the harness of Ring-LWE and Ring-LWR problems. Although the security ground of ring variant of this scheme is weaker than that of the original scheme based on LWE and LWR, the ring variant exploits better key sizes, plaintext expansion rate, and Enc/Dec speed.

For the simplicity of ring operations, we choose a power-of-two degree in the following description.

1. *RLizard.Setup*(1^λ): Choose positive integers q, p, and t. Let $n \in \mathbb{Z}$ be a power of 2 and $\Phi(X) = X^n + 1$ be the $2n$-th cyclotomic polynomial. Choose h_s, h_r less than or equal to n, a private key distribution $\mathcal{D}_s$ over R^n, an ephemeral secret distribution $\mathcal{D}_r$ over R^n, and parameter σ for discrete Gaussian distribution $\mathcal{D}G_\sigma$. Output $params \leftarrow (n, q, p, t, \mathcal{D}_s, \mathcal{D}_r, \sigma)$.

2. *RLizard.Gen*($params$): Generate a random polynomial $a \leftarrow R_q$. Sample a secret polynomial $s \leftarrow \mathcal{D}_s$, and an error polynomial $e \leftarrow \mathcal{D}G_\sigma^n$. Let $b = a \cdot s + e \in R_q$. Output the public key $pk \leftarrow (a, b) \in R_q^2$ and the secret key $sk \leftarrow S \in R$.

3. *RLizard.Enc*$_{pk}$(m): For a plaintext $m \in R_t = R/tR$, choose $r \leftarrow \mathcal{D}_r$ and compute $c_1' \leftarrow a \cdot r$ and $c_2' \leftarrow b \cdot r$. Output the vector

---

[7]i.e., R_q is a polynomial whose orders are less than n to represent q^n elements, and each coefficient have the element over $\mathbb{Z}_q$. E.g., when $n = 3$ and $q = 5$, the element over R_q can be $3x^2 + 4x + 2$.

$\mathbf{c} \leftarrow (c_1, c_2) \in R_p^2$, where $c_1 \leftarrow \lfloor (p/q) \cdot c_1' \rceil \in R_p$ and $c_2 \leftarrow \lfloor (p/t) \cdot m + (p/q) \cdot c_2' \rceil \in R_p$.

4. $RLizard.Dec_{sk}(\mathbf{c})$: For a ciphertext $\mathbf{c} \leftarrow (c_1, c_2)$, compute and output the polynomial $m' \leftarrow \lfloor t/p \cdot (c_2 - c_1 \cdot s) \rceil (\mathrm{mod}\ t) \in R_t$.

Note that all the polynomial multiplications with s or r required in key generation, encryption, and decryption phases can be done very efficiently by shifting and adding vectors.

Parameter consideration Since the best known attacks do not utilize the ring structure so far, the authors analyze the hardness of Ring-LWE as the LWE problem without ring structure. By setting $\mathcal{D}_s = \mathcal{D}_r = \mathcal{HWT}_n(128)$, they recommend to use the parameter $n = 1024, q = 2^{10}, p = 2^8, t = 2, \alpha^{-1} = 154$ to resist all known quantum attacks for the security parameter $\lambda = 128$.

Hardness of ring-LWR There have been a lot of progresses in studying the hardness of the ring-LWR problem. Banergee et al. [7] proved that the decision version of the ring-LWR problem is harder than that of the ring-LWE problem for large modulus. Bogdanov et al. [18] extended the scope of the modulus, but the extension holds only for the search version of the ring-LWR problem. They stated that the search version of the ring-LWR problem is not easier than that of the ring-LWE problem when the number of samples is bounded with a flexible upper bound in Theorem 3 in [18].

24

Introduction to Linear Codes

CONTENTS

Along with lattice-based cryptography, code-based cryptography has emerged as one of the strong candidates which seems to be secure against quantum computer attacks. This chapter mainly introduces the coding theory and code-based cryptography. The basics of linear codes are first presented for understanding the next sections. The types of decoding are then explained with main focus on unique decoding. The next part presents the types of codes that are efficiently decodable. The final part of the chapter discusses hard problems from the coding theory that can serve as basis for cryptographic primitives.

24.1 Fundamentals of Coding Theory

Coding theory originated from digital communication systems, where data are easily corrupted by noise during transmission. Now error-correcting codes have been not only in telecommunication, and computer system including data storage and data compression, but also in theoretical implications such as cryptography and complexity theory. A general coding-theoretical model assumes that a sequence of symbols called message is transmitted over a noisy channel and the received message is likely to become corrupted with a non-zero probability. To overcome this problem, the transmitted information will not only contain the message, but also include some redundancy based on the message symbols. Generally, we send k bits of data in n bits, where $r = n - k$ are redundant bits. For example, 64 bits are stored as 72 bits, where extra 8 bits are used for check and recovery. We classify a wide range of code families into two types of codes: block codes encode information block by block, while convolutional codes encode a continuous stream of information bits.

24.2 Basics of Linear Codes

In this section, basics of linear codes have been introduced. A linear code which we denote $\mathcal{C}$, is a linear subspace. The elements of the code are called codewords.

Definition 1 (Linear Code) *An $[n,k]_q$ linear code $\mathcal{C}$ is a linear subspace over $\mathbb{F}_q$ of length n and dimension k.*

The cardinality of $\mathcal{C}$ is $|\mathcal{C}| = q^k$ and the (information) rate, denoted R, of an $[n,k]_q$ linear code is $\frac{n}{k}$. We sometimes omit the subscript and simply write $[n,k]$ linear code, which implicitly means that the code is binary, i.e., $q = 2$.

Definition 2 (Hamming Distance) *The hamming distance between two words in $\mathbb{F}_2$ is the number of coordinates or places in which they differ.*

Example(Hamming Distance)

$$d_H((1,1,0,1,1),(1,0,0,1,1)) = 1$$

Definition 3 (Hamming Weight) *The hamming weight of a word is the number of non-zero coordinates.*

Example (Hamming Weight)

$$w_H(1,0,0,1,1) = 3$$

Note that the hamming distance between $\mathbf{x}$ and $\mathbf{y}$ equals the hamming weight of $\mathbf{x} + \mathbf{y}$.

Example

$$d_H((1,1,0,1,1),(1,0,0,1,1,)) = w_H(0,1,0,0,0) = 1$$

Definition 4 (Minimum Hamming Distance) *The minimum hamming distance of a linear code C denoted by d_{min} is the minimum distance of its codewords:*

$$d_{min} = \min_{c,c' \in C} d_H(c,c') \tag{24.1}$$

$$= \min_{c,c' \in C} w_H(c - c')$$

$$= \min_{c \in C, c \neq 0} w_H(c)$$

If C has minimum distance d_{min}, then we say that C is an $[n,k,d_{min}]$ linear code over $\mathbb{F}_q$. From the above, we see that the minimum distance is equal to the minimum of codeword weights in C. A linear code C can be expressed as the image of a matrix, and as the kernel of another matrix explained in the subsequent section. Furthermore, the minimum distance of a code is fundamental to determine its error-correction capabilities. Imagine a codeword $\mathbf{x}$ is transmitted over a noisy channel, and errors occur in a certain number of positions, say w. We represent this as an error vector $\mathbf{e}$ of weight w having non-zero positions where the errors occur. The received word will then be $\mathbf{z} = \mathbf{x} + \mathbf{e}$. We say that a code C is able to correct w errors if, for each codeword, it is possible to detect and correct any configuration of w errors occurred during transmission. The following theorem holds.

Theorem 1 Let C be an $[n,k]$ linear code over $\mathbb{F}_q$ having minimum distance d_{min}. Then C is able to correct at most $t = w = \lfloor \frac{d_{min}-1}{2} \rfloor$ errors.

Proof is omitted.

24.2.1 Generator Matrix and Parity-Check Matrix

Let $\{x_1, x_2, ..., x_k\} \in \mathbb{F}_2^k$ denote the k information bits encoded into the codeword $C \in \mathbb{F}_2^n$. Thus the vector of k information bits into the encoder is denoted by

$$\mathbf{x} = \{x_1, x_2 \cdots x_k\} \in \mathbb{F}_2^k \tag{24.2}$$

and the output of the encoder is the vector

$$\mathcal{C} = \{c_1, c_2 \cdots c_n\} \in \mathbb{F}_2^n. \tag{24.3}$$

The encoding operation performed in a linear binary block encoder can be represented by a set of n equations of the form as

$$c_j = x_1 g_{1,j} + x_2 g_{2,j} + \dots + x_k g_{k,j} \quad (j = 1, 2, \dots, n), \tag{24.4}$$

where $g_{i,j} = 0$ or 1 and $x_i g_{i,j}$ represents the product of x_i and $g_{i,j}$. The linear equations may also be represented in a matrix form as

$$\mathcal{C} = \mathbf{x}\mathbf{G}, \tag{24.5}$$

where $\mathbf{G}$, called the generator matrix of the code, is defined as

$$\mathbf{G} = \begin{bmatrix} \leftarrow \mathbf{g}_1 \rightarrow \\ \leftarrow \mathbf{g}_2 \rightarrow \\ \vdots \\ \leftarrow \mathbf{g}_k \rightarrow \end{bmatrix} = \begin{bmatrix} g_{11} & g_{12} & \cdots & g_{1n} \\ g_{21} & g_{22} & \cdots & g_{2n} \\ \vdots & \vdots & & \vdots \\ g_{k1} & g_{k2} & \cdots & g_{kn} \end{bmatrix}. \tag{24.6}$$

Note that each codeword is simply a linear combination of the vectors $\{\mathbf{g}_i\}$ of $\mathbf{G}$, i.e.,

$$\mathcal{C} = x_1 g_1 + x_2 g_2 + \dots + x_k g_k. \tag{24.7}$$

Since the linear $[n, k]$ code with 2^k codewords is a subspace of dimension k, the row vectors $\{\mathbf{g}_i\}$ of the generator matrix $\mathbf{G}$ must be linearly independent, where they must span a subspace of k dimensions, i.e., $\{\mathbf{g}_i\}$ must be a basis for the $[n, k]$ code. We note that the set of the basis vectors is not unique because $\mathbf{G}$ is not unique. Also, the subspace has dimension k, and the rank of $\mathbf{G}$ is k. Any generator matrix of an $[n, k]$ code can be reduced by row operations to the systematic form as

$$\mathbf{G} = [\mathbf{I}_k \vdots \mathbf{P}] = \begin{bmatrix} 1 & 0 & 0 & \dots & 0 & \vdots & p_{11} & p_{12} & \cdots & p_{1n-k} \\ 0 & 1 & 0 & \dots & 0 & \vdots & p_{21} & p_{22} & \cdots & p_{2n-k} \\ \vdots & \vdots & \vdots & & \vdots & \vdots & \vdots & \vdots & & \vdots \\ 0 & 0 & 0 & \dots & 1 & \vdots & p_{k1} & p_{k2} & \cdots & p_{kn-k} \end{bmatrix}, \tag{24.8}$$

where $\mathbf{I}_k$ is a $k \times k$ identity matrix and $\mathbf{P}$ is a $k \times (n - k)$ matrix that determines the $n - k$ redundant bits or parity check bits. Note that a generator matrix of the systematic form generates a linear block code in which the first k bits of each codeword is identical to the information bits to be transmitted, and the remaining $n - k$ bits of each codeword are linear combinations of the k information bits. These $(n - k)$ redundant bits are called parity check bits and the resulting $[n, k]$ code is called a systematic code. An $[n, k]$ code generated by a generator matrix that is not in the systematic form (Eq. 24.8) is called non-systematic. Such a generator matrix is equivalent to a generator matrix of the systematic form in the sense that one can be obtained from the other by elementary row operations and column permutation. The two $[n, k]$ linear codes generated by the two equivalent generator matrices are said to be equivalent, if one can obtain from the other by a permutation of the places of every element. Thus, every linear $[n, k]$ code is equivalent to a linear systematic $[n, k]$ code. Now, on the basis of the above argument, we define the generator matrix and parity-check matrix as follows.

Definition 5 (Generator matrix and parity-check matrix) *Let $\mathcal{C} \subseteq \mathbb{F}_q^n$ be a linear code of dimension k. If $\boldsymbol{G} \in \mathbb{F}_q^{k \times n}$ is a basis matrix of $\mathcal{C}$, i.e.,*

$$\mathcal{C} = \{\mathbf{uG} : \mathbf{u} \in \mathbb{F}_q^k\} \tag{24.9}$$

then we say that $\boldsymbol{G}$ is generator[1] matrix for $\mathcal{C}$. Therefore, $\mathcal{C}$ has an encoding map $f : \mathbb{F}_q^k \to \mathbb{F}_q^n$ which is $\boldsymbol{u} \mapsto \boldsymbol{uG}$. If $\mathcal{C}$ is the kernel[2] of matrix $\boldsymbol{H} \in \mathbb{F}_q^{(n-k) \times k}$, i.e.,

$$\mathcal{C} = ker(\boldsymbol{H}) = \{\boldsymbol{v} \in \mathbb{F}_q^n : \boldsymbol{Hv}^T = \boldsymbol{0}\}$$

then we say that $\boldsymbol{H}$ is a parity-check matrix of $\mathcal{C}$. It follows that $\boldsymbol{GH}^T = \boldsymbol{0}$.

Now suppose that the linear $[n, k]$ code is systematic and its generator matrix $\mathbf{G}$ is given by the above systematic form. Then, since $\mathbf{GH}^T = 0$, it follows that

$$\mathbf{H} = [-\mathbf{P}^T \vdots \mathbf{I}_{n-k}]. \tag{24.10}$$

Here, the negative sign may be dropped[3] when dealing with the binary codes.

Example Consider a $[7, 4]$ code with generator matrix

$$\mathbf{G} = [\mathbf{I}_k \vdots \mathbf{P}] = \begin{bmatrix} 1 & 0 & 0 & 0 & \vdots & 1 & 0 & 1 \\ 0 & 1 & 0 & 0 & \vdots & 1 & 1 & 1 \\ 0 & 0 & 1 & 0 & \vdots & 1 & 1 & 0 \\ 0 & 0 & 0 & 1 & \vdots & 0 & 1 & 1 \end{bmatrix}$$

---

[1] In other words, let $\mathcal{C}$ be an $[n, k]$ linear code over $\mathbb{F}^k$. A $k \times n$ matrix $\mathbf{G}$ whose rowspace equals $\mathcal{C}$ is called the generator matrix of $\mathcal{C}$.
[2] A vector v is in the kernel of a matrix A if and only if $Av = 0$.
[3] Since modulo-2 subtraction is identical to modulo-2 addition.

and its corresponding parity-check matrix

$$\mathbf{H} = [\mathbf{P}^T \vdots \mathbf{I}_{n-k}] = \begin{bmatrix} 1 & 1 & 1 & 0 & \vdots & 1 & 0 & 0 \\ 0 & 1 & 1 & 1 & \vdots & 0 & 1 & 0 \\ 1 & 1 & 0 & 1 & \vdots & 0 & 0 & 1 \end{bmatrix}.$$

A typical codeword may be expressed as

$$C = [x_1 \ x_2 \ x_3 \ x_4 \ c_5 \ c_6 \ c_7],$$

where the x_j are the four information bits and the c_j represents the three parity check bits generated as

$$c_5 = x_1 + x_2 + x_3,$$

$$c_6 = x_2 + x_3 + x_4,$$

$$c_7 = x_1 + x_2 + x_4.$$

This linear systematic $[n, k]$ binary block encoder may be implemented by using a k-bit shift register and $(n-k)$ modulo-2 tied to the appropriate stages of the shift register. The $(n-k)$ adders generate the parity check bits, which are subsequently stored temporarily in a second shift register of length $(n-k)$. In this way, k-bit of information bits shifted into the k-bit shift register and then $(n-k)$ parity check bits are computed as shown in Figure 24.1.

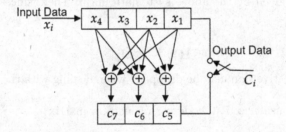

FIGURE 24.1
A linear shift register for generating a $[7, 4]$ binary code.

Definition 6 (Dual Code) *Let C be an $[n, k]$ linear code over $\mathbb{F}_q$. The dual code of C is the set $C^\perp = \{x \in \mathbb{F}_q^n : x \cdot y = 0 \forall y \in C\}$.*

Theorem 2 *Let C be an $[n, k]$ linear code over $\mathbb{F}_q$. Then the dual code $C^\perp$ is an $[n, n-k=r]$ linear code. Moreover, if $\mathbf{G} = (\mathbf{I}_k|\mathbf{P})$ is a generator matrix in systematic form for C, then $H = (-\mathbf{P}^T|\mathbf{I}_{n-k})$ is a generator matrix for $C^\perp$.*

Proof is omitted.

24.3 Types of Decoding

There are many types of decoding. Different approaches of decoding are briefly introduced in this section. The main focus will be on the unique decoding, i.e., when one desires a unique solution to the decoding problem. In unique decoding, the number of errors that an $[n, k, d_{min}]_q$ linear code is able to correct is given by the error-correction capability

$$t = \left\lfloor \frac{d_{min} - 1}{2} \right\rfloor. \tag{24.11}$$

24.3.1 Maximum-Likelihood Decoding

Given an $[n, k]_q$ code $\mathcal{C}$ and a received word $\mathbf{r} \in \mathbb{F}_q^n$, a maximum-likelihood decoding procedure chooses the most likely codeword $\mathbf{c} \in \mathcal{C}$, i.e., it will find a solution to the maximization problem

$$\underset{\mathbf{c} \in \mathcal{C}}{arg} \; (max(Pr(\mathbf{r}_{received} \mid \mathbf{c}_{sent}))). \tag{24.12}$$

If all codewords are sent according to a uniformly random distribution, it allows for a reformulation of the maximization problem. Using the Bayes' rule, we obtain

$$Pr(\mathbf{r}_{received} | \mathbf{c}_{sent}) = \frac{Pr(\mathbf{r}_{received}, \mathbf{c}_{sent})}{Pr(\mathbf{c}_{sent})}$$

$$= Pr(\mathbf{c}_{sent} | \mathbf{r}_{received}) \cdot \underbrace{\frac{Pr(\mathbf{r}_{received}, \mathbf{c}_{sent})}{Pr(\mathbf{c}_{sent})}}_{\text{constant}},$$

which in turn yields the maximization problem

$$\underset{\mathbf{c} \in \mathcal{C}}{arg} \; (max(Pr(\mathbf{r} \; received \mid \mathbf{c} \; sent))). \tag{24.13}$$

This reformulation of the maximum-likelihood decoding problem is called ideal observer decoding.

24.3.2 Minimum-Distance Decoding

A minimum-distance (or nearest neighbor) decoding procedure chooses the codeword $\mathbf{c} \in \mathcal{C}$ closest to the received word $\mathbf{r}$. More specifically, a minimum-distance decoding procedure solves the minimization problem

$$\underset{\mathbf{c} \in \mathcal{C}}{arg} \; (min(d_H(\mathbf{r}, \mathbf{c}))). \tag{24.14}$$

When the error model is a binary symmetric channel $\mathsf{BSC}_\rho{}^4$ with $\rho < \frac{1}{2}$, minimum-distance decoding is equivalent to maximum-likelihood decoding. This follows from that the probability-distribution function of the error

$$Pr(\mathbf{r}_{received}|\mathbf{c}_{sent}) = (1 - \rho)^{n-d} \cdot \rho^d \qquad (24.15)$$

obtains its maximum when $d = d_H(\mathbf{r}, \mathbf{c})$ is minimal.

24.3.3   Syndrome Decoding

A vector $\hat{c} = c + e$ with an error vector e of $w_H(e) > 0$ added to the codeword c can be interpreted as an erroneous codeword.

Definition 7 (Syndrome) *The syndrome of a vector $\hat{c} = c + e$ in $\mathbb{F}_q^n$ is the vector in $\mathbb{F}_q^{n-k}$ defined by*

$$S_{\hat{c}} = H \cdot \hat{c}^T = H \cdot (c^T + e^T) = H \cdot e^T. \qquad (24.16)$$

24.4   Hamming Geometry and Code Performance

In the previous section, we have seen the Hamming distance and Hamming weight. There is an interesting relationship between Hamming Geometry of a code and its ability to correct errors. Let $\mathcal{C} = \{\mathbf{x}_1, \mathbf{x}_2, ..., \mathbf{x}_M\}$ be a code of length n. Suppose that we want $\mathcal{C}$ to be capable of correcting all error patterns of Hamming weight $\leq e$, that is, if $\mathbf{x}_i$ is sent, $\mathbf{y} = \mathbf{x}_i + \mathbf{z}$ is received, and $w_H(z) \leq e$, we want our decoder's output to be $\hat{x} = \mathbf{x}_i$. It is easy to see that if each codeword is sent with probability $\frac{1}{M}$, then the receiver's best strategy for guessing which codeword was sent is to pick the codeword closest to $\mathbf{y}$, that is, the one for which $d_H(\mathbf{x}_i, \mathbf{y})$ is the smallest (Note that $d_H(\mathbf{x}_i, \mathbf{y}) = w_H(z)$). It follows that syndrome decoding for the linear codes described before is equivalent to a decoding process that "finds the closest codeword." It is clear that if this geometric decoding strategy is used, the code will be capable of correcting all patterns of weight $\leq e$ iff the distance between each pair of codewords is $\geq 2e+1$. For Figure 24.2 (a), if $d_H(\mathbf{x}_i, \mathbf{x}_j) \geq 2e+1$, that is, if the hamming spheres of radius e around $\mathbf{x}_i$ and $\mathbf{x}_j$ are disjoint, then if $\mathbf{x}_i$ is sent and $d_H(\mathbf{x}_i, \mathbf{y}) \leq e$, $\mathbf{y}$ cannot get closer to $\mathbf{x}_j$ than it is to $\mathbf{x}_i$, and so geometric decoder will not prefer $\mathbf{x}_j$ to $\mathbf{x}_i$. On the other hand, if $d_H(\mathbf{x}_i, \mathbf{x}_j) \leq 2e$, that is, if the hamming spheres of radius e intersect (see Figure 24.2 (b)), then it is clear that, if $\mathbf{x}_i$ is sent, there exists a $\mathbf{y}$ that has $d_H(\mathbf{x}_i, \mathbf{y}) \leq e$, but is at

---

[4]If the channel is discrete and memoryless with a constant crossover (bit error) probability $\rho \in [0, 1]$, we say that it is a binary symmetric channel denoted BSC_ρ.

least as close to $\mathbf{x}_j$ as it is to $\mathbf{x}_i$. Therefore, we are led to define the minimum distance of the code $\mathcal{C}$ as

$$d_{min}(\mathcal{C}) = min\{d_H(\mathbf{x}, \mathbf{x}') : \mathbf{x}, \mathbf{x}' \in \mathcal{C}, \mathbf{x} \neq \mathbf{x}'\}$$

and we have the following theorem.

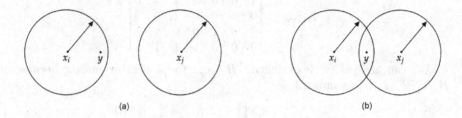

(a)   (b)

FIGURE 24.2
Hamming sphere of radius e around adjacent codewords.

Theorem 3 A code $\mathcal{C} = \{\mathbf{x}_1, \mathbf{x}_2, ..., \mathbf{x}_M\}$ is capable of correcting all error patterns weight $\leq e$ iff $d_{min}(\mathcal{C}) \geq 2e + 1$.

Proof is omitted.

For example, a code with $d_{min} = 7$ can correct all error patterns of weight ≤ 3; if $d_{min} = 22$, all patterns of weight ≤ 10 and so forth.

24.5 Types of Codes

A family of codes is said to be efficiently decodable if there exists a polynomial time (PPT) machine that can solve a problem related to minimum distance decoding for all given instances in the particular encoding. A lot of progress has been made in constructing efficiently decodable (and encodable) codes with good error-correction properties.

24.5.1 Hamming Code

The Hamming codes are a kind of (binary) linear error-correcting (block) codes that are able to correct one error and able to detect up to two errors. Hamming codes are perfect in the sense that that they attain the Hamming bound and thus achieve the highest possible rate for a certain block length and minimum distance $d_{min} = 3$. For any integer $r > 1$, there is at least one Hamming code of length $n = 2^r - 1$ and dimension $k = 2^r - r - 1$.

Example A very simple example of $[7, 4]$ Hamming code is

$$(u_1 \; u_2 \; u_3 \; u_4) \mapsto (u_1 \; u_2 \; u_3 \; u_4 \; v_5 \; v_6 \; v_7)$$

Here $(u_1 \; u_2 \; u_3 \; u_4)$ are information bits and $(v_5 \; v_6 \; v_7)$ are parity bits. Generator matrix form for this example is

$$\mathbf{G} = [\mathbf{I}_k \vdots \mathbf{P}] = \begin{bmatrix} 1 & 0 & 0 & 0 & 1 & 1 & 0 \\ 0 & 1 & 0 & 0 & 1 & 0 & 1 \\ 0 & 0 & 1 & 0 & 0 & 1 & 1 \\ 0 & 0 & 0 & 1 & 1 & 1 & 1 \end{bmatrix}.$$

We can get parity-check matrix H from the generator matrix because $H = [P^T : I_{n-k}]$ as shown below

$$\mathbf{H} = [\mathbf{P}^T : \mathbf{I}_{n-k}] = \begin{bmatrix} 1 & 1 & 0 & 1 & 1 & 0 & 0 \\ 1 & 0 & 1 & 1 & 0 & 1 & 0 \\ 0 & 1 & 1 & 1 & 0 & 0 & 1 \end{bmatrix}.$$

24.5.2 Cyclic Codes

Cyclic codes are attractive in achieving a good error-correction capability. Many codes (e.g., BCH, Reed-Solomon codes, Euclidian geometry codes, and quadratic residue codes) belong to the family of cyclic codes.

Definition 8 (Cyclic Code) *Let C be a $[n, k, d_{min}]_q$ linear code. If every circular shift of a codeword $c = (c_1 \; c_2 \cdots c_n) \in C$ again is a codeword $c' = (c_n \; c_1 \cdots c_{n-1}) \in C$, we say that C is a cyclic code.*

The description of cyclic code may become easier to understand if we see them as polynomials, i.e.,

$$(c_1 \; c_2 \cdots c_n) \mapsto c_1 + c_2 x + \cdots c_n x^{n-1} \in \mathbb{F}_q[x] / < x^n - 1 > . \qquad (24.17)$$

If so, then every right-circular shift in codeword space corresponds to a multiplication by x in the polynomial counterpart, i.e.,

$$(c_n \; c_1 \cdots c_{n-1}) \mapsto c_n + c_1 x + \cdots c_{n-1} x^{n-1} \qquad (24.18)$$

$$= x \cdot (c_1 + c_2 x + \cdots c_n x^{n-1}). \qquad (24.19)$$

24.5.3 Generalized Reed-Solomon (GRS) Codes

GRS codes are a generalization of Reed-Solomon (RS) codes. GRS codes are maximum distance separable codes, i.e., the minimum distance has the maximum value possible for a linear $[n, k]$ code, where $d_{min} = n - k + 1$.

For some polynomial $f(x) \in \mathbb{F}_{p^m}[x]_{<k}$, pairwise distinct elements $\mathcal{L} = (\alpha_0, \ldots \alpha_{n-1}) \in \mathbb{F}_{p^m}^n$, a non-zero elements $V = (v_0, \ldots, v_{n-1}) \in \mathbb{F}_{p^m}^n$ and $0 \leq k \leq n$, GRS code of order $[n, k]$ over $\mathbb{F}_{p^m}$ for a certain prime power p and extension degree $m > 1$ can be defined as

$$GRS_{n,k}(\mathcal{L}, V) = \{c \in \mathbb{F}_{p^m}^n | c_i = v_i f(\alpha_i)\}. \tag{24.20}$$

24.5.4 Goppa Codes

Goppa codes are alternate codes over $\mathbb{F}_q$ that are restricted to a Goppa Polynomial $g(x)$ with degree $\deg(g) = t$ and support $\mathcal{L} = (\alpha_i, \ldots, \alpha_n)$ of n distinct elements in $\mathbb{F}_1$. Note that $g(x) \in \mathbb{F}_q[x]$ is a square-free polynomial of degree t such that $g(\alpha_i) \neq 0 \ \forall \alpha_i \in \mathcal{L}$. Here, g is another representation of the previously defined (in Section 24.5.3) tuple of non-zero elements V and polynomial $f(x)$. Therefore, Goppa code can be derived from the definition of GRS codes as

$$Goppa_{n,k,p}(\mathcal{L}, g) = GRS_{n,k}(\mathcal{L}, g) \cap \mathbb{F}_p^n. \tag{24.21}$$

24.5.4.1 Construction of Goppa Codes

Goppa codes are one of the most important code classes in code-based cryptography because they resist all critical attacks so far.

24.5.4.2 Binary Goppa Codes

First, we will give the definition of the binary Goppa codes.

Definition 9 (Binary Goppa Code) *Let m and t be the positive integers and the Goppa polynomial*

$$g(x) = \sum_{i=0}^{t} g_i x^i \in \mathbb{F}_{2^m}[x] \tag{24.22}$$

be square-free polynomial of degree t and let the support

$$\mathcal{L} = \{\alpha_1, \ldots \alpha_n) \in \mathbb{F}_{2^m}^n, g(\alpha) \neq 0 \forall \alpha \in \mathcal{L}\} \tag{24.23}$$

be a set of n distinct elements of $\mathbb{F}_{2^m}$. For any vector $\hat{c} = (c_1, \ldots, c_n) \in \mathbb{F}_{2^m}^n$, we define the syndrome of c as

$$S_{\hat{c}}(x) = -\sum_{i=1}^{n} \frac{\hat{c}_i}{g(\alpha_i)} \frac{g(x) - g(\alpha_i)}{x - \alpha_i} \bmod g(x). \tag{24.24}$$

We now define a binary Goppa code over $\mathbb{F}_{2^m}$ using the syndrome equation, where $c \in \mathbb{F}_{2^m}^n$ is a codeword of the code, as

$$Goppa_{n,k,2}(\mathcal{L}, g(x)) = \{c \in \mathbb{F}_{2^m}^n | \mathcal{S}_c(x) = \sum_{i=1}^{n} \frac{c_i}{x - \alpha_i} \equiv 0 \ mod \ g(x)\}. \quad (24.25)$$

Note: If $g(x)$ is irreducible over $\mathbb{F}_{2^m}$, then $Goppa(\mathcal{L}, g)$ is called an irreducible binary Goppa code. If $g(x)$ has no multiple roots, then $Goppa(\mathcal{L}, g)$ is called a separable code and $g(x)$ a square-free polynomial.

24.5.4.3   Parity-Check Matrix of Goppa Codes

According to the definition of syndrome in Goppa codes, every element $\hat{c}_i$ of a vector $\hat{c} = c + e$ is multiplied with

$$\frac{g(x) - g(\alpha_i)}{g(\alpha_i) \cdot (x - \alpha_i)}. \quad (24.26)$$

Given a Goppa polynomial $g(x) = g_s x^s + g_{s-1} x^{s-1} + \cdots + g_0$, the parity-check matrix H can be constructed as

$$H = \begin{pmatrix} \frac{g_s}{g(\alpha_0)} & \frac{g_s}{g(\alpha_1)} & \cdots & \frac{g_s}{g(\alpha_{n-1})} \\ \frac{g_{s-1}+g_s \cdot \alpha_0}{g(\alpha_0)} & \frac{g_{s-1}+g_s \cdot \alpha_0}{g(\alpha_1)} & \cdots & \frac{g_{s-1}+g_s \cdot \alpha_0}{g(\alpha_{n-1})} \\ \vdots & \ddots & & \vdots \\ \frac{g_1+g_2 \cdot \alpha_0+\cdots+g_s \cdot \alpha_0^{s-1}}{g(\alpha_0)} & \frac{g_1+g_2 \cdot \alpha_0+\cdots+g_s \cdot \alpha_0^{s-1}}{g(\alpha_1)} & \cdots & \frac{g_1+g_2 \cdot \alpha_0+\cdots+g_s \cdot \alpha_0^{s-1}}{g(\alpha_{n-1})} \end{pmatrix}. \quad (24.27)$$

This can be simplified to

$$H = \begin{pmatrix} g_s & 0 & \cdots & 0 \\ g_{s-1} & g_s & \cdots & 0 \\ \vdots & \ddots & & \vdots \\ g_1 & g_2 & \cdots & g_s \end{pmatrix} \times \begin{pmatrix} \frac{1}{g(\alpha_0)} & \frac{1}{g(\alpha_1)} & \cdots & \frac{1}{g(\alpha_{n-1})} \\ \frac{\alpha_0}{g(\alpha_0)} & \frac{\alpha_1}{g(\alpha_1)} & \cdots & \frac{\alpha_{n-1}}{g(\alpha_{n-1})} \\ \vdots & \ddots & & \vdots \\ \frac{\alpha_0^{s-1}}{g(\alpha_0)} & \frac{\alpha_1^{s-1}}{g(\alpha_1)} & \cdots & \frac{\alpha_{n-1}^{s-1}}{g(\alpha_{n-1})} \end{pmatrix} = H_g \times \hat{H}, \quad (24.28)$$

where H_g has a determinant unequal to zero.

Then, $\hat{H}$ is an equivalent parity check matrix to H, but has a simpler structure. Using Gauss-Jordan elimination[5], $\hat{H}$ can be brought to systematic form. Note that for every column swap in Gauss-Jordan, the corresponding elements in the support $\mathcal{L}$ have also to be swapped. The generator matrix G can be derived from the systematic parity check matrix $H = (P|I_{n-k})$ as $(I_k|-P^T)$.

---

[5]http://www.math.udel.edu/ angell/Gausjor.pdf

24.6 Hard Problems

Code-based cryptography has been based on hard problems that arise from coding theory. We start with the so-called the general decoding problem (GDP). This corresponds to correcting a certain number of errors occurred on the codeword $\mathbf{x}$, represented by an error vector $\mathbf{e}$, that is, $\mathbf{y} = \mathbf{x} + \mathbf{e}$.

By Theorem 1, a unique solution exists if the weight of $\mathbf{e}$ is less than or equal to $t = wt = \lfloor \frac{d_{min}-1}{2} \rfloor$, where d_{min} is the minimum distance of $\mathcal{C}$. This problem is well known and was proved to be NP-complete by Berlekamp et al. in [13].

An alternative formulation is given in terms of the parity-check matrix, and is known as the syndrome decoding problem (SDP) as we have seen syndrome decoding in the previous sections. Sometimes, this is also referred to as computational syndrome decoding problem. Both problems are summarized below.

General Decoding Problem

    Given An $[n, k]$ linear code $\mathcal{C}$ over $\mathbb{F}_q$ and a vector $\mathbf{y} \in \mathbb{F}_{\mathbf{q}}^{\mathbf{n}}$

    Goal Find $(\mathbf{x}) \in \mathcal{C}$ such that $d_{min}(x, y)$ is minimal.

Syndrome Decoding Problem

    Given An $[n - k, n]$ parity-check matrix for an $[n, k]$ linear code $\mathcal{C}$ over $\mathbb{F}_q$ and a vector $\mathbf{s} \in \mathbb{F}_{\mathbf{q}}^{\mathbf{n-k}}$ and an integer $w \in \mathbb{N}^+$

    Goal Find $(\mathbf{e}) \in \mathbb{F}_{\mathbf{q}}^{\mathbf{n}}$ of weight $\leq w$ such that $\mathbf{s} = \mathbf{H}\mathbf{e}^{\mathbf{T}}$.

Exercises

24.1 Calculate the Hamming distance d for the codes below.

1.

$$(1\ 0\ 1\ 1\ 0\ 0\ 1\ 1\ 1\ 1), (0\ 1\ 0\ 1\ 0\ 0\ 0\ 0\ 0\ 1)$$

2.

$$(1\ 0\ 1\ 0\ 1\ 1\ 1\ 1\ 0\ 1), (0\ 0\ 1\ 0\ 0\ 1\ 0\ 0\ 0\ 0)$$

3.

$$(1\ 1\ 0\ 1\ 0\ 1\ 1\ 0\ 0\ 0), (1\ 0\ 1\ 1\ 0\ 1\ 1\ 1\ 1\ 1),$$
$$(0\ 0\ 0\ 1\ 0\ 1\ 0\ 1\ 0\ 1)$$

4.

$$(1\ 1\ 0\ 0\ 0\ 1\ 0\ 1\ 0\ 0), (1\ 1\ 0\ 0\ 0\ 0\ 0\ 0\ 1\ 1)$$
$$(1\ 1\ 0\ 1\ 1\ 0\ 0\ 1\ 0\ 0), (0\ 0\ 1\ 0\ 0\ 1\ 1\ 1\ 1\ 0)$$

24.2 Calculate the Hamming weight w_H for the codes below.

1.

$$(0\ 1\ 1\ 1\ 0\ 1\ 0\ 1)$$

2.

$$(1\ 0\ 1\ 1\ 0\ 0\ 1\ 1\ 1\ 1) + (0\ 1\ 0\ 1\ 0\ 0\ 0\ 0\ 0\ 1)$$

3.

$$(1\ 0\ 1\ 1\ 0\ 0\ 1\ 1\ 1\ 1) - (0\ 1\ 0\ 1\ 0\ 0\ 0\ 0\ 0\ 1)$$

4.

$$(1\ 0\ 1\ 1\ 0\ 0\ 1\ 1\ 1\ 1) \oplus (0\ 1\ 0\ 1\ 0\ 0\ 0\ 0\ 0\ 1)$$

24.3 Calculate the maximum errors t that can be corrected by the codes below.

1.

$$(1\ 1\ 1\ 0\ 0\ 0\ 1\ 1\ 1\ 0)$$

2.

$$(0\ 1\ 0\ 0\ 1\ 0\ 0\ 1\ 0\ 0)$$

3.

$$(1\ 1\ 1\ 1\ 0\ 1\ 1\ 0\ 1\ 0)$$

4.

$$(1 \quad 1 \quad 0 \quad 0 \quad 1 \quad 1 \quad 0 \quad 1 \quad 1 \quad 1)$$

24.4 Calculate the codeword C for the following.

1.

$$x = \{101\}, \ G = \begin{bmatrix} 0 & 1 & 0 & 0 & 0 & 1 \\ 1 & 0 & 0 & 1 & 1 & 0 \\ 0 & 1 & 1 & 0 & 0 & 0 \end{bmatrix}$$

2.

$$x = \{1011\}, \ G = \begin{bmatrix} 1 & 0 & 0 & 0 & 1 \\ 0 & 1 & 0 & 1 & 0 \\ 0 & 0 & 1 & 0 & 0 \\ 0 & 0 & 0 & 1 & 0 \end{bmatrix}$$

3.

$$x = \{100\}, \ G = \begin{bmatrix} 1 & 0 & 1 & 0 & 1 & 0 & 1 \\ 1 & 1 & 0 & 0 & 0 & 0 & 1 \\ 0 & 0 & 1 & 1 & 0 & 0 & 0 \\ 1 & 0 & 0 & 1 & 0 & 1 & 0 \end{bmatrix}$$

4.

$$x = \{100\}, \ G = \begin{bmatrix} 1 & 0 & 1 & 1 & 0 & 0 & 0 \\ 0 & 1 & 1 & 0 & 1 & 0 & 1 \\ 0 & 1 & 0 & 1 & 0 & 1 & 0 \\ 0 & 1 & 0 & 0 & 0 & 0 & 1 \end{bmatrix}$$

24.5 Convert the generator for every C in Exercise 24.4 to the systematic form.

24.6 Find the parity-check matrix for every C in Exercise 24.4.

24.7 Given a code $C = \{c_1, c_2, c_3, c_4, c_5\} \in \mathbb{F}_2^5$, where each word has different probability of being bit 1 as $\{0.7, 0.9, 0.5, 0.6, 0.8\}$: Using the maximum-likelihood decoding, which is the most likely code that has been received:

1. If you received a word $r = 0$.
2. If you received a word $r = 1$.

24.8 Given a code $C = \{11001, 00000, 01010, 10101, 11110\}$ and a received code 10010, decode the received word by using the minimum-distance decoding.

24.9 Given the parity-check matrix $H = \begin{bmatrix} 1 & 1 & 1 & 0 & 1 & 0 & 0 \\ 1 & 0 & 1 & 1 & 0 & 1 & 0 \\ 1 & 1 & 0 & 1 & 0 & 0 & 1 \end{bmatrix}$ for a $[7, 4]$ code:

1. Encode the message $\{0110\}$.

2. You received a word {0100011} with one error in a message bit. Decode the transmitted word.

3. You received a word {0110001} with one error in a parity bit. Decode the transmitted word.

24.70 Given a code $C = \{10110, 01101, 10001, 01010\}$:

1. Find the Hamming sphere with radius $e = 1$ for every word in C.

2. Give two Hamming spheres that intersect for radius $e = 2$.

3. Draw the Hamming sphere of radius $e = 2$ for the code C.

24.11 Given the generator for a $[7,4]$ Hamming code as $G =$
$$\begin{bmatrix} 1 & 0 & 0 & 0 & 0 & 1 & 1 \\ 0 & 1 & 0 & 0 & 1 & 0 & 1 \\ 0 & 0 & 1 & 0 & 1 & 1 & 0 \\ 0 & 0 & 0 & 1 & 1 & 1 & 1 \end{bmatrix}:$$

1. Encode the message $x = \{1101\}$.

2. Find the parity-check matrix H.

3. Decode the word from (1).

4. Show how to detect an error in a corrupted received word $c = \{1111001\}$.

5. Decode c.

24.12 Given the generator for a $(7, 4)$ cyclic code as $g(x) = 1 + x + x^3$.

1. Encode the message $x = \{1101\}$.

2. Find the parity-check matrix H.

3. Decode the word from (1).

4. Show how to detect an error in a corrupted received word $c = \{1111001\}$.

5. Decode c.

25

Code-Based Cryptography

CONTENTS

An overview of the classic code-based cryptography is provided including the McElice cryptosystem and Niederrieter Cryptosystem. The next section presents the McElice cryptosystems using binary Goppa codes. Similarly, the Niederreiter Cryptosystem along with the algorithms involved are then discussed in detail. The next part of the chapter discusses the MDPC codes and QC-MDPC McElice cryptosystem. The explanations start with the formal definitions of MDPC codes followed by the construction for the algorithms involved in the MDPC and QC-MDPC codes. The work proposing QC-MDPC code to instantiate McEliece cryptosystem is presented in the next section.

25.1   McEliece Cryptosystem [75]

For the purposes of the McEliece encryption, the generator matrix G of a linear code over $\mathbb{F}_q^k$ should be seen as a map $\mathbb{F}_q^k \to \mathbb{F}_q^n$ sending a message m of length k to an element in $\mathbb{F}_q^n$. McEliece proposed code-based cryptography using binary Goppa code. The McEliece public-key cryptosystem is set up as follows.

25.1.1   Key Generation

The secret key consists of a random classical Goppa code $\Gamma = \Gamma_q(\alpha_1, \cdots, \alpha_n, g)$ over $\mathbb{F}_q$ of length n and dimension k with an error-correction capability of w errors. A generator matrix G for the code Γ as well as an $n \times n$ permutation matrix P, and an invertible $k \times k$ matrix S are randomly generated and kept secret as a part of the secret key. In particular, an efficient decoding algorithm for Γ is known. All steps of key generation are formally explained as in Construction 1.

Construction 1. ClassicMcElice : Gen

Input System parameters t, n, p, m

Output Public key K_{pub}, and secret key K_{sec}

1. Choose a binary $[n, k, d]$-Goppa code $\mathcal{C}$ capable of correcting up to t errors.
2. Compute the corresponding $k \times n$ generator matrix G for code $\mathcal{C}$.
3. Select a random non-singular binary $k \times k$ scrambling matrix S.
4. Select a random $n \times n$ permutation matrix P.
5. Compute the $k \times n$ matrix $\hat{G} = S \cdot G \cdot P$.
6. Return $K_{pub} = \hat{G}$ and $K_{sec} = (\Gamma, G, S^{-1}, P^{-1})$.

25.1.2 Encryption

Information needs to be embedded in a length-k word $m \in \mathbb{F}_q^k$ in order to be suitable for the encryption algorithm. Then m can be encrypted with the following algorithm in Construction 2.

Construction 2. Classic McElice : Encryption

Input: Public key $Key_{pub} = (\hat{G})$, message M and the parameter w

Output Ciphertext $y \in \mathbb{F}_q^n$

1. Compute $m\hat{G}$.
2. Hide the message by adding a random error vector e of length n and weight w.
3. Return $y = m\hat{G} + e$.

25.1.3 Decryption

The decryption algorithm as shown in Construction 3 needs to decode the ciphertext y, i.e., determine the error vector e. The legitimate receiver of y, i.e., the owner of the private key, can make use of the hidden Goppa-code structure, in particular, of the decoding algorithm for Γ.

Construction 3. Classic McElice : Decryption

Input A vector $y = m\hat{G} + e \in \mathbb{F}_q^n$ and private key $K_{sec} = (\Gamma, G, P, S)$ corresponding to $\hat{G}$

Output Message m

1. Compute the syndrome $\hat{y} = y \cdot P^{-1}$.
2. Compute the syndrome s corresponding to y.
3. Obtain $\hat{m}$ of length k from s using decoding algorithm Γ.
4. Compute $m = \hat{m} \cdot S^{-1}$.
5. Return m.

The decryption algorithm works for any McEliece ciphertext y, i.e., for any y which is an output of the encryption algorithm. Indeed, in this case, y is known to be at distance w from a vector mSG which is a codeword in Γ. The permutation by P^{-1} of the errors in the error vector does not change the weight of this vector, so it does not affect the decoding algorithm for Γ.

25.2   Niederreiter Cryptosystem

Niederreiter's cryptosystem, a variant of the McEliece cryptosystem, uses the Goppa codes as the McElice crytosystem but differs from it in public-key structure, encryption mechanism, and decryption mechanism. Note that the specific system in [72] with Goppa codes replaced by generalized Reed–Solomon codes was broken. The Niederreiter public-key cryptosystem is set up as follows.

25.2.1   Key Generation

The secret key consists of an $n \times n$ permutation matrix P, a non-singular $(n - k) \times (n - k)$ matrix S, a parity-check matrix H for a Goppa code $\Gamma = \Gamma_q(\alpha_1, \cdots, \alpha_n, g)$ of dimension k and error-correcting capability w. In particular, an efficient decoding algorithm for Γ is known. As in the McEliece cryptosystem, the sizes n, k, w are public system parameters, but $\alpha_1, \cdots, \alpha_n, g, P$, and S are randomly generated secrets.

Construction 4. Niederreiter : Gen

Input System parameters t, n, p, m

Output Public key K_{pub}, and secret key K_{sec}

1. Choose a binary $[n, k, d]$-Goppa code $\mathcal{C}$ capable of correcting up to t errors.

2. Compute the corresponding $(n - k) \times n$ parity-check matrix H for code $\mathcal{C}$.

3. Select a random non-singular binary $(n - k) \times (n - k)$ scrambling matrix S.

4. Select a random $n \times n$ permutation matrix P.

5. Compute the $k \times n$ matrix $\hat{H} = S \cdot H \cdot P$.

6. Return $K_{pub} = \hat{H}$, and $K_{sec} = (\Gamma, H, S^{-1}, P^{-1})$.

25.2.2 Encryption

Information needs to be embedded in a length-n word $x \in \mathbb{F}_q^n$ with w nonzero entries in order to be suitable for the encryption algorithm. Then x can be encrypted with the following algorithm in Construction 5. The output is the syndrome of x with respect to the public matrix $\hat{H}$.

Construction 5. Niederreiter : Encryption

Input A message $x \in \mathbb{F}_q^n$ of weight w and Public key $Key_{pub} = (\hat{H})$

Output Ciphertext $c \in \mathbb{F}_q^{n-k}$

1. Represent message m as a binary string x of length n and weight t.
2. Compute the syndrome $c = \hat{H} \cdot x^T$.
3. Return c.

25.2.3 Decryption

In order to decrypt the message, one has to find a weight-w vector x having syndrome s with respect to $\hat{H}$. As in the McEliece cryptosystem, the owner of the private key can make use of the hidden Goppa-code structure, in particular, of the decoding algorithm for Γ.

Construction 6. Niederreiter : Decryption

Input: A syndrome $s = c = \hat{H} \cdot x^T \in \mathbb{F}_q^{n-k}$ and private key $K_{sec} = (\Gamma, S, H, P) = (H, S^{-1}, P^{-1})$ corresponding to $\hat{H}$

Output Message x

1. Compute $\hat{c} = S^{-1} \cdot c$.
2. Use the decoding algorithm Γ to find $\hat{x}$.
3. Computer $x = P^{-1} \cdot \hat{x}$ of length n and weight t.
4. Return x.

The decryption algorithm works for any Niederreiter ciphertext c, i.e., for any c which is an output of the encryption algorithm.

25.3 Security Analysis of McEliece and Niederreiter

- There are two computational assumptions underlying the security of the McEliece scheme.

Assumption 1 (Indistinguishably) *The matrix $\hat{G}$ output by* Gen *is computationally indistinguishable from a uniformly chosen matrix of the same size.*

Assumption 2 (Decoding Hardness) *Decoding a random linear code with parameters n, k, w is hard.*

The computational assumptions for Niederreiter are almost the same, except for Assumption 1, that changes as follows.

Assumption 3 (Indistinguishably) *The $(n - k) \times n$ matrix $\hat{H}$ output by* Gen *is computationally indistinguishable from a uniformly chosen matrix of the same size.*

McEliece and Niederreiter are one-way secure under passive attacks, but not indistinguishably secure under chosen ciphertext attacks as well as chosen plaintext attacks. It is easy to show that McElieceis is not IND-CPA secure. An adversary $\mathcal{A}$ is given a public key G; it then chooses two plaintexts m_0, m_1, submits them to the encryption oracle and gets back $\psi^* = \mathsf{Enc}_\mathsf{G}^\mathsf{McE}(m_b)$. To win the game, $\mathcal{A}$ chooses a random $b \in \{0, 1\}$, encodes m_{b^*}, then checks the weight of $\psi^* - m_{b^*}G$; clearly $b = b^*$ if and only if $w_H(\psi^* - m_{b^*}G) = w$. The attack is trivial for Niederreiter since the scheme is deterministic. Furthermore, it is easy to show that both McEliece and Niederreiter are not IND-CCA secure.

25.4 QC-MDPC McEliece Cryptosystem

As discussed in the previous chapter, the security of code-based cryptography is based on two hardness assumptions: the indistinguishability of the code family and generic decoding.

Many articles have shown that the indistinguishability problem for Goppa codes might not be always sufficiently hard. Although it does not necessarily lead to a practical attack, it suggests that Goppa (and more generally, algebraic) codes may not be the optimal choice for code-based cryptography. Therefore, we can conclude that codes that do not have any algebraic structure would completely prevent this practical threat. One of the good alternatives is low density parity check (LDPC) codes [47] that are commonly used in the telecommunication, since they have no algebraic structure. However, such code is also vulnerable to attacks, as the low weight codewords can be easily found in polynomial time. To avoid such problem, McEliece schemes based on moderate density parity-check (MDPC) codes [76] are being proposed. As the name implies, they introduce moderate density parity-check (MDPC) codes of higher density than what are normally adopted for telecommunication applications. MDPC codes lead to a worse error-correction capability, but they ensure an adequate security level in the code-based cryptography. More efficient variants employ quasi-cyclic MDPC (QC-MDPC) codes, wherein each row of the code matrix is the cyclic rotation of the row before it, except the first row. In other words, we can compress the code into a single row vector, which greatly reduces the public/private key size compared to the Goppa codes.

25.4.1   MDPC and QC-MDPC Codes

The definitions and constructions of both MDPC and QC-MDPC codes are presented.

25.4.1.1   MDPC Code

Given an $[n, k]$-linear code, the value n is usually referred to as the length of the code, and k is referred to as the dimension. In what follows, the value $r = (n - k)$ is referred to as the co-dimension of the code.

Definition 1 (MDPC code) *An $[n, r, w]$-MDPC code is a linear code of length n, co-dimension r which admits a parity-check matrix of a constant row weight $w = \tilde{\mathcal{O}}(\sqrt{n})$ or $w \in \mathcal{O}(\sqrt{n \cdot log(n)})$.*

Definition 2 (Quasi-Cyclic Code) *A linear code $C \subseteq \mathbb{F}_2^n$ is quasi-cyclic if there exists a positive integer $n_0 \in \{1, 2, ..., n - 1\}$[1] such that for every codeword $c \in C$ the word c' obtained from a right cyclic shift of c by n_0 positions is itself a codeword of C.*

Definition 3 (QC-MDPC code) *An $[n, r, w]$-linear code is a quasi-cyclic moderate density parity-check (QC-MDPC) code if it is both an MDPC code and a quasi-cyclic code.*

25.4.1.2 MDPC Code Construction

A random $[n, r, w]$-MDPC code is easily generated by picking a random paritycheck matrix $H \in \mathbb{F}_2^{r \times n}$ of row weight w. With overwhelming probability, this matrix is of full rank and the rightmost $r \times r$ block is always invertible after possibly swapping a few columns.

25.4.1.3 QC-MDPC Code Construction

Main concern of this section is $[n, r, w]$-QC-MDPC codes, where $n = n_0 p$ and $r = p$. This means that the parity-check matrix has the form as

$$H - [H_0 | H_1 | \ldots | H_{n_0 - 1}], \tag{25.1}$$

where H_i is a $p \times p$ circulant block. We define the first row of H by picking a random vector of length $n = n_0 p$ and weight w. The other $r - 1$ rows are obtained from the $r - 1$ quasi-cyclic shifts of this first row. Each block H_i will have a row weight w_i such that $w = \sum_{i=0}^{n_0 - 1} w_i$.

In general, a smooth distribution is expected for the sequence of w_i's. A generator matrix G in row reduced echelon form ($G = [I_k | Q]$) can be easily derived from the H_i's blocks. Assuming the rightmost block $H_{n_0 - 1}$ is nonsingular (which particularly implies $w_{n_0 - 1}$ odd, otherwise the rows of $H_{n_0 - 1}$ would sum up to 0), we construct a generator-matrix as

$$G = \begin{bmatrix} [c|c] & \mathbf{I} & \begin{matrix} (H_{n_0-1}^{-1} H_0)^T \\ (H_{n_0-1}^{-1} H_1)^T \\ \vdots \\ (H_{n_0-1}^{-1} H_{n_0-2})^T \end{matrix} \end{bmatrix}. \tag{25.2}$$

25.4.2 QC-MDPC McEliece Cryptosystem [101]

The latest work deploying QC-MDPC code to instantiate McEliece cryptosystem was presented in [101].

25.4.2.1 Key Generation

Before describing the scheme, it is worth mentioning that the generator matrix G is not in general a generator matrix for a quasi-cyclic code, but rather it is isomorphic to such a generator matrix. However, as it turns out, the representation of G given above is suitable for the needs of the cryptosystem and furthermore, using this representation of G does not degrade security at all. To obtain a generator matrix G' for a QC-MDPC code from a matrix G as above, one must interleave the columns of G (a simple permutation). Note that indeed G is a $k \times n$ matrix and that for any vector $x \in \mathbb{F}_2^k$, the first k bits of xG is exactly equals to x itself.

Construction 7. QC-MDPC McEliece:Gen

Input: Security parameter n, weight w, co-dimension r, and error-correction threshold t

Output: Public key G, secret key H

1. Generate a parity-check matrix $H \in \mathbb{F}_2^{r \times n}$ of a t-error-correcting $[n, r, w]$-QC-MDPC code as described above.
2. Calculate $G = [I_k | Q]$ as described above.
3. Return (G, H).

25.4.2.2 Encryption

Encryption in the QC-MDPC McEliece scheme can be succinctly described as a matrix multiplication followed by an XOR with an error vector.

Construction 8. QC-MDPC McEliece: Encryption

Input: Public key G, message $m \in \mathbb{F}_2^k$, and error vector $e \in \mathbb{F}_2^k$ of weight at most t

Output: Ciphertext $c \in \mathbb{F}_2^n$

1. $c \leftarrow mG \oplus e$.
2. Return c.

25.4.2.3 Decryption

Decryption requires as a subroutine a t-error-correcting QC-MDPC decoding algorithm Ψ_H with knowledge of the secret key H.

Construction 9. QC-MDPC McEliece: Decryption

Input: Ciphertext $c \in \mathbb{F}_2^n$

Output: A message vector $m \in \mathbb{F}_2^k$ such that $d(mG, c) \leq t$, $\perp$

1. Compute $mG = \Psi_H(c) = \Psi_H(mG \oplus e)$. If this step fails, output $\perp$.
2. Extract m as the first k bits of mG.
3. Return m.

The QC-MDPC McEliece scheme is secure under two assumptions:

1. The randomness of the public key: given a parity-check matrix H, it is hard to tell if there exists a random vector within it.

2. The hardness of decoding QC-MDPC codes: given a parity-check matrix H, it is hard to decode it, and the best known solution is generic decoding algorithms.

These two assumptions are true in the case for non-cyclic code, but it is unknown for the cyclic case. However, general consensus agrees that the cyclic code alone does not make the problem easier [101]. Hence, QC-MDPC remains the most efficient variant of McEliece cryptosystem to date.

Exercises

25.1 Given the parameters of an McEliece encryption scheme as $m = 4$, $t = 2$, $S = \begin{bmatrix} 1 & 0 & 0 & 1 \\ 0 & 1 & 0 & 1 \\ 0 & 1 & 0 & 0 \\ 0 & 0 & 1 & 1 \end{bmatrix}$,

$$G = \begin{bmatrix} 0 & 1 & 1 & 0 & 1 & 0 & 1 & 0 & 0 & 1 & 0 & 0 \\ 0 & 1 & 1 & 1 & 1 & 0 & 0 & 1 & 1 & 0 & 0 & 0 \\ 1 & 1 & 1 & 0 & 1 & 1 & 0 & 1 & 0 & 0 & 1 & 0 \\ 1 & 1 & 1 & 0 & 1 & 1 & 0 & 1 & 0 & 0 & 1 & 0 \end{bmatrix},$$

$$P = \begin{bmatrix} 1 & 0 & 0 & 0 & 0 & 0 & 0 & 0 & 0 & 0 & 0 & 0 \\ 0 & 0 & 1 & 0 & 0 & 0 & 0 & 0 & 0 & 0 & 0 & 0 \\ 0 & 0 & 0 & 0 & 0 & 0 & 0 & 0 & 1 & 0 & 0 & 0 \\ 0 & 0 & 0 & 0 & 0 & 1 & 0 & 0 & 0 & 0 & 0 & 0 \\ 0 & 1 & 0 & 0 & 0 & 0 & 0 & 0 & 0 & 0 & 0 & 0 \\ 0 & 0 & 0 & 1 & 0 & 0 & 0 & 0 & 0 & 0 & 0 & 0 \\ 0 & 0 & 0 & 0 & 0 & 0 & 0 & 0 & 0 & 0 & 0 & 1 \\ 0 & 0 & 0 & 0 & 0 & 0 & 1 & 0 & 0 & 0 & 0 & 0 \\ 0 & 0 & 0 & 0 & 0 & 0 & 0 & 0 & 0 & 1 & 0 & 0 \\ 0 & 0 & 0 & 0 & 0 & 0 & 0 & 0 & 0 & 0 & 1 & 0 \\ 0 & 0 & 0 & 0 & 0 & 0 & 1 & 0 & 0 & 0 & 0 & 0 \end{bmatrix} :$$

1. What are the values for n, k, and d?
2. Compute $G' = S \cdot G \cdot P$.
3. Encrypt the message $\{1010\}$ with error $\{110000000000\}$.
4. Decrypt $y = \{001111011110\}$.

25.2 Given the parameters of a Niederreiter encryption scheme as $m = 6, t =$

$$2, S = \begin{bmatrix} 0 & 0 & 1 & 1 & 1 & 1 \\ 1 & 1 & 1 & 1 & 1 & 0 \\ 0 & 1 & 1 & 1 & 1 & 1 \\ 0 & 1 & 0 & 0 & 0 & 1 \\ 1 & 0 & 1 & 0 & 0 & 1 \\ 1 & 0 & 1 & 0 & 1 & 1 \end{bmatrix},$$

$$H = \begin{bmatrix} 0 & 0 & 1 & 1 & 1 & 0 & 0 & 1 \\ 0 & 0 & 0 & 1 & 0 & 1 & 1 & 1 \\ 1 & 1 & 0 & 0 & 0 & 0 & 0 & 0 \\ 0 & 0 & 1 & 0 & 0 & 1 & 1 & 1 \\ 0 & 0 & 1 & 1 & 1 & 0 & 1 & 0 \\ 1 & 0 & 1 & 1 & 1 & 1 & 1 & 1 \end{bmatrix}, P = \begin{bmatrix} 0 & 0 & 0 & 0 & 0 & 0 & 0 & 1 \\ 0 & 0 & 0 & 1 & 0 & 0 & 0 & 0 \\ 0 & 0 & 0 & 0 & 0 & 0 & 1 & 0 \\ 1 & 0 & 0 & 0 & 0 & 0 & 0 & 0 \\ 0 & 1 & 0 & 0 & 0 & 0 & 0 & 0 \\ 0 & 0 & 1 & 0 & 0 & 0 & 0 & 0 \\ 0 & 0 & 0 & 0 & 0 & 1 & 0 & 0 \\ 0 & 0 & 0 & 0 & 1 & 0 & 0 & 0 \end{bmatrix} :$$

1. What are the values for n, k, and d?
2. Compute $H' = S \cdot H \cdot P$.
3. Encrypt the encoded message $\{00100001\}$.
4. Decrypt $y = \{011111\}$.

Part IV

Implementations of Selected Algorithms

26

Selected Algorithms

CONTENTS

This chapter briefly explains implementations of some selected cryptographic algorithms. **The source code can be downloadable at https://ai-security.github.io.**

26.1   Introduction

Various popular cryptographic schemes are implemented using the MIRACL library. MIRACL is an open source software library for implementing cryptographic algorithms, which can be used for writing C or C++ program that requires elliptic curve cryptography (ECC). It also supports multi-precision arithmetic like modular multiplication, modular exponentiation, etc. These operations can work with very large integer (e.g., 1024-bit, 2048-bit, etc.) due to the efficient implementation in MIRACL. We show the steps to compile MIRACL as a static library (.lib) and use it in the Windows environment.

26.2   Boneh-Franklin IBE

Conventional public key cryptography (PKC) requires that the public keys to be exchanged before the encryption starts. Identity-based encryption (IBE) can be used to perform similar tasks offered by conventional PKC. The main feature in IBE is that it allows the user to create public key using known unique identifier such (e.g., email address). Then a third party can use this public key to create private key. In such a setting, there is no need to perform key exchange, which is one important advantage compared to conventional PKC. Boneh-Franklin IBE scheme is developed based on the Weil pairing over elliptic curves and finite fields. We show how the Boneh-Franklin IBE scheme can be implemented using the MIRACL library.

26.3   Boneh-Boyen IBE

Boneh-Boyen IBE is another popular IBE based on the well-studied decisional bilinear Diffie-Hellman assumption, which is extensible to systems with hierarchical identities (or often known as HIBE). This scheme is provably secure in the selective-identity sense without the random oracle model. It is often viewed as an improvement compared to the Boneh-Franklin IBE scheme with provable security. We show how the Boneh-Boyen IBE scheme can be implemented using the MIRACL library.

26.4   Broadcast Encryption

Broadcast encryption (BE) is a special type of encryption that controls the content accessed by a group of users. BE deals with methods to efficiently broadcast information to a dynamically changing group of users who are allowed to receive a data. It is often convenient to think of it as a revocation scheme, which addresses the case where some subset of the users (non-members) are excluded from receiving the information. We show how the BE scheme can be implemented using the MIRACL library.

26.5   Ciphertext-Policy Attribute-Based Encryption (CP-ABE)

Attribute-based encryption (ABE) is an advanced public-key cryptosystem developed recently, wherein the secret key used for decryption is dependent on the user attributes (e.g., the city in which he lives or his position in a company). The sender can encrypt the data and send to another person without relying on the certificate. In ABE, the sender can encrypt a list of attributes and broadcast it; whoever having some or all these attributes can decrypt the data successfully. CP-ABE is a variant of ABE where the policy to access the plaintext is not contained the secret key but the ciphertext. A structure of access will be built in CP-ABE, wherein only the user with the correct secret key (a set of attributes) and the access structure, can decrypt the ciphertext. We show how the Brent Waters' CP-IBE scheme can be implemented using the MIRACL library.

26.6   Predicate Encryption (PE)

Predicate encryption is an advanced public-key cryptosystem developed recently to supports attribute-hiding as well as payload-hiding, which allows high flexibility in terms of access control. Since the first PE scheme was introduced in 2008, several predicate encryption schemes have been published. However, these schemes are impractical as they require $O(n)$ pairing computations for decryption with considerably large sized public parameters, secret key, and ciphertext, where n is the dimension of the attribute/predicate vectors. Recently, I. Kim, S. O. Hwang, J. H. Park, and C. Park proposed a very efficient predicate encryption scheme that requires only n exponentiation and three pairing computations for decryption. The scheme also comes with shorter sized public parameters, secret key, and ciphertext. It is proven selective attribute-secure against chosen-plaintext attacks in the standard model under the Asymmetric Decisional Bilinear Diffie-Hellman assumptions. We show how the Kim et al.'s PE scheme can be implemented using the MIRACL library.

26.7   Rivest-Shamir-Adleman (RSA)

RSA is a popular public key cryptography that widely used by the industry for the past decades. It has a very simple structure, thus easy to understand and implement correctly. It can also be used as a digital signature generation algorithm (e.g., DSA). However, due to the advancement of the integer factorization techniques and development of powerful computers, the RSA problem can be solved easily if the key size is small. Hence, the key size of RSA is usually 2048-bit or 3076-bit, which can be very slow if it is not implemented efficiently. We start with basic approach to implement multiplication in multi-precision format, then introduce the efficient modular reduction technique (Montgomery reduction). Binary exponentiation is then introduced to improve the performance of exponentiation, which allows an efficient RSA implementation. Lastly, graphics processing unit (GPU) is being used to implement RSA in parallel form, achieving very fast RSA encryption/decryption.

26.8   Elliptic Curve Digital Signature Algorithm (ECDSA)

ECDSA was published in the early 2000 by NIST as an alternative to the DSA (based on RSA), released as FIPS-186. ECDSA relies on a elliptic curve public key cryptosystem, which is designed based on the hardness of elliptic curve discrete logarithm problem. It is able to achieve similar security level compared to RSA, with a much smaller key size. For instance, RSA requires 3072-bit key size to achieve 128-bit security, but ECC only needs 256-bit key. Hence, ECDSA is becoming popular in the past two decades as it requires much smaller key size compared to RSA. This translate directly into smaller memory cost (good for embedded system) and faster signature generation/verification. ECDSA relies heavily on the modular multiplication, which shares a lot of similarity with RSA. We explain the implementation of ECDSA as outlined in the latest revision of Digital Signature Standard (DSS) released by NIST in 2019.

26.9   QC-MDPC McEliece

McEliece cryptosystem was one of the oldest code based cryptosystems that are still secure nowadays. It is designed based on the coding theory, which is secure against the attack from quantum computers. The original McEliece cryptosystem was designed with Goppa code, which suffers from very large key sizes, causing it impractical to be implemented on embedded systems. In 2013, R. Misoczki, J.-P. Tillich, N. Sendrier, and P. S. L. M. Barreto proposed to replace the Goppa code with the QC-MDPC code, which successfully reduced the key sizes to a practical level. The encryption in McEliece is very simple, as it only involves matrix-vector multiplication and addition. The decryption depends on the bit-flipping algorithm, which is commonly used for decoding error code. The QC-MDPC McEliece cryptosystem was implemented and its speed performance was evaluated.

26.10   NTRUEncrypt

NTRU is a lattice based cryptosystem developed in 1996 and remain as one of the most promising candidates in post-quantum cryptography. It was designed based on the shortest vector problem (SVP) in a lattice, which is still not possible to be solved by quantum computers efficiently. NTRUEncrypt was included into the IEEE Std 1363.1 in 2008; this is the first post-quantum cryptosystem that was standardized. Among the two NTRU schemes proposed (NTRUSign and NTRUEncrypt), NTRUEncrypt had received more attention due to its efficiency comparable to popular public key cryptosystem like ECC. The encryption and decryption process in NTRUEncrypt are very simple, as it only involves polynomial multiplication. The polynomial multiplication was implemented with technique to exploit the sparsity in polynomials. It is also implemented on graphics processing unit (GPU) to exploit the parallel architecture for batch polynomial multiplication.

26.11   Number Theoretic Transform

Besides NTRU, there are other variants of lattice based cryptography that has special lattice structure suitable for efficient implementation; qTESLA is one of such scheme. With special lattice structure, the polynomial multiplication can be implemented more efficiently using Number Theoretic Transform (NTT). NTT is developed based on the Fast Fourier Transform (FFT), which is a popular technique used in signal processing. FFT operates over real number (floating point), but NTT operates on the integer; other than that, both techniques share a lot of similarities. We show how to implement the NTT with various techniques, including the precomputation of twiddle factors, nega-cyclic convolution, Cooley-Tukey and Stockham FFT. The implementation was performed on the qTESLA parameters to demonstrate its practicality on state-of-the-art lattice based cryptography. Lastly, it is also implemented on graphics processing unit (GPU) to exploit the parallel architecture for batch polynomial multiplication using NTT.

26.12   The Paillier Encryption

Homomorphic encryption (HE) allows computations to be performed in encrypted domain. This means that a user can encrypt the plaintext and pass the ciphertext to third party (e.g., cloud server) to compute the data on behalf of him/her, without disclosing important information. This computing paradigm is very important to protect the privacy of users in various applications. Paillier cryptosystem was standardized in ISO/IEC 18033-6:2019 recently. It allows the user to perform additive operation on encrypted domain, so it is also known as Additive HE. The main operation involved in Paillier cryptosystem is modular exponentiation, which is very time consuming. However, we can utilize the same techniques presented in RSA section (e.g. Montgomery multiplication, binary exponentiation, and Chinese Remainder Theorem (CRT)) to speed up the execution. We show how Paillier cryptosystem can be implemented efficiently using the MIRACL library.

26.13   AES Block Cipher

Advanced Encryption Standard (AES) released by NIST in year 2001 eventually became the de-facto encryption scheme for many applications. AES can be implemented easily by following the specifications, but the performance may not be optimal. On the other hand, many operations in AES can be pre-computed, so that the encryption/decryption process only requires simple table-lookup (T-box). This is essentially an example of time-memory trade-off, wherein more memory space is used to store pre-computed results for better speed performance. AES with both basic and T-box implementation are discussed.

26.14   wolfSSL

Secure Socket Layer (SSL) is a cryptography protocol used to protect the communication in networking system. Since 2015, SSL was succeeded by Transport Layer Security (TLS) protocol. Both SSL and TLS are widely used in many networking applications. We show an overview of the handshake process in SSL/TLS, which is the core operation in the protocol to protect the communication. Then, we introduce wolfSSL, a software library implementing TLS protocol in plain C language, which is widely used in many commercial products. wolfSSL is highly portable; it can be used in desktop PC, server, and embedded system. It is also smaller in code size and faster in performance, compared to another popular software library, OpenSSL. Simple client/server and bench-marking programs are shown to enable further exploration on using this commercial grade software library.

Bibliography

[1] Ethereum whitepaper, (Accessed: September 26, 2020). Available Online: $https: //ethereum.org/en/whitepaper/$.

[2] Mining hardware comparison, (Accessed: September 26, 2020). Available Online: $https : //en.bitcoin.it/wiki/Mining\_hardware\_comparison$.

[3] Nadhem AlFardan, Daniel J Bernstein, Kenneth G Paterson, Bertram Poettering, and Jacob CN Schuldt. On the security of RC4 in TLS. In *22nd USENIX Security Symposium (USENIX Security 13)*, pages 305–320, 2013.

[4] Erdem Alkim, Léo Ducas, Thomas Pöppelmann, and Peter Schwabe. Post-quantum key exchange—a New Hope. In *25th USENIX Security Symposium (USENIX Security 16)*, pages 327–343, 2016.

[5] Joël Alwen, Stephan Krenn, Krzysztof Pietrzak, and Daniel Wichs. Learning with rounding, revisited. In *Annual Cryptology Conference*, pages 57–74. Springer, 2013.

[6] Nuttapong Attrapadung, Jun Furukawa, Takeshi Gomi, Goichiro Hanaoka, Hideki Imai, and Rui Zhang. Efficient identity-based encryption with tight security reduction. In *International Conference on Cryptology and Network Security*, pages 19–36. Springer, 2006.

[7] Abhishek Banerjee, Chris Peikert, and Alon Rosen. Pseudorandom functions and lattices. In *Annual International Conference on the Theory and Applications of Cryptographic Techniques*, pages 719–737. Springer, 2012.

[8] Boaz Barak, Yevgeniy Dodis, Hugo Krawczyk, Olivier Pereira, Krzysztof Pietrzak, François-Xavier Standaert, and Yu Yu. Leftover hash lemma, revisited. In *Annual Cryptology Conference*, pages 1–20. Springer, 2011.

[9] Anja Becker, Léo Ducas, Nicolas Gama, and Thijs Laarhoven. New directions in nearest neighbor searching with applications to lattice sieving. In *Proceedings of the Twenty-Seventh Annual ACM-SIAM Symposium on Discrete Algorithms*, pages 10–24. SIAM, 2016.

[10] Mihir Bellare and Thomas Ristenpart. Simulation without the artificial abort: Simplified proof and improved concrete security for waters' IBE scheme. In *Annual International Conference on the Theory and Applications of Cryptographic Techniques*, pages 407–424. Springer, 2009.

[11] Mihir Bellare and Phillip Rogaway. The exact security of digital signatures-how to sign with RSA and Rabin. In *International Conference on the Theory and Applications of Cryptographic Techniques*, pages 399–416. Springer, 1996.

[12] Mihir Bellare and Phillip Rogaway. Probabilistic signature scheme, July 24 2001. US Patent 6,266,771.

[13] Elwyn Berlekamp, Robert McEliece, and Henk Van Tilborg. On the inherent intractability of certain coding problems (corresp.). *IEEE Transactions on Information Theory*, 24(3):384–386, 1978.

[14] John Bethencourt, Amit Sahai, and Brent Waters. Ciphertext-policy attribute-based encryption. In *2007 IEEE Symposium on Security and Privacy (SP'07)*, pages 321–334. IEEE, 2007.

[15] Frits Beukers. Lattice reduction. In *Some Tapas of Computer Algebra*, pages 66–77. Springer, 1999.

[16] George Robert Blakley. Safeguarding cryptographic keys. In *1979 International Workshop on Managing Requirements Knowledge (MARK)*, pages 313–318. IEEE, 1979.

[17] Daniel Bleichenbacher. Chosen ciphertext attacks against protocols based on the RSA encryption standard PKCS# 1. In *Annual International Cryptology Conference*, pages 1–12. Springer, 1998.

[18] Andrej Bogdanov, Siyao Guo, Daniel Masny, Silas Richelson, and Alon Rosen. On the hardness of learning with rounding over small modulus. In *Theory of Cryptography Conference*, pages 209–224. Springer, 2016.

[19] Dan Boneh and Xavier Boyen. Efficient selective-ID secure identity-based encryption without random oracles. In *International Conference on the Theory and Applications of Cryptographic Techniques*, pages 223–238. Springer, 2004.

[20] Dan Boneh and Xavier Boyen. Efficient selective identity-based encryption without random oracles. *Journal of Cryptology*, 24(4):659–693, 2011.

[21] Dan Boneh, Xavier Boyen, and Eu-Jin Goh. Hierarchical identity based encryption with constant size ciphertext. In *Annual International Conference on the Theory and Applications of Cryptographic Techniques*, pages 440–456. Springer, 2005.

[22] Dan Boneh, Xavier Boyen, and Hovav Shacham. Short group signatures. In *Annual International Cryptology Conference*, pages 41–55. Springer, 2004.

[23] Dan Boneh, Giovanni Di Crescenzo, Rafail Ostrovsky, and Giuseppe Persiano. Public key encryption with keyword search. In *International Conference on the Theory and Applications of Cryptographic Techniques*, pages 506–522. Springer, 2004.

[24] Dan Boneh and Matt Franklin. Identity-based encryption from the Weil pairing. In *Annual International Cryptology Conference*, pages 213–229. Springer, 2001.

[25] Dan Boneh, Craig Gentry, and Brent Waters. Collusion resistant broadcast encryption with short ciphertexts and private keys. In *Annual International Cryptology Conference*, pages 258–275. Springer, 2005.

[26] Dan Boneh, Amit Sahai, and Brent Waters. Functional encryption: Definitions and challenges. In *Theory of Cryptography Conference*, pages 253–273. Springer, 2011.

[27] Joppe Bos, Craig Costello, Léo Ducas, Ilya Mironov, Michael Naehrig, Valeria Nikolaenko, Ananth Raghunathan, and Douglas Stebila. Frodo: Take off the ring! practical, quantum-secure key exchange from LWE. In *Proceedings of the 2016 ACM SIGSAC Conference on Computer and Communications Security*, pages 1006–1018, 2016.

[28] Joppe W Bos, Craig Costello, Michael Naehrig, and Douglas Stebila. Post-quantum key exchange for the TLS protocol from the ring learning with errors problem. In *2015 IEEE Symposium on Security and Privacy*, pages 553–570. IEEE, 2015.

[29] Zvika Brakerski, Craig Gentry, and Shai Halevi. Packed ciphertexts in LWE-based homomorphic encryption. In *International Workshop on Public Key Cryptography*, pages 1–13. Springer, 2013.

[30] Zvika Brakerski, Adeline Langlois, Chris Peikert, Oded Regev, and Damien Stehlé. Classical hardness of learning with errors. In *Proceedings of the Forty-Fifth Annual ACM Symposium on Theory of Computing*, pages 575–584, 2013.

[31] Ran Canetti, Shai Halevi, and Jonathan Katz. A forward-secure public-key encryption scheme. In *International Conference on the Theory and Applications of Cryptographic Techniques*, pages 255–271. Springer, 2003.

[32] Ran Canetti, Shai Halevi, and Jonathan Katz. Chosen-ciphertext security from identity-based encryption. In *International Conference on the Theory and Applications of Cryptographic Techniques*, pages 207–222. Springer, 2004.

[33] Liqun Chen and Zhaohui Cheng. Security proof of Sakai-Kasahara's identity-based encryption scheme. In *IMA International Conference on Cryptography and Coding*, pages 442–459. Springer, 2005.

[34] Jung Hee Cheon, Duhyeong Kim, Joohee Lee, and Yongsoo Song. Lizard: Cut off the tail! A practical post-quantum public-key encryption from LWE and LWR. In *International Conference on Security and Cryptography for Networks*, pages 160–177. Springer, 2018.

[35] Jean-Sébastien Coron. Optimal security proofs for PSS and other signature schemes. In *International Conference on the Theory and Applications of Cryptographic Techniques*, pages 272–287. Springer, 2002.

[36] Ronald Cramer and Victor Shoup. A practical public key cryptosystem provably secure against adaptive chosen ciphertext attack. In *Annual International Cryptology Conference*, pages 13–25. Springer, 1998.

[37] Cécile Delerablée. Identity-based broadcast encryption with constant size ciphertexts and private keys. In *International Conference on the Theory and Application of Cryptology and Information Security*, pages 200–215. Springer, 2007.

[38] Cécile Delerablée, Pascal Paillier, and David Pointcheval. Fully collusion secure dynamic broadcast encryption with constant-size ciphertexts or decryption keys. In *International Conference on Pairing-Based Cryptography*, pages 39–59. Springer, 2007.

[39] Jintai Ding, Xiang Xie, and Xiaodong Lin. A simple provably secure key exchange scheme based on the learning with errors problem. *IACR Cryptology EPrint Archive*, 2012:688, 2012.

[40] Morris J Dworkin. Sha-3 standard: Permutation-based hash and extendable-output functions. Technical report, 2015.

[41] Donald Eastlake and Paul Jones. US secure hash algorithm 1 (SHA1), 2001.

[42] János Folláth. Gaussian sampling in lattice based cryptography. *Tatra Mountains Mathematical Publications*, 60(1):1–23, 2014.

[43] Marcus Frean and Phillip Boyle. Using Gaussian processes to optimize expensive functions. In *Australasian Joint Conference on Artificial Intelligence*, pages 258–267. Springer, 2008.

[44] Eiichiro Fujisaki and Tatsuaki Okamoto. Secure integration of asymmetric and symmetric encryption schemes. In *Annual International Cryptology Conference*, pages 537–554. Springer, 1999.

[45] Eiichiro Fujisaki and Tatsuaki Okamoto. Secure integration of asymmetric and symmetric encryption schemes. *Journal of cryptology*, 26(1):80–101, 2013.

[46] David Galindo. Boneh-Franklin identity based encryption revisited. In *International Colloquium on Automata, Languages, and Programming*, pages 791–802. Springer, 2005.

[47] Robert Gallager. Low-density parity-check codes. *IRE Transactions on Information Theory*, 8(1):21–28, 1962.

[48] Craig Gentry. Practical identity-based encryption without random oracles. In *Annual International Conference on the Theory and Applications of Cryptographic Techniques*, pages 445–464. Springer, 2006.

[49] Craig Gentry, Chris Peikert, and Vinod Vaikuntanathan. Trapdoors for hard lattices and new cryptographic constructions. In *Proceedings of the fortieth annual ACM symposium on Theory of computing*, pages 197–206, 2008.

[50] Craig Gentry and Brent Waters. Adaptive security in broadcast encryption systems (with short ciphertexts). In *Annual International Conference on the Theory and Applications of Cryptographic Techniques*, pages 171–188. Springer, 2009.

[51] Ryan Glabb, Laurent Imbert, Graham Jullien, Arnaud Tisserand, and Nicolas Veyrat-Charvillon. Multi-mode operator for SHA-2 hash functions. *Journal of Systems Architecture*, 53(2-3):127–138, 2007.

[52] Oded Goldreich. *Foundations of Cryptography: Volume 1, Basic Tools*. Cambridge University Press, 2007.

[53] Oded Goldreich, Shafi Goldwasser, and Silvio Micali. How to construct Randolli functions. In *25th Annual Symposium on Foundations of Computer Science, 1984.*, pages 464–479. IEEE, 1984.

[54] Oded Goldreich, Daniele Micciancio, Shmuel Safra, and J-P Seifert. Approximating shortest lattice vectors is not harder than approximating closest lattice vectors. *Information Processing Letters*, 71(2):55–61, 1999.

[55] Vipul Goyal, Omkant Pandey, Amit Sahai, and Brent Waters. Attribute-based encryption for fine-grained access control of encrypted data. In *Proceedings of the 13th ACM Conference on Computer and Communications Security*, pages 89–98, 2006.

[56] Lien Harn and Changlu Lin. Authenticated group key transfer protocol based on secret sharing. *IEEE Transactions on Computers*, 59(6):842–846, 2010.

[57] Johan Håstad, Russell Impagliazzo, Leonid A Levin, and Michael Luby. A pseudorandom generator from any one-way function. *SIAM Journal on Computing*, 28(4):1364–1396, 1999.

[58] Jeffrey Hoffstein, Jill Pipher, and Joseph H Silverman. Ntru: A ring-based public key cryptosystem. In *International Algorithmic Number Theory Symposium*, pages 267–288. Springer, 1998.

[59] Burton S Kaliski Jr and CA Redwood City. An overview of the PKCS standards. *RSA Laboratories, Nov*, 1993.

[60] Jonathan Katz, Amit Sahai, and Brent Waters. Predicate encryption supporting disjunctions, polynomial equations, and inner products. In *Annual International Conference on the Theory and Applications of Cryptographic Techniques*, pages 146–162. Springer, 2008.

[61] Jonathan Katz and Nan Wang. Efficiency improvements for signature schemes with tight security reductions. In *Proceedings of the 10th ACM Conference on Computer and Communications Security*, pages 155–164. ACM, 2003.

[62] Intae Kim, Seong Oun Hwang, Jong Hwan Park, and Chanil Park. An efficient predicate encryption with constant pairing computations and minimum costs. *IEEE Transactions on Computers*, 65(10):2947–2958, 2016.

[63] Intae Kim, Jong Hwan Park, and Seong Oun Hwang. An efficient public key functional encryption for inner product evaluations. *Neural Computing and Applications*, 32(17):13117–13128, September 1, 2020.

[64] Takashi Kitagawa, Peng Yang, Goichiro Hanaoka, Rui Zhang, Hajime Watanabe, Kanta Matsuura, and Hideki Imai. Generic transforms to acquire CCA-security for identity based encryption: The cases of FO pkc and REACT. In *Australasian Conference on Information Security and Privacy*, pages 348–359. Springer, 2006.

[65] Hugo Krawczyk, Mihir Bellare, and Ran Canetti. HMAC: Keyed-hashing for message authentication, 1997.

[66] Ben P Lanyon, Till J Weinhold, Nathan K Langford, Marco Barbieri, Daniel FV James, Alexei Gilchrist, and Andrew G White. Experimental demonstration of a compiled version of Shor's algorithm with quantum entanglement. *Physical Review Letters*, 99(25):250505, 2007.

[67] Joohee Lee, Duhyeong Kim, Hyungkyu Lee, Younho Lee, and Jung Hee Cheon. Rlizard: Post-quantum key encapsulation mechanism for IoT devices. *IEEE Access*, 7:2080–2091, 2018.

[68] Hendrik W Lenstra Jr. Lattices. 2008.

[69] Allison Lewko, Tatsuaki Okamoto, Amit Sahai, Katsuyuki Takashima, and Brent Waters. Fully secure functional encryption: Attribute-based encryption and (hierarchical) inner product encryption. In *Annual International Conference on the Theory and Applications of Cryptographic Techniques*, pages 62–91. Springer, 2010.

[70] Richard Lindner and Chris Peikert. Better key sizes (and attacks) for LWE-based encryption. In *Cryptographers' Track at the RSA Conference*, pages 319–339. Springer, 2011.

[71] Yu Liu, Kaijie Wu, and Ramesh Karri. Scan-based attacks on linear feedback shift register based stream ciphers. *ACM Transactions on Design Automation of Electronic Systems (TODAES)*, 16(2):1–15, 2011.

[72] Pierre Loidreau and Nicolas Sendrier. Weak keys in the McEliece public-key cryptosystem. *IEEE Transactions on Information Theory*, 47(3):1207–1211, 2001.

[73] Vadim Lyubashevsky, Chris Peikert, and Oded Regev. On ideal lattices and learning with errors over rings. In *Annual International Conference on the Theory and Applications of Cryptographic Techniques*, pages 1–23. Springer, 2010.

[74] Alexander May and Joseph H Silverman. Dimension reduction methods for convolution modular lattices. In *International Cryptography and Lattices Conference*, pages 110–125. Springer, 2001.

[75] Robert J McEliece. A public-key cryptosystem based on algebraic. *Coding Theory*, 4244:114–116, 1978.

[76] Rafael Misoczki, Jean-Pierre Tillich, Nicolas Sendrier, and Paulo SLM Barreto. MDPC-McEliece: New McEliece variants from moderate density parity-check codes. In *2013 IEEE International Symposium on Information Theory*, pages 2069–2073. IEEE, 2013.

[77] Satoshi Nakamoto. Bitcoin: A peer-to-peer electronic cash system. Technical report, Manubot, 2008.

[78] Dalit Naor, Moni Naor, and Jeff Lotspiech. Revocation and tracing schemes for stateless receivers. In *Annual International Cryptology Conference*, pages 41–62. Springer, 2001.

[79] Mototsugu Nishioka. Identity-based encryptions with tight security reductions to the BDH problem. *IEICE Transactions on Fundamentals of Electronics, Communications and Computer Sciences*, 91(5):1241–1252, 2008.

[80] Tatsuaki Okamoto and Katsuyuki Takashima. Hierarchical predicate encryption for inner-products. In *International Conference on the Theory*

and Application of Cryptology and Information Security, pages 214–231. Springer, 2009.

[81] Pascal Paillier. Public-key cryptosystems based on composite degree residuosity classes. In *International Conference on the Theory and Applications of Cryptographic Techniques*, pages 223–238. Springer, 1999.

[82] Jong Hwan Park and Dong Hoon Lee. An efficient IBE scheme with tight security reduction in the random oracle model. *Designs, Codes and Cryptography*, 79(1):63–85, 2016.

[83] Jong Hwan Park, Kwangsu Lee, and Dong Hoon Lee. New chosen-ciphertext secure identity-based encryption with tight security reduction to the bilinear Diffie–Hellman problem. *Information Sciences*, 325:256–270, 2015.

[84] Chris Peikert. Public-key cryptosystems from the worst-case shortest vector problem. In *Proceedings of the Forty-First Annual ACM Symposium on Theory of Computing*, pages 333–342, 2009.

[85] Chris Peikert. Lattice cryptography for the internet. In *International Workshop on Post-Quantum Cryptography*, pages 197–219. Springer, 2014.

[86] Chris Peikert, Vinod Vaikuntanathan, and Brent Waters. A framework for efficient and composable oblivious transfer. In *Annual International Cryptology Conference*, pages 554–571. Springer, 2008.

[87] David Pointcheval and Jacques Stern. Security proofs for signature schemes. In *International Conference on the Theory and Applications of Cryptographic Techniques*, pages 387–398. Springer, 1996.

[88] Oded Regev. On lattices, learning with errors, random linear codes, and cryptography. *Journal of the ACM (JACM)*, 56(6):1–40, 2009.

[89] Ronald Rivest and S Dusse. The MD5 message-digest algorithm, 1992.

[90] Adi Shamir. How to share a secret. *Communications of the ACM*, 22(11):612–613, 1979.

[91] Adi Shamir. Identity-based cryptosystems and signature schemes. In *Workshop on the Theory and Application of Cryptographic Techniques*, pages 47–53. Springer, 1984.

[92] Victor Shoup. Lower bounds for discrete logarithms and related problems. In *International Conference on the Theory and Applications of Cryptographic Techniques*, pages 256–266. Springer, 1997.

[93] NIST-FIPS Standard. Announcing the advanced encryption standard (AES). *Federal Information Processing Standards Publication*, 197(1-51):3–3, 2001.

[94] Ehsan Ebrahimi Targhi and Dominique Unruh. Quantum security of the Fujisaki-Okamoto and OAEP transforms. *IACR Cryptology ePrint Archive*, 2015:1210, 2015.

[95] Paolo Tasca and CJ Tessone. A taxonomy of blockchain technologies: principles of identification and classification. ledger 4 (2019). *arXiv preprint ArXiv:1708.04872 [Cs]*, 2019.

[96] Luuc Van Der Horst, Kim-Kwang Raymond Choo, and Nhien-An Le-Khac. Process memory investigation of the bitcoin clients electrum and bitcoin core. *IEEE Access*, 5:22385–22398, 2017.

[97] Gilbert S Vernam. Secret signaling system. *US Patent*, (1,310,719), 2016.

[98] Brent Waters. Efficient identity-based encryption without random oracles. In *Annual International Conference on the Theory and Applications of Cryptographic Techniques*, pages 114–127. Springer, 2005.

[99] Brent Waters. Dual system encryption: Realizing fully secure IBE and HIBE under simple assumptions. In *Annual International Cryptology Conference*, pages 619–636. Springer, 2009.

[100] Tsu-Yang Wu, Chien-Ming Chen, King-Hang Wang, Chao Meng, and Eric Ke Wang. A provably secure certificateless public key encryption with keyword search. *Journal of the Chinese Institute of Engineers*, 42(1):20–28, 2019.

[101] Atsushi Yamada, E Eaton, K Kalach, P Lafrance, and A Parent. QC-MDPC KEM: A key encapsulation mechanism based on the QC-MDPC mceliece encryption scheme. *NIST Submission*, 2017.

[102] Christof Zalka. Grover's quantum searching algorithm is optimal. *Physical Review A*, 60(4):2746, 1999.

Index